Volumes in the *Wars of the United States Series* published in paperback by Indiana University Press

THE AMERICAN WAY OF WAR
A History of United States Military Strategy and Policy
Russell F. Weigley

THE WAR OF AMERICAN INDEPENDENCE
Military Attitudes, Policies, and Practice, 1763–1789
Don Higginbotham

THE SWORD OF THE REPUBLIC
The United States Army on the Frontier, 1783–1846
Francis Paul Prucha

FRONTIER REGULARS
The United States Army and the Indian, 1866–1891
Robert M. Utley

The American Way of War

THE AMERICAN WAY OF WAR

A HISTORY OF UNITED STATES MILITARY STRATEGY AND POLICY

Russell F. Weigley

Indiana University Press Bloomington

Indiana University Press paperback edition published 1977 by arrangement with Macmillan Publishing Co., Inc.

Permission to quote copyrighted materials has been granted by the Council on Foreign Relations, for the quotations from Henry A. Kissinger, *Nuclear Weapons and Foreign Policy*, published by Harper & Row; by Random House, Inc., for the quotations from General William Mitchell, *Memoirs of World War I: From Start to Finish of Our Greatest War;* by Simon & Schuster, Inc., for the quotations from Alexander P. De Seversky, *Victory through Air Power;* and by the United States Naval Institute, for quotations from various articles from its *Proceedings*.

Manufactured in the United States of America

Library of Congress Cataloging in Publication Data

Weigley, Russell Frank.
The American way of war.
Reprint of the ed. published by Macmillan, New York, in series: The Wars of the United States.
Bibliography: p.
Includes index.
1. United States—Military policy. 2. Strategy.
3. United States—History, Military. I. Title.
II. Series: The Wars of the United States.
[UA23.W3695 1977] 355.4'3'0973 77-74434
ISBN 0-253-28029-X

8 86

In memory of Roy F. Nichols

Contents

Maps

It is not an easy task—to discuss the general subject of strategy, in one period, to this group of mature and educated officers. Not that nothing has been written on the subject, from which I might compile a lecture! The shelves are full of them! In serried ranks they march down through the decades, each one calling itself a treatise on "modern war." Omitting those away back there in the dim, misty light, here stalk Clausewitz, von der Goltz, and Bernhardi; Napoleon, Jomini, Foch, and Castex; Hamley, Byrd, Maurice, Fuller, Hart, and Corbett; Bigelow, Wagner, Mahan, Naylor, Meyers, and Robinson. I salute them. I make obeisance to their industry, their great learning, the vast storehouse of knowledge they have bequeathed us. I swear allegiance to all the great truths they have proclaimed. But—!!! Well, they all treat of strategy as a science (and so it is); the earlier group treats it as a problem in plane geometry, with their lines, and bases and dislocations. The best strategy was that which avoided combat; one writer of that school goes so far as to say, "If we find ourselves obliged to fight a battle, mistakes have been committed previously." The later group of writers, led by Clausewitz and based on the campaigns of Frederick the Great and Napoleon, treats of strategy as a number of principles and like unto some curator of a musty museum, armed with a butterfly net and a magnifying glass, they neatly classify every action of the commander as an observance of this principle or a violation of that. You gentlemen, who are now nearing the end of our formal system of military education, have studied this science for long years, and now, I believe, you would join me in a longing for someone who could talk to us of Strategy as an *art*. (For it is an art.) I recommend it to you as the theme of the book you are some day going to write; or better still, the theme of the campaign you are some day going to conduct. For we study strategy as a science: the application of that knowledge, is an art.

Everyone who writes on the subject of strategy finds it necessary to define his understanding of the meaning of the word. As a result there are as many definitions as there are writers. Admiral Castex, for example, quotes nineteen different definitions and then makes up one of his own.

—Colonel Ned B. Rehkopf,
to the Army War College, 1939

Introduction

As Colonel Ned Rehkopf said, we must begin with definitions. "Strategy" has always lacked something in precision of meaning. Clausewitz defined tactics as "*the theory of the use of military forces in combat*," strategy as "*the theory of the use of combats for the object of the War*."[1] This definition of strategy is too exclusively military and focuses too narrowly upon battle and war to be adequate in the discourse of the late twentieth century. As Alastair Buchan wrote in 1966 regarding the current conception of strategy, ". . . the real content of strategy is concerned not merely with war and battles but with the application or maintenance of force so that it contributes most effectively to the achievement of political objectives."[2] The *Dictionary of United States Military Terms for Joint Usage* distinguishes between "national strategy" and "military strategy" and says:

> National Strategy.—The art and science of developing and using the political, economic, and psychological powers of a nation, together with its armed forces, during peace and war, to secure national objectives.
>
> Military Strategy.—The art and science of employing the armed forces of a nation to secure the objectives of national policy by the application of force, or the threat of force.

Still, to review the history of military strategy in the United States, Clausewitz's definition conveys better than any other concise one what Americans meant by strategy when they thought about the subject in its (to them) broadest sense from the beginning of their national history through the Second World War and even through the Korean War. It should be remembered, of course, that Clausewitz was little read in the United States before the twentieth century. For that reason among others, Americans, especially American soldiers, often held to a still narrower definition of strategy than Clausewitz's, the time-worn conventional definition that calls strategy "the art of bringing forces to the battlefield in a favorable position."[3] This latter view of strategy, unlike Clausewitz's, excluded from consideration the purposes for which a battle or a war was being fought. It made the distinction between strategy and tactics merely one between the management of forces before or during the battle, and it helped convey the widespread impression that strategy was a matter of little consequence deserving little of the soldier's professional study, because it involved much less intricate and specialized problems than those of tactics (or of operations, a term the Germans and Russians came to use to apply to the planning, organizing, and direction of specific campaigns, intermediate between the tactical realm of battles and the strategic realm at the highest level of military decision making).

The narrower definition of strategy meant also that not only was the applicability of the word confined almost wholly to strictly military affairs, but military strategists gave little regard to the nonmilitary consequences of what they were doing. General Albert C. Wedemeyer of the United States Army wrote of his "education as a strategist" in the years just before World War II:

> At Leavenworth I had furthered my education in advanced military science. But my real education as a strategist, using the word in its broadest connotation, began during my two years of study at the German War College, 1936–38. This was my most professionally remunerative assignment and, no doubt, the principal reason why I was assigned to the War Plans Division of the General Staff in Washington early in 1941.
>
> . . . Thanks to my assignment in Germany, I was afforded an opportunity to acquire a broad concept of strategy embracing political, economic, and psychological means for the attainment of war aims, in place of the narrower concept of strictly military science which I had studied at Leavenworth.[4]

The idea that in 1941–45 the American government subordinated considerations of possible postwar advantage to the immediate requirements of military strategy in direct pursuit of military victory is familiar to the point of being a cliché. An emphasis in wartime on military strategy calculated to lead to military victory by the most direct means possible was not so automatically censurable as the post-1945 use of the cliché has generally implied. But it is true that during 1941–45 and throughout American history until that time, the United States usually possessed no national strategy for the employment of force or the threat of force to attain political ends, except as the nation used force in wartime openly and directly in pursuit of military victories as complete as was desired or possible. The only kind of American strategy employing the armed forces tended to be the most direct kind of military strategy, applied in war. The United States was not involved in international politics continuously enough or with enough consistency of purpose to permit the development of a coherent national strategy for the consistent pursuit of political goals by diplomacy in combination with armed force. A not unhealthy corollary of this situation was its contribution to civilian predominance over the military in the American government; when the military themselves regarded strategy as narrowly military in content, their temptations to intervene in the making of national policy were proportionately small.

During the Cold War and especially after the Korean War, the belief that the United States was involved in a protracted conflict with international Communism led to a departure from historic habits and to an effort to form a national strategy for the employment of American power in defense and promotion of the country's political values and interests. The new national strategy would be not merely a military strategy but an all-inclusive planning for the use of the nation's total resources to defend and advance the national interests, encompassing military strategy and Clausewitz's use of combats along with other means. This determination to conceive and to act upon a national strategy prompted a flow of writing and criticism concerned with strategy, including its military aspects, that was unprecedented in American history. Although by the 1970s the bipolar confrontation between the United States and Soviet Russian Communism that produced the new interest in strategy and a new concern for a broad national strategy had given way to more complex power relationships, the perils of unstable world politics, an unstable balance of nuclear force, and "wars of national liberation" are more than ample to perpetuate strategic thought and writing as a thriving American industry.

The broadening of the American conception of strategy beyond a primarily military definition and the existence of a large and active circle of strategic writers distinguish the years since the Korean War from the earlier history of American military strategy and policy.

Before the Korean War, American writers on strategy were few and, with the conspicuous exception of Alfred Thayer Mahan, their strategic writings were of limited volume. Military policy is based upon two main elements, the structure of a nation's armed forces and the strategy of their use. American writing about military policy before 1950, again with the exception of the works of Admiral Mahan, almost wholly concerned the first element, the structure of the American armed forces, and neglected the second.

The great structural question throughout most of the history of American military policy was that of the proper form of military organization in a democratic society, approached through a running debate over the proper weights to give to citizen soldiers and to military professionals in the armed forces of the United States. Colonel and Brevet Major General Emory Upton wrote his highly influential book *The Military Policy of the United States* as though the only question of military policy was the structural one. There is not much about strategy in Upton's book.[5]

I have written about the structural aspects of the history of United States military policy in my earlier books. I now turn to the history of American strategic thought, or rather, to the history of American strategy; for the evolution of American strategy before the 1950s has to be traced less in writings about strategy than in the application of strategic thought in war. It has to be a history of ideas expressed in action. This book of history, like probably most histories that look back beyond only yesterday, is based on an assumption that what we believe and what we do today is governed at least as much by the habits of mind we formed in the relatively remote past as by what we did and thought yesterday. The relatively remote past is apt to constrain our thought and actions more, because we understand it less well than we do our recent past, or at least recall it less clearly, and it has cut deeper grooves of custom in our minds.

Through the earlier era when strategy meant in America mainly the use of combats to attain the objects of war, the principal object sought was simply military victory. For American strategists, the pursuit of military victory could cause perplexities enough. What was victory? Clausewitz stated that wars are of two kinds, those that seek the overthrow of the enemy, and those that seek merely to achieve some conquests on the frontiers of the enemy's country.[6] In the earlier wars of the United States, the nation was usually too weak to pursue more than the second, limited type of victory. The War of American Independence does not fit neatly into either of Clausewitz's categories, but it fits the second better than the first. It was an effort to strip away territory from the British Empire, albeit the very large territory inhabited by the American Revolutionaries, not to accomplish the utter overthrow of the enemy, a task that would have been fantastically far beyond the Americans' means. At that, the Americans' aim was very large and ambitious by the standards of contemporary European wars; in seeking the complete elimination of British power from North America, or if not from all of North America including Canada at least from the richest parts of the whole continent, the Americans of the Revolutionary generation offered a foretaste of the later American conception of war. As time went on and the military power of the United States grew greater, Americans with increasing frequency fought wars of Clausewitz's first type, to overthrow the enemy. Indian campaigns early encouraged the notion that the object of war is nothing less than the enemy's destruction as a military power. The Civil War tended to fix the American image of war from the 1860s into America's rise to world power at the turn of the century, and it also suggested that the complete overthrow of the enemy, the destruction of his military power, is the object of war.

As Clausewitz pointed out, even wars of the second type have tendencies to evolve toward the first type. Clausewitz defined war as "*an act of violence intended to compel our opponent to fulfill our will.*"[7] The extent of the violent effort required and of the opponent's resistance varies with the object being contested. But the tendency of war is to require that in order to impose one's will upon an opponent, the opponent must be disarmed.

> If our opponent is to be made to comply with our will, we must place him in a situation which is more oppressive to him than the sacrifice which we demand; but the disadvantages of this position must naturally not be of a transitory nature, at least in appearance, otherwise the enemy, instead of yielding, will hold out, in the prospect of a change for the better. . . . The worst condition in which a belligerent can be placed is that of being completely disarmed. If, therefore, the enemy is to be reduced to submission by an act of War, he must either be positively disarmed or placed in such a position that he is threatened with it.[8]

That is, he must be overthrown or threatened with being overthrown. Given this tendency even in limited, local wars, and given also the tendency of later American wars to be aimed candidly and from the outset at the overthrow of the enemy, the main problem of American strategists was usually that of encompassing the destruction of the enemy's armed forces. In the Indian wars, the Civil War, and then climactically in World War II, American strategists sought in actuality the object that Clausewitz saw as that of the ideal type of war, of war in the abstract: ". . . the destruction of the enemy's armed forces, amongst all the objects which can be pursued in War, appears always as the one which overrules all others." "The destruction of the enemy's military force, is the leading principle of War, and for the whole chapter of positive action the direct way to the object."[9]

Drawing in part upon Clausewitz's distinction between two kinds of war, the German military historian Hans Delbrück suggested that there are two kinds of military strategy: the strategy of annihilation, which seeks the overthrow of the enemy's military power; and the strategy of attrition, exhaustion, or erosion, which is usually employed by a strategist whose means are not great enough to permit pursuit of the direct overthrow of the enemy and who therefore resorts to an indirect approach.[10] In the history of American strategy, the direction taken by the American conception of war made most American strategists, through most of the time span of American history, strategists of annihilation. At the beginning, when American military resources were still slight, America made a promising beginning in the nurture of strategists of attrition; but the wealth of the country and its adoption of unlimited aims in war cut that development short, until the strategy of annihilation became characteristically the American way in war.

The destruction of the enemy's armed force and with it the complete overthrow of the enemy is clearly no modest aim in war. To aim at the overthrow of the enemy, said Clausewitz, is to "presuppose a great physical or moral superiority, or a great spirit of enterprise, an innate propensity to extreme hazards."[11] Once American military power became great enough to make the destruction of the country's enemies an object worth contemplating, a central theme of the history of American strategy came to be the problem of how to secure victory in its desired fullness without paying a cost so high that the cost would mock the very enterprise of waging war. But another main theme of this as of any history concerned with modern war must be the growing tendency, especially after the Napoleonic Wars, for a variety of technological and social developments to deprive warfare of its ability to produce decisions. When in the most recent American wars even limited victories have threatened to demand an intolerable cost—so far have the tendencies toward indecisiveness advanced—the use of combats has had to seem less and less a rationally acceptable means for the pursuit of national objects. To add nuclear weapons to the modes of combats would add whole new dimensions of futility. Unfortunately, the preservation of national values demands that the use of combats should still be contemplated by the makers of national strategy nevertheless.

For a research grant to aid in completing this book, I am indebted to the John Simon Guggenheim Memorial Foundation. For teaching schedules and a leave of absence that made possible its completion, I must thank Temple University. And on a second occasion, I am deeply indebted to the General Editor of the *Macmillan Wars of the United States*, Professor Louis Morton, for his encouragement and constructive criticism.

PART ONE

Waging War with Limited Resources, 1775-1815

There now is the fairest Opportunity of totally destroying the British Army. . . .

—*George Washington*[1]

1. A Strategy of Attrition: George Washington

In deliberating on this Question it was impossible to forget, that History, our own experience, the advice of our ablest Friends in Europe, the fears of the Enemy, and even the Declarations of Congress demonstrate, that on our Side the War should be defensive. It has even been called a War of Posts. That we should on all Occasions avoid a general Action, or put anything to the Risque, unless compelled by a necessity, into which we ought never to be drawn.

—*George Washington*[1]

THE MOST FAMILIAR visual depiction of Washington as a general is probably Emanuel Leutze's version of him, wrapped in muffler against freezing December as he crosses the Delaware on Christmas Day, 1776. Whatever documentary or esthetic misgivings the painting may occasion, its popularity is appropriate enough, for it suggests the essence of Washington's way of war, a strategy of attrition. The passage over the Delaware to raid the Hessian barracks at Trenton was the most successful single example of his chief stock in trade of active war, the erosion of the enemy's strength by means of hit-and-run strikes against his outposts.

Washington's was a generalship shaped by military poverty. When the British arrived by sea before New York in the summer preceding the Trenton raid, General William Howe brought against Washington's defenders of the city 31,625 soldiers of all ranks, 24,464 of them effectives fit for duty when the fighting for the city commenced, well equipped, and well trained and disciplined in the arts of eighteenth-century war. Behind Howe's soldiers stood a British fleet of ten ships of the line, twenty frigates, hundreds of transports, and 10,000 seamen, commanded by General Howe's very capable brother, affording the British general the privilege of descending wherever he chose upon the American coast.

For the defense of New York against this array, Washington was able to muster only 19,000 men, only 9,000 of them troops of the Continental Line possessing some small approximation of regular military skill and discipline (the most that could be squeezed from a Congressional authorization of 20,000 Continentals), the rest short-term militiamen. The Americans had no naval power for the protection of a city of islands, and their land forces were deficient in almost every kind of equipment. By Christmas Day and the Trenton raid, successive defeats and heavy casualties at the hands of the powerful British forces had combined with expiring enlistments to reduce to some 2,400 men the force that Washington could lead across the Delaware, though this small band was the principal embodiment of the military power of the American Revolution. The Trenton raid was a stroke of desperation designed to renew recruiting, which had shrunk almost to nothing, for by New Year's Day expiring enlistments were due to bring Washington's army down to about 1,500.

The dramatic elimination of the Hessian garrison at Trenton, with the capture of most of it, produced the results Washington desired. It stimulated enlistments enough to prevent the evaporation of the army, and it inspirited enough veteran soldiers to postpone their departure from the army to permit Washington to launch a second stroke across the Delaware into New Jersey. This second venture culminated in his crushing a British detachment at Princeton early in the new year, with further benefits both to enlistment and to American morale.

Nevertheless, through the remainder of the War of the Revolution, Washington and his generals continued never to have enough men or enough armaments. The loose Revolutionary confederation and the limited resources of a scattered agricultural economy could not supply either. Such armies as the Revolutionaries did succeed in mustering and equipping, furthermore, were never able to match the British consistently in the discipline required to stand up to the open-field exchanges of volleys and bayonet fighting which characterized eighteenth-century warfare. They could not match the well-drilled British in the battlefield maneuverability and tactical articulation of their battalions. These deficiencies persisted despite the strenuous efforts of the German drillmaster Baron Friedrich Wilhelm von Steuben to overcome them, beginning at Valley Forge in 1778, and despite the real improvements that Steuben effected. The American Revolutionary armies simply never had enough officers and NCOs themselves familiar with minor tactics to inculcate among the rank and file the tactical proficiency of the British. Therefore the American Revolutionary armies were never able to meet British armies of approximately equal size on equal terms on the battlefield.

Thus the strategy of the American armies in the Revolutionary War had to be a strategy founded upon weakness. The Commander in Chief of the Revolutionary armies, General George Washington, interpreted these conditions as imposing upon him a strategic paradox. His ultimate object as Commander in Chief must be to remove the British armies altogether from the insurgent provinces; no other military outcome would be consistent with the political goal of independence. Nevertheless, Washington believed that his military method must be that of a strategic defensive. The weakness of his armies was such that in general he could not even pursue a vigorous offensive in the more limited tactical realm, for even the tactical offensive meant a battlefield attack, which his soldiers usually could not win.

To find a way out of the paradox, Washington's hopes had to lie mainly not in military victory but in the possibility that the political opposition in Great Britain might in time force the British Ministry to abandon the conflict. At the beginning, Washington did not believe that he dared hope also for foreign intervention in the Revolution's behalf. To count on foreign aid would be to nourish possibly demoralizing delusions.[2] But to depend on Great Britain's losing patience meant depending on a protracted war, with consequent severe risks for the Revolutionary cause. The Americans might well lose patience before the British. Many years later, during the Second World War, General George C. Marshall, Jr., was to remark that "a democracy cannot fight a Seven Years War."[3] If protracted war would have strained the moral resources of the American government and people in General Marshall's time, the Revolutionary coalition of Washington's day was far less equipped to endure prolonged conflict. At best, it was an active minority of the American population that nourished the Revolutionary cause. The Continental Congress and the Revolutionary governments of the states possessed none of the reserves of public allegiance that long-established sovereignties may accumulate. General Washington himself was by nature an impatient man, and the temptation and pressure for him to seek an impetuous short-cut to victory were great. But Washington believed he must accept all the risks of protracted war, because American resources permitted no other way to lay the military foundation of political independence.

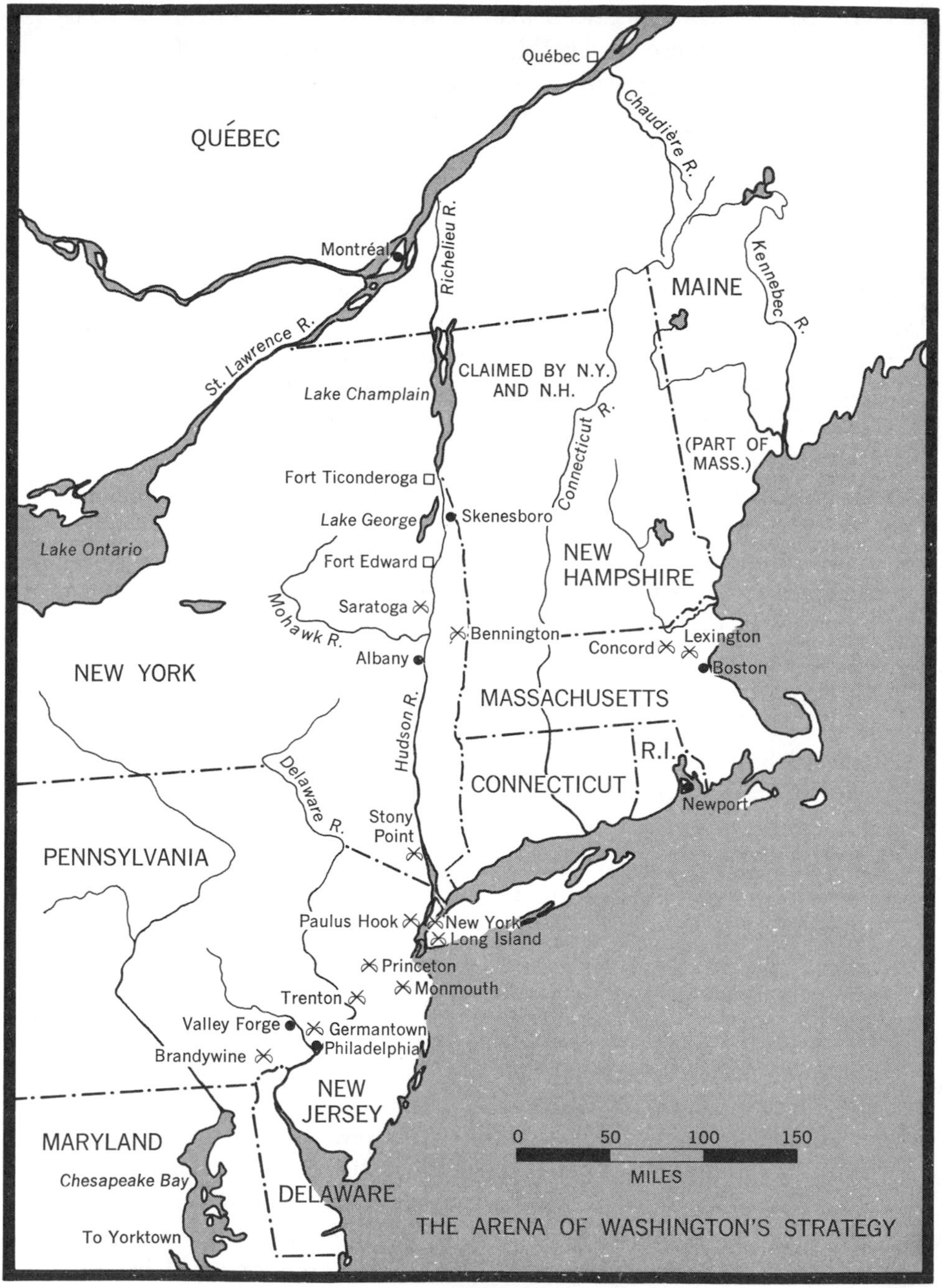
Québec
QUÉBEC
Chaudière R.
Montréal
Richelieu R.
Kennebec R.
MAINE
St. Lawrence R.
CLAIMED BY N.Y. AND N.H.
Lake Champlain
Connecticut R.
(PART OF MASS.)
Fort Ticonderoga
Lake George
Skenesboro
Lake Ontario
Fort Edward
NEW HAMPSHIRE
Mohawk R.
Saratoga
Bennington
Concord
Lexington
Albany
NEW YORK
Boston
MASSACHUSETTS
Hudson R.
Delaware R.
R.I.
CONNECTICUT
Newport
Stony Point
PENNSYLVANIA
Paulus Hook
New York
Long Island
Princeton
Monmouth
Trenton
Valley Forge
Germantown
Brandywine
Philadelphia
NEW JERSEY
MARYLAND
0
50
100
150
MILES
Chesapeake Bay
DELAWARE
To Yorktown
THE ARENA OF WASHINGTON'S STRATEGY

At first, to be sure, when revolution flared into war at Lexington and Concord, no strategy, Washington's or anybody else's, governed American military conduct; it flowed from the momentum of events. When the British garrison of Boston marched against the Massachusetts provincial military stores at Concord on April 18, 1775, the citizen-soldiers of the Massachusetts militia gathered to drive them back into the city. With conflict thus joined, the logic of the situation demanded that the Massachusetts forces remain in arms around the circumference of Boston in an effort to continue the confinement of the garrison there. Lest this Massachusetts effort fail and the British become free to ravage all New England, the other New England provinces in self-defense sent troops from their militia to join in the watch upon the Boston garrison. Without anyone's having planned it beforehand, the encirclement of the garrison became a siege.

When the Continental Congress in Philadelphia adopted the troops besieging Boston, sought to recruit reinforcements for them from provinces beyond New England, and named Washington Commander in Chief of the Continental Army, the siege of Boston persisted as the only evident strategy for the Americans to follow. At first there was no longer-range strategy or military policy, largely because in 1775 few Americans conceived of a long-range military problem. They hoped that the outbreak of open warfare in America would shock the British Ministry at once into efforts toward conciliation, and that consequently there would be no need for further campaigns after Boston.[4] Boston in its narrow peninsula was an uncomfortable and vulnerable place for the British to find themselves, however, and as the Americans persisted in the siege, the British decided to abandon the place. Their motive in the abandonment was not to yield up everything, as the Americans hoped, but to resume campaigning against the American rebels on more favorable ground.

While the siege of Boston was going on, circumstance and momentum led the Revolutionaries into another military effort, which constituted a more ambitious strategic offensive than it appears Washington would willingly have countenanced later in the war when he knew more about the relative merits of British and American battalions than he did at this early stage. The leaders of the Revolution tended to assume that given the opportunity, most Canadians would join in the effort to seek redress from the Crown. They tended to assume also that if resistance to Britain were to succeed anywhere in North America, it must succeed everywhere; a perpetual foothold of royal and ministerial power in Canada would leave self-government anywhere in America forever insecure. Therefore the Continental Congress urged and Washington joined in sponsoring a two-pronged Revolutionary march into Canada. Richard Montgomery would lead troops from Philip Schuyler's northern branch of the Continental Army down the Lake Champlain-Richelieu River route toward Montréal, while Benedict Arnold would command an expedition from Washington's main army up the Kennebec River and down the Chaudière toward Québec.[5]

In reality, Montgomery's and Arnold's expeditions proved to be overextensions of the Revolution's limited resources. They failed to precipitate a Canadian rebellion against the Crown, and they met military as well as political defeat. Their failure did much to crystallize in Washington's mind a conviction of the necessity to resign the cause to a defensive strategy. "By Reason of the Succession of Ills that has attended us" in Canada, he wrote to Major General Schuyler,

> I fear we must give up all Hopes of possessing that Country of such importance in the present Controversy, and that our Views and utmost Exertions must be turned, to prevent the Incursions of the Enemy into our Colonies. To this End, I must pray your strictest Attention and request that you use all the Means in your Power, to fortify and secure every Post and Place of Importance on the Communication.[6]

Fortifying and securing places of importance became Washington's own object of strictest attention. Hastened by the Americans' seizure of the commanding position of Dorchester Heights, the British carried out their resolve to evacuate Boston on March 17, 1776. Evidence soon accumulated that they would attempt their corollary resolve of resuming the war on better ground by means of an amphibious descent upon New York. Washington prepared to defend the city.

Except for the general idea of a strategic defensive based upon fortified posts and places of importance, Washington was still feeling his way toward the details of his military methods. In the spring and early summer of 1776 he did not yet think he knew, despite the failure of the Canadian campaign, what performance to expect of his men on the battlefield. The invaders of Canada had fought only small forces of British regulars, and the accounts of what had occurred in such encounters were unclear. The principal battle of the war thus far remained the action known as Bunker Hill, fought on June 17, 1775, just before Washington had joined the army around Boston.

There the British had allowed the Americans the privilege of fighting from behind earthworks, against which the redcoats hurled themselves in sacrificial frontal assaults. In these circumstances the Americans had performed well, holding on stoutly until an ammunition shortage obliged them to withdraw from the field. Bunker Hill encouraged Washington to believe that as long as he maintained a similar tactical as well as strategic defensive, he might hope to resist sucessfully the whole of any army the British were likely to mobilize against him, in spite of the obvious deficiencies of his troops in numbers, equipment, and training. Unfortunately for Washington, even this modest optimism was to prove unfounded; the British had so badly bungled their opportunities at Bunker Hill that the battle gave the Americans excessive hopes of what they could accomplish in full-scale battle as long as they stood on the tactical defensive.[7]

Washington could foresee that the next British move would be against New York, not only because he received hard evidence to that effect, but also because he recognized the nature of sea power enough to understand that if the British navy found a suitable base along the coast of the rebellious colonies, British sea power might permit the enemy to keep the Revolution constantly off balance by landing forces anywhere on the colonial coast. New York was the best harbor and base available. According to a strategic conception which was already taking shape in the minds of leaders on both sides, moreover, British possession of New York would also be a step toward dividing and thus perhaps fatally weakening the Revolution by separating New England, where Revolutionary sentiment was exceptionally strong, from the provinces farther south, where the spirit of rebellion was not so consistently powerful.[8]

Although Washington thus perceived the strategic advantages beckoning the British to take possession of New York, he perceived less clearly the advantages which sea power would afford the enemy in a contest for the capture of New York. Encouraged by Bunker Hill, he seems to have hoped his men would be able to hold the city from entrenchments against British attacks on the Bunker Hill model. He recognized only occasionally and ambiguously the dangers that the British would simply outflank any fortifications he might build, using their ships in the complex waterways system of New York harbor to go around his defenses. Obviously he knew that the British could sail into the rivers and bays around Manhattan and Long Island practically at will. He strengthened and built batteries of artillery overlooking various narrows, but soon after the enemy first arrived in the area, he had to report that two enemy ships had exhibited "a proof of what I had long most religiously believed; and that is, that a Vessel, with a brisk Wind and a strong Tide, cannot (unless by a chance Shott) be stopp'd by a Battery without you could place some obstructions in the Water to impede her Motion within reach of your Guns. . . ."[9] For various reasons, no obstructions were made ready or placed. In addition, Washington's intelligence sources informed him "from what they could collect from the conversation of Officers &ca. they [the British] mean to Hem us in by getting above us and cutting off all communication with the Country."[10] Nevertheless, Washington could also write that until his first setback in a land battle, "I had no doubt in my own mind of defending this place."[11]

The latter statement notwithstanding, perhaps Washington always merely hoped, rather than believed, that he could hold New York City, thinking wishfully because Congress apparently expected him to defend the place. Whatever their sources, all Washington's hopes for New York foundered. Sea power permitted the enemy to turn his defenses, and Bunker Hill proved to have been misleading evidence about American prowess in battle even when the British did offer Washington the opportunity to stand and fight on land. General William Howe chose to send his troops on an attack by land against the first line of Washington's defenses, along a ridge called the Heights of Guian on Long Island east of Gowanus Bay. Washington and his generals obtusely neglected to guard all the roads which led to the left and rear of the position, and the defense collapsed when it was assailed from three directions at once.

After the battle of Long Island, most of the fighting for New York had to be done without benefit of entrenchments, because the British refused to be drawn into another frontal assault like Bunker Hill and repeatedly turned such earthworks as Washington prepared. In these circumstances, the advantages of the tactical defensive were not enough to permit inexpert American soldiers to resist disciplined volley firing and bayonet charges from the British and their German mercenaries. Washington raged and desponded as he saw his men break and flee almost without a fight on Long Island and again at Kip's Bay on Manhattan. "Are these the men with whom I am to defend America?" he reportedly cried at Kip's Bay. "Good God, have I got troops such as those?" "Till of late," he wrote the president of Congress, "I had no doubt in my own mind of defending this place, nor should I have yet, if the men would do their duty, but this I despair of. . . ."[12]

So the British captured New York, and Washington concluded that not only must he fight on the strategic defensive, but that even on the tactical defensive he could not rely on his army against strong forces of the British. At Fort Washington on Manhattan Island on November 16, 1776, the very advantages of Bunker Hill did not suffice. With the Americans now discouraged by repeated defeat, the British overcame strong entrenchments and artillery with relative ease. "... Being fully persuaded that it would be presumption to draw out our Young Troops into open ground, against their Superiors both in number and Discipline; I have never spared the Spade and Pick Ax," Washington reported. He still met disappointment:

> I confess I have not found that readiness to defend even strong Posts, at all hazards, which is necessary to derive the greatest benefit from them. The honor of making a brave defence does not seem to be sufficient stimulus, when the success is very doubtful, and the falling into the Enemy's hands probable.[13]

After New York, therefore, Washington avoided confrontations with the main British army whenever he could do so. At the Brandywine in September, 1777, he had to fight a full-scale battle again, because the Revolutionary cause could not afford the ignominy of abandoning the Congressional capital at Philadelphia without a fight. Once more the advantages of the tactical defensive did not save Washington from losing the battle. Once more, as on Long Island, his own blunder of failing to protect an open flank contributed greatly to the result.

The battle of Brandywine was the only occasion between the campaign for New York City in 1776 and the end of the war when Washington risked his army in battle against the main British army commanded by Howe and later by General Sir Henry Clinton. His other battles, such as Trenton and Princeton, pitted his main force against only detachments of the enemy. Like Trenton and Princeton, Germantown and Monmouth were attacks by Washington's army against parts, not the whole, of Howe's and Clinton's forces, Germantown against Howe's outer defenses of Philadelphia, Monmouth against Clinton's rear guard. At Yorktown, Washington faced not the main British army in America but a weakened portion of their southern army, and he did so with French assistance by land and by sea which itself was strong enough to have overwhelmed Charles Lord Cornwallis.

After the contest for New York, indeed, Washington's first object in his defensive war was to defend not any geographical area or point but the existence of his army. He would shield the most important sections of the country as best he could, but the preservation of his army was a higher object. Washington concluded that if the army could be kept alive, the Revolutionary cause would also remain alive. Then in time it could be hoped that the British government would lose patience and abandon the war. But no other asset of the Revolutionary cause, certainly no city or even a province, seemed as necessary in Washington's view as the army.

Surely, cities and provinces would be lost anyway. With their sea power, as Washington recognized from the beginning, the British could descend anywhere upon the coast. To try to defend the whole Revolutionary seaboard would place Washington in the predicament which Major General Charles Lee had described when he attempted such a task in the Southern Department early in the war, before Washington's strategy had matured:

> I am like a Dog in a dancing school [Lee had said]. I know not where to turn myself, where to fix myself, the circumstances of the Country intersected by navigable rivers, the uncertainty of the Enemy's designs and motions, who can fly in an instant to any spot They choose with their canvass wings, throw me, or woud throw Julius Caesar, into this inevitable dilemma. I may possibly be in the North, when, as Richard says, I should serve my Sovereign in the West. I can only act from surmise, and have a very good chance of surmising wrong. . . .[14]

Or as Washington more succinctly put it: "The amazing advantage the Enemy derive from their Ships and the Command of the Water, keeps us in a State of constant perplexity and the most anxious conjecture."[15]

Therefore Washington abandoned any pretense of defending the whole coast. When state and local authorities felt threatened by British sea power and appealed to him for aid, he replied that they should build fortifications at the most critical places, and that to hold the fortifications and generally to protect themselves they must rely on their militia. Washington has often been quoted in disparagement of the part-time citizen soldiery of the militia, who were so likely to run away from open battle; but he commended the militia to the states as their best reliance against enemy incursions: "The Militia, Independent of other Troops, being more than competent to all the purposes of defensive war." He could not have believed this description, when he knew that his Continental Army though more thoroughly trained than the militia was hardly competent to all the purposes of defensive war. But he had no other choice, lest "by dividing the Army into small parties, we should have no place secure and guarded."[16]

Washington of course was not a soldier steeped in the literature of war. His knowledge of the principles of war derived almost entirely from direct observation and experience. As an alert participant on the British side in the French and Indian War, for example, he could hardly have failed to gain the appreciation of sea power which he acknowledged repeatedly during the Revolution, because it was British sea power that gave the British not only the raw strength to overcome the French in America but also the flexibility to assail them at every vulnerable point.

Though not a book-taught soldier, Washington nevertheless was a thoroughly conventional soldier in his efforts to adhere to the generally accepted and orthodox principles of war as understood in his times and by himself. While he commanded a revolutionary army, he never sought to wage a "revolutionary" kind of war, one which would overthrow the conventions of warfare itself. He tried to mold the Continental Army into as close an approximation of the British army as possible, and his methods of using his army were as orthodox as circumstances would permit. In particular, his conviction that to preserve the existence of his army must be his first object encouraged him in a thoroughly conventional belief that of the various principles governing warfare and strategy, the most important was the one which the twentieth century would call the "principle of concentration or mass":

> It is of the greatest importance to the safety of a Country involved in a defensive War [he said], to endeavour to draw their Troops together at some post at the opening of a Campaign, so central to the theatre of War that they may be sent to the support of any part of the Country, the Enemy may direct their motions against. It is a military observation, strongly supported by experience, "that a superior Army may fall a sacrifice to an inferior, by an injudicious division." It is impossible, without knowing the Enemy's intentions, to guard against every sudden incursion, or give protection to all the Inhabitants; some principal object shou'd be had in view, taking post to cover the most important part of the Country, instead of dividing our force, to give shelter to the whole, to attempt which, cannot fail to give the Enemy an Opportunity of beating us in Detachments, as we are under the necessity of guessing at the Enemy's intentions, and further opera-

> tions; the great object of our attention ought to be, where the most proper place is, to draw our force together, from the Eastward and Westward, to cover the Country, prevent the Enemy's penetration and annoy them in turn, shou'd our strength be equal to the attempt.[17]

"I cannot divide the Army," Washington said again, "not superior (from sickness and other causes equally painful when collected) to the Enemy's forces, into detachments contrary to every Military principle and to our own experience of the dangers that would attend it."[18]

The army must be kept undivided, but at the same time, and also for the army's preservation, general engagements with the enemy must be avoided, "since the Idea of forcing their lines or bringing on a General Engagement on their own Grounds, is Universally held incompatible with our Interest."[19]

Yet there remained the dangers implicit in protracted war, and the overriding problem of how to win the war and secure independence. The patience and endurance of the Revolution were far from limitless, and a mere passive defense might well cause American, not British, hope and endurance to collapse first. Washington believed he must do something more despite his army's weakness, to hasten the discouragement of the enemy and to stimulate confidence in his own cause. He could not emulate the recent campaigns of Frederick the Great of Prussia and mix major tactical attacks with the strategic defensive. That plan had carried even Prussia toward exhaustion until Frederick himself had gradually resorted to less vigorous methods, in a situation in which Frederick could call upon an army far more reliable in battle than Washington's but wherein his other weaknesses in resources and manpower resembled Washington's. Washington's program had to be less ambitious, but it had to be in some part a positive program nevertheless.

Washington's own impatient nature and combative temperament came into play. In his darkest hour of adversity, when after losing New York he retreated across New Jersey with his beaten army disintegrating around him from desertion and expiring enlistments, Washington never ceased to think of finding a way to strike back: "As nothing but necessity obliged me to retire before the Enemy, and leave so much of the Jerseys unprotected, I conceive it to be my duty, and it corresponds with my Inclination, to make head against them, as soon as there shall be the least probability of doing it with propriety. . . ." ". . . If we can collect our force speedily, I should hope that we may effect something of importance, or at least give such a turn to our Affairs as to make them assume a more pleasing aspect than they now have."[20]

From such aggressive determination finally came the movement of Christmas Day: "Notwithstanding the discouraging Accounts I have received from Col. [Joseph] Reed of what might be expected from the Operations below, I am determined, as the Night is favourable, to cross the River and make the attack upon Trenton in the Morning. . . ."[21]

It was to raids and attacks against detachments and outposts that Washington turned, a modest policy, but one which offered some satisfaction to his own and his country's aggressive impulses, and yet within the limits of the overall caution to which wisdom impelled him. To the extent that by such means Washington's strategy became at all an offensive strategy, it may be too much to call it even a strategy of attrition. Perhaps the phrase "strategy of erosion" would be more accurate; to wear away the resolution of the British by gradual, persistent action against the periphery of their armies was as much of an offensive purpose as Washington could afford.

To act offensively at all demanded the best possible intelligence system and rapid movement. To hit detachments and not the major strength of the enemy Washington must effect surprise. He must know the enemy's location and movements intimately, and the enemy must not know his. No general in American history has surpassed, and probably none has matched, the care and thought which Washington gave to his intelligence service. He was forever seeking out sources of information and good spies, he wove networks of his spies through the countryside, he diligently sought and studied maps, and he acted as his own chief intelligence officer, personally digesting the reports that came to his headquarters. This duty was one among an excessive multiplicity of staff functions that Washington imposed upon himself, but the intelligence service of the Continental Army unlike some later American intelligence agencies never suffered from a failure to communicate with the source of responsible action.

Washington enjoined a similar vigilance upon all his subordinate commanders. Typical is the directive to Brigadier General William Maxwell as Washington searched for the opportunity which was to materialize at Trenton:

> You are to be extremely vigilant and watchful to guard against surprizes, and to use every means in your power to obtain a knowledge

of the Enemy's Numbers, Situation, and designs. If at any time you should discover that they are moving from Brunswick and that Quarter towards Trenton, or the Delaware in other parts, endeavour, if it can be attempted with a probability of success, to fall upon their Rear, and if nothing more can be done, annoy them in their March.

Every piece of Intelligence which you may think of importance for me to know, communicate it without loss of time.[22]

To guard against surprise while surprising the enemy, swift movement was as necessary as good intelligence. Washington habitually insisted that his army begin its day's march early, while the enemy was still likely to be asleep in his camps. Later in the war he took a special interest in the development of light infantry formations especially designed to march fast and to hit and run quickly, encouraging his battalion commanders to detail their most alert and able soldiers into their light infantry companies and assembling the light infantry companies from the various battalions into a separate elite command.[23]

Washington has been criticized for neglecting the possibilities of cavalry for reconnaissance and raiding, and it is true that as an officer whose whole early military experience had been with infantry he neither created a strong cavalry force for his army nor made much use of the mounted troops who happened to come his way. The deficiencies in his use of cavalry are all the more regrettable and surprising because in theory he recognized its peculiar advantages for the very mode of war he felt obliged to adopt:

> The benefits arising from a superiority in horse, are obvious to those who have experienced them. Independent of such as you may derive from it in the field of action, it enables you, very materially, to controul the inferior and subordinate motions of an enemy, and to impede their knowledge of what you are doing, while it gives you every advantage of superior intelligence and, consequently, both facilitates your enterprizes against them and obstructs theirs against you. In a defensive war as in our case it is peculiarly desirable; because it affords great protection to the country, and is a barrier to those inroads and depredations upon the inhabitants, which are inevitable when the superiority lies on the side of the invaders.[24]

Washington was a conventional soldier in his efforts to make of the Continental Army a force modeled in organization, training, and tactics upon its British opponent, and in his efforts to husband the strength of his army through devout adherence to the principle of concentration. In his desire to compensate for inferiority by snapping at the enemy's outposts and flanks, however, he perceived and demonstrated the virtues of boldness and of the unconventional and unexpected.

> Enterprises which appear Chimerical [he said] often prove successful from that very Circumstance, Common Sense & Prudence will Suggest Vigilance and care, when the Danger is Plain and obvious, but when little Danger is apprehended, the more the enemy is unprepared and consequently there is the fain'd Prospect of Success.[25]

Trenton again offers the best illustration of this mode of war.

For all that, and for all the boldness and impatience of his own personality, Washington finally believed he must keep as his watchword—caution. He summed up his method of war when he wrote to Benedict Arnold about an attack Arnold was planning against the British in Newport:

> You must be sensible that the most serious ill consequences may and would, probably, result from it in case of failure, and prudence dictates, that it should be cautiously examined in all its lights, before it is attempted. Unless your Strength and Circumstances be such, that you can reasonably promise yourself a *moral certainty* of succeeding, I would have you by all means to relinquish the undertaking, and confine yourself, in the main, to a defensive operation.[26]

To be able to adhere to his own cautious advice despite all the pressures of circumstances, politics, and martial tradition probably made Washington precisely the right strategist for the American Revolution. But his cautious strategy of attrition or erosion did ensure a protracted war, and the protraction of the war itself posed so many perils for the Revolutionary cause that the question whether the Americans could find a more swiftly effective strategy had to be raised then and since.

2. A Strategy of Partisan War: Nathanael Greene

You see that we must again resume the partisan war.
—*Nathanael Greene*[1]

The Americans would be less dangerous if they had a regular army.
—*Frederick Haldimand*[2]

THE PARADOX of George Washington's mode of strategy ran deeper than its most obvious feature, the incongruity between a defensive strategy and the necessity to remove the British forces from North America in order to secure political independence. There existed a further incongruity between the eighteenth-century conventionality of the ideas about warfare entertained and applied by the wealthy and conservative Virginia gentleman turned Commander in Chief of a revolutionary army, and the incorrigibly revolutionary dimensions of the war in which Washington had to fight. For in terms of the eighteenth century's conceptions of war, the War of American Independence was indeed revolutionary. It is a commonplace of history, but a correct one, to assert that in Europe the eighteenth century was an age of limited war. Until the French Revolution at the end of the century, European armies of the period carefully restrained the destructiveness of war, and they did so because European statesmen restrained the aims of war. A variety of considerations, all involving the statesmen's and soldiers' awareness of the delicacy of the social fabric of Europe under the *ancien régime*, made European war in the eighteenth century habitually a contest for limited objectives of a fortress or province or two or of favorable dynastic alliance. The War of American Independence was revolutionary in the very scope of the Americans' objective: to eliminate British power completely from the vast extent of the thirteen rebellious colonies.

War in America had been diverging from the European pattern of limited war almost from the beginning of the American settlements. When the English colonists in America fought the Indians, they often fought in what both sides recognized as a contest for survival. In King Philip's War of 1675–76, the Indians came fearfully close to obliterating the New England settlements. When the colonists rallied to save themselves, they saw to it that their victory was complete enough to extinguish the Indians as a military force throughout the southern and eastern parts of New England, the heart of English settlement in the region. Not every Indian war was so overtly a struggle for existence as King Philip's War, because the limitations upon military power on both sides often prevented so complete a fulfillment of the logic of the contests between Indian and white societies. But the logic of a contest for survival was always implicit in the Indian wars, as it never was in the eighteenth-century wars wherein European powers competed for possession of fortresses and counties, but always shared an awareness of their common participation in one civilization, Voltaire's "Republic of Europe."[3]

In the American setting, even the contests among the European powers became less restrained than they had been in Europe. America was not Europe; when Great Britain, France, and Spain clashed in America, they struggled without the consciousness of a common interest in preserving the social fabric of the country where they fought that restrained them in Europe. When the powers fought each other in America, their governments in Europe took up some of their colonials' attitudes about the nature of warfare. Accustomed to thinking of warfare against the Indians as a struggle for existence, England's American colonists regarded the contest with New France in a similar light, believing that they could never be secure as long as they had to share North America with France, and that accordingly their security demanded the complete elimination of New France. After all, it was New France that supported the English colonists' mortal rivals among the Indians. Though seeking the removal of all the enemy's pieces from the board was alien to European warfare in the eighteenth century, London absorbed enough of the attitude of the American colonists to insist upon the extinction of New France in the Treaty of Paris in 1763.

In view of these tendencies of American warfare it was not surprising that in 1775 the rebellious colonists should have believed that they must bring Canada into their rebellion, that their success required the complete elimination of British power from all of North America, just as they had demanded and won the complete elimination of French power. If their resources proved inadequate for the conquest of Canada, still the Americans at least had to remove British power completely from the boundaries of their own provinces. Occasionally Washington himself perceived how truly revolutionary were the strategic implications of this grandiose political aim. The political aim suggested that the military power of Great Britain in America would have to be destroyed. In occasional moments of optimism, Washington responded by declaring the destruction of the British armies to be his objective. Intoxicated by his raids on Trenton and Princeton, he spoke briefly thereafter of hoping to give the enemy "a fatal Stab": "There now is the fairest Opportunity of totally destroying the British Army. . . ."[4]

Washington was too sober and conventional a soldier to entertain such optimism for long. He soon reverted to his strategy of attrition, based on the strategic defensive but hoping gradually to wear out British patience with the help of hit-and-run raids. If the objective of the War of American Independence was so unconventional and revolutionary by European standards, however, involving as it did not the accession or loss of a fortress or a province but of a whole empire, did not the objective suggest that the Americans' method of warfare ought to be revolutionary as well? Washington's application of a conventional mode of war, the application of a strategy of attrition by a conventionally trained and organized army (but an army inferior in these attributes to its opponents), ran so many risks that the method of war might prove incommensurate with the objective and that the Americans might give up before the British did, that other American leaders wondered whether they might not devise a less conventional method of war, more suited to the revolutionary dimensions of the American objective.

In the later years of the war, Washington found decreasing opportunities to employ his limited offensive raids. From the summer of 1778 until he moved southward against Lord Cornwallis in the early fall of 1781, his army and the main British army glowered at each other much but fought little, Clinton's British in their sea-girt haven at New York, Washington's Americans in their watching positions among the highlands of New Jersey and the Hudson. Washington repeated the Trenton strategy with the bayonet attack of Anthony Wayne's light infantry against Stony Point in July, 1779, and Henry Lee's similar raid against Paulus Hook the following month; but the cautious Sir Henry Clinton gave him few such opportunities.

On the other hand, Clinton by sitting securely in New York was of course accomplishing little except to hold a single American city. His situation suggests a British poverty in strategic conception comparable to the material poverty of the Americans. After France in 1778 and Spain in 1779 joined the war against Great Britain, the British had to treat the American mainland as a secondary theater. Since their global triumph in the Seven Years War, they had complacently allowed their naval strength to wither so badly that the Admiralty could no longer guarantee the home islands against invasion when threatened by the combined fleets of the Bourbon monarchies. In addition, Britain had to look to the defense of her West Indian possessions, lest her troubles in North America be compounded by loss of her island empire there to Bourbon naval power. In these circumstances, the British army in North America received few reinforcements after 1778, and Clinton's quiescence in New York in consequence was partly forced upon him. Nevertheless, it is not especially probable that Clinton would have accomplished much more without the problems of the French intervention, because bolder British generals had been able to do little more in the earlier years of the American war, when London had been generous with reinforcements and had urged the hastening of the war for the very purpose of winning it before France should come in.

Yet even before France compelled the British to turn much of their military attention away from North America, finding a design for victory over the American rebels eluded them. There was much to be said for Washington's belief that the essential element in keeping the Revolution alive was the existence of the Continental Army. The best British strategy therefore might have been to utilize superior skill and numbers to press Washington's army to destruction. General William Howe indeed began the New York-New Jersey campaign of 1776 with expressions of an intent to win decisive victories over the rebel army remarkable in light of the conventions of eighteenth-century warfare. For whatever reason, however, such an intent disappeared immediately from Howe's practice; perhaps he was stultified by his and his brother Vice Admiral Richard Lord Howe's belief that they must conciliate the rebels as well as fight them. The

New York-New Jersey campaign became less an effort to eliminate the rebel army than simply an exercise in occupying places. In the Philadelphia campaign of the following year, General Howe again sacrificed possible large strategic advantages—this time in connection with the simultaneous British invasion of the colonies from Canada—in pursuit of occupying a place.[5]

In Philadelphia, Howe took the Congressional capital and the most populous city in the rebellious colonies; but Philadelphia was not a capital city in the European sense, and the political damage that its capture inflicted upon the Revolutionary cause was minimal. For the British to occupy places might deprive the rebels of resources useful in supporting the rebel armies. But the American economy was exceedingly amorphous. To occupy the whole country or even a major part of it was beyond the British army's means, and short of that there were no vital places. The Americans were so poverty-stricken militarily that they could not be made much poorer. They could find foodstuffs for their small armies almost anywhere in an agricultural country, albeit transportation and distribution were so bad that the soldiers often came near to starving anyway. Clothing depended on scattered home industries—usually, that is, on the rebel soldier's own resources. Manufactories of weapons and powder were small and scattered, and the best sources were not anywhere in America but in France. British sea power, however formidable in comparison with anything the Americans could generate, was not sufficient to deny such imports all along the American coastline, much less so after France openly joined in the war.

Lacking strategically vital geographic objectives whose seizure might produce indirectly the destruction of the American armies, the British tended to occupy places for vaguer reasons. Their fascination with the old Champlain-Hudson route between Canada and the seaboard colonies offers an example. Probably because the route had figured so prominently in the French wars, British leaders began to think about using it again early in the contest with the rebellious colonies. Unfortunately for the British, however, going south over this route led to no objective comparable in strategic importance to Montréal and Québec, and not more readily accessible directly from the ocean. The rationale which the British gradually developed for going south from Canada to the Hudson and New York was that such a march would divide New England, the heart of the rebellion, from the colonies farther south, and by dividing the rebellion it would go a long way toward ending it. No doubt British control of the whole

Lake Champlain-Hudson River line would have imposed a severe setback to the Revolution if the British had been able to effect it. But the setback would not have been likely to be fatal, because the British could hardly have held the line in enough strength to prevent the Americans from continuing to cross it to the limited extent that was essential. The gains to be anticipated from an invasion of the rebellious colonies via the Lake Champlain-Hudson River route were in fact far from commensurate with the risk that the whole expedition might be lost in a hostile country affording few supplies. In the old French wars, the most difficult part of the invasion route, the wooded, inhospitable, largely overland trek between Albany and navigation on Lake George or Lake Champlain, had lain in British hands. Now a British invading army would have to make this part of the journey through a country full of enemies and with the line of communications already stretched dangerously long and thin.

The effort offered the rebels an opportunity to improvise less conventional modes of warfare than those practiced by General Washington. In the third week of June, 1777, a British force of about 10,000 under Major General John Burgoyne started out from St. Johns on the Richelieu for Lake Champlain. The invasion began well, with a rapid and cheap capture of the American fort at Ticonderoga, which the rebels had deluded themselves into regarding as a kind of Gibraltar of the North. Thereafter, however, Burgoyne soon ran into trouble, for the American General Schuyler diligently obstructed the already bad roads between Lake Champlain and the Hudson with entanglements of felled trees, which slowed the British pace from Skenesboro to Fort Edward to a mile a day. British invasion so close to the New England hotbed of rebellion, along with reports of atrocities by Burgoyne's Indian allies such as the Jane McCrea murder, brought out swarms of rebel irregulars. Some joined the main Northern Army; when Schuyler gave way to Major General Horatio Gates in its command, the change especially pleased and encouraged the New Englanders, among whom Gates was popular. Others hovered around Burgoyne's line of march to wage an unconventional, no-holds-barred campaign of harassment against his outposts and supplies. Already moving too slowly through desolate country, Burgoyne was soon within sight of the exhaustion of his provisions. An American army which seemed to the British to have sprung full-blown from the countryside eliminated a sideshow that was supposed to have helped Burgoyne, Lieutenant Colonel Barry St. Leger's advance toward Albany from the west. Another American force of the same kind, materializing out of the New England hills, practically wiped out two large detachments sent by Burgoyne on a provisioning raid toward Bennington, Vermont.

By mid-September, Burgoyne's army was so depleted (to about half its original numbers) and so exhausted from lack of supplies and fending off harassment all around it, that Gates with about 7,000 men dared to take a stand blocking further movement south, from a fortified position on Bemis Heights overlooking the Hudson. By now Burgoyne was desperate; he had hoped to be met around Albany by a friendly column moving up from New York City, but the government in London had neglected to coordinate its armies in America, and Sir William Howe was away to the south for his Philadelphia campaign instead. Two efforts to break Gates's defenses, the battles of Freeman's Farm and Bemis Heights, produced only further losses for Burgoyne, including some of the best of his subordinate leaders. After the second effort, on October 7, the British army was down to a bare three weeks' food supply even by calculating for very short rations. The American irregulars around Burgoyne's flanks and in his rear were threatening to recapture Ticonderoga and thus extinguish the last faint hope of resupply. On October 17, Burgoyne surrendered all that remained of his army to Gates at Saratoga. The principal cause of his ruin was his own and London's misconceived strategy, the march to nowhere through the wilderness south of Lake Champlain. What a later generation would call a "guerrilla war" by American irregulars had then exploited the strategic mistake to deliver Burgoyne's army into the hands of Gates's American army.[6]

The idea of cutting off New England from the rest of the rebellion and thus possibly killing rebellion elsewhere through lack of nourishment was related to another hope of British strategy. This was to place the British army in contact with those reservoirs of loyalty which the British felt sure must exist somewhere in America, so that the army could release the streams of loyalism to flow once more throughout the country. The search for a reservoir of loyalism apparently had been one of the motives for Sir William Howe's insistence on going to Philadelphia in 1777 rather than northward toward Burgoyne. Lacking a design for the destruction of the Revolutionary armies, even by indirect means, and lacking a better rationale for the mere occupation of places, the British from beginning to end hoped that by occupying *some place*, sooner or later they would find themselves welcomed and surrounded by Loyalists, who, encouraged by their presence, would begin the work of dissolving the opinions from which the Revolution had sprung.

Whatever the strength of loyalism might have been, a question which is still arguable, there was never enough of it to permit the British to stimulate this sort of response. They found heartening numbers of Loyalists when they took New York, and heartening numbers again when they took Philadelphia, but the Loyalists who welcomed them were incapable of initiating a broad reversal of American opinion. The nearest approach to success in the British search for the great reservoir of loyalism developed in the southern colonies, where the British did approach tantalizingly close to subduing the Revolution in several provinces. There, however, they were checked by the development to much fuller fruition of the possibilities for irregular war which the Americans had opened in the Saratoga campaign, nourished by an American strategist far subtler than General Washington.

After Burgoyne's surrender and Sir Henry Clinton's retreat from Philadelphia to New York reduced the northern war to virtual stalemate, the British decided to exploit their control of the sea to a greater extent than they had previously done and to send expeditions to the South. In the southern colonies, they soon discovered to their gratification that acute divisions between upcountry areas and tidewater over local political issues had produced unusually strong Loyalist factions, largely because the Revolution tended to be identified with the lowcountry politicians who sponsored it in the region, while the upcountry distrusted everything associated with the lowcountry.[7]

In late 1778 and early 1779 the British army reconquered thinly populated Georgia, a place where Revolutionary sentiment had always appeared brittle. On May 12, 1780, Clinton, come down from New York and acting jointly with Vice Admiral Marriot Arbuthnot, captured Charleston (until 1782 called Charles Town), and with it the whole of the main Revolutionary army in the South. Major General Benjamin Lincoln had foolishly allowed himself to be persuaded to keep this army in the city. A few days later Lieutenant Colonel Banastre Tarleton's British and Loyalist Legion defeated and dispersed a Revolutionary cavalry command at the Waxhaws settlement near the border between the two Carolinas, and with these events organized resistance to British power south of Virginia became almost extinct. The British army could now do what had never been possible in the North because there the presence of Washington's army had always forbidden wide dispersal. The British scattered their forces among a series of outposts from Charleston, Georgetown, and Beaufort on the coast of South Carolina through Camden and Rocky Mount to Ninety-Six on the western frontier, to restore and maintain the king's peace through the whole colony.

But unwonted success so infatuated both British and Loyalists that they took steps tending toward giving away the game after all. Because Loyalist sentiment had always been relatively strong in the South, the southern Revolutionaries may have been especially cruel in their harassment and repression of Loyalists as long as they had the power. The Loyalists in turn now seized the advantage of British occupation to take reprisals in violence against both persons and property. The British set them a bad example, beginning with Colonel Tarleton, who made the phrase "Tarleton's quarter" a byword by permitting his men to slaughter rebels who asked for quarter at the Waxhaws. On his way into the interior, Tarleton burned the settlement belonging to Thomas Sumter, a retired Revolutionary colonel, and thereby pushed Sumter back into active opposition to the Crown. Though the southern Scotch-Irish had often been indifferent to the war, the British angered them with a policy of deliberate hostility to the Presbyterian church, motivated by the assumption that dissenters must necessarily be rebels. Clinton acted further to force a clear choice between rebellion and loyalty, when many would have preferred neutrality, by ending a system of parole for rebels and promising punishment as enemies to any South Carolinians who failed to affirm complete loyalty. Under circumstances in which both British and Loyalist soldiers mixed indiscriminate looting with pretenses of legal seizures, Clinton's policy perversely encouraged a return to rebellion.

Parties of armed Revolutionaries coalesced and grew in havens in the sparsely populated clay hills, and they began to descend upon Loyalist outposts. The British and Loyalists responded with reprisals which provoked further restlessness. A Revolutionary convention elected Thomas Sumter brigadier general of militia, and Sumter responded by leading an attack on Rocky Mount, one of the Crown's principal garrisons. Repulsed there, he succeeded nevertheless in destroying a strong Loyalist camp at Hanging Rock. Much of South Carolina began to flare into guerrilla war. Bands of rebels converged on horseback to strike enemy outposts, then used the hard clay-and-sand roads to ride away and scatter in the abundant forests before any enemy, especially infantry, could catch them.[8]

These developments were highly exasperating to the British, the more so because their cause in the South seemed otherwise so hopeful. But the Revolutionaries were mounting only the first, preliminary phase of a guerrilla campaign, that of scattered terrorism; they can hardly be said to have had as yet a strategy; and whether they could do more was doubtful. Few guerrilla campaigns have progressed farther than the phase of terrorist raids without the assistance of at least a semblance of an organized army, which even if much weaker than the enemy's army can prevent the enemy from dispersing enough to hunt down and destroy the guerrillas. When the South Carolina Revolutionaries began their "partisan campaign"—to use the eighteenth-century term which approximates our "guerrilla war"—no organized Revolutionary army existed in the South. Major General Baron Jean de Kalb was on his way southward with a detachment from Washington's army, but the disaster of Lincoln's surrender of Charleston impelled Congress to send the victor of Saratoga, Horatio Gates, to take command instead, with orders to engage in industrious recruiting. Gates brought on a fresh disaster, by facing the British under Cornwallis in battle rashly and prematurely and throwing still another army away, at Camden on August 16, 1780.[9]

Camden left the Revolutionary cause in the South more hopeless than before, and the partisans of Sumter and similar chieftains apparently with less chance for organized support. Two days after Camden, indeed, Tarleton followed up by surprising Sumter in his camp at Fishing Creek, killing 150 of his men, wounding 300, and scattering the rest. When news of these events reached Europe, the foreign minister of France suggested that his American allies would have to make peace with Great Britain on the basis of *uti possidetis*, with the southernmost colonies in British possession.[10]

Fortunately for the Revolution, Congress now deferred to Washington's judgment by sending Major General Nathanael Greene to command the Southern Department in Gates's stead. Fortunately, too, the possibilities raised by the partisan bands were kept alive after Camden and Fishing Creek by the rise to prominence of another partisan leader more capable than Sumter, possessed of a superior sense of strategy and a superior willingness to cooperate with other leaders, the "Swamp Fox" Francis Marion. Meanwhile, the Revolutionary cause in the South received a moral stimulus when it needed it most and from an unanticipated direction. The British, more confident than ever after Camden and Fishing Creek, prepared to carry the war into North Carolina and perhaps even to the settlements beyond the Appalachian Mountains; but boastful threats about their

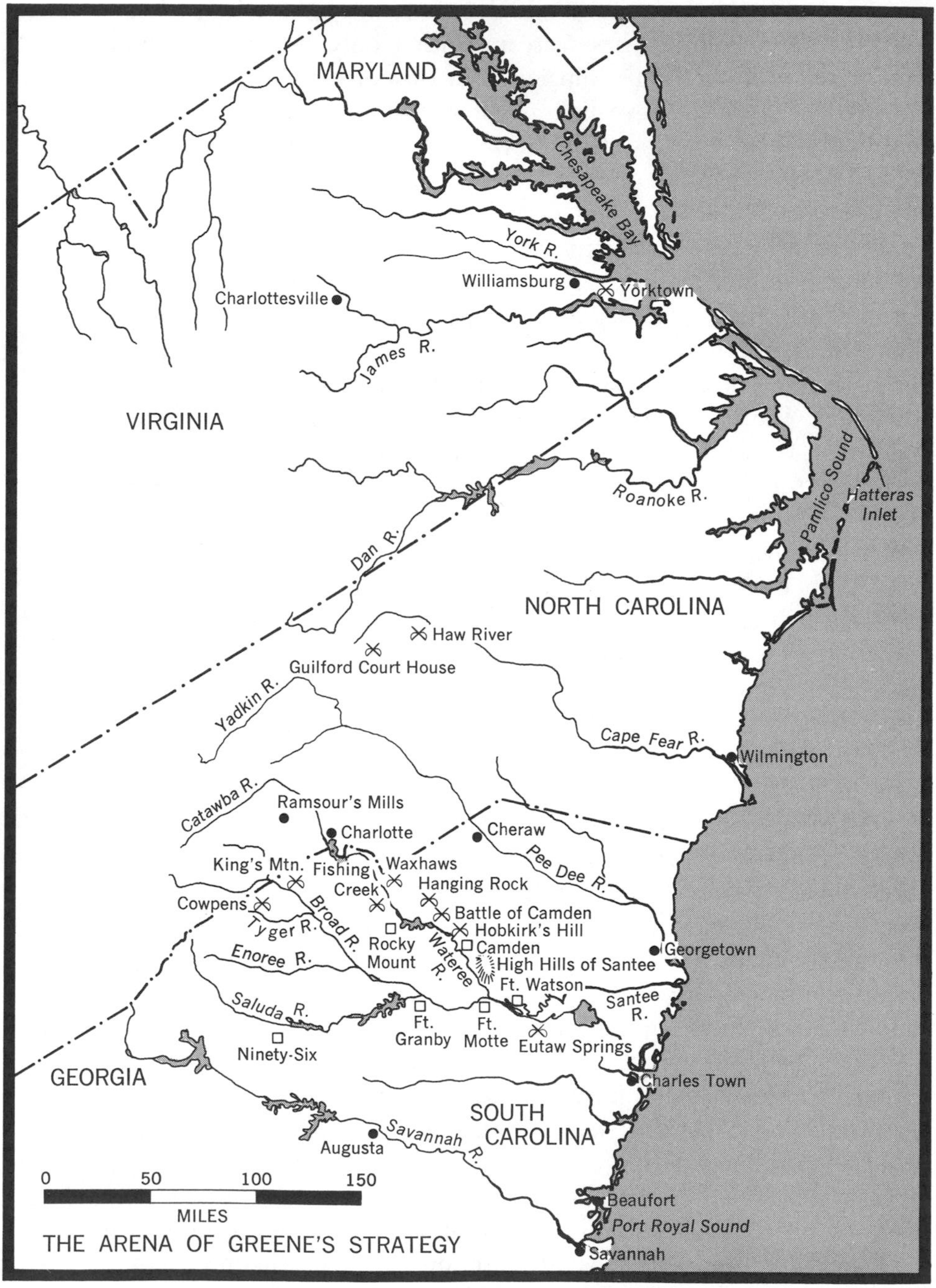
MARYLAND
Chesapeake Bay
York R.
Williamsburg
Yorktown
Charlottesville
James R.
VIRGINIA
Roanoke R.
Pamlico Sound
Hatteras Inlet
Dan R.
NORTH CAROLINA
Haw River
Guilford Court House
Yadkin R.
Cape Fear R.
Wilmington
Catawba R.
Ramsour's Mills
Charlotte
Cheraw
Pee Dee R.
King's Mtn.
Fishing Creek
Waxhaws
Hanging Rock
Cowpens
Battle of Camden
Hobkirk's Hill
Tyger R.
Broad R.
Rocky Mount
Wateree R.
Camden
Georgetown
Enoree R.
High Hills of Santee
Ft. Watson
Santee R.
Saluda R.
Ft. Granby
Ft. Motte
Eutaw Springs
Ninety-Six
GEORGIA
Charles Town
SOUTH CAROLINA
Augusta
Savannah R.
0 50 100 150
MILES
Beaufort
Port Royal Sound
Savannah
THE ARENA OF GREENE'S STRATEGY

intentions provoked the over-mountain men to hasten into the Carolinas to forestall them. Joining with Revolutionary partisans from both Carolinas, the over-mountain men and their comrades visited astonishing and complete destruction upon the westernmost British flank force in the region at the battle of King's Mountain on October 7, 1780. They killed Major Patrick Ferguson, a famous British rifleman, with 157 of his Loyalist force and captured the rest, about 800.

Greene gathered up the remnants of Gates's command and restored their energies as best he could by camping in a productive and friendly district around Cheraw Hill, just below the border between the two Carolinas. He had little more than a thousand men, Continentals and militia, and far fewer of any proven reliability in combat. He promptly began to demonstrate his unorthodoxy as a strategist, however, by violating the principle of concentration, so dear to Washington, dividing his army into three parts in the face of an already more numerous and otherwise superior enemy under Cornwallis (Clinton having returned to New York). Greene dispatched Brigadier General Daniel Morgan with about 600 men toward the west to operate in the vicinity of the British outpost at Ninety-Six. Lieutenant Colonel Henry Lee—"Light Horse Harry"—with his Legion of 280 horse and foot went eastward to cooperate with Francis Marion along the coast. With recruits and militia increments, Greene's total strength grew enough so that a few hundred men formed around the commanding general in the center.

Washington could never have attempted a similar dispersion, in the unlikely event that the idea would have appealed to him, because he did not have the partisan bands whom Greene counted on to keep the enemy enough off balance and hindered in his movements and supply to prevent the American dispersion from becoming suicidal. In part, the motive for Greene's unorthodox distribution of his forces was nothing more complex than the idea that with provisions scarce, three scattered detachments could subsist more easily than one concentrated force. More than that, however, Greene was not only depending upon the partisan bands to help protect him from disaster but exploiting their presence to move toward a strategy of unconventional war, in which he would set orthodox military dicta such as the principle of concentration on their heads. By violating the principle of concentration, Greene tempted Cornwallis to violate it also, and thus he might make the British army still more vulnerable to partisan harassment and to encounters with his own force, which was not strong enough for a major battle but which might like Washington's army be able to beat up detachments.

If Cornwallis now persisted in his evident design to advance the area of British reconquest into North Carolina, Morgan might take advantage of his northward march to capture Ninety-Six. Following upon King's Mountain, an American seizure of Ninety-Six could well raise all of western South Carolina into rebellion again. If on the other hand Cornwallis led his whole force against Morgan, then Greene, Lee, and Marion would be able to threaten Charleston. In this dilemma of Greene's devising, Cornwallis decided to divide his own force, keeping part of it in hand to watch Greene, while Tarleton moved westward with about half the force to deal with Morgan.

The outcome must have surpassed Greene's highest hopes. Daniel Morgan happened to be a superb battle captain, an inspiring leader who was able to draw from his troops battlefield performances unexcelled and perhaps unequalled by any other officer of the American cause. His force augmented by militia to about 1,040, Morgan allowed Tarleton to bring him to battle on January 17, 1781, at a place called the Cowpens. Morgan cleverly got the best out of his militia by assuring them that they would be allowed to fall back to a safe, prepared position after they had fired off a couple of good shots each. In the sequel, he won the clearest American battlefield victory of the war in a combat involving regular British forces. Tarleton lost some nine-tenths of his men in killed and wounded. The reputation he had gained at the Waxhaws and against Sumter fell deflated, and the Revolution in the South gained renewed encouragement beyond measure.[11]

By the time the battle occurred, Cornwallis had grown so nervous over the division of his forces that he was on the march to rejoin Tarleton, judging rightly that the most Greene could do against Charleston after all was to bluff. Reinforced by 1,500 men from Clinton's northern army, Cornwallis was again considerably stronger than Morgan and Greene combined, and his march placed Morgan in peril of being cornered by an army far too powerful for his magic to overcome. On the day of Cowpens, Cornwallis was as close as Morgan to the best route between Morgan and Greene, and three rivers, the Broad, the Catawba, and the Pee Dee, lay between the two principal American forces.

Nevertheless, Morgan decided he must hasten toward Greene; and Greene, learning of Morgan's situation, left his own force to ride cross-country for a meeting with Morgan to arrange a converging march of their two corps. Cornwallis missed his best chance to catch Morgan when he wrongly assumed his quarry would pause for breath at the scene of the Cowpens victory and directed his army thither. Discovering his error, the British general angrily destroyed all impediments to a swift march—all rations except such as the men could carry in their haversacks, all tents, all wagons except a handful for ammunition and hospital stores—and set out from Ramsour's Mills determined to run the rebels into the ground. Cornwallis possessed a quality hitherto rarely displayed by British generals in this war, a thirst for battle. He felt sure that if he could only compel the Revolutionaries to meet him in open combat, he could destroy them.

When Greene learned that Cornwallis had burned his stores, he is supposed to have exclaimed, "Then, he is ours!" The partisans would see that Cornwallis found no more, unless he returned to the coast. Against the advice of Morgan, who proposed taking refuge in the mountains to the west, Greene determined to lead Cornwallis on as long a chase as possible, northward across the Carolinas and their rivers, northward if need be into Virginia, until Cornwallis would regret the destruction of his stores and without them, and with the partisans biting at his heels and closing the country behind him, would exhaust himself.

The season was propitious for Greene's design. It was January 27 when Cornwallis began his chase, and cold rains were swelling the rivers and making quagmires of the clay roads. The immediate problem for Greene was to keep his own and Morgan's men, never well supplied, from falling into exhaustion first, in which case Cornwallis would catch them and force the battle he wanted. But if the Revolutionaries could remain ahead of the British into Virginia, in that state Greene would find provisions and reinforcements, and then he might be ready to let Cornwallis have his battle.

So began the race to the Dan River. Across the Catawba and the Yadkin, Cornwallis pursued Greene and Morgan, whose forces reunited at Guilford Court House. Sometimes Cornwallis drove his men thirty miles a day in bitter weather, over badly broken roads that froze by night and thawed by day. Repeatedly Greene's rear guard had to stand to prepare to fight, and several times the weary rearguard pickets barely escaped destructive surprise at the hands of the British van, led by a resentful Tarleton. Yet always Greene managed to keep his men just out of reach, and at the Dan River the fords were flooded, but Greene had boats awaiting him. The British covered forty miles in the last twenty-four hours before they reached the Dan, but the American rear guard marched the same distance in sixteen hours, and on February 14 the Americans escaped. Cornwallis's army arrived at the Dan worn to a frazzle, 500 men of 2,500 having dropped out since Ramsour's Mills, haversacks empty, and the Carolina partisans stripping away provisions from the countryside in their rear.

Cornwallis took what consolation he could in raising the royal standard over North Carolina, but it was small comfort. Almost immediately, raiders returning from across the Dan were joining the partisans in snapping at the British outposts. At the Haw River, Light Horse Harry Lee bushwhacked and massacred some 400 Loyalist recruits on their way to join Cornwallis. Continental recruits and Virginia and North Carolina militia raised Greene's numbers to about 4,300, against slightly more than 2,000 with Cornwallis. Greene decided to give battle, on the theory that he could hardly lose. If Cornwallis should win a tactical victory, he was already so far gone in exhaustion that it would probably hurt him almost as much as a defeat.

Greene recrossed the Dan to challenge Cornwallis at Guilford Court House. Here Cornwallis attacked him on March 15. The British army was no longer what it had been when it left Ramsour's Mills, but it remained an army of veteran soldiers against a force fewer than one-fourth of whom had previously seen combat. In part, Cornwallis's confidence in his veterans was vindicated and his thirst for battle slaked as he would have wished. Despite respectable fighting by most of the Americans and a superb fight by Greene's Continentals of the Maryland Line against the "Brigade of Guards," the best of Cornwallis's army, the Americans had to abandon the field.[12]

Nevertheless, Guilford also vindicated Greene's willingness to risk a battle. In capturing the battlefield, Cornwallis suffered 532 casualties, including almost 150 killed. He remained without adequate sustenance, and with his strength so low and the partisans as well as Greene in the field against him, he could not detach parties to forage. Nor could he gamble on another battle, lest even another tactical victory reduce him to impotence. He retreated to the Cape Fear River, to Wilmington, and to the ocean, where the succor of British sea power awaited him.

Greene marched forthwith into South Carolina. There British and Loyalist detachments remained scattered in the garrisons which had been established to keep the province pacified, spread all the way from Charleston to Ninety-Six. When they had formed the garrisons, the British could afford to disperse, because no American army had existed in the South to threaten them; there had been nothing but the beginnings of partisan resistance. Now Greene arrived with his American army, and it was Cornwallis's British army that was far distant. Greene was ready to gobble up the British outposts one by one and thus accomplish the reconquest of South Carolina.

The British actually had 8,000 soldiers in the province, but they were unlikely to be able to concentrate freely enough and rapidly enough to prevent Greene's beating them in detail. Greene chose as his first target the central post at Camden, which controlled communication between the coast and the West. Cornwallis made no effort to interfere; by the time his battered army might have been ready to respond, Greene was already too close to Camden. Either the British force there would be able to resist him, or Cornwallis would arrive too late to help anyway. Cornwallis decided not to return to South Carolina at all. Despite all the bright prospects with which the campaign there had begun, it had left the earl's army a ruin, and the British commander chose to make his next moves into Virginia instead. In Virginia, he could tell himself, he would be striking against a nest of rebellion almost as incorrigible as Massachusetts. He would be disrupting the principal source of Greene's supplies. And he would have the advantage also of operating in a country of deep tidal estuaries, where the Royal Navy should be always at hand.

Cornwallis's departure left a young nobleman of twenty-six, Lieutenant Colonel Francis Lord Rawdon, in command of the British field forces in South Carolina. Like Cornwallis, Rawdon was destined for a later career as an empire builder in India, and already he was a worthy antagonist.[13] But he was perhaps too youthfully aggressive a soldier for the occasion, for like Cornwallis he felt a thirst for battle otherwise rare among British officers. When Greene, with about 1,400 men, halted before Camden to await reinforcements from the partisans before taking on Rawdon's strong defensive works, Rawdon moved out from the works to mount a surprise attack against Greene's position at Hobkirk's Hill, on April 25. He succeeded in driving the Americans from the field. He also suffered losses so heavy that he decided he must evacuate Camden after all and direct the evacuation also of Ninety-Six and Fort Granby, the link between Camden and Ninety-Six, in order to collect from the garrisons a field force sufficient to handle Greene.

Unfortunately for Rawdon, the outposts had not prevented the partisans from gaining enough control of the countryside to forestall this effort. The British had fallen entrapped into the dilemmas of a war of posts conceived as a counter to a guerrilla campaign. Their posts had never been numerous enough really to control the country, because partisan raids on the smaller posts had compelled them to consolidate into fewer and larger garrisons. But the larger garrisons, too few to check the partisans' maraudings, were themselves too small against a reasonably strong field force. While Greene was facing Rawdon in the Hobkirk's Hill campaign, Francis Marion and Light Horse Harry Lee were capturing Fort Watson and Fort Motte nearer the coast. Rawdon's order to evacuate Fort Granby miscarried into partisan hands—the consequence of Revolutionary control of the countryside—and Lee captured both fort and garrison, while Sumter was taking another post at nearby Orangeburg. While Marion captured Georgetown on the coast and Lee took Augusta, Georgia, just across the Savannah River from South Carolina, Greene himself moved against the largest western post, Ninety-Six.

Here the Revolutionaries' succession of triumphs temporarily struck a snag. With a garrison of about 550 good Loyalist troops ably commanded by Lieutenant Colonel John Harris Cruger of New York, Ninety-Six was strong enough to compel Greene to resort to a formal siege. He mishandled this operation by pressing the vital points too little and too late. Greene was a self-taught soldier who lacked anything resembling Washington's experience with the British army, and he frequently showed deficiencies in tactics, the more technical side of war. While Greene was botching the siege, Rawdon received part of the first substantial troop reinforcement to reach America from Great Britain since 1778. Thus Rawdon could form a field army of 2,000 men, with which he hastened from Charleston to the relief of Ninety-Six, obliging Greene to draw away. For a time it appeared that Rawdon's aggressiveness might lead to a repetition of the race to the Dan, this time in the wilting heat of the Carolina summer, as Rawdon pursued Greene to the Enoree River and Greene raced ahead across the Tyger and the Broad toward Charlotte. But Rawdon was wise enough to have profited from Cornwallis's experience, and he gave off the pursuit.

As it was, he lost some fifty men dead of sunstroke on his fairly leisurely march back toward the coast. And the essentials of his situation had not improved. Without forcing Greene to battle, he could not prevent the Revolutionaries from resuming their reconquest of the South everywhere except where the British field army stood. With the Ministry still distracted by France and further reinforcements uncertain, even if he forced Greene to battle he might well suffer losses that would transform his prospects from merely difficult to impossible. Accordingly, the British withdrew into a coastal district centering on Charleston and extending some distance up the Santee River, the Revolutionaries returned to their attacks on vulnerable detachments, and Rawdon himself sailed home to England sickened and exhausted.[14]

Guilford and Hobkirk's Hill suggest that Greene was less chary of battle than Washington, and he apparently chaffed at his failure to win a tactical victory over one of the larger British forces. After resting his own army through the early summer of 1781 in the relatively salubrious climate of the High Hills of Santee, he decided in late August to challenge the British field force on the Santee, which still numbered about 2,000 men and was now commanded by Lieutenant Colonel Alexander Stewart. This decision was perhaps Greene's most questionable, because his numbers merely equalled the enemy's, and while a larger proportion of his force than in the earlier battles could be called "veterans," the advantages of military skill still lay with the British. Greene attacked Stewart at Eutaw Springs on September 8. For a time the Revolutionaries drove the enemy before them, and Greene seemed about to win his tactical victory at last. The rich supplies of the British camp undid him, however, for when the Americans reached them most of Greene's formations disintegrated into parties of plunderers. Thereupon Stewart counterattacked and won the field.

Even by an optimistic count, Greene suffered more than 500 casualties, more than one-quarter of his force. The British hold on the South had already been so diminished before the battle that it had to be doubtful whether even an American triumph could have offered dividends equal to the risk of such losses. On the other hand, Stewart reported casualties totaling 693, which was so appalling that he had to withdraw into the environs of Charleston. After Eutaw Springs, British control in the South was reduced to the immediate vicinity of Wilmington, Charleston, and Savannah.[15]

To drive them from those remaining strong points, where the British stood well fortified and with their backs to the sea, Greene had to await developments elsewhere which would make further reinforcements available to him and complete the ruination of the enemy's morale. Nevertheless, the achievements of Nathanael Greene and the southern partisans in reversing the greatest British success of the war, the conquest of the southernmost rebellious provinces, must rank as the war's most impressive campaign.

General Greene's outstanding characteristic as a strategist was his ability to weave the maraudings of partisan raiders into a coherent pattern, coordinating them with the maneuvers of a field army otherwise too weak to accomplish much, and making the combination a deadly one. "I have been obliged to practice that by finesse which I dared not attempt by force," said Greene, and he found that in the process, "There are few generals that has run oftener, or more lustily than I have done. . . ." (As Mao Tse-tung has said, "The ability to run away is the very characteristic of the guerrilla.") "But I have taken care not to run too far," said Greene, "and commonly have run as fast forward as backward, to convince our Enemy that we were like a Crab, that could run either way." "We fight, get beat, rise and fight again." (Or as Mao was to put it: ". . . enemy advances, we retreat; enemy halts, we harass; enemy tires, we attack; enemy retreats, we pursue.")[16] The later course of American military history, featuring a rapid rise from poverty of resources to plenty, cut short any further American evolution of Greene's type of strategy. He therefore remains alone as an American master developing a strategy of unconventional war. As a military commander of the Revolution, he claims a further distinction. His method of warmaking accorded thoroughly with the goals of the Revolution: Greene wrecked enemy armies.

By most modern standards of measurement, Greene's principal opponents, Cornwallis and Rawdon, were better soldiers than their commanding officer and contemporary in the North, Sir Henry Clinton. Modern military textbooks invariably endorse what the twentieth century calls the "principle of the offensive," the principle that to achieve decisive results in war it is necessary to seize the initiative and to strike the enemy aggressively. Even weaker armies are customarily urged to mount at least local offensives whenever they can. Certainly Cornwallis and Rawdon displayed an aggressive dedication to the offensive far surpassing the sedentary Clinton's. Greene made this very aggressiveness of his opponents an instrument of their ruination. Because Cornwallis and Rawdon were unwilling to remain passive like Clinton, because they were unwilling also to content themselves with a strategic defensive to hold South Carolina and Georgia but pursued the destruction of Greene's army with a fervor uncommon for their time, Greene was able to lead them upon exhausting marches through the partisans' country and thus to debilitate them. Knowing the superiority of their disciplined soldiers to Greene's army on the battlefield, Cornwallis and Rawdon devoutly pursued battle—so devoutly that Greene was usually able to arrange that when battle occurred, it was in circumstances wherein he could hardly fail to gain, even if he suffered the tactical defeat that proved his lot in his three major fights.

Misdirected aggressiveness carried Cornwallis also to his and the British army's final disaster of the war. Clinton in New York was British Commander in Chief for all of North America, and his orders to Cornwallis enjoined him to undertake no other ventures until South Carolina was secure. Partly because of Cornwallis's distance from Clinton, however, and partly because the Secretary of State for the American Department, Lord George Germain, did not like or trust Clinton, Cornwallis was permitted direct communication with Germain and in practice held an autonomous command. Cornwallis thus made bold to enter upon his North Carolina campaign before South Carolina could reasonably be considered secure or Clinton's orders fulfilled. When Greene frustrated him in North Carolina, Cornwallis evidently could not bear the thought of returning to Charleston, retreating and abandoning the initiative. He resolved instead to advance again and to maintain the offensive, and thus he conceived his Virginia campaign.[17]

Cornwallis spent late May and early June, 1781, operating in the interior of Virginia, with Tarleton raiding as far as the temporary state capital at Charlottesville. In early June, Clinton received several intercepted dispatches which indicated that Washington had conferred with the military and naval chieftains of the French forces in America, now allied with the Americans, and that they had agreed upon a combined land and sea operation against New York. Clinton thereupon sent Cornwallis peremptory orders to go over to the defensive and to send as many troops as possible for the reinforcement of New York. Cornwallis was highly displeased; and indeed, on the defensive he was likely to accomplish so little that Clinton might have done better to summon his whole force to New York. But neither Clinton nor Germain could bring himself to abandon Virginia completely, for they still hoped for the elusive Loyalist rising. Cornwallis arrived at Yorktown on August 1 to establish a defensive base on the Chesapeake where he could communicate with the Royal Navy. Claiming he needed all the troops he had to remain in Virginia at all, he sent Clinton nothing.[18]

Ever since he received the news of the French alliance in the spring of 1778, Washington had envisioned the means of escaping from his cautious strategy of attrition into an offensive ambitious enough to compel the Ministry in London to abandon the war as futile. He contemplated reinforcements from the French army and, yet more important, assistance from French sea power that might at least temporarily deprive the British of their greatest asset, the command of the sea. As he wrote on July 15, 1780: "In any operation and under all circumstances a decisive Naval superiority is to be considered as a fundamental principle, and the basis upon which every hope of success must ultimately depend."[19]

Washington knew and events soon proved that a decisive naval superiority should be within the allies' grasp. Especially after Spain joined in the war, the British navy was so strained by the competing demands of the home waters, the Mediterranean, the West Indies, and North America, and fear of a Franco-Spanish invasion kept so much of the fleet at home, that the French tended to acquire naval predominance in North American waters for several weeks at least once each year, when the hurricane season in the Caribbean obliged them to forgo offensive operations there.[20]

Nevertheless, after the French alliance Washington suffered three more years of frustration. In 1778 Admiral Lord Howe thwarted and kept off balance the generally superior French fleet of Vice Admiral the Comte d'Estaing, in a campaign reminiscent of Washington's own operations on land in that Howe skillfully mixed the strategic defensive with occasional audacious sallies.[21] The next year d'Estaing had no one of Howe's ability against whom to contend, but he continued to demonstrate his own feebleness by withdrawing from two opportunities for decisive victory blunderingly presented to him by Vice Admiral John Byron. The next year, 1780, Washington at last received some of the French soldiers he hoped for, more than 5,000 men under Lieutenant General the Comte de Rochambeau.

In 1781 there came to the Western Hemisphere a French admiral of boldness and breadth of strategic grasp to match the opportunities there, in the large and handsome person of François Joseph Paul, Comte de Grasse. Rear Admiral de Grasse came equipped with authority to cooperate with Washington and Rochambeau to fulfill any offensive designs they might conceive, provided he attended first to certain Spanish projects in the West Indies. When the Spanish proved to have no enterprises in immediate prospect, de Grasse persuaded them to endorse his going north as early as July, as well as to grant him financial assistance and to relieve his ships of patrolling duties, so he could take with him twenty-eight sail of the line.[22]

Through Rochambeau, Washington learned early of the brightening prospects for French naval assistance toward the major stroke he had long hoped for. It was always the main British stronghold in New York that Washington had regarded as the most likely objective of a combined land and sea operation. As recruiting failed to produce as many new soldiers as he hoped for in 1781, however, he began to incline away from New York and to look toward the South as the appropriate theater for combining with de Grasse. Meanwhile, Rochambeau corresponded with the French admiral and, though without any failure of subordination to Washington, made clear his own preference for a strike against Cornwallis on the Chesapeake as better tailored to the allies' strength than an attempt upon New York. The Chesapeake design accorded better than New York with de Grasse's own conviction that he should return to the West Indies as soon as the hurricane season ended in mid-October. Out of these motives came a plan to trap Cornwallis at Yorktown, through de Grasse's closing the entrance to Chesapeake Bay and a march by Washington and Rochambeau to bottle up Cornwallis by land.[23] Good fortune finally crowned Greene's scourging of Cornwallis's army in the Carolinas with a far larger success than reason could have anticipated; Greene had pushed Cornwallis into the vulnerable position which made possible the crowning American triumph of the war, and the decisive blow to the British Ministry's resolution to persist in fighting on which Washington had always believed the American cause depended.

3. The Federalists and the Jeffersonians

It must be superfluous to observe that this species of naval armament is proposed merely for defensive operations. . . .

—*Thomas Jefferson*[1]

I should not wish to extend the boundary of the United States by war if Great Britain would leave us to the quiet enjoyment of independence; but, considering her deadly and implacable enmity, and her continued hostility, I shall never die contented until I see her expulsion from North America, and her territories incorporated with the United States.

—*Richard Mentor Johnson*[2]

BRITISH NAVAL POWER had been the enemy's principal strategic asset in the War of the Revolution, a timely accession of allied naval power produced American victory at the end, and the major strategic preoccupations of the new United States almost inevitably became naval. A weak republic in a mainly hostile world—for hostility soon characterized the attitude even of the Republic's late ally—the United States had to rely for its security mainly upon its distance from the centers of foreign power. But to save future American generals from Charles Lee's distressed feeling that he was like a dog in a dancing school, the Republic hoped to remedy the extreme vulnerability of its coast to any naval power capable of projecting itself across the Atlantic. Because an overseas commerce, recovering remarkably from the dislocations of the war and of departure from the British navigation system, quickly became a mainstay of the national economy, and because much of the country's domestic commerce was conducted over water along the coasts, thought had to be given also to naval protection of American shipping.

Problems in the strategy of national defense existed along the country's land frontiers as well; but fortunately, foreign territory to the west and south never came under the effective control of a formidable European military power, and the defense of the land frontier with British North America was largely an extension of the naval problem. The western Indians of course posed military difficulties capable of straining the young Republic's limited capacities, the more so because they received sympathy and periodic assistance from the British territories to the north. But at first the Indians were dealt with less by direct military means than by the sheer weight of an advancing population, whose members carried guns and learned elementary tactics to be able to fight off Indian retaliation against their encroachments into the Indians' country.

Waging the War of the American Revolution had so nearly exhausted the military energies of the loose national union formed upon the Articles of Confederation that for a time after 1783 a navy and army alike could be little more than ideas, and the United States relied for national defense on distance and foreign forbearance alone. The tiny Continental Navy of the Revolution became extinct. The Army was reduced to a single regiment less than equal to the demands of the northwestern Indian frontier. Happily, the international world of the 1780s was relatively tranquil—a calm before a storm—and no threat developed to require more. Obviously any sort of assertive national policy was impossible. The United States could do nothing effective, for example, to guarantee its citizens the free navigation of the Mississippi through Spanish New Orleans.

To make possible a stronger military defense and the better assertion of national interests were among the motives which shaped the Constitution of 1787, and *The Federalist* papers have much to say about the military advantages of the proposed new frame of government.[3] The ratification of the Constitution nevertheless produced little immediate enlargement of the Republic's military forces or development of a less passive strategy of national defense. Suspicion of standing armies remained strong in all regions of the country, and of navies throughout the agricultural sections of the Union. The financial resources of the new government remained too limited, the prestige and popular standing of the government too precarious to permit ambitious military programs. The Army was recruited to somewhat over 4,000 men for Major General Anthony Wayne's campaign against the northwestern Indians in 1793–94. This campaign made the future state of Ohio relatively safe for settlement and opened the way to the provision of Jay's Treaty whereby the British evacuated the military posts they had retained on American soil despite the Treaty of Paris of 1783. Wayne's expedition, however, was a response to a particular frontier emergency and not an expression of anything that can be called a general national military policy or strategy.[4]

The first germs of such a policy and of a strategy of national defense did, however, begin to emerge about the same time, because the French Revolution reopened the ancient warlike quarrel between Great Britain and France, and the reopened quarrel threatened to envelop North America as it had done so often before the independence of the United States. Both belligerents interfered with American shipping, and both moved toward larger demands upon the conduct of the Republic, designed to make America serve their economic, if not their more active, warfare against each other. Simultaneously, the Barbary States of the North African coast increased their piratical attacks upon American commerce and demands for American tribute, because the European wars made the United States the most conspicuous neutral shipping nation.

In response to the European part of these threats, Congress voted in 1794 to rehabilitate coastal fortifications of the Revolutionary era and to erect new ones to protect sixteen principal ports and harbors. Explicitly in response to the Barbary pirates, Congress voted a navy of six frigates, but with the proviso that the building of the frigates should be suspended if the United States made peace with the Regency of Algiers. The Federalist Congressmen who sponsored the latter measure and the Federalist War Department which administered it may have had more than the Algerines in mind, however, for the Washington administration laid down six cruisers designed to meet in more than equal combat the best British or French vessels of their class, including three frigates rated at forty-four guns which would be superior to any European warships save line-of-battle ships. On March 15, 1796, President Washington had to inform Congress that the peace with Algiers contemplated by the Naval Act of 1794 had been attained—the United States having consented to pay a satisfactory amount of tribute—but Federalist advocates of a strong government and respectable armed forces were able to win Congressional approval for completing three of the frigates anyway, *United States* and *Constitution*, 44 guns, and *Constellation*, 38.[5]

These measures set the directions which American defense policy was to follow for a century, although they came as yet unaccompanied by an explicitly stated strategic rationale. The federal government would erect fortresses to guard the principal coastal cities and harbors. These fortresses, it was hoped, would protect the most important points on the coast from any sudden hostile *coup de main*, would compel any invading force which might arrive to land at less vital places while American forces assembled to deal with them, and would provide bases and places of refuge for an American Navy. It was a long established military dictum, confirmed by numerous examples, that good coastal fortresses would always repulse attacks by naval vessels. The fortresses offered stable gun platforms, while ships did not. Relatively few well placed shots from a fort could eliminate a whole ship with all its guns, while ships had to try to knock out fortress armament tediously, battery by battery, even gun by gun. Strong masonry and earthworks offered considerable proof against the solid shot of naval guns. While the fort was a stationary target, so virtually were ships, because sailing ships could not maneuver much while retaining an attacking position against forts. With the vital parts of the American coast secured by forts, the American Navy would be free to range out to sea, to threaten an invading expedition before it reached American shores and perhaps deter it from attempting to land, while also protecting the waterborne commerce so important to the growth of the economy and harassing enemy commerce.[6]

This rationale began to be articulated when American troubles with France erupted into undeclared warfare in 1798. Congress then authorized the completion of all six frigates of 1794; the construction, purchase, or rental of additional warships; and the creation of a Navy Department.[7] President John Adams appointed as first Secretary of the Navy Benjamin Stoddert, a merchant of Georgetown, who both administered competently the building of the Navy and suggested the outline of a naval strategy.

The American frigates, the first of which were launched in 1798, were expected to be the finest ships of their class anywhere in the world; but Stoddert believed that ships of their class, cruisers for commerce protection and commerce raiding, were not enough. The United States needed battleships, he believed, ships of the line to compete with the strongest warships of the French and British fleets. Stoddert recommended the building of twelve seventy-four-gun ships of the line. He eventually suggested twice that many strong frigates in addition, plus the preparation of timber, copper, munitions, and shipbuilding facilities for the rapid construction of still more warships.

Such a navy, he believed, would assure the nation against invasion and, more than that, it would deter further troubles similar to the quasi-war with France. Twelve seventy-fours was a small number of ships of the line compared with the scores kept afloat by Great Britain and France, but Stoddert pointed out that the United States could continue giving weight in its strategic considerations to the distance separating America from Europe. To dare to attempt an invasion of the United States, a European power would have to employ for the purpose more than double the American strength in ships of the line, he believed, to feel assurance of getting an invasion force safely ashore and to keep communications open across the ocean. Given the other risks of invading so extensive a country, Stoddert believed that the costs would then far outweigh the possible gains from any European invasion of the United States—all this provided that the United States built the recommended fleet of seventy-fours. "When the United States shall own twelve ships of seventy-four guns," he said, "and double the number of strong frigates, and it is known that they possess the means of increasing, with facility, their naval strength, confidence may be indulged that we may then avoid those wars in which we have no interest, and without submitting to be plundered."[8]

Congress appropriated a million dollars toward building six of the seventy-fours, but before much could be accomplished France agreed to satisfactory peace terms and the plans were suspended. At most, Congress appears to have voted the seventy-fours because to do so seemed a gesture of force and determination that might impress the French, not because Congressmen shared any general acceptance of Secretary Stoddert's idea that a fleet of battleships could keep enemy navies from American shores. The most enthusiastic Congressional friends of the Navy, from the eastern commercial states, seem to have thought generally in terms only of a commerce-protecting and commerce-raiding navy, no doubt assuming that the immense head start of the British and French made a more ambitious plan not feasible.[9]

On a small scale, nevertheless, the quasi-war with France produced the beginnings of an American Navy, in teamwork and fighting spirit beyond the mere building of warships, when Captain Thomas Truxton made an excellent fighting ship of *Constellation* and her crew and proved it in victory over *Insurgente* and a near-victory over the much more heavily gunned *Vengeance*. A naval tradition of fighting success, with disciplined, coordinated crews acting in a disciplined squadron, came still more out of Commodore Edward Preble's campaign against Tripoli in 1803–1804. But Stoddert's proposals were probably too ambitious in every way; it is unlikely that Truxton and Preble had yet developed enough officers with enough of the right combination of skills to make effective ships and an effective fleet of Stoddert's seventy-fours had they been built.[10]

Far from proceeding with the seventy-fours, the Jefferson administration, which entered office in 1801, was intent upon economy in government, emphatically including the reduction of warlike expenditures. The new administration was suspicious of all standing military forces, and as a southern and western administration it was especially suspicious of the Navy. Eventually it built its naval policy upon Jefferson's famous gunboat fleet. The Barbary powers had demonstrated the utility of small, shallow-draft vessels armed only with a single cannon or two for close-in defense of harbors. Becoming interested in such vessels, President Jefferson was able to testify to Congress that all the maritime powers made some use of similar boats, although he was unable to point to any respectable naval power that made them its major reliance in maritime defense. He believed, however, that they could serve in such a larger task for the United States. He persuaded Generals Horatio Gates and James Wilkinson, the superintendent of the Washington Navy Yard, Captain Thomas Tingey, and in a more guarded way Captain Samuel Barron of the Navy to say so, too. Thereupon he recommended building 200 of them—his Secretary of the Navy eventually called for 257—as the foundation of the American Navy. Congress authorized 25 in 1805, 50 in 1806, and another 188 in 1807. One hundred seventy-six were eventually built. They were mainly one-gun, fifty-foot craft.[11]

As Jefferson saw it, the gunboats offered flexible harbor defense, with some of the larger ones shifting from port to port as needed, and enough of them in a major harbor to swarm around any approaching enemy fleet. In time of peace, he believed, all but six or eight could be laid up on shore, to save money. One-third could be brought into service when Europe was at war, to be manned by skeleton crews of regular sailors who would be joined by naval militiamen if the emergency heightened. In wartime, when the whole gunboat fleet would be in commission, it too would be manned largely by citizen seamen of a naval militia. The simplicity of the gunboats permitted such a militia system, which accorded with Jefferson's general preference for citizen warriors over professional ones as well as with his passion for public economy. In every way, Jefferson hoped, from initial building costs onward, the gunboats would be cheap. (The next administration, less enamored of them though still Jeffersonian in ideology, found the gunboats inordinately expensive to maintain, especially as contrasted with the frigates.) Most important of all to Jefferson, however, "It must be superfluous to observe that this species of naval armament is proposed merely for defensive operations"; it could not "become an incitement to engage in offensive maritime war, towards which it would furnish no means."[12]

As the pressures of the Napoleonic Wars drove the United States closer and closer toward a new international conflict during the later years of Jefferson's administration and into James Madison's, the military policy of the United States prepared the country for little more than a strategy of passive defense against any adversary stronger than the Indian tribes. The Army was gradually restored from fewer than 3,000 men to about 6,000, and Congress voted large emergency increases on the eve of declaring war in 1812. But on land as well as at sea the Jeffersonians preferred to rely upon citizens' militia springing to arms in emergencies, and the events of war soon proved the Army even less ready for any sort of offensive operations than the Navy. The building and strengthening of the harbor fortifications had been going forward slowly since 1794, and on those fortifications and the gunboats rested the government's hopes to fend off foreign attack by sea. When the War of 1812 began, there remained sixteen ships in commission in the United States Navy exclusive of the gunboats, six of them the frigates first planned in 1794. But there was no agreed-upon design for their employment, and at least until recently Secretary of the Navy Paul Hamilton had believed that in view of the immense superiority of the British navy, the best thing to do with the seagoing vessels was to take out their masts and moor them in harbors as floating batteries.[13]

The trouble with the Jeffersonians' defensive military system was that it ensured that again in the War of 1812 as in the Revolution earlier, the military means of the United States were far from according with the country's political goals. The youth and the economic limitations of the country would almost certainly have produced this kind of situation in any event, but the Jeffersonian military system aggravated the problem. The political goals of the Jeffersonian leaders who carried the nation into a second war with Great Britain were incongruously offensive. Even short of possible motives of territorial expansion, at the least the purpose of fighting Great Britain in 1812 was to compel her to respect American neutral rights at sea, the issue upon which President Madison dwelt in his war message. Because America lacked the naval power to compel respect for neutral maritime rights by direct means, the purpose of the war had to be pursued indirectly, by punishing Great Britain at some vulnerable point until she should feel obliged to yield to the American view of international law at sea. Her most vulnerable point accessible to Americans was Canada. The United States under the most modest interpretation of its purposes thus went to war intending to attack Canada, an offensive goal. When Americans interpreted their purposes less modestly, they saw themselves as going to war for the outright conquest of Canada. Their motive was the belief developed during the colonial wars that only the complete elimination of the rival power from North America could assure the security that was desired. In words such as those of Congressman Richard Mentor Johnson quoted at the beginning of this chapter, some Americans returned to the effort begun by Montgomery's and Arnold's expeditions to Canada in 1775.

The more modest goal of injuring Canada enough to win concessions from Britain elsewhere might have been attainable despite America's lack of offensive military power. Only about 7,000 British and Canadian regulars guarded the Canadian frontier of some 900 miles' extent, and these troops could not at the outset be much reinforced from Great Britain because the American war was only a sideshow to the desperate British struggle against Napoleon. Potentially, American militia reinforcements might so outnumber British and Canadians that, with the small American Regular Army as a spearhead, they might overwhelm the enemy almost by weight alone. The less than tremendous popularity of the war kept the Americans from mobilizing the numbers of soldiers for which their leaders hoped or which Congress authorized, but despite that, enough men came forward to have injured Canada badly if they had received good leadership. But none of these ideas about the offensive purposes for which military force was now to be used was ever formulated clearly by anyone in the United States government—perhaps in part because the Jeffersonians were too deeply wedded to defensive conceptions of American military power. Consequently, the political leaders of the country never brought themselves to inform the military leaders clearly what they were supposed to be doing.[14]

There was no strategy for the war beyond general agreement in the government and the War Department that Canada ought to be attacked. The seemingly obvious line of attack against Canada would have been the historic Lake Champlain-Richelieu River route to Montréal. If the United States concentrated its forces around Albany and then pushed them forward to get astride the St. Lawrence at Montréal, everything in Canada to the westward would be deprived of aid from across the Atlantic and from the most populous part of the Canadian provinces, and should become relatively easy pickings.

For the Americans, the Lake Champlain route now possessed the advantages which the British had found in it during the French and Indian War, not the disadvantages which had developed when the British tried to use it in the opposite, southward, direction during the War of the Revolution.

But the United States failed to adopt the strategic approach which was obviously appropriate. Upon the outbreak of war, the busiest American military activity occurred not toward Montréal but at the western end of the Canadian frontier, in Major General William Hull's attempt to invade Canada from Detroit. The enthusiasm of the West in support of the war helped produce this strategic incongruity. As events turned out, Hull badly bungled even the misplaced major blow, and before the year 1812 was over, Canada was cleared of American invaders, and the whole American Northwest beyond the Ohio River was in danger of collapsing under British and Indian counterattack.

This disastrous experience still failed to instruct the Americans that they should observe the elementary strategic principle of directing their offensive efforts upon the most vital and vulnerable objective, in this instance the St. Lawrence bottleneck into the Canadian interior. Never in the war did the American Army recognize that strategic principle clearly enough to act upon it. Always the Army continued to dissipate its already necessarily limited offensive efforts in scattered sideshows along the western Canadian frontier. The best that can be said for American strategy along the border is that by 1813 the Americans perceived that if they were to save their Northwest and regain the initiative along the western reaches of the international boundary, they must capture naval control of Lakes Ontario and Erie.

Taking Montréal in 1812 would have assured them such control. Now they had to seek it in a race with the British to build warships on the lakes. In this race the Americans had a slight logistical advantage, in that it was slightly easier for them to get essential fittings to the lakes from across the Appalachians or from Pittsburgh or Buffalo than for the British to transport them across the Atlantic. Nevertheless, it required uncommon leadership and initiative from Commodore Oliver Hazard Perry in building his squadron on Lake Erie, as well as his exceptional courage and skill in battle, to win control of that lake. On Lake Ontario, the less enterprising Commodore Isaac Chauncey managed, though starting from behind, to build a squadron which at least matched and sometimes surpassed the rival British squadron, but Chauncey never achieved more than a stalemate. Perry's battle of Lake Erie on September 10, 1813, was enough, however, to restore American predominance in the American Northwest beyond the Ohio, and to permit Major General William Henry Harrison to carry the war briefly into western Canada again, at the battle of the Thames.[15]

At sea, American naval officers began the war by grasping the most promising possible strategy on their own initiative, without direction from Washington; but the inferiority of the American Navy to the British made the possibilities of accomplishment far slighter here than on land. Three days after the declaration of war, in June, 1812, Commodore John Rodgers sailed from New York with the frigates *President*, 44, *United States*, 44, and *Congress*, 38, along with two smaller vessels. He determined to protect American ships which happened to be at sea by compelling the Royal Navy to concentrate resources against him. To that end, as well as for the damage he might impose on the enemy and the valuable prizes he might win, he set out to hunt the annual plate fleet homebound from Jamaica to England. He failed to find the Jamaica convoy, partly because of a frustrating encounter with a British frigate which also escaped him. Nevertheless, he sailed well across the Atlantic and then turned southward to come home by way of the Madeiras. Learning of his cruise led the British naval commander at Halifax to send his four frigates in a squadron to look for Rodgers, cancelling the idea of scattering them to prey upon returning American merchantmen. Most of the American ships at sea when war was declared came safely into port.[16]

The Royal Navy in 1812 counted more than 600 fighting vessels, with some 120 ships of the line and 116 frigates. Upon the declaration of war, about a hundred British warships were in the western Atlantic, but only one ship of the line and seven frigates lay in American waters. As long as the European war continued, the British would have to continue holding most of their naval strength in Europe, and they delayed for a time before they shifted as much strength as the war against Napoleon permitted, hoping that their repeal of the Orders in Council would persuade the United States to make peace and remove itself as a distraction. Therefore the small American Navy could continue to put to sea during most of the first year of the war, despite British efforts at blockade.[17]

Commodore Rodgers remained an advocate of the closest possible approximation of a fleet strategy, the American warships to sail in relatively large squadrons which would oblige the British to concentrate ships against them. The British would be deterred from dispersing for attacks against American commerce, and American privateers should also have the freest possible hand. Captain Stephen Decatur preferred to send the ships out singly or at most in pairs, to increase their chances of encountering vulnerable British vessels. Rodgers's seemed the sounder plan, and the Navy Department adopted it; but there were so few ships that the result came close to Decatur's plan anyway. Three squadrons were set up: *President* and *Congress* to cruise the North Atlantic under Rodgers; *United States* and *Argus*, 16, to the Azores under Decatur; *Constitution*, *Essex*, 32, and *Hornet*, 18, to the South Atlantic and Cape Horn under Commodore William Bainbridge. *Constitution* under Captain Isaac Hull had already fought and bested H.M.S. *Guerrière* while Rodgers was completing his first cruise. The new voyages led to the victories of *United States* over *Macedonian*, *Constitution* over *Java*, and *Hornet* over *Peacock*, and to *Essex*'s destructive cruise under Captain David Porter among Britain's Pacific Ocean shipping. By distracting Britain's Halifax squadron, the voyages helped keep American seaports relatively open for several more weeks.[18]

Naturally, there was no keeping the ports open once London decided it must prosecute the war in earnest and sent enough ships to America to do so. Discussion of the Rodgers versus the Decatur strategy became academic then, for the best that could be hoped for was that individual warships might slip out to sea occasionally, and precious little of that was possible. In November, 1812, Captain Charles Stewart of *Constitution* was asked his opinion of the coming shape of the war and predicted exactly what began to happen, in a document which Captains Isaac Hull and Charles Morris also signed:

> It cannot be supposed that, in a war with a foreign maritime Power, that Power will only send to our coast frigates and smaller cruisers, because we possess no other description of vessels. Their first object will be to restrain, by ships of the line, our frigates and other cruisers from departing and preying upon their commerce; their next object will be to send their smaller cruisers in pursuit of our commerce; and by having their ships of the line parading on our coast, threatening our more exposed seacoast towns, and preventing the departure of our small cruisers, they will be capturing what commerce may have escaped theirs, and recapturing what prizes may have fallen into our hands. Thirdly: they can at any time withdraw their ships of the line, should a more important object require it, without hazarding much

> on their part; and return in sufficient time to shut out our cruisers that may have departed during their absence. Fourthly: they can at all times consult their convenience in point of time and numbers; and will incur no expense and risk of transports for provisions and water, but can go and procure their supplies at pleasure, and return to their station ere their absence is known to us.[19]

The next month, December, 1812, the British proclaimed a blockade of the Delaware and the Chesapeake, the principal nests of American privateers because New England did not favor the war. In May, 1813, the blockade was extended to the whole Atlantic and Gulf coasts except New England. American ocean commerce withered, including intracoastal commerce. Beginning in February, 1813, the Royal Navy also began raiding the seaports of the Delaware and the Chesapeake, destroying defenses, looting, burning, and further disrupting commerce. The raids demonstrated the uselessness of Jefferson's gunboats against a formidable naval power; unsupported by larger warships, the gunboats had to retire far upstream to escape British men-of-war.[20]

In 1814 Great Britain could turn its major weight against the United States. Until then British strategy had been essentially defensive, with only local offensives; but now London resolved that America should be punished for interfering while Great Britain fought not only for her own life but for the freedom of Europe from centralized tyranny. The British decided to take the offensive. At the end of May, the day after Britain signed a peace treaty with France, Great Britain proclaimed the entire American coastline under blockade. Her commanders prepared larger raids in the Chesapeake, aimed at nothing less than the federal capital and the obnoxious privateering base of Baltimore. More than that, they planned major invasions via Lake Champlain from the north and New Orleans and the Mississippi from the south, which might permanently detach parts of the United States.

By mismanaging its limited opportunities against Canada, the American government had squandered much of whatever public support the war had once commanded, and against the ominous prospects of 1814 it could do little more than trust in the regional military and naval commanders of the threatened districts to muster enough local manpower and equipment under peril of invasion and to improvise tactics which could turn the threats back. Endangered from north, east, and south, the United States did not have the capacity to apply a coordinated national strategy.

A pedantic view of strategy might have it that Great Britain was about to violate the principle of mass or concentration by taking the offensive simultaneously on several fronts from the St. Lawrence to the Gulf of Mexico rather than by concentrating strength against a single vital objective. Against an opponent as weak as the United States was in 1814 and defending so extensive a frontier, it was eminently proper, however, for a power with Britain's reserves of military strength to apply pressure all around the frontier. The United States had scarcely the resources to be strong at any one point, let alone everywhere, and seemingly the American defenses must have crumbled somewhere. Anyway, the United States was so amorphous a polity, rendered more so by the strains of the war, that there was no one vital American point against which to strike.

But while Britain's offensive strategy was sound enough, the execution proved faulty. Furthermore the United States, though strategically bankrupt, was about to enjoy the good fortune of skillful tactical improvisation by its commanders in almost all the threatened regions. In August the grand British raid up the Chesapeake carried into Washington, causing the Jeffersonian gunboat fleet in the area to be scuttled. But at Baltimore in September, Major General Samuel Smith of the Maryland militia was able to put together a successful defense compounded of citizen soldiers of the militia, fighting better than usual when they found themselves ably led in defense of their own homes, plus Fort McHenry, one of the seacoast defenses of the 1794 program which had been carried to a fair degree of completion.

Also in September, the northern British invasion under Lieutenant General Sir George Prevost overwhelmingly outnumbered and outclassed the American army in its path, but Prevost decided not to advance beyond the Saranac River at Plattsburg until his naval commander, Captain George Downie, had dealt with the American squadron which Master Commandant Thomas Macdonough had built on Lake Champlain. If Prevost had pushed forward, he would have denied Macdonough the opportunity to fight on his own terms, anchored in Plattsburg Bay where the British squadron had to come in and meet him broadside to broadside, with cables set to pivot the American ships round to present fresh broadsides when a critical moment should arrive. A British advance on land would have forced Macdonough out of Plattsburg Bay. But Prevost did not advance, Macdonough fought a naval battle on his own terms and won it, and Prevost retreated back to Canada.

At New Orleans, of course, the southern invasion force met the redoubtable Major General Andrew Jackson, who prepared for their coming by seizing Pensacola in Spanish Florida to eliminate distractions from that quarter, offset much of the effect of British naval victory over Jeffersonian gunboats on the naval approaches to the city by executing a surprise night attack on the enemy army almost as soon as they landed, and left the British so nonplussed by his boldness that they neglected opportunities to outflank him and expended their strength in futile frontal assaults.[21]

Thus American defense in 1814 came off better than the country's shortcomings in policy and strategy deserved. The only offensive efforts the United States was able to mount during the year were those of the privateers, plus a few forays by government sloops of war constructed like privateers and a couple of sallies by the *Constitution*. The British blockade practically eliminated any kind of seafaring except privateering, so the Americans built ships especially designed for the purpose, vessels based on the model of the Baltimore clippers, sleek and fast to flash out of ports past the blockaders and to outrun more powerfully gunned ships, well armed themselves because they could have no other business than raiding enemy commerce. While Britain was still fighting Napoleon, the privateers had become a serious annoyance on the line of communication with the Duke of Wellington on the Peninsula. In all, the privateers took some 1,300 prizes during the war, at an accelerating rate while the blockade was tightening. This was the most substantial injury the United States inflicted on Great Britain anywhere in the course of the war.

At the time of the quasi-war, John Adams had wanted to discourage privateering and put all maritime warfare, including commerce raiding, in the hands of the Navy. Perhaps the best course the United States could have adopted at sea in the War of 1812 would have been to follow Adams's idea, prohibit private raiding, oblige all who wished to fight at sea to join the Navy, concentrate naval building on fast raiding ships, and thus wage a planned, concerted campaign against British shipping. The haphazard campaign of the privateers accomplished much, but a planned guerrilla campaign at sea should have accomplished still more.[22]

Instead, Congress adopted a program reminiscent of Secretary Stoddert's, when it was too late to do any good in this war. In January, 1813, the legislature voted six more heavy frigates and four seventy-fours. None of them was finished in time for service in the war, an outcome which of course was not altogether predictable but which should have seemed likely. Sloops of war for commerce raiding voted at the same time could have been ready by early 1814, and four or five of them could have been built for the price of a frigate. But the frigate victories of the first year of war made Congress of a mind to do a favor for the Navy, and Captain Stewart, seconded by Captains Hull and Morris, responded to a request for advice with suggestions much like Stoddert's. A strong squadron of line-of-battle ships, they said,

> would produce one of two results—either that the enemy would be obliged to abandon our coast or bring on it a much greater force, at least double our number, out of which they will be obliged to keep on our coast a superiority, at all the hazards of the sea, and at great additional expense and risk of transports to provision and water them. But should they, from other circumstances, be unable to keep up this superiority on our coast, the door will be kept open for the ingress and egress of our cruisers and their prizes; while our other classes of ships may be sent in pursuit of their smaller cruisers and commerce. These observations will apply to all future wars in which we may be engaged with maritime Powers. . . .[23]

Under the pressures of war the Jeffersonian Congress accepted this Federalist kind of advice, but unfortunately, the advice was better for future wars than for the immediacies at hand.

A few years after the War of 1812, Secretary of War John C. Calhoun submitted to Congress his famous plan for an expansible United States Army. This plan would have had all the formations of a war army and a full wartime command and staff structure kept ready in peacetime, so that at the coming of war it would be necessary only to flesh out the full skeleton of the Army with recruits, with "nothing either to new model or to create." Calhoun stressed that one reason for favoring the expansible army plan was the desirability of developing a corps of officers well trained in the art of war, for "War is an art, to attain perfection in which, much time and experience, particularly for the officers, are necessary."[24]

Through no fault of Calhoun's, the debate over his expansible army plan, a debate which turned out to be a perennial of American military policy for the next hundred years, often tended to overlook what he said about officers and to hinge upon the question of the military training of the rank and file. It became mainly a debate over whether citizen soldiers drawn from the militia could serve the requirements of national defense as well as long-service Regulars. One side of this debate said the models for American soldiers ought to be the Regulars in gray who stood up to Wellington's Invincibles on more than equal terms in open-field fighting at Chippewa and Lundy's Lane on the Niagara frontier in 1814. The other side sang the praises of Andrew Jackson's hunters of Kentucky—and of Tennessee and Louisiana—who mowed down Sir Edward Pakenham's assault troops at New Orleans.

Unfortunately, the debate over Regulars versus militia missed the main point which the War of 1812 should have raised about the military policy of the United States. The Regulars of Chippewa and Lundy's Lane had not been in service much longer than most militiamen who fought in the War of 1812 and who did badly. The difference between the Regulars of Chippewa and Lundy's Lane and other American soldiers of the war was mainly a difference of leadership. The soldiers on the Niagara frontier in 1814 acquired the marks of Regulars in a short time because they were intensively trained in minor tactics by Brigadier General Winfield Scott, who used textbooks obtained from Europe for the purpose, and then led by an inspiring battle captain, Major General Jacob Brown. The great need of the United States Army and Navy demonstrated by the War of 1812 was more good leadership.

But the leadership needed was not simply the battlefield leadership of Winfield Scott and Jacob Brown, or the seafighting leadership of Isaac Hull or Stephen Decatur. Even more, the country needed the kind of leadership that Secretary Calhoun suggested when he spoke of war as an art: leadership with an overarching conception of war, capable of giving American warmaking the coherence of a strategic design. Strategy was the element which the United States most seriously lacked in the War of 1812. With strategy, even the ill prepared military forces of the United States might have been able to injure Great Britain severely and thus to accomplish the most basic purpose of the war, by capturing Montréal early and thus placing all of Canada to the westward at the mercy of the United States.

The military leaders of the United States went into the War of 1812 with practically no education in strategy whatever, let alone a thorough acquaintance with strategic doctrine. The United States Military Academy at West Point was a neglected foundling; there were no higher schools of war; there was no native military literature beyond a few tactical manuals; European books on the art of war were expensive and hard to procure; nothing had yet occurred to encourage American officers to become students of the art of war. The greatest military need of the United States demonstrated by the War of 1812 was an education in the principles of strategy for the American officer corps.

PART TWO

Young America as a Military Power, 1815-1890

To get possession of Lee's army was the first great object.
—*U. S. Grant*[1]

4. The Age of Winfield Scott

The capital of an ancient empire, now of a great republic; or an early peace, the assailants were resolved to win.

—*Winfield Scott*[1]

To have emerged from combat against the premier world power of the era with the status quo ante bellum preserved was not a bad result for a war fought practically without a strategic design.

Furthermore, the war did lead immediately to a clarification of the national military policy for deterrence of foreign attack and defense in case of attack. The United States had been building forts and a Navy since 1794 without much of a plan for their use or for one fort to complement another or for the forts and the Navy to work together. Without an agreed-upon plan, neither the forts nor the Navy had sufficed to prevent mortal peril of invasion in 1814. While memories of that year's alarms were still fresh, Congress authorized a peacetime Army of 10,000 men and a Navy of nine seventy-fours with frigates in proportion. President Madison appointed a Board of Engineers to propose a system of coastal defense which would utilize the forts and the Navy, including on the board Lieutenant Joseph G. Totten of the Corps of Engineers, Captain Jesse D. Elliott of the Navy, and perhaps most important, Simon Bernard, a military engineer of distinguished reputation in Napoleon's army and thus in the country which was regarded as the fountainhead of military science, appointed assistant engineer with the pay and emoluments of a brigadier general.[2]

The report of the Board of Engineers dated February 7, 1821, with a supplement dated March 1, 1826, became the basic statement of a strategy of national maritime defense and remained so until the 1880s, albeit it often represented theory rather than practice. It stated that the first reliance of the United States against attack from overseas must be upon the Navy. Assuming, however, that for the foreseeable future the United States would not possess a navy large enough to guarantee against invasion by the great naval powers of Europe, and written primarily by Army engineers, the report went on to emphasize the usefulness of a unified system of seacoast fortifications. These fortifications would be essential for the support of the Navy itself, because they would assure the protection of the bases from which it would operate. The small American Army could not possibly protect the whole length of the country's frontiers against invasion without a system of fortifications. If an enemy mustered enough naval power off the American coast to invade at all, he would have enough to compel the Army to disperse its defenders hopelessly while guessing about the enemy's landing place—unless the country built a system of strong forts. Then the vital places could be held by a minimal number of troops. The enemy would be able to get no foothold on a sheltered harbor where he might base his navy and built up a large invasion force at leisure. The cities would be safe from panic. Blockade of the coast would be made difficult, again because the enemy would not have a good harbor as a base. Intracoastal navigation might be kept open.[3]

Congress's initial postwar appropriation for coastal fortification was $38,000, a substantial sum for the time but enough to make only a beginning of the vast system of batteries, masonry-walled enclosures, and earthworks projected by the Board of Engineers from Maine to New Orleans. The work gradually went forward during the next several decades, but when Europe as well as America proved to remain at peace after 1815, Congress lost its sense of urgency in defense matters. By 1820 it was asking the Secretary of War to recommend how best the Army might be reduced from 10,000 to 6,000 men. It was in response to this request that Secretary Calhoun offered his expansible army plan; but Congress largely ignored his reasoned proposal and simply cut its authorizations.[4]

The Canadian frontier no longer received so much attention as the coasts. A general postwar settlement of outstanding problems with Great Britain included the Rush-Bagot Agreement of 1817, which limited naval armaments on the Great Lakes to stipulated small revenue cutters. The ability to reach this agreement indicated, of course, that the Congressional sense of a growing national security was well founded, and in turn it further nourished that sense. Land fortifications along the Canadian border continued to be built, especially forts similar in design to the coastal ones and located at strategic waterways, such as Fort Wayne at Detroit and Fort Montgomery at Rouses Point on Lake Champlain. But again the pace of construction was not hurried, and after the Oregon boundary dispute was settled in 1846, building ceased and the border forts fell into a slow process of decay.[5]

As for the first line of defense, the Navy, seven ships of the line had slid down the ways by the early 1820s, *Independence*, *Washington*, *Franklin*, *Columbus*, *North Carolina*, *Ohio*, and *Delaware*. The first four were not altogether successful attempts to transfer the design principles of the oversize *Constitution* frigates to battleships; the latter three proved to be the finest and most powerful seventy-fours, perhaps the best battleships of any rating, in the world. These ships, however, never got to act as a squadron such as Benjamin Stoddert and Charles Stewart had suggested. With Europe and America at peace again, the Navy's most urgent immediate responsibility became the protection of American commerce by showing the flag to powers which might otherwise discriminate against it and by suppressing pirates and quasi-pirates—the Barbary corsairs again, cutthroats who took advantage of weak and tolerant governments by basing themselves in the newly independent Latin American states, East Indian and Asian brigands who became a nuisance when American commerce with the Orient enjoyed an astonishing growth. Therefore the Navy was divided into small and scattered squadrons, Mediterranean, African, West India, Brazil, eastern Pacific, western Pacific (East India). For the patrolling and pirate-chasing work of these squadrons, small, fast vessels were more useful than battleships or even frigates. By the mid-1820s, only one of the seventy-fours remained on active duty, and President John Quincy Adams persuaded Congress to authorize ten sloops of war specially designed for the purposes at hand.[6]

An incipient revolution in naval technology brought back to mind the large strategic purposes which the Board of Engineers had suggested for the Navy and which Secretary Stoddert and Captain Stewart had discussed more explicitly. Technological change raised the hope that Britain's existing naval superiority might be cancelled overnight. Stoddert and Stewart had hoped at best to use a fleet still greatly inferior to Britain's to exploit the distances across the Atlantic in such a way that blockades or invasions in America would henceforth cost the British more than they were worth. In 1823, however, the "steam galliot" *Sea Gull*, a converted commercial sidewheel steamer, joined the American West India squadron and became the first steam warship in history to go into battle, against some of the local pirates. She proved so useful in pursuit in calm weather that she often wore the squadron commander's pendant. She also revived an interest in steam warships which had languished despite America's having launched, late in the War of 1812, the first of the species, the steam frigate *Demologos*, a center-wheeler invented by Robert Fulton and soon renamed for him.[7]

All through the 1820s successive Secretaries of the Navy called for increased experimentation with steam vessels, if not ocean-going warships then at least steam-powered batteries for mobile defense of the harbors. Even Brevet Major General Edmund P. Gaines of the Army developed an infatuation for steam batteries, seeing in them a cheaper and more effective substitute for some of the coastal fortifications. The postwar naval expansion laws had included authorization to purchase engines and materials for steam batteries. In 1835 Secretary of the Navy Mahlon Dickerson at last acted on the project his predecessors had merely talked about, using the old authorization to lay down a new steam frigate, a sidewheeler also called the *Fulton*.[8]

Launched in 1837, the new *Fulton* proved badly designed and underpowered, but she was fortunate to be commanded by Captain Matthew Calbraith Perry, an enthusiastic proponent of steam propulsion. Perry got her to perform well enough, especially on a timely trip to Washington for Presidential and Congressional inspection, that in 1839 Congress authorized three additional steam frigates. Two were begun the same year, the ten-gun sidewheelers *Mississippi* and *Missouri*. Two years later, the third received a new design. U.S.S. *Princeton* adopted an underwater screw propeller invented by the immigrant Swedish engineer John Ericsson. *Princeton* thus escaped the vulnerability of sidewheelers to crippling of the propelling wheels by enemy gunfire, put the machinery below the water line, permitted the return of broadside gun arrangements, and, with the propeller designed to be detachable, was able to cruise efficiently under sail and thus conserve fuel.[9]

Though she could carry a broadside, however, *Princeton* mounted only fourteen guns. The number was small partly because of the weight of the engine, but also because like *Mississippi* and *Missouri* she had a new and more powerful type of armament, the Paixhans shell gun. Naval guns firing explosive shells had been objects of experiment since the eighteenth century, and John and Robert L. Stevens had developed a model for the American Navy under the same stimulus that had produced the first *Fulton*, the British blockade. But when the immediate stimulus passed, so did government encouragement for the new weapon. The ideas of the Stevenses and others were then further developed and achieved their first successful application in France beginning in the 1820s, under the aegis of a former general of artillery named Henri-Joseph Paixhans. Paixhans hoped through a technological breakthrough to destroy the historic naval superiority of Great Britain. The hollow sphere fired by a Paixhans gun would explode to ignite fires fatal to wooden warships and to hurl deadly projectiles of debris all over a ship.[10]

Princeton's career began tragically with the famous explosion of one of her two twelve-inch guns in 1844, killing the Secretaries of State and the Navy and other dignitaries. The gun was a faulty wrought-iron design in which Captain Robert F. Stockton had tried to economize upon the principles employed by John Ericsson in its sister gun, which had three iron bands sweated around the breech. Nevertheless, the new steam frigates proved successful ships both in distant voyages such as Perry's expedition to Japan and in blockade work off the Mexican coast in the Mexican War. They attained what then seemed remarkable speeds against the wind, and while their shell guns found little opportunity for battle, in their exercises they demolished stout targets that would have defied solid shot. Two more sidewheel frigates, *Powhatan* and *Susquehanna*, were authorized during the Mexican War.[11]

Secretary of the Navy Abel P. Upshur, who after becoming Secretary of State perished in the *Princeton* explosion, believed that the new technology made possible a fresh start in the competition for sea power, and that the United States now could and should maintain a navy at least half the strength of the largest foreign fleet.[12] In the 1850s, President Franklin Pierce's Secretary of the Navy, James C. Dobbins, tried to develop further the strategic implications of the new armament and steam propulsion. His reasoning approximated that which had inspired Paixhans's development of the shell gun in the first place. He believed that the new naval technology, in which the United States started out on at least an even footing with the other naval powers, would permit the cancelling out of British naval superiority as it affected the United States. Steam propulsion increased the advantage the United States could find in distance from Europe, because the early steam warships were notoriously voracious in devouring fuel, and any enemy squadron trying to cruise off the American coast would be hard put to keep up steam. Even with British bases existing in Canada and the West Indies, a repetition of the British blockade of 1813–15 would probably be impossible in the face of any respectable American naval force.

Furthermore, the need to begin naval building anew with steam-powered and shell-gun vessels meant that the United States no longer faced an impossible task of catching up with the Royal Navy, but could much more closely keep pace with British building. To equal Britain's total shipbuilding would remain unnecessary, because America's maritime interests remained more limited than Britain's. But if Benjamin Stoddert could reasonably hope to counter British sea power in Western Hemisphere waters with twelve line-of-battle ships against Britain's more than a hundred, the United States could now match Britain closely enough in the building of steam warships to aspire to outright mastery of American waters. That done, and the United States invulnerable, foreign powers would be unlikely to interfere even with distant American commerce.

To begin, Secretary Dobbins recommended the building of six additional steam frigates, not paddlewheelers like the retrogressive *Powhatan* and *Susquehanna* of the Mexican War but propeller-driven like *Princeton*. For a variety of reasons—the exuberant nationalism of the "Young America" era, the success of the Mexican War, southern interest in Caribbean expansion, added to the consistent northeastern mercantile and manufacturing interest in the Navy—Congress voted the ships, the *Wabash* class. It followed up with an authorization for five steam sloops, the *Hartford* class, and then, during James Buchanan's Presidency, seven more sloops, the *Iroquois* class.[13]

This surge of naval interest and construction in the 1850s remains surprising and not altogether accountable. For all that, it was not enough to match British and French naval development in the manner that Dobbins suggested. The United States did not keep pace with the European naval powers in quantity of the new types of vessels, and despite experimentation with the ironclad "Stevens battery," it produced no equivalent of France's thirty-six-gun ironclad frigate *Gloire* (1858) or Great Britain's iron battleship *Warrior* (1859). Iron armor was the inevitable next technological advance, because nothing less could fend off the shell gun. But the American naval enthusiasm of the fifties became exhausted before this step was reached, fundamentally because there was no sufficiently important national interest to be served.

This factor was the same one that had curtailed the first naval expansion immediate after the War of 1812 and had kept American naval strength limited ever since. Not only were international affairs tranquil after the fall of Napoleon; but also, to the extent that American relations with the great naval powers did occasionally become strained, as in the Oregon controversy, the uncertainties and limitations of the first steam warships made blockades and descents upon the American coast in the manner of 1813–15 even less likely than Secretary Dobbins thought. Levi Woodbury, Secretary of the Navy under Andrew Jackson, was shortsighted about the effects of the new technology upon an ability to improvise a navy in short order. But he was at least as close as Dobbins to perceiving the realities of American security, and closer to popular convictions about defense, when he wrote:

> Though nominally, as to vessels in commission, only the fifth or sixth naval power in the world, and not expending over one-eighth of the annual amount paid by some nations to maintain a naval establishment, yet, if we look to the true elements of naval power, to our ships in ordinary and on the stocks, to our materials for building and equipment collected and collecting, to our large commercial marine, whether of merchant vessels or steamboats, to our flourishing fisheries, our extended sea-coast and inland seas, and, at the same time, to our position in regard to other nations, with few neighbors bordering us by land, and an ocean rolling between us and most of the governments with whom we are likely to have collision, it must be manifest that our greatest exposure and danger are on the waters, and that our means of attack and defence there, if duly husbanded and developed, will probably always prove equal to sustain us with credit in any hostilities into which the convulsions of the world may hereafter plunge our peaceful confederacy.[14]

On land, the preeminent figure in American military history for four and a half decades after the War of 1812, and through his campaign in Mexico the most notable American strategist of the period, was Winfield Scott. Scott emerged with Jacob Brown and Andrew Jackson as one of the most impressive of the new generals whose tactical abilities helped rescue the nation from the worst consequences of the strategic bankruptcy of the War of 1812. Promoted to brigadier general at the beginning of the campaign of 1814, he was brevetted major general for his conspicuous role in that year's battles at

Chippewa and Lundy's Lane. After Andrew Jackson retired from the Army in 1821 to leave Jacob Brown as the only full major general, and during Alexander Macomb's subsequent tenure as Commanding General of the Army, Scott alternated with Edmund Gaines in the principal field commands, the Eastern and Western Departments. When Macomb retired in 1841, Scott was advanced to major general and General in Chief of the Army, and he continued as Commanding General for twenty years, into the early months of the Civil War. For his leadership in the Mexican War he received the brevet rank of lieutenant general, the only American soldier to achieve that rank between George Washington and the Civil War.

Scott's military ideas were still largely those of the classical military age in eighteenth-century Europe. His military education was not a formal one—he did not attend the Military Academy at West Point—but came from his reading of European books. After practicing law around Petersburg, Virginia, he had secured a commission as captain of artillery in 1808, in the expansion of the Regular Army which followed the *Chesapeake-Leopard* affair. An associate in the law, Benjamin Watkins Leigh, happened to own an extensive military library, which became the foundation of Scott's study for his new career. Of course, Scott's reading in Leigh's library was mainly in a literature which antedated the wars of the French Revolution and Napoleon. His earlier conditioning and his temperament made for eighteenth-century manners, tastes, and turn of mind. Though of course he encountered the new military ideas of the Napoleonic age, in tactical manuals if not in larger military studies and in a visit to France just after the War of 1812, his conceptions of war remained mainly those of the eighteenth century. At the end of his career he had to preside over the gathering of the mammoth Civil War army of citizen soldiers, but he clearly felt most at home with a small professional army. In strategy he was at his best in a war of limited objectives which could be pursued by maneuver and occupation of territory rather than by ruthless destruction.[15]

His first major success, at Chippewa and Lundy's Lane in the Niagara frontier campaign of 1814, had an eighteenth-century quality; like Frederick the Great he won fame through his superior training and conditioning of his soldiers. In 1814 the British army was the most old-fashioned of the major armies of Europe. Despite the acceptance elsewhere of the French Revolutionary doctrine of the nation in arms, the British army remained a relatively small professional force, adhering to traditional linear tactics and reluctant to accept the growing tendency toward open-order fighting. Scott trained the newly organized Regular regiments on the Niagara frontier to fight in similar highly disciplined fashion, though the basis of his tactical system was French rather than British. His great achievement of 1814 was to do the job so well that his regiments met the British with equal tactical skill in the open field. After the war he became chairman of a board of officers to prepare a new American tactical manual. His "system of 1815," modified a decade later as the "system of 1825," remained standard until 1834, when he incorporated features of the Prussian drill system. In that version, Scott's tactics prevailed until the introduction of Captain William J. Hardee's famous manual on the eve of the Civil War.[16]

During most of the years of Scott's preeminence, the immediate problems of the American Army were less those of preparing for European-style war than of keeping peace on the Indian frontier. This mission included protecting Indians from unruly whites, but inevitably most of the Army's energies went into the historically better known task of protecting whites from unruly Indians. For Indian fighting, Scott's European tactics were not so inappropriate as they have sometimes been made to seem. When Indian opponents could be brought to stand in battle, the best way to crush them was to pour a heavy fire into them and then assault them with a disciplined charge. This method best exploited the superior cohesion of the disciplined white troops.[17]

But in other ways an army modeled on European armies, as the American Army of Scott's day was, fit less well into the requirements of Indian war. Winfield Scott's own next important venture in campaigning after the War of 1812 was his command in the Second Seminole War in 1836. The venture was not auspicious. Scott chose this occasion to essay an unwontedly Napoleonic maneuver, attempting to trap the main body of hostiles in their lair around the Cove of the Withlacoochee (modern Lake Tsala Apopka) by means of an elaborate movement of three converging columns. His heavy columns of slow-moving troops and much impedimenta marching noisily through the Florida hammocks merely served to scatter the Seminoles, so that Scott's blows landed in air. Once the hostiles were scattered, the Army never again enjoyed an opportunity to deal with them as a tangible mass.[18]

Instead the Army had to cope with guerrillas who raided outposts and white settlements, but seemed to evaporate whenever the Army thought it was about to corner any of them. The terrain and climate of Florida, tangled hammocks, insect-ridden swamps, and sawgrass-covered everglades, with debilitating extremes of temperature and humidity, assisted the Seminoles' methods. The standard strategic objectives of European war, strategically located fortresses, lines of communication, and political centers, could not be pursued because they did not exist. For seven years, from 1835 to 1842, one general after another damaged his military reputation in Florida in the frustrating pursuit of enemies who seemed solid only when they were striking out of ambush, but who apparently changed into ghosts as soon as they were struck in turn.

Of a procession of eight commanders, only Zachary Taylor, brevetted brigadier general for the battle of Okeechobee, emerged with his reputation enhanced, because at Lake Okeechobee some of the Seminoles were encouraged enough by having strong defenses to make the mistake of attempting a stand against an American bayonet charge. The Regular Army had to be enlarged from 7,000 to 12,500 men to fight the war, and some 10,000 Regulars and 30,000 volunteers fought in Florida at one time or another—their numbers sometimes making matters worse by overstraining logistical resources and making American movements still more clumsy and noisy. In the end, a kind of victory was achieved through treachery and brutality: the policy inaugurated by Brevet Major General Thomas S. Jesup of making captives of the Indians who came under a truce to parley, as Jesup captured Osceola, and the policy of destroying Indian villages and crops to deprive the enemy of sustenance. Even then, the announced object of the war was never achieved. The purpose was to remove all the Seminoles from Florida. But after seven years of guerrilla war against an enemy whose warriors may never have exceeded 1,000, and who had no industrial base, no outside aid, and no arms beyond those they possessed at the beginning of the war or could capture, the United States had to leave them in possession of a large tract extending from Charlotte Harbor down to Shark River in the Everglades, and east to Okeechobee. The experience should have served as a standing warning against the difficulties of guerrilla war, against even the most primitively equipped adversaries, in areas favoring the guerrillas and when the guerrillas are animated by an intense will to independence.[19]

On the western frontier, the Army's European conceptions of war did not serve it much better. There the policy had evolved since Confederation days of planting Army outposts along the farthest fringes of settlement to offer protection against hostile Indians. The outposts were called "forts," but rather than elaborate defenses like those on the seacoast they were usually wooden stockades surrounding a congeries of log offices and barracks; most of them were not meant to be permanent, but to be abandoned when settlement moved westward. The frontier forts at first represented no strategic plan at all, but merely a response to the demands of the pioneering western communities.

By the end of the second decade of the century, during John C. Calhoun's tenure as Secretary of War, the frontier outposts had already reached out to the confluence of the St. Peter's River with the Mississippi in present-day Minnesota and to Council Bluffs on the Missouri. This ambitious extension of the area which the Army was trying to protect tended, however, to lure white adventurers beyond the regions where the military could guard them with reasonable adequacy, thus to stir up troubles with the Indians, and to scatter the posts beyond mutual support. During the late 1820s, Secretary of War Peter B. Porter deplored such overstretching of resources, but he could do little to correct it.[20]

By the middle 1830s, the removal of large numbers of eastern Indians westward was aggravating the problems of keeping order along the boundaries between white settlement and the Indian areas. But it was also intended to create a permanent "Indian Country" beyond Arkansas and Missouri, and the War Department tried to eliminate haphazard extension of the military frontier in favor of a reasoned plan. By 1840 the removals of eastern Indians to the Indian Country in the West were almost complete, and the boundary of Indian Country was fixed along the western boundaries of Arkansas and Missouri, eastward along the northern border of Missouri, northward through eastern Iowa, and along the Mississippi and then eastward across northern Wisconsin to Lake Superior.[21]

To Secretary of War Lewis Cass, serving under President Jackson while this boundary was taking shape, the chief desideratum of military policy along the boundary was to bring the western frontier defenses into a coordinated system permitting the forts to secure the new quasi-international frontier and in doing so to give each other mutual support. To that end he recommended a cordon of posts connected by a north-to-south military road to permit rapid shifting of troops. Congress voted $100,000 to build the military road, from Fort Snelling at the junction of the St. Peter's and the Mississippi in the north to the vicinity of Fort Towson on the Red River, in modern Oklahoma, in the south.[22]

Martin Van Buren's Secretary of War, Joel R. Poinsett, objected to Cass's plan on the ground that it violated all experience and rules of war to depend on a line of communication running parallel to the potential fighting front. Reinforcements using the road would have to undergo exposed flank marches. An army's line of communication should always lead to its relatively secure rear. Therefore Poinsett proposed two lines of forts, exterior and interior, the former shielding the farthest advanced settlements, the latter serving both as shelters for threatened populations and as depots for reserves. Selected forts should contain not only their own garrisons but also "disposable" troops to act as a mobile reserve. General Gaines, proposing a similar system, suggested the building of railroad lines between the reserves in the rear and the scattered forts on the exterior line; to save money, Poinsett proposed so locating the reserve depots that river lines could be employed instead.[23]

Poinsett found himself obliged to build the military road despite his disapproval of it, and the project was carried well along during his administration and completed in 1845. Nevertheless, he also tried to effect his own system, designating Jefferson Barracks at St. Louis as the principal reserve depot for the boundary forts. Unfortunately, neither Cass's plan nor Poinsett's, both of which had merits, could ever be fully implemented. During Poinsett's term the Seminole War pulled so many troops to Florida that it destroyed any pool of reserves and so denuded the whole frontier that there could not be much mutual support over the military road either. Before the end of the term, emigration all the way across the Indian Country to distant Oregon was gathering so much momentum that Poinsett had to begin thinking about planting new forts far up the Missouri toward the Rocky Mountains. While contemplating a permanent Indian Country, the United States had reserved the right of transit through the country, and the Oregon Trail would have to be guarded if the right of transit was to remain effective. Poinsett's successor, John F. Spencer, made specific proposals for new forts in the Indian Country along the Oregon Trail. Then the Mexican War came along, adding to the United States so vast a territory west and south of the Indian Country that no feasible plan could promise the existing Army real control over it.[24]

On the eve of the Mexican War, Colonel Stephen Watts Kearny had already recommended that the whole idea of guarding the

Indian border with numerous small posts be abandoned as impractical. He would have substituted large, consolidated forces patrolling into Indian Country regularly from a limited number of major bases, to remind the Indian nations of the military might of the United States. He believed that the small garrisons of the scattered border outposts invited only contempt from the Indians. While his large columns might have impressed a tribe while they were in its neighborhood, however, the obvious objection was that they would not do so once they moved on. Consolidating the troops into a few columns would have left too much of the Indian frontier altogether unprotected.[25]

Consequently, even after the Mexican cession, Indian defense rested upon small garrisons in outposts near the Indian border but so distant from each other that support was often too long in coming to be of much use. Old fears of standing armies as a danger to republicanism, and perennial desires for economical government, kept the Regular Army pathetically small in proportion to its responsibilities both to protect whites from Indians marauding out of Indian Country and to protect the Indian Country from incursions by unauthorized and predatory whites. Too much of the troop strength that did exist was infantry, not enough cavalry, for mobility between the forts across the western plains. (There was no Regular cavalry until a battalion of mounted riflemen was authorized in 1832; before the unit was completed, the authorization was changed to create a regiment of dragoons, of which a second regiment was authorized in 1836.)[26]

All the way through the 1840s and 1850s and into the Civil War, both national policy and military strategy for dealing with the Indians continued to rest upon the idea of a permanent Indian Country boundary, even while emigration to California on top of the trek to Oregon and the Mexican War brought the concept badly unhinged. Fortunately, the number of whites who tried to settle in the Indian Country itself was still small enough, and Indian attitudes toward passage through their country were tolerant enough, so that no severe crisis arose. But by the time the nation resolved the sectional controversy between North and South, it was also to have to develop an Indian policy, and a military strategy to uphold policy, more truly capable of permanence than the Indian Country idea.

Winfield Scott's greatest campaign, from Veracruz to the halls of the Montezumas in the Mexican War, permitted him to wage limited war in the pre-Napoleonic, eighteenth-century style most congenial to him. He conducted the campaign with strict regard for the rights of the citizens of the invaded territories, with every effort to confine bloodshed and suffering to the enemy's armed forces and to avoid inflicting them upon civilians. He imposed stringent regulations to compel orderly conduct from his soldiers in their dealings with the Mexican populace and to confine the opportunities for friction to the minimum necessary for the sustenance of his army and the morale of his troops. He forbade forced requisitions and insisted upon the purchase of supplies, this despite a most precarious logistical situation at the end of a long supply line across the Gulf of Mexico and through the yellow-fever belt of the Mexican coast. After he landed near Veracruz, he eschewed the sort of costly assault which his colleague Zachary Taylor had recently employed in similar circumstances to take the fortified city of Monterrey, preferring instead to save lives through a formal siege of the eighteenth-century style (with the ironic result that because Scott's casualties at Veracruz were low, the American public inclined to believe that Taylor's capture of the weaker defenses of Monterrey was a greater achievement; after all, the price was higher). Throughout his campaign, Scott avoided all-out battle whenever it was possible to do so and husbanded lives by substituting maneuver for combat with all the frugality of a general of the *ancien régime*.[27]

In the other principal campaign of the Mexican War, General Taylor showed himself to be an altogether less thoughtful and accomplished strategist than Scott. Taylor's campaign in northern Mexico also had less strategic merit than Scott's apart from the shortcomings of the general officer commanding. Once Taylor had secured President James K. Polk's version of the new United States-Mexico frontier created by the American annexation of Texas, namely, the line of the Rio Grande, the strategic objects of his subsequent operations into Mexico were not clear. Too much difficult country intervened between the Rio Grande and the City of Mexico via the overland route for there ever to have existed any serious intention that Taylor should advance to the enemy capital. The American government's hope for Taylor's campaign of invasion across the Rio Grande into Mexico's northern states was that occupation of those states would penalize Mexico enough to compel her to make peace, recognize the annexation of Texas, and grant the United States the other territorial increments which President Polk and his fellow expansionists desired, westward to the Golden Gate. Mexico's northern states were so remote from the center of her national power, however, that General Scott was right to be doubtful from the beginning that Taylor's operations could cause the Mexican government to conclude a peace satisfactory to the United States.

Plunging into Mexico to Monterrey and beyond for strategically dubious purposes, General Taylor mismanaged his logistics so that his troops were too often sick and supply too often uncertain, allowed a relatively lax discipline in regard to plundering the inhabitants, fought battles unsubtly and expensively to clear the Mexican army from his path, and after he became angered by the detachment of 4,000 men including nearly all his Regulars for Scott's campaign, disobeyed Scott's orders to retreat to a strong defensive line around Monterrey. Instead Taylor placed his remaining troops in a position difficult to defend and dangling on a precarious supply line, eighteen miles south of Saltillo at the hacienda of Agua Nueva. His excuses for this last decision were that he understood Scott's orders only as advice, and that the Mexican army could not cross the 200 miles of barren country between San Luis Potosí and his position anyway. When General Antonio López de Santa Anna surprised him by marching 20,000 Mexican soldiers across the barren country to attack him, Taylor, now reduced to 5,000 troops, retreated three miles to a slightly better position at the hacienda Buena Vista. There he displayed his best and redeeming qualities, by so inspiring his mostly inexperienced army and so skillfully maneuvering its units from one threatened place to another, that he repulsed the Mexicans with 1,500 to 2,000 casualties to about 750 casualties of his own. Buena Vista is a deservedly famous tactical triumph of American arms; but in strategic conception and conduct, Zachary Taylor's campaign in Mexico was a throwback to the amateurishness of the War of 1812.[28]

The object of Scott's campaign was far clearer: to convince the Mexican government of the futility of prolonging the war, and perhaps to make its continued prolongation impossible, by capturing the capital and heart of the country, the City of Mexico. The territorial gains which the United States had sought in going to war against Mexico were already in American hands or about to be when Scott's campaign began. Taylor had assured American possession of Texas; and the combined efforts of the American settlers in California, the American Navy's eastern Pacific squadron, John C. Frémont's *opéra bouffe*, and Brigadier General Stephen Watts Kearny's Army of the West were capturing California. Kearny dropped off enough garrisons between Texas and California to terminate Mexican sovereignty in the intervening territory, especially when shielded by the anabasis of Colonel Alexander Doniphan's one thousand across Chihuahua. Scott's task was to persuade a Mexican government to grant formal recognition to these developments so that the United States could go about exploiting its conquests in as much peace as the resident Indians would permit.

Characteristically, Scott did not include as an object of his campaign into Mexico the destruction of the Mexican army. Even if he had thought that the destruction of the enemy army was necessary for the winning of peace, which he did not, he could not have afforded the casualties implicit in a strategy of annihilation. For his campaign inland from Veracruz he never had more than about 10,000 effectives, and to have attempted to destroy the Mexican army would have been to risk prohibitive diminution of his own limited strength. Anyway, the Mexicans had already displayed a remarkably resilient ability to raise new armies when large forces had crumbled before Zachary Taylor's bludgeon in the north. They were fighting in their own recruiting ground, and Scott would be far from his.

Scott determined upon a political strategy. He believed that unlike the American Confederation during the War of the Revolution, Mexico offered a political target analogous to European capitals. He believed that Mexican political life centered upon the City of Mexico completely enough that the conquest of the capital would paralyze the country and oblige any Mexican government to make peace in order to remain a government at all. He would aim at the capture of the City of Mexico by as direct means as possible, but with the lowest casualties commensurate with that purpose.[29]

Therefore he set out on a campaign not of great battles but of maneuver, seeking to flank the Mexicans out of successive positions at minimal cost in casualties to them as well as to his own army. He departed from a policy of avoiding headlong battle only twice, when victory at Contreras near the gates of Mexico so fired the enthusiasm of his army that the divisions swept forward in frontal assault against the Mexican line along the Rio Churubusco, and when a mistaken report of an active Mexican cannon foundry in the Molino del Rey convinced Scott he had to pay the price of assaulting that place. Otherwise his attacks and battles were the unavoidable incidents of flanking maneuvers. The one aspect of his campaign most reflecting the new influences of the wars of the French Revolution and Napoleon was his organization of his army into divisions used as autonomous units of maneuver for the purpose of his flanking operations. But even here, Scott kept his army relatively close in hand and under his constant personal control, so that his operations more closely resemble those of the unitary armies of the eighteenth century than those of Napoleonic divisions.

It is apparent that Scott wished to avoid actions which might unduly inflame Mexican emotions and prolong the war as a result. Bloody battles, even if destroying a Mexican army, might have had that counterproductive effect. Thus after the victorious day of Contreras and Churubusco, August 20, 1847, when the Mexican army was in flight before him and he might have harried it to destruction and marched into the City of Mexico forthwith, Scott halted his advance. Instead of pressing his advantage, he acquiesced in an armistice. The armistice as it turned out permitted the Mexicans to rally themselves and ended in renewed fighting at Chapultepec, and so it may have been a mistake. But it was consistent with a policy that in the end gave Scott what he wanted.

At this juncture, after Contreras and Churubusco, Scott hoped he was near enough to the City of Mexico that he need not go farther; if he could secure a satisfactory peace without the bitterness which going all the way into the capital might engender, so much the better. This particular hope failed; to win a satisfactory peace he had to display the Stars and Stripes from the Palacio Nacional. But he had to do no more than that. The Mexican army survived the loss of its capital; Scott did not crush it, but had made one position after another untenable for it. Under Scott's forbearing regime, daily life in the capital city under American occupation followed almost a normal course, without harsh punishments by the conqueror. But the national life of the country fell into the paralysis Scott had foreseen, and therefore at length the government of Mexico made peace.[30]

Though he avoided bloody battles, Scott was a bold strategist. His march from Veracruz into the interior was one of the most daring movements of American military history, for he had to capture the enemy's capital while separated from his naval support not only by the fever coast but also by more than 200 miles of mountainous, guerrilla-infested roadway. The Duke of Wellington may well have said when he learned of the beginning of Scott's campaign, as we are told he did: "Scott is lost. . . . He can't take the city, and he can't fall back upon his base."[31]

Scott could be an innovative general as well as a bold one. His amphibious landing near Veracruz, for which he shares credit with the Navy and especially with Commodore David Conner, was a model operation which might well have aroused the envy of many of those who conducted similar landings in World War II. To accomplish it, Scott ordered the first boats in American military history specifically designed as landing craft. Characteristically, he ensured the success of the landing by taking infinite pains in the planning and preparation. With all men and equipment packed in proper order for their use—in twentieth-century terminology, "combat-loaded"—in the transports which discharged them into the landing craft, the boats approached the shore in the appropriate order of battle, supported close up by the guns of shallow-draft vessels of the naval squadron. The Mexicans chose not to oppose the landing; but that mistake on their part cannot detract from proceedings which almost certainly would have been successful no matter what the enemy attempted.[32]

Nevertheless, though he was bold and when necessary innovative, Winfield Scott remained an old-fashioned general of the eighteenth-century mold. The essence of his approach to war and of the spirit in which he conducted his greatest campaign is to be found in a letter to General Santa Anna opening the negotiations that led to the armistice after Churubusco: "Too much blood has already been shed in this unnatural war between the two great republics of this continent."[33] How remarkable Scott's life-saving strategy of limited objectives was, at as late a date as 1847, the whole course of the American Civil War will reveal. That war was also to suggest that while Scott was the preeminent American strategist of the first half of the nineteenth century, he occupied a lonely plateau in more senses than one: that at the zenith of his powers he was already a museum piece, a soldier of an age gone by whose perceptions of war and strategy had little influence on most of the very graduates of West Point whose service in Mexico he so fulsomely praised, because the young graduates inhabited a new world of very different values from Scott's, the military world of Napoleon.

5. The Founding of American Strategic Studies: Dennis Hart Mahan and Henry Wager Halleck

Strategy is defined to be the art of directing masses on decisive points, or the hostile movements of armies beyond the range of each other's cannon.

—*Henry Wager Halleck*[1]

WINFIELD SCOTT COULD AFFORD to wage his old-fashioned style of campaign in part because his enemy was often inept and could be persuaded to make peace relatively easily. Scott was masterful enough to have carried through a similar campaign against a more formidable adversary; but he by no means faced so difficult a task in breaking his enemy's will to fight as did, for example, the European monarchs of the 1790s who had sought to extinguish the French Revolution. The will to resist, to fight, and to win was so great in revolutionary France that it had created revolutionary patterns of war.

When assailed by the hostile monarchs, the Revolution in France had found itself fighting for much higher stakes than the fortresses or even the provinces which were the prizes of the eighteenth-century wars. The Revolution was fighting for its very existence, and France herself fought for control of her own national destiny. For such stakes, France could mobilize resources beyond the imagination of the monarchs of the old regime: the united manpower of the nation, and all the material goods the nation's people could bring to bear. "From this moment until that in which our enemies shall have been driven from the territory of the Republic," in the words of the

Convention's decree of August 23, 1793, "all Frenchmen are permanently requisitioned for service in the armies."[2]

With the energy and the passions of France's manpower enlisted in the dual causes of the Republic and the nation, France drove her enemies from the national territory and then, to assure and complete the triumph, carried the war into the enemies' countries. In near and small neighbors, France established republican governments dependent upon her own. In more distant and larger neighbors, the French sought at least governments in complaisant alliance with them. These strokes of France against the rest of Europe aroused in time, however, nationalist fervor comparable to that first developed in France herself. If the faltering ancient monarchies could not enlist all the popular emotions mobilized by France, some of them could at least enlist nationalism, against the threat of French domination and as a source of manpower and resources sufficient to compete with the French.

Once rival nationalisms became enlisted in war, victory became harder to win for all the belligerents. Defeat in one or two campaigns would no longer persuade a government to cut its losses, make peace, and await retribution in the future. Popular emotions rallied in defense of the national destiny could not so abruptly be turned off. To break the will of the enemy to resist, the basic object of warfare, became much more difficult than before. If the ends of war were more difficult to obtain, however, the means were more abundant. The mass armies which could be enlisted or conscripted under the stimulus of nationalism provided reservoirs of manpower which by standards formed during the old regime seemed inexhaustible. Not surprisingly, governments and military commanders became tempted to spend their huge manpower reserves prodigally in quest of the victories which were ever harder to attain.

More specifically, Napoleon Bonaparte found his way to victory amid the new circumstances of war by expending manpower lavishly to impose even greater human losses upon the enemy, and an immense moral loss as well, in the military event which became his hallmark, the mighty, climactic battle. "It is upon the field of battle," he said, "that the fate of fortresses and empires is decided."[3] In battle, Napoleon compressed a strategy of annihilation into an overwhelming thunderclap of combat, combining the imposition of huge physical casualties with the dramatic seizure of a psychological ascendancy over the enemy—the latter characteristically through envelopment, *la manoeuvre sur les derrières*—so swiftly and bewilderingly accomplished that the enemy capitulated despite the profundity of the issues in contest. "There are in Europe many good generals," said Napoleon, "but they see too many things at once. I see only one thing, namely the enemy's main body. I try to crush it, confident that secondary matters will then settle themselves."[4]

To paralyze the enemy's will by crushing the main body of his army tended to require exacting from him casualties so large that, even with skillful execution of *la manoeuvre sur les derrières*, they could be purchased only with terrible casualties of one's own. This price Napoleon was willing to demand of his troops, if by doing so he could attain in a dramatic stroke of war the moral advantage of a sudden, almost instantaneous alteration of the balance of power in his favor. Through the Austerlitz type of battle Napoleon concluded he could break the enemy's will to resist despite all the reinforcement given that will by the new issues of war—and he demonstrated that he could, at least for the short run, when he knocked Austria out of the Third Coalition in the Ulm-Austerlitz campaign of October-December, 1805, and dispatched Prussia while almost literally destroying her army in the three weeks' Jena-Auerstädt campaign of October, 1806.

Napoleon had the advantage not only of deep reservoirs of manpower but also of new tactics and technology. In the late eighteenth century, and especially after becoming Inspector General of Artillery in the French army in 1776, Jean Baptiste Vaquette de Gribeauval had created a new, more mobile artillery with greater power in proportion to the weight of the guns, by reducing the length and windage of the pieces and designing new carriages which ran more smoothly. He also built carriages with interchangeable parts for quick repair, and he made soldiers of the men who drove the carriages. Simultaneously, the development of coke smelting made possible the production of increased numbers of iron guns. Gribeauval's artillery could go into action at a gallop and change positions swiftly, and with the new quantities of guns it could go far toward smothering enemy infantry under an overwhelming volume of fire. With the Gribeauval artillery system Napoleon was able to throw an immense mass of case shot from close range against critical points in the enemy's position, to stun the enemy in preparation for the infantry assault.[5]

Napoleon also had the advantages of the military innovations of the Revolution and of the years just preceding it, not only in the numbers of men the Revolution gave him but also in its organization of the men into divisions, which were small armies capable of independent maneuver. His favorite device for bringing on and winning the climactic Napoleonic battle involved advancing a web of divisions within supporting distance of each other, utilizing some of them to fix in position, hold, and batter the enemy, while he exploited the capabilities of the others for independent maneuver to accomplish the enemy's envelopment.

The mass army, the nation in arms sustained by nationalistic fervor, was the signal feature of the new Revolutionary mode of war. A strategy of annihilation employing the climactic Austerlitz kind of battle was Napoleon's characteristic means of precipitating decision out of the new mode of war. In combination, these new features of war produced a rebirth of military thought and literature. In eighteenth-century dynastic war, rival armies resembled each other so closely, and the accepted limitations upon their conduct were so confining, that strategy had come to signify little more than stratagems; the general who excelled his opponent in ruses was likely to win the contest. Revolutionary and Napoleonic war added so many complexities that military writers became hard put to define the ingredients of successful war. But amid the complexities, Napoleon so impressively exploited the Austerlitz or Jena-Auerstädt battle that this type of climactic struggle tended to emerge in the writings of Napoleon's interpreters as the essence of warfare. "We have only one means in War," said his great German interpreter Clausewitz, "—the battle."

> The combat is the single activity in War; in the combat the destruction of the enemy opposed to us is the means to the end; it is so even when the combat does not actually take place, because in that case there lies at the root of the decision the supposition at all events that this destruction is to be regarded as beyond doubt. It follows, therefore, that the destruction of the enemy's military force is the foundation-stone of all action in War, the great support of all combinations, which rest upon it like the arch on its abutments. All action, therefore, takes place on the supposition that if the solution by force of arms which lies at its foundation should be realized, it will be a favourable one. The decision by arms is, for all operations in War, great and small, what cash payment is in bill transactions. However remote from each other these relations, however seldom the realisation may take place, still it can never entirely fail to occur.[6]

Under the inspiration of Napoleon the rise in Europe of a theoretical literature of war was one of several developments of the early nineteenth century which make up the beginnings of the modern military profession. The steps which had accompanied the French

Revolution toward divorcing officership from the remnants of the feudal aristocracy and the foundation of schools for the study of officership and war were other developments in the same direction. The United States, still a colony of Europe in matters of war—for it was against the European military powers that the United States had to measure itself to prepare for any major test of its security—followed these European developments and began the professionalization of its own officer corps through the rebirth of the foundling Military Academy at West Point, under the superintendency of Sylvanus Thayer beginning in 1817. Thayer's West Point tried to stimulate a systematic American study of war, which might tie together the diverse strands of activity in maritime defense and land war into a coherent strategy for the military protection and advancement of American national interests, thus remedying the gravest American military deficiency of the War of 1812. Since Thayer and the disciples whom he brought into the West Point faculty were thoroughly conscious of the colonial relationship of the United States to European military thought and practice—indeed, extravagantly deferential to Napoleon and to France—this foundation of an American strategic doctrine presumably would take place by borrowing relevant principles from the military literature of Europe and especially of France.

West Point could devote only a small proportion of its resources to the development of American strategic thought. Despite the acuteness of the need which the War of 1812 had demonstrated for American consideration of strategy, the Military Academy had too many other things to do. In an army still lacking, as it had since its birth, enough junior officers competent to instruct the rank and file in elementary tactics, the most basic rudiments of war had to consume a large share of attention. In a country not immediately imperiled by foreign enemies and jealous of standing armies, the academy had to justify itself by preparing officers who could do useful work in peace, so it became largely a school of civil engineering. No American strategic thought comparable to that of Europe could yet emerge, still less a truly original strategic thought. Nevertheless, it is remarkable how much Thayer's academy accomplished, in the face of all sorts of distractions, toward developing among its cadets concepts of officership as a profession and of strategy as an appropriate object of reflection demanding systematic study both of its history and of its theory.[7]

Dennis Hart Mahan (USMA 1824, graduating number one in his

class), a protégé of Thayer who joined the faculty in 1832 after study in France and rose to become chairman of the academic board, became the principal instructor in warfare as well as in engineering. The attitude toward the study of war inculcated by Mahan was summed up by his student Henry Wager Halleck (USMA 1839):

> War in its most extensive sense may be regarded both as a *science* and an *art*. It is a science so far as it investigates general principles and institutes an analysis of military operations; and an art when considered with reference to the practical rules for conducting campaigns, sieges, battles, &c. . . .
>
> As thus defined, the military art may be divided into four distinct branches, viz.: 1st. *Strategy*; 2d. Fortification, or *Engineering*; 3d. *Logistics*; 4th. *Tactics*. Several general treatises on this art add another branch, called *The Policy of War*, or the relations of war with the affairs of state.[8]

For many years the standard text on the science and art of war in use at the academy was Captain J. M. O'Connor's translation of S. F. Gay de Vernon's *Treatise on the Science of War and Fortification*. This work emphasized the engineering aspects of war. To bring to the academy a larger consideration of strategy, O'Connor's translation included a summary of the strategic precepts of Antoine Henri, Baron de Jomini, prepared by the translator. Jomini, not Clausewitz, became the principal interpreter of Napoleonic strategy to Americans; Clausewitz was not translated into English until 1873.[9]

Though he was the foremost commentator on Napoleonic war writing in the language of France itself, Jomini was in certain characteristics of thought and temperament less well equipped to interpret Napoleon than was the Prussian Clausewitz. Jomini's intellectual roots were deep in the eighteenth-century Enlightenment. He was repelled when he found elements of the chaotic and the demoniacal in Napoleon's character and methods of war. He abhorred indiscriminate bloodshed. He did not approve of armies' living off the country through which they marched and spreading devastation and suffering in their paths. His mind moved in orderly and logical ways which impelled him to define the principles of war in such a manner that they would form a neat system. Though he criticized earlier military writers of the Enlightenment for system building, he was himself both a system-builder and a traditionalist, whose interpretations emphasized less what was novel in Napoleonic war than its continuity with the warfare of the eighteenth century.

To Jomini, the principles of strategy are timeless and unchanging, like the natural law of the Enlightenment universe. The basic tenet of strategy is a simple one, the necessity to bring the maximum possible force to bear against the decisive point in the theater of operations while the enemy can muster only an inferior part of his strength there.[10] To be able thus to bring superior against inferior strength depends upon the proper ordering of one's lines of communication in relation to the enemy's.[11] It is almost always preferable to operate upon interior lines, while the enemy is obliged to operate upon exterior lines. The interior position vis-à-vis the enemy will permit the parts of one's own army to unite more rapidly than the parts of the enemy, and the enemy can be beaten in detail, by turning first against one and then against another of his inferior parts more rapidly than he can unite them.[12] Jomini's preoccupation with lines of communication and with interior versus exterior lines tended to make strategic problems appear to be exercises in geometry. His emphasis on the decisive point which would permit domination of the theater of operations tended to turn warfare away from the quest for the destruction of the enemy's armed forces and back toward the contest for control of geographic places more characteristic of eighteenth-century than of Napoleonic war.[13]

On the other hand, Jomini had served both with Napoleon's armies and with their Russian opponents, it was Napoleonic war that he was attempting to interpret, and he could not be unmoved—however much he might be repelled—by the dynamic new forces unleashed by Revolutionary and Napoleonic war. In contrast to a tendency in Enlightenment military writing to dwell upon fortifications and the difficulties they posed for the attacker, Jomini was Napoleonic in his emphasis on the virtues of offensive war. Despite his general concern with the contest for control of territory, he occasionally acknowledged that Napoleon fought for larger and more brutal aims: Napoleon, he said, "seemed convinced that the first means of effecting great results was to concentrate above all on cutting up and destroying the enemy army, being certain that states or provinces fall of themselves when they no longer have organized forces to defend them."[14]

Jomini's interpretation of Napoleon became the foundation of the teaching of strategy at West Point. In addition to meeting Jomini through Captain O'Connor's summary of his principles, the cadets encountered his teachings in Dennis Mahan's explication of the art of war in the senior course which formed the principal introduction to the subject, for Mahan's ideas were formed upon Jomini's. The first American writer to attempt a systematic exploration of the principles of strategy in the form of a book was Mahan's student Halleck, with his publication of *Elements of Military Art and Science* in 1846. Halleck, who was later to translate Jomini's *Life of Napoleon*, owed his ideas on strategy mainly to Jomini, both through Mahan and directly. He took Jomini's first tenet of strategy as his very definition of the word: "*Strategy*," he said, "is defined to be the art of directing masses on decisive points, or the hostile movements of armies beyond the range of each other's cannon."[15]

The most Napoleonic feature of Halleck's theory of strategy was the emphasis upon the value of the offensive (somewhat surprisingly to those acquainted with Halleck mainly through his performance in the Civil War):

> *Offensive* war is ordinarily most advantageous in its moral and political influence. It is waged on a foreign soil, and therefore spares the country of the attacking force; it augments its own resources at the same time that it diminishes those of the enemy; it adds to the moral courage of its own army, while it disheartens its opponents . . . . if a political diversion be made in favor of the invading force, and its operations be attended with success, it strikes the enemy at the heart, paralyzes all his military energies, and deprives him of his military resources, thus promptly terminating the contest. Regarded simply as the initiative of movements, the offensive is almost always the preferable one, as it enables the general to choose his lines for moving and concentrating his masses on the decisive point.
>
> The first and most important rule in offensive war is, to keep your forces as much concentrated as possible. This will not only prevent misfortune, but secure victory,—since, by its necessary operation, you possess the power of throwing your whole force upon any exposed point of your enemy's position.[16]

Thus Halleck both praised the offensive and returned to the more specific Jominian tenet of concentration against the decisive point. Despite this bold endorsement of offensive war, however, as Halleck's book develops, it becomes both less aggressively Napoleonic and perhaps more consistent with what his future campaigns were to reveal of Halleck's own character. In the process it becomes no less Jominian, since its departures from the bold and ruthless in Napoleonic war accord with the Enlightenment moderation of Jomini himself.

As the book goes on, praise for the offensive and injunctions to attack come to be qualified by exceptions and cautionary admonitions, until the original encouragement to offensive war is almost diluted out of existence. This tendency becomes especially marked when Halleck attempts to apply Jominian strategic precepts to the military situation of the United States. Here, of course, the circumstances of the United States offered apparent reasons for a defensive approach to war. Halleck saw the military role of the United States in world affairs as primarily that of defending the resources of its continental homeland. His concern was not for a military policy to deal with the Indians or a small neighbor such as Mexico; he implied that such a policy needed little attention because against such adversaries the strength of the United States was more than adequate. The problem which drew Halleck's attention was that of the United States holding its own militarily when increasing national wealth and commerce and improving navigation brought the country into closer contact with the world of the great powers. In that arena, Halleck foresaw no aggressive role for the United States but rather a military policy of self-protection and self-preservation, with a consistently defensive strategy.[17]

Five of fifteen chapters of Halleck's book directly concern fortifications, and especially the American system of coastal fortresses designed after the War of 1812 and still building when Halleck wrote. Halleck strongly endorsed the Board of Engineers system of coastal defenses and urged its completion. He devoted a lengthy section of his book to stating the theoretical reasons why forts are always superior to attacking navies, and to cataloguing historical examples of successful defenses by apparently inferior forts against apparently superior fleets. He acknowledged that no belt of fixed defenses is impregnable, that the coastal fortifications could not guarantee against hostile landings everywhere along the Atlantic and the Gulf, and that similarly the Canadian border could not be hermetically sealed. But it was a primary element in the defensive cast of his thinking that fixed defenses could greatly ease the problems of mobile armies and fleets engaged in waging defensive war. The fulfillment of the program of powerful fortifications for every major harbor of the United States, Halleck said, echoing the old Board of Engineers, would guard the major population centers against wanton bombardment and would deny to any invader quick access to port facilities from which to support his invasion. If American harbors were well fortified, a hostile power which did seek to invade would have to base itself at first on coastal areas exposed to surf and storms and without piers, and the lack of a port might be enough to make the difference between victory and defeat for an invader. Furthermore, fortresses of all kinds are especially useful for rallying inexperienced troops, who would surely comprise the bulk of an American army early in a war; in this way the French border fortresses had been indispensable to maintaining the resistance of the raw French Revolutionary armies to the invaders of 1792.[18]

While emphasizing the values of fortifications for the defense, Halleck correspondingly feared them when he directed his thoughts to the conduct of the offensive. He was cautious in his advice on the necessity to eliminate, or to mask with absolute assurance of security, fortresses standing in one's rear when conducting an offensive. It would be folly, he conceded, to return to a medieval sort of preoccupation with fortified places, insisting upon their reduction whether or not they occupied strategic points; but in general his emphasis was on the potential for disruption which forts must represent in the plans of an invader. Halleck's whole concern with fortresses reflected also his concept of war as a contest for the possession of places, not a Napoleonic or Clausewitzian struggle for the overthrow of enemy armies.[19]

In general, Halleck shrank from the invader's role. He pointed to the dangers which await an invading army deep in hostile territory even when the defender lacks adequate fortresses: Moscow became Napoleon's ruin despite the Russian neglect of its defenses and the French emperor's consequent ability to march into the city. As Halleck saw it, the invader of any country whose defenders retain a modicum of national spirit faces almost impossible dilemmas. To supply an invading army, an ancient prescription was to make war support war, to requisition necessary provisions and matériel from the occupied provinces. Not to follow this prescription, not to make the invaded people feel the harsh hand of war, is to risk leaving the spirit of resistance touched too little, to risk occupying the country without actually subduing it. But while an invader's excessive leniency is likely to be dangerous to himself, still, to deal too harshly with the occupied population, to make war feed war by requisitioning upon the country as Napoleon's soldiers did in Spain, is to risk provoking the same kind of popular resistance which the French aroused in Spain.[20]

Always Halleck diluted his offensive prescriptions. He cautioned that inside an enemy's territory celerity of movement is less important than concentration, than keeping one's own forces united and well in hand against surprise. "As a general rule the attacking force has a moral superiority over the defensive," he said "but this advantage is frequently more than counterbalanced by other conditions."[21]

Halleck's mentor, Dennis Mahan, published his own reflections on warfare the year after Halleck's book appeared, under the deceptive as well as awkward title, *An Elementary Treatise on Advanced-Guard, Out-Post, and Detachment Service of Troops, and the Manner of Posting and Handling Them in Presence of an Enemy. With a Historical Sketch of the Rise and Progress of Tactics, &c., &c.* This book, especially in its larger later editions, was more of a treatise on war in general than its long or its familiar short title—simply *Out-Post*—would imply. Its foundations remained the precepts of Jomini. To a degree, Mahan's work was both more directly Napoleonic and less ambiguous in its endorsement of offensive war than Halleck's. Mahan, significantly, chaired for a time the "Napoleon Club," in which officers stationed at the Military Academy discussed the Corsican's campaigns. He held that nothing remained to be learned of the art of war that had not been discovered by Napoleon; and he was given to rhapsodies upon both the emperor's genius and the climactic Napoleonic battle of annihilation such as the following:

> [To Napoleon] we owe those grand features of the art, by which an enemy is broken and utterly dispersed by one and the same blow. No futilities of preparation; no uncertain feeling about in search of the key-point; no hesitancy upon the decisive moment; the whole field of view taken in by one eagle glance; what could not be seen divined by an unerring military instinct; clouds of light troops thrown forward to bewilder his foe; a crashing fire of cannon in mass opened upon him; the rush of the impetuous column into the gap made by the artillery; the overwhelming charge of the resistless cuirassier; followed by the lancer and hussar to sweep up the broken dispersed bands; such were the tactical lessons taught in almost every battle of this great military period.[22]

For all such romanticism, and despite his endorsements of celerity of movement which have sometimes been quoted and emphasized,[23] Mahan was not so far removed from the cautious and defensive approach to war of his student Halleck. The material in *Out-Post* which, by the large share of the book it occupies, somewhat justifies the title concerns the necessity for careful and cautious reconnaissance and screening in the movement and posting of troops:

> Great prudence must be shown in advancing; as the troops engaged are liable at any moment to an attack on their flank. If the assailed attempts

> this manœuvre, the line of skirmishes must hold on pertinaciously to the ground gained, whilst the supports display and keep the enemy in check, until the reserves can be brought up to repel the attack with the bayonet.[24]

Mahan's other military books are about fortresses and military engineering, and the common theme among them is the strength and value of good defensive works: *Complete Treatise on Field Fortification* (1836), *Summary of the Course of Permanent Fortification and of the Attack and Defence of Permanent Works* (1850), *Descriptive Geometry as Applied to the Drawing of Fortification and Stereotomy* (1864), and *An Elementary Course of Military Engineering* (1866–67). If the offensive is attempted against a strongly positioned enemy, Mahan cautioned, it should be an offensive not of direct assault but of the indirect approach, of maneuver and deception. Victories should not be purchased by the sacrifice of one's own army; perhaps Napoleon himself erred in this respect. "*To do the greatest damage to our enemy with the least exposure to ourselves,*" said Mahan, "is a military axiom lost sight of only by ignorance to the true ends of victory."[25]

Despite the obeisance to the offensive necessitated by deference to Napoleon, the earliest attempts to systematize American strategic thought remained in harmony with the cautious, un-Napoleonic approach to war exemplified earlier by George Washington and in Dennis Mahan's day by Winfield Scott. The first American strategic writers, Mahan and Halleck, were not proponents of a strategy of annihilation except occasionally and ambiguously. Their preoccupation with fortification made them advocates to a larger extent of the strategic virtues of the well-prepared defensive. To the degree to which they endorsed offensive warfare in spite of its risks, they envisioned mainly a limited war for territorial objectives of the sort favored by Jomini himself and conducted in Mexico by Winfield Scott. If an offensive strategy was to be adopted, it was by implication to be a strategy of attrition or a political strategy, not a strategy of annihilation. One ought to seek the greatest damage to the enemy with the least exposure to oneself, as Dennis Mahan said; and one ought to seek "political diversion . . . in favor of the invading force," as Halleck said.

To this point, consequently, the mainstream of American strategy in thought and in action was cautious, an eighteenth-century rather than a Napoleonic kind of strategy, Jominian rather than Clausewitzian.

But as Clausewitz said, war is "chameleon-like in character."

> The greater and the more powerful the motives of a War, the more it affects the whole existence of a people. The more violent the excitement which precedes the War, by so much nearer will the War approach to its abstract form, so much the more will it be directed to the destruction of the enemy, so much the nearer will the military and political ends coincide, so much the more purely military and less political the War appears to be. . . .[26]

The pertinency of this observation lies, of course, in the fact that the next American test of arms was to be one which unleashed passions and called forth issues of national existence comparable to those of the wars of the French Revolution and Napoleon. In such a crisis, and with the United States by the mid-nineteenth century no longer poor but rich in the manpower and resources to make war, the caution and restraint hitherto predominant in American strategy gave way, just as the cautious strategies of attrition of Europe during the Enlightenment had fallen before the Napoleonic strategy of annihilation compressed into the Napoleonic battle.

This process was to occur the more easily because it was less anyone's academic teaching about strategy and war, Jomini's, Mahan's, or Halleck's, and less even Winfield Scott's restrained practice of war that dominated the imaginations of American military men in the nineteenth century, than the arresting image of Napoleon. American soldiers were generally not scholars anyway, and the study of strategy was a small part of the course at West Point. Without concerning themselves much with the theory of strategy, but from the kind of knowledge of Napoleon's campaigns possessed by any reasonably well-educated man in the nineteenth century, American soldiers knew that the climactic battle was the central feature of the Napoleonic art of war, with the destruction of the enemy army both physically and morally the battle's aim. And for soldiers, to emulate the great Napoleon was a much more compelling motive than to master the study of strategic theory.

It is far from the least of the many evidences of the peculiar magnetism which Napoleon exerted upon the nineteenth-century mind that soldiers could revere his methods of war despite the large, perhaps fatal, contribution of those very methods to his eventual downfall. Napoleon's greatest battlefield victories were of course never so decisive as they sometimes seemed; they produced immediately advantageous treaties, but Napoleon's enemies, especially after the French transmitted to them the virus of nationalism, developed an exasperating habit of rising to fight again, until at last it was they and not Napoleon who triumphed. They triumphed in large part because Napoleon's mania for battles eventually drained away his manpower although it had once seemed inexhaustible, and the emperor was reduced to desperate expedients to fend off combinations whose strength he could no longer match.

Napoleon's battles cost him an ultimately prohibitive price in manpower notwithstanding the advantages which the military technology of his time, especially his artillery, contributed toward decisiveness in battle. As the American Civil War approached, artillery lost its Napoleonic advantages. In 1855 the United States Army adopted the .58-caliber Springfield rifle as its standard shoulder arm. Supplying the Army with the new weapon would take time, and in 1861 many soldiers North as well as South went to war still carrying smoothbore muskets. Both belligerents in the Civil War rapidly put rifles into the hands of nearly all their soldiers, however, and both sides had enough rifles from the beginning to make Napoleonic artillery tactics impossible.

Napoleon used his concentration of artillery close up against the enemy's lines, to batter an opening into those lines through which his infantry could pour. The Model 1855 Springfield rifle had an effective range of about 400 to 600 yards as compared with 200 yards or less for smoothbore muskets. With the old smoothbore muskets, as Ulysses Grant wrote, "At the distance of a few hundred yards a man might fire at you all day without your finding out."[27] But with rifles, defending infantry could pick off the gunners of any artillery which came close up in Napoleonic fashion before the artillerists could complete their destructive work. The attacking artillery had to stand so far back that it could no longer do much damage to defending infantry to prepare for its own infantry's attack, especially if the defenders protected themselves behind earthworks. Though artillery itself adopted rifling to increase the range of its guns, it remained unable to do effective work against sheltered infantry until the invention later in the century of the modern shrapnel shell which would explode above the enemy trenches to rain down a deadly hail of pellets. Even with modern shrapnel, however, artillery did not regain its Napoleonic usefulness against a well-prepared defense.[28]

With artillery unable to prepare the way for an attacking army as it had done in Napoleon's time, decision in battle would depend upon the infantry's ability to accomplish successful attacks. But the increased range of the rifle meant that attacking infantry would be exposed much longer than before to effective fire from the defenders. With muzzleloading smoothbores, a defending force usually could fire only one useful volley against attackers; by the time the attackers came within effective range, they would be able to close the remaining distance and be among the defenders before the defenders could reload. With Civil War rifles, even though they were single-shot muzzleloaders cumbersome to reload, each defending soldier could get off multiple shots against an advancing adversary. For the defense, the longer range of the rifled artillery became useful, too; although the artillery projectiles of the 1860s could not accomplish much against defenders protected by earthworks, they could do havoc among the unsheltered soldiers of an attacking infantry force. So destructive did rifled muskets and cannons prove themselves to be against attacking infantry in the American Civil War that attackers could win battlefield decisions if at all only through immense sacrifices of their own manpower. Yet the fascination of Napoleon and the Napoleonic battle still gripped the military imagination.[29]

6. Napoleonic Strategy: R. E. Lee and the Confederacy

Under ordinary circumstances the Federal army should have been destroyed.
—*R. E. Lee*[1]

THE MILITARY TASK confronting the government of the United States in 1861 was notably similar to that which faced Great Britain in 1775: to reassert its authority over a vast territorial empire, far too extensive to be completely occupied or thoroughly patrolled, with a dearth of strategically decisive types of objectives whose seizure could produce disproportionate economic, political, or moral results. In both instances the rebels began their war in substantial control of their territory and needed only to conduct a successful defense of what they already held in order to win. The established governments had to accomplish the much more difficult feat of conquest. In both instances the prospect was further encumbered by the limitations of conquest by the bayonet as an instrument for securing the desired renewal of political allegiance. In both instances the established government could find consolation at least for some of its disadvantages in its possession of sea power, wherewith to attempt to deny the rebels succor from the world outside.

Here, indeed, the parallel begins to break down, because the Union government in 1861 enjoyed the advantage of much more complete control of the seas which washed the rebel shores than the British had held in the War of the Revolution. This mastery of the seas sprang partly from another, and obvious, asset of the Union government in 1861 not possessed by the British in the earlier contest, proximity to the areas of rebel power. On the other hand, the Union advantages of proximity and sea power were partially offset by the fact that the military strength of the rebels on land much more closely approached that of the established government than did the Revolutionary strength against the British in the War of American Independence.

Winfield Scott, aged seventy-five, remained Commanding General of the United States Army when the Civil War began with the firing on Fort Sumter on April 12, 1861. His strategy for the suppression of rebellion in the Southern states had to acknowledge a much more ambitious objective than he had pursued in Mexico, the complete overthrow of the opposing state; but granting that, his strategy remained consistent with the pre-Napoleonic conception of war which had characterized his whole career. He proposed to subject the Southern Confederacy to a gigantic siege, employing Union naval power to blockade the Southern ports and gradually to strangle the Confederate economy by preventing the export of cotton and the import of industrial products and war material. On land, he proposed to delay major actions until superior armies could be equipped and trained, whereupon he would have conducted a war of regular, deliberate approaches, using the rivers which penetrated the Confederacy, and again Union naval power, gradually to dismember the Confederacy as a besieging army might gradually chop away the bastions of a fortress. These plans the newspapers soon labeled, with a hint of derision, the "Anaconda policy."[2]

The hint of derision arose from the unwillingness of the Northern people to wage war so patiently, and for so probably prolonged a period, as old Scott suggested. Even with the Union severed, the days when meager resources compelled the United States to wage war patiently were long since gone. The image of Napoleonic war with its brief, climactic battles had impressed itself upon the popular mind as well as upon soldiers younger than Scott, and it stimulated the usual popular impatience to have wars over with promptly. So Scott had to yield to the "On to Richmond" clamor, assisting in the preparation of an army around Washington for a march across northern Virginia toward the Confederate capital a hundred miles away. Presumably, while marching across Virginia, the army would win a Napoleonic battle against the Confederate army defending Richmond.

Younger officers than Scott shared his fears that an immediate

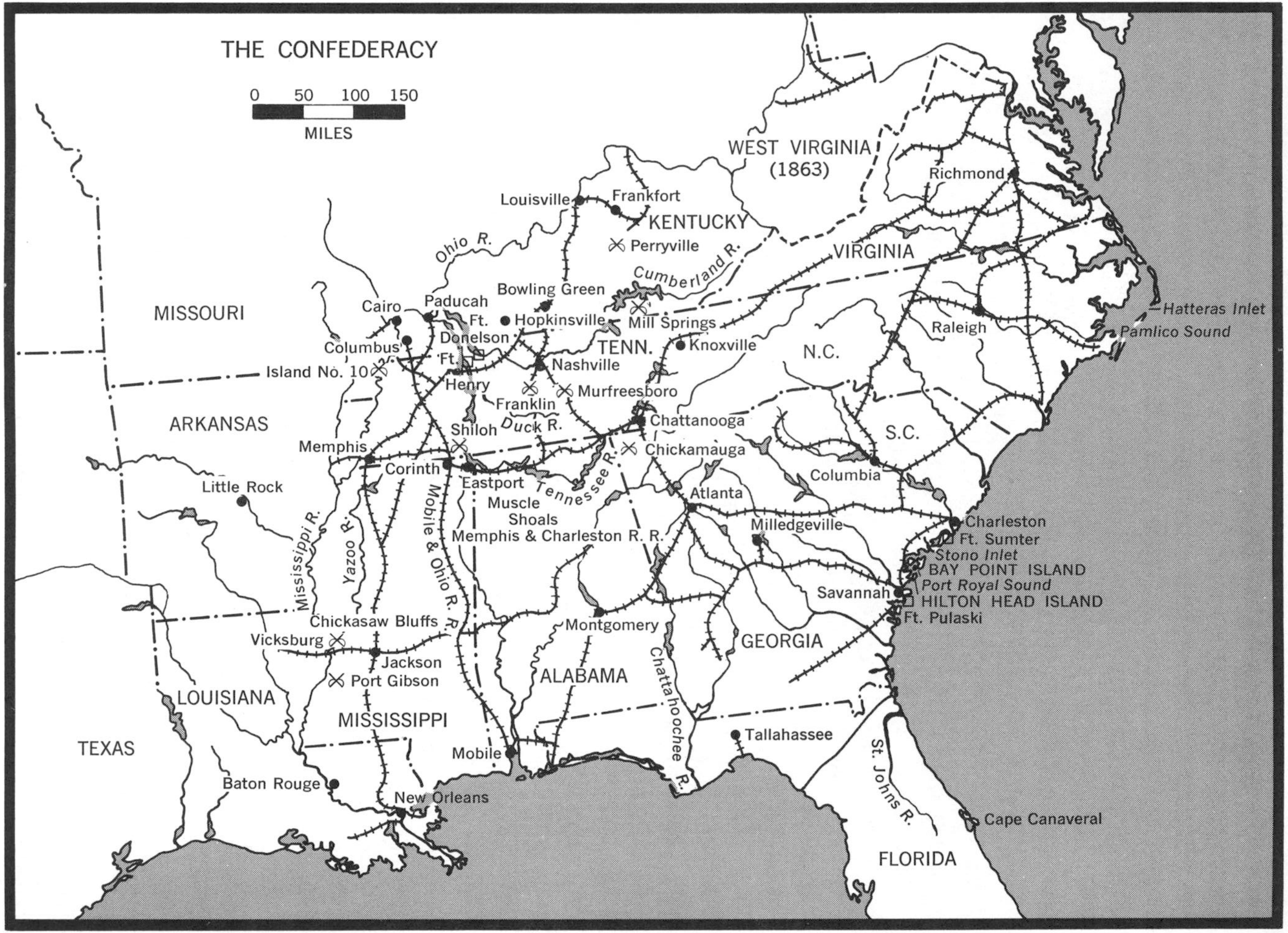
THE CONFEDERACY
0 50 100 150
MILES
MISSOURI
ARKANSAS
TEXAS
LOUISIANA
MISSISSIPPI
ALABAMA
GEORGIA
FLORIDA
TENN.
KENTUCKY
WEST VIRGINIA
(1863)
VIRGINIA
N.C.
S.C.
Richmond
Raleigh
Louisville
Frankfort
Perryville
Ohio R.
Cumberland R.
Bowling Green
Cairo
Paducah
Ft.
Donelson
Hopkinsville
Mill Springs
Knoxville
Columbus
Island No. 10
Ft.
Henry
Nashville
Franklin
Murfreesboro
Shiloh
Duck R.
Chattanooga
Chickamauga
Memphis
Corinth
Eastport
Tennessee R.
Muscle
Shoals
Memphis & Charleston R. R.
Little Rock
Mississippi R.
Yazoo R.
Mobile & Ohio R. R.
Atlanta
Columbia
Milledgeville
Charleston
Ft. Sumter
Stono Inlet
BAY POINT ISLAND
Port Royal Sound
Savannah
HILTON HEAD ISLAND
Ft. Pulaski
Hatteras Inlet
Pamlico Sound
Chickasaw Bluffs
Vicksburg
Jackson
Port Gibson
Montgomery
Chattahoochee R.
Tallahassee
St. Johns R.
Cape Canaveral
Mobile
Baton Rouge
New Orleans

march against Richmond by the largest army that could be quickly assembled would be premature. They did not, however, so much share his misgivings about the very strategy which would make a powerful offensive against Richmond the first blow to be struck. This design could well appear the fulfillment of Jomini's maxim expressed by Halleck as "*Strategy* is defined to be the art of directing masses on decisive points. . . ."

Students of Jomini on the Union side were apt to be troubled by the fact that if all the borders of the Confederacy were viewed as a single war front, geography made it inevitable that the Confederacy would enjoy the coveted advantage of interior lines, with the Union condemned to operate on exterior lines. This Union disadvantage was so crippling in the Jominian conception of war that it may help account for the persistent refusal of many Union generals to regard the whole Confederacy as a single arena of war at all. Instead, Union commanders insisted upon regarding the war as a contest waged in several theaters, where they at least might hope to secure the advantage of interior lines in a given theater. This attitude also contributed to the willingness of Union officers to concentrate upon a march to Richmond; for if a Union force advanced from Washington against Confederate defenders scattered through Virginia from the Shenandoah Valley through Manassas Junction to Hampton Roads, the Washington force appeared to possess the interior lines.

President Abraham Lincoln, thinking in strategic terms not unlike Scott's, soon developed the view that the Union armies ought to apply simultaneous pressure against the Confederate frontiers at many places throughout their length, across the whole arena of war, on the theory that because total Confederate strength was inferior to that of the Union, Union pressure applied everywhere would force the Confederates to stretch themselves too thin somewhere, and their defenses would rupture. But Henry Wager Halleck, the foremost American student of Jomini and as of August 17, 1861, a major general, dismissed such reasoning as hopeless military amateurism, because it ignored the indisputable maxim not to extend one's forces but to concentrate masses on decisive points.[3]

So the first major Union movement of the war on land became the advance from Washington toward Richmond by an army of about 35,000 under Brigadier General Irvin McDowell, which accorded both with the popular clamor and with the Jominian principles of concentration and interior lines. Unfortunately, the Confederates managed to unite their forces from the Shenandoah Valley with those in front of Washington around Manassas Junction despite their having the exterior lines vis-à-vis McDowell's force; they had the Manassas Gap Railroad instead, which suggested that railroad transportation might dilute some of Jomini's geometric principles. As much through the accidents of a battle fought by untrained troops and inexperienced commands as through these other factors, the Confederates won the battle of Manassas, or Bull Run, on July 21, 1861.[4]

Even had the Federals won it, their new army probably lacked the staying power to have captured Richmond; and even had they captured Richmond, at this early stage neither the economic nor the moral blow to the Confederacy would have been likely to be severe enough to decide the war. Richmond had not yet acquired the moral significance which the fighting of many battles for it would later give it. Even having won the first battle, meanwhile, the Confederates remained precariously situated, with armies inferior in size and equipment facing an enemy whose potential military superiority was far greater than anything yet realized, and with no Confederate navy to speak of although both the rivers of the Mississippi system in the West and coastal estuaries in the East made the Confederacy vulnerable to deep penetration by Union naval power. The Confederate President, Jefferson Davis (USMA 1828), prided himself on his military knowledge and experience. Though he spoke often of the merits of the "offensive-defensive," Davis's policies showed that in the circumstances facing the Confederacy, on the whole he believed the best strategy would be a defensive strategy reminiscent of Washington's in the similar circumstances of the War of the Revolution, if possible a strategy as frugal of manpower as Washington's.[5]

In one important regard, however, the Confederacy was incapable of duplicating Washington's strategy. Faced with the ability of British sea power to deposit hostile forces anywhere on the rebellious coast, Washington had resisted demands that he disperse his army along the coast. He kept the Continental Army concentrated, and left most of the coastal areas to defend themselves as best they could with their own fortifications and their own militia. But no part of the Confederacy's frontiers, except possibly parts of the trans-Mississippi West, was so undeveloped and so lacking in political influence that President Davis could afford to be so cavalier as that about the central government's contributions to local defense. Their states' rights sentiments notwithstanding, the Southern people had grown accustomed to a government with greater resources than any individual state possessed and which would bear the main burden of military defense; they would not accept less military protection from the new government at Richmond than they had received from the old government at Washington. Therefore Jefferson Davis had to scatter his already limited forces, to make at least an appearance of a defense of the whole many-thousand-mile circumference of the Confederacy. The pressures upon him to disperse his armies were greater than those which Washington had borne, and Davis had to yield to them.

This necessity posed a further difficulty. If the Confederacy scattered its defenses and its manpower all along its sea and land frontiers, it was bound to be too weak not only at a few points but at many places. Sooner or later the Union would probably attempt Lincoln's idea of applying pressure all along the line, military pedantry such as Halleck's notwithstanding, and then sections of the Confederate defenses were bound to collapse. What then? This unhappy prospect generated a strategic design different from the one President Davis would have preferred, a conviction among some Confederate military leaders that the Confederacy could not afford an essentially passive defense such as George Washington had employed. The only way to prevent the Union from applying fatal pressures somewhere along the Confederate circumference, the reasoning of such leaders ran, was to seize the initiative. The Confederacy ought to adopt an offensive-defensive strategy, permitting the South and not the Union to determine in which places the critical military confrontations should occur. Then the Confederacy might muster adequate numbers and resources at the critical places despite overall inferiority of strength. The principal advocate of the offensive-defensive strategy of capturing the initiative came to be General Robert Edward Lee. The great question which an offensive-defensive strategy in turn posed was that of its cost in manpower; it was Washington's defensive passivity which had made it possible for him to conserve his limited numbers of men.

R. E. Lee, son of Light Horse Harry, had been one of Winfield Scott's staff engineers in Mexico and proved to be the most outstanding member of an outstanding staff. He would have been Scott's choice to take the field command of the Union armies directly under Scott himself, had he not followed his native state of Virginia out of the Union. Lee promptly received command of Virginia's military forces during the interval between the secession of the Commonwealth and her adherence to the Confederacy, and in this post he immediately had to grapple with the defense of an extensive territory while possessing insufficient means.

For some weeks until jointure with the Confederacy was near completion, Virginia with her own resources proposed to defend her borders: along the upper Ohio River, from approximately the longitude of Columbus, Ohio, to the panhandle reaching above Pittsburgh; the mountainous country from the Ohio to the Potomac; the Potomac from beyond Cumberland to the Chesapeake; and a complex bay and ocean frontier reaching from the Potomac south beyond Norfolk to the backwaters of the North Carolina sounds. On the water frontier the Union retained a foothold at Fort Monroe. Even if Virginia found men enough, and weapons enough in her own and the Harpers Ferry arsenals, which of course was doubtful, Lee discovered that the state scarcely had transportation enough to meet the elementary logistical necessities of such a far-flung defense.

The resources of the Confederacy reinforced those of Virginia before Union arms put the Commonwealth to the test; but Lee's first field service for the Confederacy involved the same kinds of problems and ended badly. Union forces from Ohio, first led by Major General George B. McClellan and then by Brigadier General William S. Rosecrans, took advantage of the disaffection which Virginia's secession caused in the nonslaveholding western counties to penetrate deep into the mountainous district beyond the Alleghenies. After the victory at Manassas eased hostile pressure against Virginia's Potomac frontier, President Davis dispatched Lee to the western counties to try to turn back the penetration there. In a rainy autumnal campaign, Lee failed to regain the lost ground. Inept and irresolute leadership by his chief subordinates and his own overgenerous unwillingness to push them hard were the most visible causes of the failure. A more basic cause was the inability of Confederate logistics to mount and sustain an operation commensurate with the task of ejecting the Federals from territory so difficult as western Virginia, when so many more vital areas also demanded protection.[6]

Lee's next assignment seemed almost equally thankless. After Bull Run, President Lincoln's government had renewed its interest in Scott's Anaconda strategy. It collected ships to make the naval blockade of the Confederacy which it had proclaimed become more than a paper fiction, and it looked to the collecting of harbors along the Confederate coast for the same purpose. While Lee was in western Virginia, Flag Officer Silas H. Stringham of the United States Navy appeared on August 27–28 off the Hatteras Inlet to Pamlico Sound, leading a strong squadron which included two of the *Wabash*-class steam frigates, *Wabash* herself and *Minnesota*, and the veteran side-wheeler *Susquehanna*. The Confederates had earthwork forts covering the inlet; but standing mainly out of range of their guns, using his steam power to keep his ships in motion when they did approach within range, and exploiting the virtues of the shell gun, Stringham quickly battered the forts into submission. His success suggested that the old dictum about the superiority of coastal forts over ships, which had played so large a part in Halleck's book about strategy, and in American defense policy long before that, might need revision. This was a bad discovery for the Confederacy, which had inherited the traditional United States system of coastal defense. When Lee returned to Richmond from western Virginia at the beginning of November, President Davis sent him to do something about these developments.[7]

At this time the Confederate government was receiving information that the Union Navy would apply the experience of Hatteras Inlet in a more ambitious endeavor, against Port Royal Sound about midway between Charleston and Savannah. Gaining Port Royal would give the Federals a sheltered harbor big enough to float the navies of the world, on which to base themselves the better to blockade both Charleston and Savannah and the whole south Atlantic coast. From Port Royal also they could gain access to a system of interior waterways from which to blockade the coast from just below Charleston to the Saint Johns River without having to bear the risks and uncertainties of standing off at sea, in effect, blocking the neck of the bottle out of which Confederate vessels had to emerge.

Richmond's information was correct. When Lee arrived at the railroad station nearest Port Royal Sound on November 7, he learned that a battle was in progress between a Federal fleet and the earthwork forts guarding from opposite sides the entrance to the sound, Fort Walker on Hilton Head Island and Fort Beauregard on Bay Point Island.[8]

The fleet was commanded by Flag Officer S. F. Du Pont, with *Wabash*, *Susquehanna*, three steam sloops, eight gunboats, and a sailing sloop. Du Pont had studied closely both Stringham's battle and the contests between ships and forts at Odessa and Sevastopol in the Crimean War. In the Crimea the ships had failed as they had done so often in the past, apparently reconfirming the old dictum about ships versus forts. But Du Pont believed the Allies in the Crimea had come close enough to winning such duels that, along with Hatteras, they slowed the old dictum might be broken. The key elements modifying the historic balance between ship and shore were the shell gun and the steam engine. Port Royal Sound was big enough to permit maneuver, and Du Pont planned to exploit his steam engines to keep his ships moving as a protection against the forts' guns, sailing in an elliptical pattern which would hold both Confederate forts under continuous fire. The British had approached this tactic at Odessa, but they had failed to pass in front of the Russian batteries and thus had not brought the land defenses under direct fire. Du Pont would not outrange the Confederate batteries as Stringham had, so there were risks. But his plan worked. After four or five hours' bombardment, the garrisons evacuated the forts.[9]

General Lee's mission of coastal defense thus suffered a staggering blow on the day of his arrival. Accepting the lessons of Port Royal forthrightly, Lee ordered first the evacuation of all of Hilton Head and Bay Point Islands and then of the sea islands generally. He would no longer contest the islands or the deep waterways. Forts were too vulnerable, and Confederate naval strength in the area was almost nonexistent. Lee retreated inland to where the rivers emptying into the sounds became narrow and shallow enough that they could be obstructed. There he established batteries supplemented by obstructions, strong enough to hold off Union incursions until the batteries could be reinforced by reserves moving on the Charleston and Savannah Railroad, which ran just inside the defended part of the coast. Lee's father, Light Horse Harry, had campaigned in this same area in similar circumstances, and Lee probably knew that his father had believed that when defending a territory against an enemy who controls the sea, it is best to withdraw inland beyond the range of the enemy's naval guns. Charleston of course had to be defended despite its accessibility to the Federal fleet, and there Lee hurried to block the approaching interior waterways and to urge expansion of the defending batteries.[10]

Lee's measures served to protect the South Carolina-Georgia coast against a deeper Federal penetration until the close of the war, when Major General William Tecumseh Sherman's forces uncovered the coastal defenses from the rear. But the Federals achieved all they expected from the Port Royal victory. Securely based in Port Royal Sound, and controlling the interconnecting sounds and inlets, Du Pont's South Atlantic Blockading Squadron maintained an effective, if not perfect, blockade all the way south to Cape Canaveral. With Du Pont's cooperation, Federal troops under Brigadier General

Thomas W. Sherman invested the principal fortification built to defend Savannah under the old Board of Engineers program, Fort Pulaski on Cockspur Island. With that, Savannah was rather well sealed off from the ocean, but the Federals went farther. Many experts on both sides, including Lee, thought the massive masonry walls of Fort Pulaski were secure against Federal artillery on the nearest firm ground, at least a mile to a mile and a half away on Tybee Island. Brigadier General Quincy Adams Gillmore, USA, thought not. On April 10, 1862, rifled artillery carefully placed by Gillmore opened a bombardment which in two days tore away enough of the walls to impel surrender. The elaborate masonry walls of the Board of Engineers program were obsolete in the face of long-range rifled artillery.[11]

Charleston remained a tougher nut for the Federals to crack. It was the port where Du Pont's blockade leaked worst, to the embarrassment of the flag officer commanding, and of the United States government in its relations with foreign powers skeptical of the whole blockading enterprise. The Federal Army fumbled an early chance that Du Pont gave it to approach the harbor defenses by the back door through Stono Inlet, before the defenses of the inlet were properly strengthened. Afterward the Army held it could do nothing more until the Navy knocked out some of the Confederate batteries and forts in the main harbor. Du Pont was hesitant to try, because Charleston harbor would not permit the movement he had employed at Port Royal, and he feared that as stationary targets his ships would be mauled by the forts before they could do enough damage in return.[12]

Nevertheless, experience with south Atlantic coast defense troubled General Lee. To secure minimal and precarious results, the Confederacy had to keep large numbers of men in relative idleness on the seacoast. By the time Lee's defensive arrangements were well along, there were almost 25,000 coastal defenders in Georgia and the Carolinas.[13] Even then, the Confederates were back in Charles Lee's Revolutionary War situation, on the same coast, of a dog in a dancing school. The enemy, as R. E. Lee said, "can be thrown with great celerity against any point, and far outnumbers any force we can bring against it in the field."[14]

This predicament confirmed Lee in the opinion that no merely defensive strategy could suffice to preserve the independence of the Confederacy. President Davis wanted to take advantage of the fact that the Confederacy needed only to stand fast within its boundaries, while the Union faced the harder task of conquest. But the profligacy with which troops had to be dispersed to try to defend the mountains of western Virginia and then the 300-mile seacoast of the Carolinas and Georgia assured Lee that the Confederacy could not afford trying to defend itself everywhere.

On March 2, 1862, Davis called Lee back to Richmond to resume his place of the previous summer, as confidential military adviser at the President's side. The strategy of mere defense had crumbled in the Mississippi Valley during the previous month, when the Federals broke through the defensive line of the Ohio River and went far toward detaching Tennessee as well as Kentucky from the Confederacy by utilizing their naval power again, this time to steam up the Tennessee and Cumberland rivers and in conjunction with the Union Army to capture Forts Henry and Donelson which guarded the routes into the state of Tennessee. When Lee arrived in Richmond, no fewer than four separate Federal forces were forming to threaten Virginia and the Confederate capital, from Washington, from Fort Monroe at the tip of the Peninsula between the James and York rivers, from Winchester in the Shenandoah Valley, and from the western counties beyond the Allegheny Mountains. By dividing the Southern forces to try to confront each of these Federal groupings, the Confederacy with its inferior numbers merely made each detachment so thin that each was threatened with engulfment.[15]

In these circumstances, Lee concluded that the only salvation for the Confederacy was to concentrate its forces and attack. "It is only by concentration of our troops," he was to say, "that we can hope to win any decisive advantage." ". . . we must decide between the positive loss of inactivity and the risk of action."[16]

The risk of action: the Confederacy, Lee believed, must go from a defensive strategy to an offensive-defensive, attacking at some chosen point or points and causing the war to focus there in order to prevent the enemy from attacking everywhere. In Virginia's peril against multiple Federal threats in the spring of 1862, and as Federal activity on the Peninsula between the York and the James took shape as the principal threat, his solution in part was to urge a junction of as many as possible of the troops facing western Virginia and on the Rappahannock line opposite Washington with the force in the Shenandoah Valley, so that the latter might mount an offensive. This course involved the risk of action—the risk that the enemy would take advantage of a concentration in the Shenandoah to move on one of the weakened points. To offset the risk, Lee would have the Con-

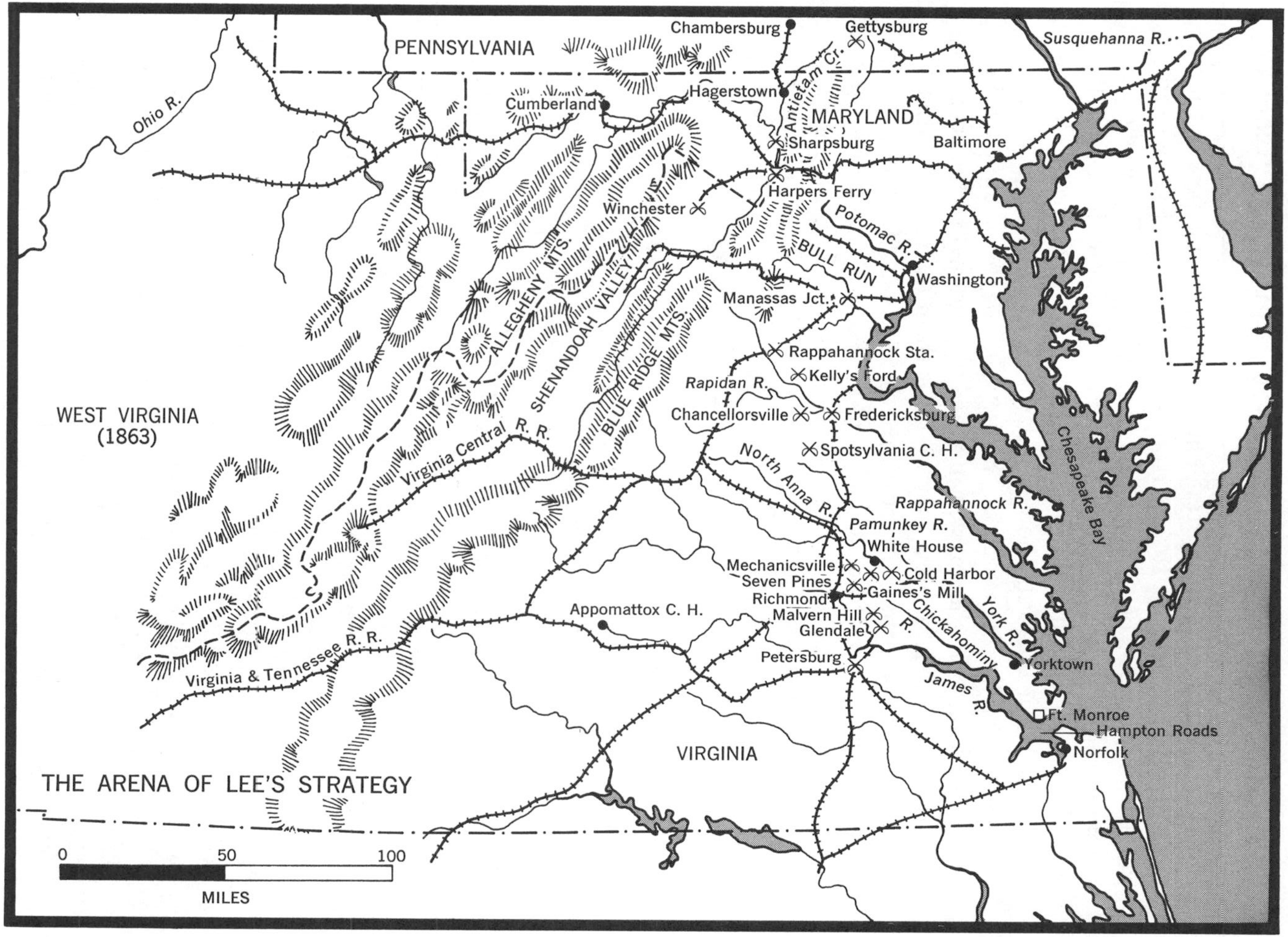
THE ARENA OF LEE'S STRATEGY
PENNSYLVANIA
MARYLAND
WEST VIRGINIA
(1863)
VIRGINIA
Chambersburg
Gettysburg
Susquehanna R.
Ohio R.
Cumberland
Hagerstown
Antietam Cr.
Sharpsburg
Baltimore
Harpers Ferry
Winchester
Potomac R.
BULL RUN
Washington
Manassas Jct.
ALLEGHENY MTS.
SHENANDOAH VALLEY
BLUE RIDGE MTS.
Rappahannock Sta.
Kelly's Ford
Rapidan R.
Chancellorsville
Fredericksburg
Spotsylvania C. H.
Chesapeake Bay
North Anna R.
Rappahannock R.
Pamunkey R.
White House
Virginia Central R. R.
Mechanicsville
Seven Pines
Cold Harbor
Gaines's Mill
Richmond
Malvern Hill
Glendale
Chickahominy R.
York R.
Yorktown
Appomattox C. H.
Petersburg
James R.
Ft. Monroe
Hampton Roads
Norfolk
Virginia & Tennessee R. R.
0
50
100
MILES

federacy depend on swiftness of action and the paralyzing effect of an unanticipated offensive stroke.[17]

Lee's office as adviser to President Davis gave him power to do little more than persuade, for the troops to be employed were mainly subject to the orders of General Joseph E. Johnston, who was taking position on the Peninsula to meet the Federal threat there. But Lee found an eager coadjutor in the commander of the Shenandoah Valley army, Major General Thomas Jonathan Jackson, known since his brigade's stand at Manassas as "Stonewall." "I have hoped," Lee wrote Jackson, "in the present divided condition of the enemy's forces that a successful blow may be dealt them by a rapid combination of our troops before they can be strengthened themselves either in position or by reinforcements."[18] Out of Lee's recommendations and urgings and Jackson's brilliant application of them came the Valley Campaign of April–May, 1862, in which Jackson first sent the Federals in the Valley fleeing north of the Potomac, and then drew upon himself an aggregation of Federals from their Valley army, from western Virginia, and from the Rappahannock.

Lee's perception of the uses of concentration was not the simplistic kind represented by Halleck's criticism of Lincoln. He recognized that the kind of concentration that serves a defensive strategy best is that which causes the enemy to draw strength away from the vital points or leads him to disperse his forces. Lee saw the object of the Valley Campaign as fulfilled when the Federal concentration against Jackson kept reinforcements away from the main Union force on the Peninsula. Thereupon Lee turned his attention to the Peninsula, and obeying his theory of concentration, he hurried Jackson's Army of the Valley southeastward to join the direct fight against those Federals whom Jackson's indirect action had just weakened.[19]

By now Lee could order Jackson, not merely recommend. In the battle of Seven Pines on the Peninsula on May 31, General Johnston fell wounded, and President Davis put Lee in Johnston's place at the head of the Confederate force which Lee now designated the Army of Northern Virginia. For all the success of Jackson's Valley Campaign in diverting Federal troops away from the Richmond area, this army and the Confederate capital remained in a dangerous situation. Reinforced by 18,500 men under Jackson, Lee could hope to muster somewhat over 80,000 men in his army; but he faced a Federal force, the Army of the Potomac under Major General George B. McClellan, estimated to approach 150,000 despite Jackson's diversions. (McClellan actually had 117,000.) When Lee took command, McClellan's army already stood within sound of the church bells of Richmond, the Confederates paying the penalty for having placed their capital in so exposed a state as Virginia and almost within reach of Union sea power on the tidal estuaries. McClellan's approach march up the Peninsula had been ponderous, but Lee believed that unless the Confederates grasped the initiative from him, he would eventually push his way into Richmond through sheer weight. If he should clamp Richmond into a siege, in time the city would fall. Therefore Lee again resolved upon the risk of action, determining to attack McClellan despite his inferiority in numbers.[20]

He also displayed again his mastery of the strategic uses of concentration. Both the opposing armies outside Richmond were divided by the Chickahominy River, a stream formidable enough to require bridges for military crossings. McClellan's weaker wing, his right, lay north of the Chickahominy, but so did his line of communication, the York River Railroad, and the base from which he was supported by sea, the White House on the Pamunkey River, a tributary of the York. Lee proposed to concentrate the great bulk of his own army north of the Chickahominy and to attack McClellan's weak wing, thereby Lee hoped wrecking that wing and compelling McClellan either to shift all his forces north of the Chickahominy to defend his communications or to withdraw everything south of that stream and to establish a new base on the James River. Either defensive reaction would force McClellan into awkward crossings of the Chickahominy which should render him vulnerable to further offensive strokes.

The risk, of course, was that McClellan would not merely react defensively, but would take advantage of Lee's drastic weakening of the Confederate forces south of the Chickahominy to plunge directly into Richmond, which itself lay south of the stream. To guard against that risk, Lee had his men strain themselves in the unpopular work of digging trenches in front of the city, until they called him unkindly "the King of Spades." While the strong trenches helped, Lee again had to count on striking swiftly and on the unsettling effect of his blow to assure that once he seized the initiative, he could keep it.[21]

Lee's plan opened the Seven Days' Battles for Richmond, June 25–July 1, 1862. His capture of the initiative by attacking McClellan's weak right wing north of the Chickahominy did have the paralyzing effect upon the enemy's will on which he counted. McClellan did not move against the weakened defenses of Richmond south of the Chickahominy, but instead went over to the defensive and tried to reestablish the security of his army by setting up a new base on the James. In the process of pulling back all his forces to the south side of the Chickahominy and of retreating to the James, McClellan opened himself to further Confederate offensive blows as Lee had hoped he would. While McClellan was entangled in the Chickahominy crossings and the adjacent swamps, Lee hoped for nothing less than to destroy the Federal army: to find the opportunity for an Austerlitz battle which would effect a strategy of annihilation. He had carried Confederate strategy a long way from President Davis's defensive.[22]

But Lee's plan did not work out so neatly as had Stonewall Jackson's Valley Campaign. The initial onslaught to ruin McClellan's exposed right wing involved closely coordinated converging movements by a number of Lee's divisions. The Confederate commanders and staffs proved as yet not skillful enough to achieve the coordination desired. Jackson himself failed to perform his assigned role in the opening action, probably in part because of fatigue after a long forced march from the Valley, in part because of ambiguity in Lee's orders. The tactical means wherewith to strike the enemy had to be the close-order infantry assault; no other method of attack permitted adequate communication among the attacking troops or could hope to muster enough weight to break the enemy's lines and achieve Napoleonic results. But the war was beginning to reveal that rifled weapons extracted horrendous losses from the makers of such attacks. One of Lee's division commanders, Major General A. P. Hill, impatiently began the assault upon McClellan's right before Jackson was on hand to join in. Although A. P. Hill eventually received support from James Longstreet's and D. H. Hill's divisions, his close-ordered attacks suffered a bloody repulse, known as the battle of Mechanicsville, on June 26.[23]

Mechanicsville removed the element of surprise from Lee's intentions against McClellan's right wing, and the next day the Federal right was strongly placed in a new position, still north of the Chickahominy, along Boatswain's Swamp near Gaines's Mill, the place which gave its name to the June 27 battle. Lee persisted in the attack. He did so partly because poor intelligence work by his staff and cavalry, and poor maps, misled him about the location of the Federal position and the direction of Federal retreat, so that he thought he enjoyed opportunities to outflank and cut off the Federal right which in fact did not exist. More than that, Lee persisted in the attack because his belief in the offensive-defensive as the only strategy which could save the Confederacy compelled it. He believed that if he did not retain the initiative he had grasped, Richmond and in time the Confederacy would fall. He believed he must hold on to the initiative, though Gaines's Mill became a battle of Confederate frontal assaults, still poorly coordinated, which at length drove the Federal right wing from its position, but at a cost of some 8,000 Confederate dead and wounded against lesser Federal losses.[24]

By that time McClellan was ready to give up the position anyway, as he prepared to shift his base from the York River southward to the James. Through the next several days Lee continued to assault the rear and the western flank of the retreating Federal army, hoping that while it was strung out along the roads to the James and hindered by another watercourse, White Oak Swamp, he could deal it a mortal blow. A major action developed on June 30 at Glendale, or Frayser's Farm, where Longstreet and A. P. Hill attempted to break the Federal army in two while Jackson was to fall upon its rear. Longstreet and Hill fought hard, but again other divisions failed to coordinate their actions properly, and again Jackson failed to display the vigor expected of him. Glendale was Lee's last chance to inflict major damage before McClellan's army consolidated itself on the James. The next day, July 1, the Federals stood fast in an excellent defensive position on Malvern Hill. Frustrated by the repulse of his previous attacks, again as at Gaines's Mill not altogether informed about the Federal position or that of his own troops, with his staff again dispensing ambiguous orders, Lee allowed another series of frontal assaults to take place. At a cost of 5,500 casualties, they hardly shook the Federals.[25]

To the government and people of the Confederacy, the main result of the Seven Days' Battles was that the Federal grip on Richmond was broken. The months since Manassas had brought the Confederacy so many reverses, McClellan had approached so close to the capital, and the Federal army had seemed so strong, that this result appeared almost miraculous. Lee, so recently in eclipse after his western Virginia campaign, became the hero of the Confederacy to remain so forever, and already the new name he had given his army, "the Army of Northern Virginia," became charged with evocative magic.

It was a great achievement indeed, but the price was 20,141 casualties out of somewhat over 80,000 men with whom Lee had opened the contest: 3,286 dead, 15,909 wounded, 946 missing.[26] A humane and Christian gentleman, Lee grieved over the casualties; but as a soldier, he was troubled less by them than by his conviction that "Under ordinary circumstances the Federal army should have been destroyed."[27] What he meant by "ordinary circumstances" was a professional command and staff which would not have been guilty of the lapses he suffered during the campaign. He resolved to improve the organization of his army before the next campaign.

Clearly, lapses had occurred. Clearly, the commanding general of the Army of Northern Virginia had to coordinate too many separate "commands" and divisions without intermediate corps headquarters, and too many of the division commanders were not up to snuff. Staff work, intelligence gathering, even at this stage of the war the reconnaissance work of Jeb Stuart's cavalry, all required improvement. But was it realistic of Lee to hope that even the best army conceivably available to him could have achieved what he sought, not merely McClellan's withdrawal from Richmond but the destruction of the Army of the Potomac? Was not the very idea of the destruction of so mighty a host in a single campaign an illusion now that the defense had rifled weapons, but an illusion still fostered by the Napoleonic legend and the Napoleonic concept of the climactic battle? Yet Lee's thoughts dwelt upon his failure to destroy the Army of the Potomac, a state of mind which implied another similar attempt in similar battle on some future day.

"My desire has been to avoid a general engagement, being the weaker force, and by maneuvering to relieve the portion of the country referred to."[28] George Washington might have written that, but it was Lee reporting to President Davis on the morning of August 30, 1862, the second day of the Army of Northern Virginia's next great battle, Second Manassas. The Federal government had responded to Lee's checking of McClellan's offensive on the Peninsula by forming a new army of invasion in northern Virginia, under Major General John Pope. To Pope the Federals dispatched drafts from McClellan's army, on an accelerating schedule. Against Pope, Lee then directed his own attention, sending first Jackson's command to watch him and eventually following with the bulk of his army. The quotation indicates that Lee was surely not unmindful of the risks and losses of a general battle. His strategic conceptions, however, drove him into the very general engagement he professed to want to avoid and which formed the ironic setting for his dispatch to the President; for when he moved north from Richmond his avowed purpose was again to destroy the enemy army before him, first hoping to catch Pope in the cul-de-sac formed by the junction of the Rappahannock and Rapidan rivers, then, failing his first opportunity, seeking to ruin Pope by falling on his line of communication around Manassas before Pope's reinforcement by McClellan could be complete.[29]

At Second Manassas, Lee succeeded better than in the Seven Days, fixing the Federal army with Jackson's troops and then routing them with a flank attack by Longstreet's troops that would have done credit to Napoleon himself. Lee's losses this time fell short of the Federals': 9,197 Confederate casualties of all types to 16,054 Federal.[30] Lee's intelligence system functioned superbly well, the movements of his army were swift and well coordinated, and by dividing the army into two wings under Longstreet and Jackson he found the basis of an adequate system of command. He outgeneraled Pope so decisively that the Federals retreated into the defenses of Washington, where the rest of McClellan's men joined them. On the 25th of June, the United States Army had looked upon the spires of Richmond; by the end of August, Virginia east of the Allegheny Mountains was almost cleared of Federal soldiers, and it was Washington, not Richmond, that seemed threatened.

Against such achievements, Lee's mastery of the offensive-defensive mode of war he had elected to practice can scarcely be gainsaid. His Second Manassas campaign was a showpiece of Napoleonic warfare, a campaign of maneuver which drew the enemy into a disadvantageous position and then stunned him in a climactic battle. But nemesis lay in this very mode of war. Even having caught Pope in a disadvantageous position, to pursue his objective of the destruction of the enemy army Lee finally had to attack, and his losses in killed and wounded at Manassas amounted to 19 percent of his force, as against Federal losses in those categories of 13 percent.[31] As in the Seven Days, the Federal army was not destroyed; the Confederate advantage was mainly moral and psychological. The Army of Northern Virginia could not so much as follow up its triumph with a vigorous pursuit. Its triumph left it too exhausted; its own losses were too large.[32] And the logic of an offensive-defensive strategy which so much emphasized the offensive that it aimed at the destruction of the enemy army still beckoned Lee to court further losses of similar proportions.

For as soon as his army caught its breath and gathered itself together, Lee decided to invade the North, to carry the offensive into Maryland and if possible Pennsylvania. Brilliant though his achievements had been, he knew there was a hollowness about them. Not only had they failed to destroy McClellan's and Pope's armies; they had failed to weaken visibly the resolve of the North to restore the Union, and they had not halted Northern advances elsewhere into the Confederacy, especially in the Mississippi Valley. Lee could not assault the defenses of Washington; they were too rich in strongpoints and artillery. He believed he could not go over passively to the defensive. His men were hungry, and it would aid both the army and the Confederate economy to subsist his army during the harvest season in the Northern states. More than that, merely to rest now, shielding Virginia against new invasion, would have violated Lee's philosophy of war. So he saw the invasion of Maryland as the only acceptable course open to him.[33]

Again as on the morning of August 30 at Manassas, he professed to hope he could avoid a costly general engagement. His intent, he said, was to wage a campaign of maneuver north of the Potomac, which he hoped might persuade slaveholding Maryland to join the Confederacy and so discourage the North that overtures from Richmond for the recognition of Confederate independence might bring positive results.[34] But he could not hope that the Federal armies would allow him to maneuver in Maryland and Pennsylvania without challenging him to battle, and when the challenge in fact came, as usual he welcomed it.

Lincoln placed McClellan in command of the combined forces of his own army and Pope's. McClellan marched northwestward from Washington into Maryland to try to halt Lee's progress. The lucky finding of a copy of Lee's orders to his division commanders outlining his plan of campaign permitted McClellan to move against Lee with uncharacteristic swiftness and assurance. As the campaign approached its climax, Lee faced McClellan with the Army of Northern Virginia divided into five widely spaced detachments in order to try to capture Harpers Ferry, and a real prospect that the Federals' unexpectedly rapid advances might compel the detachments to fight while still dispersed. In Lee's situation, a general of even moderate caution would have pulled his forces back across the Potomac into Virginia. The strain imposed by prolonged campaigning and a weak supply system, along with a certain aversion among the Confederate rank and file to a campaign of invasion when the Confederacy claimed to be defending itself, produced unprecedented straggling in Lee's army; and at best, if he could get all his troops reunited, Lee could hope to confront McClellan with only about 50,000 men to

75,000 or more. There could be no prospect on this occasion of a battle that would destroy the Federal army.[35]

Yet Lee had already demonstrated a strain of stubbornness in his nature, pushing him beyond even the demands of his offensive strategy to offer battle once he found himself in the presence of the enemy—the stubbornness which persisted in driving the frontal attacks forward at Gaines's Mill, and which allowed the sacrifices of Malvern Hill to occur. When McClellan now closed in on him, Lee did not retreat across the Potomac. He drew in his scattered forces and, though his brigades could not all be reassembled if McClellan attacked with the most minimal promptness, he stood to fight along Antietam Creek around the village of Sharpsburg. There was no prospect of destroying the Federal army; there was a much more likely prospect of the destruction of Lee's own army, if it should be mauled by McClellan's superior numbers with the barrier of the Potomac behind it. There was only Lee's unwillingness to abandon the invasion of Maryland without a fight, the consideration of the moral loss to be suffered by throwing away the hopes with which the invasion had begun by fleeing from a Federal challenge.

For the Confederacy, in quest of foreign recognition, such a loss could not have been taken lightly. But neither could the casualties of the battle of Antietam. On September 17 McClellan attacked, and in giving battle the Army of Northern Virginia lost some 13,724 men, against 12,410 Federal casualties.[36] Lee's army was not destroyed, but on several occasions in the course of the battle its fate hung by a thread, as reinforcements reached threatened points at the last possible moment. After the battle Lee had to retreat into Virginia anyway, and Antietam consequently looked enough like a Federal victory to embolden Lincoln to issue the Emancipation Proclamation and thus to snuff out whatever prospects of foreign intervention might have existed. On Lee's behalf it must be noted that in the course of the campaign he had captured the Union garrison at Harpers Ferry, about 11,000 men, together with seventy-three guns and 13,000 small arms. Accordingly, total Federal losses in the campaign, including prisoners, were about double Lee's total casualties; and some 11,000 Federal prisoners were eventually exchanged to retrieve Confederates.[37] Nevertheless, there is much to be said for the view that counts the Maryland campaign and the battle of Antietam as the turning point of the war—in favor of the Union.

Still, in the months that followed, Lee refused to abandon the reasoning that had led him to attempt the invasion. When he first assumed command of the Army of Northern Virginia in front of Richmond, he had not thoroughly probed the question of how to achieve the ultimate purpose of winning the war; for the moment it was all he could do to liberate Richmond from McClellan's grasp and hope to destroy the enemy army immediately before him. By the time he drove Pope from Virginia, his thoughts could run beyond immediate crises to the problem of bringing the Union government to make peace with an independent Confederacy. This purpose, Lee then began to conclude, could be achieved only by moving beyond an offensive-defensive strategy, even beyond one which sought the annihilation of enemy armies as the object of its offensives, to a still more thoroughly offensive strategy that would produce victories on Northern soil. To win recognition of the Confederacy, the Northern will to pursue the war must be broken. To that end, Lee believed victories in Virginia would not suffice even if they were more complete than those he had already won. Despite his own victories, the Union continued to conquer Confederate territory in the Mississippi Valley, and the coils of the blockade continued to tighten. To convince the Union government that the war was futile, and to do so before Union successes in theaters other than his own became irreversible, Lee came to believe that he must defeat Union armies *in the North*, and perhaps march into one of the great northeastern cities, Philadelphia or Baltimore or Washington itself. Less than a week after his retreat into Virginia from Antietam, Lee was writing to Davis:

> In a military point of view, the best move, in my opinion, the army could make would be to advance upon Hagerstown and endeavor to defeat the enemy at that point. I would not hesitate to make it even with our diminished numbers, did the army exhibit its former temper and condition; but as far as I am able to judge, the hazard would be great and a reverse disastrous. I am, therefore, led to pause.[38]

But he remained impatient for the day when he would no longer need to pause, but could march northward again. Lee had never felt much hope for foreign intervention to rescue the Confederacy. He always believed the Confederacy would have to win Northern recognition through its own strength.[39] The Confederacy must conquer peace for itself. But to win peace, to break the will of the North, the Confederacy must do more than defend its capital at Richmond, more even than to smash enemy armies in Virginia. The Confederacy must *conquer*; it must win victories on Northern ground.

In the Piedmont and the Shenandoah Valley of northern Virginia in the autumn of 1862, Lee recruited and refitted his army after the losses and the strains of the summer, but he also looked forward to the time when he might resume the invasion of the North. To him, and to Stonewall Jackson at his side, the Fredericksburg campaign of the late fall and early winter was painfully frustrating. A new commander of the Federal Army of the Potomac, Major General Ambrose E. Burnside, replaced McClellan and returned to the invasion of Virginia before either Lee's preparations or the season could encourage a second Confederate invasion of the North. The route which Burnside chose brought Lee's army to face him at the crossings of the Rappahannock at Fredericksburg. There on December 13 Lee repulsed Burnside's attacks in an almost purely defensive battle. The terrain afforded no opportunity for Confederate maneuver or counterattack. Merely receiving the enemy's assaults, the Confederates suffered only 5,300 casualties to 12,700 Federal losses.[40] But Lee was sure that static victories such as this one, on Virginia soil, could not break the Northern will and win the war.

Early in 1863, Lee felt obliged to detach Longstreet with two divisions of what was now his First Army Corps to southeastern Virginia, with a third division going to North Carolina, to guard against a possible Federal amphibious threat to the railroad connections between Richmond and North Carolina. If it had not been for this development, Lee might well have begun a new invasion march northward in the spring of 1863 before the Federals opened another drive against Richmond.[41]

As it was, the Army of the Potomac under yet another new commander, Major General Joseph Hooker, crossed the Rappahannock southward again at the end of April. Hooker chose to avoid Lee's defenses around Fredericksburg by staging his main thrust farther westward, in a wooded area called the Wilderness around Chancellorsville. By doing so, however, Hooker gave Lee an opportunity to seize the initiative by means of a flanking maneuver, conceived and conducted by Lee and Jackson still more brilliantly than their Second Manassas campaign. Jackson's Second Army Corps descended upon Hooker's exposed right flank, rolled it up, and so panicked Hooker that although his men fought hard and reestablished a tenable position, on May 5–6 the Federal army retreated across the Rappahannock. In the absence of three of his divisions, Lee fought this battle of Chancellorsville with at most 60,000 men, against the Army of the Potomac in one of its most powerful phases, numbering perhaps as many as 134,000. The Confederates extracted over 17,000 casualties from the Federals, while suffering fewer than 13,000 themselves.[42]

Yet Chancellorsville cost Lee the irreplaceable loss of Stonewall Jackson, shot down by his own men in the course of a reconnaissance; and even if it had not brought that disaster, Lee would have been dissatisfied with the battle. He would have preferred using Jackson at the height of his abilities, and having the absent Longstreet with him too, to win a Chancellorsville victory on northern soil. Convinced that only victories in the North could win the war, Lee turned toward another invasion immediately after Chancellorsville, despite the death of Jackson. He recalled Longstreet to the main army, and on June 3 the Army of Northern Virginia began breaking its camps on the Rappahannock to march once more to the Potomac.

Lee's battlefield victories from the Seven Days to Chancellorsville had of course immensely enhanced President Davis's confidence in him, and Davis continued to consult Lee as a general military adviser though Lee had to give his attention principally to the Army of Northern Virginia. Despite his confidence in Lee, however, the President still inclined to favor a more purely defensive strategy, and he felt doubts especially about Lee's moving from an offensive-defensive to a candidly offensive strategy. Before Chancellorsville, Davis suggested to Lee the possibility of reinforcing the western Confederacy from Lee's army, and this idea still appealed to Davis as an alternative to an offensive north of the Potomac. Along the Mississippi, U. S. Grant's Federal army was moving toward the investment of Vicksburg at the time when the idea of Lee's new invasion of the North was germinating, and Grant's siege of Vicksburg had begun by the time Lee's army began moving northward. Between Virginia and Vicksburg, rival armies in middle Tennessee were quiescent, and their strength was balanced closely enough so that an increment to the Confederates might allow advantageous operations. Davis wondered whether the Confederacy should not exert every effort to prevent being sundered by Federal control of the entire Mississippi River, and whether exerting every effort did not imply reinforcement of the western armies, if not directly around Vicksburg, then in middle Tennessee to permit diversionary actions there which might draw some Federals away from Vicksburg.

Lee's response was that he could offer no reinforcements sufficient to turn the western balance, certainly not without incapacitating himself before the Army of the Potomac. In truth, Lee seems to have been less than fully responsive to the problems of the West, partly out of Virginia parochialism—he always regarded his sword as serving first his state of Virginia—and partly in adherence to his military philosophy. The vast expanses of the Mississippi Valley did not afford opportunity for the limited manpower of the Confederate armies to mount an offensive which could hope for decisive effects.[43]

Lee began his new offensive with skillful maneuver, placing the protective shelter of the Blue Ridge between himself and Hooker's Army of the Potomac before Hooker was certain of the nature of his movements. A head start in the march northward combined with the Blue Ridge to permit the Army of Northern Virginia to cross the Potomac and enter Maryland and south-central Pennsylvania unmolested by any Federals except small detachments and emergency levies of militia. Yet to succeed, the campaign could not remain one of maneuver; the fulfillment of Lee's design demanded a climactic, Napoleonic battle. On June 28, Lee learned at Chambersburg, Pennsylvania, that the Army of the Potomac had crossed from Virginia into Maryland and that he must concentrate his army to meet it. Such news was bound to have come. To approach the Susquehanna and move upon Washington, Baltimore, or Philadelphia, Lee had to leave the sheltering Blue Ridge behind him. His head start had never been long enough to permit his reaching one of the great Northern cities before the Army of the Potomac interposed itself. The North could not yield any of these cities without a battle; winning a decisive victory in battle was the essence of Lee's own design.

Lee counted on the prowess his troops had displayed so often in Virginia to win that battle, and with it perhaps the war; but as the Antietam campaign might have warned, the conditions of battle were not likely to be so favorable north of the Potomac as in Virginia. On this invasion Lee managed to avoid the costly straggling which had plagued him in Maryland the year before. Also, his troops were able to subsist comfortably off the rich farmlands of Pennsylvania. For replenishment of ammunition, however, he was dependent on uncertain wagon shipments over the long route through the Shenandoah Valley from the Virginia Central Railroad. This dependence meant that there would be severe risks in prolonged battle, lest his ammunition, especially his artillery ammunition, be exhausted. It also meant that his capacity to maneuver would be limited by the necessity to maintain a connection with the Shenandoah Valley route.

Longstreet, already concerned by the attrition which Lee's offensive battles had imposed on the Army of Northern Virginia, had urged that if an offensive into Pennsylvania were attempted, it should be combined with a tactical defensive. The Federals should be forced to attack, in order to drive the Confederate army from their soil. But when Union and Confederate detachments collided at Gettysburg on July 1 and the whole of both armies was drawn into battle there, the perils of maneuver with a limited ammunition supply militated against such a course. So did the Confederates' relative unfamiliarity with the terrain. So did Lee's confidence in his troops, and his belief that he must stake the results of the invasion upon a climactic battle. Because his army was living off the country, Lee could not remain long in one place inviting attack. Lee himself attacked, and attacked again, through three days of battle.[44]

In this campaign Lee again was sometimes served less than well by his corps, division, and brigade commanders. After the war he said of the campaign: "If I had had Stonewall Jackson with me, so far as man can see, I should have won the battle of Gettysburg."[45] The attrition suffered by the command structure of the Army of Northern Virginia by the time of the battle of Gettysburg, which D. S. Freeman blames for much of the failure there, was itself, however, largely a product of the casualties and strains that Lee's strategy imposed upon the army. If Stonewall Jackson had been at Gettysburg, or if his successor in the Second Corps, Lieutenant General Richard S. Ewell, had moved against Cemetery Hill on the evening of July 1, or if Longstreet had attacked the Union left as promptly as possible on July 2, it still remains highly uncertain—indeed, utterly unlikely—that Lee could have won the kind of overwhelming battlefield victory he wanted. His friends have always tended to exaggerate Union weaknesses both on Cemetery Hill, at the time on the evening of July 1 when they say Ewell should have been attacking, and on the Union left, where Union strength was already heavy at the earliest hour Longstreet could conceivably have been ready to attack on July 2. The new commander who took over the Army of the Potomac on the eve of Gettysburg, Major General George G. Meade, gave the Confederates no opening for a *manoeuvre sur les derrières* like Jackson's against Hooker at Chancellorsville. If Lee had won at Gettysburg, his ammunition would have been nearly exhausted in victory, while Federal logistics would have improved as the Army of the Potomac fell back toward the eastern cities. Lee had to stake the whole campaign on one battle; the Federals did not.[46]

Lee's efforts to roll up both Federal flanks on July 2 resolved themselves into costly frontal assaults, as they almost certainly would have done no matter how early in the day they had been launched.

They strained Lee's army at least as much as they strained the enemy, and they gave little reason to hope that renewed attacks on the following day would do better. Nevertheless, the importance with which his whole strategy had invested this battle, and the stubbornness which had driven him on at Gaines's Mill, Malvern Hill, and Antietam, impelled Lee to try still another major attack on July 3. When disagreements and reluctance among his lieutenants changed the concept of the July 3 attack from another effort against the Federal left flank to the most unsubtle of frontal assaults, Lee's stubborn pugnacity still pushed the attack forward, until three divisions totalling about 15,000 men suffered wreckage beyond recovery in the failure of Pickett's Charge. Those 15,000 Confederates who followed their red battleflags through solid shot, canister, grape shot, and minnie balls from Seminary to Cemetery Ridge on the humid afternoon of July 3, 1863, deserve all the romantic rhapsodizing they have received, for soldiers never fought more bravely to rescue so mistaken a strategic design. Much the same thing might be said for the whole tragic career of the Army of Northern Virginia.[47]

The problem of the frontal assault against rifled weapons was not simply one of inability to penetrate the enemy lines. If it had been that alone, if strong positions could never be penetrated at all, generals such as Lee might have abandoned the frontal assault as futile more quickly than they did. Despite the costs, the assailants sometimes got inside the defender's position, as George Pickett's gallant battalions did break into the Union lines near the famous copse of trees on Cemetery Ridge. The greater problem was how to stay there and exploit the advantage once the enemy's line was pierced. Almost invariably, by that time the attacker had lost so heavily, and his reserves were so distant, that he could not hold on against a counterattack by the defending army's nearby reserves. So it was with Pickett's Charge; the men of Armistead's, Kemper's, and Garnett's brigades who entered the Federal lines were too few to stay, let alone make further headway, when reserves from the whole Union center converged against them.

With that, the renewed offensive into the North of which Lee had dreamed since Antietam was dead. The Gettysburg campaign cost Lee about 23,000 casualties, and with such losses and all that had gone before, the offensive capacity of the Army of Northern Virginia was also virtually dead.[48] Lee kept the war in Virginia stalemated in a campaign of maneuver through the autumn of 1863. He could do so because Meade proved a cautious adversary who would not permit a bloody, full-scale battle unless he was sure he could win, and Lee remained too skillful to give him such an opening. On the other hand, a bungled Confederate attack at Bristoe Station, and a Federal coup which snuffed out two Confederate bridgeheads and inflicted 2,023 casualties at a cost of 419 at Rappahannock Station and Kelly's Ford showed that the fighting edge of the Army of Northern Virginia was no longer what it had been.[49]

When the Army of the Potomac crossed the Rappahannock southward once again in the spring of 1864, with the aggressive U. S. Grant directing it, the Army of Northern Virginia for two days essayed counteroffensives in the Chancellorsville manner, on May 5 and 6 in the Wilderness. These counterattacks achieved local, tactical success, but they failed to stop Grant's southward advance. Thereafter, the Army of Northern Virginia dug into entrenchments, never again to fight a campaign of offensive maneuver and general counterattack. It had bled so much that against the Army of the Potomac its offensive power was gone.

For a belligerent with the limited manpower resources of the Confederacy, General Lee's dedication to an offensive strategy was at best questionable. To be able to come to no decision between an offensive strategy such as Lee's and a strategy of defense such as Jefferson Davis favored and to waver between the two was still worse. Yet the course of indecision was the one followed by the Confederacy in the West. Indecision, as usual, offered the worst of both worlds; it produced casualties comparable to Lee's, combined with territorial and logistical losses which began to stagger the Confederacy before the dust had settled from the first campaign.

At the beginning of 1862, President Davis's defensive strategy had the Confederate armies trying to hold the entire Confederate state of Tennessee and as much as possible of the politically divided state of Kentucky. General Albert Sidney Johnston, the Confederate commander in this theater, had forces totalling about 43,000 scattered across a front of about 300 miles, following a line of highlands from Mill Springs, Kentucky, in the east, through Bowling Green and Hopkinsville, to Columbus, Kentucky, on the Mississippi River. There were good military reasons to try to hold all this ground, apart from the obvious political ones. Not only did the Confederacy need every reservoir of military manpower it could get, but Tennessee was the South's principal granary and source of meat.[50] The trouble, of course, was that with Confederate forces scattered so thinly in passive defense, the Federals were almost certain to concentrate superior force for a breakthrough somewhere, and the effort to hold everything would end by holding nothing. We have returned to the dilemma which pushed Lee toward his offensive strategy in the first place.

Between Hopkinsville and Columbus, the Confederate military frontier dropped down just below the Tennessee border, where earthworks called Fort Henry and Fort Donelson guarded the Tennessee and Cumberland rivers. There were few good roads or railroads by which Northern invaders might pierce Johnston's lines; but the penetration of the frontier by the Tennessee, the Cumberland, and the Mississippi was an additional crippling weakness, because the North with its industrial and naval resources could put gunboat fleets on the waterways. At the beginning of February, 1862, Henry W. Halleck, now major general commanding the Union Department of Missouri with some 91,000 troops, authorized U. S. Grant, a brigadier commanding at Paducah, to attempt to take Forts Henry and Donelson in cooperation with Flag Officer Andrew H. Foote of the Navy and seven gunboats. Grant's force on land eventually numbered about 23,000. Fort Henry surrendered after a short bombardment from the boats; it was indefensible and its garrison had already been reduced to 100 men. Fort Donelson was harder to take, but it surrendered with about 11,500 troops on February 16.[51]

The fall of Forts Henry and Donelson turned the Confederate positions in western and central Kentucky, especially because it permitted the Federals to cut the railroad connection between Memphis and Bowling Green. Before the capture of the forts and the railroad, the Confederates might have been able to concentrate against Grant's relatively small force and check it. Now such opportunity was lost. Union gunboats could range up the Tennessee River as far as the Muscle Shoals in Alabama, far enough to bombard thc Memphis and Charleston Railroad around Eastport, Mississippi, and thus jeopardize direct communication between the Confederate East and West. The opening of the Cumberland River to the gunboats uncovered Nashville. General Johnston had to fall back to the Memphis and Charleston rail line, roughly along the northern border of Alabama and Mississippi. Thus the strategy of passive defense had thrown away most of the logistically crucial state of Tennessee.

Consequently, General Johnston switched strategies, to attempt a counterattack and a redemptive Napoleonic battle. At Corinth, Mississippi, on the Memphis and Charleston Railroad, he assembled

40,000 or more men by drawing troops from all over his theater and from as far away as Louisiana and Pensacola. With this army he proposed to attack Grant's force, now reinforced to 35–40,000, as it lay encamped near Pittsburg Landing, Tennessee, before Grant could be joined by Major General Don Carlos Buell's army of 50,000 which was marching toward it from Nashville.[52] Grant presented a tempting target, because he had prepared no defensive works and his troops lay encamped helter-skelter, the most exposed of them around a little church called Shiloh. He also conducted no patrolling to speak of, and Johnston was able to achieve complete surprise. But Johnston managed the tactics of his assault badly, and the rifle proved to make a frontal assault even against surprised and unentrenched troops a costly experience for the attacker. The next day, April 7, the Confederates had to retreat, having suffered more than 10,000 casualties, including Johnston himself killed, with nothing to show for it.[53]

Had the attack gone better, the rewards available to the Confederates at Shiloh would still have been limited by Buell's arrival. After the Confederates' first mistake in their western theater, that of dispersing their forces across too wide a front, this kind of outcome continued to plague them again and again: their concentrations, when they did accomplish them, invariably came too late. General P. G. T. Beauregard held together the army which Johnston had assembled for Shiloh and drew to it additional reinforcements from Arkansas, the Gulf coast, east Tennessee, and the Carolinas, until he raised the total to about 70,000. But by that time Halleck had added an army from the Mississippi River under John Pope to Grant's and Buell's forces, so that the Federals opposed Beauregard's 70,000 with 120,000. Beauregard conducted an admirable, cautious, life-saving defense of Corinth, the junction where the Memphis and Charleston Railroad met the Mobile and Ohio line which ran on southward. But he could not prevent Halleck from pushing into the town by means of traditional siege methods reflective of the military scholar.[54]

Halleck then made the mistake, curious in a student of Jomini, of dispersing his own troops in turn, scattering some 67,000 of them under Grant's command in driblets all along the Memphis and Charleston line from Memphis into Alabama, and back along the Mobile and Ohio from Corinth to Columbus. Buell with another 56,000 troops began a slow progress eastward toward Chattanooga, laboriously repairing the Memphis and Charleston Railroad as he went. General Braxton Bragg, who succeeded Beauregard in the Southern command, might have been able to recapture much of the territory lost in the Shiloh-Corinth campaign by gobbling up Grant's detachments. Instead, he decided to play for higher stakes, by transferring his troops via the railroads through Mobile to Chattanooga, and then attempting a bold end run around Grant's and Buell's forces to carry the war back into Kentucky and, he hoped, to redeem that state for the Confederacy. Bragg's plan had the considerable strategic merit that by obliging the Federals to shift eastward to meet him, it would require them to move perpendicular to their best lines of communication. As usual in the Confederate West, however, he proved to have just not quite enough men to succeed. Buell followed him and checked him in a battle at Perryville, Kentucky, on October 8. At least Bragg's campaign compares favorably with Lee's nearly simultaneous Antietam campaign; Bragg lost only about 4,000 casualties at Perryville, because he did not persist in doing battle when he was not strong enough to win.[55]

After these frustrations in essaying counteroffensives at Shiloh and in Kentucky, the western Confederates reverted to a dispersed and all too static defensive. General Joseph E. Johnston received overall command of the Confederate troops in Tennessee and Mississippi on November 24, 1862; but his command was an anomaly, because the department commanders whom he was to supervise continued also to receive orders directly from Richmond. In the western part of the theater, Grant was remedying Halleck's post-Corinth mistakes and concentrating his Federal forces again, for a drive on Vicksburg to give the Union control of the whole length of the Mississippi River. The Confederate forces in northern Mississippi, who came under the department command of Lieutenant General John C. Pemberton, were both too weak in numbers and too scattered to resist indefinitely a skillful and determined campaign, which was the sort Grant was likely to wage. Johnston, the government at Richmond, and the other Confederate generals in the West were unable, however, to reach agreement about whose troops should reinforce Pemberton.[56]

Bragg, a man of bilious temperament, was annoyed that Lee had received more public credit for his bloody and futile Maryland campaign than he himself had gotten for his similar but considerably less expensive Kentucky campaign. His resentment of this misappropriation of applause may have contributed to his decision to attempt a Napoleonic battle of his own. When the Federal army facing his, in command of which Buell had given way to Major General William S. Rosecrans, reached Murfreesboro on the Nashville-Chattanooga railroad line, Bragg anticipated its attack upon him with an attack by his own Army of Tennessee. The outcome was the customary one for such efforts. The battle of Murfreesboro, or Stones River, fought on the last day of 1862 and the second day of 1863, produced a tactical standoff, with both armies badly bloodied, the Confederates, who could afford it less, losing almost 12,000 killed, wounded, and missing. Bragg had to retreat to the Duck River, the next defensible position in front of Chattanooga.[57]

Meanwhile Grant's campaign against Vicksburg was developing so far and so little impeded by the quarreling Confederate commanders in the West that by mid-May Grant had invested Vicksburg with some 20,000 of Pemberton's men inside its defenses. Against him Pemberton and Johnston together were remarkably inept, able neither to concentrate their dispersed forces nor to maneuver effectively with those bodies which they did contrive to assemble.

In accordance with the now well-developed western Confederate strategic pattern of alternating a weak, static, and dispersed defensive with an equally futile but more costly offensive, the next major act of the drama was another effort at Napoleonic offensive battle by Bragg. In mid-summer Rosecrans maneuvered Bragg out of Chattanooga; this was the season when President Davis thought that Lee's most appropriate move, rather than an offensive in Pennsylvania, might have been to reinforce Bragg. Failing reinforcement from Lee at that juncture, another opportunity seemed to come to the Confederacy later. After entering Chattanooga, Rosecrans grew overconfident and careless, dispersing his troops recklessly as his Army of the Cumberland advanced into northwest Georgia. He gave Bragg hope and opportunity for a counterattack. Lee, his invasion of Pennsylvania defeated but with the cautious Meade in front of him, agreed now to send Longstreet and two of his divisions to reinforce Bragg's Army of Tennessee. Bragg struck Rosecrans on September 19 and 20 in the battle of Chickamauga; but still again the Confederate concentration was too little and too late to produce a decisive advantage. A miscarriage of Federal orders permitted the Confederates to maul Rosecrans's army badly, but it got away to Chattanooga substantially intact though weakened in morale. For this result Bragg paid with 18,000 casualties out of some 66,000 engaged.[58]

The price was too high and the result not enough. Grant's earlier success at Vicksburg permitted the Union to concentrate the bulk of its western forces at Chattanooga, along with two corps from the Army of the Potomac, all under Grant's command. With superior strength thus assembled, Grant broke Bragg's half-hearted siege of

Chattanooga late in November, opening the way to a campaign into Georgia the following spring.

The new campaign in the spring began with another change in the cast of characters. In March, Grant went east to assume command of all the Union armies, leaving his longtime lieutenant William Tecumseh Sherman in charge of the West. Bragg gave way to Joe Johnston in command of the Army of Tennessee. The student of war may speculate over what would have happened had this Johnston received command in the West, with more ample powers than he had held in 1863, early in the contest. For Johnston now proceeded to conduct the first western campaign of the Confederacy to be marked throughout by a coherent strategy appropriate to the Confederacy's resources.

Johnston kept his Army of Tennessee well concentrated; the days of the dispersed defensive were over, as far as he could control matters. But he did not attempt an ambitious counteroffensive which might cost heavy casualties beyond the Confederacy's ability to pay. Instead, like George Washington he eschewed general engagements altogether, unless they could be fought on terms wholly favorable to himself. He fought a war of defensive maneuver, seeking opportunities to fall upon enemy detachments which might expose themselves and inviting the enemy to provide him with such openings, meanwhile moving from one strong defensive position to another in order to invite the enemy to squander his resources in frontal attacks, but never remaining stationary long enough to risk being outflanked or entrapped. Few campaigns of the war saw an army kept so well in hand, so precisely controlled, so adroitly maneuvered, as Joe Johnston's defense of northwest Georgia in the spring and summer of 1864. Starting with some 62,000 men against 100,000, Johnston required one of the enemy's most capable commanders to consume seventy-four days in advancing a hundred miles, holding casualties to a minimum so that after nearly three months of campaigning his army remained almost as strong as when it came out of winter quarters.[59]

But Johnston did retreat. Applied with similar skill early in the war, his strategy of defensive maneuver might have so postponed substantial Federal triumphs and made the price for them so high that by 1864 and its Presidential election the Northern people might have lost patience and a political upheaval in the North might have awarded the Confederacy its independence; by 1864 the North was verging fairly close to that as matters stood. Yet the time was growing late for Johnston's strategy. He needed plenty of space for maneuver—space in which to wear the enemy down, space in which to extract losses from the enemy while never stopping to fight so stubbornly for a given position that Confederate losses themselves might become excessive. By 1864, there was not enough space left. On July 9, Johnston retreated behind the Chattahoochee River, the last important obstacle facing the enemy before the defenses of Atlanta, themselves less than five miles away.

Already a flanking arm of Sherman's Union forces was also across the Chattahoochee. President Davis, for all his belief in a defensive strategy which would not carelessly expend Confederate lives, thought the Confederacy could not afford to yield Atlanta without fighting a major battle in its defense. The moral damage would be too great. The physical damage, too, would be insupportable if Atlanta fell; it was one of the last industrial centers remaining to the Confederacy, the last important railroad center between the East and what remained of the Confederate West. In front of Atlanta, the space necessary for Johnston's war of maneuver ceased to exist. On July 17, the President replaced Johnston with General John Bell Hood, who was sure to fight.[60]

This change of command was a gesture of despair. If it was too late for Johnston's frugal, life-saving strategy to work, it was too late for anything to work. Hood attacked Sherman as expected. In the battles of Peachtree Creek, Atlanta, and Ezra Church, he poured away the strength of the Army of Tennessee in bloody assaults, until the army no longer had enough strength remaining to hold on to Atlanta. Though Confederate losses in the campaign had run behind Federal while Johnston was in command, Hood increased them so that they totaled over 27,000 to about 22,000 Federal for the campaign. After Atlanta fell on September 2, Hood was so weak that Sherman believed the bulk of the Union army could afford to ignore him. Sherman with the major part of his forces struck off on the march from Atlanta to the sea, leaving Major General George H. Thomas to gather up some 50,000 troops, some of them from scattered garrisons, to counter whatever Hood might do. Daring and aggressive to the last, Hood marched back into Tennessee. There he lost 5,550 more at Franklin and 4,462 in prisoners alone at Nashville, the Franklin losses mainly in as hopeless an assault as any of the war, across two miles of open ground against well prepared earthworks. He pushed on to the defenses of Nashville, but there Thomas counterattacked to wreck the already shattered Army of Tennessee and eliminate it from the war.[61]

To all these events in the West, Lee remained remarkably indifferent, despite President Davis's continuing to call upon him as a military adviser. He persistently underrated the strength and importance of Federal offensives in the West. As late as the spring of 1864, when Sherman faced Johnston with a larger numerical advantage than Grant's over Lee, Lee argued that "the great effort of the enemy in this campaign will be made in Virginia," and accordingly urged Johnston to take the offensive.[62] Lee persistently neglected also the logistical implications of the western campaigns, the loss of the granary of the Confederacy when most of Tennessee fell to Union arms so early, the threat to the Confederacy's most important iron mines and to one of the South's two main munitions centers (Richmond being the other) in Sherman's campaigning southward from Chattanooga into the Georgia-Alabama mining, industrial, and transportation complex. The only occasion when Lee consented to a major reinforcement of the West, Longstreet's trip to Bragg for the Chickamauga campaign, occurred after Gettysburg had left Lee's own offensive strategy in ruin. The West probably would have benefited from Lee's application of his strategic perceptions to it; almost any consistent strategy would have been better than vacillation between a dispersed defensive and hasty, belated counteroffensives. Thinking consistently about the West might also have encouraged greater realism in Lee's own mind.[63]

In the spring of 1864 Lee remarked to Major General Jubal Early: "We must destroy this army of Grant's before he gets to James River. If he gets there, it will become a siege, and then it will be a mere question of time."[64] Still, as on the day of Seven Pines when he first commanded the Army of Northern Virginia, at this late date Lee's hope and aim continued to be the destruction of the Federal army. But by the time he spoke to Early, his pursuit of that aim had already exhausted his army far beyond any capacity to accomplish such a purpose. He spoke to Early about the time when he repulsed Grant's attacks at Cold Harbor; by then, the siege warfare which made the outcome a mere question of time had already begun. The Army of Northern Virginia could no longer maneuver or mount a general offensive against its major adversary. It could hope only to hold off superior numbers from behind strong entrenchments and to make occasional diversionary sallies against exposed places and detachments.

Forced to confine himself to this type of warfare, Lee waged it with a skill at least comparable to Johnston's in Georgia. He had shown himself exceptionally talented in the use of field fortifications since those early days of his command when his men called him "the King of Spades"; and he had acknowledged the effects of rifled firepower enough to fight increasingly from trenches whenever his strategy permitted it from Chancellorsville onward.[65] He and the lieutenants trained in his and Stonewall Jackson's school of war could still achieve spectacular diversionary effects with minimal numbers, as when Early made the city of Washington tremble in the summer of 1864 with a new campaign down Jackson's old Shenandoah Valley route, and then across the Potomac into Maryland. But as soon as substantial Federal armed strength confronted a diversion such as Early's, the Confederates had to retreat; and attempting battle outside entrenchments during the autumn, Early was crushed.

No feasible diversion could effect more than a momentary interruption in the now inexorable course of the war toward Confederate defeat. The siege warfare which Lee had always feared began as early as May, at Spotsylvania Court House. Confederate and Federal armies both fought from trenches, with the Federals constantly shifting toward their left, first from Spotsylvania toward the North Anna and the James rivers, then across the James and southward beyond Richmond toward Petersburg, and on toward the railroads which served Richmond and Petersburg from the south. Unable to maneuver or attack, Lee could merely reach out with his own right flank in response, until at last in the trenches around Richmond and Petersburg he stretched his army to the breaking point. Then the enemy both broke into his trenches and cut the indispensable railroads.

In the spring of 1865 Lee's army had to march out of its trenches to undertake a war of motion once more—but the effort sapped its last strength and killed it. Johnston's war of flexible defense failed in Georgia because the Confederacy no longer had enough space for the necessary maneuver; Lee's attempt at a flexible defense in 1864–65 ran out of space and also out of men and commanders able to maneuver enough to make such a defense successful.

Of many of the arts of war, R. E. Lee was a consummate master. He organized his army to extract the best possible efforts from his men and his lieutenants. Within his immediate theater of war, his logistical management was excellent. His famous victories rightly made him the Southern commander most feared by his enemies. In one of them, Second Manassas, he came as close as any general since Napoleon to duplicating the Napoleonic system of battlefield victory by fixing the enemy in position with a detachment, bringing the rest of the army onto his flank and rear, and then routing him front and flank. But Lee was too Napoleonic. Like Napoleon himself, with his passion for the strategy of annihilation and the climactic, decisive battle as its expression, he destroyed in the end not the enemy armies, but his own.

7. A Strategy of Annihilation: U. S. Grant and the Union

It was indispensable to annihilate armies and resources; to place every rebel force where it had no alternative but destruction or submission, and every store or supply of arms or munitions or food or clothes where it could be reached by no rebel army.

—*Adam Badeau*[1]

Ulysses S. Grant believed that the strategy followed by Joe Johnston in the Atlanta campaign was the one that would have been best for the South generally. ". . . I think that his policy was the best one that could have been pursued by the whole South—protract the war, which was all that was necessary to enable them to gain recognition in the end." "For my own part, I think that Johnston's tactics were right. Anything that could have prolonged the war a year beyond the time that it did finally close, would probably have exhausted the North to such an extent that they might then have abandoned the contest and agreed to a separation."[2]

For Grant and the other Northern generals, the problem was always more complex. Not only did the North have to conquer the Confederacy, while the Confederacy only had to maintain itself. For the reason expressed by Grant in his evaluation of Johnston, the North in pursuit of conquest could not simply be content with Scott's Anaconda policy. The North had to win the war as quickly as possible. Northern sentiment in support of the Union's war of conquest against the South was much more divided than Southern sentiment supporting the defense of the Confederacy. The very fact that the principal object of the North was aggressive while that of the

South was not made for divisions of opinion in the North which were not duplicated in the South. The Democratic party in the North, over which the electoral margins of Lincoln's Republican party were never decisive enough for comfort, suffered mixed feelings about the war from the beginning, and its members tended increasingly to fear that the war was both subverting the Constitution as written by the founding fathers and becoming a partisan effort to assure Republican political ascendancy. The abolition of slavery, eventually established as a second Northern object in the war, threatened to produce intensely divisive effects in Northern opinion, touching as it did the always inflammable American race issue.

All these factors made not merely victory, but victory with the least possible delay, imperative to the Lincoln government. Even after Gettysburg, the Confederacy still retained hope of survival if the Democrats could win the Presidential election of 1864. Scott's Anaconda, the blockade and gradual military pressure against the Confederate land frontiers, seemed sure to produce military victory if the North had enough time; but Lincoln was never certain of having enough time. The impatience which produced First Bull Run was implicit in the Northern situation.

General Lee adopted an offensive strategy for his part of the Confederate armies by debatable choice. The North accepted a similar strategy by necessity. But a pursuit of rapid offensive success implied for the North many of the same problems that such a quest produced for Lee and the South. The effort to fulfill an offensive strategy by means of decisive Napoleonic battle bled Lee's army to exhaustion. Similar efforts by the North could bleed the Union armies too, if not so quickly to physical exhaustion, then at least to the loss of a divided section's will to continue the struggle, the very loss which rapid victory and therefore a resolute offensive strategy were supposed to avert.

The North's manpower and material resources were superior to the South's, a fact which is proverbial; but they were not limitless. To quote comparative population statistics is customary but misleading. The twenty-three states remaining in the Union had a population of about 23,000,000 in 1860, as against some 9,000,000 in the eleven seceding states, 3,500,000 of whom were slaves. The slaves at the beginning had to be counted in favor of the South, because their labor made possible a remarkably complete military mobilization of Southern white men—although it is true that this Southern asset partially wasted away as Northern armies advanced and black men fled into their lines. Some 3,000,000 of the population of the non-seceding states, including over 400,000 slaves, were in the border states and could not be counted wholly for the Union. To be sure, some division also existed within the Confederacy, especially in Virginia, whose western counties split away, and in Tennessee; but the combination of the border states with a generally less unified public opinion than existed in the Confederacy meant that the North could not translate its potential into actual military manpower as fully as the South. At one time or another, about 2,100,000 men served in the Union armies, with a peak strength at any given time of about 1,000,000; perhaps 900,000 served in the Confederate armies, with a peak strength of about 600,000.[3]

Allowing for the tendency, and in large part the necessity, for the Southern armies to disperse to defend the wide territory of the Confederacy, the South nevertheless made a larger proportion of its potential manpower felt on the decisive battlefronts than did the North, especially as the war went on. The North, aiming at permanent conquest, had to establish occupying garrisons in the Southern territories which its armies overran. When the Confederate armies occasionally invaded the loyal states, in contrast, they did not face the same necessity to drop off detachments to hold the places they took; their aim was not permanent occupation but the moral effect of victories on the enemy's soil. General Grant estimated that by the final campaigns of the war, at least half and probably more of the soldiers in the Union armies were not in the main field armies but on some kind of garrison or occupation duty or otherwise unavailable for service with the armies' cutting edge. On the eve of Sherman's Atlanta campaign in the spring of 1864, the muster rolls of his three armies showed an aggregate of 352,265 men, with 180,082 actually present for duty; but with reductions to meet demands for garrisons in occupied territories and guards for lines of communication, the force Sherman led into the field totaled only about 100,000.[4]

This dispersion of Union manpower was accentuated by the proportionately greater logistical apparatus of the Union as compared with the Confederate armies. The mass armies introduced by nationalism and the French Revolution and now employed for the first time in America made logistics an increasingly important element of strategy by their size alone. Other factors added to the dimensions of the Northern armies' logistical problems. Union soldiers by and large were accustomed to a higher standard of living than Confederate soldiers, and the greater divisions within Northern public opinion demanded that to maintain Union morale the living standard of the Union armies should continue at a higher level than the Confederate. The Confederates had the advantage of operating usually within their own, friendly territories, while each Union advance into the South lengthened and made more vulnerable the Union supply lines. When the Confederate armies did make forays into the loyal states, they mainly subsisted off the country; their invasions always included the replenishment of supplies from Northern stores among their purposes. But Confederate invasions of the North were always in the nature of raids, while once again the fact that the Union armies went into the South to stay meant that they could not be so casual and opportunistic about their supply arrangements. The United States armies of the Civil War were the first in history to be supplied over long distances and for a long period of time by railroads; without the invention of the railroad, Union operations over the extensive territory of the South might well have been impossible. But the railroads were as vulnerable as they were indispensable. The Confederates invariably broke them up in retreat, so that the Federals had to rebuild them as they advanced; and once they were rebuilt, detachments had to be dropped along their length to protect them from Confederate cavalry and guerrilla raids.[5]

Logistical support of the Union armies was conducted less by soldiers permanently assigned to service organizations such as the Quartermaster's Department than by men detailed from line regiments. Thus it is difficult to know just how large a proportion of the armies' personnel were doing jobs which in World War II would have placed them in the Army Service Forces. But Union strength returns, such as those for Sherman's armies in the spring of 1864, suggest that the expansion of the logistical and administrative tail of the army at the expense of the fighting battalions already had a large beginning toward its twentieth-century dimensions. Support of the army limited at the same time its sustained fighting capacities, and logistics increasingly limited the calculations of strategy.

In general, Union supply operations were well managed but difficult, and as Union conquests grew they became increasingly so. Confederate logistics were less well managed, but were aided by the proximity of the Confederate armies to their bases, by the Confederates' fighting usually in friendly territory. Despite the limitations of Southern industry and agriculture, despite Confederate losses of logistically critical areas, despite indifferent management of the Confederate armies' supply systems, despite the gradual breakdown of the

Confederacy's internal transportation system, and despite the blockade, the Confederacy did not lose a battle or campaign from a shortage of supplies until the very end, when supply failures converged with multiple additional causes of defeat to produce a disintegration of the Confederate armies.

Northern manpower and material advantages, then, were not so great as they might have seemed. The Northern reservoir of manpower was not inexhaustible, even apart from the moral consideration that excessive losses in battle might destroy the relatively fragile Northern will to continue the war. With that moral consideration added to the physical ones, the Northern generals faced perplexing problems in waging an offensive war of conquest, in pursuit of rapid victory, without suffering casualties so severe that they would destroy the very resolution which the quest for rapidity of conquest was supposed to sustain.

Abraham Lincoln perceived still another reason why the North must pursue rapidity of conquest. To subdue the South and all its white population militarily would be difficult enough. But Lincoln did not seek mere military conquest. The primary object of his government was the restoration of the Union, the achievement of which demanded that sooner or later the South must yield to the Union with some measure of voluntary consent. The South could not be held forever with the bayonet. The longer the war went on, however, the more bitterness it seemed likely to nourish, and the more difficult a true restoration of the Union might become. The longer Southerners fought Northerners as enemies, the less able they might be to accept each other once again as friends. More than that, the longer the war went on, the more likely would it become that accumulating Northern frustrations would push Lincoln's government into harsher and more vindictive policies, which might multiply the sources of Southern enmity by geometric progression. Lincoln did not wish to defeat the Southern armies only to have an embittered South shift into guerrilla warfare, which might perpetuate itself indefinitely.

> In considering the policy to be adopted for suppressing the insurrection [Lincoln said], I have been anxious and careful that the inevitable conflict for this purpose shall not degenerate into a violent and remorseless revolutionary struggle. . . . The Union must be preserved, and hence, all indispensable means must be employed. We should not be in haste to determine that radical and extreme measures, which may reach the loyal as well as the disloyal, are indispensable.[6]

The most important specific meaning which the phrase "remorseless revolutionary struggle" could imply in the Civil War was the possible elimination of slavery, with all the immense corollaries that such a step might entail. The moral desirability of the elimination of slavery cannot detract from the wisdom of Lincoln's hope and effort to maintain a rational control over the course and direction of the war. In recognizing the danger of the war's degenerating into "remorseless revolutionary struggle," Lincoln acknowledged that by waging war he was not merely pursuing political ends by different means, but rather that war tends to take shapes and create purposes of its own. He hoped to restrain that tendency, to keep control of the war and its purposes. Therefore he announced from the beginning that while he was obliged to wage war, he would do so in as humane and conciliatory a manner as he could. "We are not enemies, but friends," he told the seceded states in his first inaugural address.[7] In the proclamation of April 15, 1861, in which he called for troops to suppress rebellion, he promised to wage a limited war, engaging in no unnecessary punishment and destruction:

> I deem it proper to say that the first purpose assigned to the forces hereby called forth will probably be to repossess the forts, places, and property which have been seized from the Union; and in any event, the utmost care will be observed, consistently with the objects aforesaid, to avoid any devastation, any destruction of, or interference with, property, or any disturbance of peaceful citizens in any part of the country.[8]

No general of Lincoln's Army more clearly recognized this particular dimension of policy, and consequently of the factors which must influence strategy, that the way in which the war was fought would certainly shape its ends, or more thoroughly sympathized with Lincoln's wish to prevent "remorseless revolutionary struggle," than did Major General George B. McClellan. McClellan came to the head of the army around Washington, and soon, when Scott retired from age, to the head of all the Union armies, after leading in the implicitly revolutionary work of detaching the nonsecessionist western counties of Virginia from the Confederate portion of the state. But McClellan was anything but a friend of war as revolution. He was a Democrat in politics, of no antislavery proclivities. He believed firmly that to win the war it was necessary to accomplish the difficult balancing act of combining military victories, to convince the South that it must return to its old allegiance, with restraints upon destruction and an attitude of conciliation, to persuade the South that it ought to do so.

"I have not come here to wage war upon the defenseless, upon non-combatants, upon private property, nor upon the domestic institutions of the land," McClellan told a Virginia gentleman in apologizing for the loss occasioned by the presence of the Union army upon the gentleman's plantation. "I and the army I command are fighting to secure the Union and maintain its Constitution and laws, and for no other purpose."[9] Such, McClellan advised the President in his famous Harrison's Landing letter—that very controversial departure from his military role—ought to be the whole policy of the government. There should be no alliance of the administration with radicalism, no warfare against the civilian population of the South, no forcible abolition of slavery.[10]

McClellan's military strategy was consistent with his view of the policy which ought to govern the conduct of the war. By conserving life as well as property, he sought to wage war with the least possible destructiveness, to occasion the least possible bitterness on both sides. The South must be convinced by military means that secession could not succeed, but the South must also be conciliated. For a general who chose to clothe himself in a Napoleonic *persona* ("Soldiers! I have heard that there was danger here. I have come to place myself at your head and to share it with you."[11]), McClellan was a notably un-Napoleonic strategist. In his western Virginia campaign and thereafter he held to the "intention of gaining success by maneuvering rather than by fighting."[12] He won the enduring affection of his soldiers not least because they believed he cared about their lives and would not waste them in reckless adventures. When confronted with the apparently formidable defenses of Yorktown at the beginning of his Peninsular Campaign, he did not rush into assault but resorted to a siege, a method which later provoked ridicule but which ensured a low butcher's bill.

Though he had a hand in hastening Scott's retirement so he could become Commanding General himself, his military methods made McClellan more nearly the heir of Winfield Scott than any other general who followed in high command in the Union armies. Like Scott he hoped to reach his objective by maneuver rather than by fighting, and like Scott he chose a political objective, the enemy's capital city. He hoped that by capturing Richmond he would accomplish what Scott had done by capturing the City of Mexico, to convince the enemy of the military futility of the war, but without excessive bloodshed or bitterness. By June 25, 1862, he was closer to Richmond than any other Union general was to come for another two years—and closer also to embracing Lee and the defending army in the siege which Lee thought would prove fatal. The Peninsular Campaign which carried him to that point was, notwithstanding its fault in seeming to expose Washington, an admirable exploitation of sea power and maneuver to bring McClellan to the verge of his objective with minimal costs in resources and lives.

With so much to be said for McClellan's generalship, it is a pity that he was no Winfield Scott when it came to the execution of his strategy in the cash payoff of battle. When Lee aggressively forced him to do battle before finally reaching his goals, he could not cope with the Confederate Napoleon. Probably it was impossible to conquer the Confederacy with the minimal destructiveness for which McClellan hoped, even had McClellan been an abler commander on the battlefield. The more is the pity that he was not, however, because once Lincoln removed him from command, the experiment in a war of restrained rationality was dying.[13]

For almost a year after McClellan's departure, his successors in the eastern Federal command gave themselves over to the Napoleonic mania for the climactic battle. The mystique of the battle—the idea that the battle was the natural object and climax of any military campaign—was so pervasive and powerful in the military world of the post-Napoleonic era that all the Federal commanders in the East between McClellan and Meade—Pope, Burnside, Hooker—were incapable of perceiving any strategic design beyond either the capture of Richmond or the grand battle in which they hoped to win their Austerlitz victory over Lee. So much did these generals regard "the battle" as synonymous with "the campaign" and even "the war," that when they lost a battle they never knew what to do next and withdrew into paralysis until their replacement came along. It is difficult to believe that they would have demonstrated a much clearer notion of what to do next had they ever been fortunate enough to win their battles.

In June, 1862, Lincoln brought Halleck eastward from the Mississippi to replace McClellan as Commanding General of the Army, surely hoping that this military scholar would produce some strategy of longer range and greater foresight that would involve a cumulative design for winning the war. But it was one of the several failures of Halleck's tenure as Commanding General that he did not. Perhaps Lincoln should have been forewarned, in that before Halleck came to Washington he had already interrupted the working out of one of the obvious strategic designs which had occurred to Lincoln from the beginning, the use of Federal naval power to split the Confederacy in two by controlling the Mississippi River. This design had taken two long steps forward in April, 1862, when Flag Officer David G. Farragut captured New Orleans and the Union won the Island No. 10-Memphis and the Shiloh campaigns. But the effort stalled when Halleck dispersed the western armies on garrison and railroad-building work after the capture of Corinth. Instead of being helpful with grand strategy, it was Halleck who sneered at Lincoln for wanting to violate the principle of concentration by maintaining pressure against the Confederacy everywhere.[14]

Therefore Lincoln found it hard to do much for military victory beyond encouraging the tightening of the naval blockade and offering support to the successive generals who gained notoriety, hoping that one of them would conceive a design to win the war or at least prove capable of winning battles. The President did not have the time or the staff to become a general himself; as it was, he went remarkably far in that direction, showing no mean military ability. After McClellan was removed as Commanding General of the Army in March, 1862, and until Halleck took up that post in July, Lincoln and Secretary of War Edwin M. Stanton personally directed the armies. They conceived and supervised the plan for trying to trap Jackson after his northward surge down the Shenandoah Valley in May by bringing converging columns from the east and west against the southern part of the Valley. This plan nearly worked, and it might have succeeded altogether had it not encountered bad weather and disobedience of orders by Major General John C. Frémont.[15] When McClellan was repulsed on the Peninsula, Lincoln with characteristic balance refused to be stampeded by the general's pleas for reinforcements and did not remove troops from the more successful campaigns in the West. He made the decision, not so common among strategists as it should be, not to reinforce failure but to press harder where there already was success, in the West. With Halleck's guidance and support, Lincoln made the courageous decision to remove McClellan's army from the Peninsula after the Seven Days, thus publicly writing off the campaign as a failure.

None of Lincoln's efforts as an active Commander in Chief, however, not even the one strategy that was steadily pursued, the tightening of the blockade, brought the kind of tangible and swift achievements that Lincoln needed to offset the effects of futile battle casualties upon Northern morale or to keep the war from degenerating into remorseless revolutionary struggle. McClellan's military failures produced the very political results that McClellan as self-appointed policy adviser most deplored. Through 1862 Lincoln's statements reflected a troubled, growing sense of losing control of the momentum and direction of the war. "If, however, resistance continues," he said on March 6, "the war must also continue; and it is impossible to foresee all the incidents, which may attend and all the ruin which may follow it."[16] When citizens of Union-occupied Louisiana complained that already the conduct of the Union armies was departing harshly from Lincoln's first assurances of protection for property and liberties, Lincoln felt obliged to warn that worse might come:

> . . . I never had a wish to touch the foundations of their society, or any right of theirs. With perfect knowledge of this, they forced a necessity upon me to send armies among them, and it is their own fault, not mine, that they are annoyed by the presence of General [John Wolcott] Phelps [who wanted to recruit Negroes from New Orleans]. They also know the remedy—how to be cured of General Phelps. Remove the necessity for his presence. And might it not be well for them to consider whether they have not already had *time* enough to do this? If they can conceive of anything worse than General Phelps, within my power, would they not better be looking out for it?[17]

About the same time there appeared indications that such a warning might have implications for strategy as well as for policy. A harsher conduct by the Federal military toward rebel property and liberties might begin to be employed as a weapon with which to attack the Confederate will to persevere in the struggle, and the Confederate means to do so. Lincoln acquiesced in measures involving the civil population of Virginia announced by General Pope, though General Lee and other Southerners considered these measures barbarous. While enjoining against pillaging, Pope directed his forces to live off the country, with his authorized officers to requisition supplies and to reimburse *only loyal citizens*. He announced stern penalties for "evil-disposed persons in rear of our armies"; Virginia communities must pay compensation for any damage done by marauders or guerrillas within their bounds, and Pope threatened to destroy any house from which a Union soldier was shot. So far Pope was within the limits of the recognized practices of warfare, but he was clearly departing from McClellan's conciliatory policies. He went still further, and to positions that were legally dubious or worse. He ordered that an oath of allegiance be administered to all disloyal male citizens within his lines, he directed the expulsion beyond his lines of any such who refused to take the oath, and he threatened the death penalty for any who returned after expulsion or any person who from within his lines communicated with the enemy.[18]

A mild, conciliatory policy had failed to bring the South back into the Union, and with the bitterness engendered by prolonged war many Republican party leaders were demanding a sterner policy of punishment for secessionists. Lincoln's acquiescence in Pope's decrees suggests that he reflected that since mildness had failed, harshness might help his armies as well as his position within his party. If conciliation could not persuade the South to return to the Union, punishment and an application of the harsh hand of war might undermine the Southern will to remain out of the Union. Punishment might become an element of military strategy.

Certainly the Emancipation Proclamation issued on September 22 involved strategy as well as national policy. It was, among its other purposes, an instrument designed to deprive the South of the black labor supply which enabled the Confederacy to maintain the industry and agriculture of war and to build fortifications while still retaining an extraordinary proportion of its white population in the front lines. Henceforth more than before, as Union armies advanced into the South, they would act as magnets drawing black laborers away from their Confederate masters.

Lincoln moved to these harsher measures of war with reluctance, but he asked: "What would you do in my position? Would you drop the war where it is? Or would you prosecute it in future, with elder-stalk squirts, charged with rose water? Would you deal lighter blows rather than heavier ones? Would you give up the contest, leaving any available means unapplied?"[19]

Meade won at Gettysburg, but he supplied no long-range strategy for winning the war. At least he did not suffer from the battle mania, but the kind of campaign of maneuver in which he engaged during the autumn of 1863 was not going to overcome the Confederacy, or as shrewd a veteran general as R. E. Lee. Meade himself seems to have sensed that he was only marking time, until a general promising a better plan might be brought to the East from the western theater. The portents suggested that Meade was too old-fashioned a soldier and Philadelphia gentleman to have the ruthlessness necessary for the better plan in this war.

By the time Meade turned Lee back at Gettysburg, the lineaments of the next Union general were becoming evident enough. Ulysses Simpson Grant had earned the major share of the credit for capturing Forts Henry and Donelson in February, 1862. At Shiloh he gave himself no opportunity to display distinction in the intellectual aspects of generalship, but he did show a stubborn pugnacity which could stand firm against reverses. As an officer who ranked low in his class at West Point and who claimed little knowledge of the literature of war, he was not the type to appeal to Halleck. Halleck appears to have been jealous of him for his early successes as well, and he did all that he could to deny Grant full credit for his achievements at Henry, Donelson, and Shiloh and kept him under a shadow as second in command in the West, practically a supernumerary, through the Corinth campaign.[20]

After Halleck went to Washington, however, Grant began to demonstrate that his stubbornness at Shiloh was related to more nearly intellectual qualities. He showed himself free from the common fixation of his contemporaries upon the Napoleonic battle as the hinge upon which warfare must turn. Instead, he developed a highly uncommon ability to rise above the fortunes of a single battle and to master the flow of a long series of events, almost to the point of making any outcome of a single battle, victory, draw, or even defeat, serve his eventual purpose equally well.

His Vicksburg campaign, which extended from the autumn of 1862 into the summer of 1863, was a model of persistent long-range planning. He did not draw inflexible plans, because war is too unpredictable for that, and his progress toward Vicksburg did suffer many reverses. But while always retaining a variety of options in preparation for the unexpected, nevertheless Grant kept pursuing consistently a well-defined strategic goal, the opening of the Mississippi; and viewing battles as means rather than as ends, he refused to be diverted from his goal by the temporary fortunes of any given battle.

Grant's popular reputation remains that of an unsubtle general who bulled his way to victories over the butchered bodies of his troops. Yet few campaigns in history have accomplished so much at so low a cost in lives as Grant's for Vicksburg, against great obstacles of geography if not of enemy generalship. In the most active part of the campaign, when after a variety of experiments and frustrations Grant had contrived to place his troops on dry ground on the Vicksburg side of the Mississippi River, between May 1 and 19, 1863, his army marched 180 miles, fought five battles, split the forces opposing them in two, clamped Vicksburg into a siege, and imposed over 7,000 casualties upon the enemy while suffering fewer than 4,500 themselves.[21]

After the siege began, Grant sought to hasten victory by means of several assaults which proved to be mistakes, and his army suffered 4,910 casualties in the course of the siege to 2,872 Confederate. But with the Confederate surrender on July 4, Grant gathered in 2,166 officers, 27,320 enlisted men, 115 civilian employees of the Confederate Army, 172 artillery pieces, and between 50,000 and 60,000 muskets and rifles.[22] Beyond that, of course, he ensured the reopening of the whole length of the Mississippi River to Union navigation, divided the Confederacy, deprived the eastern Confederacy of all but a trickle of the foodstuffs of the trans-Mississippi states and the war supplies imported through Mexico, and dealt a moral blow probably more destructive than the measurable losses.

Grant prided himself especially upon what he considered the most important innovation of his Vicksburg campaign, his bold expedient in cutting loose from his line of communication, the Mississippi River, and living off the country from the time he left the river to deal with the Confederate forces in the interior of Mississippi at the beginning of May until he returned to the river by encircling Vicksburg three weeks later. This gamble made possible the whole campaign on the good dry ground south and east of Vicksburg, and it contributed greatly to the befuddlement of the enemy. Grant was able to keep the two main enemy forces under Joe Johnston and John Pemberton separated largely because Pemberton became too preoccupied with trying to cut Grant's nonexistent line of communication with the river to march to a junction with Johnston. Nevertheless, breaking away from the line of communication was not so much an innovation as Grant's accounts of it make it seem. Scott had essayed a similar gamble in Mexico. Bragg's and Lee's Confederate forays into the North depended upon their armies' living off the country.[23]

Grant's losses were slight because he fought no battle between Port Gibson and the beginning of the siege in which he did not have the enemy already off balance and outnumbered before the action began. This result he accomplished despite possessing no significant numerical advantage over Pemberton and Johnston if the Confederate forces had united. He waged successfully the kind of campaign of maneuver, and eventually of siege, at a low cost in lives, that McClellan had only hoped to wage. He was able to do so in part because of the unsettling effect upon the enemy of his departure from his line of communication. He was able to do so mainly because he kept his ultimate object constantly in view, while in the face of Lee's activities McClellan had constantly yielded his attention to distractions. Yet while retaining his focus upon the ultimate object, Grant also kept in mind every optional means of pursuing it, so that whatever countervailing means the enemy employed, he was always prepared to circumvent them. The long view toward his object had enabled Grant to rise above the initial reverses at Shiloh, and again above the initial reverses of the Vicksburg campaign, when the Confederate repulse of Sherman's attack on Chickasaw Bluffs in December, 1862, had been as bad a defeat on as ill-chosen a field as Fredericksburg. To keep the long view and to retain options may seem simple things, but no Federal commander in the East had yet managed to accomplish them, and they were the keys to the success of Grant's campaign for Vicksburg.[24]

So little was Grant influenced by the Napoleonic infatuation with the battle as the supreme means in war that he believed even Winfield Scott had fought too many battles. "In later years, if not at the time," Grant said, "the battles of Molino del Rey and Chapultepec have seemed to me to be wholly unnecessary." Grant believed that Scott's troops could have moved out of range of the Mexican guns at those places and onto an optional road—the aqueduct road—into Mexico City at a point where the mill and the castle which were the objects of the battles would have been turned and would have had to be evacuated. Indeed, Grant believed that Scott had chosen the wrong route from Veracruz to Mexico and should have gone by a more circuitous route swinging north of the city of Puebla, which would have avoided easily defensible mountain passes and thus avoided some of the battles and losses.[25] Grant did not much like battle; he was never distracted by the panoply and drama of battle.

But while charging even Scott with having incurred unnecessary casualties, Grant did not believe the Civil War could be won without heavy loss of life. For although he rejected the Napoleonic glorification of the battle, Grant accepted a Napoleonic strategy of annihilation as the prescription for victory in a war of popular nationalism. In the Vicksburg campaign he had pursued mainly a geographical objective, which by skillful maneuver he was able to attain without much bloodshed, while gathering in large numbers of enemy soldiers as an incident of attaining the territorial objective. When Vicksburg and his subsequent victory at Chattanooga led to his appointment to succeed Halleck as Commanding General of the Army, however, with responsibility to accomplish the complete and final conquest of the Confederacy, he believed that different methods became appropriate. For the final defeat of the Confederacy it would be necessary to destroy the two principal Confederate armies, Lee's Army of Northern Virginia and Joe Johnston's Army of Tennessee. The commanders of both these enemy armies were too capable to permit the elimination of their armies by mere maneuvers and stratagems. Hard fighting would be necessary. Grant proposed a strategy of annihilation based upon the principle of concentration and mass, hitting the main Confederate armies with the concentrated thrust of massive Federal forces until the Confederate armies were smashed into impotence.

Unlike Lee, Grant entertained no illusions about being able to destroy enemy armies in a single battle in the age of rifled firearms. Unlike Lee, he possessed enough resources to make a strategy of annihilation feasible and not chimerical. In the spring of 1864 he took the field with the Army of the Potomac, while retaining Meade in immediate command of that army.

> Soon after midnight, May 3d–4th [Grant wrote], the Army of the Potomac moved out from its position north of the Rapidan, to start upon that memorable campaign, destined to result in the capture of the Confederate capital and the army defending it. This was not to be accomplished, however, without as desperate fighting as the world has ever witnessed; not to be consummated in a day, a week, a month, or a single season. The losses inflicted, and endured, were destined to be severe; but the armies now confronting each other had already been in deadly conflict for a period of three years, with immense losses in killed, by death from sickness, captured and wounded; and neither had made any real progress toward accomplishing the final end. . . . The campaign now begun was destined to result in heavier losses, to both armies, in a given time, than any previously suffered; but the carnage was to be limited to a single year, and to accomplish all that had been anticipated or desired at the beginning in that time. We had to have hard fighting to achieve this. The two armies had been confronting each other so long, without any decisive result, that they hardly knew which could whip.[26]

It was the grim campaign to destroy the Confederacy by destroying Lee's army that was to give Grant his reputation as a butcher. His answer to criticism was that it was better to suffer heavy losses to achieve the object of the war than to suffer heavy losses for the stalemate in which the eastern armies had floundered for three years. His method of achieving the destruction of the enemy army was not to seek the Austerlitz battle, a method which had been tried in the East for three years by both sides and found wanting, but rather an extension of the concept of battle until the battle became literally synonymous with the whole campaign: he would fight all the time, every day, keeping the enemy army always within his own army's grip, allowing the enemy no opportunity for deceptive maneuver, but always pounding away until his own superior resources permitted the Federal armies to survive while the enemy army at last disintegrated. "Lee's army," he told Meade, "will be your objective point. Wherever Lee goes, there you will go also."[27] When Sheridan went to deal with Early's Confederate force in the Shenandoah Valley, Grant gave similar instructions: ". . . I want Sheridan put in command of all the troops in the field, with instructions to put himself south of the enemy and follow him to death. Wherever the enemy goes let our troops go also."[28]

To pursue the destruction of the main Confederate armies, Grant's plan "was to concentrate all the force possible against the Confederate armies in the field."[29] He sought to apply the principle of concentration by eliminating as many as possible of the garrisons scattered for defensive purposes along the Confederate borders and throughout the occupied parts of the South.

> . . . as the Army of the Potomac was the principal garrison for the protection of Washington even while it was moving on Lee, so all the forces to the west, and the Army of the James, guarded their special trusts when advancing from them as well as when remaining at them. Better indeed, for they forced the enemy to guard his own lines and resources at a greater distance from ours, and with a greater force.[30]

As Grant's own previously cited testimony shows, this kind of concentration could not be effected to the extent Grant would have liked. So extensive was the territory already occupied and so exposed were the rear areas to enemy cavalry raiders and guerrillas that about half the manpower of Grant's armies had to remain in garrison and supporting duties.[31] To make his own concentration against Lee and Johnston more effective, however, Grant also saw to it that the principle of concentration was not narrowly applied. To force the Confederacy to disperse its limited resources as much as possible, Grant sent his main armies forward against both Lee and Johnston simultaneously, and at the same time he also advanced lesser forces from the James River against Richmond, up the Shenandoah Valley, and against the Virginia and Tennessee Railroad from West Virginia. He hoped to mount an expedition also against Mobile, Alabama, a task which eventually the Navy had to initiate. As his land campaigns progressed, the tightening of the naval blockade and the seizure of the Confederacy's remaining seaports also continued. "I arranged for a simultaneous movement all along the line," said Grant.[32] This method was the one Lincoln had urged on other generals throughout the war, without success.

While aiming at the destruction of the enemy armies, Grant could not ignore the Jominian territorial objectives. It was threats against the political and logistical centers of Richmond and Atlanta that compelled Lee's and Johnston's armies to fight. In the early part of his campaign with the Army of the Potomac, Grant forced Lee into combat by continually threatening to interpose the Federal army between Lee and the Confederate capital. In the siege of Petersburg, he forced Lee into debilitating activity by means of threats to the railroads which connected Lee with his supplies. But territorial objectives and Jominian considerations of interior and exterior lines became secondary to the object of destroying the enemy armies by clinging to them and not letting go, and in large part the object of destroying the enemy armies translated into the raw purpose of fighting and taking lives.

> The criticism [Grant said] has been made by writers on the campaign from the Rapidan to the James River that all the loss of life could have been obviated by moving the army there on transports. Richmond was fortified and intrenched so perfectly that one man inside to defend was more than equal to five outside besieging or assaulting. To get possession of Lee's army was the first great object. . . . It was better to fight him outside of his stronghold than in it.[33]

The human cost of Grant's strategy of annihilation had to be large. In the first month of the 1864 campaign, from the Wilderness through Cold Harbor, the Army of the Potomac and the various forces attached to it suffered 55,000 casualties, not far from the total strength with which the rival Army of Northern Virginia began the month. In the process the Federals inflicted 32,000 casualties upon Lee's army, a loss which following upon the already severe bleeding of that army obliged the Confederacy to rob the cradle and the grave in desperate efforts to replenish the ranks.[34] Under such losses the Confederacy could not endure, and Grant did in time destroy Lee's army and end the war. Battles had lost their Napoleonic decisiveness because rifled weapons multiplied casualties so much on both sides in every battle that neither contestant could win a clear enough advantage to produce decisive effects. Grant never gained decisive results in any single battle, and he did not expect to. He returned decision to the war by prolonging battle through the whole campaign, inflicting casualties until he won not a dramatic Napoleonic victory but the peace of exhaustion.

Grant returned decision to the war, but trading casualties was hardly a satisfying means to the end. With the armies driven by rifled weapons into entrenchments to protect themselves from the weapons' full effects, and with Lee and Johnston skillfully delaying the outcome, the process became depressingly prolonged, aggravating all the tendencies of the war to grow into an uncontrollable juggernaut which would ruin everybody's reconstruction plans. The outcome itself remained doubtful until Lincoln's reelection in November, and the heavy price that Grant paid to advance no closer to Richmond than McClellan had gone two years before enhanced the doubtfulness of the election.

Napoleon had achieved decision in war less by the literal destruction of the enemy's armies than by his destruction of the enemy's will through the psychologically paralyzing effects of his dramatic battlefield victories. With Napoleonic decisiveness in battle no longer possible, Grant became the prophet of a strategy of annihilation in a new dimension, seeking the literal destruction of the enemy's armies as the means to victory. So appalling were the costs, however, that Grant's strategy of annihilation entailed, that inevitably the question arose: Could there not be some better means of extracting decision from war now that battles no longer offered Napoleonic decisiveness?

Grant himself suggested a possible way. His order to Sherman in the West equivalent to the order which told Meade go go wherever Lee's army might go included an interesting additional instruction: "You I propose to move against Johnston's army, to break it up and to get into the interior of the enemy's country as far as you can, inflicting all the damage you can upon their war resources."[35]

To strike against war resources suggested an indirect means of accomplishing the destruction of the enemy armies. If the enemy were deprived of the economic means to maintain armies, then the armies obviously would collapse. This idea of course was not startlingly new; it was implicit in the blockade from the beginning of the war, as it had been one of the objects of blockades in times past.

In the modern Western world, however, war by land armies waged directly upon the enemy's economic resources had been attempted only very charily and within narrow limits imposed by the accepted rules of war. For the European states of the eighteenth century to have waged economic war against each other by destroying each other's resources would have endangered excessively the whole precarious financial and economic stability of early modern Europe and thus would have imperiled everybody, including the first state to initiate such war. Furthermore, not even the passions loosed by the wars of the French Revolution produced economic war against enemy resources as a general practice of armies on land, because there was still another reason not to practice such warfare. The wars of early modern Europe, even the wars of the French Revolution, were not contests in which economic strength was decisive. They were not "gross national product wars" such as World War II, in which the contest did largely turn upon the question of which rival coalition of powers could outproduce the other. The products and resources needed to sustain armies in early modern history and through the wars of the French Revolution were still limited enough and simple enough that a relatively limited economy could sustain war.

By the time of the American Civil War, this condition was beginning to change. The Civil War was still far from being a contest of rival productive capacities on the model of World War II, but the logistical requirements of armies had become large enough and complex enough that making war against the enemy's resources did begin to appear a tempting prospect, especially because other means of attaining decision in war were becoming so unsatisfactory.

Because modern European nations had gone so long without warring upon each other's resources, except through naval blockades, steps in that direction were bound to appear shocking. Pope's decrees in 1862 about living off the country remained within the accepted rules of war, but they nevertheless departed so far from the customary practices, or at least threatened to do so, that Lee spoke of their author as "the miscreant Pope."[36] Still, the unromantic Grant early began to reflect upon the utility and perhaps indeed the necessity of a war against Confederate resources:

> Up to the battle of Shiloh [he said] I, as well as thousands of other citizens, believed that the rebellion against the government would collapse suddenly and soon, if a decisive victory could be gained over any of its armies. Donelson and Henry were such victories. An army of more than 21,000 men was captured or destroyed. Bowling Green,

Columbus and Hickman, Kentucky, fell in consequence, and Clarksville and Nashville, Tennessee, the last two with an immense amount of stores, also fell into our hands. The Tennessee and Cumberland Rivers, from their mouths to the head of navigation, were secured. But when Confederate armies were collected which not only attempted to hold a line farther south, from Memphis to Chattanooga, Knoxville and on to the Atlantic, but assumed the offensive and made such a gallant effort to regain what had been lost, then, indeed, I gave up all idea of saving the Union except by complete conquest. Up to that time it had been the policy of our army, certainly of that portion commanded by me, to protect the property of the citizens whose territory was invaded, without regard to their sentiments, whether Union or Secession. After this, however, I regarded it as humane to both sides to protect the persons of those found at their homes, but to consume everything that could be used to support or supply armies. Protection was still continued over such supplies as were within lines held by us and which we expected to continue to hold; but such supplies within the reach of Confederate armies I regarded as much contraband as arms or ordnance stores. Their destruction was accomplished without bloodshed and tended to the same result as the destruction of armies. I continued this policy to the close of the war. Promiscuous pillaging, however, was discouraged and punished. Instructions were always given to take provisions and forage under the direction of commissioned officers who should give receipts to owners, if at home, and turn the property over to officers of the quartermaster or commissary department to be issued as if furnished from our own Northern dépots. But much was destroyed without receipts to owners, when it could not be brought within our lines and would otherwise have gone to the support of secession and rebellion.[37]

Grant told a story of his application of this policy when his troops captured Jackson, the capital of Mississippi, on their way to investing Vicksburg:

. . . Sherman was to remain in Jackson until he destroyed that place as a railroad centre, and manufacturing city of military supplies. He did the work most effectually. Sherman and I went together into a manufactory which had not ceased work on account of the battle nor for the entrance of Yankee troops. Our presence did not seem to attract the attention of either the manager or the operatives, most of whom were girls. We looked on for a while to see the tent cloth which they were making roll out of the looms, with "C. S. A." still woven in each bolt. There was an immense amount of cotton, in bales, stacked outside. Finally I told Sherman I thought they had done work enough. The operatives were told they could leave and take with them what cloth they could carry. In a few minutes cotton and factory were in a blaze. The proprietor visited Washington while I was President to get his pay for this property, claiming that it was private. He asked me to give him a statement of the fact that his property had been destroyed by National troops, so that he might use it with Congress where he was pressing, or proposed to press, his claim. I declined.[38]

Grant further developed the war on the enemy's resources when in 1864 he instructed Sheridan regarding the farms in the Shenandoah Valley: "If the war is to last another year, we want the Shenandoah Valley to remain a barren waste."[39] Sheridan responded proficiently: "I have destroyed over 2000 barns filled with wheat, hay and farming implements; over 70 mills, filled with flour and wheat; have driven in front of the army over 4000 head of stock, and have killed and issued to the troops not less than 3000 sheep. . . . The people here are getting sick of war."[40]

By that time, laboring under the heavy losses and the public dismay occasioned by Grant's campaign for the direct destruction of the enemy armies, all of the Union high command had become impressed with the possible advantages of the war upon resources. Halleck in his prewar writings expressed distaste even for subsisting off the country, let alone spreading calculated ruin: "The inevitable consequences of this system," he said then, "are universal pillage and a total relaxation of discipline; . . . and the ordinary peaceful and non-combatant inhabitants are converted into bitter and implacable enemies."[41] But in 1864 Halleck urged upon Sherman in Georgia the very policies he had once deplored, and with a vengeance:

> . . . I am fully of opinion that the nature of your position, the character of the war, the conduct of the enemy (and especially of non-combatants and women of the territory which we have heretofore conquered and occupied), will justify you in gathering up all the forage and provisions which your army will require, both for a siege of Atlanta and for your supply in your march farther into the enemy's country. Let the disloyal families of the country, thus stripped, go to their husbands, fathers, and natural protectors, in the rebel ranks; we have tried three years of conciliation and kindness without any reciprocation; on the contrary, those thus treated have acted as spies and guerrillas in our rear and within our lines. . . .We have fed this class of people long enough. Let them go with their husbands and fathers in the rebel ranks; and if they won't go, we must send them to their friends and natural protectors. I would destroy every mill and factory within reach which I did not want for my own use. . . .[42]

Thus encouraged, Sherman designed his campaign "for me to destroy Atlanta and march across Georgia to Savannah . . . breaking roads and doing irreparable damage,"[43] and thence proceeding northward through the Carolinas on the same destructive mission.

But Sherman's marches were not aimed against the enemy's resources alone. In Halleck's advice to Sherman and in Sheridan's comment that the Valley people "are getting sick of war," there was a suggestion of a further target beyond the enemy's economy, in the minds of the enemy people. Sherman scarcely needed Halleck's advice. He not only carried on war against the enemy's resources more extensively and systematically than anyone else had done, but he developed also a deliberate strategy of terror directed against the enemy people's minds.

". . . we are not only fighting hostile armies, but a hostile people," said Sherman, "and must make old and young, rich and poor, feel the hard hand of war, as well as the organized armies." When after taking Atlanta he compelled the evacuation of its civilian population, he did so in part to avoid detaching still more troops for unproductive garrison duty. But he did so also because "I knew that the people of the South would read in this measure two important conclusions: one, that we were in earnest; and the other, if they were sincere in their common and popular clamor 'to die in the last ditch,' that the opportunity would soon come."[44]

To fight the enemy armies was immensely expensive, above all in lives; but Sherman came to believe that if the terror and destruction of war could be carried straight to the enemy people, then they would lose their zest for war, and lacking the people's support, the enemy armies would collapse of their own weight. So he made of his marches campaigns of terror and destruction, with his armies ordered to forage liberally on the country, with all war industries and transport his target, and with greater depredations by his men treated leniently. He followed the prescription of the *United States Service Magazine*, an Army and Navy journal which had already written: "It will be different when it is realized that to break up the rebel armies is not going to bring peace, that the people must be influenced. . . . They must feel the effects of war. . . . They must feel its inexorable necessities, before they can realize the pleasures and amenities of peace."[45] "If the people raise a howl against my barbarity and cruelty," said Sherman, "I will answer that war is war, and not popularity-seeking. If they want peace, they and their relatives must stop the war."[46]

We cannot very well measure the effectiveness of campaigns waged against men's minds. Sherman ran the risk which Halleck had recognized before the war, of so infuriating the enemy people that they would turn more than ever into bitter and implacable foes. Whatever the effects of his campaign upon the long-run prospects for reconciliation between North and South, however, apparently Sherman did not suffer an immediate counterproductive result. Apparently his marches through Georgia and the Carolinas had the desired effects of causing some soldiers to desert the Confederate armies so they could go home to protect families and property, and of undermining Confederate morale by fixing the impression that the Southern cause was hopeless. Apparently Sherman was mainly right when he said:

> I know that this recent movement of mine through Georgia has had a wonderful effect. . . . Thousands who have been deceived by their lying newspapers to believe that we were being whipped all the time now realize the truth, and have no appetite for a repetition of the same experience. To be sure, Jeff. Davis has his people under pretty good discipline, but I think faith in him is much shaken in Georgia, and before we have done with her South Carolina will not be quite so tempestuous.[47]

Sherman's war against the enemy's mind like Grant's war for the complete destruction of the enemy armies was a recipe for the achievement of total victory. The Northern generals were pulled toward both methods because their aim was the utter and complete conquest of the South. By the time Grant and Sherman reached the two most powerful positions in the Army, the descent of the Civil War into remorseless revolutionary struggle was nearly complete. Lincoln had had to abandon nearly all his hopes for reconciliation, and even for rational control over the shape and momentum of the war. Considerations of the possibly dangerous effects of military means upon the ultimate ends of postwar sectional understanding had to be sacrificed to the immediate quest for victory, because nothing less than total victory seemed to offer any prospects for reunification at all.

Grant's semiofficial biographer Adam Badeau argued that Grant's greatness lay in his measuring these new circumstances of the war and in formulating his strategy accordingly:

> But above all [said Badeau], he understood that he was engaged in a people's war, and that the people as well as the armies of the South must

> be conquered, before the war could end. Slaves, supplies, crops, stock, as well as arms and ammunition—everything that was necessary in order to carry on the war, was a weapon in the hands of the enemy; and of every weapon the enemy must be deprived.
>
> This was a view of the situation which Grant's predecessors in the chief command had failed to grasp. Most of the national generals in every theatre, prior to him, had attempted to carry on their operations as if they were fighting on foreign fields. They sought to outmanœuvre armies, to capture posts, to win by strategy pure and simple. But this method was not sufficient in a civil war. The passions were too intense, the stake too great, the alternatives were too tremendous. It was not victory that either side was playing for, but for existence. If the rebels won, they destroyed a nation; if the government succeeded, it annihilated a rebellion. It was not enough at this emergency to fight as men fight when their object is merely to outwit or even outnumber the enemy. This enemy did not yield because he was outwitted or outnumbered. It was indispensable to annihilate armies and resources; to place every rebel force where it had no alternative but destruction or submission, and every store or supply of arms or munitions or food or clothes where it could be reached by no rebel army.[48]

There is much merit in such a view of Grant's generalship; Grant not only waged war to exterminate armies and resources, but played a part in encouraging Sherman toward Sherman's strategy of terror. Still, it was Sherman much more than Grant who developed the implications of seeing the war as a contest between peoples beyond the contest of armies. In 1864–65, it was distinctively Sherman's strategy "to follow them [the enemy people] to their inmost recesses, and make them fear and dread us. 'Fear is the beginning of wisdom.' "[49] Sherman's strategy of terrorizing the enemy people obviously goes yet further than Grant's strategy of annihilation of armies toward turning any war into remorseless revolutionary struggle—and of course, despite Badeau's emphasis on the peculiarities of *civil* war, the considerations he noted could shape strategy in any war, in which "the passions are too intense, the stake too great, the alternatives are too tremendous."

In the twentieth century the British military critic Sir Basil Liddell Hart was to draw a contrast between Sherman and Grant in another way. Liddell Hart praised Sherman as a primary exponent of his own favorite strategy of the "indirect approach." Grant perpetuated "the battledore and shuttlecock tournament in Virginia—which . . . [British and European generals] faithfully imitated with even greater lavishness and ineffectiveness on the battlefields of France from 1914 to 1918."[50] Sherman made "the indirect approach to the enemy's economic and moral rear" which permitted him to "claim, as truly as Napoleon in Austria—'I have destroyed the enemy merely by marches.' "[51] The weakness in Liddell Hart's view of Sherman is that Sherman's indirect strategy of marching through Georgia and the Carolinas was possible only because the main Confederate armies either had already been destroyed by a direct strategy of annihilation or were otherwise occupied—by George Thomas's large share of the troops of Sherman's own Military Division of the Mississippi, who prevented Hood's Confederate army from reaching the Ohio River after Sherman turned his back on it, and by Grant in Virginia. Despite the desertions from Lee's army that Sherman may have stimulated, there is no good reason to believe that the Army of Northern Virginia could have been destroyed within an acceptable time by any other means than the hammer blows of Grant's army.[52]

Sherman's marches through Georgia and the Carolinas nevertheless retain a fascination for military students in America and abroad, a fascination which has not declined but grown with the twentieth century and goes well beyond Liddell Hart's special theories. If the total submission of the enemy had to become an object of war, Sherman's design for pursuing the object by attacking the enemy's resources and will could well appear preferable to Grant's method of destroying the enemy armies by direct means, a process almost certain to cost heavy casualties among one's own soldiers. When a new technology of war, offered by the internal combustion engine in the airplane and the tank, seemed to promise new ways of invoking Sherman's strategy, then its appeal rose especially high. If Sherman had had the airplane, then he might indeed have been able to deprive the Confederate armies of the economic resources they needed to continue the fight, while destroying popular morale as well. So the fascination with Sherman has lived on, however much his design for war reflected his stark belief that "war is simply power unrestrained by constitution or compact": "You cannot qualify war in harsher terms than I will. War is cruelty, and you cannot refine it."[53]

8. Annihilation of a People: The Indian Fighters

I want you to be bold, enterprising, and at all times full of energy, when you begin, let it be a campaign of annihilation, obliteration and complete destruction. . . .

—*Philip H. Sheridan*[1]

If the conduct of the Civil War had prepared the United States Army to employ a strategy of annihilation, sometimes with frightful literalness, in its wars against the Indians, the strategy was much in harmony with post-Civil War national policy. Hitherto, in the dealings of the United States with the Indian nations a considerable amount of temporizing had always been possible. Until the time of the Civil War, the conscious purpose of the United States government in its relations with the Indian nations was not to eliminate them but to move them, out of territory desirable to the white man and into lands where the white man was not yet ready to venture, or where it was assumed he would never settle.

The military power of the Indians east of the Mississippi was already well on its way to breaking when the American Republic came into existence, as a result of the strains imposed on the Indians by long involvement in the colonial wars of the British, French, and Spanish. Consequently, even the feeble young Republic of the 1790s was able to administer a severe defeat to the Indians of the Old Northwest, in Anthony Wayne's battle of Fallen Timbers in 1794. In the course of rallying to fend off British threats to its national integrity in the latter part of the War of 1812, the United States also contrived to win battles against Great Britain's Indian allies, and thus to carry much further the process of eliminating the military power of both the northwestern and southwestern Indians east of the Mississippi. Thereafter, white population growth was sufficient to keep the cis-Mississippi Indians in check and eventually to smother their independence and culture. The overwhelming effects of white population growth were demonstrated in 1832, when old Black Hawk of the Sauks and Foxes attempted to lead a band of his people from exile west of the Mississippi back into their old country, in Illinois east of the river. Black Hawk had only about 400 warriors, and a motley white force consisting largely of untrained militia, but aggregating about 4,000, was able to crush him and slaughter many of his followers.[2]

That same year, an office of Commissioner of Indian Affairs was created in the War Department, and a policy was taking shape for the office to administer. The explorations of Zebulon Pike, Stephen H. Long, and other Army officers west of the Mississippi had convinced most white Americans that the land beyond the ninety-fifth meridian was generally unfit for agriculture, and Major Long had fixed upon the area the phrase "the Great American Desert." In 1825 Secretary of War Calhoun had recommended that this "desert" area be set aside as a permanent Indian Country, and that the eastern Indians be moved there to find a permanent home. In 1830 Congress authorized the President to exchange land beyond the Mississippi for lands held by the Indian tribes in the states and territories. President Andrew Jackson, nothing if not a westerner with western hostility to Indians, began a vigorous program of negotiating removal treaties with the eastern nations, and by now most of those nations were too enfeebled and too hemmed in by overpowering numbers of whites to resist. The Cherokees caused some trouble, and the resistance of the Seminoles which brought on the Seminole War of 1836–42 was a major exception to the general acquiescence. But most of the eastern tribes were escorted westward by the Army during the 1830s, with immense suffering and appalling loss of life on the way.[3]

To underwrite the idea of the permanency of the Indian Country, the Indian Intercourse Act of 1834 forbade the intrusion of unauthorized white men into Indian Country, while providing government agencies and schools to assist the Indians. By 1840 the boundary of the Indian Country was, as we have seen before, reasonably well fixed, and for the time being the strategic problem of the Army regarding the Indian nations became that of guarding a border which amounted almost to an international frontier.[4]

The United States government established the permanent Indian Country essentially in good faith. Through the 1850s, the idea of the Great American Desert was as alive as ever, and most Americans still believed that the bulk of the Great Plains which made up the Indian Country was unsuitable to agriculture and therefore to white settlement. But during the 1850s, the policy of a permanent Indian Country nevertheless became rapidly eroded. After the Mexican War and the Oregon settlement, the Indian Country no longer marked the effective western boundary of the United States, but divided two parts of the United States from each other. No such arrangement was likely to remain permanent. The California gold rush immensely increased white emigration over the trails westward through Indian Country, so much that the buffalo herds began to avoid the trails and the ecology and Indian economy of the country were consequently altered.

In 1849 the Office of Indian Affairs was transferred to the new Department of the Interior, which was to be customarily dominated by westerners less sympathetic to the Indians than the War Department might be. White men along the border of the Indian Country and travelers passing through it were learning that much of it was not so unsuitable to white settlement as had been believed, especially the well-watered grasslands in the eastern part of it. Consequently, treaties drawn up with the Indian nations during the 1850s to define the boundaries between the various nations also were used sometimes to nibble away at the Indian Country. The Sioux in Minnesota were restricted to a reservation 150 miles long but only 10 miles wide along the Minnesota River. The discovery of the agricultural properties of the grasslands combined with the pressures of the sectional controversy to create the new territories of Kansas and Nebraska in 1854, sprawling across the northern part of the Indian Country. On the other hand, the whites did not yet contemplate early settlement beyond the eastern fringes of Kansas and Nebraska, and until the Civil War the Indians remained sufficiently undisturbed in Indian Country that only a few serious armed clashes between Indians and white soldiers marred the decade of the fifties.[5]

Then the rebel guns fired on Fort Sumter early in 1861, and the white soldiers mostly left their posts on the Indian border to travel eastward and fight in the Civil War. Local volunteers from the western states and the territories replaced the Regular Army in garrisoning the border forts, and the volunteers might seem more vulnerable than the professionals in the Indians' eyes, at the same time that they were more likely than the professionals to bear malice toward the Indians. These developments occurred just as the Sioux in Minnesota were nourishing their anger over their growing recognition of the significance of how the whites had limited their territory during the fifties, and as the Cheyenne and Kiowa between the Arkansas and South Platte rivers were feeling the consequences of white emigration across their ranges to the gold fields in the central Rockies discovered during the late fifties.

In August, 1862, the anger of the Sioux erupted in a massacre of whites in the neighborhood of their reservation along the Minnesota River. Minnesota volunteers were able to repulse Sioux attacks on Fort Ridgely and New Ulm and then to repress the uprising; here the weight of white population was already great enough to be decisive as it had earlier been east of the Mississippi. In the new territory of Colorado in the Rocky Mountains, misunderstandings and then armed clashes between the Indians and the settlers provoked the raising of regiments of Colorado volunteers who not only pacified the Indians but massacred many of them in the process.[6]

By the time the Regular Army returned to the Indian frontier in 1865 and 1866, the policy of a permanent Indian Country was clearly obsolete. The Homestead Act of 1862 opened the prospect of cheap farmsteads throughout the national domain; whatever the agricultural deficiencies of the Great Plains, more conventional agricultural lands were largely taken up, and consequently the homestead policy made the Indian Country beckon. (With the prospect of almost free land, the old notion of the Great American Desert yielded to the opposite extreme of an excessively hopeful estimate of the potential for traditional agriculture in the semiarid sections of the Plains.) By 1865, the Union Pacific and Kansas Pacific Railroads were working their way westward from Omaha and Kansas City into the Indian Country, to carry the homesteaders and revolutionize the Army's old problems of mobility and logistics in the West.

Federal policy could no longer be one of removal of the Indians to some distant place, because with the Indian Country dissolving there was no place left to which to remove them. The remaining options were extremely difficult. White men who knew the Indians and were well disposed toward them, such as William Bent at Bent's Fort and Kit Carson, were coming to believe that if the Indians were to live close to white men, they must abandon their own way of life and take up the white man's. Otherwise there could be no lasting peace between white men and red, for their cultures and their economies clashed too much; and if the white men continued coming into the Indian Country without the Indians' adopting white ways, the red men eventually would be exterminated.[7]

The immediate military problem after the Civil War, demanding attention while long-range policies were being worked out, was the relatively familiar one of protecting the white man's trails through the Indian Country, though the problem was immensely enhanced by the increasing numbers of white men traversing the trails, the presence of the new railroads among the trails, and the consequent growing restlessness of Indians who could now begin to discern the coming calamity to their independence and their way of life. During the war, John M. Bozeman had opened a trail which came to bear his name, to take miners from the Oregon Trail on the North Platte River through the Powder River country and up the Yellowstone to newly discovered gold fields around Virginia City, Montana Territory. Unhapply, the trail led through the domain of perhaps the most powerful in war of all the Plains Indian nations, the Teton Sioux or Teton Dakotas.

With the other Sioux these westernmost Sioux had been pushed out of the forest country of Minnesota by the Chippewas in the early days of the white man's westward pressure upon the Indians, when the Chippewas had acquired firearms, but the Sioux had not. The Teton Sioux had adapted superbly to the Plains and had become excellent horsemen and mounted warriors. The Sioux made the Bozeman Trail an extremely perilous path, and during the Civil War the Army was not able to do much to protect it. In 1866 the Regular Army opened a major effort to safeguard the trail, strengthening Fort Reno at the crossing of the main branch of the Powder River and building Fort Philip Kearny and Fort C. F. Smith farther up the trail. The Sioux were fierce indeed, however, and ably led by Red Cloud they were determined to keep white travelers out of their range, while the Army was reduced to some 57,000 officers and men and stretched thin in its efforts to police the conquered South and defend the Indian border and the trails through Indian Country. The Bozeman Trail had to be guarded mainly by about 700 men of the Second Battalion, 18th Infantry, with a few additional companies and little cavalry. Red Cloud's Sioux put the soldiers effectively under siege, and on December 21, 1866, the Indians wiped out all eighty men of a detachment under Captain William Fetterman who ventured out from Fort Phil Kearny to protect a woodcutting party.

The commanding general of the Military Division of the Missouri, encompassing the Indian Country, was Lieutenant General Sherman. Sherman reacted to the Fetterman fight with a characteristic proposal for a long-range policy to deal with the Sioux: "We must act with vindictive earnestness against the Sioux, even to their extermination, men, women and children."[8] Sherman spoke in anger and embarrassment over Fetterman's defeat, but his subsequent policies made it clear that despite later denials he was not simply speaking in the heat of the moment.

Still, a nation weary from one war fought with a strategy of annihilation wanted to continue reducing its Army and was not yet ready for another, yet more literal campaign of annihilation. Instead of following Sherman's prescription, Congress responded to the Fetterman fight by creating in 1867 a Peace Commission to negotiate for the restoration of order. The commission was expected to deal both with the Sioux and other restless northern tribes and with the Cheyenne and other southern tribes still active in the hostilities which had erupted in Colorado during the Civil War. But the means of restoring peace proposed by Congress nevertheless implied the elimination of the Indian nations as sovereign polities and and military powers. A Congressional Committee on the Condition of the Indian Tribes created at the end of the Civil War recommended dealing with the Indians as individuals rather than as nations and eliminating the Indian Country by concentrating the Indians on much more restricted reservations. The Peace Commissioners spent the summers of 1867 and 1868 on the Plains attempting to persuade the Indians to retreat into reservations, whose boundaries would open a large central area of the old Indian Country to white settlers and their railroads.[9]

Enough Indian leaders had some inkling of the whites' potential power that the Peace Commissioners enjoyed considerable success, at least in securing agreement to treaties. Red Cloud of the Sioux, however, signed a treaty on November 6, 1868, only after the Army had abandoned the Bozeman Trail and the United States had agreed that the Powder River country should remain unceded Indian country, not a mere reservation, and closed to whites.[10]

The Army remained as undermanned as before the Civil War in proportion to the vastness of the Indian territory it had to police. The immediate postwar reduction in strength was followed by another in 1869, which kept its numbers in the neighborhood of 25,000 until the Spanish-American War. The new policy of abolishing the Indian Country and forcing the tribes into limited reservations eased, however, the military problems of strategy. Before the Civil War, the Army largely had to confine itself to passive patrolling of the Indian boundary, and in passivity the disproportion between its small numbers and the extent of territory to be patrolled imposed special hardship. The new policy, in contrast, implied that the Army would be mainly on the offensive, to force the Indians into their reservations, and to punish them if they did not go promptly or if they wandered astray. On the offensive, the Army could choose its targets, and by concentrating its limited strength make that strength count for more.

For weaker tribes, the implications of the reservation policy quickly began to be demonstrated. Having accepted limited reservations, they must now confine themselves to the designated limits. They must not venture across the emigrant routes westward. General Grant, still the Commanding General of the Army, said in 1868 that the emigrants would be protected "even if the extermination of every Indian tribe was necessary to secure such a result."[11]

In the fall of 1868, the commander of the Department of the Platte, Major General Philip Sheridan, prepared to force into the reservations to which some of their leaders had agreed the Indians of four principal southern nations, the Southern Cheyenne, the Arapaho, the Kiowa, and the Comanche. The strategy Sheridan chose was an innovative one for an Indian campaign, reflecting his and Sherman's experience in carrying war to the enemy's resources and people. He would wage a winter campaign, thus striking when the Indians' grass-fed war ponies were weak from lack of sustenance and the Indians' mobility was at a low ebb. He would strike against the fixed camps in which the Indians huddled against the rigors of winter. The camps would then either submit to him, or if their occupants fled he would destroy the provisions they had accumulated for the winter and thus starve them into helplessness. To execute this strategy, Sheridan planned for three columns to converge upon the Indian camps scattered through the northern Texas panhandle and the extreme western part of Indian Territory (present Oklahoma). The plan succeeded with brutal efficiency. It included Lieutenant Colonel (Brevet Major General) George Armstrong Custer's destruction of the camp of the friendly Cheyenne chieftain Black Kettle on the Washita River on November 29. Sheridan's immediate superior, General Sherman, was pleased. Just before the campaign opened he told his brother: "The more we can kill this year, the less will have to be killed the next war, for the more I see of these Indians the more convinced I am that they all have to be killed or maintained as a species of paupers. Their attempts at civilization are simply ridiculous." After the campaign, Sherman told his officers he was

> well satisfied with Custer's attack. . . . I want you all to go ahead; kill and punish the hostile, rescue the captive white women and children, capture and destroy the ponies, lances, carbines &c &c of the Cheyennes, Arapahoes and Kiowas; mark out the spots where they must stay, and then systematize the whole (friendly and hostile) into camps with a view to economical support until we can try to get them to be self-supporting like the Cherokees and Choctaws.[12]

The reservation system of dissolving tribal sovereignty and military power and reducing the Plains tribes to the helplessness of the previously broken eastern tribes was abetted by the destruction of a mainstay of the Plains Indians' economy, the buffalo herds, from which the Indians took food, clothing, and shelter. The advance of the railroads into the Plains greatly increased the opportunity for indiscriminate white hunting of buffalo as a sport. In 1871 a tannery discovered a way to turn buffalo hides into good leather, whereupon the white man's slaughter of the buffalo was redoubled to obtain the hides. The consequent threat to their livelihood set the southern Plains Indians to moving again and to attacking white buffalo hunters off their reservations. The Army responded with another campaign aimed at the destruction of the Indians' military power and their ability to live their independent way of life, the Red River War of 1874–75.

Sheridan, now a lieutenant general commanding the Division of the Missouri, again ordered a cold-weather campaign. Again he sent converging columns against the north Texas panhandle, this time from the south as well as north, east, and west. Again the Indians' winter camps were destroyed to deprive them of sustenance and shelter. This time the Army's attacks were followed up by shipping Indian leaders—and sometimes warriors simply chosen arbitrarily—to exile in Florida. In one of the final actions of the war, a detachment of the 6th Cavalry slaughtered a hundred or more fugitive Cheyennes at the Sappa River in northwestern Kansas. The Red River War, combined with the extermination of the buffalo, fulfilled its purpose. The independence of the southern Plains tribes was destroyed.[13]

That of the northern tribes, even of the redoubtable Sioux, was shortly to follow. In 1864 President Lincoln had signed a bill chartering a second transcontinental railroad, the Northern Pacific. The road began building in 1870, and by 1872 it was approaching Montana Territory. A preliminary survey indicated that the most feasible route through the territory was the course of the Yellowstone River, within the unceded domain of the Sioux. Commissioners sent to negotiate with the Sioux early in 1873 found them unwilling to grant a right of way. Nevertheless, a column of more than 1,500 soldiers under Colonel (Brevet Major General) D. S. Stanley escorted surveyors as far up the Yellowstone as Pompey's Pillar during the summer. The Panic of 1873 kept the railroad temporarily at Bismarck, Dakota Territory. But the next year Lieutenant Colonel Custer, who had been with Stanley, led ten companies of the 7th Cavalry and two companies of infantry into the Black Hills to find a suitable site for a fort to protect the railroad.

The Custer expedition also included geologists to investigate rumors that there was gold in the Black Hills, and Custer sent back somewhat overenthusiastic reports that there was. These reports naturally touched off a gold rush, which sent hundreds of prospectors into the Black Hills by the following summer. All of this was dangerous business, because the Black Hills were not only part of the unceded Sioux territory; their watered, wooded glades were also sacred to the Indians.[14]

In September, 1875, federal commissioners made another effort to persuade the Sioux to open their country to white men, and this time to sell the Black Hills as well. The commissioners accomplished nothing and were lucky to escape a threat against their lives. Their angry report encouraged the Commissioner of Indian Affairs to order in November that all Indians must return to their reservations and report to their agencies by January 31. The order should hardly have been applicable to the Sioux, for those Sioux bands that were not on reservations were in their own unceded country. Furthermore, the months from November to January were the wrong time for Plains Indians to travel. Nevertheless, those Indians not on reservations by January 31, 1876, were assumed to be at war with the United States, and General Sheridan planned a punitive expedition, three columns, from east, south, and west, to converge on the Sioux and drive them into reservations.[15]

The southern column, under Brigadier General (Brevet Major General) George Crook, met a repulse when its advance guard attacked a camp of Northern Cheyennes on March 17 and suffered defeat. This action also had the effect of pushing the previously quiet Northern Cheyennes into throwing in their lot with the Sioux. The other Army columns did not get moving until the return of warm weather, and then they found even more trouble. With the heart of their homeland under attack, the Sioux and Northern Cheyennes rallied perhaps 5,000 warriors and produced a leadership capable of tactical skill and of inspiring the warriors to fight with a determination and resolution uncommon in Plains Indians, who tended to view war as a kind of game and often missed opportunities because they lacked the white man's ruthless persistence. Under Crazy Horse of the Oglala Sioux, Gall and Sitting Bull of the Hunkpapas, Hump of the Minneconjous, and Two Moons of the Northern Cheyennes, among others, the Indians turned back another advance by Crook's southern column at the Rosebud River on June 17. On June 25, Custer recklessly led the 7th Cavalry into the Indians' camps ahead of the remainder of the eastern and western columns under Major General Alfred Terry and Colonel (Brevet Major General) John Gibbon. Custer died with much of his regiment in the battle of the Little Big Horn.

Even now, however, the Indians lacked the white man's sense of closing in for the kill. They might well have overpowered Terry's and Gibbon's troops when those soldiers reached the Little Big Horn battlefield the day after Custer's defeat. But the Sioux and Cheyenne had demonstrated their prowess in battle to the whites and hoped that doing so would be enough to discourage them as Red Cloud had discouraged them before. The Indians themselves had suffered heavy losses, and rather than fight Terry and Gibbon they withdrew into the Big Horn Mountains to celebrate their successes. The white soldiers accomplished little during the rest of the summer, though after licking their wounds Terry and Crook resumed the campaign. For the Army, the Custer disaster only reconfirmed the necessity of eliminating the military power of the Sioux. Sheridan accordingly ordered another winter campaign, to repeat the now familiar pattern of forcing either submission or debilitating, starvation-inducing movement when the Plains offered blizzard winds but no sustenance.

Crook and Colonel (Brevet Major General) Nelson A. Miles harried the Sioux and Cheyennes through the cold months, winning some battles, losing a few, but always driving the Indians toward exhaustion. In February, Sitting Bull and a few of his followers fled into Canada. By spring, Crazy Horse alone held a reasonably formidable band together, but it numbered only some 800 men, women, and children, and Crook persuaded Crazy Horse to surrender. Crook tried to win honorable and generous treatment for the Oglala chieftain, but in the course of a disagreement during negotiations one of Crook's soldiers bayoneted the chief. Meanwhile, more docile Sioux leaders had signed away the previously unceded Powder River country and the Black Hills, and it was thus with a show of legality that the Army forced the Sioux into reservations. The Sioux could no longer offer effective resistance; Crook's and Miles's winter campaign had broken their military power.[16]

The lance of the mightiest Plains Indian nation was shattered, and thereafter no Indians retained enough military power to resist the writ of Washington for long. In 1877, a year after the Little Big Horn, Chief Joseph led the Nez Percé on their famous anabasis; but the Nez Percé were a small tribe, and though they resisted the white Army with amazing success until winter closed in, the most they could have hoped for was to reach Canada. In the 1880s the Apaches fought to deny the white man the mountains of the Southwest; but Apache numbers also were small, and against them Crook showed a skill in guerrilla war uncommon among United States soldiers. He kept his own expeditionary forces small to avoid telegraphing his moves, he made excellent use of Indian scouts who knew the country as well as the hostiles, and he left only the rags and tatters of a guerrilla band—thirty-three Indians, thirteen of them women—for Nelson Miles to run to ground in a five months' campaign to gain the final glory of capturing Geronimo.[17]

The final Sioux uprising of 1890 was no real uprising but a last, desperate bid for freedom to roam the Plains and search for the lost buffalo as of old. The 7th Cavalry ended it with a massacre of Indians at Wounded Knee Creek. By the turn of the century, the whole culture of the American Indian seemed about to be extinguished, in the wake of the Army's annihilation of the Indian nations' military power.

PART THREE

Introduction to World Power, 1890-1941

Jomini's dictum that the organized forces of the enemy are the chief objective, pierces like a two-edged sword to the joints and marrow of many specious propositions. . . .

—*Alfred Thayer Mahan*[1]

9. A Strategy of Sea Power and Empire: Stephen B. Luce and Alfred Thayer Mahan

. . . knowing ourselves to be on the road that leads to the establishment of the science of naval warfare under steam, let us confidently look for that master mind who will lay the foundations of that science, and do for it what Jomini has done for the military science.

—*Stephen B. Luce*[1]

FOR A MOMENT in 1865, before the armies and fleets dispersed, the United States was the strongest military power on the planet. Even the Navy, despite the limited seaworthiness of its most powerful ships, the ironclad monitors, and the diversity of the rest of its blockading squadrons, could have given hard knocks to any other navy, at a time when steam, iron, and shell guns had thrown naval architecture into confusion and wiped away the old insurmountable supremacy of the wooden walls of England.

But in a twinkling the tents were struck and the Grand Army faded away, leaving barely enough soldiers in blue to police the southern states and the Indian frontier. The United States returned to the ancient scheme of military defense inherited from the Presidency of George Washington: coastal fortification to protect the seaboard cities from naval raids and to restrict foreign invasion to areas not vital until the citizenry could arm; the Navy, to the extent that the forts could free it for duties other than coastal defense, to guard American maritime commerce and raid the commerce of the enemy. Not even that: Quincy Adams Gillmore's rifled guns at Fort Pulaski had shown the masonry forts of the Bernard-Elliott-Totten Board of Engineers program obsolete, but for twenty years more they remained the country's reliance on the coastal frontier; the Navy reverted to squadrons of wooden sailing cruisers which used their steam engines only in emergency and at the risk of reprimand, because such was the cheapest means of reestablishing the squadrons scattered around the whole globe to show the flag in consular disputes.[2]

In the Army, the intense and humorless Lieutenant Colonel Emory Upton (USMA 1861 and Brevet Major General at the age of twenty-six) began to write books grumbling over this ingratitude of democracy to its military saviors and commending the Prussian military system. His standing in the service was high enough, his research and writing persuasive enough, and the mood of officers doomed to a lifetime as lieutenants and captains gloomy enough that he helped instill a distrust of democracy and of the American principle of civilian control of the military in a generation of professional soldiers.[3]

But except for internal police duties, what more of a defense policy did the country need? Steam power and dependence upon coal so limited the range of warships that no great power, not even Britain with her Canadian bases, could have maintained a close blockade of the War of 1812 type or risked a large-scale invasion of America. The tensions within the European state system accompanying the transformation of the Prussian Kingdom into the German Empire precluded the diversion of any large European force to the Western Hemisphere anyway. The United States could safely concentrate upon its domestic affairs, which were difficult enough. Its international security was even more complete than in the period from 1820 to 1860, which is saying a great deal.

> Excepting for our ocean commerce and our seaboard cities [General Sheridan said in his report as Commanding General of the Army for 1884], I do not think we should be much alarmed about the probability of wars with foreign powers, since it would require more than a million and a half of men to make a campaign upon land against us. To transport from beyond the ocean that number of soldiers, with all their munitions of war, their cavalry, artillery, and infantry, even if not molested by us in transit, would demand a large part of the shipping of all Europe.[4]

In the late nineteenth century, two steamers were considered to be required to transport a regiment of infantry on a long voyage. For a division of 10,000 men, at least thirty steamers were calculated to be required; for a corps of 33,000 men, 135 steamers. No nation except

Great Britain and possibly France possessed enough ships to carry 50,000 troops across an ocean. In theory, Great Britain might have transported 500,000 men; but that would have required nearly all her shipping, which she could not have afforded because of her economic needs. An invasion of the United States by a European power was out of the question.[5]

For all that, the post-Civil War indifference to military affairs could not last. Emory Upton, suffering from a brain ailment, committed suicide in 1881 just on the eve of a military revival that might have moderated his professional discontent.[6] In 1883 Congress voted appropriations for three light cruisers (*Atlanta*, *Boston*, and *Chicago*) and a dispatch vessel (*Dolphin*), which became the "White Squadron" and the beginning of a new steam and steel Navy. By the end of the decade, Congress added other cruisers and authorized two large armored cruisers or small battleships, *Maine* and *Texas*. The Naval Appropriation Act of 1883 also established the Army-Navy Gun Foundry Board, to study how the United States could make up for time lost over nearly twenty years in the technology of producing both modern naval armor and armor-piercing guns.[7] Two years later another board was established, under the chairmanship of Secretary of War William C. Endicott, to study the rehabilitation of the coastal fortifications.[8] The work of the Endicott Board led to a permanent Board of Ordnance and Fortification, created in 1888, and to a gradual supplementation and replacement of the old masonry forts with earthworks, armor-plated concrete pits, and ten- and twelve-inch breechloading rifles.[9]

Although these initial symptoms of reviving military interests apparently served the traditional purposes of continental defense, and certainly no responsible governmental official of the 1880s was willing to acknowledge any but a defensive military intent, the underlying motives harbored something new. There was still no threat to American security from overseas, and none was rationally conceivable, although the Endicott Board dispensed bloodcurdling fantasies of foreign warships arriving in American ports to offer a choice of ransom or destruction.[10] Within the United States, however, there were forces stirring which would push the interests of the country outward, and which through the projection of American ambitions and activities overseas might involve the country in international competition, perhaps including military competition.

The American military might of 1865 had been in part an expression of an industrial and business growth which in the succeeding decades became so prodigious that it looked increasingly beyond even the huge American market and investment arena for places in which to sell and to make capital multiply. In an era of national pride stimulated by reunion and then by observances of the centenary of the Revolution, the American people felt eager to express their sense of the greatness of their country by showing that the country could excel in anything the other great nations might do. When the other powers embarked upon a new round of economic and colony-building competition overseas, the United States grew tempted to join in the game. Whatever the varied motives, the fact of a new American ambition seeking influence beyond the North American continent was clear enough, as the United States secured from the Kingdom of Hawaii in 1887 the exclusive right to use Pearl Harbor and to establish coaling and repair stations there, or as in 1889 three United States Navy vessels became victims of a typhoon while trying to protect American interests against German rivalry in Samoa.[11]

In the 1880s, when the cruisers of the White Squadron first reflected an American military revival which the new overseas ambitions would make largely naval, the strategy of war at sea lacked a systematic analyst comparable to Jomini. The importance of command of the sea to national commercial and military greatness, and the necessity for a power aspiring to its command to acquire not just commerce-destroying cruisers but a navy of battleships able to overawe or overpower any rival battle fleet in the waters in contest—these matters had been commented upon by a host of writers, especially in the English-speaking world, at least as early as Sir Walter Raleigh, and including in America Benjamin Stoddert and James Dobbins. But in spite of the command-of-the-sea ambitions (at least for American seas) of Stoddert and Dobbins, in spite of the British navy's demonstration of the advantages of command of the sea and American testimony to those British advantages reaching back to George Washington, and in spite of the fact that in the Mexican and Civil Wars the United States itself had benefitted greatly from command of the sea against its opponents, official American naval theory still produced in the 1880s the building of a new navy in the form of cruisers good for commerce raiding if they were good for anything in naval war. It should be remarked, however, that the combined advent of steam power, shell guns, and iron and steel armor had so confused naval architecture and with it naval theory, that in France the *jeune école* of navalists was making a beginning of modern systematic naval thought by proclaiming that the supremacy of the battle fleet was dead, British naval supremacy dead with it, and the future belonged to the commerce-raiding *guerre de course*.[12]

In the United States, the twenty years of neglect of the armed services following the Civil War produced the somewhat surprising result of a cultivation of professional military study and discussion among the officers. In a time of civilian indifference and slow promotion, professional officers could apparently salvage some satisfaction from their careers through the more intense pursuit of the special knowledge and attributes which set them apart from the civilians. Knowing the inner mysteries of their calling, they could explain away civilian neglect by pointing to civilian ignorance. Emory Upton was a prime exemplar of these tendencies in the Army, and he encouraged others in them. The Navy showed the same tendencies. The 1870s and 1880s witnessed a remarkable flowering of military professional associations and a military periodical literature, notably the founding of the United States Naval Institute in 1873 and the prompt beginning of publication of its *Proceedings*, and in the Army the beginnings of the modern professional school system, the post-graduate officer schools beyond the Military Academy, especially with the School of Application for Infantry and Cavalry founded at Fort Leavenworth in 1881.[13]

One of Upton's correspondents was Commodore Stephen B. Luce of the Navy, who had spent most of his senior career at the Naval Academy at Annapolis but had also commanded a monitor off Charleston. Charleston had been the Navy's great frustration of the Civil War. In the constricted harbor of Charleston, ships could not maneuver as Du Pont had maneuvered at Port Royal; to engage the forts they had to stand under the forts' guns. In April of 1863 Du Pont had led into the harbor a fleet built around seven of the new ironclad monitors, moving against his own better judgment but under urgent pressure from the victory-starved Lincoln administration. The monitors' armament, generally one fifteen-inch and one eleven-inch gun in the turret of each, did not match their defensive strength; and with so few guns, the defensive strength of their iron plates was not enough to prevent their vulnerability from exceeding the damage they could inflict on the Charleston forts. The attack failed, and the failure ruined Du Pont's career. Rear Admiral John A. Dahlgren replaced him, and Dahlgren spent much of the rest of the war in further futile battering away at the Charleston defenses. An old masonry fort like Sumter could be pounded into rubble, and was; but the Confederates compensated with new batteries behind earthworks all around the harbor.[14]

Luce served under Dahlgren and shared his frustration. After the war Luce pondered on the contrast between the Navy's expensive and ineffectual frontal attacks upon the Charleston defenses and the ease with which the city at last was taken when Sherman's armies in its rear snapped its communications with the interior. It seemed obvious then to Luce that the proper way to approach Charleston would have been to operate against its communications from the first, and he concluded that the struggle for Charleston showed that naval officers ought to give more study to strategy. Encouraged by Upton and by similar developments in the Army, he persuaded the Navy Department to establish the Naval War College at Newport, Rhode Island, in 1884. He became the college's president.[15]

> But there is another branch of his profession which the naval officer should study [Luce said]: he should not only know how to fight his own ship, and how to form and carry several ships into action, but having a certain force at his disposal, he should know where to place it that it may do the most good. In other words, he should have some idea of the principles of strategy, that he may be able to comprehend the strong points within the field of operations, and either hold them or prevent an enemy from holding them. . . .
>
> It is the part of the naval student to prepare himself by study and reflection for these higher duties of his profession; and the only way to do that is to study the science of war as it is taught at our military schools [i.e., the schools the Army had already established], and then to apply the principles to the military operations conducted at sea. He should be led into a philosophic study of naval history, that he may be enabled to examine the great naval battles of the world with the cold eye of professional criticism, and to recognize where the principles of the science have been illustrated, or where a disregard for the accepted rules of the art of war has led to defeat and disaster. Such studies might well occupy the very best thoughts of the naval officer, for they belong to the very highest branch of his profession.[16]

"Now, it must strike any one who thinks about it as extraordinary," Luce also said, "that we, members of a profession of arms, should never have undertaken the study of our real business—war."[17] So much was this statement true, so much had naval officers studied seamanship—on which Luce had written the outstanding American text[18]—but not naval strategy, that Luce's Naval War College was the first institution of its type anywhere in the world. While Luce gave the war college its general direction, the key position among its faculty would in his judgment be that of the lecturer on naval history, who would lead officers into the "philosophic study" of that subject. ". . . knowing ourselves to be on the road that leads to the establishment of the science of naval warfare under steam," said Luce, "let us confidently look for that master mind who will lay the foundations of that science, and do for it what Jomini has done for the military science."[19]

Needless to say, the Jomini whom Luce found was Captain Alfred Thayer Mahan. This Mahan was the son of West Point's Dennis Hart Mahan. He chose a naval career against his father's wishes and graduated from the Naval Academy in 1859. To the time in 1884 when Luce invited him to lecture at the Naval War College his naval career was not outstanding, and in fact he possessed only middling talents in seamanship and had developed an aversion to sea duty. He had not yet shown outstanding qualities as a naval thinker either, winning only third prize when he entered the Naval Institute essay contest of 1878, with a conservative paper on naval education that applauded the old-fashioned sailing skills he would have liked to enjoy in fuller measure in himself. But he was beginning to take an interest in improving the Navy's antiquated ships, and most to Luce's point, he had come to show a taste for the study of naval history and naval strategy, with a book on *The Gulf and Inland Waters* in the Civil War.[20]

In the course of preparing his lectures for the Naval War College, Mahan somehow found himself, rose above a career which until now he himself acknowledged had been nearly wasted, and exceeded Luce's expectations by developing his famous trilogy to inaugurate a philosophical study of naval history: *The Influence of Sea Power upon History, 1660–1783* (1890); *The Influence of Sea Power upon the French Revolution and Empire, 1793–1812* (1892); and *Sea Power in Its Relation to the War of 1812* (1905).[21] The first of these three books won Mahan an international reputation as indeed the Jomini of naval strategy. He achieved also the presidency of the Naval War College in succession to Luce in 1886, retirement as rear admiral in 1896, a return to duty with a prominent place on the Naval War Board in the War with Spain in 1898, and a prolific career as a speaker and the writer of more than 120 articles and seventeen additional books on current naval policy and the principles of naval war.[22]

Mahan poured through the pages of Jomini in his effort to formulate a new science of naval strategy, and many of the principles of naval war which he suggested are naval applications of Jomini's precepts. Mahan regarded lines of communication as retaining at least as great an importance in naval war as Jomini believed they had on land. In fact, the great advantage that sea power can offer the nation possessing it is control over communications, with sea power of worldwide dimensions offering control over communications throughout the world. One of the first clues that led Mahan to his theories of sea power and naval strategy was his reading of Theodor Mommsen's *History of Rome*, and his reflection that everything might have been different in the great struggle between Rome and Carthage if Carthage had controlled communications across the Mediterranean and Hannibal could have gone directly to Italy by sea instead of using the long land route through Spain. Sea communications, Mahan concluded, are the most important single element in national power and strategy. The ability to insure one's own communications and to interrupt an adversary's is at the root of national power, and is the prerogative of the sea powers.[23]

Sea power confers control of maritime communications in general, but in a contest between rival naval powers control of favorable lines of communication in the more specialized strategic sense is a major goal. In naval war as on land, a principal desideratum of strategy is control of the interior lines, because the possessor of interior lines will be able to threaten the enemy upon several fronts and to concentrate his forces more quickly than the enemy upon any one of them. Certain geographic points are strategic points for naval war because they command interior lines. Certain places on the globe are strategic points of lasting worldwide importance, such as Suez, on the interior line from Europe to the East as opposed to the exterior line via the Cape of Good Hope, and Panama, which especially with the building of an isthmian canal would represent an interior line connecting the Atlantic and the Pacific. The possession of such strategic points affords great advantage in any contest between rival naval powers. In naval strategy as on land, a strategic point should possess intrinsic strength and access to military resources as well as a favorable geographic location. In naval strategy as on land, the strategist seeks to throw the greatest possible concentration of his own force against the enemy's vital points. The principle of concentration most emphatically carries over from land to maritime war.[24]

Mahan was not indebted only to the Jomini of geometrical principles of strategy, of diagrams of interior and exterior lines. He seized upon the more truly Napoleonic aspects of Jomini and pushed them further than Jomini himself had done. "Jomini's dictum," he said, "that the organized forces of the enemy are the chief objective, pierces like a two-edged sword to the joints and marrow of many specious propositions. . . ." In naval strategy, Mahan believed, ". . . the enemy's ships and fleets are the true objects to be assailed on all occasions."[25]

> It is not the taking of individual ships or convoys, be they few or many, that strikes down the money power of a nation; it is the possession of that overbearing power on the sea which drives the enemy's flag from it, or allows it to appear only as a fugitive; and which, by controlling the great common, closes the highways by which commerce moves to and from the enemy's shores. This overbearing power can only be exercised by great navies. . . .[26]

The purpose of naval strategy is to gain control of the sea. "Naval strategy has for its end to found, support, and increase, as well in peace as in war, the sea power of a country." To control the sea in war it is necessary first to destroy the enemy's fleet. The destruction of the enemy fleet is the first task of a navy in war. Everything else is a sideshow. Once the enemy fleet is destroyed, the victorious navy can exploit its resulting control of the sea for any further purpose that is desirable. In particular, having won control of the sea a navy can advance its nation's economic power by keeping open its access to the resources of the world, while correspondingly strangling the enemy economy by depriving it of such access. Ultimately, Mahan believed, "War is not fighting, but business."[27] But control of the sea must come first, and that could be achieved only by a great navy which could overthrow the enemy navy.

Not the least Napoleonic aspect of Mahan's thinking was his belief that the essential decision in war could be achieved quickly, in the dramatic Austerlitz battle transferred to the sea. Wars might be prolonged over many months or even years, because the workings of sea power upon an enemy economy though inexorable might be long in taking full effect. But the decision could be achieved rapidly, in the contest between the opposing fleets to determine which of them should control the seas. Once this contest was decided, everything else would follow irresistibly, no matter how lengthy the process of fulfillment.

It followed from Mahan's emphasis on the destruction of the enemy fleet that he rejected commerce-raiding warfare, whether of the haphazard type practiced by the Americans in the War of 1812 or the more systematic type advocated by the *jeune école*, as an instrument to achieve decision:

> Such a war cannot stand alone; it must be *supported*, to use the military phrase; unsubstantial and evanescent in itself, it cannot reach far from its base. That base must be either home ports, or else some solid outpost of the national power, on the shore or on the sea, a distant dependency or a powerful fleet. Failing such support, the cruiser can only dash out hurriedly a short distance from home, and its blows, though painful, cannot be fatal.[28]

Commerce raiding alone could not win control of the sea; and control of the sea remained the object of all naval strategy:

> He who seeks, finds, if he does not lose heart; and to me, continuously seeking, came from within the suggestion that control of the sea was an historic factor which had never been systematically appreciated and expounded. Once formulated consciously, this thought became the nucleus of all my writing for twenty years then to come. . . .[29]

Mahan's strategic precepts are scattered throughout his works, and it was less a naval strategy that he offered his readers than a national policy for the pursuit of national greatness.

> From Jomini also [he said] I imbibed a fixed disbelief in the thoughtlessly accepted maxim that the statesman and general occupy unrelated fields. For this misconception I substituted a tenet of my own, that war is simply a violent political movement. . . .
>
> It was with such hasty equipment that I approached my self-assigned task, to show how the control of the sea, commercial and military, had been an object powerful to influence the policies of nations; and equally a mighty factor in the success or failure of those policies. This remained my guiding aim; but incidently thereto I had by this time determined to prepare a critical analysis of the naval campaigns and battles, a decision for which I had to thank Jomini chiefly.[30]

The central theme of Mahan's histories is that it was through sea power that Great Britain in particular had achieved her preeminence among the nations of the world.

> . . . For the twenty-five years following the Peace of Utrecht, peace was the chief aim of the ministers who directed the policy of the two great seaboard nations, France and England; but amid all the fluctuations of continental politics in a most unsettled period, abounding in petty wars and shifty treaties, the eye of England was steadily fixed on

the maintenance of her sea power. . . . While England's policy thus steadily aimed at widening and strengthening the bases of her sway upon the ocean, the other governments of Europe seemed blind to the dangers to be feared from her sea growth. The miseries resulting from the overweening power of Spain in days long gone by seemed to be forgotten; forgotten also the more recent lesson of the bloody and costly wars provoked by the ambition and exaggerated power of Louis XIV. Under the eyes of the statesmen of Europe there was steadily and visibly being built up a third overwhelming power, destined to be used as selfishly, as aggressively, though not as cruelly, and much more successfully than any that had preceded it. This was the power of the sea, whose workings, because more silent than the clash of arms, are less often noted, though lying clearly enough on the surface. It can scarely be denied that England's uncontrolled dominion of the seas, during almost the whole period chosen for our subject, was by long odds the chief among the military factors that determined the final issue.[31]

Mahan implied that sea power mobilized by another nation would probably do for that nation much the same thing that sea power had done for Great Britain. He emphasized repeatedly Great Britain's advantage of location. Nevertheless, though he similarly recognized certain handicaps impeding the American development of sea power, among them the absence of so strategic a location on world sea routes as that of Britain and the existence of a continental territory whose very vastness tended to absorb American energies, he believed the United States might yet prove to be the next inheritor of Great Britain's naval and therefore economic and political predominance.

If the United States were to achieve such a destiny, obviously certain steps must be taken. The harbors must be made secure through an improved program of defensive armament. As the foundation of maritime strength, as the nursery of naval attitudes and aptitudes, international trade must be cultivated and carried on by America's own mercantile fleet. To overcome the handicap to an American navy of the long and dangerous sea voyage between the Atlantic and Pacific coasts and to command the most strategic interior line of sea communication in the Western Hemisphere, a canal must be built across the isthmus of Central America under United States control. To protect the approaches to the canal, the United States must prevent foreign powers from acquiring or developing new naval bases and coaling stations in adjacent waters and must meanwhile acquire and develop bases of its own in the Pacific and the Caribbean. Above all, the United States must build a modern navy, a great fleet, "the arm of offensive power, which alone enables a country to extend its influence outward."[32]

Mahan's main purpose clearly was to provide the rationale for an enlargement of his service, the Navy, and in particular for the transformation of the commerce-raiding Navy into a battleship navy. He wrote at the right time. When his books began appearing during the 1890s, his ideas soon received the acceptance of thoughts whose hour had struck. The need for expanded overseas commerce and for overseas possessions to stimulate it could well be endorsed by business leaders, restless to explore opportunities for investment and markets beyond the American continent. Nationalists ambitious to enhance the national greatness, especially young political leaders of that type such as Henry Cabot Lodge and Theodore Roosevelt, could respond to Mahan's prescription of the means of fulfilling a noble national destiny. A self-consciously patriotic public was prepared to applaud the expansion of the White Squadron and the planting of the Stars and Stripes on distant shores. There was an appropriate irony in the fact that only after Great Britain acclaimed Mahan as the premier historian of British sea power did his influence reach full flower at home, but after that the captain was a prophet thoroughly honored in his own country.[33]

Nevertheless, Mahan was deficient in the role for which Stephen Luce had cast him, that of a maritime Jomini. He was better as a propagandist for a policy of sea power than as a strategist. Perhaps Mahan was also too much the historian to be all Luce might have hoped for in a strategist. Not only were his strategic precepts scattered unsystematically through his histories—an arrangement which concealed inconsistencies—but they were uniformly conservative, more appropriate to the age of wood and sail than that of steel and steam.

They were also too much bound up with Great Britain's special geographic position. While Mahan acknowledged that geography contributed much to British naval predominance, he did not make fully clear how much of what the Royal Navy accomplished was possible only because of Britain's geography. Mahan frequently reiterated the importance of the Jominian principle that the fleet must be kept concentrated, and he offered as illustration the ability of the British fleet concentrated in European waters to protect the whole vast empire. "Postponing more distant interests, she [Britain] must concentrate [in the home waters] an indisputable superiority. It is, however, inconceivable that against any one power Great Britain should not be able here to exert from the first a preponderance which would effectually cover all her remoter possessions."[34] In the heyday of British sea power, however, there had existed no effective naval power outside Europe. Therefore by concentrating her fleet in home waters, in her favored position astride the European routes to the outside world, Britain was able to keep in check all the navies that counted and to protect her possessions everywhere. The United States enjoyed no such favored geographical position. No American bases in which the United States fleet could concentrate could afford naval security for both American coastlines, let alone the overseas interests of the United States.

By the time Mahan was writing, even Great Britain was losing her ability to protect all her maritime and colonial interests with a fleet concentrated in European waters. The White Squadron and the Naval War College were a small beginning, but they did prove to be the beginning of the rise of an American naval power capable of challenging and then excelling Britain's in Western Hemisphere waters. Simultaneously, and with British assistance, Japan was beginning to emerge as an independent naval power in the western Pacific. Unless Britain dispersed her fleet into American and western Pacific waters, her interests in those areas would become dependent upon the good will of the United States and Japan. Because of rivalry first with France and then, more ominously, with the German navy, the British fleet could not be so dispersed. Great Britain established an informal entente with the United States and an alliance with Japan to protect interests and possessions which the British navy could no longer secure.

This dispersal of world sea power complicated and indeed undermined Mahan's strategic prescriptions for the United States. He insisted that the American fleet should be kept concentrated; the essence of sea power was a concentrated battle fleet able to assume the primary strategic task of confronting and defeating an enemy battle fleet in order to assert control of the sea. At the same time, he said that American sea power demanded an isthmian canal—to assist concentration—and bases on both its eastern and western approaches to protect the canal, with outlying bases and coaling stations to permit patrolling to protect the first bases. But in a period witnessing the development of several centers of sea power, the canal and its outlying defenses could be given a semblance of protection only by dispersing, not concentrating, the American fleet. No concentration in home waters in the traditional British fashion could meet the needs of the United States.[35]

Apart from the difficulties for the United States in maintaining a concentrated battle fleet, the battle fleet was losing its ability to command the strategic results which Mahan described from the past. Technological developments occurring while Mahan wrote were making it possible for a battle fleet to destroy the enemy's rival battle line and yet not be able to exercise full control of the sea in order to bring economic pressures against the enemy homeland. These developments included the explosive floating mine, its offspring the self-propelled torpedo, and a new instrument for carrying the torpedo, the submarine. With these devices a defeated or otherwise inferior navy might render at least the waters adjacent to its own coast so precarious that control of the sea might be diluted beyond meaning and recognition. Close blockades could become highly dubious and dangerous enterprises. In any event, blockades applied to powers of any considerable territorial extent, especially the larger European powers, no longer had the same potential for imposing economic ruin as in the past. Railroad systems had too much replaced coastal waterways as the medium of transportation within Europe. Mahan did not concede that the change since Napoleon's day was so drastic, but his failure to do so is another evidence of his excessive reliance on the past to guide the strategy of the future.[36]

In yet another way he failed to appreciate the possible strategic importance of the torpedo and the submarine. Mahan may have been unduly contemptuous of the possibilities of a strategy of commerce raiding even in the past. The *jeune école* could point to the Southern Confederacy's resort to this naval strategy in response to the Union blockade, and to the success of the famous Confederate commerce raiders in driving American merchant ships into foreign registry and almost eliminating the United States flag from international maritime commerce. Similar accomplishments against Great Britain, argued the *jeune école*, could ruin British finance and through finance the British economy, because Great Britain depended so much more than the United States upon the national merchant marine. But brushing aside this argument, Mahan also ignored the greatly enhanced possibilities for commerce raiding implicit in the torpedo and the submarine. For a power not itself dependent on maritime commerce, investment in a commerce-raiding navy to injure those who did need maritime commerce could pay off much greater dividends than an unnecessary effort to achieve control of the sea. The torpedo and the submarine were about to make the dividends grow into nothing less than a new kind of blockade which might strangle the very powers which maintained the traditional kind of control of the sea. By overlooking the new technology, Mahan contributed to the maritime powers' ignoring the emergence of a threat which in 1917 was to come close to ruining Great Britain and thereby gravely endangering the United States.[37]

Sea power in the twentieth century would not accomplish even for Great Britain all it had accomplished in the past. For the United States, a pursuit of Mahan's ideal of sea power would lead into dilemmas from which Mahan offered no escape, involving how properly to concentrate the fleet while defending widely dispersed territories and interests. Nevertheless, in the 1890s the United States was ready to extend its economic and political influence beyond the North American continent, the Navy would surely be a convenient if not essential means of assisting such extension, and the United States accordingly proceeded to build a navy which fit the teachings of Mahan.

This meant a navy of battleships. A navy according to Mahan must be able to face and defeat the main battle fleet of an enemy. Any other activity is a sideshow, and therefore any ships except those capable of standing in the line of battle against the enemy's first-line fleet are mere auxiliaries, and squadrons comprised of them cannot be called a navy. Hitherto the United States Navy had been built around cruisers, with occasional line-of-battle ships of the old three-decker sailing type as impressive showpieces to wear the pendants of squadron commanders. Now there must be many battleships, organized into a fleet.

There must be enough battleships to control at least the waters adjacent to the United States. Because he wrote off the importance of mere commerce raiding, Mahan did not see much use in building a fleet of acknowledged inferiority to its rivals. His strategy for an inferior fleet was partly that it should remain sheltered and play the role of a fleet-in-being, that is, one which by its mere existence compels the enemy to divert forces and expend resources to watch against its possible forays upon his shipping. To a greater extent, Mahan favored the idea that the inferior fleet should attempt an offensive-defensive, emerging from its sheltered harbors from time to time to grasp measured opportunities against detachments of the superior enemy fleet, in the hope of gradually whittling the enemy down. All in all, however, Mahan did not express much confidence in any possible line of action open to an inferior fleet. Sooner or later, he believed, the superior fleet would almost surely eliminate the inferior.[38]

These doctrines did not imply that the United States Navy had to be superior to every other navy in the world, including the British, to be worth building at all. Mahan recognized, though not always so clearly as he might have, the distractions with which European politics would influence any European fleet attempting operations in American waters. He also recognized, again not always so clearly as he might have, the effects of an Atlantic crossing in reducing any fleet's effectiveness, even the effectiveness of the British fleet despite its Western Hemisphere harbors. Therefore the United States Navy would not have to equal the greatest navy in the world to achieve command of American waters.

> In truth, a careful determination of the force that Great Britain or France could probably spare for operations against our coasts, if the latter were suitably defended, without weakening their European position or unduly exposing their colonies and commerce, is the starting-point from which to calculate the strength of our own navy. If the latter be superior to the force that thus can be sent against it, and the coast be so defended as to leave the navy free to strike where it will, we can maintain our rights; not merely the rights which international law concedes, and which the moral sense of nations now supports, but also those equally real rights which, though not conferred by law, depend upon a clear preponderance of interest, upon obviously necessary policy, upon self-preservation, either total or partial.[39]

The United States Navy must not be the greatest in the world in order to be worth building, but it must be a battleship navy. Mahan's major books had not yet been published and he was not yet famous when President Benjamin Harrison's Secretary of the Navy, Benjamin F. Tracy—in a Republican administration with expansionist tendencies—issued his annual report for 1889; but Mahan's ideas and echoes of his phrasing are evident in the report, which called for a fleet of twenty armored battleships "to raise blockades," to "beat off the enemy's fleet on its approach" to the American coast, and to divert him from the American coast "by threatening his own, for a war, though defensive in principle, may be conducted most effectively by being offensive in operations."[40]

Congress was not yet ready at the beginning of the decade to enter fully into the spirit of these Mahanian concepts. It confined itself to authorizing, in the Naval Act of 1890, three "sea-going, coast-line battleships," with a stipulated fuel endurance of only 5,000 nautical miles to emphasize their defensive purposes: *Indiana*, *Massachusetts*, *Oregon*, each of 10,288 tons, with main batteries of four 13-inch guns.[41]

By the time Grover Cleveland's Secretary of the Navy, Hilary A. Herbert, offered his report for 1893, the Secretary had read the second of Mahan's books about the influence of sea power on history and was explicitly denigrating commerce raiding and the construction of cruisers rather than battleships. Herbert was a Democrat and so were the majorities in Congress, and the Democrats were supposed to be cool to overseas expansion, as they illustrated by dropping the Harrison administration's effort to annex the new Hawaiian Republic. But enough members of Congress were now both aware of Mahan and in a nationalist mood receptive to his ideas that they voted two more battleships in 1895 (*Kearsarge* and *Kentucky*, 11,520 tons each; *Iowa*, 11,346 tons, had been authorized in 1892), and three more again in 1896 (*Alabama*, *Illinois*, *Wisconsin*, 11,552 tons each).[42]

Of these battleships, *Indiana*, *Massachusetts*, *Oregon*, and *Iowa* were ready by 1898 to form the backbone of the fleet for the Spanish-American War. *Oregon* offered a dramatic object lesson in the peculiar American problem of keeping the fleet concentrated by having to make the long voyage from the Pacific coast through the Straits of Magellan after war was declared. She did it in grand style and record time, some 13,000 nautical miles in sixty-eight days, although she had to be accompanied much of the way by a coal-carrying gunboat because she was a "coast-line" battleship.[43]

The American press and public demonstrated that however much they shared the ideal of Mahanian sea power, they did not understand its principles, because they pressured the McKinley administration to scatter the fleet among the coastal cities to defend them against the Spanish naval squadron which crossed the Atlantic to help protect Cuba from the United States. Once *Oregon* had joined the Atlantic fleet and enough old monitors were put on exhibition in the principal harbors to assuage the cry for coastal defense, however, the directors of the war—President William McKinley, the War Department, and the Naval War Board on which Mahan served as adviser to Secretary of the Navy John D. Long—did not face any especially difficult strategic problems. Despite an absence of adequate contingency planning apparatus, the Navy had planned before the war to begin by attacking the decrepit Spanish naval squadron in the Philippines, to gain a makeweight for the eventual peace negotiations. Commodore George Dewey's Asiatic Squadron promptly executed this plan. As if in vindication of Mahan's emphasis on battleships, the battleships of the American Atlantic fleet quickly bottled up in the harbor of Santiago de Cuba the four cruisers that were the strongest vessels Spain could send to the assistance of Cuba. When the United States Army invaded Cuba under the Navy's protection and approached Santiago, the Spanish cruisers had to leave the harbor, and the American fleet destroyed them.[44]

The only really delicate strategic problem was that posed by a fleet in being not present at either the Caribbean or the Philippine scene of action. Before their squadron in Cuba was destroyed, the Spanish sent eastward into the Mediterranean toward the Suez Canal a force of cruisers large enough to have troubled Dewey's small squadron in the Philippines if it should get there. The danger was not large, especially because the Spanish no longer had a base from which to operate in the Philippines, Dewey being in control of the only developed naval facilities. But Mahan delighted in the way in which he saw to it that the threat was countered, as an illustration of the very kind of indirect approach whose neglect by the Navy in the Civil War had interested Stephen Luce in the Naval War College and the study of naval strategy in the first place. Instead of hastening to reinforce Dewey, Mahan and the Naval War Board suggested the detachment of several cruisers which could be spared from the Santiago blockade and their conspicuous preparation for a voyage across the Atlantic to threaten the coasts of Spain itself. Thereupon the Spanish squadron in the Mediterranean promptly returned home.[45]

Although the inferiority of the Spanish warships helped a lot, the war showed that the revived American Navy had good ships. The cruise of the *Oregon* was an achievement combining speed and endurance in remarkable proportions. There had been good fortune, certainly for the American taxpayer, in the Navy's having been able to sit out the worse period of confusion in the efforts of the naval architects to weld steam power, improved guns, and metal armor into an acceptable new standard of naval design. By the time the American Navy began to rebuild, much had been clarified after costly experiments and false starts, conducted mainly by other navies. At the turn of the 1880s into the nineties, some officers were still reluctant to abandon sails, and the White Squadron had full sail rigging. But H.M.S. *Devastation* had evidenced the feasibility of a battleship powered by steam alone as long ago as 1873, everyone else was abandoning sails on battleships, and so sails could be eliminated from the major ships of the new American program. The guns, it was by now agreed, had to be breechloading rifled shell guns firing conical projectiles. By the 1880s the muzzleloading gun had reached the limit of its development, but was failing to keep pace with improvements in naval armor. In other ways the guns would be of a new type, much longer than had been possible with the technology of iron castings as it had existed only a few years before, burning a larger charge of slower burning powder which exerted a continuous accelerating effect upon the projectile during its whole course through the long barrel, the whole producing greatly enhanced ranges and penetrating power. The contest between guns and armor which had begun with the first shell guns and iron plating persisted; the new Navy began late enough so that the United States could run tests among the three favored types of armor, standard steel plate, a compound plate of steel and wrought iron bolted together, and a new nickel alloy steel, choosing the last on a basis of demonstrated superiority.[46]

This is not to say that the new American warships were perfect instruments of their kind. The American warships of the 1880s were built largely from plans purchased abroad, and the designs of the nineties were still derivative, in some ways badly derived. The battleships had too low a freeboard—they rode too low in the water. Consequently, the guns sometimes could not be worked in a heavy sea. The gunports were too large to give adequate protection to the crews and to the guns' own machinery. The straight vertical ammunition hoists were so designed that a powder flash in a turret was likely to ignite a magazine. The turrets were not well placed to command the widest possible field of fire. The armor belts did not extend low enough into the water. For guns with a range of several miles, improved spotting and aiming techniques would have seemed mandatory, but the techniques actually in use during the Spanish War differed little from those of the sailing ship era; they involved the gunner's touching off his charge as his target passed through his field of vision with the rolling of the ship. Before the war, Lieutenant Bradley A. Fiske had invented an optical rangefinder, a telescopic gunsight, and other devices to cope with the aiming problem, but he had to sell them to other navies because his own showed little interest.[47]

The new Navy also had problems of command. Since the dissolution of the short-lived Board of Navy Commissioners (1815–42), the Navy had been administered under the "bureau system" of five to eight separate bureaus each responsible for some aspect of naval activity, such as Navy Yards and Docks or Construction, Equipment and Repairs. After the Civil War the Bureau of Navigation, controlling ship movements and personnel, acquired a kind of primacy; but there was no coordination of the bureaus' activities below the level of the Secretary of the Navy, and therefore no professional coordination at all. No professional officers conducted centralized planning to estimate the strategic needs of the country and to develop ships and naval organization accordingly. In the nineties, Captain Henry C. Taylor, for a time president of the War College, and the retired Rear Admiral Stephen Luce campaigned for centralized professional administration and planning as a necessary concomitant of a Mahanian vision of sea power; but by 1898 all they got was a makeshift Naval War Board of three advisers to the Secretary, including Mahan.

A more permanent improvement came with the creation of the General Board in 1900. As much as anything, Secretary Long established the General Board to find a suitable position for the prestigious naval hero of Manila Bay, Admiral George Dewey, who became the board's president and served as such until his death in 1917. The General Board was charged, however, with preparing plans for the defense of the nation and its dependencies, with gathering relevant information, and with effecting cooperation with the Army. The extent of its authority was not clear, it remained principally an advisory body, and it was never a true "general staff" even though Admiral Dewey liked to use that term. Still, Dewey and Taylor, now a rear admiral and chief of the Bureau of Navigation during the board's early years, made the board at least the beginning of an agency for naval strategic planning.[48]

When the accident of assassination carried Theodore Roosevelt into the Presidency, the Navy gained a famous champion well able to exploit the Spanish War triumphs of the service to win more ships and to remedy some of the technical deficiencies. The Spanish War and Rooseveltian enthusiasm made Mahan a prophet so thoroughly honored that hardly anyone continued asking the questions that could have been raised about the applicability of his strategic ideas to the United States, except for those Congressmen and publicists who were opposed to a strong Navy of any type. Instead, ideas lifted from Mahan became shibboleths, such as Roosevelt's parting injunction to his successor in the White House, never to divide the fleet between the Atlantic and Pacific before the Panama Canal was completed;

itself an oversimplification of a strategic principle, this notion was soon further reduced to a fetish, "Never divide the fleet."[49]

Roosevelt easily persuaded Congress to authorize ten first-class battleships within four years, and thus he hurried the Navy on its way toward second place in battleship strength among the fleets of the world. It was an embarrassment when the British navy in 1906 launched H.M.S. *Dreadnought*, the first battleship to have a primary armament consisting uniformly of big guns, ten 12-inch guns in five turrets. Although this idea had been anticipated when the American battleships *South Carolina* and *Michigan* were laid down in 1905 (each of 16,000 tons, with eight 12-inch guns), and although Mahan surprisingly was skeptical and critical of the *Dreadnought* idea, citing Japanese success with smaller guns at close range in the Russo-Japanese War, *Dreadnought* nevertheless rendered all previous battleships at least obsolescent. The trouble for Roosevelt's program was that for all the naval and nationalist zeal of the time, it was difficult to have to begin the building program all over again in response to *Dreadnought*, especially since Roosevelt himself had just offered assurance that with the ten battleships of his first term his program was complete and only replacement would be necessary.

By now the Spanish War was fading into the past, and the country was focusing its attention upon the domestic issues of the Progressive Era, which had the additional effect of driving a wedge between the progressive Roosevelt and a more conservative Congress. Still, Roosevelt managed to wrest four more battleships from Congress, all to be of the *Dreadnought* class, *Florida* and *Utah*, 21,825 tons, ten 12-inch guns, and *Arkansas* and *Wyoming*, 26,000 tons, twelve 12-inch guns. Roosevelt's successor, William Howard Taft, in his single term got six more, *New York* and *Texas*, 27,000 tons, ten 14-inch guns; *Nevada* and *Oklahoma*, 27,500 tons, ten 14-inch guns; and *Pennsylvania* and *Arizona*, 31,400 tons, twelve 14-inch guns.[50]

The Philippines, of course, had not served merely as the makeweight originally planned in the peace negotiations with Spain. In its imperialist mood, the United States had kept them. After Roosevelt became President he urged the construction of a system of naval bases in the new possessions, including the Philippines. The Navy eventually proposed that a major Pacific Ocean naval installation be located at Olongapo, on Subic Bay on the island of Luzon. By the time of the proposal, however, Japan had certified herself as an independent center of sea power through her naval victories over Russia in the war of 1904–1905, and as a military power on land as well. The

United States Army therefore objected to the Subic Bay site as indefensible against Japan. The Navy, concentrated in American waters in accordance with Mahan's dicta, could not guarantee against a swift Japanese attack upon an archipelago some 7,000 miles distant from the United States. The Army, with a total authorized strength of less than 100,000, could not create a garrison strong enough to defend a Philippine base until the fleet could arrive. In 1909 the Navy perforce withdrew the site of its projected major Pacific base to Pearl Harbor. In a remark that was to become proverbial, President Roosevelt referred to the Philippines as the "Achilles heel" of American defense.[51]

Mahan's conception of sea power and Theodore Roosevelt's application of it gave the United States a fleet of "capital ships"—to use the term that came into vogue about 1909—more than capable of controlling the waters of the Western Hemisphere. Roosevelt set in motion the building of an American-controlled isthmian canal to ease the single most difficult problem of American naval strategy, and he saw to it that the battleships became welded into a fleet, not remaining a mere aggregation of vessels. Cruisers, not battleships, patrolled on foreign stations. The first fleet maneuvers in the Navy's history took place in 1902, and they became an annual event. The voyage of the battle fleet around the world in 1907–1909 both dramatized the idea of the ships as a fleet and assisted their practice in becoming one. In regard to the technical deficiencies, Roosevelt helped give Lieutenant William S. Sims, first as Target Practice Inspector on the China Station and then as Inspector of Target Practice for the whole Navy, the encouragement and support necessary to modernize gunnery and fire control, based on a continuous aiming method as opposed to spot aiming as the ship rolled, and to install the instruments essential for the purpose.[52]

But none of these achievements solved the strategic puzzles most evident in the problem of defending the Philippines but underlying, even undermining, the whole naval program. The concentrated battle fleet as the essence of sea power simply could not do for the United States what it had done for Great Britain in another era and from a far different geographical base. Mahan's emphasis on the battle fleet and his deprecation of any kind of naval war except the contest of first-line ships for control of the sea had combined with the difficulties of extracting from Congress even the later battleships to create an unbalanced fleet. Roosevelt got most of the battleships he wanted, but the Navy did not have enough cruisers or auxiliary vessels, and especially it did not have enough ships for a fleet train to support the battle fleet on long voyages. For the cruise around the world, foreign merchant ships had to be hired to assist in supporting the fleet. This imbalance obviously aggravated the already severe difficulty of naval defense of the distant possessions.[53]

Alfred Thayer Mahan published his books when the strategic problems of the United States were changing from those merely of protecting the continental domain to those of providing military means to sustain the projection of American interests overseas. The means clearly had to be in part naval; therefore Mahan's theory of sea power seemed to appear at precisely the appropriate moment, and Mahan became a figure of tremendous influence and prestige. But the kind of sea power that Mahan described from the historic experience of Great Britain proved inadequate to the requirements of the new American empire. Pressure brought by sea power against lines of maritime commerce was no longer capable of serving any nation so well as it had served Great Britain in the past, except in the limited situations when it was applied against one of the specialized maritime powers themselves, Britain or Japan. But beyond that shortcoming in Mahan's conceptions, the American empire was to be the projection overseas of the interests not of a maritime and primarily commercial state but of a continental land mass, and the appropriate military instrument for it was to prove to be not merely a battle fleet on the British model but a more amphibious form of military power, combining warships with a capacity to place on foreign shores and support over oceanic distances large numbers of soldiers.

> It is a singular fact [wrote Lieutenant Commander James H. Sears in the Naval Institute *Proceedings* in 1901, when Mahan was at the height of his influence] that military or naval people have not yet determined with exactness the amount of tonnage required to transport a given army corps, with or without all the necessary equipage. . . . It is sufficiently apparent, however, that for the transport of an army of invasion of the size absolutely demanded under the modern conditions which so greatly favor concentration for resistance, an enormous tonnage would be required even for a short trip of a few miles, and in addition, the covering fleet would require to be fully the equal, and probably greatly the superior in strength to the opposing navy. In an expedition of sufficient magnitude to approximate success, extending over the Atlantic Ocean, the transport would need to be so numerous that its clumsiness and vulnerability can well be imagined.[54]

The problems of such uses of sea power remained neglected during all the years of Mahan's preeminence in American strategic thought until the First World War—in part, no doubt, because they suggested too much that sea power was linked in mutual dependence with land power to fit well into Mahan's calculations. Because of the neglect of careful study of the maritime capacity that might be required to transport an army overseas, President Theodore Roosevelt was able to revive outdated fears and to entertain seriously the fantasy of a German invasion of the Western Hemisphere on a scale large enough to threaten the United States. The preparedness campaigners of the early years of the War of 1914 could similarly frighten their audiences and themselves with visions of vast German columns making another Belgium of the United States.[55] Conversely, when the United States eventually entered the World War, the Navy Department and everyone else proved to have neglected both the possibilities of the submarine and the other principal American naval problem of the war, the one to which Commander Sears had referred, how to transport an army of a million men and more across the Atlantic with all its equipment and to keep it supplied.

Conservatively neglectful of these problems raised by technological change and American geography, Mahan's calculations remained conservative even with regard to the battleship; he not only continued to resist the move to the all-big-gun battleship, arguing that most of the damage done to Russian ships in the Russo-Japanese War was inflicted by intermediate-sized batteries, but he argued too against a growing emphasis on the value of speed in battleships by saying that in any event a fleet could move no faster than its slowest ship. Sims and Captain Richard Wainwright took issue with Mahan on these matters; still other and especially some younger officers, like Sears, became at least implicitly critical of Mahan. Naval strategic thought grew more analytical as it profited from the war-gaming techniques developed at the Naval War College by Lieutenant William McCarty Little, a regular part of the curriculum beginning under the presidency of Captain Henry C. Taylor in 1894. By 1907, Commander Bradley A. Fiske called openly for a book on naval strategy based not on row galleys and sailing ships but on modern conditions. Still, Mahan's books and articles provided the belaying pin by which the Navy had fastened its ambitions to the popular national mood and the expansionist policies of the Spanish War and the Rooseveltian era; the Navy was committed to him irretrievably. Even as younger and more progressive officers came to recognize the shortcomings of

Mahanian strategic thought, the Navy had to pay homage to Mahan because its public and political image depended on him. Thus his ideas survived the criticism they encountered in his later years, and after his death in 1914 he gained renewed stature as the high priest of American navalism, whose strategic teachings were its holy writ.[56]

10. Strategy and the Great War of 1914-1918

Strategy had failed in its prime object of bringing two armies into contact in such a way that the issue would not have to be decided by a frontal attack. And thus the ensuing struggle for four years became rather a test of the courage and endurance of the soldier and of the suffering civil population behind him than of the strategical skill of the general.

—*Tasker H. Bliss*[1]

AMONG THE MANY REASONS for the vogue of Mahan, one surely was that he promised a way to relatively anesthetic victory in war. However terrible a climactic battle at sea might be, with hundreds or even thousands of men consumed in the fiery explosions of warship magazines or suffocated in ironclad tombs, Mahan promised that such an event might swiftly and abruptly ensure the outcome of a war, and it was a more inviting prospect than a repetition of Grant's costly battering campaign against the Confederate armies in 1864–65. Once command of the sea was achieved, the naval siege of a blockaded foe still more excelled in attractiveness a Grant-style campaign to destroy enemy armies. Those who cast themselves in the role of blockaders could readily overlook prospective deprivation and even starvation among an enemy people while contemplating the painless course to victory that Mahan seemed to offer for themselves.

The Army remained skeptical about relatively painless ways to victory. Considering the Southern Confederacy's unusual dependence, for a large land power, upon imports from abroad, Captain John Bigelow argued in his textbook *Principles of Strategy* that the Civil War showed "that the most effective blockade should not be expected to prove decisive in itself. An entire country can hardly be starved like a city into surrendering."[2]

> The ultimate decision in war [said an editorial in the *Infantry Journal* in 1902] is gained in the contact of field armies on the field of battle. Hence as regards the ultimate object of war, the fleet is to be regarded as auxiliary to the mobile army. But the command of the sea determines whether the contact of field armies will take place on our own or on foreign territory and also which party will have access to the resources of neutral countries. It is, therefore, of immense importance. It thus becomes an intermediate objective; during the struggle to attain it, naval forces are principal and land forces, for the time being, auxiliary.[3]

By the time the United States entered the World War in April, 1917, the intermediate objective of command of the sea had in a conventional sense been achieved. The Royal Navy had the German High Seas Fleet securely bottled up in German coastal waters. Unfortunately, when the United States entered the war the German submarine campaign was making conventional command of the sea appear a very bad joke. William S. Sims, now a rear admiral, arrived in London soon after the American declaration of war to learn from the Admiralty's statistics that Great Britain was within measurable distance of strangulation. The submarines were sinking one ship of every four that left England, and the British were able to replace only one ship in ten. With the submarine and the self-propelled torpedo employed against a vulnerable maritime nation, the *guerre de course*, the commerce-raiding war, was becoming an immense German success, Mahan to the contrary notwithstanding. Indeed, one of the principal mistakes the Germans had made was to have paid too much heed to Mahan and to have built too many battleships and not enough submarines before the war.[4]

For the kind of naval campaign in which it now found itself engaged, the United States also had built the wrong warships. The Navy should have had more destroyers. The Royal Navy had almost 300, but nearly 100 of them were busy screening the Grand Fleet. The United States had seventy, only forty-four of them relatively new oil-burning ships. It was not until early July, 1917, that as many as thirty-four American destroyers reached Queenstown to reinforce the British, and the rest of the American squadrons consisted mainly of the obsolescent types, which were retained in Western Hemisphere waters. Belatedly, battleship building was pushed aside for destroyers and smaller escort craft.[5]

In this crisis, Admiral Sims's persuasions may have made at least a small contribution to the saving British decision to organize merchant shipping into escorted convoys. Despite the technical problems which had led the Admiralty to reject convoys until now, once attempted they proved a remarkable success. In April, the Admiralty's projections had British shipping ruined by November. When November came, shipping losses had fallen from April's 881,000 tons to 289,000 tons, and production was about to surpass losses. Less than 1 percent of ships in convoy were lost to all causes. Almost alone, the convoy system turned the war against the submarine.[6]

An increasing fleet of American escort vessels helped. Before the war, American warships often took notoriously long in building. But American industry now proved itself adept in conversion to the swift production of destroyers and improvised lesser antisubmarine craft. Previously, building an American destroyer normally had required more than a year; in wartime the Mare Island Navy Yard completed one in seventy days, and a civilian yard had another ready for trials in forty-five days. Such a pace now became almost ordinary. Some 248 destroyers, 60 large "Eagle boat" submarine chasers, and 116 smaller submarine chasers were built or building for the United States Navy by the end of the war, along with many additional submarine chasers built for the Allies. In June, 1918, the United States also began laying the huge North Sea mine barrage across 240 miles between Scotland and Norway, to make even entering the Atlantic a hazardous business for the submarines. With these developments, control of the sea became meaningful again; but as the *Infantry Journal* had expected, it remained only an intermediate objective.[7]

To defeat Germany, especially now that Russia was beaten and Germany could draw on the foodstuffs of the Ukraine, would require not just the application of sea power but the defeat of the German armies on land. To accomplish their defeat, no one had yet, unhappily, developed a method better than Grant's against the Army of Northern Virginia. By the time units of the United States Army began to take over sectors of the Western Front in the spring of 1918, the French and British armies on one side and the German army on the other had been spending almost four years in efforts to bleed their opponents white. But because through most of the four years the front had extended from Switzerland to the North Sea and flanking maneuvers were impossible, the only available means of bleeding the enemy was the frontal assault, and both sides had been draining each other into mutual exhaustion. The development of the internal combustion engine had advanced far enough that the deadlock might conceivably have been broken by protecting attackers in self-propelled armored weapon-carrying vehicles, and midway in the war the tank in fact began to make its appearance on the battlefield. But land war had so long been fought in much the same way that generals were unreceptive to suggestions for rapid technological change, and supporting great mass armies cost so much that both statesmen and generals were reluctant to risk large additional sums in experimental programs to build armored vehicles.

Still, because there were always political pressures demanding swift as well as complete victory, both sides took turns in staging variations upon Pickett's Charge, modernized in weaponry and minor tactics but equally futile. Or rather, since the habit of digging into the earth begun by Lee's and Grant's armies had now become universal, the belligerents alternated in repeating Grant's attack at Cold Harbor.

The Europeans had tended to regard America's prolonged blood-letting in 1861–65 as exceptional; they tended to believe that the Union and Confederate armies had remained deadlocked so long merely because the militarily unsophisticated Americans lacked the skill to overcome the admitted problems raised by rifled firepower. The European soldiers also tended to write off as exceptional the similar campaigns of trench warfare in the Russo-Turkish War of 1877–78 and the Russo-Japanese War. Europeans before 1914 generally expected a new war among first-class European armies to be a repetition of the short wars of 1866 and 1870–71, which had consolidated the German Empire. The Germans especially had expected a new war to be made another short war by repeating on a larger scale the strategy of envelopment which Helmuth von Moltke had employed against the French in 1870. In the grand envelopment of the French armies contemplated in their Schlieffen Plan, the Germans failed to pay enough regard to what would occur when their armies, dangling at the ends of overstretched communications, would at last have to do battle with French troops whose magazines and haversacks would have been replenished by their retreat into their bases. The Germans really counted on the moral effect of the great Schlieffen envelopment to destroy France's will before there would have to be a head-to-head collision of the armies. They counted on a campaign of maneuver and failed to pay enough regard to the effects of bloody collisions, because they underestimated their opponents.

All the calculations which anticipated a short war overlooked also the coming impact of the mature Industrial Revolution upon war.

Industrial productivity had increased vastly by 1914 over the productivity of 1870. At the time of the Franco-Prussian War, Germany produced 1.3 million tons of pig iron and .3 of a million tons of steel annually; by 1914, her yearly production of these commodities was 14.7 and 14 million tons, respectively. Great Britain had yielded first place among the industrial powers in the interval, but nevertheless she produced 11 million tons of pig iron and 6.5 million tons of steel in 1914 compared with 6 million and .7 of a million tons in 1870. France, which produced 1.2 million tons of pig iron and .3 of a million tons of steel in 1870, produced 4.6 and 3.5 million tons, respectively, by 1914. In 1914, the pig iron production of the United States was 30 million tons, the steel production 32 million tons, compared with 1.7 million tons of pig iron and a minuscule production of steel in 1870. These great advances in industrial productivity generated the economic surplus that permitted the powers to put into their armies in 1914–18 much larger numbers of men even than in the mid-nineteenth century. These great advances in industrial productivity, and the economic surplus that they generated, were also to prove to permit the powers to sustain war over a prolonged period of time, despite unprecedented expenditures of ammunition, equipment, and supplies, and to display an unprecedented resiliency and endurance. To exploit industrial productivity and the economic surplus fully in sustaining war, the powers had to invoke governmental control and indeed mobilization of their whole manpower and wealth more than ever before, and war took another long stride toward true totality. But after such complete mobilization occurred, the economic resiliency of the great powers became so enormous that such an economic weapon as a Mahanian naval blockade worked only very slowly and gradually against a continental power, a war of merely economic attrition was likely to persist indefinitely, and the destruction of the enemy armies became more than ever the only means of achieving victory within a tolerable time span—though at a cost approaching the intolerable in other dimensions than that of time.[8]

To some extent, American military writers, accustomed to deferring to the accumulated experience of Europe, had come to share before 1914 the European conviction that land wars in the twentieth century must be short wars. No more than the Europeans did they foresee the total war of the new industrialism. On the other hand, the Americans knew well the history of their own Civil War, and they were not convinced that either the Civil War or Russia's wars of 1877–78 and 1904–1905 departed from the mainstream of the evolution of warfare. All of the latter conflicts indicated that modern wars against reasonably determined opponents, even badly equipped opponents such as the Turks, are not easy to win. These wars did not offer much reason to believe, in the judgment of American military students, that resourceful and resolute opponents could be conquered by maneuver alone, without direct collisions of armies in which the contender undertaking the strategic offensive must accept the burdens of the tactical offensive as well. As Captain Bigelow put it in his textbook on strategy:

> There is an old theory that the offensive in strategy should be combined with the defensive in tactics, but it is rarely carried into practice. It may be generally asserted that an army cannot move upon any commanding strategic point without overcoming some resistance, and that, once in the enemy's rear, it must move against him and attack him under penalty of being overpowered or of seeing the value of its position nullified by the enemy's manœuvres. *The strategic offensive ordinarily involves the tactical also.*[9]

But the Civil War and succeeding wars did not offer glowing prospects for the tactical offensive in an age of entrenchments and rifled weapons, with the already devastating fire power of 1861–65 now vastly multiplied by magazine-firing breechloaders and by machine guns. Major General John M. Schofield, later lieutenant general and Commanding General of the Army, repeatedly stressed this lesson of the Civil War:

> Surely, twenty-two thousand men [as in Schofield's own fight at Franklin], with abundant supplies and time to select and intrench a position, need not apprehend the result of an attack by twice that number for two or three days! Was not the whole history of the war of secession full of examples of successful resistance in similar cases? Was it not, in fact, such attacks as that of Franklin, Atlanta and Gettysburg, rather than any failures of defense, that finally exhausted and defeated the Confederate Armies?[10]

"It caused a feeling of relief," said Schofield again, "rather than anything else, when Hood challenged me to a 'square stand up fight' . . . . For that was a kind of combat in which all our experience had shown that victory was almost sure to be on the side of the defense."[11]

But without attack, even frontal attack, and bloody combat, how was the enemy army to be destroyed and victory won? Francis Vinton Greene, first ranking cadet in the West Point class of 1870 and later a major general of volunteers in the War of 1898 and a reflective military writer, wrestled with this hard question in a letter to General Sherman from the Russian headquarters at San Stefano during the 1877–78 campaign against the Turks:

> . . . [The Russians Skobeleff and Gourko, said Greene, are] the only generals of this campaign of the first order. They are totally different in temperament and action. Gourko having a semi-independent army and numerically superior to his antagonist has always tried to plan in advance such combinations as would result in manoeuvering his enemy out of his position without direct attack, while Skobeleff, commanding a division or corps forming part of an army, has bent his whole mind to the problem how to storm a redoubt successfully. But for him the war would have established the principle that well built trenches with modern breechloaders can *not* be carried by direct attack—and he too would have been of the same opinion had he not succeeded so well in his last attack (at Cenovo, behind Shipka). The results of these two lines of thought are most interesting. Gourko's enemy finally escaped, dispersed and routed it is true and losing all its artillery and baggage—but still the men with most of the muskets on their shoulders did get away, and might at a future time have been reorganized into another army; whereas Skobeleff by storming Cenovo with large loss bagged the whole Shipka army, artillery, baggage, supplies *and men*. Yet there are not many Skobeleffs, and Gourko was right, for 99 out of 100 division generals will fail to carry trenches by assault.[12]

In short, to defeat and destroy an enemy might well require frontal assaults, whatever the heavy losses entailed; but at best such pursuit of victory was a highly doubtful enterprise. American observers of Russia's later war against Japan found the problem still worse aggravated:

> Formerly the battlefield was a narrow strip, the opposing forces came promptly together and brought about a tactical decision by the slaughter of the short range conflict and hand to hand fighting. An inferior force could be quickly overpowered. The men were still comparatively fresh when entering the decisive part of the action. Modern long range arms have changed all this, the fire swept zone which must be crossed by the attacker has steadily increased, has grown deeper until to-day shrapnel is used with accuracy at 6,000 yards. Modern arms give great defensive power. To get at the enemy with the bayonet may require not minutes and hours, but days of exposure to fire, coupled with immense exertions and with lack of shelter, food and water. At one point at least in the battle of Liaoyang the infantry fire never ceased for 36 hours and the Japanese infantry was lying within

> a few hundred yards of the Russian trenches. Russian non-commissioned officers who helped to repulse a night attack on the south front of the I Siberian Corps, were unanimous in stating that the Japanese soldiers seemed to be at the end of their physical strength and were slaughtered with the bayonet like sheep. Battle has become a long-enduring, nerve-racking contest, extending over days and consuming the last minim of mental and physical strength of the participants, inferior forces can no longer be quickly overpowered, an opponent attacking the enemy with equal forces ought to fail. . . .
>
> In the battle of Liaoyang 4½ Japanese divisions with 240 guns assailed the key position held by the I Siberian Corps numbering less than 15,000 men and 80 guns; in this last case the numerical superiority was not sufficient. Though smothered under a blanket of concentrated fire such as was never before known in military history, though their trenches were blown about their ears by high explosive shells, though attacked by superior numbers during three consecutive nights and two days, and suffering hunger and thirst, the I Siberian Corps repulsed all attacks. This will convey some idea of the strength of the defensive. . . .[13]

This should also have conveyed some idea of what to expect when the European powers went to war in 1914, but its effect upon the European conception of the coming war was remarkably slight.[14] Lieutenant Commander Dudley W. Knox of the American Navy erred mainly in giving the French more credit for circumspection than they deserved when he described the major belligerents' doctrines of war in 1915 by saying:

> The Germans seek the offensive blindly and vigorously at all points at all times and from exterior lines [which afford opportunity for envelopment], whereas the French aim is to husband their troops and to preserve interior lines during a period while the strength and disposition of the enemy is being ascertained. Once the necessary information is obtained however and the time is deemed by the commander-in-chief to be opportune, conservation ceases and the end in view becomes a vigorous attack by almost the whole concentrated army. . . .[15]

The common European idea that a European war would be a short war implied the continuing vitality in Europe of the Napoleonic concept of the climactic, decisive battle, the Austerlitz victory. Europeans were unwilling to concede that it was Prussia's wars of 1866 and 1870–71, not those of the United States and Russia, that were outside the mainstream of the evolution of war. But both in 1866 and in 1870–71 Prussia's opponents were too badly mismatched, and their generals too incompetent, to provide a forecast of the probable course of conflict between reasonably well-balanced opponents with reasonably good military leaders. Not recognizing this fact, the author of the Schlieffen Plan went on dreaming of a Cannae victory—the Napoleonic battle but in a different historical setting—and the French generals longed for a new Jena among the hills of Lorraine.

But in 1914, all prospect of the Napoleonic battle disappeared still faster than it had in the American Civil War. The armies were too big to be beaten decisively in a single stroke, the casualties suffered with even the best of generalship too severe to afford one side decisive battlefield advantages over the other. No longer did any contender defeat himself through the sheer ineptitude of his generalship, as the French had done in 1870. The universal adoption of the general staff system by the great powers, more or less modeled on the Prussian General Staff, ensured that through the leadership of a collective brain and the study of an accepted corpus of military doctrine, all the major armies would have, if not brilliant generalship, at least the guarantee that collectivity can offer against total incompetence. The Marne then became not a Napoleonic battle but the culmination of the progressive exhaustion of the German armies as they marched and fought incessantly on their way into France and outran both their logistical support and the ability of *Oberste Heeresleitung* to control and direct them in pursuit of the Cannae victory. Thereafter the size of the armies soon determined that there would be no more flanks for would-be Napoleons to turn, and the war degenerated into the head-on exchange of assaults and casualties, with battle not an occasional climax but an almost continuous event, that has given the phrases "the World War" and "the Western Front" their ominous connotations.

Since the establishment of the General Board of the Navy in 1900 and the General Staff of the Army as part of the Elihu Root military reforms in 1903, the United States had possessed the rudiments of strategic planning agencies. In 1903 there had also been created the Joint Army and Navy Board, the first interservice planning body, consisting of four principal officers of each service meeting under the chairmanship of Admiral Dewey, the senior member until his death in 1917. The Joint Board both set forth general principles for the defense of the United States, its possessions, and the Western Hemisphere, recommending the establishment of various bases and suitable allocations of effort and strength, and began preparing color-coded war plans for the event of conflict with certain possible enemy nations, Plan ORANGE for Japan, RED for Great Britain, BLACK for Germany. The BLACK plans envisioned the contingency of a German invasion of the Western Hemisphere, and none of this early strategic planning turned out to have much relevance to the war in which the country actually found itself in 1917.[16]

Anyway, there was not much chance for the belatedly belligerent United States to shape the military strategy of the World War. The United States fell in with the existing strategies of distant blockade at sea and frontal collision in the hope of destroying the enemy armies on land. The failure of the amphibious campaign at Gallipoli and the frustration of the Salonika expedition had long since killed whatever small interest the British and French governments had once felt in projects to circumvent the Western Front; the collapse of Russia before the United States could made a military contribution closed the question altogether by destroying the possibilities of circumvention. Theoretically it might have remained feasible to turn the German lines on the Western Front by means of amphibious landings somewhere on the north German coast, an idea which had intrigued Lord Fisher in the British Admiralty before the war. But the continuing strength of the German High Seas Fleet in its own waters and the current limitations of amphibious technique and doctrine, so glaringly revealed at Gallipoli, practically ruled out the prospect.[17]

Woodrow Wilson might have decided that the American military participation in the World War should be a limited participation; taking part only in the naval war against the submarine would have been consistent with the limited cause—Germany's resumption of unrestricted submarine warfare—that precipitated American entry into the conflict, as well as with the President's previously expressed horror at the bloodletting going on across the European battlefields. But limited American participation would not have been consistent with the deep popular emotions that President Wilson decided he must arouse to support a declaration of war, or with the plans for mass mobilization that American military planners had already made with the encouragement of such political figures as Theodore Roosevelt and Elihu Root, or with Wilson's own ideas of America's proper influence at the peace negotiations. Wilson decided to commit a mass army to the Western Front, and once he had so decided, the American Army, so dependent upon the Allies for communications and vital supplies that maintaining its own identity was a precarious effort, could do nothing but join the Allies in the attempt to destroy the

German army by accepting heavy losses in unsubtle attack and counterattack.

Within these limitations, General John J. Pershing, commander of the American Expeditionary Force, tried to exercise a modicum of strategic judgment. Circumstances decreed that if the American Army were to take over a portion of the Western Front, which Pershing insisted it must do (the alternative being to distribute American soldiers among the French and British), then the American sector should be the Allies' right, or southern, flank, from the Argonne Forest to the Vosges Mountains. Nationalism dictated that the French army retain the central part of the front directly covering Paris. Geography and logistics both demanded that the British army retain the left, or northern, Allied flank, just across the channel from England itself. Logistically it would be most convenient to establish the American sector in the south, because railroads reached that sector from France's Atlantic ports without entanglement in the already overloaded railroad complex around Paris. Pershing discerned strategic advantages in the southern sector as well:

> On the battlefront from the Argonne Forest to the Vosges Mountains [he said] a chance for the decisive use of our army was clearly presented. The enemy's positions covered not only the coal fields of the Saar but also the important Longwy-Briey iron-ore region. Moreover, behind this front lay the vital portion of his rail communications connecting the garrison at Metz with the armies of the West. A deep Allied advance on this front and the seizure of the Longwy-Briey section would deprive the enemy of an indispensable source of ore for the manufacture of munitions. It might also lead to the invasion of enemy territory on the Moselle valley and endanger the supply of coal in the Saar basin. Allied success here would also cut his line of communications between the east and west and compel his withdrawal from northern France or force his surrender.[18]

The last of these points was the critical one. No real alternative remained to a strategy which aimed at destroying the German armies by grinding them into ruin; but at least the cost to the Allies might be reduced if the Germans could be forced out of their present defenses and fought while retreating into new positions. When Pershing was able to organize the American First Army, its initial offensive was directed against the St. Mihiel salient, a German arrowhead lodged in the Allied front since 1914. Between September 12 and 16, 1918, the Americans wiped out the salient, thereby opening the Paris-Nancy railroad for the use of the Allies. In doing so, they staggered the Germans so badly that a continuation of the drive would have enjoyed excellent chances to capture Metz and to continue on up the Metz-Thionville railroad to the Thionville-Longuyon-Sedan railroad without which, as Pershing said, the Germans could not remain in France.[19]

It happened, however, that the Allied Supreme Commander, Marshal Ferdinand Foch, had yielded to Field Marshal Sir Douglas Haig's importunities that the direction of the main American effort be shifted westward and northward toward Sedan and Mézières. This shift would produce an American offensive tending toward convergence with Haig's British offensive from around Cambrai. In time it might also carry the Americans to the strategic railroad. But it meant abandoning the opportunity opened by the dislocation of the German troops from the St. Mihiel salient and attacking instead through extremely difficult territory, a rugged ridge reaching northward between the valleys of the rivers Meuse and Aire, commanded by the Argonne Forest to the left and the Heights of the Meuse to the right, protected by a German defense system some twelve miles deep.

Still, Foch directed that the Meuse-Argonne attack should be the primary American effort even before the St. Mihiel offensive had gotten under way. Between September 26 and the Armistice on November 11, the Americans in the Meuse-Argonne battered some forty-seven German divisions, captured 16,059 prisoners and many guns, and eventually brought the railroad at Sedan under their own guns, but at a cost of 120,000 casualties.[20] Insisting upon this offensive against perhaps the strongest German defenses on the Western Front was a folly which gave ample credence to an observation of Brigadier General William Mitchell of the American Army Air Service: "The art of war had departed. Attrition, or the gradual killing off of the enemy, was all the ground armies were capable of."[21]

It was not necessary to accompany General Mitchell to his subsequent conclusions about the supremacy of air power to agree with him that land war had descended into futility. Soon after the war General Tasker H. Bliss, the scholarly American military member of the Allied Supreme War Council, reached similarly pessimistic conclusions about the possibilities available for strategy to produce decision at an acceptable price in modern land war. Bliss still believed that sound prewar planning might permit initial decisive strategic advantages to be gained, an idea the Germans were especially to explore as they attempted to digest the experience of the war just ended, and from which they were to profit in France in 1940. But failing a coup which might be gained from a brilliant initial strategic plan, for which Bliss did not hold much hope, General Bliss feared that the War of 1914–18 had set a pattern for strategic futility that would be difficult to break:

> The paucity of scientific strategical combinations in the military operations of the World War has often been commented upon. To whatever extent it is true—and to a large extent it is true—is due to the radical change in recent years in the conditions under which war is waged.
>
> . . .
>
> One other only, of many things that limit the exercise of strategy, need be mentioned here. It is the limitation imposed by the great size of modern armies. The essential element of strategy is surprise. Under modern conditions this element is most likely to be found, on a strategic as distinguished from a tactical scale, in the initial war plans. . . . If both initial plans fail in their object these huge masses cannot be readily manoeuvred into new strategical combinations. The tendency then is for the two sides to take offensive-defensive positions which from the magnitude of the forces engaged, may extend across the entire theatre of war. This theatre, which is the field for strategy, then becomes one great battle-ground, which is the field for grand tactics. . . .
>
> [At the outset of the World War] Strategy had failed in its prime object of bringing two armies into contact in such a way that the issue would not have to be decided by a frontal attack. And thus the ensuing struggle for four years became rather a test of the courage and endurance of the soldier and of the suffering civil population behind him than of the strategical skill of the general.[22]

No more perceptive American naval critic of the strategy of the World War appeared than young Commander Halloway Halstead Frost. In 1916 at the age of twenty-seven H. H. Frost (USNA 1910) had been the youngest officer ever ordered to the Naval War College. Through the 1920s he contributed stimulating and often prize-winning papers to the Naval Institute *Proceedings*. In 1925, discussing "National Strategy" in that journal, Frost argued that in its indecisiveness the World War had in fact been typical of warfare, and therefore it was all the more likely to indicate the pattern of future war. The few decisive wars fought during the nineteenth century, Frost argued, had been rendered decisive only by circumstances that were now exceptional in contests between great powers: marked inferiority in numbers, efficiency, or leadership on the part of one of the contenders; technical developments temporarily favoring offensive tactics, such as had prevailed in the Napoleonic wars; little or no use of permanent or field fortifications; armed forces too small to form a continuous front. "Where these conditions have not been present," said Frost, "rapid and purely military decisions have seldom been the rule," at any time in military history.

> . . . While it might have been possible for the Germans to have gained a decisive military success in the French campaign of 1914, this is now beginning to appear more and more doubtful. Two great armies, when their morale is unbroken, tend to reach a state of equilibrium. . . .
>
> It was only where a lesser power, Belgium, Serbia, or Rumania, was attacked that a purely military decision could be won, although even here brilliant leadership was usually necessary to supplement superior resources.
>
> From the above facts it may be deduced that when a great power is at war with a small power it will probably still be possible to win a purely military decision by destroying the enemy field armies; but when great nations are at war with approximately equal military forces it will seldom be possible to win a purely military decision.[23]

Clearly, the decision of 1918 seemed to have been not purely military but economic, political, and moral as well. The German Empire had collapsed not through military defeat alone but because the ability of the German army to resist and the vitality of German public morale and of the German political system were mutually dependent, and all collapsed together and influenced each other. The frustrations and disappointments of a prolonged war, the pressures of blockade and of economic strains and deprivations, and weaknesses that were inherent in the German political system but aggravated by war had all contributed to the political and moral collapse. If military strategy alone could no longer achieve acceptable decisiveness, then military men had to expand their conception of strategy to include more than military factors. The title of Commander Frost's article, "National Strategy," suggested his effort to broaden the military man's definition of strategy. In part, Frost envisioned the military in future wars as waging war not only against the enemy's armed forces but against his economy and political system as well, in the manner of Sherman in the Civil War.

> Sherman's march from Atlanta and Sheridan's devastation of the Shenandoah Valley were both direct attacks on the enemy economic forces. The organization of a nation is now so strong and complex and the economic forces of the world are so interwoven that sometimes a mili-

tary decision will not in itself bring about the defeat of the enemy nation.[24]

Frost increased the objectives to be sought by armed forces in war, but he still emphasized the strategic action of armed forces, and he was dubious of most diversions from a strategic focus on the destruction of the enemy's armies and navies as sideshows. Other military writers still more enlarged the definition of strategy, to emphasize not only action by the armed forces but political, diplomatic, and economic action as well. As Commander George J. Meyers, USN, told an Army War College audience in the 1923–24 course:

> The application of strategy to the armed forces is not something separate and distinct from other war activities, but is part of a whole which we may call national strategy. The modern conception that "war is a mere continuation of policy by other means" changes the aspect of the whole question from one of purely naval or army considerations to one embracing the fields of all three means designed to further national policies, not only armed forces of the army and navy, but diplomacy as well. However much we of the military services may strive to strengthen our hands in war operations by making proper strategic dispositions, our efforts are weakened and sometimes nullified if diplomacy and statesmanship do not work hand in hand with us, particularly during peace time, to support our national strategy. Sound national strategy builds up during times of peace a structure that will strengthen in the future sea and land forces when policy passes from the realm of persuasion by minds to the operations of war where decisions are obtained by force.

Promoted to captain, Meyers published in 1928 a book on *Strategy* in which he defined the term as meaning "the provision, preparation, and use of diplomacy and of the nation's armed forces in peace and in war to gain the purpose of national policy."[26]

Captain Meyers stressed the strategic functions of diplomacy. More frequently, military writers seeking to enlarge the scope of strategy in light of the World War stressed the economic and logistical dimensions of strategy, and modern war as an economic well as a military contest. The cost of maintaining and equipping armies of millions of men over four years had turned the World War into a contest of the productivity and endurance capacities of the rival economies, and the economic strains which Germany had to undergo did much to undermine her moral and political as well as military vitality and to produce her collapse.

> We cannot blame the General Staffs of 1914 [said Lieutenant Colonel A. L. Conger at the General Staff College in 1920] for not knowing the economic possibilities and consequences of making war on a large scale. . . . To try to visualize a world war in 1914 was almost to leave the world of fact and enter the realm of fiction. Bernhardi's "Germany in the Next War" was read with the same amused smile as "A Trip to the Moon" by Jules Verne. . . .
>
> But, although we cannot condemn any General Staff before 1914 for not correctly appraising the economic factors of war, we can say today that the General Staff which has not learned how to appraise them and does not correctly appraise them is not to be taken seriously; for on the one hand we have had a complete demonstration of the operation of all these factors in a great war and on the other in the decision reached, we have, at least as regards the defeated countries, a measuring stick by which to compute their relative importance.
>
> A very important difference to note, in estimating the economic factor, between a war of today and any previous war is that whereas formerly an army went out to fight for the nation, while the nation abided by the result of the armed conflict without much suffering except on the part of the unfortunate people who lived in the immediate theatre of operations, nowadays it is not the army but the nation which bears the brunt of the struggle and undergoes the hardships and suffering, the army and navy being merely the weapons with which the nation delivers its blows or wards off the blows of its opponents. This altered factor is due to the fact that the powerful transportation systems and highly organized and efficient systems of government now make it possible to mobilize and concentrate in the organized armies a vastly greater percentage of the nation's resources than was formerly possible.[27]

In the aftermath of the World War, little was done to apply to practice such observations as Captain Meyers's on the interdependence of armed forces and diplomacy. It was not until 1938 that the State, War, and Navy Departments established a Standing Liaison Committee for mutual consideration of policy, and the committee achieved only limited success. It focused mainly on Latin American policy and hemisphere defense, it met irregularly, and it was not distinguished for its members' trust of each other.[28] The armed forces showed much more interest in following up observations such as Colonel Conger's on the economic dimensions of war.

Before 1917, planning by the armed forces for the economic demands of war was even more conspicuously and completely absent in the United States than strategic planning. The subsequent dependence of the American Army on French and British artillery, ammunition, tanks, and aircraft on the Western Front was in part a result of this absence. The first important step in the direction of economic war planning occurred in 1916, when observation of the importance of industrial production in the European war led to inclusion in the National Defense Act of that year of provisions empowering the President to place orders for defense materials and to require compliance from the industries involved, charging the Secretary of War to make a survey of industries concerned with the manufacture of arms and ammunition, and authorizing the President to establish government-owned nitrate plants. A rider attached to the Army Appropriation Act of 1916 followed up by creating a Council of National Defense to consider especially the problems of economic mobilization. Little could come of these measures before the United States entered the war in 1917, and despite the industrial preeminence of the United States, lack of industrial preparation for war then caused many false starts and disappointing output, with the consequent large dependence on the Allies.[29]

To prepare better for the economic demands of future war, in 1922 the American armed forces established the interservice Army and Navy Munitions Board. The Navy, however, believed it would still have to depend mainly on warships constructed in peacetime, because building capital ships was a work of years; therefore the Navy concentrated its efforts in the industrial procurement field on trying to prevent excessive peacetime curtailment of naval building. But the Army knew its wartime equipment would have to be manufactured largely after war began, and so it developed a strong interest in industrial mobilization planning. Indeed, the most probable enemy of the United States after the defeat of Germany was Japan; the principal strategic planning conducted during the 1920s and until the late thirties concerned a primarily naval war against Japan, and consequently the Army showed rather greater interest in economic mobilization planning than in the strategic plans in which its contemplated role was relatively small.[30]

The National Defense Act of 1920 created the post of Assistant Secretary of War, with responsibility for assuring "adequate preparation for the mobilization of material and industrial organizations essential to war-time needs."[31] The Harbord Board of 1921, studying the reorganization of the War Department General Staff, recommended that the General Staff prepare estimates of required materials and that the Assistant Secretary of War plan how the materials were to be procured. The General Staff proceeded to develop a series of mobilization plans, principally those of 1923, 1924, 1928, 1933, and 1936. Meanwhile the Assistant Secretary of War established within his office a Planning Branch to cooperate with the supply departments of the Army special staff in procurement planning. Every officer assigned to the Planning Branch was required to read the records of the mobilization agencies of the World War. To provide for fuller and more systematic study of industrial mobilization planning, in 1923 the War Deparement established the Army Industrial College.

By the 1930s, the War Department had an Industrial Mobilization Plan that received generally favorable reviews by the potentially critical members of President Herbert Hoover's War Policies Commission and the Nye Committee of Congress. Unfortunately, while the plans were technically sound, they developed a political and social insensitivity to the subsequent events of the 1930s. Not only did they predictably propose a large role for the armed forces in governing a wartime national economy; they also proposed to concentrate more power in the hands of business than President Franklin D. Roosevelt could well accept—thus foreshadowing the later evolution of a military-industrial complex—and in their provisions for manipulation of the labor force they failed to take into account the likely wishes and the rising political power of organized labor. President Roosevelt inevitably refused to accept the War Department mobilization plans as a blueprint for industrial mobilization when a new war emergency developed, and the Army's post-1918 mobilization planning received application only in administrative and technical details and at that only gradually and after much trial and error. The planning process had utility in acquainting a new generation of officers with the economic dimensions of war; its utility might have been greater if Army economic planners in the 1920s and 1930s had been more politically and socially aware.[32]

The limitations of vision were not surprising in an armed force which before 1917 had interpreted strategy almost wholly in military terms[33] and had lived in its posts inherited from the Indian wars in considerable physical and intellectual isolation from civilian America. Still, the Army went on with its efforts to take a larger view of war. The recognition that the decision in 1918 had not been "purely military," and that "purely military" decisions in war were probably a thing of the past if they had ever existed at all, led from consideration of the role of diplomacy in war and economic mobilization planning to a wider philosophical view of the nature of war. When Commander Meyers spoke of the "modern conception that 'war is a mere continuation of policy by other means,'" he echoed Clausewitz; and a vogue of quoting Clausewitz—if not of studying that difficult writer thoroughly—was another consequence of the frustrations encountered in attempting to reach a "purely military" decision in the Great War, as well as of the war's stimulating an interest in military things German.

Carl von Clausewitz's *Vom Kriege*, left incomplete at his death in 1831, had been published as the first three volumes of a ten-volume German-language edition of his military works beginning the year after his death. Although Halleck cited Clausewitz's work in his *Elements of Military Art and Science*, American acquaintance with it was small throughout the nineteenth century. Until 1870, Americans looked to France, the country of Napoleon and one with which the United States had strong historical military ties, as the principal source of military wisdom. Like Jomini, Clausewitz found his point of departure in Napoleonic war; but he was concerned less with the particulars of the Napoleonic campaigns than with a search for the inner nature of war, and his consequent abstractness diminished his appeal for those caught up in the cult of Napoleon.

The military prestige of Germany soared in America as everywhere during and after the Franco-Prussian War and was soon abetted in the United States Army by Emory Upton's admiration for the German military system. Colonel J. J. Graham's English translation of Clausewitz's *On War* became available in 1873. Nevertheless, interest in Clausewitz among American officers continued to grow very slowly. Clausewitz's writing is difficult, circumlocutory, often apparently self-contradictory, thoroughly Germanic, full of distinctions between "absolute war" as an ideal type and war as an individual process modified by the frictions of reality, and altogether a less satisfactory guide to the practical-minded seeker of strategic precepts than Jomini's work. Near the end of the nineteenth century, Alfred Thayer Mahan's ambition was to become the Jomini of maritime war, not its Clausewitz. But the World War did turn American and British attention to the Prussian military philosopher. American and British digests of Clausewitz appeared during the war. The first edition of *On War* to originate in America did not arrive until the publication of the translation by O. J. Matthijs Jolles of the University of Chicago in 1943. But by 1928, Clausewitz's stature as an oracle had already risen so rapidly and so far in the United States that Lieutenant Colonel O. P. Robinson could write:

... a little research, a little study and reflection brings out the fact that Clausewitz's book on war, published in 1832, occupies about the same relation to the study of the military profession as does the Bible to all religious studies. Most books on strategy for the past one hundred years are in great part a compilation or an attempt to reduce to simpler form and to explain Clausewitz.[34]

Despite his subtleties, the most evident thrust of Clausewitz was to support the kind of strategy of mass and concentration in furtherance of the goal of destroying the enemy army that U. S. Grant had relied on in 1864–65 and both sides had fallen back on in 1914–18. One of the distinctions drawn by Clausewitz was that between "two kinds of war," limited war and war whose object is to overthrow the enemy. Clausewitz argued that after the French Revolutionary and Napoleonic wars had broken the bonds that for some centuries had limited war and in doing so had carried war into the second category and toward its absolute nature, to confine war again within its earlier limitations would be difficult. Modern democratic wars tend to be sustained by powerful popular emotions, and "The greater and the more powerful the motives of a War," Clausewitz said, ". . . by so much the nearer will the War approach to its abstract form. . . ." And in its abstract form, "War is an act of violence pushed to its utmost bounds. . . ." "*War therefore is an act of violence intended to compel our opponent to fulfil our will.*" "In order to attain this object fully, the enemy must be disarmed, and disarmament becomes therefore the immediate object of hostilities in theory."[35]

Now, philanthropists may easily imagine there is a skilful method of disarming and overcoming an enemy without causing great bloodshed, and that this is the proper tendency of the Art of War. However plausible this may appear, still it is an error which must be extirpated; for in such dangerous things as War, the errors which proceed from a spirit of benevolence are the worst.[36]

These dicta pointed to the strategic value of concentration and mass with which to overwhelm the enemy and thus disarm him: "Every combat is therefore the bloody and destructive measuring of the strength of forces, physical and moral; whoever at the close has the greatest amount of both left is the conqueror."[37] To destroy the enemy, it is necessary to fight him:

Let us not hear of Generals who conquer without bloodshed. If bloody slaughter is a horrible sight, then that is a ground for paying more respect to War, but not for making the sword we wear blunter

> and blunter by degrees from feelings of humanity, until someone steps in with one that is sharp and lops off the arm from our body.[38]

Thus Clausewitz directed the military attention back again from diplomacy and economics to the necessity to fight wars in order to win them.

The cast of mind of the American Army in the aftermath of the World War was not conducive to an appreciation of the subtler qualities of Clausewitz at the expense of his striking pronouncements about bloodshed, concentration, and mass. The American military in the 1920s and 1930s was concerned with survival in the face of postwar and depression budgetary stringencies, and the military mood of the period was to value and cling to basic essentials. A much more striking feature of American military thought than the new popularity of quoting from Clausewitz was a tendency quite different from any that a careful reading of Clausewitz would encourage, the habit of attempting to encapsulate the major ideas of all military philosophy in a handful of terse "principles of war." The ideas of Clausewitz as well as those of Jomini were supposed to be among those that the "principles of war" condensed, though Clausewitz's Hegelian reasoning defies condensation and compression.

One military reaction to the prolonged indecisiveness of the War of 1914–18 was characteristic of a bent of thought inherited by the early twentieth century from the nineteenth. Stephen B. Luce had hoped that the Naval War College would become not only a school of strategy but a school of "scientific" strategy; he believed that a proper study of naval history would yield strategic generalizations comparable to the conclusions of the physical sciences.[39] We have seen General Bliss remark that "The paucity of scientific strategical combinations in the military operations of the World War has often been commented upon."[40] The World War, this reasoning ran, had been fought inefficiently and thus inconclusively because it had not been fought "scientifically" enough. The proper application of science to the study of war ought to reveal universally applicable principles of war. American methods of warmaking in particular, military writers had begun to say even before the Great War, were inefficient because the American armed forces lacked unity of doctrine, unity of acceptance of basic military principles. Acceptance of common doctrinal principles throughout the armed forces was essential to coherent strategy and tactics.[41]

In an attempt both to apply "scientific" combinations to war and to make a beginning toward a unified military doctrine, the War Department in 1921 published its first list of the "principles of war," in *War Department Training Regulations No. 10-5* of that year:

a. The Principle of the Objective.
b. The Principle of the Offensive.
c. The Principle of Mass.
d. The Principle of Economy of Force.
e. The Principle of Movement.
f. The Principle of Surprise.
g. The Principle of Security.
h. The Principle of Simplicity.
i. The Principle of Co-operation.

The first list appeared without comment, but lecturers in the military schools offered elaborations of a type that remains familiar in the courses of the schools and in military manuals today. The first of the principles is supposed to remind the military officer that every military operation ought to be directed toward a clearly defined, decisive, and attainable objective. In American commentary on the principles, the ultimate objective has consistently been held to be the destruction of the enemy's armed forces and of his will to fight; every operation and every subsidiary objective ought to contribute to the attainment of the ultimate objective.

The principle of the offensive refers to the traditional dictum of Western military thought that the objective of war is best pursued through offensive action; the offensive is necessary to maintain an army's own freedom of action and to achieve decisive results. The defensive should be adopted only as a temporary expedient, and the commander obliged to take the defensive should seek every opportunity to capture the initiative. Clausewitz, it might be noted, was much more ambivalent about the value of the offensive. While he believed that the defender must usually go over to the offensive to bring war to a satisfactory conclusion, he repeatedly emphasized the advantages of the defensive and called the defensive the strongest form of war.

The principle of mass, sometimes called the "principle of concentration," reasserts the central dictum of Jomini, emphasized also by Clausewitz and necessarily by all strategists, that the strongest part of one's forces must be brought to bear upon the decisive objectives in the theater of war, and in such a manner that one's own strongest forces will encounter only inferior parts of the enemy. Halleck, it will be remembered, defined strategy as "the art of directing masses on decisive points." The principle recalls also the Mahanian dictum of sea power that the fleet must not be divided.

The principle of economy of force, as Colonel W. K. Naylor pointed out in his exposition of the principles at the Army War College soon after their first publication, appears in the writings of the German strategist General Colmar von der Goltz as the "rules for detachments," a phrase which conveys some further idea of its meaning. It refers less to the modern sense of "economy" implying minimum expenditure of resources than to the judicious employment and distribution of force. Still, in time it has been taken to mean that the most discerning use of combat power will permit the commander to accomplish his mission with minimum cost. The principle of mass notwithstanding, combat power is not simply to be hoarded; it must be allocated to accomplish secondary tasks while insuring the presence of enough power at the point of decision.

The principle of movement, today called the "principle of maneuver," is a reminder to the commander of the need for enough flexibility in his force structure and his designs to permit maneuvers that will place the enemy at a relative disadvantage and thus achieve results that would otherwise be costly.

Surprise, the commander is to be reminded, can bring success out of proportion to the effort expended and may shift the balance of combat power decisively.

Security is necessary to prevent being surprised and to preserve freedom of action.

Simplicity minimizes confusion and misunderstanding; other things being equal, the simplest plan is held to be the best plan.

The principle of cooperation has now come to be called the "principle of unity of command," which suggests the theme. Decisive application of combat power demands at least cooperation among the relevant commanders; since World War II, when the American armed forces came to accept unified interservice area and tactical commands, decisive application of combat power can be said to demand unity of command, which is better.[42]

The principles of war tended during the 1920s, and still do today, to receive inordinate attention. Amid the harsh pressures of war and combat it is surely helpful to have at hand such straightforward guides to conduct, but the principles are so straightforwardly simple and general that they can lead astray almost as easily as they can assist. It might be better to pay proportionately less attention to the principles and more to the warnings about rules included in a handbook on *Infantry in Battle* based on studies of World War experiences and first prepared under the direction of Colonel George C. Marshall:

> The art of war has no traffic with rules, for the infinitely varied circumstances and conditions of combat never produce exactly the same situation twice. . . .
>
> It follows, then, that the leader who would become a competent tactician must first close his mind to the alluring formulæ that well-meaning people offer in the name of victory. To master his difficult art he must learn to cut to the heart of a situation, recognize its decisive elements and base his course of action on these. The ability to do this is not God-given, nor can it be acquired overnight; it is a process of years. He must realize that training in solving problems of all types, long practice in making clear, unequivocal decisions, the habit of concentrating on the question at hand, and an elasticity of mind, are indispensable requisites for the successful practice of the art of war.
>
> The leader who frantically strives to remember what someone else did in some slightly similar situation has already set his feet on a well-traveled road to ruin.
>
> . . . Every situation encountered in war is likely to be exceptional. The schematic solution will seldom fit. Leaders who think that familiarity with blind rules of thumb will win battles are doomed to disappointment. Those who seek to fight by rote, who memorize an assortment of standard solutions with the idea of applying the most appropriate when confronted by actual combat, walk with disaster. Rather, is it essential that all leaders—from subaltern to commanding general—familiarize themselves with the art of clear, logical thinking. It is more valuable to be able to analyse one battle situation correctly, recognize its decisive elements and devise a simple, workable solution for it, than to memorize all the erudition ever written of war.[43]

In the effort to digest the military experience of the World War, and to try to find means of avoiding its "paucity of scientific strategical combinations" for the future, it is perhaps surprising that the most motorized society in the world contributed little to the theories and experimentation which looked to restoring decisiveness to land war through the application of the internal combustion engine.

The tank could excel the foot soldier in its armor protection, in the weight of the weapons it could carry, and in its mobility. When tanks made their slow and grudgingly accepted appearance on the battlefields of the World War, it was the first of these three qualities that received the armies' principal attention. In the deadlock which rifled weapons and the machine gun imposed on the Western Front, soldiers usually saw the tank's armor as its most valuable feature. Its potential gun power was neglected, the British often arming even their heavy tanks only with machine guns rather than cannon; the tank's speed was still slight. The tank was employed mainly as a heavily armored mobile fortress, to rumble through the enemy's barbed wire and machine-gun nests in the hope of making a path for the infantry and, the generals continued to hope, for eventual exploitation by horse cavalry.

As the number of tanks available increased and soldiers gave more thought to the devising of a doctrine for their most effective employment, some officers considered making greater use of the tank's potential in weapons power and mobility, especially the latter. With greater speed and endurance, tanks themselves might assume the task of exploitation which horse cavalry proved no longer able to manage. They should no longer be held in virtual lockstep with the infantry, as they were on the Western Front. Using heavier weapons of their own as well as their armor protection, they could break through the enemy's defenses; with sufficient mobility through speed and endurance, they could push on to the sensitive headquarters, communications, and supply depots in the enemy's rear and restore decision to war. Such ideas were developed most fully by Colonel J. F. C. Fuller, chief of staff of the Tank Corps which the British army created in 1917. Fuller's plan for 1919 contemplated the use of 5,000 Allied tanks for both breakthrough and exploitation.[44]

In 1918 the United States Army also established a Tank Corps, and for a time it appeared that the corps would develop ideas similar to Fuller's. Speaking to a General Staff College audience in 1919, its commander, Brigadier General S. D. Rockenbach, argued that the United States was more likely than its Allies to realize the full potential of the tank:

> 1. All that is claimed for the Tank Corps is that it is not fettered by English ideas in operation which are applicable only by the English or by their clumsiness in design; nor by French low mechanical knowledge which makes the self-starter too complicated and unreliable to be employed; nor by our own abnormal use of Tanks with the First American Army [in driblets and in close infantry support]. It has resisted entangling alliances and to date is not Infantry, Artillery, Motor Transport, Engineers or even Aviation, notwithstanding its great value to each of these services, causing deep thought as to which of them it should be.
>
> . . .

2. Ludendorff's ignorance of Tanks caused the death of many German soldiers and the stampede of many more. [But] He is correct in stating that Tanks should be used in masses or not at all. . . [45]

The possibilities for such American development somehow failed to survive the dissolution of Rockenbach's Tank Corps under the National Defense Act of 1920 and the assignment of the tanks to the infantry. Here the tanks continued to be regarded as moving fortresses tied to the pace of infantry advance. The dependence of the Army on slow-moving tanks inherited from the Great War until 1930, except for a few experimental prototypes, encouraged a restricted view of tank utility. "A tank is a mobile armored attack unit, designed to assist the advance of the infantry and the tank service is a branch of the infantry": this became the basic American tank doctrine.[46]

It remained for the British strategic writers Fuller and B. H. Liddell Hart to develop Fuller's 1919 plan into a theory of mechanized land war in which mobility gained by tanks and by motorized infantry and artillery, integrated in a new mobile force, was to overcome the battlefield deadlock. It remained for the Germans led by Heinz Guderian to put Fuller's and Liddell Hart's ideas into practice in the Panzer divisions and to improve upon the ideas by adding to the British strategists' emphasis on mobility Guderian's concern for the gun power of the armored forces and a marriage of armored forces to tactical air power developed as an immensely mobile form of artillery.

In 1927 Secretary of War Dwight F. Davis visited England and witnessed maneuvers of the Experimental Mechanised Force at Aldershot, where some of Fuller's theories were being tried out. Davis was impressed enough that he asked the American General Staff to undertake similar experiments, and in 1928, consequently, there were assembled at Camp Meade, Maryland, two tank battalions, a platoon from another tank company, the Army's only motorized cavalry troop, a battalion of infantry, a battalion of artillery, a company of engineers, a signal company, a medical detachment, an ammunition train, and a squadron of observation planes, to form the American experimental mechanized force. The available tanks, British-type Mark VIII heavies and M1917 American versions of the French Renault F. T., were too cumbersome to be suitable for experiments in armored mobility, and after three months the mechanized force disbanded.

The experiment was fortunate in its commanding officer, however, for Major Adna Romanza Chaffee perceived some of the possibilities of armored mobile warfare, and he did what he could to revive the experiment. A second mechanized force was assembled at Fort Eustis, Virginia, in 1930. That year General Douglas MacArthur became Chief of Staff of the Army, and for armored, mechanized developments his accession was a mixed blessing. Certainly he did not accept Fuller's and Liddell Hart's ideas. In his first annual report he said:

> There have been two theories advanced to govern the application of mechanization. . . . The first is that a separate mechanized force should be so organized as to contain within itself the power of carrying on a complete action, from first contact to final victory, thus duplicating the missions and to some extent the equipment of all other arms. The other theory is that each of the older arms should utilize any types of these vehicles as will enable it better and more surely to carry out the particular combat tasks it has been traditionally assigned. . . . In the initial enthusiasm of postwar thought the first method was considered as the ideal one. . . . Continued study and experimentation have since resulted in its virtual abandonment. . . . Accordingly during the last year the independent "mechanized force" at Fort Eustis has been broken up. The cavalry has been given the task of developing combat vehicles that will enhance its powers in roles of reconnaissance, counter-reconnaissance, flank action, pursuit and similar operations. One of its regiments will be equipped exclusively with such vehicles. The infantry will give attention to machines intended to increase the striking power of the infantry against strongly held positions.[47]

While this statement ruled out the appearance of an American Guderian while MacArthur commanded the Army, what made MacArthur's impact on mechanization mixed was his encouragement of more use of the internal combustion engine by the cavalry. In 1931 part of the Fort Eustis force was reorganized at Fort Knox, Kentucky, as a mechanized cavalry unit, and two years later this unit was amalgamated into the 1st Cavalry Regiment to form the 1st Cavalry Regiment, Mechanized. This regiment in turn became the nucleus of the 7th Cavalry Brigade, Mechanized, of which Chaffee was the executive officer and later commanding officer. The mechanized cavalry organizations received tanks, called "combat cars" at first to evade the regulation assigning tanks to infantry. With MacArthur's encouragement and Chaffee as guiding spirit the mechanized cavalry left well behind them the World War notions which had restricted tank motion to the speed of infantry. American mechanized cavalry began to prepare the American Army to exploit mechanized forces' potential for mobility and for ranging widely behind the enemy's lines among his headquarters and communications. During the 1930s the Army also began to develop new tanks, with an emphasis on speed consistent with the mechanized cavalry developments and accounting for the interest in the fast tanks of the eccentric engineer J. Walter Christie, until Christie was given up as impossible to work with. To range widely, tanks also had to be mechanically reliable, and the models developed during the thirties prepared the way for the American tanks of World War II whose reliability was their outstanding feature. With the most energetic American tank development taking place in the cavalry, however, American tanks sought mobility rather than heavily weaponed fighting power, and the beginning of the next war was to find them too light and too lightly armed to stand up to the best German tanks.[48]

Perhaps part of the explanation for the absence of an American Fuller, Liddell Hart, or Guderian after the World War is that, despite some worrying about the futility of warfare on the Western Front, the brief American participation in the war, with no Verdun or Passchendaele, did not provide so much inducement to American soldiers as to British or German to look for ways to avoid repetition of the deadlock in the trenches. Fuller and Liddell Hart proposed to restore decisiveness without excessive cost by using mechanized mobility to reintroduce maneuver. Liddell Hart especially urged a return to maneuver because he saw the acme of strategy as the "indirect approach," which had been disastrously abandoned in 1914–18. With mechanized mobility, maneuver and the indirect approach could reappear; armies need not expend themselves in frontal assaults against the enemy's strongest defenses, but with mobile columns could maneuver against his vulnerable rear areas. By this method the enemy would be forced to fight on terms disadvantageous to him; blows against his headquarters would dislocate him psychologically as well as physically; and the indirect approach to victory could be taken by relatively small, well-trained mechanized groups which would eliminate the necessity for mass armies and mass slaughter. Liddell Hart proposed abandonment of the conscript army for a smaller, highly trained, well-paid professional army, highly mobile, whose "Armoured Force might achieve the ideal which was the ambition of Marshal Saxe, that connoisseur of the art of war, when he argued that a really able general might win a campaign without fighting a battle at all."[49]

The American Army, less battered by the World War and with deeper reserves of manpower than the British, doubted such prophecies of victory to be achieved with small mechanized armies perhaps without battle at all. In his exposition of the principles of war at the Army War College in 1922, as in his text *Principles of Strategy* published by the General Service Schools Press, Colonel Naylor reaffirmed the Grantian convictions that the objective of warfare is the destruction of the enemy's armed forces, and that this objective can be attained only by fighting. A War College student, Naylor said, had recently suggested substituting a different first principle: "Decide on practicable vital areas, choose the one which offers greatest promise of successful penetration, and then throw all your offensive strength against that area." Naylor rejected the suggestion; the idea of substituting presumably vital areas for armies as the first objective, he said, was one of the mistakes that had undone the French in 1870, while the Germans had concentrated upon the destruction of the French army. In the third Serbian campaign of the Great War, moreover, August von Mackensen had overrun Serbia itself—surely an apparently vital area for the Serbians—but had failed to destroy thereby the Serbian army.

> I wish to stress this point [Colonel Naylor went on]; that warfare means fighting, and that war is never won by maneuvering, not unless that maneuvering is carried out with the idea of culminating in battle. . . .
>
> Disabuse your mind of the idea that you can place an army in a district so vital to the enemy that he will say "What's the use" and sue for peace. History shows that the surest way to take the fighting spirit out of a country is to defeat its main army. All other means calculated to bring the enemy to his knees are contributory to the main proposition, which is now, as it has ever been, namely; the defeat of his main forces.[50]

Of the two classical types of strategy Naylor said:

> The controversy between strategy of attrition and the strategy of annihilation is of long standing. . . . The great generals of history were not per se proponents of the strategy of attrition or of the strategy of annihilation, did not belong to one or the other school of thought, but acted, if they were real generals, according to circumstances. They always endeavored to encompass the annihilation of the enemy, if their available forces sufficed therefor.[51]

Colonel Naylor's strategic precepts remained those of the American Army. On the eve of the next war, FM 100-5, the *Field Service Regulations (Tentative), Operations, 1939*, reiterated as the Army's doctrine that "The *ultimate objective* of all military operations is the destruction of the enemy's armed forces in battle. Decisive defeat breaks the enemy's will to war and forces him to sue for peace which is the national aim." Commenting on this affirmation, Captain Reuben E. Jenkins of the First Section, Command and General Staff School, wrote in the *Military Review*:

> It should be remembered that the price of victory is hard fighting and that no matter what maneuver is employed, ultimately the fighting is frontal. The whole art in defense is to make the attacker expend himself in frontal attacks. . . .
>
> And finally, although "An objective may sometimes be attained through maneuver alone; ordinarily, it must be gained through battle" (Par 413 [of FM 100-5]). Blood is the price of victory. One must accept the formula or not wage war.[52]

In another great war, American strategic doctrine would require another great army of the 1917–18 type. The General Staff mobilization plans which followed the World War emphasized the manpower requirements of a mass army as much as the economic requirements of another world war. Around the question of meeting the manpower requirements there broke out again within the Army an old argument between the followers of Emory Upton, who wanted the largest possible cadre of professional soldiers in skeletonized regiments into which wartime recruits could be absorbed, and the champions of the citizen soldier, who preferred that the Regular Army be a compact force in readiness while citizen soldiers should receive peacetime training to prepare for the rapid mobilization of new fighting units in war. The plan presented by the wartime Chief of Staff of the Army, General Peyton C. March, for the postwar national defense bill was Uptonian; but the National Defense Act of 1920 as finally written reflected rather Major John McAuley Palmer's ideas for a citizen army.

Palmer continued through the 1920s and 1930s as an articulate champion of a "democratic" army of citizen soldiers with citizen-soldier officers in National Guard and Reserve formations, while the War Department diluted Palmer's intentions as written into the National Defense Act and turned the small Regular Army (usually of less than 150,000) into a set of skeletonized formations which might be expanded in Uptonian fashion. Both Palmer and the Uptonians, however, by their different routes pursued the goal of preparation for a massive wartime army, with enough men to confront and destroy in head-on combat the army of a major European land power. The General Staff mobilization plans, for their part, came by the 1930s to envisage an Instant Readiness Force or Protective Mobilization Force of Regulars and National Guards large enough and ready enough to serve as a shield behind which mass conscript armies could form. A Selective Service Branch in the new G-1 (Personnel) Division of the War Department General Staff kept a conscription plan up to date.[53]

The economic and manpower mobilization plans looked to a repetition of the war of 1917–18; so did the organizational details of mobilization planning, with the same strategic assumptions. The United States Army was expected to concentrate the bulk of its forces in a single theater to collide with the main mass of the enemy and overwhelm him. Under plans developed when General Pershing was Chief of Staff of the Army just after the World War and revised during General MacArthur's tenure in the thirties, mobilization for war was to coincide with the establishment of an Army operational general headquarters on the model of Pershing's GHQ, American Expeditionary Force. The Chief of Staff of the Army would then assume Pershing's place as Commanding General, Field Forces, and the War Department General Staff would provide the nucleus of the Field Forces staff. The implication was that again as in 1917–18, the commander in the field and his GHQ would overshadow the headquarters remaining in Washington, and that field command would be concentrated in a single theater of war for the massing of the Army there to overwhelm a continental adversary. Despite the horrors of the Western Front, the United States Army believed it must face up to the prospect of a repetition of a face-to-face grappling of armies, as the only sure means of destroying the enemy army and winning victory.[54]

11. A Strategy of Air Power: Billy Mitchell

The advent of air power, which can go straight to the vital centers and either neutralize or destroy them, has put a completely new complexion on the old system of making war. It is now realized that the hostile main army in the field is a false objective, and the real objectives are the vital centers.

—*William Mitchell*[1]

EVEN IN AMERICA, whose sufferings had been light, the prophets of air power could hardly have failed to rise from the ashes of the Great War. Years before the war, man's first ascents from the ground in flimsy boxes of wood and canvas—nay, the first balloon ascensions and before them the oldest dreams of taking flight—had stirred visions of wars hurried to swift conclusions when a few armed men in the sky would paralyze whole armies, cities, and peoples on the ground below. For a hundred years between Waterloo and the Argonne, men dreamed of flight with quickening hopes and then at last took wing, while through the same span of time warfare on the surface of the earth lost the attribute which had made it endurable, its capacity to produce decisions at a tolerable cost. In 1815, military decisions of surgical swiftness and completeness could still be hoped for from a single battle. By 1918, rifles and machine guns had reduced to futility a hope like Schlieffen's for a Cannae victory; and the most likely optional road to victory on land, a U. S. Grant kind of campaign for the destruction of the enemy army, had to seem repelling even in fortunate America, if not to hardened officers of the ground forces who could see no alternative, then nevertheless to prospective citizen soldiers and their families. For officers of the new

Army Air Service seeking freedom from the preconceptions of the ground soldiers, self-interest seemed to converge with humanity in the search for an alternative to the brutal futility of the Western Front by turning to the air.

Against a continental adversary such as Germany, Mahanian sea power had not worked satisfactorily either, at least not well enough to produce decisive results within an acceptable length of time. On the ground, of some 65,000,000 men mobilized into all the armies which fought the Great War, almost 9,000,000 died and 22,000,000 were wounded in battle.[2]

> One flight over the lines gave me a much clearer impression [said Brigadier General William Mitchell of the American Army Air Service] of how the armies were laid out than any amount of traveling around on the ground. A very significant thing to me was that we could cross the lines of these contending armies in a few minutes in our airplane, whereas the armies had been locked in the struggle, immovable, powerless to advance, for three years. . . . It was as though they kept knocking their heads against a stone wall, until their brains were dashed out. They got nowhere, as far as ending the war was concerned.
>
> It looked as though the war would keep up indefinitely until either the airplanes brought an end to the war or the contending nations dropped from sheer exhaustion.[3]

The airplane did not develop rapidly enough or appear in numbers enough to put an end to the war before the Germans' exhaustion did so, but its technological and tactical advancement was rapid enough to encourage such thinking. At St. Mihiel, Mitchell himself, commanding the First Army Air Service, led the largest aggregation of air strength assembled for any operation of the war, an impressive foreshadowing of still greater possibilities: twelve pursuit, three day bombardment, ten observation, and one night reconnaissance squadrons from the American Army Air Service; forty-six pursuit and day bombardment, two night bombardment, and twelve observation squadrons from the French; eight British and two Italian night bombardment squadrons, altogether including 701 pursuit, 323 day bombardment, 91 night bombardment, and 366 observation aircraft. This force effectively harassed the enemy, attacked his communications and line of retreat, and tactically supported the American ground advance. For the next year, had the war continued, Mitchell planned parachute drops behind the German lines, envisioning 1,200 Handley-Page bombers carrying a division of troops.[4]

Often seeming still more fascinating were the possibilities opened by the airplane for the Sherman strategy of carrying war to the enemy's economy and people. During the war the Germans conducted about a hundred air raids against England, first mainly with dirigibles but then increasingly with less vulnerable heavier-than-air craft. They cut deeply into the output of some factories, killed about 1,400 people, and injured over 3,000.[5] The British responded by preparing for still more severe air attacks against Germany, developing the four-engine Handley-Page bomber, which was the structural prototype of the heavy bombers of World War II. British raids were principally against military targets not far behind the German lines, but for 1919 they planned a bombing campaign across Germany to Berlin. F. W. Lanchester, a mathematician, and General Sir David Henderson, commander of the Royal Flying Corps, had moved toward a conception of aerial bombardment as an independently decisive weapon of war. Henderson advanced this idea to Jan Christiaan Smuts, the active head of a commission studying the question whether the air service should be separated from the traditional armed forces, and Smuts accepted both Henderson's concept and the desirability of air service independence:

> Air service on the contrary can be used as an independent means of war operations. Nobody that witnessed the attack on London on 11th July [1917] could have any doubt on that point. Unlike artillery an air fleet can conduct extensive operations far from, and independently of, both Army and Navy. As far as can at present be foreseen there is absolutely no limit to the scale of its future independent war use. And the day may not be far off when aerial operations with their devastation of enemy lands and destruction of industrial and populous centres on a vast scale may become the principal operations of war, to which the older forms of military and naval operations may become secondary and subordinate.[6]

Early in the war General Mitchell met General Hugh Trenchard, then commander of Royal Flying Corps units in France, and at St. Mihiel he had the cooperation of Trenchard's new command, the Independent Bombing Force of the recently established—separate from the old services—Royal Air Force. It is uncertain how much Mitchell was impressed by any acquaintance with the concept of air power as a weapon of independent decision gleaned from Trenchard or other British sources, especially because in 1918 Trenchard was somewhere in transition from advocacy of tactical bombing in support of the battlefield to the championship of independent air power, which was to distinguish him as Chief of Air Staff from 1919 to 1929.[7]

Mitchell also conducted a correspondence with Gianni Caproni, the Italian designer of bombing aircraft, and through Caproni and other acquaintances in Italy or who traveled there he surely obtained some awareness of the air power theories of Caproni's friend and countryman Giulio Douhet. Douhet was in prison at the time of American entry into the war, after having been court-martialed for his criticism of the Italian government's war policies. His criticism was based on a theory of air operations which reached well beyond Trenchard's current thinking in its confidence that air power was about to become the supreme weapon of war. Douhet was also in advance of anything Mitchell was to say publicly for some years to come, and the extent of his and Caproni's influence on Mitchell, too, is uncertain.[8]

Whatever Mitchell might have learned of Douhet's theories during the war would already have anticipated Douhet's book entitled "The Command of the Air": *Il Dominio dell' Aria: saggio sul' arte della guerra aerea*, published in 1921 after Douhet had been released from jail, rehabilitated by appointment as head of Italy's Central Aeronautical Bureau, and seen his court-martial record expunged. Douhet argued that air power ought to be used to carry war beyond the enemy's armed forces to the "vital centers" of the enemy's country, not simply the military installations behind the lines, but the industries and the cities. Under the destruction and terror of bombardment from the air, he believed, the morale and the will to war among an enemy people could not survive. Then the enemy armed forces would collapse without the necessity to fight a single land or sea battle. Decisiveness would return to war, swiftly and surely.

The instrument of air attack upon the enemy's vital centers should be a fleet of attack aircraft so designed that every plane would be capable of performing all the functions of military aviation, but would be especially suitable to attack bombing. No effort should be expended on the design and production of pursuit or fighter aircraft intended for the interception of the enemy's attackers, because with air power the initiative and the choice of time and place of attack and route of approach gave a strong attacking force so great an advantage over any defending aircraft that the attack could not be prevented or interrupted. Escort fighters to guard the attack aircraft might be useful, but Douhet did not think they were essential. Antiaircraft artillery was as futile as defensive fighter planes in the effort to turn back the enemy's attackers. The attacking force would always get through to its target. The only defense against an enemy's attacking air force was a stronger attacking air force. Only with such a force could a nation gain command of the air and with that go on to win the war by destroying the enemy's factories and morale in his vital centers.[9]

Douhet's belief that the attackers would always get through had some foundation in the experiences of the World War, in the disappointing performance of early and improvised antiaircraft artillery and in the difficulties of intercepting an approaching enemy air strike without radar. But his theories grew less from experience than from the dreams of a visionary appalled by the futility of ground warfare and impatient with practical obstacles to the fulfillment of his own design. In these latter qualities of Douhet, Mitchell was a kindred spirit. Like Douhet, Mitchell had the temperament of an enthusiast, so much so that the extravagances of his enthusiasm eventually injured his propagation of the cause he adopted. But unlike Douhet, Mitchell at least for some years confined his extravagances mainly to the zeal of manner and the excesses of language with which he came to publicize his ideas about war in the air. He kept the substance of his ideas more closely tied than did Douhet to the technological realities of aviation and to the specific military problems confronting his country.

As Mitchell developed his own thoughts about the uses of air power, for example, he did not share Douhet's conviction that against attacking aircraft no defense is possible. He did, like Douhet, undervalue antiaircraft artillery, both on land and in naval war; but he believed a strong force of good pursuit planes combined with adequate reconnaissance patrolling might successfully intercept and substantially blunt a bombing attack. Therefore he did not believe that all military aircraft should be multipurpose attack planes. He urged the development of specialized pursuit planes and of a variety of bomber types for various missions, including dive bombers as well as heavy bombers of the Handley-Page type and low-level attack planes. His efforts after the return of peace to improve the design of American planes contributed to the transformation of the fabric-covered, fixed-landing-gear, multistrutted biplane of World War I into metal-covered, retractable-landing-gear, cantilever-wing monoplane prototypes of the warplanes of World War II.[10]

After the Armistice, Mitchell's thinking about the future of the military airplane focused specifically on problems of the defense of the United States. Thus he turned his attention to the perennial question of how to guard the American coastline against attack from the sea. The proper defense for the future, he decided, was the airplane. To demonstrate the truth of his proposition he fought his way past a multitude of obstacles, thrown up both by his own service and by the Navy, to stage the famous Air Service bombing attacks against former German warships off the Virginia Capes in 1921. He began with the sinking of a submarine by Air Service bombs and progressed through successful bombings of a destroyer and a cruiser to the destruction of the "unsinkable" battleship *Ostfriesland*. He continued his demonstrations with bombing attacks on the obsolete battleship *Alabama* and in 1923 on *Virginia* and *New Jersey*, amid increasing efforts by a disconcerted Navy to muddy and conceal the significance of the results he obtained. He did his work with a growing self-confidence and brash flamboyance, ignoring his superior officers' acceptance of restrictions which might have hampered his display of air power and giving short shrift to the possibilities that antiaircraft artillery and other defensive capacities of an active fleet might in real war have detracted from the effectiveness of his aerial attacks. With more than a little reason, he evidently concluded that the Navy's obfuscation of his accomplishments justified his own oversimplifications.

The conclusion to be drawn from his aerial sinkings of battleships, he said, was that the defense of the coast should be entrusted primarily to the Air Service. Furthermore, the coastal defense of the United States was impeded by a faulty organization which divided responsibilities among land, sea, and air forces; the organization itself must be improved, preferably through the creation of a unified department of defense bringing together all the services. The basic fact hereafter shaping coastal defense was that "Aircraft now in existence can find and destroy all classes of seacraft under war conditions with a negligible loss."[11]

Because other nations would recognize this fact, the principal threat to the defense of the United States would no longer come from hostile navies but from hostile air forces. "The problem of the destruction of seacraft by air forces has been solved and is finished. It is now necessary to provide an air organization and a method of defending not only our coast cities but our interior cities against the attack of hostile air forces."[12]

These developments, said Mitchell, also had obvious and important implications for the defense of America's overseas possessions. If airplanes could nullify the offensive power of foreign navies approaching American shores, foreign planes could do the same thing to American ships. The American Navy could no longer be the principal means for the projection of American military power overseas and therefore for the defense of the insular possessions. These circumstances were especially disturbing because Mitchell came to believe, like many Americans after the defeat of Germany, that the most likely enemy in a next war would be Japan. Against Japan, the vulnerability of sea power to air attack gravely weakened the American strategic position in the Pacific Ocean. Already the Philippines and Guam, and to a degree even Hawaii, had been dangerously exposed to Japanese naval power. Now the most distant possessions, the Philippines and Guam, became more than ever vulnerable, because they lay under the threat of Japanese air power based near the heart of the Japanese Empire. The difficulties of defending Hawaii also became compounded. Mitchell did not believe that airplanes based on ships—on the aircraft carriers newly developed late in the war and just afterward—would ever be able to compete on equal terms with land-based aircraft; too many limitations had to be built into planes to permit their taking off and landing within the restricted space of a ship's deck. Any American naval expedition across the Pacific to go to the defense of the Philippines or to attack Japan would henceforth have to sail into the teeth of Japan's land-based air power. It would be extremely difficult hereafter to defend the Philippines; to carry offensive war to Japan would be worse.[13]

Mitchell wavered in his estimates of the potential of the aircraft carrier. Great Britain had developed the first ones, and the United States followed suit by converting the collier *Jupiter* and commissioning it as the carrier *Langley* in 1922. On the one hand, Mitchell saw the carrier's planes as sharing in the ability of land-based aircraft to conquer ships: "Aircraft acting from suitable floating airdromes can destroy any class of surface sea craft on the high seas."[14] On the other hand, the carrier itself would be more vulnerable to enemy air attack than the battleship. The United States Navy would be well advised to transfer some of its enthusiasm for battleships to carriers. Nevertheless, to Mitchell the basic condition remained the inherent inability of carrier planes, with the extra weight of equipment for shipboard take-off and landing, to match the speed and maneuverability of land-based aircraft. He did not feel much confidence in the carrier as a vehicle for projecting American offensive power toward Japan.[15]

The principal hope for the protection of American possessions and interests in the Pacific seemed to him to lie in Alaska. If bases to support land-based aircraft could be developed there, then long-range bombers from Alaska should be able to threaten both Japanese sea power in the northern and central Pacific and, more important, the Japanese home islands themselves. With this threat, the United States should be able to deter Japan from attacking the Philippines, Guam, and Hawaii. An early tour of duty in Alaska had convinced Mitchell of the strategic importance of this territory long before he acquired his interest in air power: Alaska, after all, was the meeting place of the Japanese, Russian, and American spheres of power. With the coming of aviation, Mitchell believed, man's general conception of geography would be changed by the development of the northern "great circle" routes between the continents; and the great circle routes enhanced Alaska's strategic importance by placing it directly between the centers of Japanese and American industrial and military power.[16]

Alaska in the early 1920's was further from development as a major base for air power than the bombing planes of the day were from the radii of striking power which Mitchell anticipated; thus Mitchell saw the United States as abysmally open to military attack in the Pacific. In the autumn and winter of 1923–24 he was able to combine a wedding trip following his second marriage with a trans-Pacific tour to Hawaii, Guam, the Philippines, Japan, China, India, Java, and Singapore. As far as China, the trip was an official inspection tour; from there on, Mitchell traveled at his own expense, but he reported on the military problems of the whole area in a 323-page document. He found the Japanese alarmingly interested in air power and active in its development; he estimated, perhaps rightly, that Japanese military air strength ranked second in the world. In contrast, he found military aviation almost nonexistent in the American possessions. The American Army and Navy commanders in the Pacific possessions seemed to him ignorant of how weak they were and indifferent to the air power problem. He predicted that one day Japan would go to war against the United States for supremacy in the Pacific. She would begin the war, he believed, with a surprise strike just after dawn some morning by carrier-based airplanes against Pearl Harbor, Schofield Barracks, and the related American aviation facilities.[17]

So menacing did he find the attitudes and activities of Japan that Mitchell returned from his Far Eastern tour with a new sense of urgency, that he must convince America to recognize an enormous peril in Japanese air power in the Pacific and to accelerate enormously the growth of American military aviation in response. His urgency encountered little but frustration. During the administration of President Warren G. Harding, the highest echelons of the executive branch of government had been sympathetic enough to permit Mitchell's bombing demonstrations against warships in 1921 and 1923 despite the misgivings of the Navy. But the administration of Calvin Coolidge was willing to give Mitchell practically no hearing at all. With the Coolidge administration, cutting the federal budget became almost an obsession, and the President established an attitude of opposition to possibly expensive innovation which permeated all the executive departments. After Mitchell completed his report on the Pacific and the Far East in October, 1924, the report was buried in the War Department and ignored.[18]

Mitchell's was not a temperament to tolerate being ignored, most especially when he felt sure that his neglected message was one on which the whole future of his country might depend. Furthermore, he found indifference to his report matched by indifference to the physical condition of the Air Service. Development of new planes and equipment seemed to be barely crawling; maintenance of old equipment was not adequate to keep the planes safe. Since the end of the war, Mitchell had been second in command of the Army Air Service; but when his complaints about the neglect of aviation made him increasingly a nuisance to the Coolidge administration, he was exiled to the position of air officer at Fort Sam Houston, Texas. There he had little to do and no direct means of effecting reforms.

Apparently he decided that on the first suitable public occasion he would speak out for military aviation in such a way that the government and the public would have to hear him. Within a few days in early September, 1925, three Navy seaplanes failed in an attempted flight from California to Hawaii, one of them with its crew disappearing for a time in the Pacific, and the Navy dirigible *Shenandoah* crashed near Cambridge, Ohio, killing thirteen out of a crew of forty-two. Here was Mitchell's public occasion. On September 5 he gave a statement to the press reading:

> I have been asked from all parts of the country to give an opinion about the reasons for the frightful disasters that have occurred during the last few days.
>
> My opinion is as follows: These accidents are the result of the in-

> competency, the criminal negligence, and the almost treasonable administration of our national defense by the Navy and War Departments.[19]

Thereupon and inevitably, Mitchell was charged before a court-martial under the 96th Article of War with "disorders and neglects to the prejudice of good order and military discipline, . . . conduct of a nature to bring discredit upon the military service." Almost as inevitably, the court convicted him. It sentenced him to suspension from rank, command, and duty with forfeiture of all pay and allowances for five years. His response was to resign from the service, as of February 1, 1926. He had used his trial as much as possible as a forum for publicizing his views on air power, an opportunity which naturally he welcomed; but apparently he did not welcome the martyrdom which came to him, nor wholly foresee that the intemperance of his statement about the Navy's Pacific flight and the *Shenandoah* disaster would lead to it. There was in him a curious mixture of extravagance and caution; not only did his extravagance thus far lie less in the substance of his beliefs than in his manner and language, but it was a quality of which he seems to have been not altogether aware, so that while he intended to arouse people, he was also surprised by the extent to which a statement such as the one about "almost treasonable administration" angered and upset them.[20]

The admixture of caution in Mitchell's attitudes and statements up to and through his court-martial appears especially in his emphasis on the special formidability of air power against ships, navies, and sea communications. This emphasis was cautious in an expedient sort of way; it was safer for Mitchell himself to attack the deficiencies of the Navy in the dawning air age than to emphasize deficiencies in the Army, his own branch of service whose commanders had much more direct power over him than did Navy officers. But emphasis on the vulnerability of sea power to aerial attack was also cautious, and realistic as well, in a more substantive sense. Although Mitchell underestimated the worth both of antiaircraft artillery on warships and of carrier-based airplanes, naval vessels were indeed more vulnerable to aerial attack than were land armies, and lines of communication at sea were more vulnerable than communications on land. No land army could be crippled from the air as quickly as the bombing of a few battleships might in fact cripple a navy. No line of communication on land could be interrupted with the completeness with which command of the air could interdict sea lanes to all but the most heavily defended warships. These things being true, Mitchell perceived aright many of the strategic problems which aviation created for the United States in the Pacific.

It was not only his prophecy about the attack with which Japan would begin the next war that proved correct, both in details of time and geography and in the fact that the battle line of the United States Pacific Fleet was knocked out by a single blow from the air. His larger assessment of the impact of air power upon American defensive or offensive action in the Pacific was also essentially right. In World War II, command of the air did prove to be the most critical element in every Pacific campaign. No defense of an island position could survive without it. Unlike continental land war, where some supplies could reach the defenders of an area despite enemy control of the air, without air power the defenders of an island position could be cut off from assistance with virtual completeness. Similarly, no offensive movement could be made by the battle fleets without the cover of air power. Only in his underestimation of the aircraft carrier did Mitchell notably miss the mark. Alaska did not figure so prominently in Japanese-American war as he predicted, but while favoring the Alaskan great circle route from which to strike Japan, Mitchell conceded that a southern island-to-island route would be feasible—provided with adequate air cover.[21]

After his court-martial and resignation from the Army, however, Mitchell's predictions about the future of air power veered closer to Douhet's "command of the air" doctrines and became progressively inflated and less realistic. Whether he had harbored all along more extravagant ideas than he had previously thought it wise to voice, whether day-to-day acquaintance with the Air Service had kept a rein upon his imagination, whether bitterness now tempted him into fantasy, his motives and the evolution of his thinking are not clear. But immediately after the Army accepted his resignation, *Liberty* magazine appeared with an article in which Mitchell took up Douhet's "vital centers" theme. He now argued that future wars would be won by air power alone, through bombing campaigns reaching over the enemy's armies and navies to his vital centers of production and population, paralyzing the vital centers, making productive activity in them impossible, and destroying the enemy people's will to resist.[22]

Until his death in 1936, Mitchell continued to develop this new and wider argument for air power in magazine articles and in books published or projected: in a spate of articles during the first few years after his trial, while public interest in his case was still fresh; in less frequent articles during the 1930s; in *Skyways*, published in 1930; and in a memoir, "From Start to Finish of Our Greatest War," which reached publication only in 1960 long after his death.[23]

> The advent of air power [Mitchell now said], which can go straight to the vital centers and either neutralize of destroy them, has put a completely new complexion on the old system of making war. It is now realized that the hostile main army in the field is a false objective, and the real objectives are the vital centers. . . . The result of warfare by air will be to bring about quick decisions. Superior air power will cause such havoc or the threat of such havoc in the opposing country that a long-drawn-out campaign will be impossible.

> No nations ever want war; they do not resort to war unless all other means of attaining their ends have been exhausted. War itself is a continuance by physical means of an altercation between nations, and its object is to impress one's will upon the enemy. This can only be done by seizing, controlling or paralyzing his vital centers, that is, his great cities and the sources of raw materials, his manufactories, his food, his products, his means of transportation and his railway and steamship lines.
>
> The old theory, which has been followed for centuries, has been to protect these vital centers against the enemy by covering them with the flesh and blood of the people, putting out in front of them what we call armies. So it was supposed heretofore that in order to obtain victory, this hostile army had to be destroyed, so as to open an avenue to the vital centers. In times past, when the only avenue of approach was over the land, the axiom that the object of war was the destruction of the hostile army in the field was sound.
>
> For an army to obtain victory, according to the methods employed in the European war, it was necessary to kill off the opposing army slowly, and in doing so, to destroy all the resources, material and personal, of the other country. In accomplishing it, the attacker suffered even more greatly than the one attacked. The result of the European war was a more or less lasting exhaustion for all those that participated in it, except the United States which came in at the very end and used up very little of its vital force.
>
> Should a war take place on the ground between two industrial nations in the future, it can only end in absolute ruin, if the same methods that the ground armies have followed before should be resorted to. Fortunately, an entirely new element has come into being, that of air power. Air power can attack the vital centers of the opposing country directly, completely destroying or paralyzing them. Very little of a great nation's strength has to be expended in conducting air operations.

> A few men and comparatively few dollars can be used for bringing about the most terrific effect ever known against opposing vital centers.[24]

So, while predicting that air power applied against the enemy's vital centers could make victory in future war relatively cheap and easy, Mitchell also returned full circle to the disgust with the indecisive bloodletting of the armies in the Great War which had prompted his speculations about air power in the first place.

In the manuscript of his war memoirs the futility of the ground campaigns became a pervasive theme. "We [airmen] could see the utter helplessness of the armies on the ground," he said. "They were merely thousands of men led to the shambles, as the result of a faulty system which was entirely oblivious to the meaning of modern war."[25]

> Progress on the ground by the armies had come to a practical stalemate as early as 1916; neither side could advance or retreat. . . . The art of war had departed. Attrition, or the gradual killing off of the enemy, was all the ground armies were capable of. The high command of neither army could bring about a decision, and the alarming conviction was beginning to dawn on the world that it must stand by and witness European civilization being destroyed or ruined for many years, if not for all time.[26]

> What a foolish kind of war this seemed, where an army could not advance twenty or thirty miles for months, even with nobody opposing them! How could such an army ever possibly end a war, except by indirect pressure? It seemed to me that the utility of ground armies was rapidly falling to about zero, due to the great defensive power of modern firearms.[27]

"Bit by bit the army was losing its mobility and, therefore, becoming incapable of quickly obtaining a decision over the enemy."[28] In bombing attacks, many of course would die; but the effect would be gained less by killing than by disrupting the economy and by simply instilling terror; and especially because terror implied rapid demoralization and quick results, the war of air power would be more humane than bloody, indecisive ground campaigns. Traditional warfare had reached an impasse. But men were still likely to fight wars, and so a desperate need existed to escape the impasse. Mitchell convinced himself that air power offered the escape.

In such thinking, he was hardly alone. Douhet had opened the route before him, and in the twenties and thirties Trenchard became a much more outspoken and categorical proponent of the air power war of "strategic bombing" than he had been when Mitchell met him in 1917. At the same time Liddell Hart was carrying his exasperation over the generalship of the Great War into advocacy of a short, ultimately life-saving strategic bombing war, especially in his book *Paris: Or the Future of War.*[29] The major role of the air force, Liddell Hart believed at this time, "should be to strike at the nerve-system of the enemy nation, in which 'its industrial resources and communications form its Achilles heel.' "[30]

However natural, even necessary, it may have been to hope for an escape from the futility which had overtaken warfare in 1914–18 and which had been in the making for more than a century, wishing for a short, decisive war would not make war become short and decisive. Mitchell's latter-day prophecies about war against the vital centers lacked the technological and strategic grasp of his earlier work. Too many assumptions about strategic bombing were accepted though untested. No one knew the effects of concentrated bombing upon the densely packed steel and concrete buildings of modern cities; the effects obviously were less readily tested than bombing attacks on battleships, and eventually urban construction would prove to muffle much of the force of bomb blasts and to make bombing less destructive physically than the prophets of air power expected. The resilience of human energies and spirit could still less be tested, and against them too the effect of aerial bombing was to prove far less destructive than the air power enthusiasts imagined. Too much, the prophets of strategic bombing could do no more than imagine; too much of their prophecy of war could be only conjecture.

There were two Billy Mitchells, the Mitchell of 1917–26, whose theories were closely tied to technology and to tactical as well as strategic knowledge, and the post-1926 apostle of the war of swift decision against the enemy's vital centers. Since World War II, those who have sought to vindicate Mitchell against the conviction of what they regard as an unjust court-martial tend, significantly, to offer for scrutiny mainly the Mitchell of the battleship bombings and the forecasts of the Pacific war with Japan, not the Mitchell who believed that the bombing of the vital centers—indeed, "a few gas bombs" per city—could alone win a war.[31]

President Woodrow Wilson had said: "I desire no sort of participation by the Air Service of the United States in a plan . . . which has as its object promiscuous bombing upon industry, commerce, or populations in enemy countries disassociated from obvious military needs to be served by such action."[32] There was always a paradox within the air power idea that war would become more acceptable and humane if it were carried beyond the enemy's armed forces to his population centers. The idea clearly ran counter to the previously accepted rule of international law prohibiting bombardment of noncombatant populations in unfortified places; to argue that when in the face of a threat of aerial bombardment, antiaircraft batteries were mounted in or near a city and fighter plane protection was provided, the city thus became a fortified place and eligible for the bombardment of noncombatants was to stretch the hitherto accepted meaning of fortification beyond recognition. Only the blurring of morality induced by a nightmare of the dimensions of the Great War could have made the destruction of cities and the killing of noncombatants seem humane, however swift and surgical the operation was intended to be.[33]

When put to the test in World War II, the process did not prove to be swift and surgical. Douhet and Mitchell believed that both modern industrial economies and civilian morale in modern cities are extremely brittle, and that both would crack quickly under aerial bombardment, to bring swift victory to the belligerent who possessed command of the air. Douhet said that bombardment from the sky would promptly cause a complete breakdown of the social structure and a popular demand for peace before an army and navy could mobilize.[34] Mitchell thought "a few gas bombs" would paralyze a city, and the paralysis of several cities would win the war. Along with the warping of moral standards by conventional warfare's loss of the power to achieve decision, it was this promise of swiftness which made the air power idea seem morally and militarily acceptable. But by 1942, when Alexander De Seversky, a Russian émigré aircraft designer in the United States and friend and associate of Mitchell, again took up the cudgels for Douhet and the latter-day Billy Mitchell, he had to concede that the decisions achieved by aerial bombardment might not, after all, be swift. Two years of new war were already demonstrating the contrary:

> Another vital lesson [of the current war, Seversky admitted], one that has taken even air specialists by surprise, relates to the behavior of civilian populations under air punishment. It had been generally assumed that aerial bombardment would quickly shatter popular morale, causing deep civilian reactions, possibly even nervous derangements on

> a disastrous scale. The progress of this war has tended to indicate that this expectation was unfounded.
>
> On the contrary, it now seems clear that despite large casualties and impressive physical destruction, civilians can "take it." Provided they have the necessary patriotism and the will to fight, they can adjust themselves to the threats and the sacrifices much more readily than had been foreseen. . . .[35]

". . . The 'panic' that was expected to spread through a city or even a nation as bombs began to fall has turned out to be a myth," Seversky also conceded. Writing of his own reporting during the battle of Britain in 1940, he said in 1942: "Because of the general expectation of a quick decision I added that 'this air engagement . . . may not be decided for weeks or even months.' I might have been bolder and said 'years.' "[36]

If air power could not achieve swift decision, aerial bombardment of cities and noncombatants might have been expected to lose much of its charm. For Seversky it did not; he called his book *Victory through Air Power*. With World War II in progress by the time he wrote, and with President Franklin D. Roosevelt and Prime Minister Winston Churchill soon to sponsor a demand for the "unconditional surrender" of Germany, Italy, Japan, and their allies, strategic bombing instead acquired a new attraction. If it could no longer promise swift decisions, it now promised complete ones. Air power to Seversky was the instrument for achieving true total war; it alone offered the totality of victory to which the United States and its allies aspired in the early 1940s. If desired, air power could produce the total annihilation of the enemy's capacity to make war.

Because civilian populations did not panic under aerial bombardment as anticipated, Seversky argued that precision bombing with a careful choice of targets must be substituted for indiscriminate bombardment of population centers. ". . . the will to resist can be broken in a people only by destroying effectively the essentials of their lives —the supply of food, shelter, light, water, sanitation, and the rest."[37] Wars are fought, Seversky said, for two basic reasons: to gain possession of the enemy's territory, or to eliminate his power. The United States and its allies fought Germany and Japan for the latter purpose; they did not seek to possess German or Japanese territory, but to eliminate those two powers as menaces to their own freedom and national aspirations. Against Germany, this purpose was especially clear-cut. It would do no good to gain physical possession of Germany; the Germans were not a docile people in the hands of foreign conquerors anyway. But after Germany with its industrial capacity had risen so rapidly out of a previous defeat, it became necessary to eliminate more completely than in 1918 Germany's potential power. The war against Germany and Japan was a war for the destruction of their power.[38]

Air power is especially suitable for a war of destruction, annihilation, elimination. When possession of the enemy's territory is not desired, the ground fighting which is necessary to gain possession of territory becomes unnecessary in an age of aerial warfare. Thus air power makes victory easier to win after all, despite the loss of the promise of swift decision:

> Obviously the war of possession is more difficult, more costly in man power, more hazardous for the nation undertaking it. . . . Hitler's troubles multiplied as his armies plowed more deeply into enemy territory, thus extending lines of communication to unwieldy length. . . . that is a consideration which should not be overlooked by those of our strategists who think only in terms of wars of possession—that is to say, great invasions of enemy-held regions all over the world by American man power.[39]

Therefore the war of elimination waged from the air offers economy after all, and it offers totality of victory as well:

> Once control of the air over hostile territory is assumed, the further disposition of that area is normally at the will of the conqueror. . . . he may find the elimination of the country as a world factor more desirable, or more expeditious, than its actual subjugation. . . .
>
> The deeper the civilization and the national pride of a people, the more likely it is to be subjected to the method of extermination, since such a people cannot be reconciled to living the life of the vanquished. . . . Because they represent a constant source of danger to the conqueror, through the threat of a 'come-back,' advanced peoples must, if possible, be reduced to impotence beyond easy recovery, through the annihilation of the industrial foundations of their life.[40]

When the skies over a nation are captured, everything below lies at the mercy of the enemy's air weapons. There is no reason why the job of annihilation should at that point be turned over to the mechanized infantry, when it can be carried out more efficiently and without opposition from overhead. Indeed, the kind of large-scale demolition which would be looked upon as horrifying vandalism when undertaken by soldiers on the ground can be passed off as a technical preparation or "softening" when carried out by aerial bombing. The technique of three-dimensional blockade—cutting off exterior contacts and continuously demolishing internal communications and economic life—can be applied for a protracted period. Only when the master of the skies wishes to conserve the property and the man power below for his own use or for some other reason will he, normally, need to take possession of the surface through employment of armies brought by land, sea, and air.[41]

Seversky sometimes lifted ideas almost verbatim from Douhet. Despite Mitchell's court-martial, the Army Air Corps during the 1930s often did the same thing. During the decade, Air Corps officers, though now less reckless than Mitchell, continued to seek a larger and larger autonomy for their service. Advancing technology and the fascination of flight helped them make considerable progress in that direction. The best argument they could offer for the creation of an autonomous or even independent air force would be the existence of an independent strategic mission in war, a means by which an air force could win victory apart from the Army and Navy. This mission Douhet described. Much of the second edition of Douhet's *Command of the Air* became available in 1932 in a French translation, a version much more accessible to American officers than the original Italian. A mimeographed English-language version of the French translation began to be distributed in the Army Air Corps the next year. General H. H. Arnold, who became commander of the Army Air Forces in World War II, said of Air Corps thinking during the 1930s: "As regards strategic bombardment, the doctrines were still Douhet's ideas modified by our own thinking in regard to pure defense."[42] As a member of the Joint Chiefs of Staff in World War II, General Arnold still echoed Douhet and Mitchell:

> America's air doctrine for years has been based solidly on the principle of long-range bombardment. Air forces are strictly offensive in character. . . .
>
> . . . *War has become vertical.* We are demonstrating daily that it is possible to descend from the skies into any part of the interior of an enemy nation and destroy its power to continue the conflict. War industries, communications, power installations and supply lines are being blasted by attacks from the air. Fighting forces have been isolated, their defenses shattered and sufficient pressure brought by air power alone to force their surrender. Constant pounding from the air is breaking the will of the Axis to carry on. . . .
>
> Strategic air power is a war-winning weapon in its own right, and is capable of striking decisive blows far behind the battle line, thereby destroying the enemy's capacity to wage war.[43]

The air officers' desire for an autonomous or independent service stimulated their acceptance of Douhet's doctrine; the doctrine in turn demanded an airplane promising its fulfillment, an attack plane capable of penetrating an enemy's air space without fighter escort and dropping heavy bomb loads upon his vital centers. In August, 1934, the Army Air Corps was able to invite contractors to submit designs for a multiengine bombing aircraft with a range of 1,020 miles, able to carry a 2,000-pound bomb load at a speed of at least 200 miles per hour. One year later the Boeing Aircraft Corporation flew its four-engine Model 299 the 2,100 miles from the factory in Seattle to Wright Field in Dayton for testing. The average speed on the flight was 252 mph; with the desired bomb load, the plane could fly almost as fast. Unfortunately, it crashed during final testing. But the model had struck air officers as so fully the aircraft they needed to realize the Douhet and Mitchell theses that they insisted to the General Staff it must be purchased despite the crash. In 1936 the Army agreed to buy thirteen such planes, which it designated the B-17 and called the Flying Fortress, in politically expedient but ironic suggestion that the purpose was thoroughly defensive.[44]

12. A Strategy for Pacific Ocean War: Naval Strategists of the 1920s and 1930s

An Orange War is considered the most probable. It is by far the most difficult for the Navy. It will require the greatest maritime war effort yet made by any nation.

—*Commander R. B. Coffey, USN*[1]

THE DEMOCRATS TRADITIONALLY were the small-navy party, and they had provided much of the Congressional opposition to Theodore Roosevelt's and William Howard Taft's naval building program. Nevertheless, Woodrow Wilson's Democratic administration brought hardly an interruption in the pace of battleship construction, and eventually a more ambitious program than even Roosevelt had dared to advocate. The troubled world conditions of the time were one obvious reason for these somewhat unexpected developments. The presentation of a persuasively planned building schedule by the General Board of the Navy was another, reinforced by the accelerated obsolescence of the predreadnought battleships in the context of the Anglo-German naval race. In 1914, after much debate and parliamentary wrangling, Congress voted the battleship *New Mexico* and a new *Idaho* and *Mississippi* to replace the predreadnought ships of those names (all three of 32,000 tons, with twelve 14-inch guns). The next annual authorization produced *Tennessee* and *California* (32,300 tons, twelve 14-inch guns).[2]

Late in 1915 President Wilson's policy of defending the letter of American neutral rights under international law was producing friction with Great Britain as well as with Germany. Wilson thereupon decided to encourage the General Board to prepare a statement calling for a Navy "ultimately . . . equal to the most powerful maintained by any nation of the world," and he followed up by submitting an appropriate legislative program to Congress. After further prolonged debate and especially bitter divisions within the President's own party, but spurred by the great preparedness campaign of the middle years of the European war and by the battle of Jutland, Congress passed the Naval Act of 1916, actually exceeding the General Board proposals. Where the General Board had called for ten battleships, six battle cruisers, and a balanced assortment of supporting vessels to be built within five years, Congress voted for the same number of ships to be built within three. Theodore Roosevelt while he was President had proposed no more than the second largest navy. After reaching that rank in Roosevelt's time, the United States Navy had fallen back to third during the Anglo-German race. Incomparably the largest rapid naval building program to its time, the Wilson program of 1916 was designed to carry the American Navy swiftly to first place.[3]

"Let's build a navy bigger than hers [Great Britain's] and do what we please," Wilson told Colonel E. M. House.[4] Unfortunately, the strategic rationale behind the Wilson program was not much clearer than that statement. After Germany bowed to the *Sussex* ultimatum in the spring of 1916 and for the second time forswore unrestricted submarine warfare, Great Britain's restrictions upon American maritime commerce became for a while more irritating than anything Germany was doing. If the United States were to insist upon neutral rights, a Navy which Great Britain would have to fear even after the German navy was gone seemed a good idea. On the other hand, when friction with British maritime policy was at its worst, the possibility of war between the United States and Britain was still absurdly remote; and while the 1916 program at last included fifty destroyers, most of the program would not fit the United States Navy for the war with Germany which was a possibility by no means remote.

The war with Germany came before the new building had well begun, and in the months of American belligerency the 1916 program was suspended so that shipyards could concentrate on antisubmarine vessels. A naval building program based on little strategic purpose from the beginning proved, however, able to move along on inertia and with even less of a purpose after the Great War ended; after the Armistice, work on the 1916 battleships and battle cruisers resumed. In 1920 and 1921 *Tennessee* and *California* from the last pre-1916 program were completed. Work progressed on the "super-dreadnoughts" of the 1916 authorization, *Colorado*, *Maryland*, *West Virginia*, and *Washington*, all of 32,500 tons and mounting eight 16-inch, not 14-inch, guns. Coming along, too, were the mammoth *Iowa*, *Indiana*, and *Massachusetts*, replacing the predreadnoughts of those names, along with *Montana*, *North Carolina*, and *South Dakota*, 43,000 tons, twelve 16-inch guns.[5]

In a reversal of roles, it fell to the Republicans to overcome the inertia of motion propelling the Democratic naval program. The dedication to fiscal economies which was to become so pervasive in the Coolidge administration had its beginnings under Harding; the Republicans seem to have experienced certain guilt feelings over their part in rejecting American membership in Wilson's League of Nations, or at least they felt obliged to offer a public demonstration that they were not wholly opposed to international cooperation in the name of peace; the resumption of the 1916 program prodded a jealous Britain into new battleship building of her own, to try to hold first place among the navies even if it broke her treasury, but meanwhile the British also tried to persuade the United States to curtail naval building; the Republicans hoped to internationalize and thereby reduce the American share of the obligations in the Pacific which had carried over from the McKinley and Roosevelt years of imperialism, notably the Open Door policy and its embellishments in China. Out of these factors came the Washington Conference of 1921–22 and American agreement to join with Great Britain, Japan, France, and Italy in a ten-year moratorium on capital-ship construction and a limitation of total tonnage. For the American Navy, the tonnage limitation involved scrapping fifteen battleships and battle cruisers on which over $300 million had already been spent, to achieve the 5:5:3:1.7:1.7 capital-ship tonnage ratio among the five principal postwar navies. Of the 1916 battleships, only *Colorado*, *Maryland*, and *West Virginia* joined the fleet.[6]

The ten-year moratorium was extended another five years by the London Naval Treaty of 1930, but the resulting long drought in battleship construction did not change the predominant American naval opinion that battleships were "the monarchs of the sea."[7] Instead, the drought caused a growing concern among American seamen that the naval limitations made impossible the fulfillment of American responsibilities in the Pacific Ocean, by denying the United States enough capital ships and enough bases supporting them to permit defense of the Pacific island possessions against Japan.[8] To gain Japanese acquiescence in an inferior naval ratio, and also to persuade Japan to forgo the Anglo-Japanese Alliance of 1902 and 1905, the Washington Treaty limitations included an American pledge to refrain from strengthening fortifications west of Pearl Harbor, and a corresponding British pledge regarding fortifications east of Singapore. This limitation upon the development of bases combined with the principle that a battle fleet lost efficiency in direct proportion to its distance from its bases, to make the Washington Treaty a confirmation of that new order of sea power which had been developing since the initiation of the modern American and Japanese fleets.

Henceforth, no one navy could dominate all the oceans of the world as the Royal Navy had done through most of the three previous centuries. Each major navy would dominate its own geographic sphere; and specifically, naval predominance in the western Pacific was assigned to Japan, the inferior ratio of the Japanese fleet being balanced out by the distance separating the western Pacific from the home bases of the American and British fleets and by the inability of the Americans and British to strengthen their Pacific bases.[9]

After the Armistice of 1918 a reorganized Joint Board resumed the work of preparing color-coded war plans involving the potential adversaries of the United States. The Joint Board was reconstituted on July 25, 1919, to consist of the Chief of Staff of the Army, the Chief of Naval Operations, the chief of the Operations Section of the General Staff, the Assistant Chief of Naval Operations, and the chiefs of both the War Department and the Navy War Plans Divisions. The reorganization added to the Joint Board a Joint Planning Committee, which bore the primary initial responsibility for strategic contingency planning. After the defeat of Germany, Japan was far and away the most likely adversary the United States might confront in war, and through the 1920s and until the late 1930s the color plan which most interested the joint planners naturally was War Plan ORANGE, in fact a series of evolving Joint Board plans for war against Japan, with various detailed Army and Navy supplements.[10]

Through the twenties and thirties the ORANGE Plans continued to envision a Japanese-American war as beginning with a desperate holding action by the garrisons of the most distant American island possessions, to be followed by the battle fleet's fighting its way across the Pacific to relieve the beleaguered garrisons and by defeating the Japanese fleet to win the war. "Our principal war plan is the Orange Plan," a naval officer correctly told an Army War College audience in 1924. "An Orange War is considered the most probable. It is by far the most difficult for the Navy. It will require the greatest maritime war effort yet made by any nation."[11]

So great and difficult were the problems of the ORANGE Plans, especially after the Washington Treaty of 1922, that the planners of the twenties and thirties never had much confidence in their handiwork. The Army planners felt little hope that the garrison of the Philippine Islands could hold out, even in such a restricted area as the Bataan Peninsula and the island of Corregidor, until the fleet arrived with reinforcements. The 1928 version of War Plan ORANGE predicted that Japan could mobilize and transport to the Philippines a force of 300,000 men within thirty days; 50,000 or 60,000 Japanese might be secretly mobilized to appear off Luzon seven days after the beginning of war, 100,000 within fifteen days. The United States Army had only 11,000 troops in the archipelago, 7,000 of them Filipinos, along with 6,000 Filipinos in the islands' constabulary.[12] The Navy planners, on the other hand, held that:

> Unless there is a harbor in readiness to receive the fleet in the Far East in time of war, the arrival of the fleet in the war area will be indefinitely delayed. I know of no way to do the fleet and its operations in the Western Pacific more injury than to deprive it of a base from which it may operate in those distant waters. I believe it to be an essential of our peace strategy that every effort be made to retain possession of Manila Bay under all circumstances. . . .
>
> Without a secure harbor in the Far East, the superiority of capital ships which we now possess under the treaty may disappear in seizing and occupying a harbor. . . .[13]

Pessimism over the ORANGE Plans had to grow as the likelihood itself grew that the next major war would indeed be a war against Japan. As the Japanese army and navy leaders more and more seized an ascendancy within the Japanese government after the outbreak of the Manchurian Incident in 1931, and as they propelled Japan toward an ambitious program of military expansion, the most influential Japanese naval leaders envisioned, interestingly, a coming Pacific war which would follow much the same scenario foreseen by their American counterparts. Both Japanese and Americans anticipated an initial Japanese conquest of the islands of the western Pacific, including the Philippines. Both anticipated an eventual effort by the United States fleet, despite the loss of its western Pacific bases, to fight its way back across the ocean toward the Japanese home islands. Both anticipated that the climax of the war would come in a Jutland type of contest between the rival battle lines. Despite their advantages of position,

Japanese naval officers therefore also worried lest they not have enough battleships for the Jutland action, while the Americans worried about Pacific distances and lest "the superiority of capital ships which we now possess under the treaty may disappear in seizing and occupying a harbor." By the middle thirties, naval officers on both sides of the Pacific were impatient for a resumption of battleship construction.

The national traditions of Japan permitted Japanese naval officers to express their discontents in ways alien to the United States. In the May 15 incident of 1932, young Japanese naval officers participated in assassinations of moderate political leaders. Under the shadow of the May 15 incident, the more militant Japanese naval leaders steadily pushed aside the "treaty faction" of officers favoring continued friendship with the Anglo-Saxon powers. During 1933 and 1934 many "treaty faction" leaders felt obliged to go into retirement. In preliminary talks during 1934 looking toward another London naval conference, the Japanese demanded naval parity with the United States and Great Britain. When they failed to win acceptance of their demand, they gave notice that they were denouncing the Washington Naval Treaty effective December 31, 1936. In January, 1936, they walked out of the main London Naval Conference. By that time they had already embarked on a 1934–37 construction program, which had already carried them beyond their Washington Treaty quota. The Japanese naval militants' ambition was especially to steal a march on the Anglo-Saxon powers with the gigantic *Yamato* battleships of more than 72,000 tons, with nine 18.1-inch guns; the rough blueprints for *Yamato* were ready in 1934.[14]

The Japanese placed special confidence in the *Yamato* class because they knew the United States still limited itself to battleships capable of passing through the Panama Canal; so strong was the legacy of Mahan's dictum that the fleet must be kept concentrated or at least capable of rapid concentration through the canal. Therefore the largest battleships which the United States laid down after the dissolution of the Washington Treaty were the 45,000-ton *Iowa*-class ships, with nine 16-inch guns, including *Iowa*, *New Jersey*, *Missouri*, and *Wisconsin*. The 108-foot beam of these vessels just permitted them to squeeze through the 110-foot width of the Panama Canal locks. The initial American battleship response to Japan's denunciation of the treaty was the smaller *North Carolina* class (*North Carolina*, *Washington*, *South Dakota*, *Indiana*, *Massachusetts*) of 35,000 tons, also with a main battery of nine 16-inch guns. Though still larger American battleships were planned, the *North Carolina* and *Iowa* classes proved to be the final American repositories of the ancient tradition of the ship of the line. For the new Jutland envisioned by both the American and Japanese navies was never to occur.[15]

It was a paradox: the Japanese navy, with its confidence in the battleship so great that it built the mightiest super-dreadnoughts of them all, threw all such warships into eclipse in the process of demonstrating its respect for the American battleships by attacking them at their Pearl Harbor anchorage on December 7, 1941—attacking them with carrier-based airplanes.

The paradox was one of several related paradoxes. At the London preliminary naval talks in 1934, Japan was represented by Rear Admiral Yamamoto Isoroku,[16] who on instructions forced the talks to fail by insisting on naval parity. Yamamoto was personally unhappy with this development, however, and when Japan walked out of the main London conference in 1935 he protested his government's policy, saying that "there was no appearance whatsoever of two powers combining to oppress the third at the talks."[17] Yamamoto belonged to the "treaty faction" of the Japanese navy, which had seen the Washington limitations as essentially favorable to Japan and desired their continuation. He also opposed the militant naval officers over the issue of the battleship as the mainstay of the fleet. He believed the aircraft carrier would become the principal naval weapon of a Pacific war, and that construction, strategy, and tactics must be altered accordingly. Though he lost out on the naval treaties, and though the monster battleships *Yamato* and *Musashi* were built in spite of his advice, he retained enough influence to be principally responsible for Japan's entering the next war with greater carrier strength than any other power, and he designed the carrier-based attack on Pearl Harbor.

During the 1930s, Yamamoto also helped see to it that Japan's carrier-based aviators were the best trained in the world, averaging 700 hours training in the air before assignment to the fleet, as contrasted with 305 hours for American carrier pilots in December, 1941. He was largely responsible for Japan's developing better carrier planes than America, with the possible exception of dive bombers. The Mitsubishi S-00 "Zero" fighters were to outperform and outgun the Grumman F4F Wildcats which were the standard American carrier fighters when war came, and the Japanese excelled in both carrier- and land-based torpedo planes. Yamamoto always emphasized the value of aerial torpedo-bombing against ships, and for his aircraft and for their surface ships and submarines the Japanese developed the best torpedoes in the world, their oxygen-propelled "long lances," which were far superior to American compressed-air torpedoes in range, accuracy, and reliability.[18]

When Japan's Nakajima B5N torpedo bombers and Aichi D3A dive bombers rose from their carrier decks to attack Hawaii on December 7, 1941, the United States was to have seven carriers, four of them in the Atlantic, to Japan's ten: *Lexington* (CV-2) and *Saratoga* (CV-3), each of 33,000 tons, 33 knots speed, which joined the fleet in 1927 and were products of a clause in the Washington Treaty permitting each signatory to transform two of its uncompleted battle cruisers into carriers; *Ranger* (CV-4), commissioned in 1934, the first American carrier to be built as such from the keel up, but a retrogression to a smaller, slower ship, 14,500 tons, 29.5 knots; *Yorktown* (CV-5), 1937, and *Enterprise* (CV-6), 1938, each of 19,900 tons, 34 knots; *Wasp* (CV-7), 1940, 14,800 tons, 32 knots; and *Hornet* (CV-8), 1941, 22,000 tons, 33 knots. Building were the first carriers of the *Essex* class, 27,000 tons, 33 knots. Most of these ships carried slightly more than eighty airplanes each.[19] Happily, the three American carriers which were in the Pacific were all away from Pearl Harbor on December 7, 1941.

A school of carrier- and aviation-oriented officers had emerged in the American Navy during the First World War and managed to sustain itself against the adverse pressure both of battleship admirals within the Navy and of the extreme air power enthusiasts outside. As early as 1919 Lieutenant Commander H. T. Bartlett wrote in the *Proceedings* of the United States Naval Institute that "Any fleet which has a number of aircraft squadrons will have a tremendous advantage over one which is not so equipped. We must get carriers in our fleet and aircraft bases at strategical points or we will invite disaster when the next crisis comes." Among the duties of naval aircraft, Bartlett listed as first in importance bombing the enemy's warships and bases, and second the protection of the American fleet. He saw aviation and carriers primarily as offensive weapons. "Offensive action against surface craft was not of much use in the war" just ended, said Bartlett, because of the technical limitations of existing airplanes and weapons, "but [it] will become increasingly important, and, it is believed, to an extent that will revolutionize the construction of men-of-war." The same issue of the *Proceedings* offered the promise of Henry Woodhouse, vice-president of the Aerial League of America, that the torpedo-carrying airplane would "revolutionize" naval tactics.[20]

In 1921 the Navy established the Bureau of Aeronautics and placed as its chief an able opponent of both the battleship admirals and the air power extremists, Rear Admiral William A. Moffet. Unfortunately, Moffet died in an airship accident in 1923. After Billy Mitchell's bombing tests, Lieutenant Commander H. B. Grow contributed to the *Proceedings* a series of conclusions seeking to open an appropriate sphere to naval aviation even while reaffirming the primacy of the battleship. In their ambiguity, his conclusions showed the tendency of naval thought:

> (a) That the battleship today, unprotected, is in grave danger;
> (b) That in spite of this danger the battleship must remain as the first line of the Navy;
> (c) That, should an enemy be able to gain control of the air at sea, victory for them is almost assured;
> (d) That one or two hits from a 2,000-pound bomb would put any ship in existence out of the battle;
> (e) That, to preserve the safety and integrity of our ships, Naval Aviation with the fleet must at once be expanded and developed to the maximum consistent with the terms of the [Washington] treaty and the size of the fleet; and that, unless this is done, our fleet will have to go to sea under such a serious handicap that defeat would be probable.[21]

In 1923 the Navy held Fleet Problem I in the Pacific, in which two battleships simulating aircraft carriers suggested some of the potential for carriers in a Pacific war. The next March, Lieutenant Forrest P. Sherman, who was to become a principal carrier strategist in the 1941–45 war and later Chief of Naval Operations, emphasized again the doctrine that the primary mission of carriers should be an offensive one against the enemy's aviation and fleet:

> To secure control of the air over a sea area it is necessary:
> 1. To locate all enemy carriers which are in a position to launch aircraft which may in any way dispute our control of the air.
> 2. To attack and destroy the effectiveness of such carriers by heavy bombing and torpedo attack against the carriers themselves, and by light bombing, incendiary, and gas attacks against flying-off decks and planes and personnel thereon.
> 3. To maintain either in the air or in readiness for flight sufficient fighting planes to defeat any air forces which the enemy can later bring into action.

The fleet, which in the early stages of an engagement secures control of the air as defined above, will find itself with the enormous advantages of aircraft spotting, the ability to use aircraft in smoke tactics, and the ability fully to utilize offensive aviation at will in bombing, torpedo, and gas attacks against the enemy battle line.[22]

The next year, 1924, little *Langley* participated in Fleet Problem V. In 1925 the Navy began the systematic formulation of air tactical doctrine, and in 1926 the first dive-bombing exercises occurred. With the arrival of *Lexington* and *Saratoga* in 1927, experiments in carrier tactics could take a long step forward. Naval aviation, lacking the ambitions of Army aviation to become a separate service and to win wars by itself, could be more readily integrated into the tactics of the fleet than could Army aviation into the ground tactics of the Army.

By 1929, the year when *Lexington* and *Saratoga* first participated in the now annual fleet problems, Lieutenant Franklin G. Percival, a student of the use of carriers who would continue to comment astutely into the years of the war of 1941–45, could write that certain premises had by now become "generally accepted":

1. The airplane is essentially an offensive weapon.

2. If we attempt to use our planes defensively, they will not only fail to defend the fleet, but will probably be destroyed in detail.

3. The logical primary objectives for the opposing forces are each other's carriers.

4. The ideal attack is one which destroys the hostile carriers, while their planes are still aboard. Hence, it must be launched at the earliest possible moment.

5. The enemy air force will observe the principle of concentration of forces and launch the majority of its planes in a simultaneous attack, calculated to reach home by sheer weight of numbers.

6. An air force, *if unopposed,* could inflict serious, possibly fatal damage upon a fleet. An *adequate* defense must, therefore, be provided against aircraft.

7. Aside from the defense afforded by the offensive operations of our planes, the gun is the most powerful weapon so far produced for this purpose.

If we accept these premises, several obvious conclusions follow. First of all, the battleship, which represents the highest development of the floating, mobile gun platform, will constitute the backbone of our aërial defense. It is also apparent that, since the composition of any ship's battery should be decided by the relative effectiveness of the weapons which may be brought to bear upon that ship, the increased

> potency of aircraft calls for corresponding increases in antiaircraft batteries. Another conclusion is that the gun defense against aircraft will require a tremendous expenditure of ammunition. Previous ideas on ammunition allowances will have to be entirely recast. Finally, while the basis of our gun defense will probably be a system of zone fire, we must be able to fire in any direction without worrying too much about where the shrapnel will fall. This means that all the personnel on our ships must be housed in shelters which are, at least, shrapnel-proof. The danger from the machine-gun bullets of attack planes further reënforces the requirement.
>
> Another change is that the torpedo and bombing planes of the carriers constitute a striking force of great power and of speed incomparably higher than anything seen heretofore. Their attacks will not only be delivered with amazing swiftness, but can be concentrated at any desired point within the radius of the planes. Entirely new vistas are opened up in applying the principle of the concentration of forces. Isolated units of the fleet will be pounced upon and annihilated as a hawk swoops down upon a stray duckling. . . . Do not these considerations necessitate the substitution of submarines for cruisers in the advance screen or for any detached duty in waters where large hostile air forces may be encountered? . . .
>
> Increased effectiveness will be seen in control operations. Airships patrolling hundreds of miles offshore will add greatly to the hazards of coastal raids. The presence of aircraft carriers with hunting squadrons will increase not only their range of vision but their range of striking. The great speed of their planes will enable them to attack promptly anything sighted, without a long stern chase, heretofore so frequently broken off by nightfall. This means that control of the sea will be more nearly absolute, and hence the value of sea power will be greater than ever. In other words, air power, instead of superseding sea power, merely adds to its effectiveness.[23]

As a description of the conditions of the Pacific war when at last it came, these comments could scarcely have been better had Percival written them sixteen years later, with all the experience of the war to guide him. This was as true of his comments on battleships and their armament and role as of his remarks on carriers. One of the reasons for Japan's success in the Pearl Harbor attack was to be the American Navy's failure to heed the kind of warning Percival gave on the antiaircraft armament of battleships. The battleships attacked by the Japanese on December 7, 1941, had at most twelve 5″/25 dual purpose guns (in the *Maryland* class) and an assortment of 3-inch and 1.1-inch machine guns, neither of which latter types worked very well in action. Later, *Iowa*-class battleships were to have twenty 5″/38s and 128 40mm and 20mm Bofors and Oerlikon guns, the result of Pearl Harbor and other bad experiences.[24] Unfortunately, though he spoke of his conclusions as "generally accepted," Percival had overleaped the thinking of most of the naval command about the importance of aircraft, aircraft carriers, and antiaircraft guns, and the command was not to catch up until adversity compelled it.

In the fleet when Percival wrote his analysis, confidence in the gun still overshadowed confidence in the airplane. "If navies should scrap their battleships and battle cruisers," wrote Captain Yates Stirling, Jr., under the title "Some Fundamentals of Sea Power," "replacing them with airplane carriers . . . we shall find that airplane carriers soon will be 'dressing themselves up' with big guns."[25] In Fleet Problem IX in 1929, *Saratoga* launched a highly effective attack against the Panama Canal, but she was judged to be sunk by the big guns of the opposing battleships. The Commander in Chief of the Fleet, Admiral Henry V. Wiley, wrote that there was "no analysis of Fleet Problem IX fairly made which fails to point to the battleship as the final arbiter of Naval destiny."[26] In Fleet Problem XVIII in 1937, the fleet commander refused to allow the commander of *Langley*, *Lexington*, and *Saratoga* to act on the doctrine that carriers must first take the offensive against hostile carriers; he compelled the three carriers to confine themselves to covering his battleships and an amphibious landing, and in the upshot *Langley* was judged sunk and *Lexington* and *Saratoga* heavily damaged.[27] Relatively few aviation officers attended the Naval War College in the 1930s, and as late as 1939 the only advocate of aviation on the staff of the college was an aviator with the rank of lieutenant commander.[28]

In the 1941 edition of his *The Navy: A History*, the popular naval historian Fletcher Pratt correctly wrote: ". . . Ours [is] primarily a gunnery navy; that is, a fleet which depends in the last analysis upon heavy artillery and good shooting. . . ." The same year the young strategic writer Bernard Brodie published his generally excellent study of *Sea Power in the Machine Age*. In it he wrote: "The carrier . . . is not likely to replace the battleship. . . . she cannot strike with the accuracy and forcefulness that is characteristic of the large naval gun within the limits of its range."[29] Seven American carriers were built by 1941 and carrier tactics substantially advanced, but in the predominant American naval thinking the battle line remained paramount.

In the fleet problems, in the game board problems at the Naval War College, in all the deliberations of the Navy's strategic problems it was always the ORANGE war whose perplexities were examined and reexamined through the 1920s and into the 1930s. The idea of a rapid strike by the battle fleet westward across the Pacific, to avenge the expected initial loss of American possessions to the Japanese, became ever more plainly unacceptable. "Our own great weakness in the Far East . . . is the extreme length of our lines of communication," said an American naval officer in 1923.[30] A steam-powered navy had never fought across distances matching those of the Pacific. From Honolulu to Yokohama by the standard sea route was about 3,400 miles; from Honolulu back to San Francisco was over 2,000 miles more. Without bases along the way, the Navy could not fight at such distances. If the Philippines and Guam fell early in an ORANGE war, even those who foresaw a super-Jutland as the climax of the war feared that first, "the military and naval approach to the Far East should be made in a step-by-step mopping-up process by which all the islands en route would be taken and occupied in passing."[31] Forward bases would be needed before the fleet could fight its super-Jutland battle; even more, forward island bases would be needed to support the economic strangulation of Japan by surface and submarine blockade which the Navy planners came to foresee as the means to compel Japan's final capitulation.

At some time before 1919, Major Earl H. Ellis of the Marine Corps delivered a lecture on "Naval Bases: Their Location, Resources, and Security," in which he discussed both the familiar difficulties of defending America's Pacific bases against Japanese attack and the hitherto less discussed problem of capturing Japanese bases in the course of a counteroffensive across the Pacific. In 1920 Major General Charles G. Morton of the Army examined Japanese landing operation procedures and, briefly, the Gallipoli campaign, in an *Infantry Journal* article the assumption of which was that landing operations against hostile shores would prove an important part of the future activity of the United States Army.[32]

Notwithstanding General Morton's article and occasional other evidences of Army interest, and notwithstanding the Navy's growing conviction of the need for forward bases in an ORANGE war, it was the Marine Corps that did most to follow up these lines of thought and, in fact, made ship-to-shore landing operations a particular specialty. The Marine Corps had existed since almost the first military laws of the Continental Congress in 1775, an adjunct of the Navy providing shipboard police (disliked by the Navy's bluejackets), boarding parties, small landing parties, some gun crews, legation and embassy guards, and increasingly in the twentieth century, police for restless underdeveloped areas of the world where there were American citizens, investments, and imperial interests. In the First World War a quirk of censorship, identifying the presence of the Marines while concealing the designations of Army units, had combined with Marine Corps valor to make the Marine Brigade of the Army's 2nd Division famous in the battle of Belleau Wood. In France, however, the Marines fought just as though they were Army infantry, although perhaps an elite formation, and their historic duties had never quite given the Corps a clear *raison d'être*. Ship-to-shore attacks seemed to offer a major military mission for which the Marines were peculiarly suited; perhaps the prospect of an island-hopping war against Japan might at last provide the Marine Corps with a distinctive reason for existing.[33]

As early as 1906, Major Dion Williams of the Corps had begun to advance the idea of the Marine Corps "as that branch of the service most likely to be called upon to take the initiative in such operations," and Williams continued to be a major advocate of Marine Corps preparation for landing missions. Major Ellis in his speech of the World War era urged his Marine Corps comrades to make the capture as well as the defense of island bases their specialty.[34]

Alfred Thayer Mahan's ideas and the acquisition of overseas possessions during the Spanish War had begun to encourage a Marine Corps interest in obtaining and protecting "advance bases" for the Navy as early as the beginning of the century. A temporary Marine Corps school for "advance-base" work was established at Newport in 1901, and in the winter of 1902–1903 a Marine battalion participated in naval exercises around Puerto Rico by defending an advance base on the offshore island of Culebra. In 1910 a more formal school of instruction in advance-base work was organized at New London, to be moved to Philadelphia the next year and to Quantico in 1920. In 1914 additional exercises took place at Culebra. This early activity was more concerned, however, with the defense of distant bases already in American hands than with the seizure of bases from an enemy by means of amphibious attack.[35]

In part, a defensive emphasis prevailed because the prospects for ship-to-shore attack against fortified places were regarded with much skepticism. Well they might have been; if the American Civil War suggested the futility of frontal assaults against strong positions on land except possibly with overwhelming force, then frontal assaults out of the water, with all the complications of forming up in and disembarking from boats and moving through surf, and with limited possibilities of initial overwhelming force, seemed so much more futile.

> If, in violation of precedent, a landing be made in the face of strongly posted troops or fortifications [said Captain Asa Walker, USN, in 1900], it must be regarded in the light of a forlorn hope. All the chances are against success and attempt is but courting disaster. Modern armaments serve to accentuate this fact, since the range of death-dealing weapons has been so wonderfully increased. The landing of vast bodies of men and horses, with the artillery and stores, even under the most favorable circumstances and with the most perfect organization, presents great difficulties. If, then, we complicate these difficulties by subjecting the troops to the fire of a determined enemy, begun at long range and continued during the confusion attendant on disembarking, what but pre-eminent disaster can be the result?[36]

The Gallipoli disaster of World War I appeared to many military critics to seal this judgment. B. H. Liddell Hart believed that amphibious assaults had become impossible. Admiral Mahan's biographer Captain W. D. Puleston doubted that Great Britain could survive another Winston Churchill, since Churchill had led her to the amphibious disaster at Gallipoli. The British armed forces generally doubted the future possibility of amphibious assaults.[37] Writing on "Joint Army and Navy Operations" in the Naval Institute *Proceedings* in 1926, Captain W. S. Pye observed:

> As a consequence of the greater effectiveness of modern weapons, modern ships, air scouting, and radio communication, and of the increase in the size of armies and of the complexity and amount of their equipment, large joint [amphibious] operations are becoming increasingly difficult.
>
> . . .
>
> The chances for success of an invasion by forces transported overseas are becoming smaller and smaller. The greater facility of movement of forces on shore by railroad and motors; the rapidity of communication; the increase in power of mobile artillery; the increased efficiency of the submarine and aircraft, and the increase in size and effectiveness of regular armies and navies, have made invasion by sea almost an impossibility, at least until bases near to the scene of landing operations have been permanently secured, and command of the sea is permanently assured.[38]

Of course, those were large loopholes that Captain Pye opened up at the end of this statement; and he also observed that the Gallipoli failure alone was not an adequate reason for discounting amphibious operations. Gallipoli was too badly handled to serve as a useful object lesson, except in how not to conduct an amphibious attack:

> In the Dardanelles campaign [Pye said] there was a thorough absence of cooperation between the Admiralty and the War Office, including the failure to determine a definite objective, and a woeful misconception of the force required for the success of the expedition.
>
> . . . The failure should be attributed to the Admiralty and the War Office, because of their failure to determine the forces required for the task and for their lack of support of the forces in the theater of operations.[39]

Such types of failures were especially critical in amphibious operations, Pye believed:

> Although it is well recognized that preparation for any and all of the operations of war is frequently the determining factor in victory, there is no type in which efficient preparation is so thoroughly rewarded as in joint operations. Judging by history there is probably no type in which, in the past, preparation has been less thorough. This condition, although regrettable, is not strange. Cooperation within a single department is very frequently hard to obtain and between two departments many times as difficult.
>
> This lack of thoroughness has been due largely to the haste with which joint expeditions have been organized and started upon their operations. Haste in decisions requiring such complicated and difficult operations is usually a result of absence of plans, and absence of plans is due to lack of foresight or administrative inertia, neither of which is justifiable or excusable.[40]

So Pye was not wholly pessimistic. And other military writers interesting themselves in the problem of amphibious attack argued that there was as yet inadequate reason for either pessimism or optimism; experience and study in amphibious war were both too limited. Military men simply did not know what could be expected and attempted in amphibious war.

> . . . There is a lack of historical data and experiences [Captain Thomas C. Hart of the Navy told the Army War College in 1925]. The student of war finds a wealth of history from which to draw lessons applying to land warfare and a lesser but seemingly adequate bibliography on war at sea. All of us have been brought up to study only the one or the other, and we do not ordinarily note how sketchy

> and incomplete the descriptions of the few combined operations of history really are. No writers have handled the subject with the ability and authority that has been brought to bear on strictly land and sea warfare.
>
> Experience itself is comparatively very limited; as a result of which it is to be expected that development in combined operations has been backward. Such is submitted to be the case; we are lacking in knowledge and the development in organization, administration, tactics and materiel necessary for successful combined operations. For instance:—navies have given little thought to their own tactics for supporting landings against opposition; no one has paid much attention to even designing the equipment specially adapted for the purpose; and the instances of actual exercise of troops in making landings are certainly few.[41]

It was just this sort of thought, matériel development, and experience that Marine officers such as Majors Williams and Ellis sought to have the Corps provide. Since the Corps was a branch of the Navy Department, Marine Corps planning for amphibious operations could proceed with relative freedom from the interservice disharmonies to which Captain Pye alluded.

In 1921, Major "Pete" Ellis followed up his earlier lecture with a paper projecting the amphibious strategy of a Japanese-American war and an outline procedure for amphibious assault operations to acquire bases across the Pacific. In those details which were not outmoded by technological developments over the next twenty years, Ellis's paper proved notably prescient, even to estimates of the number of troops likely to be required for successful amphibious assault against an island of a given size. On July 23, 1921, the Commandant of the Corps, Major General John A. Lejeune, gave his official approval to Ellis's paper, and it became the foundation of subsequent planning for amphibious war in the Pacific. Ellis's work was soon cut short, however, by his mysterious and probably sinister death while visiting the Japanese-mandated islands of Palau in 1923.[42]

The advance-base unit at Quantico was reorganized in 1921 as the Expeditionary Force, and its troops participated in new landing operations on Culebra in 1922 and in the first large-scale landing exercises, in Panama and again on Culebra in 1924. The latter were notable because they witnessed the first serious modern American experiments with landing vessels specifically designed for the purpose, in place of ships' boats towed by launches. Brigadier General Eli K. Cole, commanding the Expeditionary Force, supervised the development of a twin-motor fifty-foot landing craft with armor protection and a bow ramp, designated "Troop Barge A." The controversial tank designer J. Walter Christie produced an amphibious tank. Unfortunately, Christie's amphibian proved unseaworthy; still more unfortunately, and despite fiscal stringencies somewhat unaccountably, this line of experiment thereafter fell into a long interval of neglect. Meanwhile, as tactical exercises the 1924 landings were unsatisfactory, serving mainly to confirm what the various writers and speakers on amphibious assault were saying about ignorance of the subject. General Cole's description of the landings was "chaos reigned."[43]

The Army attempted landings in Hawaii in "Grand Joint Army and Navy Exercise No. 3," and in 1925 the Marine Corps set up a West Coast Expeditionary Force at San Diego; but in general the amphibious activity of the remainder of the 1920s and of the early thirties was theoretical rather than practical. The day-to-day concerns of the Marine Corps were mainly diverted to guerrilla warfare against the followers of Augusto César Sandino in Nicaragua, a still more chaotic and frustrating experience.[44] Nevertheless, Marine and other service officers issued increasingly frequent statements to the effect that amphibious operations were the logical primary mission of the Marine Corps, and this view culminated in a Joint Board paper of 1927 on "Army-Navy Joint Action" which said that the Corps "will be given special preparation in the conduct of landing operations."[45] In January, 1933, the Joint Board issued another paper outlining the main problems of amphibious war, suggesting the elements of answers, and defining an amphibious landing as "in effect the assault of an organized defense position modified by substituting naval gunfire support for divisional, corps, and army artillery, and generally navy aircraft support for, the army aircraft support."[46]

This document and the Marines' disengagement from Latin America in accordance with President Franklin D. Roosevelt's Good Neighbor Policy prompted both renewed practical experiments and more intense theoretical activity. In 1933 Major General John H. Russell, Assistant Commandant of the Marine Corps, was instrumental in establishing the Fleet Marine Force as the amphibious arm of the Corps. Supposedly a brigade, the Fleet Marine Force was in fact only a reinforced regiment; but its establishment was accompanied by an implicit commitment of the Corps itself to amphibious war as its principal mission. Also under Russell's impetus, the next year the Corps schools at Quantico concentrated the efforts of faculty and students upon the elaboration of the Joint Board paper of 1933 into a tactical manual, which became the *Tentative Manual of Landing Operations* (1934). The historians of the Marine Corps role in amphibious war have called this publication the Pentateuch and the Four Gospels of amphibious warfare; it became the doctrinal foundation of all Marine landings in World War II.[47]

The Marine planners were proceeding from the premise that landing attacks against Japanese-held islands would often have to be amphibious *assaults*—that is, tactical assaults out of the surf against defenses immediately on the beaches. Conducting ship-to-shore landings had been difficult enough in the past against beaches defended lightly or not at all. In the past, however, it was customary and usually possible to exploit the mobility of sea power and the attacker's possession of the initiative to surprise the enemy about the precise location of the landing, and thus to avoid his strongest defenses. The Pacific islands which the United States might have to seize from Japan offered a different problem: many of them were so small that there could be little deception about where an attack might fall, and the only defense the Japanese could make might be directly on the beaches. Even if they wished it, the defenders might not be able to employ a mobile defense somewhere behind the beaches; they might have no choice but to resist a landing directly, and the attackers then would have no choice but to fight while in the process of landing. Therefore every aspect of the ship-to-shore movement had to be conducted on the assumption that the landing force was going immediately into action. Even on occasions when the enemy had enough ground for maneuver, the only safe assumption was to be prepared for his resisting on the beaches. Every effort should of course be made to achieve strategic surprise; the enemy should be deceived as to the itinerary of islands chosen for attack. But with Japanese defenders likely to be dug in on any beach, effective tactical surprise was likely to be practically impossible, and therefore attempts to achieve it should be sacrificed to thoroughness of preparation.

The *Tentative Manual of Landing Operations* listed six points which must be considered for thorough preparation, and it offered suggestions, though not yet definitive answers, for dealing with them. The six points are:

Command relations. Relying on mere army-navy cooperation without unity of command had been one of the sources of disaster at Gallipoli. There must be a unified command of landing operations and a precise allocation of subordinate responsibilities, together with an adequate communications network to bind sea, land, and air portions of the amphibious force together.

Naval gunfire support. The assault force would be so vulnerable as it reached the beach, and so likely to be badly outnumbered, that heavy support by naval guns would be required to suppress the defenders as much as possible. Such support would, to a degree, require utilizing modern naval armor and armaments to overcome the ancient principle that ships cannot fight forts. Such support would also require adjustments in naval gunnery. The low trajectory of naval gunfire, designed for ship-to-ship action on the surface of the sea, would call for the development of special procedures for dealing with targets on the reverse slopes of hills; and ordinary slow-fused armor-piercing naval ammunition would not be suitable for use against most shore targets. As naval gunnery developed suitable tactics and ammunition, however, the Marine Corps came to favor a prolonged preliminary bombardment to smother defenses despite the obvious loss of tactical surprise.

Aerial support. The *Tentative Manual* envisioned aerial gunfire and bombing support as especially necessary at the critical moment when the troops would touch ashore, when naval gunfire support would have to cease and the ground troops' artillery would not yet be in action. As the Pacific war actually developed, however, air attack against the defenders became a major part of the action preliminary to landing simultaneous with naval bombardment. In addition, as the war actually developed, aviation came to operate in close support of the landing force much nearer the front lines than the planners of the 1930s thought feasible or safe.

Ship-to-shore movement. This movement must be in tactical formation to lead directly into the assault; it is not a mere ferrying operation.

Securing the beachhead. The initial assault must capture a zone large enough to permit continuous landing of troops and supplies without serious interference and to make possible maneuver toward further advance. There must be well-trained beach parties and shore parties. The beach party would buoy channels and erect markers for incoming craft, dispose of beach obstacles, maintain communications between troops ashore and incoming boats and nearby ships, and direct incoming boats to the proper places for unloading. The shore party would unload boats and ships at the shoreline and prepare for the support of further movement inland.

Logistics. The key principle of amphibious logistics came to be known as "combat loading": everything must be accessible at the time of landing in the order in which it would be needed for the amphibious assault.[48]

The Marine Corps schools continued to stress theoretical and historical study of the problems of amphibious assault through the rest of the 1930s. Meanwhile the suggested solutions were tested in a new series of annual landing exercises with elements of the fleet and at extensive new training grounds for amphibious war at New River, North Carolina, and at San Diego. At one time or another the 1st and 9th Infantry Divisions of the Army on the East Coast and the 3rd and 7th Divisions on the West Coast joined in the exercises.

Despite all its preoccupation with an ORANGE war, the Navy's planning for a super-Jutland of the battle fleets left it strangely indifferent to cooperation with the Marine Corps in developing amphibious assault technique and doctrine. The Army remained more interested in another continental war in Europe, in which the presence of allies would presumably guarantee unopposed landings. With the Marine Corps thus having to carry the ball almost alone, the amphibious exercises of the late thirties and the beginning of the forties still were not all they might have been. An excess of artificiality usually marked the circumstances of the landing, naval gunfire techniques were developed with less than overwhelming enthusiasm, aerial support techniques lagged even more, everything suffered from a shortage of adequate communications equipment, and logistical support was haphazard and inadequate. As late as May, 1941, the Navy had only six and the Army only four transport ships fitted for combat loading, though the joint plan merely for a landing in the Azores—which President Roosevelt now ordered the services to prepare to execute—called for forty-one combat-loaded transports and cargo ships.[49]

Perhaps the worst deficiency was continued neglect of landing craft. In 1934 the Marine Corps had begun to work with Andrew Higgins, who had developed shallow-draft boats capable of easily landing on and retracting from beaches, for use by oilmen and fur-trappers in the Louisiana bayou country. Higgins boats with flat bottoms and tunnel-shaped sterns provided the basic design for the LCVP, Landing Craft—Vehicle, Personnel; but it was not until 1939 that the Marine Corps urged Higgins to equip his boats with a hinged ramp in the bow so that troops and equipment could exit as swiftly as possible and perhaps dry-shod. The Japanese had used more than 400 ramp-boats as early as their assault on Tientsin in 1937. As late as the spring of 1941, American Marines were still going over the bows of conventional ships' boats.

Still more neglected were beaching ships of ocean-going size to carry tanks and heavy equipment. The British began to think about such things after their ejection from the European continent in 1940 strengthened the amphibious-minded minority in their services, and in 1941 they asked the United States to supply them under the Lend-Lease program. Captain T. A. Hussey, Royal Navy, offered sketches of a "Landing Ship, Tank," of a smaller "Landing Craft, Tank," and of a "Landing Ship, Dock." The Navy Department rejected the request for such craft because American yards were already overworked with orders for conventional warships and merchant ships; but Captain Hussey through a mutual friend got Justice Felix Frankfurter to interest Harry Hopkins and General George C. Marshall in the project, and then the attack on Pearl Harbor came along to direct everyone's interest abruptly to the islands of the Pacific. Belatedly, the United States decided to spend large sums to build these big landing craft for itself as well as for the British.[50]

In 1938 the Navy incorporated the basic precepts of Marine Corps amphibious doctrine into its own *Fleet Training Publication 167*, and in 1941 the Army followed suit in *Field Manual 31-5*. Nevertheless, the specifics of the doctrine based on the *Tentative Manual of Landing Operations* were to receive their most faithful application in war in the South Pacific and Central Pacific operations of 1942–45, where the Marines themselves carried out many of the landings under direct Navy command. In Europe and the Southwest Pacific, where the Army commanded, each theater tended to develop amphibious techniques of its own. In the European theater the amphibious landings in North Africa, Sicily, and Italy took place without benefit of prolonged preliminary bombardment. Against large land areas from which the enemy might bring up strong reserves, the commanders in this theater preferred to give up a thorough softening of the defenses in order to hope for tactical surprise. The results were dubious, since all of these landings save the ones in Sicily flirted with disaster; but not until the Normandy invasion and the development of overwhelming air strength which promised to isolate the beaches from enemy reinforcement did the European theater opt for a thorough preliminary campaign from the air, and even then it did not employ prolonged naval bombardment. In the Southwest Pacific theater, there was a similar problem of large land masses containing hostile reinforcements, along with the consideration that for many of the landings friendly air and sea power were both very limited. Rear Admiral Daniel E. Barbey, General Douglas MacArthur's amphibious commander in the Southwest Pacific, became a specialist in putting troops and essential supplies ashore quickly and quietly and then getting his ships out of the exposed area before the enemy's air and navy got around to counterattacking. In both Europe and the Southwest Pacific, furthermore, amphibious warfare doctrine had to be adjusted to dependence on the Army Air Forces for aerial support; the AAF generally did not believe in close support of any ground operations, including amphibious assaults.

For all that, every amphibious operation conducted by the United States and its allies in World War II was to owe a large debt to the Marine Corps and the interest of the Corps in a war through the island steppingstones on the way to Japan. After Gallipoli, almost every armed service in the world felt pessimistic about the future of amphibious assaults. But simply by defining the specific problems into which amphibious operations divided themselves, the Marine Corps made it evident that the problems most likely were not insoluble; and the Corps went on to delineate many of the solutions. There is more truth than exaggeration in the statement made by General Alexander A. Vandegrift when he was Commandant of Marines after World War II was over: "Despite its outstanding record as a combat force in the past war, the Marine Corps' far greater contribution to victory was doctrinal: that is, the fact that the basic amphibious doctrines which carried Allied troops over every beachhead in World War II had been largely shaped . . . by the U. S. Marines."[51]

When Rear Admiral William V. Pratt was president of the Naval War College from 1925 to 1927, the war games problems obliged the students to think about amphibious warfare, and Pratt also introduced a course in logistics, both steps with an eye to an ORANGE war and the difficulties of a naval campaign across the immense Pacific distances. After Pratt left the War College, however, the logistics course was dropped and amphibious warfare came to be dealt with perfunctorily, by occasional Marine Corps lecturers.[52] Despite Pratt's eventual tour as Chief of Naval Operations in the thirties, the neglect of these topics by the War College reflected their relative neglect by the Navy at large. For all the preoccupation of the Navy planners with an ORANGE war and the interminably repeated BLUE-ORANGE war games at the Naval War College, too much of the planning focused on a Mahanian clash of battle lines. With amphibious warfare and trans-Pacific logistics as with carrier war, the basic problems were delineated during the twenties and thirties, but too much remained to be improvised when war finally came.

In 1965, one of the victorious American admirals of the Pacific war, the wartime commander of the Pacific Fleet, Chester W. Nimitz, wrote to the president of the Naval War College a letter which has often been quoted, about his days as a War College student of the class of 1923:

> The enemy of our games was always—Japan—and the courses were so thorough that after the start of WWII—nothing that happened in the Pacific was strange or unexpected. Each student was required to plan logistic support for an advance across the Pacific—and we were well prepared for the fantastic logistic efforts required to support the operations of the war—The need for mobile replenishment at sea was foreseen—and even practiced by me in 1937. . . .[53]

Like many postwar reminiscences of victorious commanders, this one claims a somewhat exaggerated prescience. Still, that the American tactical and strategic improvisations of the Pacific war succeeded so well testifies that Admiral Nimitz was not merely exaggerating.

PART FOUR

American Strategy in Global Triumph, 1941–1945

Our strategy in this war was developed according to the manuals and fought along the lines for which we trained in our military schools. I don't think we learned anything new—anything that should have changed the course of our strategy in the campaign during which we crushed the German Army.

—*General Wade H. Haislip*[1]

13. The Strategic Tradition of A. T. Mahan: Strategists of the Pacific War

In case opportunity for destruction of major portion of the enemy fleet is offered or can be created, *such destruction becomes the primary task.*

—*Chester W. Nimitz*[1]

WHEN JAPAN ALLIED HERSELF with the European Axis powers, Germany and Italy, she took what proved to be a crucial step toward the long anticipated war with America. Once Japan became a partner of Adolf Hitler's Germany, Japanese ambitions to which the United States might otherwise have reacted with mere expressions of displeasure—as had occurred so often in the past—appeared to demand stronger American responses, lest in partnership with the Nazis the Japanese should turn the whole world balance of power irrevocably against the United States and the other Western democracies. The United States therefore applied an ascending series of economic penalties against Japan, which finally provoked the Japanese into attacking the battle fleet at Pearl Harbor. This attack was intended to clear the way for Japan's forcible acquisition both of required resources in Indonesia and of a Pacific island empire to shield the Japanese homeland and Japan's Asian conquests from American wrath.

Just as the American actions which helped lead to the Pacific war were taken, however, less out of fear of Japan alone than out of fear of Japan's partnership with Germany, so in war itself Germany seemed the more fearsome enemy, and the United States resolved to dedicate its primary military efforts to defeating Germany first. This policy had been decided upon in the ABC-1 conversations between American and British military leaders in early 1941, almost a year before the Pearl Harbor attack pushed the United States into open war. The chiefs and planners of both American services were so impressed, in fact, with the overriding military dangers posed by Germany, that in 1941, within the guarded limits permitted by the then prevailing American traditions of civil-military relations, they cautiously urged the President not to invoke against Japan economic penalties that might provoke Japan to attack the United States.[2]

Pearl Harbor fulfilled the service chiefs' fears of simultaneous wars against Germany and Japan, and the attack presented the first of several severe tests for the planned resolve to regard Japan as a secondary enemy. The emotional response of the American public to the "day which will live in infamy" favored the speediest possible revenge against Japan. Pearl Harbor set in motion a succession of Japanese conquests, partially foreseen in prewar planning but unexpectedly and frighteningly rapid and extensive, which carried the armed forces of the island empire through Malaya, Burma, Indonesia, the Philippines, and the western Pacific islands until they threatened India in the west, Australia in the south, and Midway and Hawaii in the east. Against the rush of Japanese conquest, even the British government in its island fortress hard by Hitler's Europe agreed that the priority of the European war over the Pacific could not become effective until India and Australia and the lines of communication thereto were secure against Japan. The United States, fronting on the Pacific, was so much more inclined to forgo the previously proclaimed European priority.

Consequently, through more than a year after Pearl Harbor, schedules calling for shipment of American military manpower and matériel to Europe were continually being scrapped for emergency, *ad hoc* efforts to shore up the Pacific against Japan. The Navy, and especially its Chief of Naval Operations and Commander in Chief of the Fleet, Admiral Ernest J. King, continually urged upon the more Europe-minded Army the necessity to halt Japan in the Pacific and in particular to preserve a line of communications with Australia. But not only did the American Navy concentrate its strength against its long awaited enemy of the ORANGE Plans; by late 1942, the Army responded enough to the Navy's urgings and to the evident necessities of halting Japan before she advanced to Australia that more than half the American Army divisions overseas and one-third of the air groups were in the Pacific. As late as September, 1943, there were as many Army divisions opposing Japan as there were opposing Germany—thirteen in each conflict—and while total Army personnel in Europe then considerably outnumbered the total committed against Japan, Navy and Marine Corps contributions still made the Pacific by a small margin the area of greater American manpower commitment. On December 31, 1943, 1,878,152 members of the American armed forces were deployed against Japan, 1,810,367 against Germany. Though the manpower balance soon shifted, the initial crisis of the Pacific war created so great a pull of American resources toward Japan that the European war never did recapture the clear strategic priority which had been planned for it in 1941.[3]

On May 3–8, 1942, the United States won its first strategic victory in the effort to stay the tide of Japanese conquest, in the battle of the Coral Sea. With its battle line knocked out at Pearl Harbor, the United States Navy had to improvise a campaign built around aircraft carriers. In the effort, the Navy enjoyed the priceless advantage of reading the principal Japanese codes, and by mid-April, 1942, its Pacific planners had penetrated a Japanese design to advance around the eastern extremity of New Guinea into the Coral Sea and thence to Port Moresby on New Guinea's southern coast, where the Rising Sun would directly threaten Australia itself. Against an enemy force including the large carriers *Shokaku* and *Zuikaku* and the small carrier *Shoho*, the United States dispatched Task Force 17, built around the carriers *Lexington* and *Yorktown*. Above the Coral Sea their aircraft fought the first major naval battle between ships that did not see or fire upon each other. Both sides mishandled this novel engagement, but the Japanese scored a tactical success by sinking *Lexington* while losing only little *Shoho*. Still, *Shokaku's* flight deck was bent and would take two months to repair, and *Zuikaku* would need a month to replace lost planes; so the Japanese abandoned the Port Moresby advance, at least for the time being.

Shokaku and *Zuikaku* would also be absent from a yet more important enterprise. Admiral Yamamoto, now commanding the Japanese Combined Fleet, was also planning, for the beginning of June, a mighty attack upon Midway and the western Aleutians, which would both provide eastern bastions for the defense of Japan's conquered empire and much more important, Yamamoto hoped, compel the remaining ships of the United States Pacific Fleet to give battle so that he could add the destruction of the American carriers to that of the battleships and achieve the Mahanian objective of the elimination

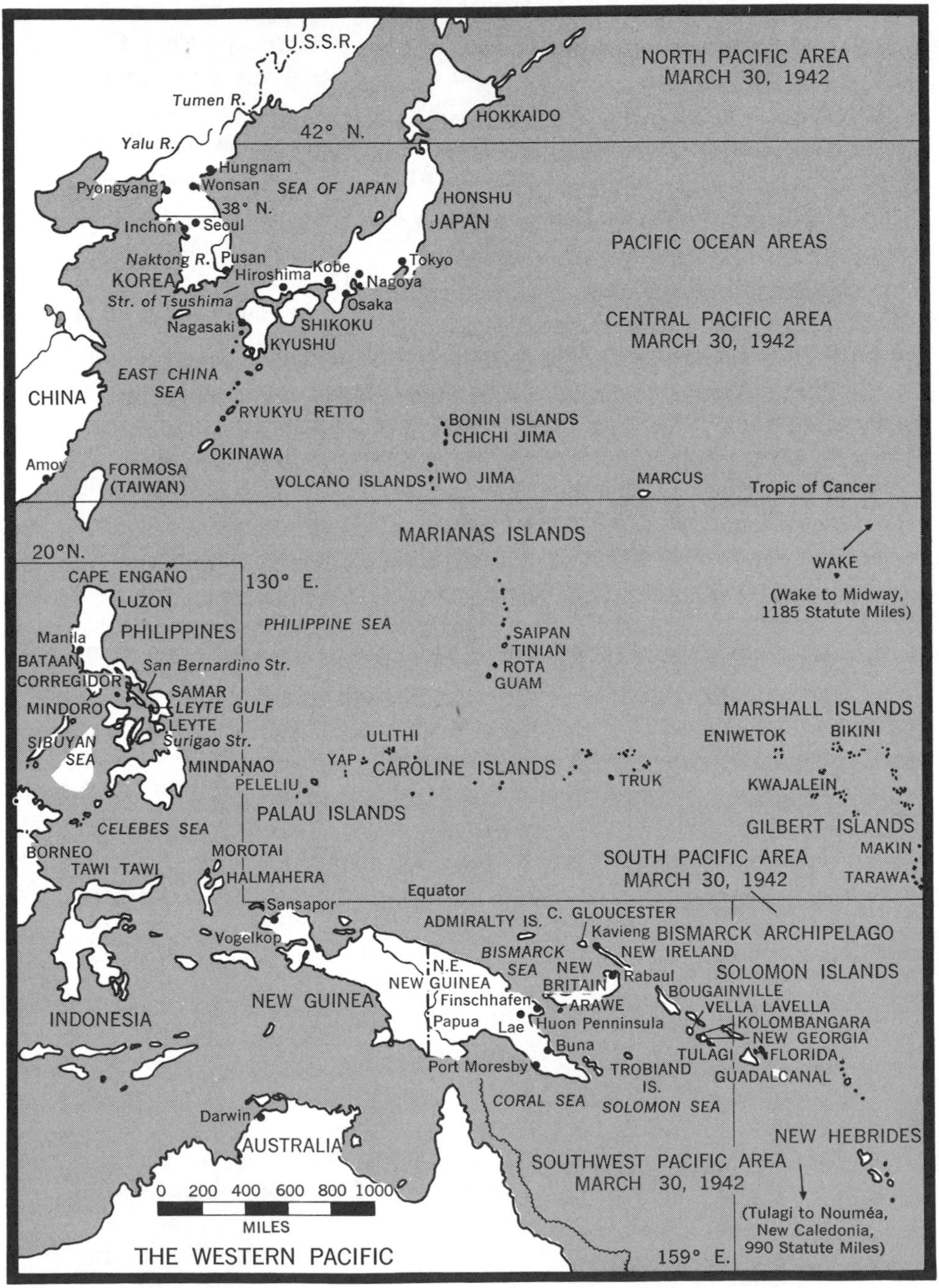
U.S.S.R.
NORTH PACIFIC AREA
MARCH 30, 1942
Tumen R.
Yalu R.
HOKKAIDO
42° N.
Hungnam
Pyongyang
Wonsan
SEA OF JAPAN
HONSHU
38° N.
JAPAN
Inchon
Seoul
PACIFIC OCEAN AREAS
Naktong R.
Pusan
Tokyo
Kobe
KOREA
Hiroshima
Nagoya
Str. of Tsushima
Osaka
SHIKOKU
CENTRAL PACIFIC AREA
MARCH 30, 1942
Nagasaki
KYUSHU
EAST CHINA SEA
CHINA
RYUKYU RETTO
BONIN ISLANDS
CHICHI JIMA
OKINAWA
Amoy
FORMOSA (TAIWAN)
VOLCANO ISLANDS
IWO JIMA
MARCUS
Tropic of Cancer
MARIANAS ISLANDS
20°N.
WAKE
CAPE ENGANO
130° E.
(Wake to Midway, 1185 Statute Miles)
LUZON
PHILIPPINE SEA
Manila
PHILIPPINES
SAIPAN
TINIAN
BATAAN
San Bernardino Str.
ROTA
CORREGIDOR
GUAM
SAMAR
MINDORO
LEYTE GULF
MARSHALL ISLANDS
LEYTE
SIBUYAN SEA
Surigao Str.
ULITHI
ENIWETOK
BIKINI
YAP
MINDANAO
CAROLINE ISLANDS
TRUK
PELELIU
KWAJALEIN
PALAU ISLANDS
CELEBES SEA
GILBERT ISLANDS
BORNEO
MOROTAI
SOUTH PACIFIC AREA
MARCH 30, 1942
MAKIN
TAWI TAWI
HALMAHERA
TARAWA
Equator
Sansapor
ADMIRALTY IS.
C. GLOUCESTER
Kavieng
BISMARCK ARCHIPELAGO
Vogelkop
BISMARCK SEA
NEW IRELAND
N.E. NEW GUINEA
NEW BRITAIN
Rabaul
SOLOMON ISLANDS
BOUGAINVILLE
NEW GUINEA
Finschhafen
ARAWE
VELLA LAVELLA
INDONESIA
Papua
Lae
Huon Penninsula
KOLOMBANGARA
NEW GEORGIA
Buna
TULAGI
FLORIDA
Port Moresby
TROBIAND IS.
GUADALCANAL
CORAL SEA
SOLOMON SEA
Darwin
NEW HEBRIDES
AUSTRALIA
SOUTHWEST PACIFIC AREA
MARCH 30, 1942
0 200 400 600 800 1000
MILES
(Tulagi to Nouméa, New Caledonia, 990 Statute Miles)
THE WESTERN PACIFIC
159° E.

of the enemy fleet. For this grand design, however, Yamamoto planned strangely. With *Shokaku* and *Zuikaku* undergoing repairs, he could still have concentrated five fleet carriers, two light carriers, and one small and obsolescent carrier against Midway, along with considerable battleship strength. Instead, Yamamoto sent fleet carrier *Junyo* and light carrier *Ryujo* off to the Aleutians in a futile effort to divert a large proportion of the American strength; dispatched light carrier *Zuiho* away from his main fleet to accompany the Midway landing force; kept small and old *Hosho* with his battleships well behind his advance; and thus had only four carriers remaining to concentrate for the principal battle.

This dissipation of resources permitted the Americans to make the odds in the main battle almost even. Again they divined the enemy's plan, and they concentrated all the carrier strength available in the Pacific to meet it: *Enterprise*, *Hornet*, and, by dint of extraordinary labor to repair damages incurred in the Coral Sea, *Yorktown*. Not suspecting that the Americans had discerned their plan and therefore anticipating a naval battle only after they had advertised themselves by landing troops on Midway, the Japanese were slipshod in their searches for American ships, failed to discover the American carriers off Midway, and concentrated the first efforts of their carrier planes against the atoll. With a combination of superb timing and luck, a strike from the American carriers on June 4 found Yamamoto's *Akagi*, *Kaga*, *Soryu*, and *Hiryu* refueling and rearming their planes. Thirty-three of forty-one slow Douglas TBD Devastator torpedo bombers sacrificed themselves while accomplishing no important damage against the Japanese ships, but they brought the enemy's fighter cover down to low altitudes and diverted his antiaircraft gunners, just before the Douglas SBD Dauntless dive bombers arrived for a deadly attack which set *Akagi*, *Kaga*, and *Soryu* to sinking. *Hiryu* soon followed, though not before her planes had crippled *Yorktown* for a fatal submarine attack the next day. Though the Americans were down to two active carriers in the Pacific, Yamamoto was stunned by the elimination of the heart of his carrier force. The Japanese turned back without attempting a landing, and they had lost control of the momentum of the war.[4]

They might regain it, though, if the United States did not do something to keep them off balance. Through the six months since Pearl Harbor, the United States had been hastily patching together resources to shore up Pacific defenses wherever the Japanese tide pounded most strongly at any given moment, sacrificing to immediate desperation any long-range strategy, including the plan to give priority to the war in Europe. The improvised defense had at last stemmed the hostile tide. Though available Japanese strength still remained superior, Admiral King, the leading champion of action in the Pacific theater, believed the American strategy of improvised defense must now go over quickly to a strategy of limited offensives —equally an improvised strategy, because resources must still be scraped together from the bottom of the barrel and the transition must occur immediately. Clausewitz had written that when a conqueror is not strong enough to subdue his adversary completely, "Often, in fact almost universally, there is a culminating point in victory." Continued advance places "a fresh load on an advancing Army at every step of its progress," until the conquering force will feel itself "at last in a state of uncertainty and anxiety as to its situation," and until at the culminating point of victory any additional effort by the conqueror serves only to expose him to the defender's riposte. "This point may be very near at hand, and is sometimes so near that the whole of the results of a victorious battle are confined to an increase of the moral superiority."[5] Admiral King believed the Japanese advance had reached the culminating point of victory, and that the United States, though its resources remained desperately small, must seize the opportunity for the riposte.

In the Solomon Islands during the summer of 1942, Japanese from a seaplane base at Tulagi prepared an airfield on Guadalcanal, twenty miles farther on. Once completed, this airfield would imperil the American line of communication to Australia and pose a new threat to Port Moresby. Rear Admiral Richmond Kelly Turner, recently director of the War Plans Division of Naval Operations and newly designated commander of the South Pacific Amphibious Force, had already on July 3 submitted a project for an amphibious offensive against Tulagi and Guadalcanal. Admiral King insisted that the United States must land troops on Guadalcanal and Tulagi and eliminate the Japanese air bases there. Admiral Chester W. Nimitz, commanding the Pacific Fleet and the interservice Pacific Ocean Areas, agreed. The Army members of the American high command in Washington, the new interservice Joint Chiefs of Staff, were reluctant to accede to the urgings of their naval member King, both because of the general shortage of resources and because America's first major operation in the priority European theater was impending, the invasion of North Africa. But King was adamantine and he demanded the riposte at Guadalcanal, and the Joint Chiefs acquiesced.[6]

The 1st Marine Division, under Major General A. A. Vandegrift, assembled at Fiji in July. More than half its members had worn a uniform less than a year; General Vandegrift had hoped to have it fit for amphibious assault operations merely by early 1943; the division had to be pieced together in Fiji from New Zealand, Australia, San Diego, and Nouméa; Fiji proved an unsatisfactory place for landing rehearsals; but nevertheless the division was the most readily available embodiment of the Marines' long interest in amphibious war. The large landing ships and craft, LSTs and LSMs that were fully seaworthy and could contain and tend smaller craft, and the LCTs for tanks and heavy equipment, were not yet available. Two-thirds of the smaller craft in which the Marines would go ashore were primitive Higgins boats without ramps; about one-third of the Marines would have new landing craft with ramps. For tanks and trucks, medium landing craft, forty-five-foot LCMs, had become available. Some amphibious tractors had arrived in the South Pacific, but not enough. Little was known about the terrain of the southern Solomons, and the photographs taken by several aerial reconnaissance missions suffered a variety of misadventures, so knowledge of the landing areas had to be pieced together largely from a thirty-two-year-old Navy hydrographic chart, conversations with Australians who had lived in the islands, and Jack London's short story "The Red One." Carriers *Enterprise*, *Saratoga*, and *Wasp* were assembled for the invasion, but Vice Admiral Frank Jack Fletcher informed Admiral Turner, commanding the amphibious force, that he could not risk his carriers against superior Japanese sea and air power by remaining in the vicinity later than the fourth day after landing; Fletcher had been in command of both *Lexington* and *Yorktown* when they were lost, and he was determined not to lose more. Softening up consisted mostly of B-17 attacks from the New Hebrides, beginning seven days before D-day, which was August 7, 1942.[7]

It was fortunate that American amphibious assault technique and equipment turned out to be not severely tested. Bad weather grounded the enemy seaplanes at Tulagi for two days before the invasion, and the approach went undetected. The Guadalcanal landings were almost unopposed. On Tulagi, resistance was as tenacious as the garrison could make it, but the island was so small and the Japanese on it so few that it was overrun by the end of the second day.[8]

Only after the beachheads were secured did the shoestring nature of the operation begin to cause trouble. The proximity of land-based

Japanese aircraft, two-day losses of 21 percent of his fighters, and low fuel supplies made Admiral Fletcher so nervous that he announced on August 8 he would withdraw his carriers even earlier than originally planned; they began moving out that night. Admiral Turner then had to consider whether without air cover he should not withdraw his partially unloaded transports. He called a conference to discuss the problem with General Vandegrift and Rear Admiral Victor Crutchley of the Australian navy, who commanded the cruiser and destroyer screen for the northern approaches to the landing area. Although a heavy force of Japanese surface ships was reported steaming through the Solomons down the interior passage soon to be called the "Slot" and in the direction of his screen, Crutchley made no battle plan and was off talking with Turner when the reported enemy column, cruisers and destroyers, struck his screen.

The night action which followed, the battle of Savo Island, revealed that among the Japanese navy's superiorities over the American Navy was its remarkable skill in night gunnery. The Japanese "long lance" torpedos also worked havoc, the more so because Japanese cruisers had torpedo tubes while American cruisers did not. Three American cruisers and one Australian were sunk and another American cruiser had its bow blown off, with little damage to the Japanese. Luckily, the Japanese failed to press their victory and go in among the transports, because they feared the carrier planes which they did not know had departed. But the next day Turner pulled out his transports and the remaining escorts, and the Marines were left out on a limb.

Something over 16,000 of them were ashore, with ammunition for less than four days of heavy combat, less than half their supplies and equipment, no radar, no coast defense guns, and no heavy construction equipment. To make morale worse, they found themselves in one of the most inhospitable settings in the world, a stinking, humid island where the rains were so heavy that they were constantly rotting and decaying some portions of the very life which simultaneously they nourished abundantly, full of loathsome crawling things, and with the razor-sharp *kunai* grass and the malaria, dysentery, and various exotic tropical diseases likely to be as fearsome an enemy as the Japanese. Short rations had to be in effect from the beginning, and starvation would soon have threatened had it not been for finding large though wormy stocks of Japanese rice. Naturally, the Japanese prepared to use their command of air and sea to bring in reinforcements while the Marines were isolated. The Japanese Seventeenth Army was to be assembled to recapture Guadalcanal. The Marines formed a loose, five-mile-long defense perimeter anchored on the Tenaru (actually the Ilu) River and the Kukum hills and hastened to use abandoned Japanese equipment to complete the airstrip, which they named Henderson Field for a Marine aviator killed at Midway.

Perhaps the Americans' only salvation was Japanese overconfidence in their ability to remove the Guadalcanal thorn from their side at leisure. The Japanese did not exploit their air and sea power to throw in quickly as many reinforcements as they could have, and they committed their reinforcements piecemeal. On the night of August 20–21 they attacked the Marines along the Tenaru (Ilu) River in the first of a series of grim jungle battles; but they threw themselves into this effort when they had only about 1,000 men ashore, and the Americans repulsed them with a loss of only 34 killed to some 816 Japanese dead.

Vice Admiral Robert L. Ghormley, commanding the South Pacific Area from Nouméa, had begun to get a trickle of supplies to the Marines beginning August 15, with night runs of APDs, high-speed transports which were converted destroyers. Still, even when transports began to arrive, "the biggest logistical bottleneck," in the well-supported judgment of Admiral Turner's biographer, Vice Admiral George C. Dyer, "was the basic lack of know-how by the Navy concerning logistical support for a big operation six thousand miles away from a United States source of supply."[9]

By August 20 the Marines had Henderson Field in limited operating condition, and nineteen Wildcat fighters and twelve Dauntless dive bombers came in from the escort carrier *Long Island* (CVE-1). On the 22nd, part of the 67th Fighter Squadron of the Army Air Forces arrived, and two days later the Navy flew in some planes from *Enterprise*. This restoration of even minimal air power was all-important. By the 24th also, the American Navy had resumed risking forays into the Solomons, enough to provoke that day the first of a series of sea-air battles to accompany the accelerating pace of combat ashore. In the naval battles the Americans generally suffered heavier losses than the enemy, including *Wasp* and *Hornet* sunk and *Saratoga* and *Enterprise* badly damaged, but they managed to gain a measure of control of the sea during the daylight hours. Thus the Marines could be strengthened by day, occasionally and still with great difficulty—the 7th Marine Regiment arrived in September

—while at night the "Tokyo Express" ran in Japanese reinforcements and shelled the Americans ashore.

October was a bad month for the Americans. It brought endless monsoon rains; heavy attacks by large enemy reinforcements; the arrival of "Pistol Pete," Japanese 150mm guns; and intensified shelling by Japanese warships at night, including the "night of the battleships," when *Kongo* and *Haruna* hurled 14-inch shells at the Marines' foxholes and nearly wrecked Henderson Field and its airplanes. By mid-month American morale was probably at its lowest ebb.

On the 13th, however, the first Army reinforcements landed, the 164th Infantry of the Americal Division. On the 16th, Nimitz replaced Admiral Ghormley as South Pacific commander with Vice Admiral William F. Halsey. The press took to calling "Bill" Halsey "Bull," which aptly described the tenacity he brought to the job of hanging on in the Solomons; the choice was a fortunate one. In Washington, Admiral King insisted that Guadalcanal must be reinforced enough to be held, whatever the disruption of the American buildup in Europe; the opportunity to recapture the initiative in the Pacific must not be lost. King won President Franklin D. Roosevelt to his side. The 25th and 43rd Infantry Divisions were dispatched to the South Pacific. To join *North Carolina*, already in the area, the Navy sent out two more of the fast new battleships that had joined the fleet since Pearl Harbor, *South Dakota* and *Washington*. In the final days of the month, the Marines and infantry stood fast against the most sustained enemy attacks yet and tore apart the Japanese 2nd (Sendai) Division.

In early November, the 182nd Infantry of the Americal Division arrived on Guadalcanal. In the Naval Battle of Guadalcanal through November 12–15, the Japanese sank the cruisers *Atlanta* and *Juneau* and four destroyers while badly shooting up other cruisers and destroyers; but they lost the battleship *Hiei*, and in a brilliant exercise of radar-directed night gunnery *Washington* knocked out the Japanese battleship *Kirishima*. On the 14th, planes from Henderson Field, from Espiritu Santo in the New Hebrides, and from *Enterprise* caught eleven Japanese transports bringing down the 38th (Nagoya) Division, sank seven of them, sent the others ashore in flames, and left fewer than 5,000 of the division's 12,000 men alive. By the turn of the year, the Japanese on Guadalcanal were going over to the defensive, and in early February they skillfully evacuated Guadalcanal by night.[10]

They could afford their losses in ships and airplanes far less than the

Americans, because by late 1942 the United States was beginning to realize the full advantages of its much superior industrial base. Still, with the insistent demands of the European theater and of less affluent Allies as well as the Pacific to be met, many months would elapse before America's industrial productivity could make itself felt decisively against Japan. In the summer of 1943, the United States had to ask the British to send their carrier *Victorious* to the Pacific so that *Saratoga* would not be alone while *Enterprise* underwent repairs and until the new *Essex*-class carriers began to arrive.[11] While Vandegrift and Halsey were clinging to Guadalcanal, General Douglas MacArthur's Southwest Pacific forces were locked in similarly desperate battle, over even worse terrain, for the Papuan tip of eastern New Guinea. Both the Papuan campaign and Guadalcanal were aimed ultimately toward Rabaul at the northeastern tip of the island of New Britain, which the Japanese had made into a mighty sea and air base. Despite the American victories at the end of 1942, it required almost all of the next year to fight on up the Solomons chain northwestward from Guadalcanal to Bougainville, where the 3rd Marine Division of Lieutenant General Vandegrift's I Marine Amphibious Corps landed November 1, and from Papua into the Huon Peninsula of Northeast New Guinea, opposite New Britain. Not until December 15, 1943, did the 112th Cavalry Regiment of the 1st Cavalry Division make the first landing on New Britain, at Arawe, while the 1st Marine Division went ashore in a larger operation at Cape Gloucester the day after Christmas.[12]

The New Guinea advance would not have been possible at all if General MacArthur had had to proceed principally by frontal assaults against the large numbers of Japanese soldiers on that big island. Beginning with small-scale landings on the Trobriand Islands on June 30, 1943, however, MacArthur's amphibious force under Rear Admiral Daniel E. Barbey developed proficiency and flexibility in remarkably short order; and despite a short supply of the new amphibious landing craft, MacArthur was able to move by amphibious end runs up the northern coast. For short hauls such as those up the New Guinea coast, landing forces no longer had to go to sea in large transports, to climb down nets into landing boats when they approached the assault areas. Instead, they could make the whole trip in the big new ocean-going landing ships, either to have their LCVP(R)s, LCMs, and LCTs discharged from the LSTs for the landing or to go ashore directly from the LSTs.[13]

MacArthur wanted to have carriers to increase the range of his air support and thus the distance his amphibious end runs could leap, but the Navy would not entrust its scarce and precious carriers to an Army general in the narrow waters of the Solomon and Bismarck seas. So MacArthur had to depend on Lieutenant General George C. Kenney's Allied Air Force, built around the American Fifth Air Force, which both had to strain itself sometimes to cover the distances MacArthur wanted to travel and initially displayed the usual Army Air Forces aversion to anything except "strategic bombing." This meant that Kenney thought the best way to give air cover to an amphibious assault was to attack enemy air bases, and that he long thought that if he bombed the air bases, then it was enough to protect amphibious convoys by holding fighters on standby alert. Not until the Finschhafen landing on September 22, 1943, was MacArthur able to nudge Kenney—Admiral Barbey's word—into providing two layers of air cover directly over the landing troops.

In time, however, Kenney's Fifth Air Force became probably the best of AAF units in rendering tactical support for amphibious assaults. And throughout the Southwest Pacific campaigns, Kenney's air power was as indispensable as Barbey's amphibious force to MacArthur's leapfrogging advance, while it contributed much also to the conquest of the Solomons.[14] MacArthur saw the New Guinea campaign as a demonstration of "the enormous flexibility of modern air power."

> The calculated advance of bomber lines through seizure of forward bases [he said] meant that a relatively small force of bombers operating at short and medium ranges could attack under cover of an equally limited fighter force. Each phase of advance had as its objective an airfield which could serve as a steppingstone to the next advance. . . .
>
> It was the practical application of this system of warfare—to avoid the frontal attack with its terrible loss of life; to by-pass Japanese strongpoints and neutralize them by cutting their lines of supply; to thus isolate their armies and starve them on the battlefield; to, as Willie Keeler used to say, "hit 'em where they ain't"—that from this time forward guided my movements and operations.[15]

But MacArthur also had to say of his indirect, leapfrogging approach: "The paucity of the resources at my command made me adopt this method of campaign as the only hope of accomplishing my task."[16] The Solomon Islands and New Guinea campaigns were gradually wrestling the initiative away from the Japanese forever, but to sustain the campaigns King and MacArthur were also wrestling into the Pacific men and resources that most of the British-

American Combined Chiefs of Staff would have preferred to see going to the presumably primary war in Europe.

In March, 1943, the Army had planned to have 753,440 of its men deployed against Japan at the end of the year; by December 31, the actual deployment of Army manpower against Japan was 912,942.[17] King and MacArthur continued to insist that now that the Pacific initiative was passing into America's hands, it was vital not to abandon it. The Japanese must be kept under continuous pressure and continuously off balance. Otherwise, even if they could no longer extend their conquests they would be able to consolidate their hold upon the vast empire they had already conquered. If they were allowed time for consolidation, the task of recapturing the territories they fortified and of projecting American power near enough to the home islands to compel Japan's submission would surely require years and a huge expenditure of casualties. To fortify her initial conquests in this manner, and behind the mobile Japanese fleet supported by those defenses to hold the Americans and their Allies away from the "Inner Ring" of Japan's most valuable territories until the Americans lost patience, was indeed Japan's strategy for the war.

Like Lincoln's government before it, President Roosevelt's in World War II labored under an acute awareness that the American electorate might not show patience with a prolonged war. General Marshall had made his observation that a democracy cannot fight a seven years' war. President Roosevelt and Prime Minister Winston Churchill had announced, however, that the object of the war was to be the unconditional surrender of the Axis powers, a characteristically American war aim but one generally accepted among the Allies in order to ensure that the aggressor governments and societies could be so completely reshaped that they would never endanger the Western democracies again. If the American people were to remain patient enough to see the Pacific war through to the unconditional surrender of Japan, then the pace of the war must not be allowed to lag. The supposedly secondary war persisted in demanding the resources of a primary war. This was the more true because the pace of the war up the Solomons and New Guinea in 1943 remained exasperatingly slow; at such a rate, the Japanese would have all too much time to fortify their Inner Ring.[18]

Some American military planners for a time nourished fond hopes for the development of China as a source of growing pressure against Japan. At the Casablanca conference of the American and British civil and military chiefs early in 1943, Admiral King said:

> In the European theater Russia was most advantageously placed for dealing with Germany in view of her geographical position and manpower; in the Pacific, China bore a similar relation to the Japanese. It should be our basic policy to provide the manpower resources of Russia and China with the necessary equipment to enable them to fight.[19]

The Army and the Army Air Forces hoped at least to make China a base for heavy bomber attacks against the Japanese homeland, since China now represented the Allied territory nearest to Japan. But by late 1943, American hopes for China as a source of effective armies or even as a site for bomber bases were collapsing on the twin obstacles of China's internal disorganization and the logistical difficulties of supplying either Chinese armies or American air power in China by air lift from India over the "hump" of the Himalayas. The American Army tried in vain to persuade the British to launch a major offensive for the reconquest of Burma and the reopening of effective land communication with China. But British resources were of course strained worse than American; and if the British were to muster any large effort in Southeast Asia, which at this point they were not prepared to do, they would have preferred to recapture their imperial outposts in Singapore, Malaya, and Borneo rather than pull Chinese chestnuts out of the fire. They procrastinated over doing anything in particular in Southeast Asia until the Americans at length also lost interest in that region and hope for China as an active ally.[20]

If continuous pressure were to bear against Japan, it would have to come not from China but from the United States; but if possible it must come without demanding so much American manpower and equipment that the theoretical priority of the European war would have to be altogether sacrificed. The interwar planning studies for an ORANGE war had contemplated three possible routes of approach to the Japanese homeland: from the South Pacific northward through the Philippines; by the northern route through Alaska and the Aleutians; and directly westward from Hawaii through the Japanese-mandated islands of the Central Pacific. Attu and Kiska in the Aleutians were recaptured from the Japanese during 1943, but the Alaska-Aleutians route seemed too difficult logistically, with too many weather problems, and with its bases too distant from the home islands, Billy Mitchell notwithstanding. The advance from the South Pacific, now the South Pacific and Southwest Pacific Areas under interservice and Allied command arrangements, was actually going forward but with the slowness that was one of the American planners' problems in 1943. Accordingly the planners in Washington turned toward the Central Pacific route, in Admiral Nimitz's Pacific Ocean Areas. When he learned they were doing so, General MacArthur naturally offered ardent objections to an emphasis on Nimitz's theater at the expense of his own:

> From a broad strategic viewpoint [MacArthur cabled to General Marshall] I am convinced that the best course of offensive action in the Pacific is a movement from Australia through New Guinea to Mindanao. This movement can be supported by land-based aircraft which is utterly essential and will immediately cut the enemy lines from Japan to his conquered territory to the southward. By contrast a movement through the mandated islands will be a series of amphibious attacks with the support of carrier-based aviation against objectives defended by naval units and ground troops supported by land-based aviation. Midway stands as an example of the hazards of such an operation. Moreover no vital strategic objective is reached until the series of amphibious frontal attacks succeed in reaching Mindanao. The factors upon which the old Orange war plans were based have been greatly altered by the hostile conquest of Malaya and the Netherlands East Indies and by the availability of Australia as a base.[21]

By late 1943, however, it was precisely the fact that the Central Pacific would feature carrier warfare and amphibious landings that made it attractive. The new *Essex*-class fast carriers, along with the lighter *Independence* class, were beginning to arrive in the Pacific. *Essex*, of 27,000 tons, 33 knots top speed, and a capacity of up to 100 planes, had been authorized in 1938 and laid down in April, 1941. Ten more carriers of the same class had been authorized in June and July, 1940, and two more just after Pearl Harbor. For more rapid construction, Congress had also authorized in the first three months of 1942 six light carriers to be converted from light cruisers. Numerous carriers would soon join the Pacific Fleet, enough so that on June 10, 1943, a new statement of fleet doctrine, PAC 10, reversed a ruling of the scarcity days of the previous year and prescribed concentration of carriers in multicarrier task forces. The British had enjoyed success with such tactical concentration of carriers in the Mediterranean. Franklin G. Percival, so prescient about carrier operations in the 1920s, wrote in the May, 1943, Naval Institute *Proceedings* that "The outstanding unsolved problem is the defense of aircraft carriers. . . . This urgency is rendered acute by the fact that there can be no sustained offensive until an adequate solution is found." Percival again urged using battleships as floating antiaircraft platforms and strengthening the carriers' own antiaircraft batteries, but to complete the solution he argued it was necessary to pool the carriers' antiaircraft defense and their fighter cover in a single tactical formation for mutual support. New radar devices would enable such a formation to maintain high speed at night or in any weather. Multi-carrier task forces began to go into action when Rear Admiral Charles A. Pownall's Task Force 15, with the new *Yorktown* (CV-10), *Essex* (CV-9), and *Independence* (CVL-22), raided Marcus Island in August, 1943.[22]

By mid-1943, the Marine Corps had three divisions in the Pacific trained in its doctrine of amphibious war and laced with veterans of Guadalcanal. In August the Corps added fifty pages to its *Landing Operations Doctrine* to incorporate lessons gained from experiences in the South Pacific and exercises under wartime conditions.[23]

To support operations across the vast distances of the Central Pacific, the Navy had abandoned its interwar neglect of logistics and, sustained by mobilized American industrial productivity, was readying an unprecedented array of at-sea logistical services. In October, 1943, Admiral Nimitz ordered the formation of two mobile service squadrons for the Central Pacific. For operations at the close of the year, thirteen oilers were available, each carrying 80,000 barrels of fuel oil, 18,000 barrels of aviation gasoline, and 6,800 barrels of diesel oil. The floating logistical bases came to include floating drydocks, floating cranes, repair barges, salvage barges, provisions stores ships, ammunition barges, and rearming barges, all calculated to permit American warships to remain at sea for months, while previous modern fleets had measured their cruising capacities by a few weeks.[24]

In June, 1943, Admiral King proposed for about November 1 an attack against the Marshall Islands, the most easterly of the Japanese mandates. General Marshall and the Army planners objected that such an offensive would require the diversion of too many resources from MacArthur's drive toward Rabaul, in particular the 1st Marine Division, which was in Australia undergoing retraining for MacArthur's use in the Southwest Pacific Area. The Army believed pressure should be maintained along MacArthur's route toward Japan. Nevertheless, the interservice Joint Strategic Survey Committee strongly recommended development of the Central Pacific route as well, as the only route along which the newly available American naval forces could be utilized to their best advantage. As for the strategic objectives which MacArthur claimed were lacking in the Central Pacific, an advance there, threatening the Japanese naval base at Truk in the Carolines, might force the Japanese fleet to offer a decisive battle. Victory in such an action could almost ensure winning the war and would free all further amphibious operations from the threat of naval interference. The Navy planners had not forgotten the strategic teachings of Admiral Mahan.

As the Joint Chiefs came to view Pacific strategy, furthermore, an advance across the Central Pacific would converge with MacArthur's advance somewhere in the bottleneck through which Japanese communications with the southern part of the empire passed between Luzon and Formosa and the China mainland. Once established there, the United States could cut off the flow of oil and other vital raw materials from the East Indies to the home islands.[25]

In July and August, 1943, the Joint Chiefs accordingly decided upon a dual advance against Japan, MacArthur to continue through New Guinea and Halsey through the Solomons toward Rabaul, Nimitz's forces in the Central Pacific Area to move toward Truk, postponing the attack on the Marshalls to early 1944 but beginning with landings about November 15 in the Gilbert Islands, taken from the British after Pearl Harbor, farther east than the Marshalls and thus offering both less immediate logistical strain and good bases for a subsequent move into the Marshalls. These offensives would require resources which were also needed in Europe, especially landing craft, which were in short supply everywhere; but they would also employ naval resources which could not so well be used elsewhere, the Central Pacific campaign might pay large dividends for a relatively small investment of troops, and at least the Japanese would be prevented from strengthening their defenses at leisure. Most important in the minds of the prime movers of the Central Pacific advance, Admirals King and Nimitz, this offensive would lead to the destruction of the enemy resource on which everything else depended, the Japanese fleet. As Nimitz said: "When conflicts in timing and allocation of means exist, due weight should be accorded to the fact that operations in the Central Pacific promise at this time a more rapid advance toward Japan and her vital lines of communication; the earlier acquisition of strategic air bases closer to the Japanese homeland; and, of greatest importance, are more likely to precipitate a decisive engagement with the Japanese fleet."[26]

With this decision to press forward along the Central Pacific route toward Japan, and not to give primary emphasis to MacArthur's advance through the large islands of the Southwest Pacific Area, the Pacific war was reconfirmed as preeminently a naval war. Henceforth the United States would wage against the island empire of

Japan a maritime war according to the precepts of Alfred Thayer Mahan. Its strategy would aim at depriving the Japanese navy of its bases and when possible striking for destruction at the Imperial Navy itself. Once the Japanese navy had been conquered in a Mahanian battle, then American command of the sea could be employed to strangle the Japanese economy, an island economy still vulnerable to sea power as continental economies were not. But with the American Navy ascendant both against its Japanese rival and in the command of the Pacific war, and with the strategic precepts of Mahan guiding the Navy's leaders, first must come the destruction of the Japanese battle fleet, a strategic objective which henceforth became increasingly the focus of American naval planning.

The principal immediate objective chosen in the Gilberts was Tarawa Atoll, where Betio Islet was large enough to support an airfield. The landing of parts of the 2nd Marine Division there on November 20, 1943, demonstrated that imperfections still remained in American amphibious technique, especially in close air support from the carriers and in naval bombardment. The preliminary bombardment attempted to saturate the defenses, dropping 2,000 tons of shells and bombs on Betio's 291 acres; the results suggested that concentration upon specific targets in the defense system was preferable to saturation, and preparation for subsequent landings was modified accordingly. Subsequent landings were also preceded by increasingly longer preliminary naval gunfire bombardment than the two and a half hours on the morning of D-day that Tarawa received; but at Tarawa the Americans were not sure how badly attrition in the South and Southwest Pacific had eroded Japanese naval surface and air strength, and it seemed important to get as much strength ashore as possible after giving the Japanese as little warning as possible, in anticipation of heavy aerial counterattacks on the invasion shipping and very likely a foray by the Japanese fleet. These counterstrokes never came, but at the time the American planners thought they had better expect them than risk the sinking of crowded transports.

The Japanese chose to resist the Tarawa landings as they had never resisted on the beaches before. They foresaw the assault on Tarawa because the atoll was the best of the Gilberts for support of further American advances. But the atoll was so small and Betio so plainly the key to the atoll that they had no space for maneuver or for defense in depth. They therefore covered Betio with guns of every kind emplaced in ferro-concrete bombproofs and coconut-log-and-concrete pillboxes. They surrounded the islet with a coconut-log seawall three to five feet high. They made the ocean approach impassable with horned concrete tetrahedrons wired together with mines among them. The Americans arrived before they could similarly obstruct the northwestern approach through the atoll's lagoon, but covering the lagoon was a reef some 500 to 1,000 yards offshore. If the Americans tried to come in at high tide to float over the reef, there would be no beaches on which to land, get organized, and sort out supplies, because the high tide reached the seawall. If the Americans tried to come in at low tide, as they probably must, their landing craft were expected to ground on the reef.

The Marines had enough information about the reef that they refused to attempt the assault unless they were equipped with enough amphibious tractors—until recently a great unforeseen requirement of amphibious war—capable of running over the reef to carry the first three waves. They got that many amtracks, but still the supply was not large enough. This first stoutly opposed amphibious assault went badly. So few of the Japanese guns were silenced by the preliminary sea and air bombardment that they disabled many of the amtracks before they reached the beach. Few of the amtracks could return to the reef to pick up troops from the fourth wave onward, and so these men had to leave their grounded landing craft at the reef and wade through half a mile or more of waist-deep water with treacherous potholes, under fire all the way. By the time the survivors of this ordeal got to the beach, the first three waves remained mostly pinned down behind the seawall and were decimated. A few tanks, reinforcements brought from the attack on Makin Atoll elsewhere in the Gilberts, and much courage and tenacity overcame the defenses and overran the islet by the third day; but the 2nd Marine Division lost 991 dead or mortally wounded and 2,311 wounded in the capture of Tarawa.[27]

Some two and a half months later, at Kwajalein Atoll in the Marshalls, Rear Admiral Richard L. Connolly staged a three-day bombardment against the northern islets of Roi and Namur, as compared with the few hours' bombardment at Tarawa, and Admiral Turner pounded Kwajalein Island in the southern part of the atoll almost as long. LCIs converted to gunboats and armored amphibious tractors mounting 37mm guns preceded the assault troops to the beaches. After Tarawa, amphibious tractors were supplied to the Central Pacific as rapidly as possible, and along with the Army's new amphibious two-and-one-half-ton truck, the Dukw, making its first

Central Pacific appearance at Kwajalein, they made impressive contributions both to landing tactics and to ship-to-shore logistical support. Meanwhile the work of airplanes based on the Gilberts in softening the defenses amply justified the decision to take those islands before entering the Marshalls. During the assault, Admiral Turner, in general charge of the landings as commander of V Amphibious Force, recommended applying close air support techniques demonstrated by some carrier aircraft in the Gilberts, continually strafing from very low altitudes as little as ten feet ahead of the infantry. A new amphibious command ship (AGC) developed from experience in the Mediterranean had communications gear for centralized control of the whole ship-to-shore operation, including control of air support. The 4th Marine and 7th Infantry Divisions took Kwajalein Atoll with a loss of only 372 killed out of 41,000, compared with 7,870 of 8,675 Japanese.[28]

Kwajalein collapsed so readily under the bombardment of surface gunnery and the fast carrier air strikes and improved amphibious techniques that Nimitz proposed advancing D-day for Eniwetok, also in the Marshalls, from May 1 to February 17, using the reserve troops already afloat and not needed for Kwajalein. The relevant commanders in the Central Pacific and in Washington agreed, and agreed also to conduct in conjunction with the Eniwetok assault a fast carrier raid against Truk originally scheduled for March. The strategic motives were the consistent ones of the Central Pacific campaign; the raid on Truk, said Vice Admiral Raymond A. Spruance, "it was hoped, might enable us to bring on an engagement with the Japanese fleet." Against Truk went three three-carrier task groups of Rear Admiral Marc A. Mitscher's Task Force 58, part of Admiral Spruance's Fifth Fleet. They destroyed some 200,000 tons of merchant shipping, two destroyers, and 275 enemy aircraft in the air and on the ground, losing seventeen airplanes themselves. They thus confirmed the superiority of newly available American carrier aircraft, spearheaded by the Grumman F6F Hellcat fighter and including the Curtiss SB2C Helldiver and the Grumman TBF Avenger, over any Japanese airplanes as long as the numerical balance was anywhere near equitable. Years of concealment behind the curtain of secrecy enshrouding the Japanese mandates had given Truk a fearsome reputation as an impregnable Gibraltar; the American carriers found it far from that, and in fact, they discovered that the Japanese navy had grown so respectful of the American Fast Carrier Task Force that its main elements had withdrawn westward from Truk. The hope for a Mahanian fleet engagement was not yet to be fulfilled.[29]

The Eniwetok invasion proceeded as scheduled and with success, and the evidence of enemy weakness produced by the Truk raid inspired new and bolder improvisations in strategy. In November, 1943, the carriers *Saratoga* and *Princeton* (CVL-23) had entered the South Pacific—the first fast carriers to do so in nearly a year—to raid Rabaul in support of the Bougainville landings; they had mauled a big Japanese cruiser force at Rabaul so badly that it sailed away. A subsequent November strike in which *Bunker Hill* (CV-17), *Essex*, and *Independence* joined with *Saratoga* and *Princeton* helped add the finishing touch to beatings which General Kenney's land-based air power had already inflicted upon the enemy's air strength at Rabaul. Significantly, much of the damage was done by the carriers' anti-aircraft guns. When MacArthur learned in February that Truk as well as Rabaul was stripped of Japanese offensive strength and that daring moves on his part therefore could not be countered either from the Carolines or New Britain, he hastened an impromptu landing in the Admiralty Islands west of New Britain on February 29. Admiral Barbey's amphibious force was up to the challenge of scrapping the necessary materials together. More Japanese ground strength turned up on Los Negros in the Admiralties than MacArthur expected, but troops of the 1st Cavalry Division fought them off and made the general's gamble a success. The Admiralties encircled and thus went far toward neutralizing Rabaul. In Seeadler Harbor, they provided MacArthur with a huge anchorage comparable to the one at Rabaul.[30]

At least since mid-1943 the Joint Chiefs of Staff had been hoping that Rabaul could be bypassed and neutralized rather than subjected to a direct assault, because there was still a strong Japanese ground force in the area. Hitherto, MacArthur insisted that he needed to take Rabaul for its harbor; but prodded by the Central Pacific advance and fearful of diversion of resources to Nimitz, he had now applied the principle of "hitting 'em where they ain't" on a bolder scale than he had ever done before.

The weakness of the Marshalls and of Truk suggested a similar strategy in the Central Pacific. From the earliest considerations of an advance across the Pacific through Japan's island chain, the idea that certain of the enemy's island strongpoints might be bypassed intrigued some of the planners. Unless some of the islands could be leaped over, there would have to be an interminable series of frontal assaults with little opportunity for strategic surprise. Until the arrival of the new fast carriers, however, few islands could be bypassed because each island or group of islands was likely to be needed as an air base against the next. Thus the Solomons campaign of 1942–43 was a straightforward slugging match from one island to the next, with only a limited experiment in leapfrogging when Kolombangara was omitted to hop from New Georgia to Vella Lavella. MacArthur in New Guinea and the neighboring islands had practiced "hitting 'em where they ain't" as much as his dependence on short-range land-based air power would permit; but that dependence made even the jump to the Admiralties a relatively short leap in terms of distance.

Now planners in Washington and the Central Pacific were suggesting that the fast carriers might make it possible to bypass Truk and to leap all the way from Eniwetok to the Marianas, a distance of a thousand miles. The Marshalls operation and the raid on Truk convinced Nimitz it could be done and should be attempted. Nimitz and his chief planner, Rear Admiral Forrest P. Sherman, traveled to Washington to meet with the Joint Chiefs on March 11 and 12. Out of the conference came a JCS directive of March 12 instructing Nimitz to continue neutralizing Truk and to make the big leap to Saipan in the Marianas on June 15. This advance in turn would open a whole new range of possibilities. From Saipan, 1,500 miles from Tokyo, the Army Air Forces' new very-long-range Boeing B-29 Superfortress bombers would be able to attack Japan itself.[31]

The JCS directive of March 12 also instructed MacArthur to carry forward his campaign to secure New Guinea and then to assault Mindanao in the southern Philippines on November 15, 1944. With the completion of the reconquest of the Solomons in the spring of 1944, the South Pacific Area was liquidated as a combat area, the bulk of its Army forces going to MacArthur, the bulk of its Navy and all its Marine forces to Nimitz. But through MacArthur's Southwest Pacific Area, the offensive thrust which had been improvised in 1942 to capture the initiative from the enemy continued to move, though the initiative was now securely in American hands and traditional conceptions of strategy would have frowned on the two American offensives from the Southwest and the Central Pacific as awarding the enemy the advantage of the interior lines. Expediently, there seemed to be no way of managing the Pacific war except by continuing to allow the Army and the Navy each to dominate a part of it. MacArthur was too egotistical and in public and political esteem too powerful a personage to be subordinated to a Navy theater command, especially since Admiral King apparently disliked as well as distrusted him; while the Navy understandably refused to give control of the fast carriers and the ocean war in the Central Pacific to an Army general. If it did not conform to classical, Jominian strategy, the dual-offensive Pacific strategy born of improvisation and expediency had by 1944 a superior virtue: America's mobilized resources were now so much greater than Japan's that, as with Lincoln's and Grant's strategy of pressing the Confederacy everywhere, the enemy was bound to be too weak to hold on some fronts if not on all.[32]

The JCS directive of March left open the question whether the Southwest Pacific and Central Pacific drives would converge on Luzon or on Formosa. The Army chiefs in Washington had once preferred Formosa, while they still cherished illusions about China and hoped to link up with its manpower, and after that while they hoped to mount a B-29 offensive from China. Admiral King and the Navy more clearly persisted in preferring Formosa, as a better place than Luzon from which to plug the bottleneck between Japan and the Indies as well as a steppingstone to the whole China coast. MacArthur insisted on Luzon and on a high priority for the liberation of all the Philippines. He believed that the route to Luzon was strategically the best because the most direct route from his area to Japan. He also believed that he personally and the United States nationally owed the swiftest possible liberation as a debt of honor to the Filipinos, for their long-suffering loyalty to the United States, their sacrifices in the campaign of 1941–42, and their unbroken resistance to the Japanese occupation. He had pledged to return, and he must fulfill his pledge. Though honor alone should be a decisive consideration, he believed too that the United States would suffer an irreparable loss in prestige and influence throughout the Orient if it did not rescue the loyal Filipinos as soon as it had the resources and the strategic position to do so. If the Filipinos were bypassed and left to liberate themselves from the remnants of Japanese power in the backwash of the Allies' advance, the United States would never be able to claim their friendship again, and rightly so; and although MacArthur was not at this time making a public issue of it, the Filipinos' self-liberation might then be taken over by Communist leadership.[33]

In July, 1944, President Roosevelt met with MacArthur and Nimitz at Pearl Harbor to discuss Pacific strategy and particularly the question of Luzon versus Formosa. The conference was not decisive, but it helped tip the balance in MacArthur's favor and toward Luzon. By the summer of 1944 the Army increasingly saw an approach to China as a strategic dead-end, with accumulating evidence of Chinese political weakness and Japan's extension of her control over the Chinese coast. With the promise of getting the Marianas, and much difficulty developing over B-29 bases in China, the Army Air Forces no longer so much counted on bombing Japan from the China mainland. Chinese weakness and Japanese activity on the China coast raised the danger that to establish secure American bases in any part of Formosa the whole island would have to be conquered; Nimitz came to believe that Amoy on the mainland would have to be captured as well. Such tasks of conquest and occupation would demand more American troops than Luzon and probably more than would be available in the Pacific until after the defeat of Germany. On July 30 an amphibious landing by MacArthur's forces at Sansapor on the Vogelkop Peninsula signalized the imminent windup of the New Guinea campaign and impelled some kind of decision. In September, the Joint Chiefs set December 20 for a landing by MacArthur's forces on Leyte in the central Philippines, with Nimitz's fleet in support, and following upon Mindanao. Preparations were to proceed for a landing on Luzon on February 20, 1945, or on Formosa on March 1. Not until October 3, 1944, did Admiral King at last capitulate to the Army and to the growing doubts of his own service, to agree that between Luzon and Formosa, it should be Luzon.[34]

So persistent an indecision about where the Southwest and Central Pacific offensives should converge was bound up with the larger question of how the final defeat of Japan was to be accomplished. The Navy clung to the Formosa objective because it believed that a blockade of Japan firmly clamping shut the Formosa-Luzon bottleneck from bases on Formosa and perhaps the China coast would suffice, along with sea and air bombardment of the home islands, to complete a Mahanian strangulation and compel Japan to surrender without need for an invasion. The Army Air Forces agreed that no invasion of the home islands would be necessary; with the coming of the B-29 the AAF hoped to vindicate the prophets of air power through the obliteration of Japanese industry, cities, and morale from the sky. The Army disagreed; its doctrine remained that the defeat of a nation required the destruction of its armed forces, and its planners believed that the destruction of the Japanese armed forces could be accomplished within an acceptable span of time only by coming to grips with the great military reserves which Japan still hoarded in the home islands. In this strategic debate, the Navy hoped to advance its case for a strategy of sea power by achieving the first object of Mahanian strategy, the destruction of the enemy fleet.[35]

According to Admiral Mahan, because the true end of a navy "is to preponderate over the enemy's navy and so control the sea, then the enemy's ships and fleets are the true objects to be assailed on all occasions."[36]

Alone among the great navies of the world, the United States Navy entered World War II never having fought a fleet action against capital ships for the fulfillment of Mahan's strategic principles, for the destruction of an enemy battle fleet and the establishment of undisputed control of the sea. Perhaps the absence of a decisive capital-ship engagement from its tradition despite its long history made the American Navy of the 1920s and 1930s regard with all the more fascination the prospect of the climactic duel between the battle fleets in the anticipated struggle against the victors of Tsushima. During the years between the world wars and amid the diligent planning for the coming ORANGE war, the officers of the American Navy poured over the record of the battle of Jutland with religious persistence, to draw from the lessons of Jutland guidance for their own expected super-Jutland in the prospective war with Japan.

No officer did more to crystallize the American understanding of the lessons of Jutland than the young and precocious Navy strategic student and writer of the interwar years, Commander H. H. Frost. For the last eighteen years of his life Frost examined Jutland microscopically to produce a history of the battle which still ranks among the best studies of a much studied subject. The book appeared posthumously, following Frost's death from meningitis while he was on the staff of the commandant of the Command and General Staff School at Fort Leavenworth in 1935. Beyond Mahan's injunction that the enemy's ships and fleet are the true object to be assailed in naval war, Commander Frost drew from the frustration of the British Admirals Jellicoe and Beatty in the great battle of May 31, 1916, the lesson that to ensure Mahanian success, Nelsonian boldness is indispensable.

Frost believed that a Trafalgar victory at Jutland could have produced immeasurably beneficial results for Great Britain, including the forestalling of Germany's unrestricted submarine warfare and the opening of a route through the Baltic for the sustenance of Russia.

He believed that a Trafalgar victory eluded the Grand Fleet at Jutland because Sir John Jellicoe, in part under the influence of the British naval historian and contemporary of Mahan Sir Julian Corbett, forsook the Nelsonian tradition that "Something must be left to chance; nothing is certain in a sea fight beyond all others," for a cautious, negative strategy based on the proposition that nothing must be left to chance. The best that Frost could say for Jellicoe was that "Jellicoe executed a poor conception of war excellently. . . . Jellicoe had skill, but as the Spartan said, 'Skill that can not fight is useless.' "[37]

> There was the choice: to fight or not to fight. Ours, in the place of the Admiralty, would have been to fight. Theirs was not to fight. That decision fastened upon the British Navy an incubus of which it will not rid itself for many a year. Every British commander with an instinctive willingness to assume risks, which is the very foundation of naval and military greatness, will be confronted with a formidable library purporting to prove by every form of skillful plea and clever argument that Jellicoe won the World War without "leaving anything to chance."[38]

Looking to the future, Frost conceded that in coming naval wars it might prove even more difficult to compel the enemy battle fleet to engage in a decisive combat than the British had found it in the Great War:

> This is due to the special circumstances of naval warfare which allow an enemy fleet to decline action by remaining in a defended port or so close to it that an assured line of retirement is always available. This means that a fleet action could take place only:
>
> *a*) When both fleets were willing to fight, or
>
> *b*) One was lured to sea and its retreat cut off, or
>
> *c*) It was forced out of port by pressure other than that exerted by our battle fleet.
>
> Due to these facts, fleet actions have rarely occurred, and of these very few have been decisive.[39]

But the decisive fleet action is so essential to naval strategy that it should be pursued despite grave risks:

> Nevertheless, despite these difficulties, the importance of decisively defeating the enemy battle fleet is so great that every opportunity for action should be seized; in addition, we must endeavor in every possible way to bring about and force such opportunities, which must not be missed just because all the conditions are not in our favor. These op-

> portunities occur so seldom to a superior fleet that they should be regarded as absolutely priceless and distinctly unfavorable battle conditions should be accepted if necessary.[40]

"Every mistake in war is excusable," said Frost, "except inactivity and refusal to run risks."[41]

To bring the Japanese fleet to decisive battle was a main strategic goal of the American Navy's Central Pacific advance. The Marianas were part of Japan's "Inner Ring," and the American Navy believed that the assault upon Saipan might well prove to be the thrust that would provoke the enemy fleet to come out to fight. To meet the enemy if he did come out, America's Pacific Ocean naval strength was concentrated in Vice Admiral Spruance's Fifth Fleet. On June 11, four days before the scheduled landing, Vice Admiral Mitscher's Task Force 58 of the Fifth Fleet began the preliminary bombardment with its carrier aircraft. On June 13 seven new battleships of Vice Admiral Willis A. Lee's Task Group 58.7 joined the bombardment. The next day seven old battleships repaired from the Pearl Harbor disaster and commanded by Rear Admiral Jesse B. Oldendorf took up the bombardment; these older and slower battlewagons were ideal for such work, and the Gilberts and Marshalls operations had given them thorough practice in it.

On June 15 Vice Admiral Turner sent ashore the 2nd and 4th Marine Divisions, spearheads of the V Amphibious Corps of Lieutenant General Holland M. Smith, a pioneer of Marine amphibious doctrine and technique. Amtracks carried the invaders over the barrier reefs. Escort carriers provided better close air support than ever before, though the Marines complained about Turner's overcentralized control of it. The assault waves secured their beachheads without undue difficulty; but they did not reach their first day's objectives. During the night, they had to stand on the exposed beaches to fight off a stout Japanese counterattack. The enemy attacked with a resolution redoubled by the knowledge circulating among them that their fleet was on its way to destroy the American Navy.[42]

The Japanese fleet would not be so difficult to invite to decisive battle as H. H. Frost had feared. It too was conditioned by the Mahanian doctrine of seeking a decisive engagement to win control of the sea. Admiral Yamamoto, now dead, victim of an AAF P-38 attack on his plane during a visit to Rabaul, had looked for the decisive encounter at Midway. Admiral Toyoda Soemu, in Yamamoto's place as Commander in Chief Combined Fleet, received word of the June 15 landing on Saipan and promptly told his commanders: "The Combined Fleet will attack the enemy in the Marianas area and annihilate the invasion force." He followed up by repeating to the fleet the orders issued by the revered Admiral Togo Heichiro on the occasion of the battle of Tsushima thirty-nine years before: "The fate of the Empire rests on this one battle. Every man is expected to do his utmost."[43]

The Combined Fleet had not sortied against the Gilberts or Marshalls operations, in part because its aircraft and pilot strength had been shattered after being shuttled to land bases to provide the aerial defense of Rabaul. For months the Japanese carriers had been almost without planes. Now the carriers were filled with aircraft again and had the best trained pilots available. At Toyoda's order the First Task Fleet under Vice Admiral Ozawa Jisaburo set sail from Tawi Tawi, its anchorage in the Celebes Sea between Mindanao and Borneo. Against Admiral Spruance's Fifth Fleet of seven fleet carriers, eight light carriers, and seven new battleships, Ozawa could bring five fleet carriers, four light carriers, and five battleships. To compensate for the American edge in naval strength, Toyoda and Ozawa counted on over 1,600 land-based airplanes in the Marianas or within striking distance. They also counted on a carefully planned submarine campaign, which American patrols and hunter-killer groups turned into one of the first fizzles of their effort.

The Japanese had the additional advantage of longer-range carrier aircraft, thanks to their planes' lack of armor and of self-sealing fuel tanks, which gave them lighter weight. They could search out and attack the American carriers before the Americans could retaliate, and they could enhance this advantage by shuttling their carrier planes in and out of the Marianas airfields. As early as June 15, however, Spruance received word from the submarine *Flying Fish* that a Japanese carrier force was heading toward him from San Bernardino Strait in the Philippines, and the next day submarine *Seahorse* reported a second enemy naval force moving northward off Surigao Strait. Thus Spruance was promptly advised; but submarine sightings could not adequately determine the size and composition of enemy forces. Spruance allowed Rear Admirals Joseph J. "Jocko" Clark and W. K. Harrill with the seven carriers of Task Groups 58.1 and 58.4 to proceed north for scheduled strikes against the land-based aircraft on Iwo Jima, Chichi Jima, and other islands in the Bonins and Volcanos on June 16 and 17, thereby reducing the enemy's supplementary threat, and set June 18 160 miles west of the Marianas island of Tinian as a safe time and place for a rendezvous before the enemy's fleet should arrive.

Spruance also conferred with Admiral Turner, who lent him five heavy cruisers, three light cruisers, and twenty-one destroyers from the V Amphibious Force. While Spruance turned west, Turner arranged to land General Smith's reserve division on Saipan and then to retire eastward with all transports on the night of the 17th, ordering Oldendorf with the seven old battleships and three cruisers to form battle line just west of Saipan as a screen for the escort carriers and the invasion force in case the enemy should get around Spruance's flank.

In his contribution to the victory at Midway, Admiral Spruance had earned a place, in Samuel Eliot Morison's words, as "one of the greatest fighting and thinking admirals in American naval history."[44] A cold, studious, thinking admiral, Spruance as a student and faculty member at the Naval War College in the twenties and thirties had formed conclusions about decisive naval battles somewhat at variance with those of H. H. Frost and the predominant opinion. He admired especially Admiral Togo's conduct of the battle of Tsushima, in particular Togo's coolness, patience, and refusal to attack impetuously. "The way Togo waited at Tsushima for the Russian fleet to come to him has always been on my mind," Spruance said.[45] Nevertheless, Spruance's orders to Admiral Mitscher were now both Mahanian and Nelsonian:

> Our air will first knock out enemy carriers, then will attack enemy battleships and cruisers to slow or disable them. Battle Line will destroy enemy fleet either by fleet action if the enemy elects to fight or by sinking slowed or crippled ships if enemy retreats. Action against the enemy must be pushed vigorously by all hands to ensure complete destruction of his fleet. Destroyers running short of fuel may be returned to Saipan if necessary for refueling.
>
> Desire you proceed at your discretion selecting dispositions and movements best calculated to meet the enemy under most advantageous conditions. I shall issue general directives when necessary and leave details to you and Admiral Lee.[46]

Jocko Clark was so imbued with the Nelsonian spirit that he proposed to take advantage of his independent status on his detached mission to move in so southwesterly a direction from the Bonins and Volcanos that his and Harrill's task groups would cut in behind the advancing Japanese fleet and block its retreat, so that it could be annihilated between his fast carriers and the carriers and battleships of the main body of Task Force 58. Harrill refused to cooperate in this daring idea, and his and Clark's task groups consequently rejoined at the appointed rendezvous early on June 18.[47]

If Task Force 58 continued steaming westward during the 18th, it should be able to launch planes to locate Ozawa's fleet before sunset. Then Admiral Lee's battle line could close in during the night for a gunnery duel. The risks of a night gunnery action had deterred Jellicoe from seizing his final opportunity at Jutland. But Lee had performed masterfully in the nighttime action of *Washington* versus *Kirishima* in the Naval Battle of Guadalcanal, the new American battleships had excellent radar-directed fire control, in the age of the aircraft carrier a battle-line gunnery duel was likely to be possible only at night, and as H. H. Frost had written, one of the lessons of Jutland was that the technical weaknesses which had dogged Jellicoe's fleet there must be overcome in order to capture "the aggressiveness, initiative, and technical proficiency necessary for the proper exercise of commands in a fleet henceforth to be dominated by the doctrine of Nelson."[48]

Nevertheless, in response to a signal from Mitscher, Lee indicated he did not wish to commit his battle line in a night engagement. "Possible advantages of radar," he said, "[are] more than offset by difficulties of communications and lack of training in fleet tactics at night."[49] This, after twenty-eight years of studying Jutland. Spruance himself was a battleship officer, and Lee's caution abruptly damaged his hitherto Nelsonian response to the enemy's foray. He received no new reports regarding the Japanese fleet all through the 18th, and he was worried about the more southerly enemy force of which he had received uncertain word. He did not know that Ozawa in his own pursuit of a super-Jutland had concentrated the Japanese Mobile Fleet; Spruance remembered that it had become standard Japanese practice in this war to divide their fleet, as at Midway, for purposes of deception. His first responsibility, he believed, and his orders from Nimitz seemed to confirm it, was to ensure the safety of the amphibious force and the invasion of Saipan. Spruance feared that either a Japanese southern force or Ozawa's whole fleet might be turning Task Force 58 to strike Saipan. At nightfall, June 18, Spruance turned his fleet eastward, back toward Saipan.[50]

The next morning Ozawa's search planes found Task Force 58, and in the course of the day the Japanese carriers launched four big raids against it. By now the American carrier pilots averaged 525 hours of training to 275 hours for the Japanese, and the Americans also had the better planes. The resulting battle of the Philippine Sea became "the Great Marianas Turkey Shoot," in which Ozawa's fleet and the neighboring land airfields lost 346 planes and the Americans a mere 30. During the course of the day American submarines sank the Japanese carriers *Shokaku*, a Pearl Harbor veteran, and *Taiho*, Ozawa's flagship and the biggest and newest carrier in his fleet. No American ships were lost or badly hit. While Mitscher's fighters dealt with the Japanese raids, his bombers further diminished the supplementary threat by attacking the airfields on the neighboring islands of Guam and Rota.

By darkness the Japanese had obviously spent their attack, but the limitations of American night scouting equipment obliged Mitscher to postpone new air searches for Ozawa's fleet until morning of the 29th. Because the American carriers meanwhile were receiving their planes in an easterly wind, they could not begin sailing westward toward the Japanese again until 10 P.M. of the 19th. A discouraged Ozawa retreated, and no American plane found him until 3:40 P.M., June 20. In late evening attacks at extreme range, Mitscher's planes sank the light carrier *Hiyo*. The rest of the Japanese fleet got away.[51]

Spruance had sunk two fleet carriers and one light carrier without losing a ship, and subsequent events were to prove that the Marianas Turkey Shoot had ruined Japanese carrier aviation for the rest of the war. Whether Spruance could have won a proportionately greater victory by displaying Nelsonian aggressiveness—by persisting in his westward movement on June 18—has to be highly debatable at least. Still, his conduct was awkwardly at variance with his own directive to Mitscher: "Action against the enemy must be pushed vigorously by all hands to ensure complete destruction of his fleet." After more than a quarter century of American criticism of Jellicoe at Jutland, Spruance had behaved like Jellicoe and had violated the dictum that "Every mistake in war is excusable except inactivity and refusal to run risks." For all the Americans knew, the Japanese might yet have hundreds of carrier planes and carrier pilots, the extent of the damage done to Ozawa's carriers themselves was uncertain, and new Japanese carriers were building. The threat of the Japanese fleet had not been eliminated. The chance for a Trafalgar seemingly had presented itself and been lost.

Some of the American strategic planners had advocated bypassing not only Formosa but the Philippines as well and thus all large land masses before Japan itself, proceeding instead from the Marianas to the Bonins and the Ryukyus and thence to Japan.[52] Whatever opportunity for acceptance this suggestion might have had, the continued existence of the Japanese fleet killed it. After the conquest of the Marianas, the acquisition of large fields for American land-based aircraft closer to Japan and the closing of the Luzon-Formosa bottleneck continued to be judged necessary preliminaries to an attack on the home islands. After the battle of the Philippine Sea, furthermore, any American admiral inclined toward boldness was likely more than ever to be intent upon grasping an opportunity to fight a decisive naval battle for the destruction of the Japanese fleet.

An admiral inclined toward boldness beyond the point of recklessness was scheduled to command the Fast Carrier Task Force in its next operations: unsubtle "Bull" Halsey. After the fighting ended in Halsey's South Pacific Area, Nimitz decided to alternate Spruance and Halsey in command of the main striking force of the Pacific Fleet. This system would help maintain a rapid pace of operations, because while one of the admirals and his staff were in action the other and his staff could be busy planning for subsequent offensives, and thus return to command ready to execute their plans. Under Spruance's command, the principal striking force would remain designated the Fifth Fleet; under Halsey's command, the same force became the Third Fleet. Under Spruance, the Fast Carrier Task Force was Task Force 58; under Halsey, Task Force 38. Halsey would command for the cooperative attack with MacArthur against the Philippines.

In preliminary air strikes against the Philippines in early September, Halsey discovered astonishingly little Japanese air strength in the archipelago. He therefore proposed advancing the invasion date for the Philippines from November 15 to as soon as possible, and he advised bypassing Mindanao for Leyte in the central Philippines. With air support from the fast carriers, MacArthur's step-by-step advancement of his land bases was no longer necessary, especially in view of the advantage of striking while Japan's aerial weakness in the islands seemed abysmal. Nimitz and MacArthur promptly agreed. Invasions of Morotai, by MacArthur's command, and of Peleliu in the Palaus, by Nimitz's command, would go forward as scheduled on September 15, to secure advance bases for and protect the flanks of the Philippines invasion; but MacArthur's Sixth Army would land on Leyte on October 20, with Admiral Halsey's Third Fleet providing overall cover.[53]

Proceeding with the Peleliu invasion was probably a mistake. The

Philippine invasion could have gotten along without it, and the Japanese garrison had adopted a new defensive technique which cost the invaders, the 1st Marine and 81st Infantry Divisions, 7,919 casualties, including 1,500 killed. Instead of attempting to destroy the invasion on the beaches, the Japanese pulled back into an intricate tunnel system burrowed several layers deep into the island's mountains, where they kept up a fight until November 25.[54]

The Japanese had hoped that the Americans would not invade the Philippines at least until November, when they would have a new batch of carrier pilots trained to a fair measure of proficiency and several new carriers would join the fleet, including the huge 68,059-ton *Shinano*, converted from a *Yamato*-class battleship hull. Nevertheless, they decided they could not afford the loss of the Philippines and the closing of the Luzon-Formosa bottleneck on their lifeline to the Indies. It would be better to sacrifice their fleet than to suffer such a loss, for if the lifeline closed, the fleet would run out of fuel and become immobile anyway. When the Americans moved toward Leyte, Toyoda and Ozawa agreed to execute their "SHO-1"—"VICTORY"—plan for the destruction of the invasion force.

Unlike the concentrated movement of Ozawa's fleet toward the Marianas, the SHO-1 plan reverted to intricate division for the sake of deception in the manner of Yamamoto's Midway operation. Briefly stated, it called for separate forces to converge on the invasion beaches in Leyte Gulf from San Bernardino Strait to the north, under Vice Admiral Kurita Takeo, and from Surigao Strait to the south, under Vice Admirals Nishimura Shoji and Shima Kiyohide. Meanwhile Vice Admiral Ozawa would advertise his presence well north of Leyte in the Philippine Sea with carriers *Zuikaku*, *Zuiho*, *Chitose*, and *Chiyoda* and the half-carrier half-battleships *Ise* and *Hyuga*. The carriers were almost without planes; such aircraft and pilots as remained after the battle of the Philippine Sea were mainly committed to land bases in the Philippines. For Ozawa's mission was to sacrifice himself by diverting Halsey northward away from the invasion beaches, so that the forces coming out of Surigao Strait, with two battleships, and San Bernardino Strait, with five battleships including *Yamato* and her sistership *Musashi*, could fall upon the American escort carriers and invasion shipping in Leyte Gulf, destroy them, and wreck the invasion.

In accordance with the strategic doctrine of Mahan and with the Nelsonian spirit in which the American Navy between the wars had hoped to interpret that doctrine, and in response to Spruance's un-

Nelsonian conduct of the battle of the Philippine Sea, Admiral Nimitz included in Halsey's orders for the Philippine campaign this injunction: "In case opportunity for destruction of major portion of the enemy fleet is offered or can be created, *such destruction becomes the primary task.*"[55] An admiral of Halsey's character probably needed no such encouragement.

The Sixth Army went ashore as planned on October 20, against initially light opposition because the early landing on Leyte had accomplished strategic surprise. The landing on a two-corps front was so large that it was conducted both by MacArthur's own VII Amphibious Force under Rear Admiral Barbey and by Nimitz's III Amphibious Force under Vice Admiral Theodore S. Wilkinson, both under Vice Admiral Thomas C. Kinkaid's Seventh Fleet from MacArthur's Southwest Pacific Area.

Following early warnings of Japanese fleet movements from American submarines and a very successful strike by the submarines against Admiral Kurita's cruisers, American carrier search planes spotted both Kurita's and Nishimura's forces in motion early on October 24. Admiral Oldendorf, assigned to the Seventh Fleet and with six old battleships as the nucleus of his force, prepared to plug Surigao Strait against Nishimura and Shima. The aircraft of Mitscher's Task Force 38 promptly attacked Kurita's force in the Sibuyan Sea, sinking superbattleship *Musashi* and, in the fashion customary among airmen, claiming devastating hits against the rest of the force. In the meantime Japanese planes based on Luzon struck hard at Task Force 38 and sank light carrier *Princeton.* This was a disturbing blow which may have whetted Halsey's appetite for Japanese carriers still higher. But in terms of prewar discussion of the vulnerability of surface ships in general and carriers in particular to aerial attack it was a significant event, because *Princeton* on October 24, 1944, was the first major American warship to be sunk by enemy aviation since cruiser *Chicago* on January 30, 1943, and the first carrier since *Hornet* on October 26, 1942.[56]

Late in the afternoon Halsey's fliers located Ozawa's carrier force several hundred miles to the northward. Under Halsey's blows Kurita's force had begun to retreat westward, and Halsey allowed himself to be convinced that Kurita was too badly damaged to be able to do much harm if he should turn around again and arrive in Leyte Gulf anyway. Halsey decided to take Task Force 38 northward to destroy Ozawa. This move, he said, "preserved my fleet's integrity [Mahan had warned never divide the fleet], it left the initiative with me, and it promised the greatest possibility of surprise." He persisted in this decision after he learned from search planes that Kurita had in fact turned eastward again toward San Bernardino Strait and Leyte Gulf. "We will run north at top speed and put those carriers out for keeps": under Bull Halsey, the United States Navy would not again betray the spirit of Nelson.[57]

Unfortunately, it was not Ozawa who was destined to be surprised. Unfortunately also, Halsey's execution was from the beginning less Nelsonian than his intentions; the "run" northward by Task Force 38 was a slow, cautious progress, hampered by the Navy's persistent deficiency in night maneuvers and by Halsey's decision to have Admiral Lee form battle line in the midst of the movement and the darkness.

During the night, Oldendorf's old battleships crossed the T on Nishimura's force in Surigao Strait and sank both its battleships and eventually the whole force except one destroyer. Shima's force, following and uncoordinated with Nishimura's, retreated in disarray. Oldendorf pursued.

This pursuit of a retreating and ruined force was ill advised, though also perhaps Nelsonian. It deprived the amphibious force and the escort carriers in Leyte Gulf of Oldendorf's as well as Halsey's protection when Kurita's big surface force, still with four battleships, emerged from San Bernardino Strait on the morning of October 25. Kurita's arrival was the great surprise of the naval actions, and the surprise fell not upon the Japanese but upon the Americans. A misunderstood radio signal had caused Admiral Kinkaid and most of his subordinates in the Seventh Fleet to believe complacently that Halsey had left Lee behind with the new battleships to bottle up Kurita. In addition, Kinkaid's search planes failed to spot Kurita until some of the escort carriers could confirm the sighting by looking at the pagoda masts of Japanese battleships and cruisers piercing the horizon. Nothing except three destroyers and a few destroyer escorts of the Seventh Fleet stood between Kurita's battleships and cruisers and Kinkaid's escort carriers and amphibious shipping. Ozawa's decoy had worked, and the American invasion of Leyte was close to the disaster on which Japan's remaining hopes hinged.

It was saved by luck and by the sacrificial fighting of the destroyers and destroyer escorts and the planes from the escort carriers. Kurita steamed on southward toward the beaches and in the course of his progress sank two of the destroyers, a destroyer escort, and escort carrier *Gambier Bay* (CVE-73). But the overmatched Americans managed to put three of Kurita's cruisers into sinking condition and luckily kept him convinced that he was facing battleships and fleet carriers. At 9:11 A.M. he lost his nerve and turned back toward San Bernardino Strait.

Off Cape Engaño far to the north, Halsey's slow procession at length caught up with Ozawa and sank all four Japanese carriers, although the hermaphrodites *Ise* and *Hyuga* eluded the American blows. Halsey persisted in his fight long after he learned something of the amphibious force's peril; reluctant to the last to stop anywhere short of annihilating Ozawa's fleet, under long-distance prodding from Nimitz at Pearl Harbor he finally divided his fleet after all to send Lee's battleships and one carrier task group southward to meet Kurita. Kurita reached the shelter of San Bernardino Strait before Halsey could intercept him.[58]

In the various actions of the Battle for Leyte Gulf, the American and Japanese navies at last had fought their super-Jutland; in numbers of ships engaged, Leyte Gulf was the greatest naval battle in history. With good fortune for the Americans, the Japanese had failed in their goal of smashing into the amphibious force, and the battle ended as another American victory. With better and less reckless leadership of the immense strength of the Third and Seventh Fleets—Halsey alone had sixteen carriers and six battleships after the loss of *Princeton*—the Americans should have been able to guard Leyte Gulf and beat up Kurita and yet have had enough strength to smash Ozawa too. The elimination of both Kurita's and Ozawa's portions of the Japanese fleet might have been accomplished by judicious division of Task Force 38, leaving Lee's battleships and perhaps one carrier group to face Kurita while Halsey moved northward, or probably better, by skillful utilization of the interior lines which the Americans enjoyed, to move first much more swiftly against Ozawa, to hit him perhaps at night on the 24th-25th, and then to turn back to face Kurita. Mitscher seems to have wanted to attempt such a movement.[59]

Whatever might have been done, it was wrong that the amphibious forces in Leyte Gulf should have been so dangerously exposed to the big guns of Kurita's battleships and cruisers. Though Halsey sank Ozawa's carriers, their empty flight decks were not worth the risks he took to get them. Is it true that "Every mistake in war is excusable except inactivity and refusal to run risks"?

General MacArthur said that when he met President Roosevelt at Pearl Harbor in July, 1944, he assured the President that losses in the reconquest of the Philippines would not be heavy: "The days of the frontal assault should be over. Modern infantry weapons are too deadly, and frontal assault is only for mediocre commanders. Good commanders do not turn in heavy losses."[60] But MacArthur had been able to avoid most frontal assaults in the past because the geography of the Southwest Pacific Area and the weapon of amphibious power afforded him the means to turn rather than storm strong enemy positions. In the Philippines, where the land areas were relatively large and, unlike New Guinea, where he was determined to reconquer everything, his fighting had to come down to numerous frontal assaults and the casualties that went with them after all. Though their naval efforts had failed, the Japanese still tried hard to retain the Philippines on the ground. The American Sixth Army suffered 15,584 casualties in capturing Leyte, and subsequent invasions had to be postponed while the battle dragged on.[61]

Japan's shortage of first-rate airplanes and greater shortage of well-trained pilots turned the Japanese to the suicidal tactics of the *kamikaze* against the American fleet as it stood by to support the fighting on Leyte. Vice Admiral Onishi Takejiro had begun urging bomb-laden suicide planes, boats, and men immediately after the battle of the Philippine Sea, as a means of overcoming the material superiority of the Americans. As the battle slogans of the Japanese Thirty-second Army put the idea: "One Plane for One Warship, One Boat for One Ship, One Man for Ten of the Enemy or One Tank." The first organized *kamikaze* crashes into American ships hit escort carriers in the southern area of Leyte Gulf on October 25 at the same time that Kurita was pounding down from the north, and these initial efforts sank *St. Lo* (CVE-63) while damaging other ships. *Kamikaze* damage to *Intrepid* (CV-11), *Franklin* (CV-13), and *Belleau Wood* (CVL-24) helped compel a temporary withdrawal of Task Force 38 from air support of Leyte at the beginning of November. A single airplane in unskilled hands could so readily do so much damage to a major warship in a suicide crash that mass *kamikaze* attacks demanded the development of still stronger antiaircraft fire and new screening tactics to protect the carriers before the next invasions beyond the Philippines.[62]

The prolonged fighting on Leyte pushed the invasion date for Luzon back from December 20 to January 9, and then Luzon brought so much more of the hard head-on fighting that MacArthur had said was only for mediocre commanders that the scheduled attack on Iwo Jima had to be postponed from January 20 to February 19 and the Ryukyus invasion from March 1 to April 1. Kinkaid's Seventh Fleet took another beating from the *kamikazes* while supporting the Luzon invasion; between opening bombardment for the preliminary invasion of Mindoro on December 13 and the securing of the Luzon beachheads on January 13, Kinkaid lost twenty ships and had twenty-four others severely damaged and thirty-four somewhat damaged. Ashore, the Sixth Army lost 8,140 killed, 29,557 wounded, and 157 missing by the time it turned Luzon over to the Eighth Army on July 1 for mop-up operations. From Luzon, MacArthur's forces turned to a systematic struggle for the recapture of all the Philippine Islands, in furtherance of MacArthur's moral concern about the Filipinos but without much strategic purpose toward the defeat of Japan or much strategic or tactical subtlety.[63]

The conquest of the most useful parts of Luzon did have the desired effect of helping to close with virtual completeness Japan's access to the East Indies and the other remaining southern parts of her empire. It facilitated American submarine operations against the enemy's commerce, at a time when the submarines were already scoring phenomenal successes. American submarine doctrine before the war had emphasized employment against enemy warships, including a defensive employment against invasion of oceanic possessions in compensation for the weaknesses of the prewar surface fleet. This latter idea never proved feasible, but with an eye to the distances of the Pacific the United States had designed undersea craft of extremely long range and endurance. These qualities then served well in scouting duties, which had been foreseen, and in commerce raiding, which had not been so clearly foreseen as an American submarine activity but to which Japan's maritime empire proved peculiarly vulnerable.

As early as 1943 American submarines sank 21 Japanese naval vessels and 291 merchant vessels, aggregating 1,369,179 tons. In 1944 they sank 104 warships and 529 merchant ships, aggregating 2,810,307 tons. After November, 1944, Japanese convoys from the southern outposts of empire had to crawl along the coast of China, often only a mile offshore. Still they fell victim to American submarines; and in February, 1945, the Third Fleet forayed into the South China Sea and almost extinguished Japanese commerce there.[64]

The necessity for invading Iwo Jima, after Luzon could provide bases as close to Japan, may not have been so absolute as the Joint Chiefs and the Pacific Ocean Areas planners thought it was at the time. But Iwo would be a valuable steppingstone and flank protection for the Ryukyus invasion, and it could contribute enormously to the B-29 raids already under way against Japan from bases in the Marianas. On November 24, 1944, a hundred B-29s took off from Saipan to attack Tokyo, and the frequency and intensity of such raids increased steadily through the following months. The Superfortresses suffered heavily, however, from Japanese fighter defenses and antiaircraft fire. The 1,500-mile trip to Japan gave the enemy plenty of warning. The long trip back to the Marianas imposed a heavy toll on damaged planes, and when they had to splash down, the B-29s were altogether lost even if Navy patrol planes could rescue their crews. Iwo Jima would give the bombers a landing place and refuge only half as far from Japan as the Marianas. With Japanese radar removed from Iwo, the warning of B-29 raids would be much abbreviated. Perhaps most important, from Iwo long-range fighters would be able to escort the bombers to their targets. In time Iwo might become an intermediate stop for the B-29s themselves, to permit refueling and thus heavier bomb loads.

So on February 19 the V Amphibious Corps sent the 4th and 5th Marine Divisions ashore on Iwo Jima, with the 3rd Marine Division in reserve. The Japanese had carried to near-perfection the new system of dug-in tunnel and cave defenses first demonstrated at Peleliu, relatively impervious to preliminary air and sea bombardment and indeed to any attack except direct fire by tanks and infantry. The Seventh Air Force based in the Marianas attacked Iwo for seventy-two days before the landings, and the Navy conducted three days' preliminary shelling, but all this effort accomplished little. The foot soldiers' battle for Iwo lasted from February 19 to March 11 and was the most bitter in Marine Corps history. To capture the island's eight square miles cost 24,891 casualties, including 6,821 killed.[65]

To divert Japanese attention from Iwo, Mitscher's Task Force 58 of Spruance's Fifth Fleet on February 16 staged the first raid of the Fast Carrier Task Force against Tokyo itself. It played a series of return engagements in Japan until the final week of March, when it shifted its attention to Okinawa in preparation for the April 1 landings on that most important island in the Ryukyus, the final island steppingstone to Japan.

Okinawa, "the Great Loo Choo" of nineteenth-century navigators, is a large island, some sixty miles in length and eighteen miles in breadth at its widest. The invasion was considered to require a full field army, the Tenth, consisting of the III Marine Amphibious Corps and the XXIV Army Corps. A field army was not excessive, for again the Japanese dug deep into all likely strong points. Behind the landing force stood the most powerful fleet ever assembled in support of an amphibious operation. The landings were the best conducted of the war, as they should have been. The air support was the best of the war, not only at the initial landings but throughout the campaign. Tactical Air Force, Tenth Army, under the command of Major General Francis P. Mulcahy of the Marine Corps, applied Marine methods of close air support throughout, and Army troops getting their first experience with such support became "insatiable in their demands" for it. Naval gunfire support was also continuously available, and the teamwork among Army, Navy, Marines, and Army Air Forces was the most impressive feature of the campaign. Without excellent support by aviation, naval gunfire, artillery, and tanks, the infantry could have made little progress at prohibitively high cost against the Japanese defense network in the southern part of the island. The interlocking of naval, air, and tank and artillery support and the interchangeability of Marine and AAF aviation and Marine and Army artillery demonstrated that the American services had made tremendous progress in joint operations during the course of the war.[66]

Still, the Tenth Army reported casualties of 7,374 killed, 31,807 wounded, and 239 missing. The supporting fleet also suffered heavy casualties: 4,907 seamen killed or missing and 4,824 wounded. The fleet losses were mainly the result of a hail of *kamikaze* attacks. Japanese strategy called for the defenders of Okinawa to hold out as long as possible to give the *kamikazes* time to ruin the American fleet as it stood off the island in support; here was Japan's last hope of countering American naval power before that power strangled or destroyed directly the home islands themselves. In support of the aerial *kamikazes*, and in testimony to the desperation of Japan's last effort to destroy the American fleet, mighty *Yamato* sortied from the Inland Sea on April 6 on her own suicide mission. Accompanied by the light cruiser *Yahagi* and eight destroyers—the Japanese probably would have sent more ships had they had fuel to spare, but the American blockade of the Luzon bottleneck prevented it—*Yamato* was to steam to Okinawa and there to bombard the invaders to her last gasp; she was fueled only for a one-way trip.

Her pitiful two-plane air cover soon had to turn back, however, and in the East China Sea she came under repeated attack from Helldivers and Avengers of Task Force 58. On the afternoon of April 7, far short of her destination, Avenger torpedos sank her, and her consorts were similarly disposed of.

The aerial *kamikazes* did better, imposing a horrible ordeal especially on the destroyer picket ships which were flung out to screen the main American fleet. The *kamikazes* sank thirty-six ships and damaged 368; but none of the ships lost was larger than a destroyer, and the *kamikazes* alone could not stop the American fleet now that there was no effective Japanese fleet to back them up. The Japanese lost 7,830 aircraft in the campaign, in both *kamikaze* and orthodox missions.[67]

American submarines and surface craft continued their campaign against the remnants of Japanese shipping. During the first seven months of 1945, the submarines sank another fifty-six warships and 205 merchant ships, aggregating 498,993 tons. At the beginning of the war, Japan had about 6 million tons of merchant shipping. Despite 3.3 million tons of construction and the capture by conquest of 800,000 tons, by August, 1945, the country was down to 1.8 million tons, mostly small vessels plying the Inland Sea. Japan was as completely a maritime power as England, as completely dependent as Britain upon the open use of the sea, and with a smaller base of shipping tonnage from the beginning. With the destruction the Americans inflicted on her shipping, her defeat was assured, her war economy ruined, even before the strategic bombing from the Marianas began in November, 1944.[68]

When beyond the strangulation of Japan's maritime commerce the B-29s and other American aircraft began to range regularly through her skies, delivering a more concentrated aerial attack than was ever mounted against her Axis partner Germany, cutting into industrial production which had already fallen to about half its prewar level through lack of imports, and terrorizing the inhabitants of the cities with fire-bomb raids, Japan ceased to be an industrial-military power. By the beginning of August, 1945, the remaining army detachments outside the home islands were long since isolated. The only war activity in the home islands retaining any efficacy was preparation to resist invasion.

With the weapons at hand, the leaders of armed forces which had shown often how literally they interpreted resistance to death prepared nevertheless to fight the coming invaders. The United States planned to invade the southern island of Kyushu in the fall of 1945, sending ashore the Sixth Army of ten infantry and three Marine divisions with MacArthur in command of all land operations, Nimitz in charge of naval operations, General H. H. Arnold of the Army Air Forces directly commanding the strategic bomber offensive from Washington, and the Pacific war command problem thus still unresolved. The Japanese anticipated invasion of Kyushu, and against the invasion fleet off that island they planned to hurl 3,000 *kamikaze* planes before troops and cargo could get ashore. If that initial wave of *kamikazes* failed, 3,500 additional planes were ready to proceed to the invasion area, along with over 5,000 suicide boats. Beyond the *kamikazes*, more than a million Japanese soldiers still stood to arms in the homeland, with ample supplies of ammunition. Without a navy, without much air cover in the conventional sense, without adequate reserves of food, the Japanese retained enough strength to make the invasion of their homeland a horrendously costly endeavor, as the American Army planners feared while to the end believing invasion a likely necessity.[69]

By all indices of national power customarily consulted in the industrial age, the American Navy and Air Force planners should have been right in their growing conviction that no invasion of the Japanese home islands would be necessary, that Mahanian maritime strangulation and aerial obliteration of the cities doubly assured Japan's defeat. But the Japanese defenders of Peleliu, Iwo Jima, and Okinawa had amply demonstrated that to them, indices normally consulted in the West and normal limits upon the capacity to resist did not apply. Some powerful Japanese civilian leaders, notably Togo Shigenori, had for years been working for peace, albeit with an obliquity enjoined by hostile military power, the threat of assassination, and in some, the national penchant for deviousness. Since April 7, 1945, the cabinet of Baron Suzuki Kantaro, with Togo its foreign minister and strongest personality, had joined in the search for peace. On August 6 and 9, B-29s dropped atomic bombs upon Hiroshima and Nagasaki; but despite the desires of the Suzuki cabinet, even then it required a singular and in some measure heroic intervention of the Emperor into the political process to precipitate a decision to make peace.

At that final crisis, reverence for the Emperor was not enough to prevent an attempted revolt among the military extremists to compel the continuation of the war. Admiral Toyoda and General Umezu Yoshijiro, Chief of the General Staff, pleaded with the Emperor to persist in the fight, members of the imperial family had to be dispatched to military bases to ensure compliance with the imperial rescript ordering surrender, and altogether the avoidance of *kamikaze* attacks on the first American ships and planes to arrive in Japan and of a resumption of fighting appears to have been a perilously near thing. It may be that the shock of the first atomic bombs was an indispensable component of the narrow margin by which the balance of Japan's political forces shifted in favor of peace.[70]

Nevertheless, the United States had gone very far toward accomplishing the total defeat of Japan by August 6, 1945, without the atomic bomb and without invasion of the home islands. The American victories before Hiroshima combined decisiveness with limited casualties and costs in proportions which had eluded every power since Prussia's victories of 1866 and 1870–71; and the American victories over Japan were won against a brave and skillful antagonist, not a decayed or incompetent power such as Prussia had overcome. After the war General Tojo Hideki told General MacArthur that three main factors accounted for those victories: the success of American submarines against Japanese commerce, the ability of the American Navy to operate for long periods far from its bases, and the leapfrogging and neutralizing of major Japanese bases. These three factors were all expressions of American sea power. The American victory over Japan was a Mahanian triumph of sea power, that power rendered immensely more formidable through its acquisition of aerial and amphibious dimensions. To be sure, it was a triumph against one of the two great powers uniquely vulnerable to sea power; against a continental adversary its strategy would have limited relevance.[71]

14. The Strategic Tradition of U. S. Grant: Strategists of the European War

We've got to go to Europe and fight—and we've got to quit wasting resources all over the world—and still worse—wasting time. If we're to keep Russia in, save the Middle East, India and Burma; we've got to begin slugging with air at West Europe; to be followed by a land attack as soon *as possible.*

—*Dwight D. Eisenhower*[1]

WHEN THE TANK and *Stuka* spearheads of the Nazi *Blitzkrieg* plunged into Poland and France, decisiveness seemed at last to have returned to ground warfare. The proponents of the mechanized armored column which could penetrate the enemy lines and strike vital areas far in his rear seemed greater prophets than they themselves had reckoned; the swiftness of the German conquest of France stunned even its authors.

But when the Germans invaded Russia and encountered for the first time a resolute enemy possessing armored strength and organization able to compete with their own, the *Blitzkrieg* lost its lightning. Against good opposing tanks and antitank weapons, used with determination and sound tactics, tanks could neither force breakthroughs without strong infantry cooperation nor range far into the enemy's rear areas without courting disaster.

After the Russians rallied in the late fall of 1941 from the effects of initially faulty armored organization and the mistakes of inept commanders, the Russo-German war settled down into an approximation of the Eastern Front campaigns of 1914–17: advances and retreats on a far grander scale than those of the Western Front in the First World War, because the vastness of the theater precluded stability, but essentially a stalemated war, with neither army able to win a decisive advantage until one was able to bleed the other into weakness through the sheer accumulation of losses and fatigue.

By the time the United States prepared to play its part in the land warfare of the Second World War in Europe, therefore, the American Army's interwar emphasis on hard fighting as the only sure road to victory (though not of course its neglect of tanks) seemed once again sound. Colonel Naylor's old discussion of the merits of a strategy of annihilation versus a strategy of attrition summed up the convictions of American Army planners of World War II; an army strong enough to choose the strategy of annihilation should always choose it, because the most certain and probably the most rapid route to victory lay through the destruction of the enemy's armed forces. To destroy the enemy army, the only proven way remained the application of mass and concentration in the manner of U. S. Grant.

Most American strategic planning in the 1920s and 1930s, in the Joint Board and its staffs and in the individual services, focused on the color plans for possible war against various individual countries, especially, as we have seen, on the ORANGE Plans for war against Japan. In the late 1930s, however, it became increasingly evident to the planners that the most likely war would be not against a single enemy country but against a combination of enemies. Specifically, it would be a two-ocean war against the Axis combination of Germany, Italy, and Japan. In late 1939, therefore, the Joint Planning Committee produced five plans for dealing with a combination of enemies, thus not simple color plans but RAINBOW plans. Unable to secure clear guidance from the civilian branches of the executive regarding the national policy which military strategy would be attempting to implement, the planners looked toward five possible situations in which a war against the combined Axis adversaries might be fought.

RAINBOW 1 was a defensive plan for preventing the violation of the Monroe Doctrine by protecting the United States, its possessions, its maritime commerce, and the portions of the Western Hemisphere from which the vital interests of the United States could be jeopardized. RAINBOWS 2 and 3 both emphasized the Pacific front in a two-ocean war. RAINBOW 2 called for the armed forces to "sustain the interests of the democratic powers in the Pacific, and defeat enemy forces in the Pacific." RAINBOW 3 envisioned a vigorous offensive in the Pacific to "insure the protection of United States vital interests in the western Pacific by securing control there." RAIN-

BOW 4 provided for Western Hemisphere defense on a more aggressive scale than RAINBOW 1 by including the dispatch of American task forces wherever necessary to South America or the eastern Atlantic. RAINBOW 5 emphasized aggressive transatlantic operations to defeat Germany and Italy in the eastern Atlantic, Africa, and Europe.

Initially, RAINBOW Plans 2 and 3, emphasizing a Pacific war against Japan, were to have priority in preparation of their details just after the defensive RAINBOW 1, as their numerical sequence implies. This sequence assumed that in a two-ocean war against the Axis combination the United States could count on both France and Great Britain to stand firm against Germany and Italy in Europe. When instead France quickly collapsed under the German onslaught in 1940, the joint planners shifted their attention from RAINBOW Plans 2 and 3, first to RAINBOW 4 and then, as confidence grew that Britain would fight on despite France's failure, to RAINBOW 5.

The strategic situation produced by the fall of France suggested a combination of circumstances familiar to the planners from their old color-plan studies. At the beginning of the 1920s, when the color plans had to be revised to fit post-World War I conditions, the Joint Board had dealt with RED-ORANGE Plans against the contingency of war with Great Britain and Japan, the only remaining potent foreign sea powers, in combination. The dissolution of the Anglo-Japanese Alliance at the Washington Disarmament Conference and the growing farfetchedness of the idea of war against Britain and Japan combined led to a gradual neglect of the RED-ORANGE Plans. But those plans included an assumption which the fall of France again made relevant: that if the United States had to fight simultaneously across both oceans, the concentration of American cities and industries upon the Atlantic coast, much closer to Europe than the Pacific coast was to Japan, decreed that the United States should concentrate upon the transatlantic enemy first. The transatlantic enemy was likely to be more menacing and formidable in other ways as well. Therefore in a two-ocean war the United States should content itself with a defensive stand against Japan until the transatlantic threat had been eliminated and the American armed forces could safely turn the bulk of their strength to the Pacific.

These old assumptions of the RED-ORANGE Plans seemed more cogent than ever if the transatlantic enemy was to be not Britain but Germany, a power of frightening military potential in every way, including a scientific aptitude which might well produce German

THE EUROPEAN THEATER

weapons of transatlantic range. Therefore the old RED-ORANGE Plans led readily into the decision after the conquest of France to regard the Pacific as a secondary arena of war in which the United States should maintain a defensive posture against Japan until the much more dangerous German military menace was disposed of. In late 1940 and early 1941 the American planners consequently devoted most of their efforts to developing RAINBOW 5. In the ABC-1 conversations with British planners beginning in January, 1941, there was no question regarding American agreement to the principle that first priority should be given to the defeat of the European Axis powers and especially to the defeat of Germany. On August 6, 1941, the Joint Board explicitly cancelled RAINBOW Plans 2 and 3.[2]

With this decision to concentrate against Germany, and because the entrance of the United States into an anti-Axis coalition would afford the manpower and resources to make possible a strategy of annihilation against Germany, the American planners even before Pearl Harbor were contemplating a direct thrust into northern Europe by American and British ground and air forces to bring the German army to battle and destroy it, in accordance with the Army's favored strategic doctrine. During 1941 the conflicting claims of American rearmament and of Lend-Lease aid to various anti-Axis belligerents led Under Secretary of War Robert Patterson to propose a study which would estimate the total resources ultimately likely to be required to defeat the Axis, in order to provide consistent formulae for resolving the appeals of rival supplicants for America's wealth. Out of Patterson's proposal came the Victory Program, the most influential parts of which were prepared under the direction of Major Albert C. Wedemeyer of the War Plans Division of the War Department General Staff.

Wedemeyer believed that before material resources required for victory could be estimated, it was first necessary to estimate American military manpower requirements, and to do that it was necessary to develop a basic strategy:

> We must first evolve [he said] a strategic concept of how to defeat our potential enemies and then determine the major military units (Air, Navy, and Ground) required to carry out the strategic operations.
>
> It would be unwise to assume that we can defeat Germany by simply outproducing her. One hundred thousand airplanes would be of little value to us if these airplanes could not only be used because of lack of trained personnel, lack of operating airdromes in the theater, and

> lack of shipping to maintain the air squadrons in the theater. Wars are won on sound strategy implemented by well-trained forces which are adequately and effectively equipped.[3]

Wedemeyer estimated from studies of past and other countries' experience that the maximum mobilization of manpower into the armed forces possible without excessive disruption of the economy is about 10 percent of a country's total population. With the 1940 population, by this reasoning the United States could mobilize some 13,500,000 men. The Navy's concurrent study led it to estimate that the defeat of the Axis would require total American naval forces numbering 1,500,000 (an underestimate of considerable proportions, since the Navy and Marine Corps of World War II eventually reached 3,400,000). Thus Wedemeyer seemed to be able to count on 12,000,000 men for the Army and Army Air Forces. If Russia fell, this number would not be enough to provide the two-to-one superiority over the Germans usually considered necessary for an offensive strategy; but, said Wedemeyer, "We counted on our advanced weapons systems—technical prowess and stupendous production capabilities—to enable us to win the war with a total of approximately ten million Americans under arms."[4] The Victory Program called for an army of 8,795,658 men, a figure remarkably close to the Army's eventual strength of 8,291,336 on May 31, 1945. Wedemeyer overestimated the number of divisions that would be required—he figured on about 200—and underestimated the proportion of service troops that would be necessary to keep combat divisions in the field. But the basis of his calculations was a strategy of direct confrontation with the German armies to destroy them and thereby to break the German will to resist.[5]

Though Pearl Harbor and its aftermath showed that prewar planning had underestimated the Japanese menace and therefore upset in fact if not in theory the plans for priority to the European war, nevertheless American strategic doctrine and prewar strategic planning combined led the American Army to propose from the moment of American entry into the war that the means by which to wage the European war ought to be to invade northern France, putting armies into the European continent in the accessible area closest to Germany's own heartland and offering the best terrain for an advance into Germany. Here German resistance was sure to be strong, but the principles of the strategy would be exactly those of the doctrines to which the American Army had consistently adhered since the time of U. S. Grant.

American strategic doctrine could not, however, so thoroughly control the course of the American war effort in Europe as it did in the Pacific. In the European war, the United States was dependent on Britain as a base and until late 1944 on British military contributions which in 1942 surpassed and then long equalled America's own. The strategy of the European war had to be a coalition strategy, shaped by British-American military and political diplomacy. At the Anglo-American ARCADIA Conference in Washington just after Pearl Harbor, Great Britain and the United States established a combined military command, the Combined Chiefs of Staff, to shape their coalition strategy and conduct their coalition war effort. The CCS consisted of the army, navy, and air force (for the United States, the Army Air Forces) chiefs of the two countries, meeting together periodically and functioning continuously through the stationing of representatives of the British chiefs with the American chiefs in Washington. The CCS exercised a general control over American and British war efforts around the globe, including the Pacific. But in fact, the CCS allocated direct operational control of the Pacific Ocean theaters to the American Joint Chiefs of Staff, and the United States usually had its way in shaping Pacific strategy. More specifically, the United States Navy so dominated the Pacific theaters that Admiral King and the American naval planners usually had their way there, despite misgivings of the American Army planners in Washington as well as any doubts the British might have. In the broadest lines of Pacific war strategy, in keeping offensives moving against Japan despite formal commitments to give strategic priority to Europe, Admiral King could also count on the considerable help of General MacArthur against the Army planners in Washington and the British. But in contrast to the Pacific, the European war had to be a war not of American strategy but of Anglo-American coalition strategy.

From the beginning of American participation in the European war, the American Army pressed for a cross-channel invasion of northern France at the earliest possible date. President Roosevelt was eager to bring American troops into action against Germany and readily persuaded of the wisdom of the Army's plan. On March 9, 1942, he cabled Prime Minister Churchill:

> I am becoming more and more interested in the establishment of a new front this summer on the European continent. . . . And even though losses will doubtless be great, such losses will be compensated by at least equal German losses and by compelling Germans to divert large forces of all kinds from the Russian fronts.[6]

The next month Harry Hopkins, the President's personal representative, and General Marshall traveled to England to reinforce the President's proposal. Marshall insisted that "the final blow against Germany must be delivered across the English Channel and eastward through the plains of western Europe."[7] The British government and military leaders stated their acceptance of this proposition. But the British were much less receptive to Marshall's additional proposal that a foothold on the French coast ought to be established as soon as possible in 1942, to be built up for a major offensive to be launched in 1943. Because Marshall had to concede that minimum requirements for such an effort could not be assembled before the autumn, when good campaigning weather would be ending, and because most of the resources for a 1942 landing would have to be British, he acquiesced in a decision to plan for a 1942 invasion, under the code name SLEDGEHAMMER, only as an emergency measure, to be applied in case either Germany or Russia should be about to collapse. Meanwhile plans would proceed for a major landing to be effected in 1943, the buildup under the code name BOLERO, the landing to be code-named ROUNDUP.[8]

Nevertheless, in May President Roosevelt appeared to say to Foreign Minister V. M. Molotov of the Soviet Union, albeit he hedged his words with various qualifications, that Molotov could inform Premier Joseph Stalin of the Western Allies' expectation to form a second front against Germany in 1942.[9] Concern about confronting enough of the German army to assure that the Russians would survive was a major motive in the President's and the Army planners' thinking. But Roosevelt's hasty commitment alarmed the British and helped bring Churchill and part of his military retinue to Washington in June to dissuade the Americans from an early cross-channel invasion. Weighing the current limitations of Anglo-American resources and the formidability of an invasion of Europe against prepared German defenses across the channel, the British were returning to thoughts of a project they had suggested to the Americans at the ARCADIA Conference, just after Pearl Harbor: combined Anglo-American action to clear the Axis forces from North Africa. The new, June visit to America happened to coincide with a British disaster in Libya and Egypt, with Field Marshal Erwin Rommel's German *Afrika Korps* and its Italian allies hurling the British Eighth Army back dangerously close to the Nile and toward Suez. Churchill now proposed a western front for 1942 not in Europe but in Africa, an Anglo-American invasion of French North Africa to threaten the rear of the enemy forces assailing the Eighth Army and finally to catch them in a pincers and end the seesaw campaign in the North African desert once and for all.[10]

Meanwhile, after Marshall's own visit to England in April he had sent eastward across the Atlantic in May Major General Dwight D. Eisenhower, head of the Operations Division (OPD) of the War Department General Staff, to investigate ways to hasten the American buildup of forces in Great Britain and to push the cross-channel invasion project. Eisenhower reported that additional energy was required in England, which led to Marshall's choosing him to go there again in June, this time as Commanding General, European Theater of Operations. Eisenhower soon discovered that the prospects for a cross-channel invasion in 1942 were even less sanguine than the Americans had thought. Everyone already knew that British ground forces were spread thin. Eisenhower learned that the Royal Air Force did not possess the right kind of equipment to mount adequate air support for an amphibious assault upon the Continent, if only because the range of its fighters was too limited, and the Royal Navy could not offer adequate gunfire support, because it believed it must hold its main strength in reserve against a possible foray by the German surface fleet. Furthermore, Allied shipping losses to German submarines were growing much worse than anticipated, reaching a total of 856,044 tons from that and other causes in June, the heaviest monthly loss of this war or the previous one. The submarine would almost certainly have to be contained before Allied shipping could support a cross-channel invasion. In addition, Eisenhower reluctantly had to conclude:

> Production limitations alone ruled out any possibility of a full-scale invasion in 1942 or early 1943. Indeed, it soon became clear that unless practically all American and British production could be concentrated on the single purpose of supporting the invasion of Europe that operation could not take place until early 1944.[11]

At the same time, Eisenhower and other Americans were developing "a lively suspicion that the British contemplated the agreed-upon cross-channel concept with distaste and with considerable mental reservations concerning the practicability of ever conducting a major invasion of northwest Europe"[12]—that with their memories of the Somme and Passchendaele, they would have preferred never to fight a major ground campaign in Europe again. Eisenhower was too polite to say so, but it did not ease American suspicions of Britain's true intentions that in Allied strategic discussions the British planners seemed to condescend to Americans in a manner appropriate to the guileless children they evidently thought the American military planners were. As Wedemeyer, now a brigadier general and chief of the Policy and Strategy Group of OPD, said:

> This attitude was a trifle odd, not to say presumptuous, for in 1941 the British themselves had had very little experience in offensive strategical maneuver. After all, they had been rapidly driven off the Continent in 1940; and from then on they had had little opportunity except in the air and on the sea to gain the experience Sir Alan Brooke [Chief of the Imperial General Staff] talked about. . . . the British army, aside from the small forces engaged in North Africa, was surely no more combat-effective than our own.[13]

The British misgivings about the whole cross-channel enterprise almost boomeranged, by tempting Eisenhower to advocate seizing a foothold in northern France during 1942 despite the hazards, in order to avoid indefinite postponement. Eisenhower later admitted that such an effort would have been a mistake; but it is not so clear that Marshall did not forever regard its abandonment with regret. In the discussions with Churchill and the British leaders in Washington in June, Marshall argued stoutly for the earliest possible cross-channel invasion, emphasizing the grave dangers that faced the Russians as the Germans mounted a second year's summer offensives, and calling for a maximum effort to keep Russia in the war lest later German transfers of troops from a defeated Russia to the West make Hitler's channel defenses impregnable. The best Marshall could secure was agreement to keep the BOLERO preparations going at full steam until September, when there would be a review of the situation. Shortly after Churchill's return to London, he cabled Roosevelt that the British Chiefs of Staff agreed that SLEDGEHAMMER was impossible, and that he himself believed the obvious alternative was to invade French North Africa.[14]

The President believed that American troops must fight Germans on the ground in 1942, for political reasons as well as to open direct American military pressure. In response to the latest word from Churchill, he decided to send Marshall, King, and Harry Hopkins to England again, with instructions to agree on "the immediate objective of U.S. ground forces fighting against Germans in 1942," if need be in Africa.[15] In England, Marshall did battle again for SLEDGEHAMMER, with Eisenhower assisting in the preparation of the arguments. But the British rejection of SLEDGEHAMMER was conclusive. Roosevelt then instructed Marshall to choose among an attack on French North Africa, an attack on Norway, sending American troops into Egypt to join the British Eighth Army, or an expedition through Iran into the Caucasus to aid the Russians, but to choose something. Asked by Marshall for a recommendation, Eisenhower stressed the danger that opening a new line of action would not only kill SLEDGEHAMMER but force the postponement of ROUNDUP, at least to the autumn of 1943 if not longer.

"We believe that no avoidable reduction in preparations for ROUNDUP should be considered as long as there remains any reasonable possibility of its successful execution," said Eisenhower. Therefore he recommended "That no major operation which will interfere with BOLERO-ROUNDUP be launched until the result of the Russian campaign can be estimated with reasonable accuracy." Plans should be made for an Anglo-American invasion of French North Africa in the fall of 1942 in case of a Russian collapse. But if no such collapse occurred, there should be no diversion from BOLERO-ROUNDUP, and meanwhile, to satisfy the President's demand for immediate action, an American armored division should reinforce the British in Egypt.[16]

Eisenhower's recommendation might have averted the postponement, perhaps even abandonment, of ROUNDUP which he and Marshall feared from a turn to a major invasion in the Mediterranean. Marshall nevertheless preferred the risks of invading French North Africa, probably because he remembered Pershing's long fight to prevent the scattering of American divisions among foreign armies in the First World War. Formally, Marshall secured agreement that the final decision on postponing ROUNDUP should be put off until September 15, and then be made according to the Russian situation. Practically, he agreed to Operation GYMNAST, presently to be renamed TORCH, the invasion of French North Africa expanded to aim at the complete expulsion of the Axis from Africa. Roosevelt eagerly snapped up the decision and ignored Marshall's insistence on its continued tentativeness. The President, Lieutenant General Joseph T. McNarney told Marshall, "could see no reason why the withdrawal of a few troops in 1942 would prevent BOLERO [i.e., ROUNDUP] in 1943."[17]

On Marshall's recommendation, Eisenhower became the Allied commander for TORCH.[18] American and British troops went ashore at Casablanca, Oran, and Algiers on November 8, 1942, and achieved the minimum results anticipated from the operation. They effected the landings without stirring up excessive French resistance and without large casualties, and the North African French soon for the most part came over to the Allied side. The landings secured a firm base for further operations eastward against Tunisia. Unfortunately, a hoped-for thrust immediately into Tunis faltered just short of its goal, for lack of strength and logistical support. If the initial landings had occurred farther eastward, as the British generally had desired, the goal of capturing Tunis quickly might have been achieved. But air support for the landings had to be based almost entirely on Gibraltar—not much carrier strength was available—and the limited range of Gibraltar-based fighters seemingly made it too dangerous to venture landings beyond Algiers in the face of German air power in the central Mediterranean. In the sequel, the Germans were able to pour enough troops into Tunisia to assure that the Allies would not capture that country until the late spring of 1943, even with simultaneous pressure from Eisenhower's forces on the west and General Bernard Montgomery's rejuvenated Eighth Army on the east. On the other hand, by fighting for Tunisia the Axis eventuall sacrificed more than 250,000 troops.[19]

These circumstances meanwhile assured the further postponement of the cross-channel invasion, as the American planners had feared. Roosevelt and Churchill and their advisers met at Casablanca in January, 1943, to plan the next moves. The principal next move they agreed upon was to be Operation HUSKY, an invasion of Sicily in July, also to be commanded by Eisenhower. The American planners, and especially Marshall, predictably argued that the purposes which had brought American troops into the Mediterranean would be served well enough by clearing out North Africa. Suez would be secure, and Britain's Mediterranean lifeline could be kept open enough by protecting it from bases on the North African coast—not perfectly open, but adequately so in view of the more urgent missions awaiting in northern Europe. The British prevailed with different arguments, and the discussions clearly indicated that ROUNDUP was off at least until 1944. Wedemeyer thought the British got their way with another peripheral operation because their military staffs arrived much more experienced, if not in "offensive strategical maneuver" then in military diplomacy, than the Americans, with much better advance preparation to support their arguments. "They swarmed down upon us like locusts," he said, "with a plentiful supply of planners and various other assistants with prepared plans to insure that they not only accomplished their purpose but did so in stride and with fair promise of continuing in their role of directing strategically the course of this war." ". . . we lost our shirts and . . . are now committed to a subterranean umbilicus operation in midsummer. . . . we came, we listened and we were conquered."[20]

The Americans thereupon set out to improve their organization for international military diplomacy. But an improved performance in this activity would not have been likely to prevent the Casablanca decision to undertake HUSKY, given Churchill's enthusiasm for assuring command of the Mediterranean and Roosevelt's desire to keep some kind of offensive moving forward. At the time of the Casablanca meeting, Eisenhower expected the Tunisian campaign to go on until about May 15, and with that it would not be until very late in 1943 that a cross-channel invasion could be attempted, even had shortages not persisted both in properly trained troops and in equipment, especially shipping to support the operation and landing craft to mount it. Allied shipping remained desperately scarce in relation to the worldwide demands upon it, including the demands of the huge distances in the Pacific where the American planners were determined to retain the initiative which they had just regained. Losses to enemy submarines in the Atlantic in 1942 had amounted to 1,027 ships and over 5,700,000 tons; the battle of the Atlantic sea lanes was not destined to begin turning clearly in the Allies' favor until after April, 1943.

General Marshall's acquiescence in HUSKY was produced almost by shipping considerations alone. To invade Sicily would strain the available shipping resources only minimally, while to shift the bulk of the troops now in the Mediterranean to England might strain shipping resources beyond the breaking point—which was another score against the original North African decision, but it was too late for regrets now. In addition to the shortage of shipping in general, the available supply of landing craft did not appear adequate for a cross-channel invasion. Although the American Army had acted to stimulate landing-craft production as early as February, 1942, a shortage was to plague the Allies almost to the end of the war. On the other hand, the shortage in Europe in 1943 was mainly in the larger landing vessels, APDs and LSTs, and Admiral King could probably have produced enough of them from the Pacific to support ROUNDUP if there had ever been any prospect that the British would agree to putting them to that good use. Failing a 1943 ROUNDUP, King preferred to keep them where they could be aimed at an enemy's jugular.[21]

So at Casablanca, President Roosevelt again concluded that the choice lay between a Mediterranean operation and leaving the Anglo-American ground troops in the European theater idle for about a year, from the projected end of the African campaign in May, 1943, until ROUNDUP the next spring. Even at the risk of still further postponement of ROUNDUP, Roosevelt decided, and his principal military advisers acquiesced in it, that Mediterranean action seemed the better choice. It would serve the Allies, especially the British of course, by further assuring an open Mediterranean for their shipping, and it might knock wavering Italy out of the war.

Marshall and the American planners could console themselves by reflecting that a limit upon Mediterranean operations was implicit in the choice of Sicily rather than Sardinia or Corsica. The latter islands would have been better bases for attacking Italy itself, because they would have encouraged landings well up the Italian boot. Sicily would serve less to encourage an invasion of Italy than simply to open the Mediterranean. In this view the proponents of a prompt cross-channel invasion found such solace as they could, and some of them also in the "unconditional surrender" declaration delivered by Roosevelt and Churchill at Casablanca, stating an Allied policy objective which accorded thoroughly with the preferred American military strategy of annihilation.[22]

For all that, Sicily led on to an Italian campaign after all. Churchill was soon regaling Americans with promises of the golden advantages to be derived from attacks against the southern European "soft underbelly" of the Axis crocodile rather than against its snout in northwestern Europe. Allied airmen, including the chief of the Army Air Forces, General Arnold, felt tempted by the prospect of bomber bases in Italy from which they could mount a new aerial campaign against Germany and better strike the Axis's Rumanian oil fields as well. At the TRIDENT Conference of the Anglo-American leaders in Washington in May, Churchill secured an agreement that made the Sicilian campaign open-ended:

> That the Allied Commander-in-Chief, North Africa will be instructed as a matter of urgency, to plan such operations in exploitation of HUSKY as are best calculated to eliminate Italy from the war and to contain the maximum number of German forces. Which of the various specific operations should be adopted, and thereafter mounted, is a decision which will be reserved to the Combined Chiefs of Staff.[23]

The British expectation was that Eisenhower should seize any opportunity to rush into Italy and especially to capture the airfields at Foggia in southeastern Italy. When the HUSKY landings on July 10 succeeded and led into a reasonably rapid conquest of Sicily despite difficult terrain, the Fascist regime in Rome visibly began to totter. Then even Marshall agreed that prompt landings in the Naples area would be desirable, not to impede the cross-channel invasion but to support it by winning rapidly and cheaply a position in Italy perhaps as far north as Rome. After Mussolini fell from power on July 25, Marshall decided that yielding to the British desire for a descent upon the Italian mainland would be not a further danger to the cross-channel invasion but a "conservative and orthodox" move.[24]

But the transition from HUSKY into AVALANCHE, the amphibious landing at Salerno below Naples, consumed more time than Marshall had hoped, and AVALANCHE occurred not in August as Marshall wished but on September 9. By that time negotiations with the new Italian government of Marshal Pietro Badoglio had produced an Italian surrender, but not rapidly enough to forestall strong German occupation of the country. Perhaps the Allies should have pressed the Badoglio government harder; more likely, there was no chance of getting Allied forces well up the Italian peninsula before the Germans came. A planned American airborne descent upon Rome to seize the capital before the Germans got there in force had to be called off when German troops approached and the Italians who were supposed to help the Americans got cold feet. The Salerno landing proved to be not an advance into a friendly Italian welcome but an amphibious assault which the Germans nearly threw back into the sea.

Part of the trouble was that Salerno was all too obviously the best landing site on the Italian west coast within range of Allied fighter aircraft; a few carriers in addition to the two British ones employed would have given the invasion much more flexibility, but there were never enough carriers in the European theater. Once the American Fifth Army, including the British 10 Corps, managed to get itself firmly ashore, and the British Eighth Army drove up the toe from the Straits of Messina and from Taranto in the east, the Italian campaign remained a fulfillment not of General Marshall's momentary hopes for it but of the gloomy assessment which General Wedemeyer had offered just before Sicily:

> Even though HUSKY is successful after a bitter struggle, we could never drive rampant up the boot, as the P.M. so dramatically depicts in

> his concept of our continued effort over here. . . . If we could only convince our cousins that this European theater struggle will never be won by dispersing our forces around the perimeter of the Axis citadel.

By the time the Anglo-Americans finally got to Rome the following June 4, Italy had absorbed thirty Allied divisions against twenty-two German, with an Allied margin of about two-to-one in actual troop strength, a disproportionate investment for the Allies. The campaign did not prevent the Germans from reinforcing the French channel coast while it was going on. It tied down Allied troops in mountainous terrain where the Allied advantage in mobile equipment, firmly based now on immense American productivity in trucks and tanks, was virtually cancelled.[25]

But the British cousins could not be convinced of the dubiety of peripheral adventures. The Mediterranean had long held infinite significance for Great Britain as the link which bound the British Empire together. It was also a traditional base for the advancement of long-standing British interests in southern Europe and the Balkans. It could not hold comparable policy significance for the Americans, not because the United States government and its military planners looked at all wartime questions from the simple military perspective of which they have often been accused, but because for American goals and policy the Mediterranean could not have the priority rightly accorded to restoring democracy in the northern European industrial zone or indeed to coming to grips with Japan in the Pacific.

Even when the British were thinking mainly not of policy goals but of military strategy for the immediate pursuit of victory—and in interallied strategy conferences, they never couched their arguments in any other terms—a peripheral strategy emphasizing the Mediterranean "soft underbelly" appealed to them far more than the American strategy of annihilation through a war of mass and concentration and direct confrontation with the enemy. To them such a war in northwestern Europe meant a return to the old battlefields of France, where Britain had bled too much in 1914–18 to risk a repetition. War on the north European plain meant a war of mass armies, when British resources were already spread too thin to permit reconstruction of anything like the great British army of 1918. In this connection, to Churchill, war on the Axis periphery, and especially in the Mediterranean, meant war involving small enough armies that Great Britain could still contribute and claim a lion's share of victory; in a war of mass armies in northern Europe, the Americans inevitably would overshadow the British contribution.

After the evacuation of the British Expeditionary Force from Dunkirk in 1940, Prime Minister Churchill hoped that the British army would never again have to return in massive force to the Continent. He hoped that by closing a ring of successes around the perimeter of Hitler's Europe, relatively small British forces could inspire and sustain rebellions of the conquered European populations, until when the time came for the British army to cross the English Channel it would be only to deliver the *coup de grace* to a Germany already mortally wounded. Once Italy had surrendered and the Allies were ashore on the Italian peninsula, Churchill looked hopefully to the continuation of the Italian campaign as a means of fighting in a narrow arena where manpower commitments had to be limited and as a base from which to stimulate anti-Nazi uprisings throughout southern Europe. With his memories of Gallipoli always a spur to him, he hoped that Allied operations in southeastern Europe might bring Turkey into this war on the Allied side, to open another new front against the Germans not requiring large numbers of British soldiers.

As soon as Italy surrendered, Churchill saw to the dispatch of British troops to take over from Italian garrisons the islands of Leros and Kos in the Dodecanese. These islands he hoped would become a springboard to the larger island of Rhodes and thence to a campaign to set southeastern Europe afire and bring in Turkey. As usual he sought to win the support of the Americans by mesmerizing them with visions of golden prospects, if only the cross-channel invasion might be postponed long enough to provide landing craft and equipment to seize the brilliant opportunities which now beckoned from the southeast. The Americans were horrified. They saw Churchill's eastern Mediterranean schemes as threatening even the hard-pressed front in Italy, let alone the cross-channel invasion. On this occasion, furthermore, the Prime Minister's passion for what Wedemeyer called "nit-picking operations" exceeded the susceptibilities of his own chiefs of staff. The Americans vetoed any Balkan adventures, and the British lost their foothold in the Dodecanese to German counterattack, while Churchill deplored his ally's inflexibility.[26]

When Churchill and Roosevelt prepared for their first combined meeting with Premier Stalin at Teheran in November, 1943, the Prime Minister hoped for Russian reinforcement of his designs for activity in the eastern Mediterranean. He hoped they would regard such activity as strengthening their southern flank as they drove the Germans westward, especially since they had recently thrown out some hints that they wanted assistance in that direction. If Stalin had been as fixedly concentrating on postwar Soviet advantage as he is now commonly believed to have been, he might well have fulfilled Churchill's hopes; apparently some of his advisers thought the Western Allies should be encouraged to go into the southeastern European mountains, where they would become entangled while the Russian tide swept farther westward in the more important zone of industrial Europe. Stalin, however, was dedicated first to victory and to escaping the risks of war. He wanted the Western Allies in northern Europe whatever the chances that they might consequently foreshorten the Russian advance into Germany. At Teheran he pressed for the cross-channel invasion as soon as possible, as the only satisfactory second front which could draw acceptable amounts of German strength away from the Soviet Union. He importuned the Western Allies to name a specific date and a commander for the operation, now code-named not ROUNDUP but OVERLORD.[27]

With the American strategy thus reinforced, Churchill had to acquiesce. Stalin was promised OVERLORD with a target date of May 1, 1944, and Eisenhower was soon removed from Italy to Britain to become Supreme Commander, Allied Expeditionary Force, in preparation for the great invasion.[28]

But Churchill remained obsessed with the Mediterranean, and as Eisenhower wrote of him, "If he accepted a decision unwillingly he would return again and again to the attack in an effort to have his own way, up to the very moment of execution."[29] He next resisted Operation ANVIL, and sought to retain its resources in Italy. At Teheran, Stalin had suggested that the cross-channel invasion of Northern France be coupled with an invasion of southern France from the Mediterranean. The Russians, he said, had learned that an envelopment succeeds better than a single punch. This suggestion revived an idea which the Americans had entertained long before, and Roosevelt promised Stalin that the suggestion would be carried out. It became Project ANVIL.

The Americans favored it for various reasons, which deserve various weights. The promise to Stalin, once Roosevelt had given it, itself became a justification for persisting in the idea. After the North African invasion in 1942, the Americans had diverted precious equipment from the rebuilding of their own army to reorganize French divisions with modern equipment. Having done that, they did not want the French divisions to go wasted. Located in the Mediterranean, the French divisions could best be employed, the Americans thought, to invade southern France. They would be more useful militarily there than in Italy, and French political leaders might well insist that French soldiers should fight mainly in the liberation of their own country. Altogether, the American planners believed that eight to ten American and French divisions in the Mediterranean would not be used to best advantage unless a new front were opened in southern France.

Furthermore, Eisenhower and his planning staff in England concluded that ANVIL was essential to protect the southern flank of the cross-channel invasion forces once they broke out of their proposed beachheads in Normandy. Without ANVIL, Eisenhower believed, large numbers of his forces in the north would be obliged to maintain a static defense line facing southward from the Loire. ANVIL would clear out the Germans from southern France, and the OVERLORD and ANVIL forces could link up for an advance against the Rhine along the whole length of that river. ANVIL would open seaports in the Mediterranean which the Allies might well need to keep their offensive across France and into Germany adequately supported, especially since fighting in northern France was likely to leave the northern ports heavily damaged. Finally, and no small consideration to the Americans in their debates with Churchill, ANVIL would turn the participating divisions toward the decisive objective of Germany, and away from southeastern European sideshows.[30]

Trying to stage ANVIL simultaneously with OVERLORD raised the perennial problem of landing craft. American shipbuilding facilities had concentrated on destroyer escorts and escort carriers for the antisubmarine war too far into 1943 for the Allies ever to have as many landing craft as they would have liked in 1944. The landing-craft problem for OVERLORD and ANVIL combined became almost insoluble when Eisenhower's headquarters decided that to ensure success the OVERLORD invasion must take place on a five-division front, rather than the three-division front previously planned by Lieutenant General Sir Frederick Morgan, Chief of Staff to the Supreme Allied Commander (designate) (COSSAC), who had conducted earlier planning for ROUNDUP-OVERLORD with narrower limitations than Eisenhower had to apply.[31]

The problem was worsened by the landing of the American VI Corps, initially two divisions (one of them British) with reinforcements, at Anzio about fifty miles north of the Allied front in Italy on January 22. This effort to turn the Germans' Cassino position and break the stalemate in Italy developed out of Eisenhower's departure from the Mediterranean, his succession by General Sir Henry Maitland Wilson, and the consequent transfer of the Mediterranean theater to the executive control of the British Chiefs of Staff. Churchill, stopping off in Italy to recuperate from an illness after Teheran, thus had a free enough hand to insist on an amphibious effort to get his favored campaign moving again. Anzio was Churchill's project. Eisenhower acquiesced in the plan before he left the Mediterranean because he felt he should not interfere with an action scheduled to take place under his successor. General Marshall later said that he, Marshall, had nothing to do with it. General Wilson went along with it partly because he was new to the command. Unhappily, Anzio was too far north for mutual support between the beachhead and the main Allied front. Even with much more shipping and manpower than the Allies had available to put into it, it would have been a difficult venture. With the resources available it needed exceptional leadership and perhaps a miracle to succeed, and it did not get either. The Germans skillfully contained the beachhead and held on around Cassino as well. Churchill himself said: "I had hoped we were hurling a wildcat on the shore, but all we got was a stranded whale."[32]

This fizzle required that landing craft be retained to reinforce and supply Anzio, where Allied strength was eventually built up to six divisions just to hold the beachhead. Between the landing-vessel requirements of the broader front for OVERLORD and of Anzio, ANVIL had to be postponed, at first indefinitely, then, renamed DRAGOON (because Churchill was dragooned into it), until August 15, when at last it was accomplished.

Until the troops went ashore, Churchill continued to resist ANVIL-DRAGOON and to hope for heartier nourishment of the Italian campaign. When Roosevelt told him the American people would not tolerate even a slight setback to OVERLORD "if it were known that fairly large forces had been diverted to the Balkans," Churchill then and later denied that the discussions over ANVIL had ever involved a thought of going into the Balkans. But in his postwar memoirs the Prime Minister also said: "It was his [Roosevelt's] objections to a descent on the Istrian peninsula and a thrust against Vienna through the Ljubljana Gap that revealed both the rigidity of the American military plans and his own suspicion of what he called a campaign 'in the Balkans.'" Churchill believed that his eastward plans "might exercise profound and widespread reactions, especially after the Russian advances."[33]

By the spring of 1944 Churchill was thinking increasingly about "the Russian advances" as well as the defeat of Germany, and thus he had a new motive of policy to encourage his interest in the eastern Mediterranean: to retain a foothold for British interests and influence in southeastern Europe despite the advance of the Soviet juggernaut. Unfortunately, the Prime Minister's sense of military practicality did not consistently match his political aspirations. The American General Wedemeyer, a political conservative, was earlier and at least as deeply alarmed as Churchill over Soviet penetration into Europe; but he rejected Churchill's ideas for offensives toward the Danube by way of Turkey, Istria, the Ljubljana Gap, or some other Churchillian hobbyhorse, because he simply believed they would not work. With good reason. By late 1944, Yugoslavia was already well on the way to its own liberation by Marshal Tito's Communist-led partisans, who would have regarded an Anglo-American march through their country with deep suspicion at the very least. It was doubtful that a force of more than six divisions could have been sustained through the Ljubljana Gap to invade the Danube Valley; perhaps not that many, because the railroad through the gap had plenty of tunnels for the delectation of German demolitions experts, and there was only a two-lane road.[34]

No feasible means existed for the Western Allies to have retained substantially more postwar influence in southeastern Europe than they actually did. The Russians thought they needed their own *cordon sanitaire* on their western borders to replace the anti-Communist one that had been put there in 1919, and if they wanted something this close to home in 1944 and 1945 they were too powerful to be denied it. The champions of Churchill's Mediterranean strategy are apt to neglect questions of which was more vital, a Western foothold in southeastern Europe or the Western Allies' advance into central Germany which only OVERLORD no later than the spring of 1944 made possible. General Wedemeyer, who never ceased worrying about the postwar position of the Russian Communists, rightly said of American strategy: "We also had our own national interest to protect; and as I saw it, it was certainly to the interest of Americans to adopt a strategy of concentration for decisive operations, decisive not only in a military sense but also in a political sense." So Wedemeyer consistently was among the American planners pushing for a cross-channel invasion: ". . . I gave free rein to my view that it was vitally important that Anglo-American forces should get to Europe as fast as possible with 'the mostest men,' in order to prevent the Communists from winning control of the European heartland."[35]

Once OVERLORD was firmly decided upon, Wedemeyer wrote home to Washington:

> Both [Anthony] Eden and the P.M. reflect confidence relative to OVERLORD. The P.M. did state that if he had been able to persuade the Chiefs of Staff, the Allies would have gone through Turkey and the Balkans from the south and into Norway on the north, thus surrounding the enemy and further dispersing his forces. He added, however, that the die is cast and that we must carry OVERLORD through vigorously to a successful conclusion.[36]

Assistant Secretary of War John J. McCloy wrote similarly about Churchill:

> I asked him how he *really* felt about it [OVERLORD] now and he said that if he had been responsible for the planning, he would have done it on a broader front and he would have liked to have had Turkey on our side and the Danube under threat as well as Norway cleaned up before we undertook this, but he was satisfied and all would find him completely committed with all his energy and all his spirit to the battle.[37]

If Churchill had had his way, there might have been stranded whales like Anzio all around the perimeter of Europe. The British Chiefs of Staff did not wholly share Churchill's passion for a peripheral strategy. But their desire to maintain British leadership in the Anglo-American coalition, their consequent desire for a British strategy independent of the American, the limitations of their resources, and the condescension toward American generalship so apparent throughout Lord Alanbrooke's memoirs, all made them Churchill's strategic coadjutors most of the time. By way of TORCH they had diverted the Americans from ROUNDUP, the cross-channel invasion in 1943. If ROUNDUP had occurred, obviously it would have had to be on a considerably weaker scale than OVERLORD in 1944; but the German defenses in France would also have been weaker than in 1944, to a degree that would probably have more than compensated for the Anglo-Americans' inability to achieve their strength of OVERLORD as early as 1943. By postponing the cross-channel invasion, TORCH and its aftermath had squandered an opportunity for an early ending of the war. If Marshall and the American planners had not stoutly and persistently demanded it in interallied councils, and perhaps if Stalin had not reaffirmed his own demand for it at Teheran, the cross-channel invasion of Europe would not have occurred even in the spring of 1944.

The fundamental reason why American Army strategists clung to their insistence that a cross-channel invasion of Europe must take place as promptly as possible lay in their belief that the destruction of the enemy's armed forces ought to be the first object of strategy, and that northern Europe was the best place to confront and destroy the German army. In the Pacific war, the destruction of the Japanese navy was a similarly consistent strategic first purpose of the American Navy, in accordance with Admiral Mahan's teaching that to win the rewards of sea power it is necessary first to secure command of the sea by defeating decisively the enemy fleet.

It was implicit in the hope that air power offered a revolutionary means of winning wars, one which could ignore traditional obstacles to victory, that the strategists of the Army Air Forces in World War II were less agreed than their counterparts in the Army and Navy that the initial object of their strategy must be to destroy the enemy armed forces which opposed them. As their wartime commander General H. H. Arnold recorded, their strategic doctrine was formed during the 1930s upon the ideas of Giulio Douhet, and Douhet believed that air power should strike directly against the enemy's vital centers without expending energy and resources upon a preliminary contest with the enemy's airplanes for command of the air. For Douhet, a battle between airplanes for control of the air analogous to the Mahanian combat of rival warships for command of the sea was a needless diversion, for attack aircraft sent to bomb the enemy's vital centers would always get through to complete their attack. Adequate interception of attacking bombers was impossible, and the way to win command of the air was the same as the way to win everything in war: to destroy the enemy's vital centers by aerial attack before his air force could destroy yours.

The air power apostles had not consistently accepted this part of Douhet's teaching, that in air war there need not be a Mahanian struggle between rival air fleets for command of the air. The legacy of Mitchell's thinking on the subject was ambiguous, with the latter-day Mitchell as usual leaning toward Douhet, but with an undercurrent of respect for the capacities of the fighter-interceptor airplane always present in what Mitchell said and wrote. Seversky, though more extreme than Mitchell in some of his enthusiasms, was conservative on this issue: he believed that rival air fleets would have to fight it out for command of the sky, and he especially stressed the value of long-range fighter escorts to a bomber offensive. Within the Army Air Corps, maneuvers held in Ohio in 1929 established to the satisfaction of some officers that interceptors could so little disturb bombers that Douhet must be accepted as right: "A well organized, well planned, and well flown air force attack will constitute an offensive that cannot be stopped."[38]

On the other hand, through the late 1930s the Air Corps contracted for a number of long-range fighters to escort the B-17s on their way to their targets. But none of these experiments panned out, and the Army Air Corps entered World War II generally though not absolutely committed to the full Douhet thesis: with its own defensive armament and flying in close formations difficult for enemy interceptors to penetrate, the B-17 was to carry destruction directly to the enemy's vital centers, without pausing to fight a battle for command of the air along the way. In general, the strategists of the Army Air Corps did not regard the destruction of the enemy air force as a necessary preliminary to the destruction of the vital centers through air power.[39]

Even when the idea of a cross-channel invasion of Europe in 1942 still seemed feasible, it was apparent that the American role in any ground offensive against Germany that year would have to be small. Eager to begin American assaults upon the primary enemy, President Roosevelt and the American military planners had to invest their hopes for a strong and early American offensive in air power. Partly for that reason, an extensive reorganization of the United States Army on March 9, 1942, went far toward granting the Army's air arm the autonomy the air power enthusiasts had long desired. The new Army Air Forces were not yet wholly divorced from the Army, among other reasons because AAF leaders themselves agreed that they did not yet possess the logistical apparatus necessary for status as a separate service. But they had their own Air Staff to conduct their planning and their own chief, General Arnold, who was directly responsible to General Marshall but who was also recognized with the chiefs of the Army and Navy as a member of the Joint Chiefs of Staff.[40]

The AAF dispatched bombardment planes to England to prepare to cooperate with the Royal Air Force bomber offensive against Germany as soon as possible. In June the AAF units in Great Britain became the Eighth Air Force, commanded by Major General Carl A. Spaatz. In collaboration with the RAF, the mission of the Eighth Air Force was to secure "air supremacy over Western Continental Europe in preparation for and in support of a combined land, sea, and air movement across the Channel into Continental Europe." Here was a suggestion of a Mahanian strategy to engage the enemy force, if not as a preliminary to attacking the vital centers, then nevertheless as a preliminary to protecting the surface forces' cross-channel invasion. At the same time, the Eighth Air Force was also to pursue an earlier stated mission to strike "primarily against German Military Power at its source." Here was the Douhet doctrine.[41]

In the autumn of 1940, Germany had attempted to drive Great Britain at least to the verge of defeat through the application of air power alone, but the disciples of air power did not regard the battle of Britain as a true test of the theories of Douhet. The Germans did not conduct a "well organized, well planned, and well flown air force attack." The German *Luftwaffe* was designed primarily for tactical support of German ground forces, and its airplanes possessed neither the bombload capacity nor the protective armament to make them fit weapons for a campaign against Britain's vital centers. In the Hurricane and more especially the Spitfire, the RAF had the best fighter planes in the world in 1940, and they tore apart both the Junkers 88 and Heinkel 111 bomber formations and their Messerschmitt 109 and 110 escorts.

The AAF and RAF hoped to make a better test of strategic bombardment. But they disagreed about methods. After a brief but costly test of daylight bombing early in the war, mainly with twin-engine Wellingtons, the RAF had concluded that bombers lacked the speed and maneuverability to fend off enemy interceptors by daylight and that no feasible amount of defensive armament could compensate for their disadvantages. In short, on one very important point, that the bombers would always get through, Douhet was wrong; but the RAF was not willing to abandon strategic bombing on that account. The British turned to night bombing, and they built four-engine bombers, the Stirling, the Halifax, and the Lancaster, that were designed primarily for maximum range and maximum bomb capacity. Their method would be to saturate target areas with great 2,000- and 4,000-pound bombs—eventually 12,000- and 22,000-pound bombs—dropped by hundreds or even more than a thousand aircraft per raid. Against evidence that night bombing was highly inaccurate—it required painstaking development of pathfinder devices and techniques even to assure hitting chosen cities—the RAF came to reply with a candid avowal that its target was first the morale of the enemy population.[42]

The AAF, in contrast, determined to mount a campaign of daylight raids. Douhet had said that the selection of the proper targets was the most difficult and delicate task in aerial warfare, and the AAF strategists agreed. In August, 1941, the Air War Plans Division had completed a document designated AWPD-1 which set forth basic doctrine on priority of targets in strategic bombing. AWPD-1 affirmed that economic targets should be regarded as the key targets for aerial attack—the true vital centers—and accorded first importance to the enemy's electric power, transportation, and petroleum. The air planners also acknowledged that a campaign might have to be mounted against targets associated with neutralizing the *Luftwaffe*. The means they suggested was to bomb air bases, aircraft factories, and aluminum and magnesium production. A third possibility was that to protect its own air bases and logistics the AAF might have to attack submarine bases, surface seacraft, and invasion ports. But the enemy economy was to be the target of highest priority. The Air War Plans Division opposed attacks against cities unless their inhabitants were known to be already low in morale, so that air attacks might cause the final abandonment of an already shattered will to fight; by August, 1941, the American air planners had observed enough of other countries' experiments to be suspicious of Douhet's and Mitchell's ideas about the extreme fragility of civilian morale under aerial attack.[43]

Effective attack against economic targets, the American air planners believed, demanded daylight precision bombing. As General Arnold stated it: "The Army Air Forces' principle of precision bombing . . . aimed at knocking out not an entire industrial area, nor even a whole factory, but the most vital parts of Germany's war machine, such as the power plants and machine shops of particular factories. . . ."[44] To that end, the Army Air Corps had acquired in 1933 the supposedly highly precise Norden bombsight, tested earlier by the Navy. AWPD-1 envisioned bombers relying on speed, massed formations, high altitude, their own armament and armor, and simultaneous strikes from many points to be able to penetrate deep into Germany. Its authors believed that such raids intensively bombing the selected targets for six months might defeat Germany without need for a surface invasion.[45]

The British remained skeptical both of daylight bombing and of the American instrument for it, the B-17, in particular. They relegated B-17s turned over to them to Coastal Command and other secondary work, maintaining that even the B-17E with heavier armament than earlier models was deficient:

> (a) defensive fire power is too weak to afford reasonable protection, the tail-gun position being cramped and the belly turret so awkward as to be useless. . . . (b) 4000-lb. bombs cannot be installed and bomb loads in any case are small unless the bomb-bay fuel tanks are removed at the expense of range.[46]

These criticisms had some merit. B-17 armament did prove inadequate for the unescorted penetration of Germany that the AAF planners intended. While bombload was increased, up to 17,600 pounds for short ranges, B-17 bombloads remained well below those of the late models of the Lancaster—which, to be sure, was designed for different purposes and a more indiscriminate kind of bombing.

Against RAF pleas that attempted daylight bombing would end in no effective American bombing campaign at all, the AAF persisted in its plans. It received the full support of General Eisenhower, in his first tour of duty in England before the North African invasion, because he believed that without precision bombing of German defenses and the transportation system behind the invasion beaches, the cross-channel invasion might well be impossible. At the Casablanca Conference, the American and British leaders agreed to give the name "Combined Bomber Offensive" to what became in many ways less combined than competitive programs whereby the British would continue bombing by night and the Americans would try bombing by day. The directive ordered "the progressive destruction and dislocation of the German military, industrial and economic system, and the undermining of the morale of the German people to a point where their capacity for armed resistance is fatally weakened"—attacks on the favored targets of each Allied air force. A more specific consideration of targets responded to the crises of the moment, the beginning of 1943, by reversing the priorities of AWPD-1, which was to prove unfortunate: German submarine yards became the target of first priority, followed by the aircraft industry, transportation, oil, and war industry in general, in that order.[47]

As with most projects in this and other wars, it took longer than the Americans had hoped to begin any American aerial offensive whatever. The first AAF B-17 reached England only on July 1, 1942 —inauspiciously; three other Fortresses were forced down by mechanical trouble around Greenland on the way.[48] The first American bombing mission occurred three days later, on the 4th of July, when six American crews joined six RAF crews in flying twelve American-built RAF Boston light bombers (the RAF version of the Douglas A-20) against German airfields in Holland. Only two of the American-operated planes reached the target, two were shot down, and one was badly damaged. The first B-17 raid sent twelve Fortresses against railroad marshaling yards at Rouen on August 17. Three ME-109s came up to intercept, and neither the B-17s nor the German fighters suffered any damage. This raid and other American raids to the end of the year were designed cautiously, to test daylight bombing without much risk of losses that might discredit the concept. The targets were close enough to the British Isles that the enemy could not get much warning from his radar screens, and that short-range RAF, and gradually AAF, fighters could protect the bombers all or most of the way. Unfortunately, these methods required bombing not Germany but friendly German-occupied countries, with sometimes deplorable results because high-altitude bombing under combat conditions was less precise than the Americans would have liked it to be. Still, targets were hit with what both British and Americans regarded as acceptable accuracy, and in twenty-seven missions in 1942 the Eighth Air Force suffered losses of less than 2 percent—partly because the Germans at the end of the year were just beginning to take the daylight bombing threat seriously enough to respond with strong interceptor protection for the targets.[49]

The decision to invade North Africa severely slowed the American aviation buildup in England, another deleterious effect of that sideshow and one that made Churchill's eventual complaints about the delays in the American bomber campaign peculiarly graceless. Nevertheless, on January 27, 1943, ninety-one bombers set out for the first American raid into Germany itself, against U-boat targets at Wilhemshaven. On this raid, distance required that the bombers fly much of the way and hit the target without fighter escort. Fifty-three planes reached the target, and they escaped without excessive losses from more than fifty enemy fighters.[50] Still, the raid was small potatoes compared with the thousand-plane raids the British had staged over Cologne and Bremen on May 30 and June 25, 1942, and even with the several hundreds of planes of major but more routine British raids.

As American attacks grew more frequent and heavier, furthermore, the Germans of course responded with stronger fighter interception, until the outcome cast additional doubt on the thesis that air power could go straight to the vital centers without fighting a preliminary battle for command of the air. On June 13, 1943, the Germans sent a swarm of interceptors heavier than any before against American bombers to deal with sixty B-17s over Kiel, and they downed twenty-two of the Fortresses. On July 28 a force of 120 bombers aimed for aircraft factories ninety miles from Berlin, but only twenty-eight reached the target, and twenty-two were shot down. On August 17, 516 B-17s set out to raid the Messerschmitt factories at Regensburg and ball-bearing factories at Schweinfurt; sixty bombers were lost. On September 6, 262 bombers flew into Germany, and 45 went down. In the second Schweinfurt raid on October 10, the attackers lost sixty aircraft, 30 percent of their planes, and during six days of that second week of October the AAF lost 148 bombers altogether. These losses, with a minimum of ten officers and men in every airplane, were too large to tolerate, specifically so in that the *Luftwaffe* was destroying Allied airplanes at a rate that Allied damage against the *Luftwaffe* could not match.[51]

By now German aircraft production had become the first priority target of the Combined Bomber Offensive, eventually code-named POINTBLANK. The Combined Bomber Offensive Directive on May 14, 1943, based on an AAF effort toward scientific target analysis and selection, thus modified the Casablanca Directive in stating significantly that "*If the growth of the German fighter strength is not arrested quickly, it may become literally impossible to carry out the destruction planned and thus to create the conditions necessary for ultimate decisive action by our combined forces on the Continent.*" Invasion as well as the bomber offensive hung on the outcome of the air battle. Submarine yards and launching bases had proven almost impervious to air attack, but by May and June of 1943 the Allied naval and aerial antisubmarine campaign had at last turned the corner toward success. From that season onward, the Allied air forces attacked with mounting intensity the German aircraft industry and factories associated with it such as the ball-bearing works, until the campaign culminated in the "Big Week" of February 20–26, 1944. On February 20 the AAF's first thousand-plane raid struck fighter aircraft factories in central Germany. Until bad weather cut off the operation on February 26, the AAF sent 3,800 bombers over Germany and dropped almost 10,000 tons of bombs. The RAF joined in at night.

The *Luftwaffe* was hurt enough that henceforth it conserved its fighters to challenge only major Allied sorties, and the Germans further dispersed their aircraft industry, thus delaying production. But the bombing campaign against the aircraft industry was not enough to overcome the German interceptors and reduce losses to an acceptable level. Two hundred twenty-six American bombers, twenty-eight fighters, and about 2,600 American crewmen were lost during "Big Week." Improved German night fighting was even throwing into question the RAF's assurance that the bombers could always get through in the protection of darkness. The RAF bomber offensive's loss rate rose to 5.2 percent in the spring of 1944, and in a raid on Nuremberg on March 30 the British lost 94 bombers out of 795 employed.[52]

The achievement of command of the air was growing doubly urgent, furthermore, because the date for the cross-channel invasion was now imminent. On December 27, 1943, General Arnold had ordered the Eighth Air Force in Britain and the Fifteenth Air Force in Italy: "It is a conceded fact that OVERLORD and ANVIL will not be possible unless the German Air Force is destroyed. Therefore, my personal message to you—this is a *MUST*—is to, '*Destroy the Enemy Air Force wherever you find them, in the air, on the ground and in the factories.*' "[53]

Efforts on the ground and in the factories had fallen short, and until now the Allies lacked the means to destroy the aerial defenders of *Festung Europa* in the air. The B-17's own armament was not enough, even if the tight formations prescribed for mutual protection could have been maintained. Good fighters had not been able to accompany the Fortresses into Germany to do battle with the *Luftwaffe*. AWPD-1 had repeated the suggestion that a long-range escort fighter would be helpful, but such experiments as occurred had continued to strike dead ends.

In the standard American fighters at the beginning of the war, the Curtiss P-40 Warhawk and the Bell P-39 Airacobra, short range was merely one of numerous shortcomings; they were badly outmatched against Germany's ME-109s and FW-190s. The British Spitfire remained the best fighter in the world for its range, but it could not venture far beyond the English Channel. The Republic P-47 Thunderbolt, which arrived in Europe in April, 1943, was the first American fighter to meet Messerschmitts and Focke-Wulfs on at least equal terms; but even with jettisonable fuel tanks the combat radius of the early models was only 350 miles, just across the Rhine. The Lockheed P-38 Lightning could reach 500 miles by straining, but without allowance for fuel consumption in combat; and the Lightning was inferior to the German fighters in maneuverability.

The solution to the problem came mainly from happy historical accident, and just in time. The first North American P-51 Mustang groups to go into escort service did so in December, 1943. The P-51 had been developed in the United States to British specifications to provide a replacement for the Kittyhawk, the British version of the P-40, in secondary duties. It was designed, built, and tested in record time, but in its early editions it seemed destined for secondary roles, such as low-level attack, and nothing else. Then a superior Rolls-Royce Merlin engine replaced its original power plant—whereupon its performance became so good that the Mustang began to be recognized as perhaps the fighter that everyone wanted but nobody had designed. With jettisonable fuel tanks it had a radius of 850 miles; it could accompany bombers to almost any target in Germany, and in combat it could best any German interceptor except the jets which were coming into service in fortunately limited numbers.[54]

At the crisis of American bombing losses in October, 1943, General Arnold ordered that no P-38s or P-51s be shipped anywhere in the world during the rest of the year except to England. After the first P-51 escort missions, General Spaatz ordered that all P-51s reaching the theater remain with the Eighth Air Force. Not until March, 1944, did the P-51s go into action in large numbers. Thereafter every fighter group in the Eighth Air Force except one was converted to Mustangs. Meanwhile P-51–escorted bombers on March 4, 1944, began the first American raids against Berlin. The purpose was to choose targets that would bring the *Luftwaffe* into the air, so that the P-51s could shoot it down. The AAF had gone over to the traditional military strategy of courting battle with the enemy's main rival force in order to destroy it.[55]

Through the rest of the year and practically to the end of the war, German fighter production increased, despite the bombing offensive. But by the end of March, 1944, the *Luftwaffe* was evidently going into decline, its rising success against unescorted British night bombers notwithstanding. Following upon the temporary setbacks to German fighter production inflicted by "Big Week," the Mustangs shot too many planes and pilots out of the air, and good pilots could no longer be trained in large enough numbers to meet the demand. With the Allies winning command of the air, after an interlude devoted to bombing in France in preparation for D-day the bombers could return to their original target priorities, the economic targets of prewar planning. Their attacks on German petroleum supplies then left too little gasoline for either pilot training or adequate interception.

The appearance of the Mustang fortunately coincided with other events which contributed to the fighter-escort's success. Earlier, American air officers had been reluctant to use auxiliary fuel tanks, because they were thought to be a fire hazard and because their fittings might interfere with the performance of the plane; the crisis of the bombing offensive overcame such judgments. The commander of the *Luftwaffe*, *Reichsmarschall* Hermann Goering, helped the Mustangs by issuing orders in December, 1943, for his pilots to concentrate their attacks on bombers and to avoid combat with the escort fighters. This order ignored the fact that the crucial battle for command of the air would now be one of fighter versus fighter, and in this battle those seeking combat were almost certain to best those trying to avoid it. About the same time, *Luftwaffe* fighters were fitted with rockets, which were effective against bombers but not so effective in duelling with fast and maneuverable fighters. Goering curiously failed to act in accord with a statement he made to General Spaatz after the war, when Spaatz asked him when it was that he realized Germany had lost the war, and he replied: "When I saw your bombers over Berlin protected by your long range fighters. . . ."[56]

From 1942 until well into 1944, German war production in general had continued to rise. A large amount of slack had remained in the German economy as late as 1942, to be taken up for war purposes during the next two years. Until the arrival of the Mustang and the Mustang's battle for control of the air, the Allied bomber offensive could not concentrate upon the economic targets which the Combined Bomber Offensive Directive, modifying AWPD-1, had declared vital. As the Allied ground forces prepared to begin at last their battle of mass and concentration to destroy the German army, the air forces prepared to test whether the command of the air which they had at last achieved could now provide the decisive avenue to victory forecast by the air power prophets.

Whatever the eventual outcome of the strategic bomber offensive, without Allied air power the losses likely in an invasion of northern France could scarcely have been contemplated, and if the Allies had nerved themselves to accept staggering casualties, the outcome nevertheless might well have been disaster. The battle for command of the air over the German homeland drew the *Luftwaffe* away from support of the German ground forces and the defenses of northern France. In the spring of 1944 all Allied air power in Britain was placed temporarily under the direction of General Eisenhower, and he instructed it to isolate the proposed invasion beaches—and for purposes of security and deception, other beaches where the Germans might expect landings—from assistance from the interior of France and Europe, by ruining the transportation systems. American precision bombing had proven to be not so precise as had been hoped, and experience after as well as during World War II was to demonstrate the limitations of even the strongest air power in attempting to interdict land communications. But for a brief period of time, as in the weeks just before and after the OVERLORD invasion, and against the sophisticated and therefore delicate transport network of an industrialized country such as France, air power could do much to strangle movement. To give it an additional month to accomplish its work, as well as to provide additional time for training troops and accumulating landing craft, Eisenhower postponed the target date for invasion, D-day, from May 1 to the beginning of June.[57]

To defend an area as large as the coast of northern France against amphibious invasion, the best method historically had not been the method used by the Japanese on a tiny atoll such as Tarawa. The defender should not attempt more than a delaying action against the initial assault waves, because the beaches of a long coastline could not be made strong everywhere. The classic method of defense rather was to maintain a strong mobile reserve ready and able to fall upon a landing wherever it might develop, bringing superior strength against it before the beachhead could be expanded adequately and thus pushing the invader back into the sea. In the nineteenth-century defense plans of the United States, this method was the one contemplated should an invader ever set foot on American shores. The coastal fortresses were to keep an invader away from the most sensitive points, and the Army supported by a mobilization of citizen soldiers would eject him from any lodgement elsewhere. With moile reserves rather than an effort to hold all the beaches, the Turks had turned back the British from Gallipoli. In 1943, Field Marshal Gerd von Rundstedt, German Commander in Chief in the West, planned a similar defense for the coast of France, based upon counterattacks by a mobile reserve.

But even before Eisenhower set Allied air power to its intensified pre-invasion offensive, air power threw this classic defense plan into question. In late 1943, Hitler gave Field Marshal Erwin Rommel command of Army Group B, the headquarters which was to control the German strategic reserve for western Europe. Rommel decided that Rundstedt's plan for the defense of France against invasion would not work. Allied aviation would prevent a mobile reserve from counterattacking against a beachhead until it was too late, if the reserve could run the gauntlet of aerial attacks at all. Whatever the disadvantages, the only hope for the defense of the channel coast lay in defending the beaches themselves so stoutly that the Allies could never secure their beachhead.

In January, 1944, Rommel asked for and received command of the Fifteenth and Seventh Armies in northern France. His Army Group B headquarters would be nominally subordinate to Rundstedt, but he would have the right to report directly to OKW, *Oberkommando der Wehrmacht*. Rommel set out to transform the defenses into a thick crust directly along the beaches, with underwater mines, underwater and beach obstacles, and well-emplaced artillery. Air power impelled him to it, and under the threat of air power his strategy was probably the best one possible. But Rommel did not have enough time remaining to do what he wanted with all the possible invasion beaches, and he and most of the rest of the Germans, except Hitler, expected the invasion to strike the Pas de Calais, so they devoted their best efforts to the wrong place. Of the five beaches in Normandy where the Allies landed on June 6, 1944, only at Omaha Beach in the American sector were the German defenses complete enough to make the landing a difficult amphibious assault. Elsewhere the British and Americans secured their beaches relatively easily, and Rommel's plan failed.[58]

Allied air power accomplished all that could reasonably have been hoped for toward isolating the beaches on D-day, and it also contributed airborne landings in both the British and American sectors. The dropping of the American 82nd and 101st Airborne Divisions was especially valuable, because they helped prevent the Germans from blocking the causeways which led inland from Utah Beach, at the base of the Cotentin Peninsula, toward Cherbourg, on which the Allies counted as the first developed seaport they could seize.[59]

Thanks to Allied air power and the disagreement between Rundstedt and Rommel over basic strategy, the major German counterattack which the Allies feared never materialized. Nevertheless, almost complete command of the air could not prevent the Germans from bringing to bear four *Panzer* divisions against the British on the Allied left flank within a few days of the invasion, and additional enemy armored divisions soon followed. It was fortunate for the Allies that Rommel threw his reinforcements into action piecemeal, instead of husbanding them for a major stroke. Fortunately, too, Allied deceptions helped lead the Germans into holding their Fifteenth Army in the Pas de Calais until July, in expectation of additional landings.[60]

"In all the campaigns, and particularly in western Europe," said General Eisenhower, "our guiding principle was to avoid at any cost the freezing of battle lines that might bog down our troops in a pattern similar to the trench warfare of World War I"—or in a pattern similar to that of the Italian campaign, he might have added.[61] Everyone knew that a period of static warfare would have to follow D-day, until enough troops and equipment could be accumulated to accomplish and sustain a breakthrough. The buildup progressed remarkably well despite having to rely on two artificial harbors, called "mulberries," and after a fierce channel storm struck on June 19, on only one. Not any failure in the buildup but stout German resistance abetted by the difficult hedgerow country of Normandy made the initial fighting more static, and Allied efforts more frustrating, than had been foreseen. At length, the concentration of German *Panzers* against the British in the better tank country around Caen, and the battering of that armor by General Montgomery's British forces, permitted Lieutenant General Omar Bradley's American First Army to break through the German defenses around St. Lô toward the end of July and initiate a mobile campaign. But when the breakthrough began on D-day plus fifty, it was from a line the Allies had hoped to occupy by D plus five.[62]

Once the breakthrough occurred, the campaign became highly mobile. Hitler judged both Rommel and Rundstedt failures and put the new C-in-C West, Field Marshal Günther von Kluge, under the *Führer*'s customary orders to give up nothing. Following Hitler's directions, Kluge threw away whatever chance the Germans might have had to halt the Allied advance at the line of the Seine by expending the German Seventh Army in futile counterattacks against the Allied breakthrough columns. These counterattacks permitted the newly committed American Third Army of Lieutenant General George S. Patton, Jr., nearly to encircle the Germans between Patton's advancing spearheads on the Allied right and Montgomery's British moving toward a junction with Patton between Argentan and Falaise. Only after the Seventh Army was nearly ruined and in headlong retreat did the Germans belatedly commit their Fifteenth Army to the battle. Even then, the Allies had picked up so much momentum and the Germans were so unbalanced that the Allies pressed forward without pause across the old battlefields of the static warfare of a quarter century before.[63]

The DRAGOON landings on August 15 precipitated a hasty collapse of whatever German strength remained on the southern flank of the Allied advance. Not until almost all of France was liberated and the Allies had penetrated into the Low Countries and at several points into Germany itself did the pursuit of the fleeing Germans cease and the lines stabilize themselves again. By that time the Allies had outrun their logistical support, still funneled in through excessively few usable ports (German garrisons were hanging on tenaciously though isolated in the ports of Brittany).

So again as in 1940, the campaign in France had brought no repetition of Verdun, the Somme, and Passchendaele. The American strategy of concentration and mass against the main German armies vindicated itself by producing decisive effects with only limited casualties, wrecking at least one German field army in the process. As in 1940, however, the rapid thrust of armored spearheads across France could not be taken as a sure indication that decisiveness had returned to warfare. Too many special circumstances favored the Allies. The Normandy landings and a successful buildup on the beachheads would almost certainly have been impossible if the bulk of the German army had not been committed in Russia. Allied planning for the Normandy invasion predicated its success on the presence of only twelve mobile German divisions in France. If without the existence of the Russian front the Allies somehow had been able to lodge themselves upon the European continent at all, surely their battles would have resembled those of World War I in cost and indecisiveness despite the presence of armor and air power. Such was the pattern of war on the Russian front itself, until the last battles when Germany suffered pressure from west and east alike and tottered at the limit of her resources. Even after the battle of Stalingrad in the fall and winter of 1942–43 ended the seesawing of the Eastern Front and brought in a Russian tide, the advances of the Soviet armies became repetitive processes of grinding down German defenses at the price of heavy casualties, only to have the Germans fall back to additional prepared positions, the Russian advance soon expend its momentum, and the expensive grinding efforts begin all over again.[64]

By D-day in Normandy, the Russians' grinding down of the German army had already gone far toward ruining the mighty war machine of 1940 and 1941. The air battles over Germany had stripped the German ground forces in France of all but minimal support from the *Luftwaffe*. All through the battle for France, the Germans maintained a superiority over the Anglo-American armies in numbers of men; but Allied air superiority was so overwhelming in what Eisenhower rightly called the "air-ground battle" (and in Major General Elwood R. Quesada the IX Tactical Air Command had an AAF officer who actually believed in tactical air support), while Allied armor was so superior not in quality but in quantity of tanks, that the German resistance cannot be compared with what might have been accomplished by an enemy confronting the Allies with approximately equal strength. At that, the Germans prolonged static warfare in Normandy beyond the time the Allies had expected, and they might well have reestablished themselves along the Seine had not Hitler's faulty strategy expended their Seventh Army uselessly.

Once that expenditure occurred and the Germans had to retreat all the way to the Low Countries, the immensely greater mechanization of the Allied armies—despite the Germans' pioneering of the *Blitzkrieg*, their ordinary divisions remained dependent on horse transport and walking infantry, and even their armored divisions mostly were not completely motorized like the American—made movement across France much more exhausting for the Germans than for the Allies, apart from the demoralizing effects of defeat.

Nevertheless, when Montgomery attempted to leap across the lower Rhine with the combined airborne and armored stroke of Operation MARKET-GARDEN in September, German resistance proved to have consolidated itself again with amazing rapidity and completeness. MARKET-GARDEN failed to hold a bridgehead across the Rhine, and the autumn fighting settled down to a prolonged British struggle for the islands of the Scheldt estuary, so the port of Antwerp might be opened, while the Americans jabbed at the ramparts of the Siegfried Line. Eisenhower believed the Allies would need Antwerp to sustain a new advance across Germany. While he waited for its opening, he also busied himself with the accumulation of supplies all along his line from the North Sea to Switzerland, hoping that this effort plus Antwerp would ensure that it would not be logistical problems that would stop him again.[65]

The enforced return to static warfare embittered a new strategic debate between the Americans and the British, this one involving British contentions that the Americans had brought on the stalemate by violating their own cherished principle of concentration and mass. While the Allies were yet moving in headlong pursuit across France, Montgomery had asserted that if Eisenhower's strained and limited logistical resources were concentrated in support of Montgomery's Twenty-first Army Group, he would be able to plunge all the way to

Berlin, by using his concentration of supplies and troops to keep the Germans on the run without respite. Only on the Allies' northern flank, Montgomery believed, across the north European plain, would such a thrust be possible, because the Siegfried Line and broken country precluded a similar quick stroke by Bradley's Twelfth Army Group or Lieutenant General Jacob L. Devers's Sixth Army Group to the south. Montgomery and his proponents have continued to assert that static warfare would never have returned to the Western Front and Allied victory would have been won in the fall of 1944, if Eisenhower had concentrated his logistical support behind Montgomery and thus allowed the Twenty-first Army Group to drive on to Berlin without pause.

In his explanations of his strategy at the time and after the war, the amiable Eisenhower became unduly defensive in replying to the tactless and supercilious Montgomery, and somehow the tone set by General Eisenhower has persisted through much of the subsequent debate among military critics and historians. Eisenhower then and later defended the principle of advancing to the Rhine and into Germany on a broad front. If Montgomery had attempted to push on across the Rhine and across Germany on a narrow front, Eisenhower believed, the Twenty-first Army Group would have had to drop off so many flank guards that it would soon have lost its punch. Once that happened, and the concentration of logistical support in Montgomery's favor had deprived the American armies farther south of their power of moving to help him, Montgomery's advanced position could have become disastrous. Apart from the merits of this argument, however, the fact is that Eisenhower gave Montgomery his chance, as much as he reasonably could have.

He did concentrate his logistical support behind Montgomery as much as he dared to do. He could not imperil his southern armies by immobilizing them completely in Montgomery's favor, but he came close to it. In late August, the American First Army, which Montgomery wanted to keep moving apace with him to shield his right flank, received an average of 5,000 tons of supply per day. Patton's Third Army on the right of the First was restricted to 2,000 tons a day. On August 30 Patton's army received 32,000 gallons of gasoline, of its normal daily requirement of 400,000 gallons. The speed of the advance from Normandy had carried the Allied armies so far beyond their ports of entry and their depots and so overstrained the intervening transportation that for any of the armies to have advanced far into Germany was probably impossible. In these circumstances,

Eisenhower favored Montgomery with a more than generous proportion of the supplies that could be hurried to the front. If with such a share of the available support, any general could have dealt the Germans a knockout blow, the man to do it was not Montgomery. He squandered Eisenhower's logistical generosity in listless failure to push on across the Albert Canal and to the Rhine with the first momentum of his advance into Antwerp, and then he blamed Eisenhower for the failures implicit in the whole logistical situation and aggravated by his own insufficiently aggressive generalship.[66]

Fortunately for the Allies, the Germans' opportunity to pause and regroup and the consequent resurgence of their power to resist misled Hitler into another desperate strategical gamble, which restored mobile warfare but ultimately not in the direction the *Führer* desired. Hoping to keep the Western Allies stalled and thus possibly to split the coalition opposed to him by playing upon American and British fears of excessive Russian success, Hitler concentrated his best remaining armored strength in the west during the fall respite of 1944. The Sixth SS Panzer Army and the Fifth Panzer Army were to strike against a lightly held portion of the Allied front in the Ardennes, where the Germans could muster three-to-one numerical superiority in the sector and six-to-one superiority at key points, to break through to the Allied supply depot across the Meuse River at Liége and beyond that, Hitler extravagantly hoped, to Antwerp.

The Ardennes was the same area where the Germans had mounted their principal thrust in the spring of 1940, while the French had neglected it because the east-west roads there were few and poor and the country much broken. Knowing that, the Allied command in 1944 again counted on the difficulty of the Ardennes to make a German counterattack there unlikely, and after their race through France they still did not believe the Germans had enough strength left for a strong counterattack at all. Eisenhower did not have enough men to be secure all along his front and still mount even limited offensives, as he had been doing through the autumn. He had to be weak somewhere, and the Ardennes seemed the best place. He believed that in the unlikely event of a German counterstroke there, he could contain it within acceptable limits.[67]

The Germans moved forward on December 16 and achieved surprise, partly because bad weather had limited Allied aerial reconnaissance for several days. Persistence of the bad weather kept Allied planes grounded until a temporary clearing on December 23, and this good fortune for the Germans helped them advance their spearhead some fifty miles behind the original American positions. Ultimately, however, Eisenhower's calculations proved good enough. Aided by desperate fighting by various outnumbered American formations to hold key road junctions, the Americans held the Germans far short of Liège or any other significant objective.

The American First Army in the north and the Third Army in the south wheeled to press in the flanks of the bulge created by the German advance. In the "Battle of the Bulge" the Americans suffered about 77,000 casualties, but the Germans later admitted losing 90,000, and the Allies estimated a German loss of 120,000, along with hundreds of now irreplaceable tanks and airplanes and thousands of other vehicles. Like so many past offensive adventures by armies whose basic strategy had to be defensive, the Ardennes attack bled away energies and resources the Germans could not spare.[68]

With the Germans exhausted by their own exertions, the Allies were able to pry them out of the Siegfried Line and close up to the Rhine River in March. At that point the windfall of capturing the Ludendorff Bridge at Remagen on March 7 permitted the American First Army to cross the river immediately. By April 1, the Allies were over the Rhine at a multitude of places from Philippsburg almost to Arnhem, including a large-scale crossing of the wide lower river on March 23–24 by Montgomery's forces, assisted by airborne landings, in what was practically an amphibious assault.

These Rhine crossings involved the final debate of the long series between British and Americans over the proper application of the principle of concentration and mass. All parties in the Anglo-American forces agreed that a major offensive directly into the Ruhr Valley should not be attempted. The Germans would fight hard in defense of that primary industrial area, and fighting in so congested an urban region was bound to degenerate into house-to-house struggles in which Allied mobility could not be used to best advantage. Therefore the question was whether to make a major effort on only the northern or the southern flank of the Ruhr, or on both flanks simultaneously. Montgomery and Field Marshal Sir Alan Brooke contended that the principle of concentration required Eisenhower to mass the largest possible force for a single blow against the most critical area, namely, the north German plain downriver from the Ruhr, earlier the proposed scene of Montgomery's projected autumn offensive. Eisenhower, now wielding power to spare and characteristically concerned lest he be trammeled by excessively narrow logistical channels, decided to go around both sides of the Ruhr.[69]

Sometimes British critics have argued that Eisenhower's refusal to concentrate his strength for a single massive blow was inconsistent with the Americans' earlier demands for concentration for a cross-channel invasion rather than multiple attacks around the German perimeter. At least one British critic of American strategy has used the same charge of inconsistency against the two-pronged American offensive of Nimitz's and MacArthur's forces in the Pacific, as compared with the American insistence on a concentrated cross-channel invasion in Europe.[70] But the crucial difference between the various American offensive strategies in Europe and the Pacific, on the one hand, and the British peripheral strategy, on the other, was that the unvarying purpose of American strategy was to aim for the enemy's vitals. The cross-channel attack in Europe, the dual offensives in the Pacific, and Eisenhower's proposed dual offensive from the Rhine into the interior of Germany all aimed at the enemy's vitals and all were appropriate to a strategy of annihilation. British Mediterranean strategy, in contrast, diverted forces away from the critical places where they could strike decisive blows.

To gain a foothold across the English Channel, the difficulty of amphibious operations and the lavish resources necessary to support them dictated a single concentrated assault against the beaches. Once the Allies were securely ashore in France, however, the principle of mass or concentration hardly required them to stage only single-thrust offensives on narrow fronts. The principle of concentration is applied most effectively by commanders who vary their own concentrations enough to cause the enemy not to concentrate, so that concentrated strength can oppose itself to relative weakness. When a belligerent possesses strength as superior to the adversary's as the Allies did in Europe and the Pacific, the whole history of American strategy since U. S. Grant confirmed that the enemy can be hit with advantage at several places and thus forced to accentuate his weakness through dissipation—as long as strategy aims at decisive objectives and does not waste itself in sideshows.

Supported by the American Joint Chiefs, Eisenhower refused to accede to Brooke's objections to his planned dual advance across the Rhine. He believed that through the corridor north of the Ruhr the Allies could sustain only about thirty-five divisions advancing across Germany. To launch only a single major blow through that corridor would enforce idleness upon large numbers of troops. It would also fail to deprive the Germans of the remaining industrial production of the Ruhr by the most efficacious method, that of encircling the Ruhr.

Eisenhower's plan called for forces from the Twenty-first and Twelfth Army Groups to converge east of the Ruhr to accomplish that encirclement, after which Bradley's army group would strike with three armies—the Ninth, First, and Third—across the center of Germany toward the remaining major industrial area, around Leipzig and Dresden, and to divide the country in two and meet the Russians.[71]

The best means of ensuring against last-ditch fanatical resistance, Eisenhower believed, was to overrun the country as rapidly as possible before such resistance could be organized. The broad-front offensive would also accomplish that purpose. While Bradley was splitting German resistance into two parts, Montgomery's forces could thrust to the Baltic coast to secure the north German seaports and isolate the enemy troops remaining in Denmark and Norway. In cooperation with Patton's Third Army on Bradley's right, Devers's Sixth Army Group in the south would overrun the Bavarian mountains, where some reports had the Germans preparing a "National Redoubt," and push across western Austria to a junction with the Allied armies coming northward through Italy.

This design ignored Berlin, which Eisenhower believed no longer of military significance, which an Anglo-American spearhead could have reached if at all only by damaging the logistical support of the effort to occupy as much of Germany as possible, and to which eventual access was promised by four-power agreements anyway. When Churchill importuned him to take Berlin, Eisenhower said to General Marshall:

> I am the first to admit that a war is waged in pursuance of political aims, and if the Combined Chiefs of Staff should decide that the Allied effort to take Berlin outweighs purely military considerations in this theater, I would cheerfully readjust my plans and my thinking so as to carry out such an operation.[72]

The American members now thoroughly dominated the British-American Combined Chiefs of Staff, for the United States contributed about three-quarters of the Allied armed strength in Europe, and therefore the Combined Chiefs did not direct a necessarily narrow spearhead toward Berlin. Under President Roosevelt's direction, and then under President Truman's in his first days in office as the heir of Roosevelt, American policy was to use strategy to gain a strong position astride Germany, but not to do anything that the Russians could construe as merely going out of the way to offend them. Under this policy, and against an enemy who had shot his last bolt in the Ardennes, Eisenhower's final strategy worked to perfection, pinching out the Ruhr early and carrying American troops far into the already agreed-upon Russian zone of occupation in Germany.[73]

The American air planners in AWPD-1 had rejected one major phase of Douhet's proposed employment of air power. They did not favor a general policy of terror bombing of civilian populations. The air planners doubted on the experience of the war that terror bombing would break civilian morale as Douhet and Mitchell had predicted. Throughout the subsequent participation of the United States in the European war, Army Air Forces officers, especially General Spaatz, consistently expressed moral revulsion at the wholesale slaughter of noncombatants which terror bombing of cities obviously entailed. Strategic judgment and morality seemed to point to a common conclusion.[74]

It was not so with Britain. The Royal Air Force had been the one armed service of a major European country to embrace strategic bombing theory between the wars, as the most appropriate modern expression of Great Britain's traditional avoidance of large-scale ground combat. From the beginning of the war in 1939 the Germans had shown noteworthy restraint in refraining from indiscriminate aerial attacks on nonmilitary targets; the famous bombing of Rotterdam was a mistake. The *Luftwaffe* was not designed for strategic bombing, and Hitler, believing the "stab-in-the-back" legend and that the collapse of German civilian morale had caused Germany's defeat in 1918, preferred not to give his enemies an excuse for attacks against his cities and that same civilian morale.

On August 24, 1940, however, several *Luftwaffe* planes happened to bomb London. Prime Minister Churchill seized the occasion to send ninety-five RAF Bomber Command aircraft against Berlin the next night—for precision bombing of industrial targets (though darkness made precision dubious), but also candidly as a retaliatory stroke. Hitler replied, "If they attack our cities, we will rub out their cities from the map," and the *Luftwaffe* shifted its main bombing efforts from British airfields and fighter defenses to London. The results proved fortunate for Britain despite the pain of "the Blitz," because the Germans' earlier efforts had so weakened the RAF that, as Churchill said, "It was therefore with a sense of relief that Fighter Command felt the German attack turn to London on September

7. . . ." The defense installations themselves could enjoy a respite from direct attack.[75]

Having thus done much to introduce city bombing into the war, Churchill and his advisers remained fascinated by its possibilities for punishing the loathsome Nazis, especially when in so many ways Britain was too weak to carry the war to the enemy. The night bombing which the RAF decided was the only feasible kind of bombing seemed to have to be indiscriminate area bombing anyway; efforts at night bombing of precision targets such as German synthetic oil facilities in 1941 failed. Churchill was by no means without misgivings about terror bombing; but his somewhat sinister—at least to many—scientific adviser Lord Cherwell (Professor F. A. Lindemann) favored it, and together Churchill and Cherwell gave a rather free hand to its foremost apostle in the RAF, Air Chief Marshal Sir Arthur Harris, after February 22, 1942, the head of Bomber Command. They often let Harris have his way when the RAF Air Staff itself felt qualms about his city-bombing enthusiasms. Harris's elevation to the leadership of Bomber Command followed immediately after and coincided in purpose with a directive to the command on February 14 to open a new offensive aimed primarily at the homes of the German people. Cherwell argued in April that this campaign, striking Germany's fifty-eight largest cities, would render one-third of the German population homeless within fifteen months and that there was no better way to break their spirit.[76]

Lack of planes had hitherto restrained the British, but they were now on the verge of their ability to mount at least occasional thousand-plane raids. From 1942 to 1944, while the American Eighth Air Force was enduring its growing pains and the losses of its daylight raids, the British carried on a sustained area bombing campaign with cities and their people candidly its primary targets. The campaign began with raids on Essen in March, 1942, and reached one of its climaxes in the fire raids on Hamburg at the end of July, 1943, when in four days the RAF killed about 42,000 people, more than had died in the whole "Blitz" against Britain.[77]

By the time Bomber Command was diverted temporarily to support of OVERLORD, the British might have felt misgivings about their bombing strategy on other accounts than their recent heavy losses to *Luftwaffe* night fighters, for two years of sustained terror bombing had conspicuously failed to destroy German morale or the German war effort. Exact evidence of the effects naturally was lacking, but already there were indications of a tendency to push the enemy people more deeply into the arms of Hitler's government, on which they became more dependent as other bonds of community were blasted away.

Nevertheless, when Bomber Command returned from OVERLORD to the German cities, Harris refused not only the invitations of the AAF but also the advice of the Air Staff and its chief, Marshal of the RAF Sir Charles Portal, and refused to join in the AAF precision bombing campaign. The interval since March had afforded time to consolidate Allied command of the air, and the RAF's crisis of German interception did not recur. By now, furthermore, the OVERLORD activities had stimulated development of ingenious RAF precision capacities in night bombing. But Harris returned to city bombing, and for the most part he kept Bomber Command on that line to the end of the war. In the last days of the conflict the terror bombing of Germany reached its final dreadful climax in the Dresden raids of February 13–14, 1945, which killed some 35,000 people, supposedly in order to assist the Russians by destroying what Churchill called "a centre of communications of Germany's Eastern Front."[78]

To General Spaatz's subsequent embarrassment, the AAF followed up the RAF strike against Dresden with a daylight raid of its own, presumably against its customary precision targets but inspiring newspaper reports that the AAF had gone over to terror raids and Soviet charges to the same effect ever since. Spaatz explicitly denied that the AAF had done anything but pursue the campaign in which it had been engaged since the OVERLORD diversion had ended: the campaign of precision bombing against economic targets which AAF chieftains regarded as the true test of American strategic bombing doctrine at last.[79]

On March 5, 1944, the AAF bomber offensive had shifted its first priority target from German fighter production to oil production. The full-scale aerial attack against German petroleum got under way soon after the Normandy beachhead was secure, and it continued until the Allied armies crossed the Rhine. In that time the AAF, with some British participation, mounted 555 attacks against 135 different targets in the German oil, synthetic fuel, and refinery industries. The devastating effect was to cut German oil production to 12 percent of its pre-attack level. By early 1945, the *Luftwaffe* had plenty of planes, but could not get them off the ground. It could not train new pilots, and the best it could manage was to fly occasional ineffectual sorties against the Allied bombers. While high-octane aviation gasoline suffered worst from the aerial assault, just as surely though a bit more slowly the vehicles of the German army halted for lack of fuel. Efforts to burn wood or coal in trucks and tanks achieved only limited success. Many German tanks could not fight in the last battles because they could not move.

The same attacks that knocked out the German oil industry also ruined the chemical industry, because it was closely integrated with petroleum production. The destruction of just two crucial plants cost Germany 63 percent of its synthetic nitrogen production, and before the end of the war the loss in synthetic nitrogen reached 91 percent. With this development, Germany was about to run out of ammunition.

In retrospect, it is evident that the earlier departure from the 1941 AWPD-1 plan to make German aviation production the primary target of the bomber offensive was a mistake, occasioned by the pressures of the air war and the possibly inescapable limitations of Allied knowledge of the German war economy. An initial concentration on petroleum probably would have grounded the *Luftwaffe* and won command of the air earlier than did direct attacks on plane and engine production, and the same concentration might well have brought also much earlier decisive effects upon the whole German war effort. ". . . The Allies would have been able to end the war sooner," Field Marshal Erhard Milch of the *Luftwaffe* said, "had they started their attacks against the German petroleum refineries earlier; in fact they would have shortened the war by the exact number of months (or weeks) it would have taken (and took) to carry out these attacks effectively."[80]

In September, 1944, the bomber offensive also commenced heavy attacks on the whole German transportation network. This campaign virtually isolated the Ruhr from the rest of Germany by a month before the capture of the Remagen bridge over the Rhine. By March 15, German railroad car loadings were cut by 85 percent. Apparently aerial attack upon a delicate modern transportation system could have combined with the raids on the petroleum industry to immobilize Germany by the summer of 1945 even if the Allied armies had never crossed the Oder or the Rhine.[81]

> The military successes of the American daylight operations [said Milch] were considerably more productive than those of British night flying operations, but the "combined" method of American daylight operations and British night flying operations successfully complemented each other to achieve the ultimate success. The greater volume

of bombs dropped by the Lancasters and other British aircraft was compensated for by the lesser number of target hits and by the, at least 30%, decrease in finding the assigned targets during night operations.[82]

Albert Speer, Hitler's Minister of Armaments and Munitions, gave a similar German view of the relative effectiveness of American and British strategic bombing: "The American attacks, which followed a definite system of assault on industrial targets, *were by far the most dangerous. It was in fact these attacks which caused the breakdown of the German armaments industry*. The night attacks did not succeed in breaking the will to work of the civilian population."[83]

The achievements of the daylight bombing offensive against well-selected targets went far toward substantiating the prewar prophecies of the air power enthusiasts after all. Still, the ground and the aerial campaigns against Germany were so closely interdependent that it is impossible to judge what either of them might have accomplished if it had gone unassisted by the other. If the Germans had been able to devote resources to aerial warfare without concern for the protection of France against amphibious assault and then their western frontiers against ground attack, they might have been able to muster enough fighter and antiaircraft strength to turn back the bomber offensive. Earlier production of jet fighters might have made a decisive difference. Spared the distractions of ground defense, the Germans also would have been likely to muster a stronger strategic bombing attack of their own, against the very vulnerable confines of Britain. The advance of the Allied ground offensives materially aided the bomber offensive by reducing the German early warning system and the number of airfields from which the *Luftwaffe* could intercept.[84]

Without the investment of Allied resources in the bomber offensive, greater means obviously would have been available for the ground offensive. Without the diversion of the *Luftwaffe* to combat the bomber offensive, and its losses in the attempt, however, the invasion of France and the final ground campaign against Germany would have been immensely more costly and perhaps not possible at all. If there is no telling what the Germans might have accomplished in the air if they had not been distracted by the requirements of the ground campaigns, there is also no telling what they might have accomplished on the ground, against Russia as well as in the west, if they had not been distracted by the bomber offensive.

Amid these puzzles, it is certain that for reasons of policy the Western Allies could not have afforded to rely on air power alone, with no ground offensives at all, however efficacious such a plan might have proved in beating Germany. The effect would have been to leave too much of the European continent open to Soviet occupation and to liberation by resistance groups which were often led by Communists. The Western Allies from the SLEDGEHAMMER planning onward had stand-by programs for hurrying their troops into the Continent and into Germany in case air power or other means should have induced a rapid Nazi collapse. Whether in that event American and British troops could have gone far enough fast enough to assure the Western orientation of as much of Europe as they eventually occupied must be doubtful.

Air and ground together amply achieved the goals of the Americans' strategy of annihilation against Nazi Germany. With the indispensable contribution of the Russians, who always confronted the bulk of the German army and suffered a terrible toll in casualties as a result, the strategy of annihilation did not exact excessive and intolerable costs from the Anglo-American armed forces. Persistence in a peripheral strategy of closing the ring around Hitler's empire would almost certainly have accomplished much less to make Britain and America decisive contributors to German defeat and to bring their armies into the European heartland, at a higher cost if not absolutely at least in proportion to the results. In all these features of the eventual victory the American strategists could find gratification.

To reflect that the costs of the strategy of annihilation and of the war of mass and concentration were limited to tolerable levels for the Western Allies only by the sacrifices and the hard fighting of the Russians was less gratifying, especially because of the implications of this fact for the postwar balance of power. To reflect that to the extent that the strategic bombing campaign contributed to decisiveness and minimal casualties in the ground war, it did so by extending the reach of war even farther and more terribly than Sherman had done could be a still less gratifying thought. Even the relatively precise bombing of industrial targets inevitably killed and maimed large numbers of civilians hitherto exempt from the most direct horrors of war. The Allied bomber offensive killed some 305,000 Germans and injured about 780,000.[85]

PART FIVE

American Strategy in Perplexity, 1945–

War for a nonaggressor nation is actually a nearly complete collapse of policy.

—*Rear Admiral J. C. Wylie*[1]

15. The Atomic Revolution

Strategy is the theory of the use of combats for the object of the War.
—*Clausewitz*[1]

THE LAST MENTIONED FEATURES of the strategy of annihilation as applied against Germany in World War II so added to the brutalizing of war that apparently they could not but blur the moral vision of their authors. Thus, unhappily, whatever moral restraint the United States had shown in refraining from participation in Britain's deliberate campaign of terror bombing against Germany disappeared with astonishingly few regrets in the Pacific. There, ironically, at the very time when General Spaatz in Europe was denying that there had been AAF terror bombing of Dresden, the United States Army Air Forces were opening against Japan a terroristic city-bombing campaign which was to surpass even what the RAF had done in visiting concentrated destruction upon thousands of noncombatants within a limited span of time.

The circumstances of the departure from the AAF's previous restraint are not altogether clear. There had always existed among the AAF planners a group more literally subscribing to Douhet and the later Mitchell than the principal authors of AWPD-1, and therefore inclined toward attacking civilians and civilian morale. In the spring of 1945 it was not yet evident how little the British campaign of terror bombing had contributed to the defeat of Germany. Anyway,

Japan was a different enemy. Her population was more deeply concentrated in cities than Germany's; her industries were less clearly separated from residential areas, since they were organized often on a smaller scale than Germany's and in smaller craft shops; her cities were highly inflammable and thus temptingly vulnerable to attack. Perhaps the bitterness of Pearl Harbor still made for a harsher American resentment toward Japan than toward Germany. Certainly far fewer Americans had ethnic ties to Japan than to Germany, and the displacement of Japanese-Americans from the West Coast revealed an American capacity for casual cruelty toward these Orientals which carried frightening implications.

In any event, the AAF gave wide discretion in the determination of bombing strategy for Japan to Major General Curtis E. LeMay's XXI Bomber Command, the B-29s in the Marianas operating under the Twentieth Air Force whose commanding general was Arnold himself. High-level precision attacks against Japanese industry brought results disappointing both to LeMay and to AAF headquarters in Washington. LeMay consequently decided to attempt nighttime area bombing with incendiary bombs dropped from low levels, using the advantage of darkness to reduce the B-29's defensive armament and increase its bombload. Such an attack against Kobe on February 3, 1945, produced impressive fires and considerable industrial damage as well. On February 19 General Arnold directed further experiments with area fire raids. At this point the Japanese aircraft industry was the first-priority target of the B-29s, but Arnold now designated urban centers as secondary targets. LeMay moved toward making the cities the primary targets. On March 9 he sent 334 B-29s, carrying some 2,000 tons of bombs, on an incendiary-bomb raid against Tokyo. In loss of life this was the most destructive air raid in history, without exception; it killed 83,793 people, while injuring 40,918, destroying about a quarter of Tokyo's buildings, and leaving more than a million homeless.

LeMay followed up with similar raids: against Nagoya on March 11, with a heavier weight of bombs than had fallen on Tokyo; against Osaka, Kobe, and Nagoya again. The Joint Chiefs were now prevailed upon to designate thirty-three Japanese cities as major targets, along with certain key industries. To accelerate the disruption of Japanese life, American bombers began dropping leaflets listing cities likely to be destroyed "in the next few days." Thousands fled their homes, dislocating war industry more than the terror bombing of Germany had ever done, swelling the ranks of an eventual eight and a half million refugees of the American aerial campaign, and spreading fear throughout the land. The hope of both AAF and Navy leaders that Japan could be brought to surrender without invasion was probably decisive in producing Washington's endorsement of LeMay's bombing methods. In that, it seemed merely a logical extension of policy to employ the two atomic bombs, which killed from 70,000 to 80,000 at Hiroshima and 35,000 at Nagasaki, with higher numbers of injured.[2]

Yet if employing the first atomic bombs could seem at the time a mere extension of a strategy already in use, it soon became evident that by carrying a strategy of annihilation to the literalness of absurdity, the atomic bomb also represented a strategic revolution. The atomic explosions at Hiroshima and Nagasaki ended Clausewitz's "the use of combats" as a viable inclusive definition of strategy. A strategy of annihilation could now be so complete that a use of combats encompassing atomic weapons could no longer serve "for the object of the War," unless the object of war was to transform the enemy's country into a desert. The rational purposes of statecraft could not be thus served. Furthermore, if the United States should lose the monopoly of atomic weapons it possessed in 1945, "the use of combats" with atomic weapons would almost certainly destroy not only America's enemies beyond rational purpose but the United States as well. In 1945 most Americans, even informed ones, optimistically exaggerated the likely duration of their atomic monopoly; but from its beginning, the monopoly was insecure enough that the American government sought a program of international control of atomic energy through the new United Nations Organization at the same time that it also attempted to invoke its atomic weaponry for postwar military purposes of its own.[3]

If the atomic bomb could not be used in combat without risking an annihilation of the enemy too complete to serve the objects of war or policy, and in time without risking America's own annihilation as well, then the definition even of military kinds of strategy had to be expanded beyond "the use of combats for the object of the War." Strategy would have to be redefined to encompass achieving the prevention of atomic combat as well as the use of combats.

Other factors in addition to the atomic bomb made obsolete an American definition of strategy as the use of combats. Until the Second World War, the United States had been involved only sporadically in international politics with its vital national interests at stake. With only intermittent involvement in international politics, the United States had had to make only intermittent active use of its armed forces in other than internal police functions. Strategy defined as the use of combats and coming to express itself as a quest for the annihilation of hostile armed forces which threatened American national interests had been a workable enough means of employing American military power for the advancement and protection of American policies. Victory in the Second World War and a consequent role as one of only two world superpowers gave the United States new international responsibilities, however, which entailed permanent participation in world politics and permanent, not intermittent, employment of the armed forces to serve national policies.

Specifically, the leaders of the United States government at the close of World War II believed that the United States must contain what they perceived as a remorseless expansionist tendency in the policies of the other superpower, the Soviet Union, lest the Soviet maw consume so much of the world that the closest friends of the United States, the other Western democracies, and the United States itself be mortally imperiled. The policy of containment of Soviet expansionism took shape in disagreements with the Soviets during the summit and foreign ministers' conferences of the last days of the war and the first days of the postwar era, found clear enunciation in the Truman Doctrine in March, 1947, and received its rationale in George F. Kennan's article, "The Sources of Soviet Conduct," published anonymously in *Foreign Affairs* the following July.[4] The policy of containment apparently necessitated a continuous reliance on the military forces of the United States as one of the means for the curbing of Soviet expansionism; but the military forces would be used not in combat, it was hoped, but rather in the support of American policy aims without recourse to combat. Containment and the Cold War as well as atomic weapons demanded a new American definition of strategy, to encompass the employment of the armed forces for the object of national policies but without resort to combats and wars.

To be sure, American military policy had always encompassed some reliance on the armed forces for purposes not adequately delineated by defining strategy as the use of combats. The coastal fortifications which were so constant a feature of American military policy from 1794 through 1945 were intended not only for use in combat but also to ward off combat, by persuading prospective enemies that descents upon the American coast would be more costly than they could be worth. The coastal fortifications in part embodied a strategy not of the use of combats but of deterrence of combat. Similarly, the early and puny American Navy had embodied a strategy not only of the use of combats but of deterrence. The early Navy could not control the seas, not even the seas adjacent to the American coast, but its founders hoped it might deter an enemy from attacking the American coast, or American interests of any kind, by threatening him with shipping losses that might make the effort too costly to be worth attempting.

Before 1945, these elements of a strategy of deterrence in American military policy had always been secondary to a view of strategy which regarded the armed forces as instruments to be employed in combat in pursuit of the objects for which the country intermittently went to war. After 1945, a strategy of deterrence would have to become not secondary but uppermost in American military policy. Furthermore, as the strategic writer Bernard Brodie was to point out, the new weapons would make atomic deterrence qualitatively different from any past strategy of deterrence, in that:

> For one thing, it [the new strategy of deterrence] uses a kind of threat which we feel must be absolutely effective, allowing for no breakdowns ever. The sanction is, to say the least, not designed for repeating action. One use of it will be fatally too many. Deterrence now means something as a strategic policy only when we are fairly confident that the retaliatory instrument upon which it relies will not be called upon to function at all.[5]

Yet to make post-1945 strategic problems all the more difficult, the strategy of atomic deterrence, while operating within the dangerous and delicate constraints Brodie suggested, was also expected to provide the military means to achieve positive objects in American policy. According to Secretary of War Henry L. Stimson, President Truman postponed meeting with Premier Stalin until he was about to have in hand his "master card" of diplomacy, the atomic bomb. Truman's Secretary of State at the time of the Potsdam meeting with Stalin, James F. Byrnes, said that he thought the bomb would make the Russians more manageable in central and eastern Europe. According to Stimson, Byrnes "looks to having the presence of the bomb in his pocket, so to speak, as a great weapon to get through the thing he has."[6]

To shift the American definition of strategy from the use of combats for the object of wars to the use of military force for the deterrence of war, albeit while still serving the national interest in an active manner, amounted to a revolution in the history of American military policy. The revolution is easier to perceive in retrospect than it was during the late 1940s, when the government and the armed forces had to digest a new view of military strategy and thus of the whole employment of military power amid the immediately pressing issues of demobilizing the World War II armies and navies, a structural reorganization of the military establishment, and the hasty invoking of military power to buttress the containment policy. For the time being, as Henry A. Kissinger was to say, "we added the atomic bomb to our arsenal without integrating its implications into our thinking. Because we saw it merely as another tool in a concept of warfare which knew no goal save total victory, and no mode of war except all-out war."[7] Lieutenant General James M. Gavin was to write of the atomic bomb "that military thinking seemed, at the outset, to be paralysed by its magnitude."[8]

In keeping with the traditional American view that military strategy and the armed forces are employed intermittently to destroy occasional and intermittent threats posed by hostile powers, the American public clamored for rapid demobilization after the Axis surrenders, just as wartime forces had been demobilized quickly after all previous American ventures in the use of combats. American GIs were eager to go home after a long war and sometimes demonstrated in support of the civilian clamor for their return.[9] Taxpayers called for reduced federal expenditures and severe limits on military spending. Despite the beginnings of the Cold War and the requirements of military occupation in the defeated countries, and buoyed by confidence in his "master card," President Truman proposed on September 25, 1945, to reduce the war Army of over 8,000,000 to 1,950,000 by June, 1946, with Navy and Air Force reductions in proportion. By January 1, 1946, the Army had been cut about in half, to 4,228,936, and by June 30 it was slightly below Truman's earlier projection, numbering 1,891,011. By that time the Navy and Marine Corps totaled 1,139,077, from a wartime high of about 3,400,000. In March, 1946, the War Department had announced a proposed Army of 1,070,000 for July 1, 1947, 400,000 of that total to represent the Air Force; it was evident that the latter service was about to be divorced from the Army in accord both with wartime experiences and with the prominence of the air arm as the deliverer of the bomb.[10]

Even a projection of modest postwar strength implied a calculation of the purposes that the strength was to serve. In the immediate postwar years there was a tendency for both Army and Navy to try to escape whatever threat the atomic bomb and the new strategy of deterrence might hold for their accustomed roles—and thus perhaps for their very existence—by denying that the changes in strategy implied by atomic weapons were so fundamental as civilians and airmen seemed to assume. Both of the traditional services emphasized that if American military strategy was to count on the bomb to deter wars or to win them if deterrence failed, there would still be a need for bases from which to launch atomic strikes. Operational aircraft of the first postwar years still lacked intercontinental range. The Army would have to take and hold overseas bases; the Navy would have to carry American strength across the seas to the bases.

As the Army viewed the problems of conflict with America's great postwar rival, war with the Soviet Union would require immense quantities of military manpower even if the decisive blows should be struck by atomic bombs from the air. At the least, vast territories would have to be occupied by great numbers of American troops to be brought under control; at worst, if atomic weapons failed to achieve a decision, then still greater numbers of American troops, heavily equipped with armor and artillery, would be required to cope with the Soviet Army. In a future world war, the United States could no longer be shielded by powerful allies and would have to participate fully from the outset. Therefore American mobilization would have to be extremely rapid. War with the Soviet Union would require rapid industrial mobilization and rapid mobilization of another mass army.

A new mass army would again have to be a conscript army. To mobilize it rapidly, the conscripts should be trained in peacetime to take their place in war units almost overnight. During the war just ended, General Marshall had formed a War Department group to prepare a plan for just such military training of the citizenry. The group was headed by Brigadier General John McAuley Palmer, the long-time advocate of citizens' military training. On August 24, 1944, Marshall issued War Department Circular 347, prepared for him by Palmer, in which he proposed as the foundation of postwar military policy a system of universal military training. Among the Army planners, this proposal survived the atomic bomb.[11]

As the Army disentangled itself from demobilization, it therefore supported the Gurney-Wadsworth Bill, which called for one year of military training for all young men at some time between the ages of eighteen and twenty-one, to be followed by four years in a reserve. General Palmer helped prepare the bill. Agreeing that in future war the United States would have to mobilize swiftly at the outset, and not certain that the atomic bomb would solve all the problems of conquering the Russian land mass, various civilian leaders endorsed the idea of universal military training, notably including a committee of prominent educators, the Post-War Military Policy Committee of the House of Representatives, and President Truman. The better to appeal to war-weary opinion, UMT was sweetened by its advocates through emphasis on the alleged virtues of the proposed training in fostering good citizenship and national good health through physical fitness. But Congress as a whole wisely cast a jaundiced eye on the latter, subsidiary arguments; and as for the main arguments, its members mostly doubted that a plan for a mass army met the strategic requirements of the atomic age, and that in any event a mass but necessarily half-trained army met the requirements of rapid mobilization.

The Army and the President both urged UMT upon an indifferent and unwilling Congress and public with remarkable persistence; but the attitude of Congress did not change. On the other hand, impelled by the rise of the Cold War, Congress did feel obliged to extend wartime selective service legislation to March 31, 1947, and then to restore it in June, 1948, in response to the Communist coup in Czechoslovakia and concurrent instances of Soviet truculence.[12]

The Navy had the advantage over the ground Army of being able to offer itself as a possible deliverer of the bomb. Nevertheless, like the Army it still stressed its contribution to the acquisition of bases near enough to the enemy to hit him. To be able to deliver the atomic bomb to any point in the world with no exceptions, there was still required the global mobility afforded only by sea power. Against some targets, the bomb might best be carried by the Navy's own carrier-based planes. But even the B-29 had required sea power to secure for it the bases from which it carried atomic bombs to Hiroshima and Nagasaki, and bombers of longer range than the B-29 yet within the limits of practicality would also need overseas bases supported by sea power to be able to mount a sustained campaign against Soviet targets. To mount air-atomic attacks or to follow them up by occupying enemy territory, sea power remained indispensable to the strategic mobility without which the United States could not remain a superpower. In this reasoning the Navy found confidence for its future.

While the Army during the war years had begun to plan for its future bigger and better mass armies through universal military training, the Navy similarly had planned for the postwar era bigger and better versions of its weapons of World War II. While that war continued, the Navy took advantage of the success of the fast carrier task forces to go on persuading Congress to vote additional carriers well beyond those likely to be completed in time to fight Japan. The carrier building of the late war years was intended less to fight Japan than to preserve the Navy through the predictable budget stringencies of postwar times. The building program included both a continuing procession of *Essexes* and the first of a new class of very large 45,000-ton vessels designated first as "battle carriers" (CVB) and then, after the war, as "attack carriers" (CVA). The keels of the first two of this class were laid down late in 1943. They were launched in March and April, 1945, as *Midway* (CVB-41) and *Franklin D. Roosevelt* (CVB-42) Others of the class had to be cancelled during the last months of the war, but *Coral Sea* (CVB-43) was also pushed to completion, due in 1946.[13]

Because the AAF and after 1947 the newly independent Air Force pressed the development of bombers of intercontinental range, the Navy believed that to assure its role in the new strategic circumstances the mobility promised by fleets of fast carriers was not enough. The aircraft launched from the carrier decks had to be able to deliver the bomb; the Navy had to be capable of its own "strategic bombing" with atomic weapons. To that end, the Navy formed new Heavy Attack squadrons, to be equipped with high-altitude planes able to carry a heavier bombload than its traditional single-engine carrier-based craft. The first such plane to become available was the twin-engine, but carrier-based, North American AJ-1 Savage, first flown in 1948 and delivered for service a year later. The Savage was given a bomb capacity of up to six tons by stripping it of other armament and depending on speed alone for protection. But with jet fighters becoming common, that was hardly enough for a propeller-driven plane. A more satisfactory attack craft was expected in March, 1949, when the Navy ordered the first prototypes of what was to be the Douglas A3D Skywarrior. This was to be a twin-jet aircraft with ample bomb capacity and a remote-control radar-aimed twin 20mm gun turret in the tail.[14]

The Skywarrior called for bigger carriers than the *Essex* class, preferably bigger even than the *Midway* class. A necessary corollary of the Navy's strategic bombers therefore was a Navy demand for still larger carriers: for the largest warships ever built, supercarriers of 80,000 tons. In the postwar era of budget stringency, the obvious trouble with this fact was that the immense cost of such leviathans would collide with the also immense costs of an air armada, and the naval aircraft operational in the late 1940s seemed unlikely deliverers of the atomic punch compared with multiengined Air Force strategic bombers.

For the Air Force held the master card indeed in the postwar effort of the armed services to justify themselves to Congress and the public. Its bombers were the most evident means of delivery of atomic weapons of annihilation. When Japan surrendered, the AAF had forty B-29 groups equipped with 2,132 of the world's most advanced operational heavy bomber. B-29 production continued after the war's end until May, 1946. As postwar international rivalries polarized into the Cold War confrontation between the two superpowers, however, an apparent disadvantage of the B-29 was its effective radius of about 1,500 miles. Great as this range was by the standards of other World War II bombers, it would make the B-29 highly dependent in a clash with the Soviet Union upon bases that might by overrun by the Soviet Army. Therefore the Air Force hastened development of an intercontinental bomber able to reach targets up to a distance of 4,000 miles. The first prototypes of the intercontinental bomber, the XB-36, had been ordered from Consolidated Aircraft about a month after Pearl Harbor. The contractor's commitments to build B-24s slowed development, but General Arnold stimulated new work on the project in 1943 when he feared that bases within B-29 range of Japan might not be secured early enough. The first XB-36 flew about a year after Japan's surrender, on August 8, 1946. It was a huge aircraft with a gross weight of 276,506 pounds (the B-17G had grossed 55,000 pounds, the B-29 140,000 pounds), powered by six 3,000-horsepower engines in pusher position on the trailing edge of the wings. The bomb bay could accommodate 84,000 pounds of bombs, and the airplane was designed for a defensive armament of five 37mm and ten .50-caliber guns. Naturally, the plane was costly as well as huge. The two prototypes cost more than $39 million, and the first ninety-five production models cost $6,248,686 each. The plane was accepted, and regular delivery of B-36As began in 1948. The B-36 did much to upset the postwar balance of power among the services by undercutting Army and Navy insistence on the value of overseas bases. So did increasingly successful experiments in mid-air refueling.[15]

Just after the bombing of Hiroshima, on August 9, 1945, an AAF

Air Staff conference recommended a postwar Air Force of seventy groups, to include four groups of B-36s. The seventy-group recommendation could hardly be based on a rational tailoring of strategic means to strategic needs, because at so early a date in the atomic age and with international power alignments still uncertain, no such tailoring was possible. Rather, seventy groups represented the strength the Air Force might hope it could get if it began asking in the immediate aftermath of its atomic triumph over Japan. Once stated, the seventy-group objective inevitably tended to take on a life of its own. On July 18, 1947, President Truman appointed an Air Policy Commission headed by Thomas K. Finletter, which on December 30 also recommended a seventy-group Air Force, to be achieved by 1950 and to include five groups of B-36s and sixteen groups of B-29s and their similar offspring the B-50. A Congressional Aviation Policy Board, usually called the Brewster-Hinshaw Board, endorsed the same recommendation.[16]

Meanwhile the domestic political situation was one in which a Republican Congress, elected in 1946 by voters intent on a respite from the prolonged strenuosities of depression and war, determined to fulfill its constituents' wishes for tranquility and "normalcy" and thus to recapture the White House for the GOP in 1948. After prolonged skirmishing between the President and Congress over a Congressional desire for tax reduction, in the Presidential election year Congress at length passed over the President's veto a bill which it was estimated would reduce revenues by about $5 billion. Against this background, and "determined not to spend more than we take in in taxes," President Truman limited defense spending to $14.4 billion in fiscal year 1947 and $11.7 billion in fiscal 1948 and proposed a defense budget of $11 billion for fiscal 1949. His proposals would allow for only a fifty-five–group Air Force, but they would permit the Navy to begin building one supercarrier. Thereby they set the stage for a bitter interservice debate about roles, strategy, and finance.[17]

By now the predictable divorce of the Air Force from the Army and "unification" of the three services under a single cabinet head had occurred, under the National Security Act of July 26, 1947. This act proved to be of little help in resolving interservice debate. The Army and Air Force had favored a relatively strong unification plan, the latter because it was confident of its future, the former because it thought it could better protect its interests against the more glamorous rival services within a centralized defense department rather than in competitive appeals to Congress and the public. The

Navy, however, feared subordination to commanders who did not understand sea power in a defense establishment which it thought an Air Force-Army partnership would dominate. Also, it did not want to lose its own air arm to the Air Force. Navy misgivings combined with Congressional fears of "Prussian" military centralization to produce a "coordinated" but not unified National Military Establishment under the National Security Act of 1947.

Behind problems of interservice unity or coordination was the doctrinally troublesome fact that the neat interservice boundaries which were formerly possible—the Army to deal with enemy armed forces on land and with anything else only to the range of its coastal guns, and the Navy to deal with enemy armed forces at sea—could no longer be drawn now that warfare had not only moved into the air, but the decisive weapons could be hurled through the air by either the Air Force or the Navy—and soon, given the pace of ballistic missile development, by the Army as well.

According to the National Security Act, a Secretary of Defense would head the National Military Establishment as the President's principal assistant in all matters relating to national security. Three service departments, of the Army, the Navy, and the Air Force, were to be administered as individual executive departments, with all powers and duties not specifically conferred upon the Secretary of Defense by the statute to be retained by the service secretaries. Each service secretary was to have a direct right of appeal to the President. The Secretary of Defense, the three service secretaries, and the three service chiefs were to make up a War Council. The three service chiefs together with a Chief of Staff to the President would constitute a Joint Chiefs of Staff organization, with an organizational joint staff of not more than 100 officers. To coordinate national security policy, linking military policy and strategy to national policy at large, the act created a National Security Council composed of the President, the Secretary of Defense, the three service secretaries, and other principal defense and foreign policy officials to be appointed at the discretion of the President. A Central Intelligence Agency was to report and make recommendations to the National Security Council and to coordinate the intelligence activities of the various departments. The act also created a National Security Resources Board, a Munitions Board, and a Research and Development Board.[18]

The Secretary of Defense lacked a staff and an executive department of his own. As Secretary of the Navy, James Forrestal as much as anyone had been the architect of the National Security Act, expressing the Navy's hesitations. As first Secretary of Defense, Forrestal found himself frustrated by the statute he had largely designed, unable to coordinate service policies and strategies by any means except force of personality, a resource he soon exhausted with consequences tragic to himself. Forrestal took office as Secretary of Defense and the new organization of the National Military Establishment began functioning on September 17, 1947. Shortly thereafter the reports of the Finletter Commission and the Brewster-Hinshaw Board brought to a head quarrels between the Navy and the Air Force over their respective strategic missions. The Air Force, encouraged by both reports, charged that the Navy with its programs for strategic bombers and supercarriers was encroaching upon the mission of the Air Force. Secretary Forrestal decided to hold a prolonged meeting of the Joint Chiefs of Staff, away from Washington, to define the respective service missions and decide "who will do what with what." If the service chiefs failed to reach agreement, said Forrestal to a press conference, "I shall have to make my own decisions."[19]

But he did not have the power to enforce his own decisions, and his Key West Conference of the service chiefs in March, 1948, resolved very little. It led to an agreement which repeated traditional but now not very relevant definitions of boundaries, stating that the primary function of the Air Force was to control the air, that of the Navy to control the seas, and that of the Army to defeat the enemy ground forces. Beyond that, a resulting Executive Order 9950 declared that in addition to the primary functions,

> . . . each service is charged with collateral functions, wherein its forces are to be employed to support and supplement the other services. . . . As an illustration of this principle, strategic air warfare has been assigned as a primary function of the Air Force, and the Navy is assigned as a primary function the conduct of air operations necessary for the accomplishment of objectives in a naval campaign . . . the Navy will not be prohibited from attacking any targets, inland or otherwise, which are necessary for the accomplishment of its mission.[20]

In accordance with the illustration, the Navy was not to be denied use of the atomic bomb, and it was "to proceed with development of 80,000 ton carrier and development of HA [high altitude] aircraft to carry heavy missiles therefrom."[21] This decision did not leave the Air Force happy, nor did the failure of the conference to give the Air Force its seventy rather than fifty-five groups as compensation for the Navy's getting a supercarrier. Furthermore, the Air Force did not much like an agreement that because UMT was unlikely to win Congressional approval, the Military Establishment should seek re-enactment of selective service; the Air Force believed that a mass army like a supercarrier would divert funds from the true weapon of a correct strategy, the heavy bomber in a seventy-group Air Force. Thereupon, Secretary of the Air Force Stuart Symington in late March resumed his advocacy of the seventy-group Air Force in testimony before the Senate Armed Services Committee. The Chief of Staff of the Air Force, General Spaatz, seconded his service secretary, calling the seventy-group Air Force a "minimum air defense." Symington also testified that resumption of the draft was unnecessary.

To Forrestal, this was insubordination; the National Security Act gave the services the right to appeal to the President, but not to advocate "unilateral" policy positions before Congress. Forrestal estimated that to add a seventy-group Air Force to the agreed requirements of the other services would raise the defense budget from $11 billion to $18 billion. Because Congress and the voters were unlikely to accept so high a cost, the other services would suffer, and the defense system would be thrown out of balance. In a supplementary appropriations bill, Congress nevertheless voted overwhelmingly for a seventy-group Air Force; but the proviso that spending the money depended on a Presidential judgment of necessity left the issue still unresolved and interservice rivalry over strategic missions still in full flood. Another Forrestal conference with the service chiefs, at the Naval War College in August, again failed to resolve their differences.[22]

The equilibrium of his intense, not to say messianic, personality eroded by nine years of government service and a year and a half as Secretary of Defense with responsibility but no commensurate power, Forrestal submitted his resignation at President Truman's request on March 2, 1949. His successor, Louis Johnson, reaped the benefit of some of Forrestal's frustrations, since on March 5 the President recommended amendment of the National Security Act to give the Secretary of Defense fuller authority. On August 10, Congress transformed the National Military Establishment into an executive Department of Defense. The service departments ceased to be executive departments and became military departments within the Department of Defense, without cabinet representation or statutory membership on the National Security Council. The Secretary of

Defense received staff assistance in a Deputy Secretary and three Assistant Secretaries. Primary budget responsibility, a critical element in control of the services, went to a Comptroller of the Defense Department, who would be one of the Assistant Secretaries. About to be thus armed, politically ambitious and heedful of opinion polls which indicated public support of both limited defense spending and the seventy-group Air Force, Secretary Johnson cancelled the Navy's supercarrier on April 23, 1949, five days after the keel was laid.[23]

He thereby precipitated the famous "revolt of the admirals." After preliminary maneuvers involving a civilian Navy employee's anonymous charges of fraud and favoritism in Air Force procurement, Captain John G. Crommelin of the Navy on October 3 released the confidential remarks of three admirals criticizing defense management in general and the favoring of the Air Force B-36 over naval aviation in particular. The remarks appeared in letters to the Secretary of the Navy, Francis P. Matthews, from Vice Admiral Gerald P. Bogan, commander of the First Task Force of the Pacific Fleet, with endorsements from Admiral Arthur W. Radford, commander of the Pacific Fleet, and Admiral Louis Denfield, Chief of Naval Operations. Their gist was that the admirals thought the Navy was being stripped of offensive power, and the nation with it. The letters precipitated an investigation by the House Armed Services Committee, at which Admiral Radford emerged as the most conspicuous Navy spokesman, calling the B-36 a billion-dollar blunder and attacking the whole Air Force strategic concentration upon atomic annihilation. Three of the Navy's leading heroes of World War II, King, Halsey, and Kinkaid, endorsed Radford's opinion that in World War II the tactical uses of air power had been more valuable than the "strategic," and that consequently the Air Force was endangering national security by neglecting tactical aircraft and fighters.[24]

Criticism of the B-36 touched the Air Force at a vulnerable point, because critics who did not have the Navy's axe to grind also felt misgivings about this piston-engined giant, especially after the unveiling of formations of Russia's MIG-15 jet fighter on May Day, 1949. On July 11, 1949, the Air Force flew a B-36D with its six piston engines supplemented by four jet engines of 5,200 pounds thrust each. All B-36s henceforth, including all on hand, were to be fitted thus with jet engines. Accordingly the chances of evading interception were improved. Meanwhile, the Air Force was also developing completely jet-powered bombers, the most immediately promising of which was a plane comparable in size and range to the B-29, the Boeing B-47, powered by six jet engines. The first XB-47 flew late in 1947, and an order for ten was placed in 1948. In January, 1946, the Air Force had also issued specifications for an intercontinental bomber on the scale of the B-36, but jet-powered; this project led to an order for the prototype of the eight-jet Boeing B-52 in July, 1948. For the present, nevertheless, the Air Force was concentrating its finances upon building its bird in hand, the B-36.[25]

The revolt of the admirals did more than call attention to the weaknesses of particular instruments of Air Force strategy. It began to call the strategic debate back to fundamental issues. "In planning to wage a war," said Admiral Radford, ". . . we must look to the peace to follow. . . . A war of annihilation might possibly bring a Pyrrhic military victory, but it would be politically and economically senseless."[26] This observation became all the more cogent because in September, 1949, the Russians achieved their first atomic explosion, and the American monopoly was no more.

Despite his general adherence to strict budgetary limitations on defense spending, Secretary Johnson decided that Russia's early acquisition of the atomic bomb demanded an American crash program to build a still more powerful weapon, a bomb whose primary principle would be not atomic fission but nuclear fusion, which was promised to be a still further superweapon with a thousand times the power of the Nagasaki bomb. David Lilienthal, the chairman of the Atomic Energy Commission, opposed such a program. Lilienthal feared that using fissionable material to try to develop the new "hydrogen bomb" would injure the production of atomic bombs. More than that, he invoked a much larger, moral argument against H-bomb development, namely, that the United States ought to forswear the imposition upon the world of weapons yet more terrible than those already available. The President appointed Johnson, Lilienthal, and Secretary of State Dean Acheson as a special committee of the National Security Council to advise him whether the United States should undertake the development of the thermonuclear superbomb. Between Johnson and Lilienthal, Acheson occupied a somewhat intermediate position, unwilling to accept the moral argument against H-bomb development, but inclined to postpone production of the bomb until further investigation of the problems of development and also until after a thorough review of foreign and military policies.[27]

The State Department, detached from the organizational insecurities of the armed services in the new defense establishment and their budgetary rivalries, proved in the immediate postwar years to be more capable than the armed forces of taking a broad view of the country's strategic needs. In June, 1948, the State Department presented a paper arguing that while war "is always a possibility," the main purpose in maintaining armed forces was to provide "support for our political position"; other purposes were to act "as a deterrent," to encourage other nations attempting to resist Soviet aggression, and to "wage war successfully if war should develop." This paper went farther than most early postwar documents toward saying explicitly that the main strategic purpose of the armed forces no longer involved directly the use of combats.[28]

The revolt of the admirals and the B-36 controversy of 1949 aroused fears in the State Department that interservice disputes were carrying the armed forces farther from, rather than closer to, a proper appraisal of strategic needs and a proper strategic posture. The Soviet atomic explosion and the Communist conquest of China naturally aggravated such fears. His own and his department's concern motivated Secretary Acheson's suggestion of an overall review of military and foreign policy in the context of the H-bomb discussion. In the sequel, Acheson decided that H-bomb research could not be delayed after all, lest the Soviets get a head start, and he and Johnson drew up a paper saying so, which Lilienthal somewhat surprisingly agreed to sign. But this recommendation was coupled with another which led the President to instruct the Secretaries of State and Defense, on January 31, 1950, "to undertake a re-examination of our objectives in peace and war and of the effect of these objectives on our strategic plans, in the light of the probable fission bomb capability and possible thermonuclear bomb capability of the Soviet Union."[29]

This instruction led to a landmark in the American government's recognition and definition of the revolution in strategy, the document eventually known as NSC-68. During the following two months an *ad hoc* State-Defense study group labored on the review of national policy and strategy. Paul H. Nitze, chairman of the State Department Policy Planning Staff, chaired the group, and as was consistent with the origins of the project and the constraints operating upon the armed services, the State Department members were most energetic in pushing forward the work. They had the cooperation, however, of Major General James H. Burns, the liaison officer of the Secretary of Defense with the State Department, and through him of the Joint

Strategic Survey Committee. When on March 22 the group presented its work to Secretaries Acheson and Johnson, Johnson left the meeting in anger, apparently in part because he thought that unauthorized people were encroaching upon the province of the Secretary of Defense, in part because the group called for a substantial increase in defense spending, with whose stringent limitation Johnson had identified himself. With the encouragement of the President the project continued nevertheless, and on April 7 Secretary Johnson felt obliged to join in signing the resulting report.[30]

NSC-68 took as its thesis, in Secretary Acheson's later words, the proposition that the Soviet Union confronted the United States with a "threat [which] combined the ideology of communist doctrine and the power of the Russian state into an aggressive expansionist drive."[31] The writers believed that to be halted, the Soviet drive must be confronted with strength including military strength—Kennan's containment thesis extended into military terms—and that the existing military strength of the United States was inadequate to the purpose. To that inadequacy, in large part, they attributed Soviet successes in extending Moscow's sphere of influence since the war. As Acheson was to put it in another later remark: ". . . what we must do is to create situations of strength; we must build strength; and if we create that strength, then I think that the whole situation in the world begins to change."[32] Unfortunately, the writers of NSC-68 believed, American strength was about to become less rather than more adequate. After the Soviet atomic explosion, they believed that Soviet nuclear development would match American by 1954. Then, with a nuclear deadlock, Soviet superiority in ground strength would count still more to the Soviets' advantage than it had before. The Soviets would be able to mount a variety of threats: general war, limited war, subversion, rupture of the Western alliance, undermining the American will.

In the face of Soviet expansionism and growing Soviet military, including nuclear, power, the group, believed the United States had four possible policy options: doing nothing; waging preventive war; retreating to the Western Hemisphere to bring its commitments into closer accord with its strength; or building up its military and general strength and that of its allies to right the power balance. The writers rejected all the options except the last, the only one which without war might both halt Soviet expansionism and by confronting the Soviets with constant strength exert a gradual persuasion to change the Soviet system. The United States ought to enlarge its capacity to wage either general or limited war. Without mentioning specific figures in their report, the State Department planners estimated a need to increase annual defense expenditures to about $35 billion. The military planners, conditioned by their budgetary experiences, estimated a much more modest increase to about $18 billion. In any event, the object of the NSC-68 prescription for national policy was to create a military balance which would employ military strength not in combat but to deter combat, and yet achieve the national policy objectives of the United States.

Receiving the report on April 7, President Truman discussed it with the National Security Council on April 25, and the council endorsed it as national policy. What that meant was questionable. A $13 billion ceiling had long since been set on defense spending for fiscal year 1951. In a Congressional election year, Congress was not receptive to increases. The hearings occasioned by the revolt of the admirals had wound down into a mood of satisfaction with current military policy after all, encouraged by the principal Defense Department spokesmen who testified. The Chairman of the Joint Chiefs of Staff, General Omar Bradley, endorsed the philosophy that had limited defense budgets since 1945. The burden of a swollen defense budget—such as $14.5 billion—would, he said, threaten the collapse of the national economy and was a danger as real as the Soviet threat. But "if the military continues to effect more economies in defense measures . . . there will be little danger of economic collapse and our over-all risk will be less and less."[33] The recommendations of NSC-68 did not seem likely to be implemented.

Certainly most members of the executive branch and Congress accepted the report's premises about the expansionist nature of Soviet power. By early 1950 the Cold War was in deep freeze. The disagreements holding back NSC-68's chances of acceptance were not with its premises but with the conclusion that containment of Communism necessarily entailed a diversified and expensive military program. The President himself was not yet altogether willing to follow in this Achesonian extension of the containment doctrine. Most Americans, in and out of government, still hoped that the master card, the atomic bomb, could take every trick militarily.

16. Old Strategies Revisited: Douglas MacArthur and George C. Marshall in the Korean War

Surprise is the most vital element for success in war.
—*Douglas MacArthur*[1]

NSC-68 SUGGESTED a danger of limited war, of Communist military adventures designed not to annihilate the West but merely to expand the periphery of the Communist domains, limited enough that an American riposte of atomic annihilation would be disproportionate in both morality and expediency. To retaliate against a Communist military initiative on any but an atomic scale, the American armed forces in 1950 were ill equipped. Ten understrength Army divisions and eleven regimental combat teams, 671 Navy ships, two understrength Marine Corps divisions, and forty-eight Air Force wings (the buildup not yet having reached the old figure of fifty-five) were stretched thinly all around the world. The Air Force atomic striking force, embodied now in eighteen wings of the Strategic Air Command, was the only American military organization possessing a formidable instant readiness capacity.[2] So much did Americans, including the government, succeed in convincing themselves that the atomic bomb was a sovereign remedy for all military ailments, so ingrained was the American habit of thinking of war in terms of annihilative victories, that occasional warnings of limited war went more than unheeded, and people, government, and much of the military could scarcely conceive of a Communist military thrust of lesser dimensions than World War III.

When troops of the Democratic People's Republic of Korea invaded the Republic of Korea on June 24, 1950, they therefore imposed upon the United States a strategic surprise in the deepest sense. Perceiving the invasion as Soviet-sponsored and believing a failure to resist would amount to a new Munich, President Truman attempted instantly to shift his military gears and to halt and punish the Communist Koreans not with all-out atomic retaliation but with military strength proportioned to the threat. To respond with atomic weaponry would have seemed indeed disproportionate both in morality and in expediency; it would have risked both a holocaust of Soviet retaliation and the possibility of using up the relatively small store of atomic bombs against a minor power, to cite only two of the considerations of expediency. To proportion the American response to the scale of the Communist challenge proved hazardous, however, not only because of the inappropriate condition of the American armed forces. Any strategy other than the now familiar strategy of annihilation proved so frustratingly at variance with the American conception of war that it upset the balance of judgment of American officers in the field and threatened the psychological balance of the nation itself.

For all that, the authors of the North Korean invasion of South Korea had also miscalculated the American response. Despite the weaknesses of the American armed forces, hardly another place on the boundary between the Communist and non-Communist worlds could have been so well selected as a setting for the frustration of a Communist military venture by the military resources of the United States. Korea is a peninsula which at the narrowest point of the Strait of Tsushima is little more than a hundred miles from Japan. Therefore Korea lay within ready reach of the largest concentration of American troops outside the United States, the four divisions of General Douglas MacArthur's army of occupation in Japan, and within ready reach also of American sea power.

The troops in Japan were not well trained, partly because Japan offered so little ground for that purpose. Like nearly all American Army formations in early 1950, their units were understrength. Infantry regiments had only two battalions instead of the standard three, and artillery battalions only two batteries instead of three. But the American troops were at least close by, and the Korean peninsula was accessible to air power vastly superior to anything the North Koreans could muster even without the atomic bomb, and to naval power which, though its ships were getting old and often had to be removed from mothballs to get into the fight, remained far and away the premier force of its kind on the globe.[3]

In fact, American naval power and the peninsular configuration of Korea for a time gave the war, from the American perspective, a heartening similarity to the Pacific war of 1941–45. The Army units thrown into Korea from Japan suffered severe initial defeats, and by late summer it was touch and go whether the Americans and South Koreans could retain a foothold on the peninsula around the port of Pusan. But even the initial defeats could be regarded with the consoling reflection that America had suffered similar defeats in the Pacific not long before and had quickly recovered, while the pattern of recovery in Korea began to become discernible even as the defeats continued. It was air and sea power that assured against complete ejection from Korea. Together the Air Force and the Navy carried enough ground troop reinforcements to the Naktong River line around Pusan to begin to equalize and then to turn the numerical balance of combat effectives against the North Koreans. Meanwhile, as long as numbers remained inadequate and combat skills and weaponry on the ground deficient, the Air Force and the Navy added enough fighting power to hold the Naktong line. The Navy anchored the flank on the Sea of Japan with offshore bombardment, and Air Force and Navy planes gave tactical support all along the line.[4]

Air Force support operations were handicapped because the newly independent Air Force had neglected tactical air support while concentrating on readiness to deliver the atomic bomb, and the Fifth Air Force and Eighth Army in Japan in particular had not carried out exercises in air-ground coordination. The speed of the new jet aircraft, the Lockheed F-80 Shooting Stars, added new complexities to the coordination problem. Nevertheless, the Air Force could break up North Korean assault concentrations and transport. It used five groups of B-29s in an interdiction campaign against the North Koreans' rail and road network. As time went on, it improved its control and communications for tactical air support, with tactical air control parties distributed down to each American regiment and ROK (Republic of Korea) division, and with Mustangs flying from Korean airstrips. Lieutenant General Walton H. Walker, commanding the Eighth Army, said: "If it had not been for the air support that we received from the Fifth Air Force, we should not have been able to stay in Korea."[5]

Meanwhile, as in the later Pacific campaigns of World War II, tactical support from Navy and Marine Corps aircraft was excellent. Before the battle for the Pusan bridgehead ended, four Navy carriers were sending their planes into the fight: first the fast carrier *Valley Forge* (CVA-45), then *Philippine Sea* (CVA-47), and the escort carriers *Badoeng Strait* (CVE-116) and *Sicily* (CVE-118). Except when they were fighting with the First Provisional Marine Brigade, Navy and Marine Vought F4U Corsairs and Douglas AD Skyraiders lacked their accustomed systems of liaison with the ground troops and maps to match the troops', but a North Korean prisoner replied when asked which American weapon he feared most by saying, "the blue airplanes."[6]

From the first, General MacArthur's experience of the Pacific campaigns of 1941–45 assured him that he would have the weapons to transform defeat into rapid and complete victory, once America flexed its muscles and ample reinforcements arrived. Since his first counteroffensive against the Japanese in New Guinea, MacArthur had made a specialty of the amphibious end run. In Korea, the initial defeats persisted longer than he expected, and the battle for the Pusan perimeter became more desperate than he anticipated; but he never removed his eyes long from his maps of the west coast of Korea and of Inchon, the port serving the capital city of Seoul.

An amphibious attack there would offer the great psychological and political reward of a possible quick recapture of Seoul. Because the main highways from north to south bunched their way through Seoul, an attack there could also disrupt the logistics of the North Korean forces on the Naktong line. Most important, MacArthur conceived a force landed at Inchon as an anvil upon which his Eighth Army and the ROK forces would break the North Korean army as his troops in the south attacked from the Naktong line to fight a battle of annihilation.

The Joint Chiefs of Staff feared that Inchon was too far away from the Naktong and that consequently a landing there would turn into another Anzio, with MacArthur's two forces too distant from each other for effective mutual support; they suggested a more shallow amphibious envelopment. But MacArthur believed that the North Korean forces had already strained themselves to the verge of collapse and that the Inchon landing with the cutting of the routes through Seoul would precipitate their disruption; a less distant landing would merely cause their withdrawal to a new line. "The amphibious landing," MacArthur said, "is the most powerful tool we have. To employ it properly, we must strike hard and deeply into enemy territory." "The deep envelopment, based upon surprise, which severs the enemy's supply lines, is and always has been the most decisive maneuver of war. A short envelopment, which fails to envelop and leaves the enemy's supply system intact, merely divides your own forces and can lead to heavy loss and jeopardy."[7]

Other factors caused the Joint Chiefs and the Navy to feel additional misgivings. Inchon might be strategically located, but it was a poor place for staging an amphibious assault. To reach it, attacking ships would have to find their way, without normal navigation lights, through a narrow and tortuous channel, where if one of them foundered the vessels ahead would be trapped and the following vessels blocked. The tides, thirty-three feet at their maximum, were the highest in the Orient and produced five-knot currents. They also deposited huge mudbanks which accounted for the difficult navigation. To ensure enough depth of water for the LSTs, an invasion would have to take place at the highest tide, which in the autumn of 1950 meant on or about September 15, October 11, or November 3. To utilize the highest tides would require a landing just before nightfall, so that the invaders would have little daylight in which to consolidate their position before they might be counterattacked. The landing would have to take place not on a beach but on a seawall, and it must proceed immediately into the streets of a city. An island, Wolmi-do, dominated Inchon harbor and would have to be bombarded and captured before the main landings, thus telegraphing what was about to happen. In any event, an amphibious operation proceeding from Japan had to be based on a country full of enemy spies, and prolonged indecision in the fighting on the Naktong line at last permitted the assembly of enough troops in time to give only three weeks of intensive preparation. Nevertheless, MacArthur persisted over the objections of the Joint Chiefs and the Navy, and as he predicted, the 1st Marine Division went ashore successfully on September 15.[8]

It was fortunate that despite all the possibilities of forewarning, Communist resistance was light. MacArthur had gauged accurately the overstretched condition of the North Koreans, as he had judged accurately every circumstance connected with the landing. The Marines' amphibious warfare skills made the tactical execution possible, but the strategy was entirely MacArthur's. Admiral Halsey telegraphed him saying: "The Inchon landing is the most masterly and audacious strategic stroke in all history."[9] However extravagant Halsey's praise may have been, MacArthur put a tiger ashore and not another stranded whale. The desired disintegration of the North Korean army occurred. That army, already overextended, collapsed between the counteroffensive of the Eighth Army from the Naktong line and the attack of the X Corps—the 1st Marine and 7th Infantry Divisions at Inchon and Seoul—on its main line of communication. After Inchon, MacArthur's forces recaptured South Korea on the run and then advanced across the thirty-eighth parallel into North Korea almost without resistance.[10]

But if Inchon was probably Douglas MacArthur's greatest single triumph, it was also his last. It was an immensely successful reapplication of his World War II experience; but after Inchon, the experience of 1941–45 too mechanically reapplied began to play MacArthur false.

The betrayal began, in a limited way, in his next amphibious operation. After he, the government in Washington, and the United Nations had agreed in deciding to continue the advance across the thirty-eighth parallel into North Korea in order to reunite the peninsula, MacArthur withdrew the X Corps from South Korea by sea for another amphibious landing, against the port of Wonsan on the east coast of North Korea. In addition to the usual advantages of the kind of amphibious envelopment he had practiced so often since New Guinea, MacArthur saw a movement against Wonsan as guaranteeing early possession of a good harbor in the North and carrying the X Corps into the North with less wear and tear on men and equipment than in an overland march across the rugged Korean terrain. Unfortunately, withdrawing the 1st Marine Division through the limited facilities of the port of Inchon, taking up half the capacity of the port for several days in October, badly hampered logistical support of the Eighth Army as it marched from Seoul into the North. Inchon had already been overtaxed, and after this disruption, the Eighth Army operated with supplies stretched dangerously thin for the rest of the campaign, partly because the inbound tonnage lost with the outloading of the 1st Marine Division was never made up. The other division of the X Corps, the 7th Infantry, marched through South Korea to Pusan and outloaded there, imposing less strain upon port facilities but more upon itself.

After all this effort, ROK troops captured Wonsan for the United Nations before the 1st Marine Division had sailed from Inchon. By the time the X Corps arrived in Wonsan harbor, the overland march of the ROK forces had already gone on to Hungnam harbor farther north, and UN troops had linked up Wonsan and Pyongyang across the peninsula.[11]

These needless difficulties produced by the stereotyped repetition at Wonsan of a previously successful strategy were minor troubles, of course, compared with those occasioned by the subsequent descent of Chinese Communist forces upon MacArthur's scattered troops farther north. But the larger troubles stemmed in part from a similarly complacent misapplication of earlier experience. MacArthur reacted with apparent indifference to a series of warnings that invasion of North Korea would provoke Chinese intervention. One of the main reasons for his lack of concern seems to have been his confidence that if the Chinese should happen to come in, his air power could effectively interdict communication between China and the battlefield, isolate the Chinese armies, and thus frustrate their efforts and expose their troops to destruction. In the Pacific war of 1941–45, air power had consistently isolated in this fashion whatever Japanese island garrisons MacArthur had earmarked for destruction. When Chinese threats were translated into the actual appearance of the first Chinese troops to challenge UN advances in North Korea, MacArthur reiterated the idea that "there are many fundamental logistical reasons against" a large-scale Chinese involvement in the Korean peninsula.[12] When the UN commander at length became convinced that nevertheless the Chinese were attempting a large-scale intervention, he ordered his air forces to destroy "every means of communication" between China and Korea, in particular the bridges across the Yalu River, the stream which forms three-fifths of the boundary between the two countries.[13]

A standard history of naval operations in the Korean War aptly states that the task which MacArthur now gave to air power was "to sever the Korean peninsula at the Yalu and Tumen Rivers, to undercut the peninsula, and to float the entire land mass into mid-ocean where interdiction, in concert with a naval blockade, could strangle the supply lines of the Communists and thereby force their retreat and defeat."[14] So far in the war the Korean peninsula, surrounded by water on three sides, had proved enough like the Pacific islands that MacArthur had grown accustomed to conquering that his World War II methods had in general served admirably all over again —cutting off the enemy from assistance by sea through naval blockade, using naval gunfire and carrier air power to supplement decisively land-based air power and the fire power of ground troops, employing the amphibious envelopment as a strategic trump card. Unfortunately, a new experience was now to demonstrate that between an island and a peninsula the strategic difference is fundamental. The Pacific war of 1941–45 could be fought to decisive victory at relatively low cost precisely because of the uniquely complete isolation that sea and air power could impose upon islands. But outside MacArthur's theater in World War II, the Italian campaign was proportionately the most bitter and costly that the Western Allies fought, because while Italy is surrounded on three sides by water, daily bombing of the Brenner Pass was not enough to isolate the German forces in Italy from assistance from the continental land mass to which Italy is joined. In Korea as in Italy, the fourth side of the peninsula was to make all the difference.

MacArthur's airmen tried heroically to isolate Korea as they would have isolated an island. The Fifth Air Force turned over to carrier-based aviation the task of trying to close the Yalu bridges. This task was bound to be extremely delicate. The Joint Chiefs of Staff insisted that MacArthur restrict his aerial attack to the southernmost spans of the Yalu bridges, which were undoubtedly in Korea and not in Manchuria. In attacking, the planes must not violate Manchurian air space or reply to any fire from the Manchurian side of the river. The Air Force had no planes that could carry a bomb load heavy enough and yet fulfill these conditions. If B-29s had attempted high-level precision bombing against the southern spans of the bridges, in the course of making their "run-ins" for adequate sightings they would have had to fly over Chinese territory as the Yalu looped far below them. Thus the Navy took on the job with the successor to the trusty old SBD Dauntless, the AD Dauntless II renamed the Skyraider, carrying two 1,000-pound bombs or occasionally a single 2,000-pound bomb, and with the F4U Corsair, carrying a 500-pound bomb or eight 100-pound bombs with various combinations of rockets. Grumman F9F Panther jets flew high cover against the possibility of interception by Russian-built MIG jets.

Against untouchable antiaircraft opposition from the north bank of the Yalu and some interference from MIGs, the Navy fliers dropped spans of three bridges and damaged four other bridges. But as World War II had demonstrated and the subsequent history of the Korean War was to confirm, permanent interruption of river crossings by means of aerial attacks on bridges is practically impossible. Anyway, the time was now November, 1950, and the Yalu soon froze so solidly that the Chinese could cross it anywhere. The Korean battlefield could not be isolated from China.[15]

The battlefield was not sealed off from enemy reinforcement and supply as MacArthur had counted on, and large Chinese forces threw MacArthur's troops into a retreat which did not halt until the armies were again south of the thirty-eighth parallel and the Communists had again captured Seoul. In the face of this unanticipated disaster, MacArthur's attitude changed abruptly from complacent optimism to the despairing belief that none of Korea could be saved unless the war were widened to include aerial attacks, employing the atomic bomb, against the sources of Chinese power and a naval blockade of China. Fortunately, a new commander of the Eighth Army under MacArthur, Lieutenant General Matthew B. Ridgway, thought otherwise. Under Ridgway's ubiquitous battlefield leadership the Eighth Army stiffened, recaptured Seoul, and slowly pushed the enemy northward toward the thirty-eighth parallel, while MacArthur's excessive pessimism on the heels of his earlier excess of optimism set events in motion toward his recall from command.[16]

For a variety of reasons, President Truman refused to accede to MacArthur's proposals for extending the war to China. The Truman administration regarded the Soviet Union as the most dangerous Communist state and Europe as the crucial arena in the confrontation between Communism and the Western world. Extension of the war in the Far East, the administration and the Joint Chiefs of Staff believed, would only weaken the West in its dealings with Russia and endanger Europe by tying up still more American forces in a secondary arena. In the words of the Chairman of the Joint Chiefs, General Bradley, extending the war to China would be provoking "the wrong war, at the wrong place, at the wrong time, and with the wrong enemy."[17] In any event, against the vast Communist mainland of China with its immense population, no decisive strategy seemed possible. To attack China might well mean losing America's own sanctuary in Japan, the great UN base which the enemy never touched. To use the atomic bomb either in China or in Korea, the administration believed, would run unacceptable risks of extending the war and of antagonizing America's allies while promising no comparable rewards, since neither China nor Korea seemed urbanized and industrialized enough to offer suitable targets. Furthermore, the atomic bomb was in short supply, which seemed to offer a highly practical reason for not expending it in a secondary theater.[18]

Yet MacArthur's proposals for the extension of the war were consistent with beliefs about strategy and military policy which had taken deep root in the preceding century of American military history. To carry the war to the Chinese mainland might open unforeseeable hazards, but once China threw its manpower into the Korean peninsula and kept its troops supplied and fighting there despite efforts at aerial interdiction, the future of the war if confined to the peninsula was all too foreseeable: stalemate was the best outcome the United States and the United Nations could well expect, except possibly at an inordinate expenditure in American manpower to drive back the Chinese through the Korean mountains toward the Yalu, where each American advance would strengthen the enemy by bringing him closer to his bases. Extending the war would be a desperate gamble, but no other means offered much hope of clear-cut decision without intolerable infantry casualties. And when MacArthur said, "There is no substitute for victory," "War's very object is victory," he was voicing a view of the nature of war that was not only a commonplace among Americans since the Civil War and the Indian wars but that could readily seem a reasonable extension of the American military's own now customary strategy of annihilation.[19]

Nevertheless, MacArthur's proposals involved risks which the President, the principal cabinet officers, and the Joint Chiefs of Staff believed too great to be run. After MacArthur had indulged his opinions too openly in defiance of orders to clear his public statements with Washington, the President on April 11, 1951, announced the general's relief from command.[20]

MacArthur's departure from the Far East did not terminate the attempt to make Korea in effect an island, where China could not reinforce or supply her armies. Apart from the question of using the atomic bomb, there could not be much strategic bombing in the World War II sense of that term, because the sources of North Korea's ability to make war, except for manpower, lay outside the country. The same thing would also have been largely true of China, if reasons of policy had not put China out of bounds for American aerial attack. But air power could attempt to prevent equipment and supplies from crossing Korea between the Manchurian and Soviet borders and the front lines. The narrowness of the Korean peninsula seemed to offer an excellent opportunity for that method of interdicting the flow of logistical support which permitted the Communist armies to function, and American strategy continued to rely on air power to turn the balance in favor of the UN ground forces.

UN air power therefore attempted to knock out the Communist transportation system south of the Yalu. The airplanes concentrated first upon North Korean railroads, the principal carriers of supplies and the most vulnerable. The Fifth Air Force gave its attention mainly to the railroads west of the central mountain ranges, naval aviation to those east of the mountains. The terrain increased the railroads' vulnerability; there were hundreds of bridges and tunnels. Nevertheless, though the UN maintained almost undisputed command of the air, months of continuous, day-by-day pounding by hundreds of aircraft failed to destroy the utility of the North Korean railroads.

When bridges were knocked out, the Communists built bypasses in less vulnerable, low places where rivers could be forded. Often the railroads had to get along with shuttle trains between breaks in the tracks, with human energy called upon to carry the loads across the broken sections. The effort imposed on the Communists was stupendous; but with their huge resources of manpower, the Communists were able to produce the necessary effort. The capacity of their eastern railroad system was reduced from 5,000 tons per day to 500 tons per day, and sometimes almost to nothing; the capacity of the western system shrank from 9,000 tons per day to 500 to 1,500 tons. Yet the Communists remained generally able to carry about half their armies' required tonnage by rail.[21]

The Communists responded to the attacks upon their rail systems by bringing more and more trucks into Korea and greatly increasing their use of the highways. The highways were bad by Western standards to begin with, merely dirt and gravel roads; but that made maintaining them according to Chinese and Korean standards all the easier. On roads and railroads both, the Communists did their repair work mostly at night. The UN command attempted night air strikes, but on a limited scale and with limited results against targets that demanded precision. When air attacks constricted every other form of movement, the Communists could still achieve remarkable results with men on foot carrying supplies on A-frames on their backs. Against a transport system that was primitive to begin with, but which had plenty of human labor to call on, aerial interdiction could not cut off the flow of supplies and reinforcements as it had around D-day in Normandy, when its target was the transport network of an industrialized society. In 1940 Alexander de Seversky had qualified his predictions about air power by saying: "Total war from the air against an undeveloped country or region is well-nigh futile; it is one of the curious features of the most modern weapon that it is especially effective against the most modern types of civilization."[22]

Still, the aerial interdiction campaign, in combination with the Communists' limited transport, did much to guarantee that the Communists would not conquer the entire peninsula. When they reached Seoul and the area of the thirty-eighth parallel, the Chinese were close to the end of their logistical tether. The primitiveness of their logistical support cut both ways. While it reduced the effectiveness of aerial interdiction, it also reduced their possibilities for accomplishment. The failure of aerial interdiction to achieve all that was hoped from it in Korea does not necessarily mean that no campaign of aerial interdiction can ever succeed, against any army or under any circumstances. Even in Korea, atomic weapons might have produced very different results. Furthermore, the aerial interdiction effort in Korea was handicapped by the fact that once the effort was well under way, the front was essentially stable, so that the Communist armies' needs were smaller than they would have been in more fluid warfare. General James Van Fleet, Ridgway's successor in command of the Eighth Army, believed that "If we had ever put on some pressure and made him [the enemy] fight, we would have given him an insoluble supply problem."[23]

The limitations of aerial interdiction in Korea are linked to another gloomy feature of the Korean War, the return of indecisiveness to the battlefield. Not until General Ridgway took command of the Eighth Army and halted its retreat just below the thirty-eighth parallel in the winter of early 1951 did the Korean War pit against each other two armies of approximately equal strength and determination. Once that occurred, fluidity disappeared from the war, and a stalemate reminiscent of World War I set in. Despite General Van Fleet's observation about air power and the Communist supply problem, it seems most likely that if the UN command had chosen to seek a decisive victory, the only available means would have been to fight bitter battles of annihilation against the Chinese and North Korean armies. The price of battles of annihilation would have been acceptance of UN casualties high enough to make the endeavor more tragic than triumphant.

Though the Korean War visited upon American strategists so many frustrations, it did reopen to the military the national purse strings. In doing so, it raised again the issues posed just before its outbreak by NSC-68, but so quickly buried by the exigencies of the budget.

Congress enacted three wartime tax increases, and the combined impact of the rate increases and an economic boom stimulated by the war was to raise federal revenues from $36.5 billion in fiscal year 1950 to $47.6 billion the next fiscal year, $61.4 billion in fiscal 1952, and $64.8 billion in fiscal 1953. Expenditures for national security purposes rose from $13 billion in fiscal 1950 to $22.3 billion, $44 billion, and $50.4 billion, respectively, in the following three fiscal years. These increased defense expenditures went first, naturally, into creating the necessary instruments to fight the war in Korea. Frightened by the unreadiness the Korean War demonstrated, however, and by its unarguable evidence that the deterrent powers of the country's atomic weaponry had not been complete, government and military leaders generally agreed that the growing funds available for national security must be used to seek a larger security beyond the immediate demands of the war.

There was less than general agreement about the methods which the quest for a larger security entailed. The Truman administration and the Joint Chiefs of Staff disagreed with General MacArthur's proposals to widen the war not so much because they did not share his philosophy of the nature of war or his penchant for a strategy of annihilation, but because they thought Korea and Asia were not the main theater of conflict with the Communists but a diversionary theater. They still feared an all-out Soviet attack on Western Europe or the United States, they feared in fact that the North Korean invasion of South Korea was a feint to draw away their attention from the vital theaters, and they did not want to be taken in by the feint. Therefore they early proposed to use much of the enlarged defense budget to make better preparation for the all-out Soviet aggression they still thought likely.

Too zealous a devotion to the President's earlier policy of defense economies made Louis Johnson expendable, and late in 1950 President Truman replaced Johnson as Secretary of Defense with the President's favorite man for all crises, General George C. Marshall. Marshall announced that the major objectives of the Defense Department's programs were to build and maintain military forces which would keep up a position of strength for a period of indefinite duration, and to aim "at greatly increasing the readiness of American industry and manpower for full mobilization." Marshall proposed to create the industrial and manpower base for rapid mobilization for all-out war. "This is a move," he said, "to place us in a strong position from which we can go rapidly to the extent that may be developed as necessary."[24]

To establish an industrial base for full mobilization, Marshall sought to distribute defense procurement in the current emergency among the largest feasible group of suppliers, "not merely to obtain as quickly as possible the matériel required for the current build-up but also to equip additional plants and assembly lines." He wanted to develop as broad a base of defense supply expertise and capacity as possible, to be able to mobilize swiftly for another war on the scale of World War II. To create the manpower reserve for mobilization on that scale and for that kind of war, Marshall took up again his old advocacy of universal military training. When the Korean War began, President Truman had shelved UMT, presumably for the duration of the immediate crisis. Marshall persuaded him to reintroduce UMT as an administration proposal to Congress in January, 1951. In June, 1951, Congress responded to the extent of passing the Universal Military Training and Service Act, which at least endorsed the principle of UMT, though it continued the immediately effective selective service system and postponed implementation of UMT.[25]

Thus Secretary Marshall used the Korean emergency to return to mobilization plans and preparations similar to those which preceded World War II and designed to permit the country to respond rapidly to a Soviet military challenge along the lines of Hitler's military challenge. By the time Congress passed the Universal Military Training and Service Act of 1951, however, the Korean truce negotiations were almost in the offing, and however trying the negotiations proved to be, their existence made the theory of the Korean War as a feint for all-out Communist aggression elsewhere seem increasingly unlikely. As the threat of a massive Soviet attack receded, so did the persuasiveness of Secretary Marshall's 1940-style mobilization strategy.

Attention turned instead to Communism as a problem likely to be present and likely to impose military challenges through a very long run, and to the deficiencies which unreadiness in Korea suggested for America's ability to counter permanent pressure and permanent menace. Attention returned, in short, to issues which had been raised by NSC-68. It returned to issues which the President had also raised in his statement accompanying his first request for a wartime tax increase in July, 1950, but which later had been obscured by Marshall's emphasis on mobilization capacity. "The purpose of these proposed estimates," Truman had said before General Marshall's return to office, "is two-fold; first, to meet the immediate situation in Korea, and second, to provide for an early, but orderly, build-up of our military forces to a state of readiness designed to deter further acts of aggression."[26] Attention turned again, especially in the months following Marshall's retirement on September 17, 1951, and replacement by Robert A. Lovett, from Marshall's mobilization strategy to a strategy of deterrence.

The difference was important. The American military posture in June, 1950, had not deterred limited Communist aggression. If it was American atomic strength that had deterred larger Communist aggression, presumably the deterrence had been possible because of the state of readiness of the Strategic Air Command. To deter acts of aggression, limited or unlimited, the Korean experience suggested that it was not capacity for mobilization that counted most, but rather the state of readiness. Potentially the United States always had possessed the ability to mobilize enough strength to roll back an Asian Communist invasion of South Korea. But apparently the Communists had gambled on an invasion because the United States in 1950 had possessed only the potentially mobilizable strength to resist in Korea, not adequate ready strength, and therefore the Communists believed they might well be able to confront America with the *fait accompli* of an all-Communist Korea before potential strength could be mobilized. If in any case deterrence failed to prevent a general nuclear war, only the forces in being at the outset would be likely to have much effect upon the course of the war anyway.

If a strategy of deterrence depended upon forces in readiness, an effort to implement deterrence of both general and local war would have to take two directions. To deter a general Communist attack, America's nuclear retaliatory force would have to be maintained and strengthened. During the period of the American atomic monopoly, the size of the American atomic striking force had not seemed of major importance, as long as the force was big enough to be likely to get through to devastate Soviet cities and industry. With the Soviets now developing their own nuclear striking capacity, however, the American retaliatory force had to be large enough and resilient enough to survive a Soviet first strike and still devastate the Soviet Union.

Anticipating Soviet nuclear parity with the United States by 1954, NSC-68 had therefore proposed a considerable expansion of American nuclear forces. When the Truman administration returned to the issue of deterrence, it decided that a deterrent nuclear retaliatory capacity demanded development of the H-bomb, an expanded stockpile of nuclear weapons, an intensified state of readiness in the retaliatory force, and a retaliatory force of greatly increased scale. The Korean War enlarged the Air Force to 95 wings by mid-1952; the administration proposed to raise it to 143 wings by the middle of the 1950s. With wartime defense budgets, the Air Force was able to accelerate its development of jet bombers. The ten B-47A Stratojets ordered in 1948 grew to a fleet of 405 B-47Bs by June, 1953. Eventually there were 1,317 B-47Es, plus 255 reconnaissance-version RB-47Es and 35 RB-47Hs. The B-47E could carry 10,845 pounds of bombs over a combat radius of 2,013 miles, at a cruising speed of 498 miles per hour; its ferry range was 4,035 miles. The first prototype of the B-52 intercontinental jet bomber flew in April, 1952, and the first production models began arriving in August, 1954. B-36 production ended that month.[27]

To deter a less than general Communist attack, the Korean experience suggested a need for conventional surface strength in readiness. The Truman administration continued to look to Europe as the most vital area of danger, and it labored mightily to create a ready ground defense there. It sought to flesh out the mutual security commitment of the North Atlantic Treaty Organization of 1949 with NATO armed forces in readiness, and to that end it secured allied agreement to the appointment of a NATO Supreme Commander and brought General Eisenhower from the presidency of Columbia University back to active military duty to fill the post. It strengthened the American Seventh Army in Germany, it tried to persuade western Europeans and Germans to accept a German military contribution to European defense, and at the Lisbon Conference of February, 1952, it won NATO endorsement of a goal of ninety NATO divisions, half on active duty, by the end of the year.[28]

The European allies never moved as rapidly as the Truman administration would have liked or the Lisbon agreement suggested, and acceptance of German remilitarization proved a predictably recalcitrant problem. The Europeans knew that their real military hopes rested not upon their own strength but upon the willingness of the United States to defend them and upon the American deterrents. Though much that the United States did in Korea made the Europeans nervous and unhappy, American intervention there served to give them symbolic assurance that the United States could in fact be counted on to fight for its allies. Assured of that, the Europeans were not prepared to strain economies just recovering from Hitler's war in a defense for which their own unaided strength would not suffice. NATO defense achievements consistently fell short of announced NATO goals.

Despite Korea, the American effort to achieve an effective strategy of deterrence was itself distorted by the same preoccupations with general rather than limited or local war and with western Europe that had perhaps tempted the Communists to strike in Asia in the first place. Nevertheless, and despite much that was reminiscent of World War II in the response to the Korean crisis, by 1952 the Truman administration and its military commanders were at last making basic intellectual adjustments to the strategic revolution ushered in by nuclear weapons. American military strategy was no longer inclusively defined as the use of combats. Rather, within the rubric of protecting and advancing the national interest, the acknowledged first purpose of American military strategy was now not to use combats but to deter adversaries from initiating combat. The Korean War rescued NSC-68 from oblivion and made it the foundation of American strategy after all.

The Korean War was so unpopular, and deterring a repetition of such a war consequently seemed so important in the early 1950s, that the problems implied in adopting a strategy of deterrence were not all immediately apparent. But problems there were. A strategy of deterrence was a thoroughly negative kind of strategy. Even granting the negativeness also of American policy as long as containment of Communism was its principal objective, policy was likely to develop positive goals which so negative, defensive, and even passive a strategy as deterrence might not adequately serve. In time, also, tensions might well develop out of the incongruity between a deterrent strategy and the historic American conception of strategy as the use of military force for offensive purposes. More promptly evident, though not immediately apparent in all its complexity, was the question of how reliably deterrence could work.

17. Strategies of Deterrence and of Action: The Strategy Intellectuals

. . . we should be as ready to profit from opportunities in the Soviet orbit as the Soviet bloc feels free to exploit all the difficulties of the non-Soviet world.

—*Henry A. Kissinger*[1]

THE NEW EISENHOWER ADMINISTRATION embraced deterrence still more enthusiastically, with fewer backward glances toward plans for mobilization on the pattern of the World Wars. Apart from the asset of Dwight Eisenhower's winning personality and prestige, the Republicans captured the Presidency in the election of 1952 largely because of voter discontent with the prolonged and puzzling Korean War. The new administration intended both to extricate the country from the Korean entanglement and to ensure against further involvements of the Korean type. It was able to succeed in the former aim, to end the fighting and the weary truce talks, for various reasons, including its political ability to be more flexible in negotiation than the Truman administration—few Americans could believe that Republicans were soft on Communism—and perhaps primarily, because Stalin soon died. Many in the new administration also believed that a threat to use atomic weapons in Korea, the message being conveyed to the Chinese through India, was decisive; this conviction was important in conditioning subsequent policy. For the second goal, guarding against a repetition of Korea, the new administration turned to an explicit strategy of deterrence, aimed at deterring local and limited as well as general wars.[2]

The instrument of the strategy of deterrence was to be an inheritance of the Eisenhower administration from the Truman administration and the Korean mobilization, unquestioned American military superiority, particularly in nuclear weapons and the means to deliver them. Thanks to the Korean mobilization and the larger military preparations which accompanied it, the prospect of Soviet nuclear parity with the United States which had frightened the framers of NSC-68 seemed to have disappeared from the horizon. Instead, the United States had pushed well ahead of the Soviets in stockpiling nuclear weapons, and by the early months of the new administration the Air Force had its more than 400 Stratojets to deliver them to the Soviet homeland from increasingly secure bases around the world. In contrast, the Soviet nuclear stockpile was reliably reported to be small enough, and perhaps more important the Soviet means of delivery were relatively so inferior, that the margin of American superiority seemed if anything greater than it had been in the days of the American atomic monopoly.[3]

On the other hand, the leaders of the Eisenhower administration perceived a danger to American security in the very plans of the Truman administration to go on enhancing American military superiority. The leaders of the new Republican administration were largely fiscally conservative businessmen, whose economic acumen the new President admired and whose cautious attitudes toward federal spending and indebtedness he shared. These leaders believed that the American contest with Communism was as much an economic as a military and diplomatic one. They believed that it was part of the Communist design that if America could not be conquered in war, the United States should be driven to strain its economy to eventual collapse by being goaded into excessive military spending over an indefinite period of time.

They feared in particular the inflation which accompanied Korean War military spending, as a dangerous symptom of the economic overstrain which the military contest with the Soviets might induce. Therefore they believed that having achieved an unprecedented military superiority, the United States must limit its further military buildup and reduce military expenditures for the sake of the economy. The time of special military danger to which the Truman administration had tended to point was no longer in the offing; the American military program accordingly should no longer be regarded as a thrust toward an immediate goal but as an effort to maintain constant readiness over a prolonged period of time. The necessity for military readiness of indefinite duration also counseled against excessive immediate financial strain. An intense push toward an immediate peak in defense spending might indeed produce an economic danger at least as bad as inflation; the achievement of the peak would have to be followed by a cutback in defense expenditures which might precipitate economic recession. To gain military security at the cost of fiscal and economic peril would be to gain no security at all, and to play into the adversary's hands.[4]

These attitudes were especially shared by the new Secretary of Defense, the General Motors executive Charles E. Wilson, and by the leading figure in the formulation of fiscal policy, Secretary of the Treasury George Humphrey. In January, 1953, the Truman administration estimated defense expenditures for fiscal year 1954 at $46.3 billion. This figure was below the 1953 peak and reflected the slackening intensity of the Korean War and the preparedness already achieved; but it seemed excessively inflationary to the new administration, and the new leaders immediately established a tentative upper limit of $41.2 billion on military spending in fiscal 1954. The Joint Chiefs of Staff protested the limit as imprudent. It ignored, they said, the continuing danger that the Soviets would acquire adequate nuclear delivery systems by the middle of the decade. The administration persisted in its attempts at reduction, principally by cutting the Air Force goal from 143 wings in the middle of the decade to 114 wings in fiscal 1954 and 120 wings in fiscal 1955.[5]

The administration hoped for a balanced federal budget by fiscal year 1955, and to that end they installed a new group of Joint Chiefs who were presumed to be more amenable to the new fiscal policies than the holdover Chiefs from the Truman period. The new Joint Chiefs immediately received the task of developing a strategy consistent with the administration assumption that the contest with the Soviets would persist indefinitely and was as much economic as military. In May, 1953, the National Security Council Planning Board, a new agency created as part of an effort by the President to regularize and make more reliable the activities of the NSC, issued a paper designated NSC-162 which helped define the boundaries of the new strategy by calling for a continuance of the containment policy, but with greater reliance on strategic air power as the means of implementing the policy. In August the Joint Chiefs offered a preliminary statement of their strategy as it had evolved from conferences aboard the Secretary of the Navy's yacht *Sequoia*. Like NSC-162, the *Sequoia* plan proposed further development of the strategic air forces, along with strengthened air defense. It looked to a money-saving deemphasis of conventional forces through reduction of overseas garrisons and creation of a mobile strategic reserve in the United States, along with greater reliance on allied forces for local defense.[6]

On October 30, the new strategic planning reached a basic conclusion when the President gave his approval to NSC-162/2. Under this document the military and economic goals of the administration were to be achieved and reconciled with each other by abandoning the idea that limited war on a large scale, presumably such as in Korea, should be waged without employing nuclear weapons. The military were to plan to use nuclear weapons whenever their use was militarily desirable. NSC-162/2 emphasized not only the delivery of nuclear weapons by the strategic air arm but also the extensive employment of new "tactical" nuclear weapons which were just beginning to come into service, such as the Army's 280mm cannon capable of firing shells with nuclear warheads. By being able to employ nuclear weapons of a wide range of magnitude and in a wide range of situations, the armed forces would not need to demand large masses of manpower or immense varieties of conventional arms, and their expenditures could thus be reduced. Potential adversaries would be deterred from aggression by the assurance that the United States would respond to aggression by means of its own choosing, primarily nuclear.[7]

On December 9 the Joint Chiefs presented to Secretary Wilson a proposal to implement NSC-162/2. They stated their assumptions that in the next few years there would be no significant change in the intensity of international rivalry or in the ratio of Soviet to American power, that American nuclear retaliatory capacity was the major deterrent to both general and limited war, and that henceforth nuclear weapons would be employed not only in general war but when they were militarily useful in limited war. These assumptions made possible a gradual reduction of American forces overseas, to be combined with strengthening of the allies and rearmament of Germany and Japan and the creation of a mobile strategic reserve in the United States. By fiscal 1957 United States military expenditures could be reduced to between $33 and $34 billion. The force level of the American services should drop from the December, 1953, strength of 3,403,000 to 2,815,000 by June, 1957. In this reduction the Army would fall from 1,481,000 men and twenty divisions to 1,000,000 men and fourteen divisions; the Navy from 765,000 men and 1,126 combat ships to 650,000 men and 1,030 combat ships; the Marine Corps from 244,000 men and three divisions to 190,000 men, with the three divisions at reduced strength. The Air Force would expand again, however, to 137 wings.[8]

The Air Force expansion indicated how much, despite the discussions of tactical nuclear weapons, the Eisenhower strategy of deterrence was to depend upon the capacity to deliver a massive nuclear strike from the air. The planned 137-wing Air Force was to have almost as many Strategic Air Command wings as the 143-wing Air Force projected by the previous administration, fifty-four rather than fifty-seven. The principal reduction from the Truman program was in troop carrier and air transport planes, with eleven rather than seventeen wings—this despite the theoretical emphasis on a mobile strategic reserve. As a further element in deterrence, continental air defense wings were to be increased from twenty-nine in the Truman program to thirty-four. The plan for fiscal 1957 could look toward the first all-jet intercontinental bomber as a principal vehicle for holding the nuclear threat over the head of the enemy. In June, 1953, the Air Force placed an order for thirty-three Boeing B-52Bs. This aircraft could carry 10,000 pounds of bombs at a radius of 3,534 miles; its ferry range was 7,343 miles, and its cruising speed 521 miles per hour. Larger orders for advanced models of the B-52 Stratofortress were forthcoming as the decade progressed.[9]

After the National Security Council, the Defense Department, and the Joint Chiefs had formulated the details of the new strategy in the *Sequoia* conferences, NSC-162/2, and the program of December 9, 1953, Secretary of State John Foster Dulles offered the most important public explication of the strategy in his "massive retaliation" address to the Council on Foreign Relations in New York on January 25, 1954. Summing up the thinking of the Eisenhower administration to this point, Secretary Dulles declared that the Soviets were "planning for what they call 'an entire historical era,' and we should do the same. They seek, through many types of maneuvers, gradually to divide and weaken the free nations by overextending them in efforts which, as Lenin put it, are 'beyond their strength, so that they come to practical bankruptcy.' " It was essential to counter this strategy "without exhausting ourselves." Therefore American ground troops should not be permanently committed to Asia to a degree that left the United States no strategic reserves; for economic as well as foreign policy reasons, the United States must not permanently support other countries; the United States must not undertake "military expenditures so vast that they lead to 'practical bankrutcy.' " The Eisenhower administration desired "a maximum deterrent at a bearable cost."

> The way to deter aggression is for the free community to be willing and able to respond vigorously at places and with means of its own choosing.
>
> So long as our basic policy concepts were unclear, our military leaders could not be selective in building our military power. If an enemy could pick his time and place and method of warfare—and if our policy was to remain the traditional one of meeting aggression by direct and local opposition—then we needed to be ready to fight in the Arctic and in the Tropics; in Asia, the Near East, and in Europe; by sea, by land, and by air; with old weapons and with new weapons. . . .
>
> But before military planning could be changed, the President and his advisers, as represented by the National Security Council, had to take some basic policy decisions. This has been done. The basic decision was to depend primarily upon a great capacity to retaliate, instantly, by means and at places of our choosing. Now the Department of Defense and the Joint Chiefs of Staff can shape our military establishment to fit what is *our* policy instead of having to try to be ready to meet the enemy's many choices. That permits of a selection of military means rather than a multiplication of means. As a result, it is now possible to get, and share, more basic security at less cost.[10]

One trouble with this strategy as a servant of United States policy was that it went far toward abandoning the use of combats as a part of strategy at all. The force on which it relied was so much the all-out nuclear destructive force of the Strategic Air Command that the strategy came close to dependence upon a force that might possibly deter but that could not be actually used, because the consequences of its use could be too terrible even granting the deficiencies of the Soviet nuclear retaliatory arm as it existed at the beginning of 1954.

At the time Secretary Dulles delivered his classic exposition of the deterrent strategy of massive retaliation, the French garrison of Dienbienphu in Indochina was preparing for a major attack on neighboring Viet Minh positions, as something of a final test of the purpose for which the French had assembled at Dienbienphu, to make it a firm base for mobile offensives designed to break the enemy's control of "Inter-Zone V" in the mountains of northwest Vietnam. The attack began on January 31, and by February 2 it had fizzled. It ended the last hope of a French offensive in the area. On January 31, furthermore, Viet Minh artillery opened fire from the surrounding hills upon the airstrips which supplied Dienbienphu. The artillery strike was the prelude to the climactic battle which began on March 13 and was to end with the fall of Dienbienphu on May 7 and the collapse of the French will to go on with the fight in Indochina.

While the battle raged and the probable lineaments of its aftermath became discernible, Secretary Dulles warned that the loss of Indochina to Communism might well lead to the collapse of all of Southeast Asia and the withdrawal of America's Pacific frontier to the Hawaiian Islands. The Secretary of State sought to utilize this dramatic warning to muster American and allied support for the application of massive retaliation to Indochina, in the form of nuclear intervention there. America's allies were fearful lest such intervention provoke at the least a Chinese counterintervention in the manner of Korea; the French would offer no assurance of persisting in the fight anyway. The American Congress was unwilling to proceed without guarantees of French persistence which the French would not give. If Dulles believed his own warnings about the consequences of French withdrawal from Indochina, he must have regarded the events in Indochina in early 1954 and the subsequent Geneva Conference as a major failure of the new strategy for the deterrence of Communist adventures.[11]

The events in Indochina and Geneva in 1954 coincided with rapid advances in Soviet nuclear capacity which upset the Joint Chiefs' assumption that there would be little change over the next few years in a balance of nuclear power which had vastly favored the United States. The Soviets achieved their first thermonuclear explosion in August, 1953. Thereafter, they accumulated a stockpile of nuclear weapons more rapidly than most American experts had anticipated. In 1955 they demonstrated a development of long-range bombers for the delivery of their nuclear weapons also in excess of American anticipations. The United States learned too that the Soviets were carrying the strategic rivalry into a new arena through extensive testing of 800-mile-range ballistic missiles.[12]

These tangible challenges to the Eisenhower strategy also coincided in time with, and lent weight to, a rising criticism of the strategy and its elements from a new quarter, not partisan foes and dissident military men—though these groups were active enough in their criticism, as will appear—but a group virtually new to American history, civilian students of strategy and of national security policy.

With military affairs relegated to the periphery of American life except for occasional wars, and with civilian Americans for historical reasons suspicious of military men and military attitudes, civilian Americans in the past had paid little attention to military strategy, except when Presidents, government officials, and Congressmen had to. American scholars and intellectuals tended to be more deeply imbued with suspicion of the military than the general run of civilians, and in the past there had been especially little scholarly investigation of military problems. The new world role of the United States after 1945 brought national security problems from the periphery to the center of American life, however, and the appearance of nuclear weaponry, especially in the hands of the country's apparent adversaries, assured that henceforth mistakes in contending with national security problems could yield horrendously disastrous consequences. By the 1950s, accordingly, civilian scholars were showing a still often reluctant but rapidly growing interest in national security issues in general and military strategy in particular.

Social scientists, economists, natural scientists, and mathematicians all began to apply their special expertise to the relevant dimensions of national security. The scientists and especially the atomic physicists were early in the field, for obvious reasons. Those who contributed to the development of atomic and then nuclear weapons felt a responsibility for what they had done that sometimes crossed the boundary into guilt. *The Bulletin of the Atomic Scientists* expressed their concerns and attempted to bring the methods and insights of science to bear upon public policy. The most spectacular weapons developments of the middle and late 1950s, the growth of missile technology, gave military problems a still more scientific tone and reinforced the growing bonds between military strategy on the one hand and physics and mathematics on the other. A mathematical approach to strategy was encouraged also by the rapid rise of computer technology after the delivery of the first commercial computer, UNIVAC-1, in 1951. Computers encouraged an attempt to resolve strategic problems into segments that could be expressed quantitatively and thus subjected to computer analysis. Allied to the growth of computers also was the continuing development of operations research and operations analysis and their evolution into systems analysis as approaches to the interlocked problems of strategy, tactics, and weapons systems. The novelty in the new strategic studies therefore lay not only in the emergence of civilian strategists but in the broadening of the roots of strategy, from history, to which military students of strategy had customarily looked for guidance, to economics, the hard sciences, and mathematics. The social scientists were prominent among the new civilian strategists, but the hard scientists and the mathematicians gave the new strategic studies a distinctive quest for precision and sometimes also a distinctive dogmatism and self-assurance.

Despite many myths to the contrary, armed forces were not closely linked to organized science and technology or sensitively attuned to scientific and technological change before World War II. But World War II so much surpassed earlier wars in the premium it placed upon possessing the highest possible quality and sophistication in weaponry, and the totality of World War II mobilization so readily suggested a mobilization of scientists and technicians to improve weaponry, that an unprecedented linkage of the military and scientific communities developed during the war in nearly every major power. In the United States, a principal means of mobilizing scientists for military research was the National Defense Research Committee, organized by President Roosevelt in 1940 under the urgings and the chairmanship of Vannevar Bush, vice president and dean of engineering at the Massachusetts Institute of Technology, and later expanded into the Office of Scientific Research and Development, still under Bush as director.[13]

One of the offspring of the new marriage between science and the military during World War II was operations research. Operations research attempted to apply systematic and especially quantitative analysis to the effort to secure optimal performance from weapons. It developed especially in Great Britain, where as early as 1937 Liddell Hart deplored that "the way that decisions are reached on questions of strategy, tactics, organization, etc., is lamentably unscientific," and urged that investigation of better ways of solving such problems "be given to a body of officers who can devote their whole time to exploring the data on record, collecting it from outside, and working out the conclusions in a free atmosphere."[14] An Air Ministry operations research unit was established in 1937. The RAF attempted to remedy the deficiencies suggested by Liddell Hart by applying scientific investigation to such problems of rapid technological change in war as the influence of radar on air tactics, the accuracy of aerial bombing attacks on various targets, the effect of antiaircraft fire on low altitude and dive bombing attacks, and the interception of enemy bombers. RAF successes were enough to stimulate the American armed forces, especially the AAF and the Navy, into similar operations research projects. Operations research contributed much to refining the methods of the antisubmarine campaign in the Atlantic, and the first major project and achievement of AAF operations research improved Eighth Air Force bombing accuracy from 15 percent in 1943 (only 15 percent of bombs dropping within 1,000 feet of the aiming point) to 60 percent in 1945.[15]

Operations research thus came out of World War II with high credit. By the end of the war, also, the term "operations analysis" was coming into vogue, intended to indicate a larger study in which the quantitative methods of operations research would be only one among all appropriate methods of systematic investigation of problems in military technology. Nevertheless, American operations research and analysis had generally followed a narrower path than the British. British operations research began with an evaluation of the operational performance of a weapon or item of equipment and then tended to go on to analyze the relationship between the weapon and tactics. From the mutual effects of weapons and tactics, the British also extended operations research into efforts to predict the course of future operations, sometimes rising from the tactical level into the strategic, and in the process they sometimes concerned themselves also with analysis of organizational structures appropriate to achieving the desired ends. American operations research tended to confine itself more severely to study of the optimal use of weapons, or at most of weapons and tactics, without the extensions that carried British operations research toward the realms of strategy and even of policy. This American tendency to keep the definition of operations research narrow and to confine the analysis to problems susceptible to quantitative measurements was reinforced by the armed forces' inclination to entrust postwar operations analysis overwhelmingly to mathematicians, physical scientists, and engineers, itself another index to the American conception of the nature of the enterprise.[16]

Nevertheless, during the 1950s there developed irresistible tendencies to broaden the scope of operations analysis. The possibility of building nuclear weapons in a wide variety of sizes with a wide variety of "strategic" or "tactical" applications joined with the rise of both guided and ballistic missile technology to open in the fifties an almost unlimited spectrum of conceivable combinations of weapons and delivery systems. But in the 1950s, the United States could not afford to permit the introduction of new weapons systems to proceed as it had in the past by trial and error. The financial investment in a new weapons system such as the B-52 bomber or a missile of intercontinental range was far too great to permit the development of all conceivable systems. The balance of military security in the thermonuclear age was also far too precarious to permit betting on the wrong systems. The techniques of operations analysis had to be applied not only to searching out the optimal uses of existing weapons, but to making choices among possible future weapons systems. Choosing among weapons systems, however, necessarily required judgments among various possible strategies. Making choices among future weapons systems and strategies would necessarily also involve choices among forms of military organization. And choices involving strategy and organization would carry the analysis far into the realms of policy. The expanded form of operations analysis which began with the effort to analyze the uses of future as well as existing weapons came to be called "systems analysis."[17]

The armed services' own operations research and analysis groups were generally too narrowly committed to a precise mathematical approach, and too far down the chain of command, to have involved themselves boldly in strategy and policy questions. Consequently the widening of operations research and analysis into systems analysis took place first mainly outside the services themselves, but in defense research organizations sponsored by the services yet established as private corporations or as parts of universities, most notably in the Air Force-sponsored RAND Corporation.

The civilian strategists of the 1950s often were based in the universities, especially in a growing group of university-associated centers for the study of national security problems. In addition, the new strategists had increasingly found their way into the federal government, both on *ad hoc* committees, which President Eisenhower chose as a favorite device for exploring and publicizing problems without having to commit himself prematurely, and in more regular appointments to executive departments and Congressional staffs. But from the beginning, still another distinctive feature of the rise of the new civilian strategists was the clustering of strategic scholars in private organizations sponsored by government agencies for the purpose of contracting with them for the study of national security problems.

In addition to offering greater freedom for research and criticism than government agencies themselves might, these organizations had been developed in part to avoid the difficulty of persuading top-flight scholars to labor for government salaries. The first such organization was the Navy's Operations Evaluation Group (OEG), founded in 1942 as the Antisubmarine Warfare Operations Group under a contract with Columbia University. In 1948 the Army established a similar Operations Research Office (ORO) under a contract with the Johns Hopkins University. The most famous of these organizations soon came to be the RAND Corporation (RAND standing for Research and Development, a misnomer in this research organization), chartered in 1948 as an outgrowth of some of the earlier AAF operations research projects and mainly involved in contracts with the Air Force, especially during its early years. In 1948–49 the Defense Department itself sponsored the Weapons Systems Evaluation Group (WSEG), and in 1956 the Institute for Defense Analysis (IDA).[18]

Systems analysis would eventually have a spectacular and publicly visible effect on strategy and policy, but in the 1950s it was still feeling its way, and the first major impact of the new strategy intellectuals came mainly from their employment of more familiar modes of thought. They required no sophisticated quantitative measurements to develop qualms about the neatness and simplicity with which Secretary Dulles had laid strategic problems to rest in his "massive retaliation" doctrine. Bernard Brodie, a forerunner of the postwar civilian strategists when he published *Sea Power in the Machine Age* in 1941, a pioneer in trying to break the paralysis in military thought initially induced by the atomic bomb when he edited *The Absolute Weapon: Atomic Power and World Order* in 1946, and now a senior staff member of the RAND Corporation, fired early salvos of criticism in RAND classified studies. He made public an abridged version of the criticism in November, 1954, in a *Reporter* article entitled "Unlimited Weapons and Limited War." In the article he expressed doubts especially about the pertinence of the nuclear retaliatory force to the deterrence of limited war, suggesting that the enemy would find it hard to believe that the United States could mean it when it threatened massive retaliation for limited provocation.[19] About the same time, William W. Kaufmann, a research associate of the Center of International Studies at Princeton University, published *The Requirements of Deterrence* as a Princeton center memorandum. In 1956 this paper reached a larger circulation as an article in a book edited by Kaufmann, *Military Policy and National Security*. Kaufmann also doubted the credibility of the massive nuclear deterrent, especially for limited-war situations, and he argued for a variety of deterrent systems.[20]

Nonspecialists in strategic thought, such as George F. Kennan and the Democratic political leaders Chester Bowles and Dean Acheson, had made public their criticisms of the massive retaliation doctrine even earlier.[21] Nevertheless, the Dulles doctrine had a measure of cogency in 1953 and early 1954 when it was announced, because at that moment the United States still possessed the ability to devastate Soviet cities, industry, and military installations with a nuclear bombardment without fear of substantial Soviet retaliation in kind. The measure of merit in the doctrine soon rapidly declined, however, under an unexpectedly swift development of Soviet nuclear stockpiles and delivery systems. By 1955, American nuclear superiority was giving way to what some strategists called a nuclear "balance of terror." If Secretary Dulles had been unable to invoke the nuclear arm of American power to prevent a Communist victory in Indochina in 1954, massive retaliation would be far less likely to deter or cope with limited, local Communist advances now. The United States would scarcely respond to Communist initiatives on the scale of Korea or Indochina with measures calculated to provoke massive nuclear retaliation against the American homeland itself.

If nuclear massive retaliation could not in fact deter all types of Communist aggression, the United States might have to return to the plans of the later Truman administration for a strategy of deterrence to be implemented not alone by nuclear power but by a balanced variety of air, sea, and ground forces, designed to deter aggression on any scale by means of readiness to make graduated responses proportioned to the scale of any enemy adventure. The new Chief of Staff of the Army, General Ridgway, had accepted the budget reductions of fiscal year 1954 only reluctantly, and he registered his objections to the plans for fiscal 1955, because he believed the "New Look" dangerously sacrificed the readiness of the Army and its capacity to deter local wars to which massive retaliation would be an incongruous response. To return to graduated means of deterrence, however, would certainly enlarge defense spending and bring back the economic strains the Eisenhower administration was determined to avoid.[22]

As the administration pondered these problems, by 1957 the new strategists' assault on the massive retaliation doctrine escalated into two widely read book-length arguments for the need for varied capacities to deter and fight limited wars. The first of these to appear was Robert E. Osgood's *Limited War: The Challenge to American Strategy*. Osgood was a political scientist and an associate of the University of Chicago Center for the Study of American Foreign Policy. He offered a historical survey of eras in the past when governments had been able to restrain the destructiveness of wars and keep wars limited, especially the eighteenth-century age of limited war and the interlude between Waterloo and World War I; he sought through history to discover the reasons why wars had sometimes remained limited and also the reasons why in the past the limitations had repeatedly broken down. Turning the focus of his historical study to the United States, he examined what seemed to be a special American tendency to allow wars to grow unlimited, a tendency whose roots Osgood believed he discerned in Americans' dissociation of the measured pursuit of policy from the unleashing of military power. He concluded that to save America and the world from nuclear destruction, in the future power and policy must be harnessed together, and that in particular, the study of limited war in the past suggested that the way to impose limits is to ensure that policy confine the warlike use of power to limited aims. Limiting the aims of war is the key to limiting war.

Limiting the aims of war should not be inconsistent with current American policy; current policy was not aggressive but rather was the limited policy of containment.

> The real strategic question facing the nation has never been whether or not to adhere to containment, for we have consistently rejected every alternative, but rather by what means to implement containment so as to be able to avoid total wars, to keep wars limited, and to fight limited wars successfully. Unfortunately, this problem has always been obscured by our profound distaste for the very notion of containment and limited war.[23]

The "urgent practical problem in contemporary American foreign policy" to which Osgood addressed himself was: "How can the United States utilize its military power as a rational and effective instrument of national policy?"[24] His answer was that "the only rational course is to develop a strategy capable of limiting warfare and fighting limited wars successfully."[25] "Perhaps the clearest lesson of the Korean War," said Osgood, "was this: that America's capacity to retaliate directly upon the Soviet Union could not deter Communist aggression in the gray areas, but that the United States was inadequately prepared to contain Communist aggression by any other means."[26]

Though "The decisive limitation upon war is the limitation of the objectives of war,"[27] a strategy making possible the utilization of military power as a rational and effective instrument of policy would also provide appropriately limited military means. Osgood would have given strategic scope to the familiar military principle of economy of force:

> An important corollary of the principle of political primacy [of political ends over military means] may be called the economy of force. It prescribes that in the use of armed force as an instrument of national policy no greater force should be employed than is necessary to achieve the objectives toward which it is directed; or, stated another way, the dimensions of military force should be proportionate to the value of the objectives at stake.[28]

"In accordance with this rationale," Osgood said, "limited war would be equally desirable if nuclear weapons had never been invented. However, the existence of these and other weapons of mass destruction clearly adds great urgency to limitation."[29] Through a strategy able to employ limited war, and through the restoration—or indeed, Osgood suggested, for America the first establishment—of a rational linkage between power and policy, America's military strength might attain a new relevance to the achievement of national purposes. "If we were to comprehend the function of diplomacy as an instrument for attaining limited political objectives in conjunction with military force, rather than as an alternative to force, we would be in a better position to cultivate useful channels of communication for keeping the present struggle for power cold and limited."[30]

Osgood was a thoroughly cautious strategist, as his emphasis on the desirability of limiting objectives and on the necessity for containment alone as the basis of policy consistently indicated. Nevertheless, the dictum last quoted suggests at least a slight implication that proper controls upon both means and ends might make possible limited American initiatives in the struggle with Communism. The question of initiatives was to become a matter of growing concern to the strategic critics.

One of the principal arguments of Dulles's massive retaliation speech, after all, was that only by application of the Dulles doctrine could the United States escape from mere reactions to the enemy's choice of times, places, and means of challenge, and recapture the diplomatic and strategic initiative. But the second of 1957's book-length works of strategic criticism displayed at least as much concern with this problem of the initiative as did Secretary Dulles himself. The book, of course, was the first strategic study in American history to approach becoming a best-seller—a remarkable testimony to the new centrality of strategic concerns among Americans

—Henry A. Kissinger's *Nuclear Weapons and Foreign Policy.* It was a publication of the Council on Foreign Relations derived from the work of a study group of the council, but it gave eloquent voice particularly to the views of the director of the study group, Professor Kissinger of Harvard, another political scientist.

As Kissinger saw it, the strategy of deterrence when expressed as the doctrine of massive retaliation was the strategy that really forswore the diplomatic and strategic initiative. It amounted to a renunciation of the use of force except to counter the most unambiguous forms of aggression, because the weapons to be employed were too horrendous to be fired in any lesser circumstances. But "A renunciation of force, by eliminating the penalty for intransigence, will therefore place the international order at the mercy of its most ruthless or irresponsible member."[31] Much like Osgood, Kissinger believed that American history had conditioned the United States to adhere to "a theory of war based on the necessity of total victory."[32] The doctrine of massive retaliation signified that the country still stubbornly held to that theory: ". . . we added the atomic bomb to our arsenal without integrating the implications into our thinking. . . . we saw it merely as another tool in a concept of warfare which knew no goal save total victory, and no mode of war except all-out war."[33] By conceiving of victory only in total terms, the United States left itself no options to pursue lesser victories by means of lesser initiatives, "no room between total war and stalemate and between complete allied support and neutrality, [and thus] we posed alternatives for ourselves which did not, in fact, exhaust the gamut of our options."[34]

Kissinger believed that other options existed—options which through military readiness to use graduated force might permit American diplomacy to take initiatives and win limited victories, and certainly options which would permit defense against local expansion of the Communist periphery without resort to general war. The first task of the United States in the age of nuclear weapons, Kissinger believed, was to free itself from the strategic preconceptions in which the country's history had bound it. The very revolution in strategic thought that had produced the strategy of deterrence had only hardened the most basic of those preconceptions, "a doctrine which left no room for intermediate positions between total peace and total war."[35] Perceiving total military victory as their own object in war, Americans projected the same conception of war into the minds of their enemies. In the past, behind the security offered by the oceans, the United States built upon this conception of war and of an enemy's intentions a refusal to respond to provocation until a threat to American security became wholly unambiguous.

"Thus we came to develop a doctrine of aggression so purist and abstract that it absolved our statesmen from the necessity of making decisions in ambiguous situations and from concerning themselves with the minutiae of day-to-day diplomacy." "In the nuclear age," however, "by the time a threat has become unambiguous it may be too late to resist it."[36] Recognizing these American characteristics, and themselves holding to a more subtle view of war and peace as gradations of a continuous spectrum of policy, America's Communist adversaries were highly unlikely to pose an unambiguous challenge, but rather would conduct their expansionist campaigns by local steps no one of which would seem to justify the unleashing of a nuclear arsenal. If the United States attempted to rely on the nuclear deterrent alone, it would have no means of checking such local advances. In Korea, to be sure, the Communists launched an aggression unambiguous enough to provoke an American military reaction, though not large enough to persuade the American government to employ nuclear weapons. Still, even in Korea, because the Korean War did not fit American preconceptions of the likely nature of Communist aggression—the Communist aim on this occasion was not all-out victory over the West—or of the nature of war, the United States had to improvise its response, and in improvising America not only underwent much torment but failed to grasp the opportunities for initiatives that the situation offered.[37]

At the least, the Korean War presented the United States with the opportunity to roll the dividing line between North and South Korea northward to the narrow waist of the peninsula, thus providing a highly defensible boundary while permanently weakening the rump of North Korea. But still thinking in terms of total victories or total defeats, after the winter of 1950–51 the United States thought that stalemate was the only alternative to total war, because Americans assumed that Russia would not tolerate a successful American initiative. "In short, we thought we could not afford to win in Korea, because Russia could not afford to lose." But while it may have been true that Russia would not have permitted an unambiguous defeat of China, "it did not follow that the U.S.S.R. would risk everything in order to forestall *any* transformations in our favor, all the more so as our nuclear superiority was still very pronounced." "A limited war is inconsistent with an attempt to impose unconditional surrender.

But the impossibility of imposing unconditional surrender should not be confused with the inevitability of a return to the *status quo ante*."[38]

The United States again required a new strategic doctrine. The "basic strategic problem of the nuclear age" was "whether it is possible to find intermediate applications for our military strength; whether our strategic thinking can develop concepts of war which bring power into balance with the willingness to use it."[39] "At a time when we have never been stronger, we have to learn that power which is not clearly related to the objectives for which it is to be employed may merely serve to paralyze the will."[40]

The search for a new strategic doctrine must not be confused with the search for a better weapons technology and with technical answers to technical questions. To seek refuge in technology from hard problems of strategy and policy was already another dangerous American tendency, fostered by the pragmatic qualities of the American character and by the complexity of nuclear-age technology. Nevertheless, Kissinger's own strategic prescriptions relied heavily on a new technology: the development of small-scale nuclear weapons of limited radioactive fall-out, suitable for use as tactical weapons. The Eisenhower administration had at times shown a great interest in such weapons, but they had tended to get lost along the way of doctrinal development in the administration's fear of any war at all resembling Korea and in its consistent preoccupation with massive retaliation. At best, administration planners saw tactical nuclear weapons primarily as a reinforcement of the massive nuclear deterrent. Kissinger emphasized their enhancement of the possibilities for flexible, graduated deterrence and flexible, graduated military action if deterrence failed or if there arose initiatives to be seized.[41]

In particular, Kissinger believed that the proper use of tactical nuclear weapons would enable the United States and its allies to offset Russian and Chinese strength in manpower. On the battlefield of tactical nuclear weapons, he believed, massive numbers would tend to become disadvantageous, in the face of the concentrated destructive firepower of the weapons. Smaller, highly mobile forces would be more effective than very large forces. Tactical nuclear weapons could make the American and NATO ground forces in Europe more than a mere "trip wire" to set off a massive nuclear response to Soviet initiatives. Tactical nuclear weapons would afford the West flexible means of response to Soviet adventures such as those to which the Kremlin was addicted in Berlin. Tactical nuclear weapons would recement the NATO alliance itself, by providing an escape from "the impasse which has been the bane of our coalition policy: the gap between the belief of our allies that they are already protected by our thermonuclear capacity to which they do not feel they have a contribution to make, and their terror of its consequences which makes them reluctant to invoke it as a strategy for fighting a war."[42]

But while he believed tactical nuclear technology could prove invaluable, Kissinger's principal concern remained with strategic doctrine. History, he said, was filled with "victories not of resources but of strategic doctrine: the ability to break the framework which had come to be taken for granted and to make the victory all the more complete by confronting the antagonist with contingencies which he had never even considered."[43] American strategic doctrine must find a place for the use of force on a scale less than absolute, a strategy that could aim at less than the annihilation of the enemy. In the nuclear age, only by this means could force, or the threat of force as an instrument of diplomacy, again serve the achievement of national purposes. A strategy capable of employing limited force could provide the indispensable defense against Communist initiatives that might erode away American strength without ever becoming unambiguous. It would also provide the scarcely less indispensable means of reopening initiatives to America and the West. "It is important for our leadership to understand that total victory is no longer possible and for the public to become aware of the dangers of pressing for such a course."[44] "Nevertheless, a strategic doctrine which renounces the imposition of unconditional surrender should not be confused with the acceptance of a stalemate."[45] Over the long run, stalemate was utterly unlikely. If the United States did not seize diplomatic and military initiatives, its allies and defenses would almost certainly be worn away: "In the process of defining our strategic interest we cannot avoid facing another fact of the nuclear age little in accord with our predilections: the difficulty, if not impossibility, of holding a perimeter of twenty thousand miles while always remaining on the defensive politically, militarily and spiritually."[46]

"To overcome this danger," said Kissinger, "requires a more dynamic conception of world affairs." ". . . we should be as ready to profit from opportunities in the Soviet orbit as the Soviet bloc feels free to exploit all the difficulties of the non-Soviet world. In foreign policy courage and success stand in a causal relationship."[47]

The writings of the civilian strategists, said General Maxwell Taylor of the Army, "represented the first public questioning of the validity of the New Look policy of Massive Retaliation and I welcomed them warmly."[48] For by now, some military leaders within the government, and especially Army leaders, were joining in the effort to break away from nearly complete dependence on massive retaliation, but were constrained in their opposition to official policy by the obligations of their own official positions. A national military policy and strategy relying upon massive nuclear retaliation for nearly all the uses of force left the Army uncertain of its place in the policy and strategy, uncertain that civilians recognized a need even for the Army's existence and uncertain therefore of the service's whole future. When the Navy found itself in similar circumstances after the Civil War, relegated to obsolete wooden hulks that could not fight the modern warships of other countries, and with the nation depending on Army forts and artillery even for coastal defense, the Navy had reestablished a role for itself by defining the Mahanian strategy of sea power. When military airmen similarly needed a rationale for existence as an independent military service, they framed the new strategy of air power. Now that the Army also needed a newly defined *raison d'être*, it joined with the civilian strategists in creating the strategy of limited war and flexible response.

To do so, however, the Army had to break drastically with its long, historic adherence to a strategy of annihilation aimed at the destruction of the enemy's armed forces. How completely it could effect such a break with so much of its past, even to save itself, was a question to which limited-war strategists might have paid more attention than they did—a question posing perils of its own for efforts to wage limited war.

The first major dissenter from the doctrine of massive retaliation within the military leadership was General Ridgway, whose counteroffensives against the Chinese in Korea, constrained though they were, had suggested some of the possibilities for seizing advantages in limited war. Now, as Army Chief of Staff, Ridgway found himself troubled by Secretary of Defense Wilson's insistence that the service chiefs must assume public responsibility for defense programs which they did not initiate, and which Ridgway considered to be based less on military than on fiscal criteria and militarily dangerous. Ridgway acknowledged his evident duty to adhere faithfully to policies determined by his civilian superiors and to implement their policies to the best of his abilities with the means they gave him. But he believed that his civilian superiors ought not to compel him to appear before the public as an author of policies in which he felt little confidence. When he had warned within the councils of the administration that he thought American military capacities were becoming inadequate to the defense of American interests, he was reluctant to have the Secretary of Defense thrust upon him the public responsibility for those very inadequacies. When questioned at length by Congressional committees, Ridgway finally felt obliged to register his misgivings. In 1955 he also felt obliged to retire from the service at the end of a two-year tour as Chief of Staff.

In his final days of duty, Ridgway summarized his objections to current defense policy in a letter to the Secretary of Defense. Secretary Wilson returned the letter with a request that it be classified and thus closed to public circulation. Shortly after Ridgway's retirement, the letter leaked to the *New York Times*, whereupon Wilson released it, dismissing it as unimportant. Ridgway followed up with a volume of memoirs published in 1956, in which the letter was reprinted as an appendix and in which the last several chapters were given over to a more extended statement of his dissent from the doctrine of massive retaliation.[49]

Ridgway was less confident than Kissinger of the probability of keeping limited war limited and of the prospects for what limited war might accomplish. Studies conducted by the Army largely at his behest convinced him that war fought with tactical nuclear weapons would not find the weapons offsetting Communist manpower. Rather, tactical nuclear war was likely to demand larger armies, not smaller: because the weapons themselves were extremely complex, because casualties were likely to be exceptionally severe, and because the depth of the combat zone would be greatly increased to make possible essential dispersal.[50] Nevertheless, Ridgway believed that only with a full spectrum of combat capacities could the United States hope to deter limited as well as general war and to defend its interests in limited war if deterrence failed.

The nuclear balance of terror, he thought, "may well result in general unwillingness to employ these [nuclear] weapons, in recognition of the mutual disaster which would follow wherein the peoples, property, and institutions of much of the world would vanish." Soviet military strength was ample enough in every way that the Soviets were unlikely to initiate the use of nuclear weapons; they could get what they wanted without them. But should the West initiate their use, the Soviets would surely reply in kind to massive devastation by devastating the United States. "In the light of this major possibility for the future, it is at least debatable whether the United States really has the freedom to rely preponderantly on nuclear weapons to exert its military power."[51]

The appropriate armed force for the United States

> must be a properly proportioned force of all arms, so deployed in danger spots around the world that each different component—land, sea, and air—can bring its own special forms of firepower most effectively to bear, as a member of a combined force of all arms. It must be adequately trained, properly armed, highly mobile, and strong in the active elements which can strike back without delay in answer to any armed attack.[52]

These views of the strategic critics in and out of the administration had enough evident merit that they were not without some effect. Before Ridgway had departed the Pentagon, the emergence of the balance of terror had already led the National Security Council to an apparent retreat from the full doctrine of massive retaliation in the 1955 version of its annual statement of "Basic National Security Policy." This document acknowledged the possibility that the United States might have to choose between massive nuclear destruction and yielding to local aggression, unless the country developed versatile, ready forces for limited war. In December, 1955, Secretary Wilson directed the Joint Chiefs of Staff to undertake a "complete and careful" study of defense programs for the fiscal years 1958, 1959, and 1960. These developments encouraged General Ridgway's successor, General Taylor, to offer a "National Military Program" calling for an enhanced readiness to fight limited wars and for a "strategy of flexible response."[53] By 1957, Secretary Dulles himself was publishing in *Foreign Affairs* an article in which he seemed to retreat from massive retaliation at least part way toward the strategists of flexible response. Dulles argued now for more emphasis on tactical nuclear capabilities, so that by the 1960s an aggressor could be confronted

> with the choice between failing or himself initiating nuclear war against the defending country. Thus the tables may be turned, in the sense that instead of those who are non-aggressive having to rely upon all-out nuclear retaliatory power for their protection, would-be aggressors will be unable to count on a successful conventional aggression, but must themselves weigh the consequences of invoking nuclear war.[54]

These tendencies toward retreat from massive retaliation collided in the administration, however, with a sharp rise in the costs of military procurement in the mid-1950s, especially in the B-52 program and the beginnings of a ballistic missile program. In 1956 the Joint Chiefs estimated that even without a change in the strategy of massive retaliation, the annual defense budget would have to rise from the neighborhood of $34 billion to $38 to $40 billion by the end of the decade. Secretary Wilson thought this estimate conservative. Under these pressures of rising costs, the administration harkened to its persistent fears of fiscal overstrain rather than to its still tentative queasiness over the possible shortcomings of massive retaliation. General Taylor, who had begun his tour as Chief of Staff feeling some optimism for the prospects of a strategy of flexible response, found himself fighting off the "Radford plan" of Admiral Arthur W. Radford, Chairman of the Joint Chiefs, for more drastic cuts of the conventional forces than the administration had yet essayed and still more reliance on massive retaliation. Early in 1957 Secretary Wilson, without recourse to the Joint Chiefs or even to their sympathetic Chairman, prepared a new defense program for the fiscal years 1959 through 1961 which would hold the budget line near $38 billion by reducing manpower from 2,800,000 to 2,200,000 by the latter year. The Secretary initiated immediate reductions of 200,000 men and of two divisions plus various other formations from the Army, twenty warships from the Navy, and even twenty wings from the Air Force.[55]

General Taylor's initial hopefulness made these developments all the more disappointing, and he ended by following General Ridgway's path into open dissent from the administration, in behalf of a strategy of limited war and flexible response. In 1956 Taylor wrote a criticism of the massive retaliation doctrine for *Foreign Affairs*, but State and Defense Department objections prevented its publication. In testimony before Senator Lyndon B. Johnson's Preparedness Investigating Subcommittee regarding a December, 1958, version of the defense budget for fiscal year 1960, General Taylor felt obliged to say publicly that he found the Army at less than adequate readiness to counter possible Communist challenges. Like Ridgway before him, once he had brought his quarrel with the administration into public view Taylor soon retired from the service, at the end of his current term (by then his second) as Army Chief of Staff. Like Ridgway also, Taylor then wrote a book: *The Uncertain Trumpet*, arguing that American defense policy was like the trumpet in I Corinthians 14:8, "For if the trumpet give an uncertain sound, who shall prepare himself to the battle?"[56]

More than Ridgway, Taylor renewed the argument that without

adequate capacities for limited war, America not only would face defensive disadvantages but would be unable to seize initiatives, unable to secure positive advantages that must be won in the battle for a better world. Massive retaliation, General Taylor reiterated, "could offer our leaders only two choices, the initiation of general nuclear war or compromise and retreat."[57] A strategy of flexible response, in contrast, "would recognize that it is just as necessary to deter or win quickly a limited war as to deter general war. Otherwise, the limited war which we cannot win quickly may result in our piecemeal attrition or involvement in an expanding conflict which may grow into the general war we all want to avoid."[58] Taylor like Ridgway believed that tactical nuclear war would require larger rather than smaller numbers of troops; therefore in limited war "primary dependence must be placed on conventional weapons while retaining readiness to use tactical atomic weapons in the comparatively rare cases where their use would be to our national interest."[59] A limited war fought with conventional weapons might not be either small or short, and accordingly Taylor believed that the country must return in some measure to General Marshall's program for the development of a mobilization capacity to sustain war for more than six months.[60] But with proper weaponry, manpower, and mobilization programs, incalculable prospects for advantage might open.

The nuclear deterrent must be maintained as "the shield under which we must live from day to day with the Soviet threat." Limited-war forces would then provide the nation with "the flexible sword for parry, riposte, and attack." "It was rather to the so-called limited-war forces that we henceforth must look for the active elements of our military strategy."[61] With such forces, "we would restore to warfare its historic justification as a means to create a better world upon the successful conclusion of hostilities."[62]

The persisting inflexibilities and budgetary limitations of the Eisenhower administration defense policies similarly precipitated the retirement of the Army's Chief of Research and Development, Lieutenant General James M. Gavin. Gavin also followed up with a book specifying the causes of his dissatisfaction, *War and Peace in the Space Age*. In a more sweeping indictment than Taylor's, Gavin argued that fiscal caution and technological and strategic inertia had caused the United States to place itself at the mercy of the Soviet Union in every crucial area of military capability, including the capacity to fight general nuclear war as well as limited war. But his concerns emphatically included the need for limited-war capacities to pursue a strategy of initiatives and of action.

General Gavin's background led him to emphasize Army mobility as a key to seizing advantages in limited war. In World War II he had been a commander of airborne troops, leading the 82nd Airborne Division in Operation MARKET-GARDEN. His postwar concentration upon technological innovation, in the Weapons Systems Evaluation Group, as president of the Army's Airborne Panel, and then as Chief of Research and Development, reinforced his concern for mobility. In 1947 he published a book on *Airborne Warfare*.[63] Among all the unfortunate effects of the budgetary limitations that the Army had experienced most of the time since 1945, Gavin especially deplored the neglect of airborne mobility, both strategic and tactical. By the time he wrote *War and Peace in the Space Age*, the United States possessed neither enough long-distance airlift capacity to move troops rapidly from its strategic reserve forces to threatened areas around the world, nor enough short-range airlift suitable for employment in battle zones. And without aerial mobility, at best limited war was likely to produce no better results than stalemate.[64]

The Korean War both demonstrated the effects of lack of aerial mobility and implied what aerial mobility might make possible. With better tactical airlift for the Army, Gavin believed, and especially with fuller realization of the possibilities of the helicopter, the history of the Korean War might have been very different:

> If we had had the vision to see, and the courage to venture in our research and development programs, we could have had a tactical mobility in Korea that would have enabled us literally to run circles around our opponents. As General Walker's armies moved north towards the Yalu, blindly going from road bend to road bend and hill to hill, they were ambushed by an army that depended largely upon foot and horse mobility. Technically, this situation was inexcusable. Tactically, with the equipment at hand, it was unavoidable.
>
> . . . From a technological point of view, the real tragedy of Korea was that this great nation, with its scientific resources and tremendous industrial potential, had to accept combat on the terms laid down by a rather primitive Asiatic army. Neither our imagination nor vision in the years since World War II had given us a combat capability that would provide the technical margin of advantage that we needed in land warfare to win decisively and quickly.[65]

To win decisively and quickly in future limited wars, the Army needed substantial forces of "sky cavalry," units converted to complete air mobility in the battle area and supported by massive strategic and logistical airlift capacities.[66] To win decisively and quickly, "to match the dynamic shifting pattern of war,"[67] the Army also needed enhanced research and development programs to produce the advanced weapons of which American technology was capable, especially missiles for the tactical battlefield.[68] But with aerial mobility and advanced weapons, limited wars could be won: "And, if in the past ten years we had spent even a small part of what we have spent in readying our forces for a one-strategy war, in developing and procuring the means of dealing with limited war, we could have settled Korea and Dien Bien Phu quickly in our favor."[69]

The capacity to make a rational use of force again and to win limited wars would in turn make possible a strategy of initiatives. "If adequate strength exists, then people will take counsel from their aspirations and not from their fears. Democracy will be more assertive, as it must be if it is to prevail against Communism." An assertive democracy would not permit repetition of the Soviet Union's destruction of the effort to free Hungary in 1956. "I do not believe that the Free World can endure many more 'Hungarys'—not and remain free." ". . . we should have sufficient force in being to enable the West, preferably as an instrument of the United Nations, to move into such a situation. . . . We were critically lacking the type of military force that would have been required to support action in Hungary."[70] General Gavin would have established a military system and a strategy consistent with his belief that democracy "is neither static nor passive. And in order to continue to serve, it must be aggressive and assert itself."[71]

The limited-war strategists might look forward to a strategy of initiatives and of action, but when General Gavin wrote in 1959, such freedom of strategic maneuver seemed yet more remote than it had when Henry A. Kissinger raised the issue in 1957. For Kissinger's *Nuclear Weapons and Foreign Policy* had assumed a reasonable stability in the nuclear balance of terror, which stability was expected to minimize danger that the limited diplomatic and military initiatives of both sides might expand or explode into nuclear war. General Gavin, in contrast, believed that the Soviets had assembled a nuclear delivery force significantly superior to the American—"a missile and space program well ahead of anything the West is capable of for many years. Under the canopy of fear created by that impressive display of global power," Gavin further believed, "they will be prepared to further the aims of the teachings of Lenin by instigating and carrying out many types of local aggression."[72]

In January, 1959, Albert J. Wohlstetter of the RAND Corporation, a pioneer in the 1950s' development of systems analysis, had made public the gist of his conclusion that the balance of terror could not be relied upon to assure stability between the nuclear powers. In his *Foreign Affairs* article "The Delicate Balance of Terror," Wohlstetter denied an idea popular since the rise of Soviet nuclear power and frequently assumed in the writings about limited war, that the United States and the Soviet Union were, in J. Robert Oppenheimer's phrase, like "two scorpions in a bottle," neither of which could assault the other without committing suicide in doing so. Rather, said Wohlstetter, the nuclear balance was unstable enough, and the technical complexities of trying to maintain a balance were so great, that relatively small technical advances of one power over the other could bring disproportionate strategic advantages. One of the nuclear powers consequently might exploit such an advantage in a preemptive strike which could disable the enemy's nuclear retaliatory force without intolerable danger to the attacker.

Wohlstetter especially warned of existing perils to the American nuclear retaliatory force in the possibility of a Soviet preemptive strike. The American defense establishment had grown complacent in its nuclear superiority of the 1940s and early 1950s and had been slow to respond to danger that Russia's nuclear warheads and long-range bombers and missiles developed during the fifties could permit a devastating Soviet first strike. In the beginnings of a recognition of danger, the Strategic Air Command had initiated an airborne alert, always keeping in the skies a part of the bomber force on which American nuclear retaliation depended. But the expenses and the demands upon crewmen of an airborne alert were so large that according to public testimony made available in 1956, the proportion of SAC bombers then in the air averaged only 4 percent, a figure which the Air Force hoped to increase within a few years to 6 percent. Wohlstetter revealed some of the difficulties raised by calculations of the effectiveness of various possible protective systems, such as dispersion of the strategic force, hardening of its bases, and advance provision of replacement vehicles, as well as varying degrees of advanced readiness. None offered much assurance of security for SAC's bombers, which when parked on the ground were extremely vulnerable to blast effects even from relatively distant bomb hits. In the face of its bombers' vulnerability, SAC had withdrawn most of its operating bases from Europe, Africa, and the western Pacific to the continental United States, retaining the overseas bases mainly as refueling installations (while also developing further its capacities for in-flight refueling). But even the bases in the United States had come within reach of long-range Russian bombers at least on one-way missions, and the advent of Russian intercontinental ballistic missiles much worsened the predicament. Nor did the liquid-fueled American ballistic missiles in immediate prospect offer significantly less vulnerability to a Soviet preemptive strike.[73]

The shift from the ebullient tone of Henry Kissinger's *Nuclear Weapons and Foreign Policy* in 1957 to the morbid notes of Albert Wohlstetter's "The Delicate Balance of Terror" at the beginning of 1959 was a rapid one, but it was reinforced by all the outward events of the strategic chess game in the interval. As the earlier mentioned decision of Secretary Wilson in 1957 to reduce the Air Force by twenty wings suggests, the Eisenhower administration was attempting to retain its budgetary limits even at the expense of the nuclear deterrent. Originally, the doctrine of massive retaliation and the "New Look" defense policies had been predicated upon the nuclear superiority of the United States. In the face of growing Soviet nuclear strength during the mid-1950s, however, the Eisenhower administration concluded that maintaining nuclear superiority could be indefinitely expensive, and that the returns would not be worth the economic strain.

A policy of nuclear superiority then gave way to a quest for merely a "sufficient" deterrent. The new administration policy, the "New New Look," was most clearly described by Deputy Secretary of Defense Donald A. Quarles in a statement of August, 1956, which argued that deterrence need not depend on the relative strength of American versus Soviet nuclear weaponry. Rather, it was the absolute power of American nuclear weapons that in this view established deterrence, and the need was not to match every gain in Soviet strength, but simply to keep American power sufficient to devastate the Soviet Union without a prospect of effective Soviet interdiction.[74]

This doctrine of a sufficient deterrent was not without strategic merit, as some of its initial critics eventually acknowledged when they found themselves approaching an endorsement of it under its later label of "finite deterrence." But the effort to apply the doctrine during 1957 to the budgets for the fiscal years just ahead proved to be unfortunately timed, when the events of 1957 made it appear part of a still further abandonment of all military and strategic initiative to the Soviets. For 1957 was the year of Sputnik, and of the onset of fear of a "missile gap" putting the Soviets in so firm a position of strategic superiority that they could cancel out the efficacy of massive retaliation altogether.

The United States had been slow to explore the prospects of transferring its nuclear delivery system from manned bombers to long-range rocket-fired missiles, partly because of the costs of the Korean War and the mobilization efforts that went with it, partly because of confidence in bombers as proven and familiar instruments, partly because early atomic and nuclear weapons were immensely heavy in proportion to the carrying capacities of the missiles of the early 1950s, partly because of all the unknowns awaiting in the world of missiles. Even when the Air Force began to acknowledge that manned bombers might someday in large part yield to missiles, Air Force judgments slowed the development of rocket-fired ballistic missiles in favor of turbojet or ramjet cruise missiles guided by extensions of familiar autopilot and autonavigational systems, because cruise missiles seemed a more natural evolution out of manned aircraft. The Air Force took much American missile development down an unproductive byway despite strong systems-analysis evidence favoring the jump to rocket-fired ballistic missiles. By 1954, however, none of the services could ignore the evidence presented by a study committee under the mathematician-economist-systems analyst John von Neumann that both a sharp reduction in the size of nuclear warheads and a rise in long-range rocket capacity were in immediate prospect; in their rivalry for control of critical weapons, all the services began major missile development programs within the next two years.[75]

By that time also, some American rocketry experts were warning the Defense Department that the Soviets appeared to be leapfrogging over an extensive manned bomber program and over cruise missiles, to hasten an early development of ballistic missiles of intercontinental range as their principal nuclear delivery system, and to steal a march on the United States. Some of the experts warned that the Soviets were likely soon to offer evidence of their missile achievements by using rocket propulsion to launch an artificial satellite into orbit around the earth. General Gavin, still the Army's Chief of Research and Development at the time, among others urged that the Army's rocket scientists at the Redstone Arsenal in Alabama, headed by the German team of Wernher von Braun, be allowed to proceed with rapid development of a satellite launching program employing the arsenal's Jupiter C intermediate-range missile, lest the Soviets score a dangerous prestige victory by being first to send a man-made satellite into space. The Defense Department chose to rely instead on a separate and leisurely satellite program, the Vanguard program. On October 4, 1957, the Soviets orbited their satellite, Sputnik I, and scored the prestige and propaganda victory predicted for them.

Beyond prestige and propaganda, the Soviet achievement suggested that the Russians had indeed successfully bypassed manned bombers to establish a dangerous superiority in missiles as their nuclear delivery system. The Defense Department responded with $1.5 billion in additional budget estimates for fiscal year 1959, including not only accelerated missile programs and efforts to reduce the vulnerability of the Strategic Air Command, but also a reduction of cutbacks in the Army the better to counter the varied Soviet challenge being lamented by the strategic critics. The Defense Reorganization Act of 1958 was another direct response to the Sputnik challenge. It sought to give new stimulus to American technical and strategic progress by awarding the Secretary of Defense additional power to overrule the disagreements among the services, by assigning development and operation of new weapons as he saw fit, consolidating, transferring, or if he chose abolishing many service functions, and exercising direct command through the Joint Chiefs of Staff over the "unified and specified" interservice commands which the President was authorized to create.[76]

These responses were too little and too late to quiet the fears of American strategic inferiority raised by Sputnik or to blunt the enhanced impact that Sputnik gave to the new strategists' criticisms. Adding further to an impression of the administration as in military and strategic disarray was the publication at nearly the same time as the launching of Sputnik of John Foster Dulles's *Foreign Affairs* article in which Dulles apparently retreated from massive retaliation. In October, 1957, also, the administration received the report of the Gaither Committee, which already embodied the thinking of Albert Wohlstetter about the vulnerability of the American nuclear retaliatory force. An example of President Eisenhower's favored device for exploring tough new questions, the *ad hoc* Gaither Committee of eleven private persons, chaired by a businessman, H. Rowan Gaither, had been established the previous spring to evaluate the need for blast and fall-out shelters to protect the civilian population against nuclear attack. The committee had decided it could not deal properly with shelter needs without reviewing the whole defense program. Its report argued that the United States was falling perilously behind the Soviet Union in both nuclear capabilities and ability to fight conventional, limited wars.

The Gaither Committee members believed that the Soviets had in fact accomplished what Sputnik was intended to imply—that they had acquired a lead in ballistic missiles that the United States would not be able to overcome until at least 1960–61 even by the most strenuous efforts. Meanwhile the vulnerability of the American nuclear force would permit a Soviet preemptive strike to cripple it. The committee believed that the American nuclear deterrent had relied too much on the initial, first-strike capabilities of SAC and had failed to pay enough attention to the question of SAC's retaliatory power if the Soviets should strike first. The report recommended that top priority be given to reducing the vulnerability of SAC and ensuring a second-strike capability, that is, a capacity to hit back after a Soviet preemptive blow. It urged accelerated development of intermediate- and intercontinental-range ballistic missiles, especially those that could be mounted on "hardened"—protected—or mobile launching pads. As for shelters, the committee urged an intensive research and preliminary civil defense planning program and a $22 billion fall-out shelter program. Against the danger that the Soviets might exploit their nuclear advantages to launch local adventures shielded by nuclear threats, the committee recommended increased capabilities for limited war fought with conventional weapons. Altogether, the report did not offer much encouragement about the immediate condition of American security. To begin remedying the deficiencies, it proposed defense spending of $46 to $48 billion annually by fiscal year 1961.[77]

The report of the Gaither Committee was and remained classified, but a report on defense policy privately sponsored by the Rockefeller Brothers Fund took essentially the same conclusions to the public in January, 1958, including the Gaither proposals for increased defense spending.[78] Despite the embarrassment of Sputnik and President Eisenhower's own sponsorship of the Gaither Committee, the responses of the administration nevertheless continued to be stubbornly slow. Fiscal caution remained an executive fixation. The administration did ask for funds to accelerate the dispersal and improve the readiness of SAC bombers, to put the Army's Jupiter and the Air Force's Thor intermediate-range ballistic missiles (IRBMs) into production, and to accelerate development of intercontinental ballistic missiles (ICBMs) and the Navy's Polaris program for launching IRBMs from nuclear-powered submarines, but all within budgetary limits of about $38.9 billion for the current fiscal year 1958 and $39.8 billion for fiscal 1959. In 1958 the Joint Chiefs of Staff divided over the limited-war issue, and though a new Secretary of Defense was in office, Neil H. McElroy, he favored the views of the Air Force and of the new JCS Chairman, Air Force General Nathan F. Twining, over those now adopted by the Navy and Marine Corps as well as the Army. McElroy announced there would be no change in national strategy. As detailed planning began in the summer of 1958 for fiscal year 1960, the Defense Department proposed both to keep close to pre-Sputnik budgetary levels and to retain the existing relative distribution of funds among the various services.[79]

Thus the strategic critics stayed in full cry, calling both for limited-war capabilities with their possibilities for a strategy of action and for a refurbished nuclear umbrella. In 1959, Albert Wohlstetter's article on the instability of the nuclear balance was followed by a study making much of the same argument at book length, Oskar Morgenstern's *The Question of National Defense.* Morgenstern was a Princeton mathematical economist who had been a leader in applying the theory of games to economics and was now extending his outlook to military strategy. "The time is with us," he said like Wohlstetter, "when even a moderate edge gained by one side over the other, coupled with a will to exploit it ruthlessly, creates new possibilities of threats, ultimatums, blackmail: open and veiled."[80] ". . . any high-level stalemate is apt to be less stable, and a nuclear one least stable, because of the ease with which the weapons can be used [to knock out the enemy's vulnerable retaliatory force by preemptive attack] and because of the rapid progress of new nuclear weapons, a process that has not yet come to end."[81]

Morgenstern argued that it would be mutually advantageous to both nuclear powers if the retaliatory forces of both were to be made relatively invulnerable, for when both parties' nuclear forces are vulnerable to preemptive attack, "The instability of the situation is increased; it is extreme."[82] To begin by remedying the vulnerability of the American force, Morgenstern recommended "the Oceanic System." He believed no hardening of existing bomber and missile bases could produce the desired invulnerability; quantitative studies indicated that it was easier and cheaper for the enemy to keep increasing the power of his missiles to overcome hardening of bases than it was to try to keep pace by means of the hardening effort. But movable bases would be more secure than fixed bases could ever be, and movable bases at sea would be more secure than movable bases on land, because at sea they could more readily adopt random patterns of movement and more easily conceal themselves. Movable retaliatory bases under the sea would be still more invulnerable than bases on the surface of the sea. Therefore Morgenstern recommended a new application of sea power: to use sea power to ensure an invulnerable capacity for nuclear retaliation against the enemy's homeland. He recommended the acceleration and enlargement of the Polaris program, so that nuclear submarines in constant movement could serve to launch the American missile force. He recommended also the development of nuclear-powered seaplanes, which could take off from anywhere in the oceans, thus being safe from preemptive strikes, and with extremely long range could carry destruction to the Soviet Union with a flexibility that manned airplanes might still in the right circumstances exploit over missiles. The endurance capacity of nuclear engines would minimize the dependence of both submarines and seaplanes on fixed bases; except for occasional refueling, their supplies could be replenished from ships themselves moving in random patterns.[83]

Morgenstern believed that Soviet nuclear accomplishments were so formidable that in 1959 the United States was "approaching a peak of danger the like of which has never been experienced by a great nation."[84] Nevertheless, like so many of the strategic critics he hoped not simply to repair the nation's defenses but with the right applications of technology and strategy to restore initiatives to American policy; he still hoped for a strategy of action. In technology itself, Morgenstern hoped through more skillful weapons development to recapture a kind of initiative from the Soviets, an initiative in weapons which would permit the United States to force the Soviets into the role of catching up, imposing costly technological burdens on them. Until 1959, he said, "As a rule, Russia has determined our armaments production by imposing plans of merely involuntary reaction upon us. Our greater wealth would have permitted us frequently to choose such weapons systems which would have imposed a great strain upon Russia."[85] "*It is good policy to choose that weapon whose anti-weapon imposes the greatest possible strain on the production facilities and military efforts of the opponent.*"[86] Morgenstern believed that his oceanic system fitted these prescriptions: in the new order of sea power, the easy access of the United States to all the oceans facilitated its adoption of a deterrent force based on the oceans, while relatively land-locked Russia would have a difficult time matching the American flexibility of maritime movement.[87]

Beyond initiatives in weapons systems, Morgenstern favored also the larger initiatives of policy, and believed that better weapons and a better military strategy could make policy initiatives possible:

> We deem it "not cricket" to use more imaginative methods in the international political struggle. We almost always leave the initiative to the opponent, under conditions where having it often gives a substantial advantage. Instead of imposing a burden upon the adversary, we adjust as best we can to the lead he so frequently assumes. Yet it is clear that without a positive program we shall be pushed back more and more.[88]

Oskar Morgenstern's hopes for initiatives revealed a basic confidence in the American future underlying his warnings of peril. In 1959, it was not every strategic writer who could feel so sanguine. The other major strategic study of the year, *Strategy in the Missile Age*, was written by that veteran among the strategy intellectuals Bernard Brodie, and the times combined with Brodie's long experience in thinking about grim military questions to make it a thoroughly disillusioned book.

Among other things, Brodie offered a seminal review of the history of strategic thought, especially that of Douhet and the air age. Brodie believed that the strategic problems posed by nuclear weapons and ballistic missiles were as revolutionary as the glib use of that word in connection with atomic strategy since 1945 suggested. But he nevertheless approached the problems by way of history, because he believed that even if we would, we could not begin thinking our strategic problems completely anew, but must be bound by our inheritance from the strategic thinking of the past.[89]

Applying the past to the present, Brodie suggested that the official American doctrine of massive retaliation was merely a variant of the old and unhonored idea of preventive war. By responding with a massive retaliatory strike to a limited Communist advance which did not immediately imperil the security of the United States, because the limited enemy advance might some day contribute to imperiling American security, the United States would wage preventive war, "save that we have waited for an excuse, a provocation. If we were really bent on preventive war, it would probably be better, at least much safer, to do it at a time entirely of our own choosing, if we could, so that our preparations could be perfected with a view to achieving the absolutely essential surprise."[90]

The vulnerability of the American strategic retaliatory force, on which Brodie cited Wohlstetter's studies, was such that American strategy could not rely on anything much better than preventive war; at the least, the United States would have to depend on preemptive war.

> Besides, preparations and concepts for the use of our retaliatory force seem always to be geared to the tacit assumption that that force will be essentially intact and unimpaired at the moment it goes into action. This situation can reflect nothing other than an abiding conviction that the enemy will not really succeed in surprising us—that it is we who will get the jump on him, and not the other way around.[91]

In short, the United States expected to be able to make a preemptive strike. Unfortunately for this expectation, Brodie found extremely unlikely the prospect that a coming Soviet nuclear strike would be signaled so unambiguously, with enough advance notice to permit the United States to forestall it. He could cite Roberta Wohlstetter's RAND study of the warnings that preceded Pearl Harbor as cogent evidence of the peril in assuming "that our commanders will be entirely alert and wise in the event of surprise attack, and also that their alertness and wisdom will be of sufficient weight to win the day for us."[92]

To remove American strategy from what amounted to dependence on a preemptive strike, the retaliatory force must be secured by concealment, dispersal, and hardening. Without securing the strategic retaliatory force, the whole strategy of deterrence was illusory. "It should be obvious that what counts in basic deterrence is not so much the size and efficiency of one's striking force before it is hit as the size and condition to which the enemy thinks he can reduce it by a surprise attack—as well as his confidence in the correctness of his predictions."[93]

And the best that Brodie thought the country could hope for with any confidence was deterrence; he did not share any expectation that strategy could promise much more positive results. In his review of the history of strategic thought he noted the consistency with which most strategists—except for the subtle and often misunderstood Clausewitz—reiterated the idea of the value of the offensive, the initiative, the attack, over the defensive. This consistent historic tendency in strategic thought had long since created among military men a suspicion of anything that resembled defensive mindedness. But Brodie believed that strategists of the nuclear age must escape the fear of defensive mindedness and the historic preoccupation with offensive strategy.

Not the least of the revolutionary implications of nuclear weapons systems was that a nation's principal offensive force could no longer serve simultaneously as its principal defense, at least not in traditional terms of defense. To deter a potential enemy from believing he could benefit from a nuclear attack, and to survive such an attack if deterrence failed, strategists had to develop a higher regard for defense—not only for measures of active defense, such as fighter interceptors and antimissile missiles, but because some nuclear carriers were likely to penetrate even the best active defenses, for measures of passive defense as well. These measures should include a shelter program for the citizenry, the presence or absence of which Brodie saw as a major determinant of how a government might feel it could afford to respond in a crisis. They should also include concealment, dispersal, and hardening of the strategic retaliatory force.[94]

The problem of limited war in Brodie's view was related to the necessity to abandon customary kinds of offensive thinking. Brodie shared the common belief of most of the new strategists that the nation must prepare to wage limited war lest enemy initiatives leave it with no choice but massive retaliation or surrender. But impressed by history with the excessiveness of men's fondness for offensive-minded strategies that promised happy solutions to problems, Brodie was not sanguine about the prospects for restoring through limited war the use of combat as a servant of policy. He was impressed instead by the difficulties of keeping limited war limited. To Brodie, it was not simply a problem of keeping rival objectives limited in order to limit wars; when the rival powers of the nuclear age resorted to combat, the objectives at least implicitly were likely to be very large. To keep wars limited it was necessary instead for the rivals to find agreement on rules limiting the conduct of a war. Though the task of finding and accepting such rules had been accomplished in the Korean War, this task was extremely difficult and delicate. Brodie thought the experience of the two world wars indicated that it was by no means nonsensical to believe, as Americans had believed before Korea, that any war tends to expand into total war, or to believe after 1950 that the Korean War was an aberration. The "all-or-nothing" belief, on the contrary, "implicitly took account of the fact that war always deeply involves the emotions and that the collapse of inhibitions in the transition from peace to war does not augur well for the containment of the succeeding violence."[95]

Concluding thus that limits upon warfare would be difficult to maintain after the outbreak of conflict, Brodie rejected the thesis that the United States ought to take the lead in employing tactical nuclear weapons in limited, local war. Once the United States used them, the enemy was likely to do so too, and "The moment we start visualizing them as being used reciprocally, their use ceases to look overwhelmingly advantageous to us. They do not make intervention cheaper, or the prospect of winning surer."[96] Army studies of the possible tactics of nuclear war continued to indicate that nuclear weapons would usually be as useful to the offense as to the defense. Furthermore, reliance on tactical nuclear weapons might weaken American deterrence of limited wars, by undermining the resolve to invoke war in the face of the terrible possibilities of such weapons. Employing nuclear weapons would be likely to devastate whatever the United States was trying to save: "A people 'saved' by us through our free use of nuclear weapons over their territories would probably be the last that would ever ask us to help them."[97] Nuclear weapons might help break down the rules of limited war, especially by tending to eliminate the kind of sanctuaries that both sides possessed and observed in the Korean War.[98] In any event, ". . . we do not even know yet whether armies can fight in a nuclear environment."[99] And above all, "it is much easier to distinguish between use and non-use of nuclear weapons than between the use of a nuclear weapon below some arbitrary limit to size and one well above that limit." The difficulty of drawing a line between "limited" and "unlimited" use of nuclear weapons once any were employed coincided with the popular moral feeling of revulsion against their use at all. If the moral feeling was in part irrational, civilization itself is held together by beliefs and customs many of which are not strictly rational; ". . . the existence of possibly nonrational feelings sharply differentiating the use of nuclear from that of non-nuclear weapons . . . ought not to be blandly waved aside as unimportant."[100]

Even without nuclear weapons, in Brodie's disillusioned thinking limited wars "can have little more than the function of keeping the world from getting worse."[101] The state of the world in the missile age was such, Brodie believed, that this modest result would be no small thing. But he pointed to too modest and negative a result to satisfy most American strategists, let alone military men, political leaders, and voters.

By the Presidential election year of 1960, the vulnerability of the American retaliatory force and the supposed Soviet lead in nuclear delivery capacities—the "missile gap"—had become staples of strategic thought and were entering the public debates of the election campaign as well. Preparing his second book on national security problems, *The Necessity for Choice*, Henry A. Kissinger wrote of the missile gap that "For all the heat of the controversy [about its significance], it is important to note that there is no dispute about the missile gap itself. It is generally admitted that from 1961 until at least the end of 1964 the Soviet Union will possess more missiles than the United States."[102] "The missile gap in the period 1961–1965 is now unavoidable."[103] "There is no dispute that the 'missile gap' will materialize in the period 1960–1964. The only controversy concerns its significance."[104] Almost all strategic writers agreed.

In the context of the missile-gap fear and the dangers of a vulnerable retaliatory force, even the Air Force at length found the occasion to join in dissent from the Eisenhower administration's strategy. The rise of Soviet missile strength and the jeopardy in which it placed the American deterrent led Air Force planners to conclude that the nation required a "counterforce" deterrent: one that could ride out a Soviet first strike and retain the capacity to destroy the Soviet nuclear forces. If the American nuclear force could not survive a Soviet first strike, then it was no deterrent against preemptive attack. If it could not survive with enough strength to destroy the Soviet nuclear forces in a retaliatory strike, then a Soviet preemptive attack would open the way to a succession of Soviet assaults or to infinite possibilities for Soviet nuclear blackmail. A counterforce deterrent obviously would be extremely expensive in its requirements for numbers, hardness, and accuracy of missiles; but the Air Force presented it as the only kind of force that could remain truly a deterrent. When the Eisenhower administration nevertheless clung to its decision for a "sufficient," finite deterrent, the Air Force sought to carry its plea for the counterforce deterrent to Congress and the public press.[105]

The missile gap and the vulnerability of the American nuclear force were bound to enter the coming Presidential campaign, especially because the Democrats, having lost in 1952 to charges that they dealt too weakly with the Communist menace, were eager to turn the tables. The limited-war strategists might find it harder to turn massive retaliation versus flexible response into a campaign issue of consequence; the arguments were sometimes abstruse, and limited war was a notion conspicuously lacking in electoral appeal. But the limited-war issue might possibly lead into another issue through the call of some of the limited-war strategists for a strategy of action. Relying on deterrence alone, the Eisenhower administration had won few positive gains for American policy around the world and had suffered embarrassing setbacks in the Middle East, in the U-2 crisis of 1960 and the cancellation of the Paris summit conference, and most damagingly, in Fidel Castro's conquest of Cuba and his turn toward the Communists. Against this disappointing foreign policy record, skillful political campaigners might convert the strategic critics' idea of a strategy of action into a call for the military means to end foreign policy defeats and get the country moving forward again.

As the election year opened, the Democratic Senate Majority Leader, Lyndon B. Johnson, made his Preparedness Subcommittee a forum for airing the dangers of the missile gap. Eisenhower's third Secretary of Defense, Thomas S. Gates, Jr., poured as much cold water on the issue as the security of American intelligence operations seemed to allow; he testified that his intelligence estimates indicated the Soviets were not pursuing a rapid program of missile emplacement that would give them the advantages suggested by the missile-gap idea. Senator Johnson refused to be mollified. As far as the administration was willing to reveal the basis of its intelligence estimates, Johnson said it seemed to him that the Defense Department was counting on the Soviet Union's presumed intentions rather than weighing its capabilities. "The missile gap cannot be eliminated by the stroke of a pen," Johnson said.[106]

Nelson A. Rockefeller, Republican governor of New York, both shared the fears of the administration's critics and wanted to avoid passing campaign ammunition to the Democrats. On the eve of the Republican national convention in July, Rockefeller's hopes of snatching the party's Presidential nomination away from Vice President Richard M. Nixon had practically evaporated. The foreign affairs crises and the defense problems of early 1960 nevertheless convinced the governor that responsibility decreed he must assert himself as leader of the Republican party's internationalist wing and of the largest state bloc of convention delegates, if not to win the nomination, then at least to assure that the Republican campaign would not rest smugly on the record of the Eisenhower administration. Rockefeller insisted that the defense budget must be increased by at least $3 billion, that missile development must be accelerated, that the strategic retaliatory force must be hardened and dispersed, and that the platform of President Eisenhower's party must assert these propositions and thus in effect censure the Eisenhower defense effort as inadequate. To avoid the risks of a convention floor fight, and probably because he shared some of Rockefeller's misgivings, Vice President Nixon proposed a meeting with the governor. Held at Rockefeller's New York City headquarters, the meeting produced a "Compact of Fifth Avenue," in which, while slightly softening Rockefeller's demands (thus eliminating the specific $3 billion figure), Nixon accepted their substance.[107]

By virtually conceding the existence of a defense emergency, the Compact of Fifth Avenue passed ammunition to the Democrats after all. The Democratic Presidential candidate, Senator John F. Kennedy, had taken a special interest in defense and foreign policy problems and was especially ready to use such ammunition. Kennedy was too responsible a man to use the idea of the missile gap recklessly, in a way that might tempt the Soviets into stepped-up bullying tactics; but he did use it. "I say only that the evidence is strong . . . that we cannot be certain of our security in the future any more than we can be certain of disaster. . . . If we are to err in an age of insecurity, I want us to err on the side of security."[108] Kennedy's supporters were often less cautious on the missile-gap issue. And the candidate himself was clear enough in his rejection of massive retaliation for the strategy of flexible response. During the campaign he agreed to review B. H. Liddell Hart's *Deterrence and Defense* for the *Saturday Review*, and he said:

> The Soviet acquisition of nuclear weapons and the means for their delivery . . . now makes certain that a nuclear war would be a war of mutual devastation. The notion that the free world can be protected simply by the threat of "massive retaliation" is no longer tenable. . . . responsible leaders in the West will not and should not deal with limited aggression by unlimited weapons. . . . the central task of American and Western military policy is to make all forms of Communist aggression irrational and unattractive.[109]

Not only that: Kennedy also accepted the strategy of flexible response because he wanted to promise the voters a strategy of action. On the campaign trail, Senator Kennedy's references to foreign and military policy dealt less with the abstrusities of deterrence than with the call for the United States to take initiatives again. For Cuba, which had fallen into hands friendly to Communism during Eisenhower's Presidency, Kennedy offered positive initiatives in place of defeat; he would "attempt to strengthen the non-Batista democratic anti-Castro forces in exile, and in Cuba itself, who offer eventual hope of overthrowing Castro." To foreign policy as well as domestic action he seemed to extend the constant reiteration of his theme, "We must move." ". . . all of us are anxious to see the United States move ahead," Kennedy said repeatedly. "If you are tired and don't want to move, then stay with the Republicans. But I think we are ready to move."[110]

On the morrow of John F. Kennedy's election victory, one of the strategy intellectuals promised at last that a certain amount of moving forward might not be incompatible even with nuclear war. The earlier strategic critics had called for a strategy of flexible response that might be able to snatch advantages from the menace of limited war. In *On Thermonuclear War*, the RAND physicist Herman Kahn said that advantages could be grasped even from a nuclear holocaust, much as the prospect was otherwise to be deplored.

Kahn joined the strategists who argued that the nuclear balance could never be stable enough to preclude altogether the possibility of nuclear war. Consequently, he believed, the nation must contemplate the possible contingencies of nuclear war unblinkingly, thinking about them enough to control the horrors if they came, to mitigate or avert some of them, and even to seize the victories that might be available in the midst of holocaust. To Kahn, it was a delusion to regard thermonuclear war as so horrible that it could never happen; but it was also a delusion to regard thermonuclear war as entailing inevitably the end of humanity or civilization, and if such war happened we must keep our wits about us to salvage from it, and even to gain from it, what we might.

In detailed calculations set forth in seventy tables, Kahn attempted to estimate the consequences of varying levels of nuclear war for life and civilization. He argued that some human beings would survive the most devastating of nuclear holocausts, and that civilization would also emerge from the fires and be rebuilt. More human beings would survive, and the future of civilization would be better assured, if the United States prepared for the possibility of nuclear war with an adequate program to shelter its people. Not only should the bases of the nuclear retaliatory force be hardened; the activities of political and economic life could and should also be given "hardened" protection.[111]

If enough people could survive nuclear war to carry on the nation and its civilization, strategy should also provide them the means to gain victory in such a war. The appropriate strategy would be a counterforce strategy, one which would afford the nation enough superiority in weapons to permit it to reply to nuclear attack not simply with a spasmodic, convulsive retaliatory blow but with a capacity to punish the enemy in such a way that he would be coerced into abandoning his aims. Both the better to assure survival even in nuclear war and to salvage victory from it, Kahn argued that plans must be prepared for "controlled (or limited) general war." The United States should be able to continue a controlled, deliberate choosing among a variety of options for military response and action in the midst of nuclear war. The national aim would still presumably be not the pointless destruction of the enemy's whole society but his coercion to the American will. The targets of nuclear retaliation should be adjusted to that aim, especially by focusing upon the enemy's strategic retaliatory forces. Depending upon the extent to which the enemy might have committed his nuclear forces and the degree of their vulnerability, the campaign against them could itself be carried on in varying degrees of intensity.[112]

Herman Kahn's *On Thermonuclear War* provoked cries of immorality from those who thought Kahn's coldbloodedness and the "grim jocularity" that attended his dissections of nuclear horror a species of encouragement to itchy nuclear trigger-fingers. The critics of his morality tended to fail to note his repeated insistence that "The greater understanding of nuclear war . . . reduces the danger of accidental war and increases the probability that any war could be conducted with restraint and terminated relatively soon," and his insistence too that nevertheless the perils were so great that we ought to strive to end the arms race through some system of the rule of law.[113] Still, by the time American strategy could begin to contemplate the possibilities for victory not only in limited wars but even in nuclear war, the strategists' sensitivities were becoming well calloused from prolonged living in the presence of nuclear weapons. In 1960, John F. Kennedy's seeming promise to encourage Cuban freedom fighters and Herman Kahn's scenarios for controlled nuclear war both suggested an adjustment to nuclear weapons that was a bit too complacent and a wish for a return to positive strategies of action that bordered on the reckless.

18. Strategies of Action Attempted: To the Vietnam War

Phase III—If the enemy persisted, a period of a year to a year and a half following Phase II would be required for the defeat and destruction of the remaining enemy forces and base areas.

—*William C. Westmoreland*,
on ending the Vietnam War[1]

THE EVAPORATION of the missile-gap scare naturally did nothing to moderate the strangely ebullient mood which many strategists shared with the nation at large upon John F. Kennedy's accession to Presidential power. The missile gap appears to have been a product of the Sputnik shock combined with selected intelligence estimates favored by those military and political leaders and strategists who desired enough American missile building to establish a counterforce strategy. The ability of the Eisenhower administration to make a case against the existence of the missile gap was crippled during the hearings of Lyndon Johnson's Preparedness Subcommittee because Defense Secretary Gates could not reveal that U-2 reconnaissance flights over Russia were going a long way toward proving Gates's assertion that the Soviets were not engaged in rapid ICBM emplacement. Gates testified in January, 1960, Francis Gary Powers and his U-2 were shot down only on May 1, and in January the U-2 overflights were still a subject of strictest silence.

Because of constant cloud cover over northern parts of the Soviet Union, the evidence from the U-2 flights was not altogether conclusive. After the Powers debacle, furthermore, U-2 flights over Russia were discontinued. Nevertheless, President Kennedy's Secretary of

Defense, Robert S. McNamara, entered office skeptical about the existence of a missile gap, and early in his term he said: "There appeared . . . no signs of a Soviet crash effort to build intercontinental missiles, though the overall Russian military preparations continue at a rapid pace."[2] By the summer and fall of 1961, the intelligence evidence, especially that derived from new earth-orbiting reconnaissance satellites, was at last incontrovertible that there existed no missile gap threatening to overwhelm America's nuclear retaliatory capacity.

During the 1950s, the Soviets had indeed pushed ahead of the United States in developing giant rockets of very great—800,000 pounds—thrust. They had invested less than the United States in bomber development, and they had also bypassed rockets of the 350,000-pound thrust of the American Atlas ICBM. With their huge rockets, they launched Sputnik and other elements of an impressive space program. But when they began to deploy their giant rockets in ICBMs, they found them too cumbersome and too vulnerable to serve as good weapons. The numbers that they mounted were insufficient to offset America's bomber superiority. The Soviets went back to the drawing boards to devise smaller, more easily handled, less vulnerable, and less costly ICBMs.

As the Kennedy administration settled itself into office, the United States soon had about seventy ICBMs deployed while the Soviet Union was still barely beginning its deployment. Lest Soviet Premier N. S. Khrushchev characteristically attempt to play upon fears of a missile gap anyway and thus increase the danger of nuclear war, the new administration decided to let the Soviets know that the United States was aware that the missile gap of the election campaign did not exist. They passed on this information both through a public statement of Deputy Secretary of Defense Roswell Gilpatric, and through briefings to representatives of foreign powers in enough detail that the Soviets would be convinced of the extent of American knowledge when the content of the briefings leaked to them.[3]

The new administration pursued an ambitious continuing missile development program despite the disappearance of the missile gap. It did so to permit it to adopt as its strategy of nuclear deterrence a counterforce strategy. In June, 1962, in a commencement address at the University of Michigan at Ann Arbor, Secretary of Defense McNamara delivered a public statement on strategy that was destined to become almost as famous as John Foster Dulles's massive retaliation speech of January, 1954. McNamara announced a counterforce strategy based on a second-strike capability and seeking to avoid the mass destruction of cities and civilian populations.

> The United States has come to the conclusion [he said] that to the extent feasible, basic military strategy in a general nuclear war should be approached in much the same way that more conventional military operations have been regarded in the past. That is to say, principal military objectives, in the event of a nuclear war stemming from a major attack on the Alliance, should be the destruction of the enemy's military forces, not of its civilian population.
>
> The very strength and nature of the Alliance forces make it possible for us to retain, even in the face of a massive surprise attack, sufficient reserve striking power to destroy an enemy society if driven to it. In other words, we are giving a possible opponent the strongest imaginable incentive to refrain from striking our own cities.[4]

Not only had the missile gap proven an illusion; the quality of the strategic nuclear weapons developed by the United States during the 1950s, despite the controversial budget limits, joined with ideas adopted from the strategy intellectuals to encourage McNamara's Ann Arbor counterforce doctrine. The Navy's Polaris program had gone forward with remarkable speed and success. The nuclear submarine *George Washington* launched the first Polaris missiles from underwater on July 20, 1960. In 1962, Secretary McNamara set a goal of forty-one Polaris submarines, each with sixteen missiles, as the American undersea attack force for the coming decade and into the next. By the beginning of the sixties, the United States was also soon to begin deployment of a "second-generation" ICBM, the Minuteman. This missile used more easily handled solid fuel in contrast to the difficult, highly volatile liquid fuel of the first-generation Atlas and Titan ICBMs, weighed only 69,000 pounds in contrast to the 269,000 pounds of the Atlas, and could be fired from underground, and thus relatively "hard," silos. McNamara soon decided on a program of 1,200 Minutemen, reduced in 1964 to 1,000. With hardened silos for the Minuteman and submarine mobility for the Polaris, these weapons represented a large advance in security for a second-strike capability. With warheads of only about one megaton (the equivalent of one million tons of TNT), great accuracy, and relatively easy controlability, they also offered the precision necessary to contemplate McNamara's Ann Arbor strategy of controlled response.[5]

Nevertheless, McNamara began to develop second thoughts about the counterforce strategy announced at Ann Arbor at least as quickly as John Foster Dulles must have begun to feel misgivings about massive retaliation. As was implied by the now current custom of calling the contrasting strategy of sufficient deterrence "finite deterrence," the counterforce strategy suggested the possibility to ride out an enemy first strike and yet to destroy the enemy's nuclear force required the solution of immense problems of intelligence and aiming. A small increase in the Soviet nuclear force could necessitate a much larger increase in the American force to assure counterforce capability in the face of the intelligence and targeting problems. A series of Soviet force enlargements thus could make the requirements upon an American counterforce truly infinite.

Furthermore, McNamara's Ann Arbor strategy harbored an incongruity between the idea of a counterforce strike focused upon the enemy's nuclear force and the avowal that the United States would never launch a preemptive first strike. To assure destruction of the enemy's missiles, they had to be hit before they were launched. Or if despite this incongruity the United States attempted to wait out an enemy first strike and then to launch a counterforce strike, the unpredictable damage done to the American nuclear force by the enemy's first strike would mean that counterforce capability was no longer assured. The Minuteman bases were not so hard that they were totally invulnerable; in the middle 1960s the country's reliance still had to be mainly on a "soft" deterrent force anyway.

These problems eventually compelled Secretary McNamara to retreat from the counterforce strategy, but he hoped to find an intermediate position somewhere between counterforce and the indiscriminate city-wrecking implications of the earlier finite deterrent. He sought his compromise ground in an exploration of a strategy of "assured destruction." The United States would attempt to maintain the capacity to inflict "unacceptable" damage upon an enemy after the enemy had launched a full-scale attack. McNamara came to define assured destruction as meaning the United States would retain a capability to destroy 25 percent of the Soviet population and a similar proportion of Soviet industry after the Soviet Union had executed a surprise attack upon the United States. The Secretary of Defense still hoped, however, to be able to use the American retaliatory force with discrimination, hitting as many Soviet military targets as possible and striking back at Soviet cities and industries only in a controlled and deliberate way, proportioning American actions to those of the Soviets, but in both American communications to the Soviets and in American actions giving the enemy as little incentive as possible for the destruction of American cities and industries.[6]

Heartened by the renewed confidence in American strategic forces that could permit such a luxury as the Ann Arbor counterforce doctrine, the Kennedy administration meanwhile turned to the pursuit of its other 1960 campaign theme concerning defense matters, the search for a strategy that would get the nation's foreign policy moving forward again. In his first special defense message after taking office, delivered on March 28, 1961, President Kennedy reaffirmed ideas of the campaign. "Our defense posture," he said, "must be both flexible and determined. Any potential aggressor contemplating an attack on any part of the free world with any kind of weapons, conventional or nuclear, must know that our response will be suitable, selective, swift, and effective."[7] In the same message, the new President reaffirmed also the need for a wider range of *usable* military power. "Diplomacy and defense are no longer distinct alternatives, one to be used when the other side fails—but must complement each other."[8]

To both President Kennedy and his Secretary of Defense, usable military power meant, first of all, stronger conventional military forces. Significantly, President Kennedy brought General Maxwell Taylor back into government as military adviser to the President. The leaders of the new administration believed that the tactical nuclear capabilities of the American armed forces must be maintained and further developed, but they felt little confidence in keeping localized a war in which tactical nuclear weapons were employed. Limited, local war should be fought with conventional weapons, or the danger would become too great that the war would not remain limited and local.

Not only did this position accord with that of General Taylor and the other later strategic critics of the 1950s, but it was the conclusion to which the original advocates of tactical nuclear war had tended gradually to turn. By the time he wrote *The Necessity for Choice*, Henry A. Kissinger, among the latter group, had shifted his view about the relative emphasis to be given conventional or nuclear forces in limited war, arguing that limited nuclear war was likely to present excessive dangers of escalation for three reasons. These were, first, disagreements within the American military and the alliance system about the nature of limited nuclear war, including disagreements stemming from the difficulty of defining the boundaries of the battlefield in the era of missiles; secondly, the growth of the Soviet nuclear stockpile, so that a limited nuclear war would now be fought against an opponent as well equipped as the United States; and, finally, the impact of recent and continuing arms control negotiations, which added to the inhibitions against any use of nuclear weapons.[9]

When Kennedy as President-elect had prepared to move toward a wider spectrum of usable military forces and a strategy of flexible response, Robert S. McNamara, president of the Ford Motor Company, had been recommended to him as a master of the new management techniques of systems analysis and cost-effectiveness comparative analysis, whose larger application to national security problems might better define the available options for American weapons and strategy. Pursuing the activities of the RAND Corporation in this area, in 1960 Charles J. Hitch and Roland N. McKean of RAND, along with other RAND economists and systems analysts, had attempted to acquaint the defense-minded public, and similarly minded political leaders, with systems-analysis methods in their book *The Economics of Defense in the Nuclear Age*.[10] Robert McNamara had been associated with the sort of quantitative-measurements approach endorsed by Hitch and McKean since his days at the Harvard Graduate School of Business Administration before the Second World War, when he had specialized in studies of statistical accounting control as an aid to management decision-making. In 1941 he became part of a group chosen to apply accounting control to Air Forces problems, and in 1943 he was commissioned a captain to continue this work. After the war, he and some of his associates formed a consulting firm specializing in statistical control, which led him into association with and then directly into Ford and finally to the Ford presidency, rising through his use of statistical methods to effect a remarkable improvement in Ford's efficiency. McNamara agreed to become Kennedy's Secretary of Defense.[11]

He took with him to the Pentagon a staff of systems analysts, including Hitch as Comptroller and Alain C. Enthoven, also of RAND, as Deputy Assistant Secretary for Systems Analysis, and a determination to apply quantitative measurements to the solution of defense problems as much as possible. "I am sure," said McNamara, "that no significant military problem will ever be wholly susceptible to purely quantitative analysis. But every piece of the total problem that can be quantitatively analysed removes one more piece of uncertainty from our process of making a choice."[12] In part, through cost-effectiveness comparative analysis attempting to compare the cost of alternative methods to secure a certain objective, or the relative effectiveness of different systems having approximately the same cost, McNamara intended to exercise negative controls over defense programs, seeking to prevent investments in ineffective programs or excessive expenditures for purposes that could be realized more cheaply by other means. But through systems analysis McNamara intended also to push forward into view options in weapons, strategies, and policies that might otherwise be neglected. "I see my position here as being that of a leader, not a judge," he said. "I'm here to originate and stimulate new ideas and programs, not just to referee arguments and harmonize interests. Using deliberate analysis to force alternative programs to the surface, and then making explicit choices among them is fundamental."[13] As a sympathetic interpreter put it, "The unique feature of Mr. McNamara's approach . . . has been his quest for alternatives and his emphasis on analysis of cost and effectiveness in deciding on the best mix of force structures and weapon systems needed for the national defense."[14]

McNamara's methods focused on the defense budget: "I consider the budget nothing more and nothing less than the quantitative expression of a plan or policy. So in developing the budget I propose to start with the plan or the policy and translate it into quantitative terms, terms of benefit and cost."[15] The Kennedy administration could not be indifferent to questions of cost as well as of defense benefit. It wanted to command adequate funds to advance the "New Frontier" at home as well as to advance the nation's security interests, and it had to contend with the limits of Congressional fiscal tolerance. Its leaders believed that their predecessors had allowed fiscal concerns to override the requirements of military balance, which were as important to national security as fiscal health, and that for the sake of military balance the country could afford to pay more for its defense programs. But revising the balance of forces within the military establishment seemed more important than large and abrupt increases in defense spending. Defense expenditures therefore showed a gradually rising curve, from $44.2, $46.5, and $45.7 billion in fiscal years 1958, 1959, and 1960, the last fiscal years to fall wholly within the Eisenhower administration, to $47.5 billion in fiscal year 1961 and $51.1 billion in fiscal 1962, the first fiscal year planned for and falling wholly within the Kennedy administration, $52.7 billion in fiscal 1963, and $54.1 billion in fiscal 1964.[16]

At the outset, Secretary McNamara suspended the program for a new intercontinental bomber, the B-70, at the development stage, with little likelihood that he would ever encourage production. He refused to put into production the Nike/Zeus antimissile system, because he did not believe it could be effective enough to justify its cost. As another means of reducing costs, he compelled the Air Force and the Navy to plan to share a common tactical airplane, the project that developed into the ill-fated TFX (Tactical Fighter, Experimental). The first increments in expenditures went largely not into the means for a strategy of flexible response but into the nuclear retaliatory systems for McNamara's counterforce strategy, especially the Polaris and the Minuteman. Initially, McNamara planned to add only 13,000 men to the three services. But eventually the new administration's commitment to flexible response and conventional forces made itself felt. The Berlin crisis of 1961 hastened matters by leading McNamara to call for an increase of the Army from 875,000 to 1,000,000 men, with an immediate enlargement through mobilization of certain National Guard and Reserve forces. As the program for a flexible strategy evolved, the Army activated two additional Regular divisions and remedied understrengths to increase the number of combat-ready divisions from eleven to sixteen. Six reserve divisions were designated high-priority units, and an effort was made to prepare them to be able to reinforce the Regular Army promptly.

The Kennedy administration insisted on a revision of European defense plans to permit reliance on conventional weapons against a conventional attack. Secretary McNamara projected a 400-percent increase in strategic airlift capacity, and to assist in the swift movement of troops to threatened areas, he "prepositioned" equipment and supplies for several divisions in Europe and in the Far East and aboard "floating depot" ships. McNamara's Defense Department held that in view of America's global responsibilities, the United States should be prepared to fight two and a half wars simultaneously—that is, a major war in Europe, a major war in Asia, and a lesser struggle elsewhere.[17]

The better still to permit the Defense Department to respond flexibly and appropriately to a full spectrum of challenges, Secretary McNamara installed at the suggestion of Comptroller Hitch the Planning-Programming-Budgeting System (PPBS). Under this system, the defense budget was reorganized around the functions of the various elements of the armed services rather than under administrative headings inherited from the past. The budget headings became "program packages," such as Strategic Offensive and Defensive Forces and General Purpose Forces, the latter for local wars. Under these headings spending for all strategic forces, the Navy's Polaris force as well as the Air Force's missiles and bombers, would be considered together as a single strategic package. The forces for local war would be budgeted for similarly. Meanwhile, McNamara used the authority to create multiservice commands under the Reorganization Act of 1958 to form analogous packages in the forces themselves, bringing all combat troops into one of the various interservice commands. The Army, Navy, and Air Force moved further toward becoming training and administrative organizations, while the fighting edge of the armed forces was embodied in the "unified and specified commands" directly under the Joint Chiefs of Staff and their superiors, the Secretary of Defense and the President.[18]

Usable military power ought to permit forward initiatives in policy. Of all the strategy intellectuals, Professor Kissinger had insisted upon a strategy of action most firmly, and he had returned to the theme strongly in *The Necessity for Choice.* In that book, Kissinger recalled that during the first crises of the Cold War, Secretary of State Dean Acheson had called for the creation of situations of military strength in order to build a foundation for favorable change in the world. "What we must do," Kissinger quoted Acheson as saying, "is to create situations of strength; we must build strength; and if we create that strength then I think the whole situation in the world begins to change." But by the time of John Foster Dulles's tenure as Secretary of State, said Kissinger, "what had originally been considered the condition of policy—security against aggression—seemed to become its only goal." Creating situations of strength became an end in itself, not a foundation for change. When American strength contributed to opportunities for policy initiatives, the opportunities consequently were lost.

The United States never exploited as it might have the possibilities in its initial nuclear monopoly. "We were so aware of the vulnerability of our allies that we underestimated the bargaining power inherent in our industrial potential and our nuclear superiority."[19] In the same way, the United States failed to exploit the disarray in the Soviet Union caused by the death of Stalin. By opening aggressive policy initiatives then, the United States should have been able to secure concessions. But, "Since Secretary Dulles was unwilling to assume the diplomatic initiative, a stalemate was the inevitable consequence."[20] "The gulf between strategy and diplomacy reduced the effectiveness of both."[21]

President Kennedy now proclaimed that diplomacy and defense were no longer to be distinct alternatives. Usable military power, the President implied again as he had done during his candidacy in 1960, would be military power that permitted forward initiatives in policy. The new President was earnest enough in pursuit of a strategy of action that he accepted the plan that led to the Bay of Pigs.

This plan had been developed during the last months of the Eisenhower administration and the first weeks of the Kennedy administration by the Central Intelligence Agency. It called for the landing of about a thousand American-armed and trained Cuban refugee opponents of Fidel Castro back in their homeland, with the idea that the Cuban populace would rise up to support them and carry the day for them against Castro's 200,000-man militia. The professional military men of the Pentagon, including the Joint Chiefs of Staff, accepted the plan despite the preposterous qualities which were to become so evident in retrospect, apparently because neither the CIA nor subordinate military officers carried full information to the Joint Chiefs, and the Joint Chiefs failed to ask the CIA and their own subordinates the appropriate hard questions. Like virtually everyone else in the American government, the leadership in the Pentagon found the Castro regime in Cuba an acute source of embarrassment and wanted to get rid of it. The State Department also shared such sentiments enough to give the invasion plan its endorsement, and President Kennedy was disturbed enough by Castro, committed enough by his election stance to try to do something to topple the Cuban dictator, and intent enough upon regaining policy initiatives that he went along.

When the CIA put the Cuban refugees ashore at the Bay of Pigs late in April, 1961, the superior military strength of the Castro government promptly smothered the attack. President Kennedy's commitment to a strategy of action did not extend to transforming covert United States sponsorship of the Cuban exiles into an overt United States assault upon a tiny Latin American state, with incalculable damage to hemisphere relations and his Alliance for Progress plan for the Americas. The President rejected suggestions of open United States aerial support, cut his losses, and withdrew.[22]

Coming as embarrassingly close as it did on the heels of his campaign promises to move forward, the Bay of Pigs fiasco created strong additional pressure upon the new President to score a success somewhere along the international horizon. The Berlin crisis of the following summer added still more pressure; the President resisted

Premier Khrushchev's efforts to bully the Western powers out of Berlin, but the Communists' building of the Berlin wall was another gain for their side, at odds with the positive turn in foreign policy that Kennedy had offered in the 1960 campaign.

In the autumn, the President turned his attention to southeast Asia and in particular to Laos, where a three-cornered struggle among Communists, neutralists, and rightists was spawning a chaos from which only the Communists could benefit. President Kennedy decided there was hope of restoring minimal political stability, and thus of scoring at least a semblance of the international success he desired, by dropping United States support for the rightists and aiding the neutralist leadership of the closest approach to a national leader available, Prince Souvanna Phouma. But restoring minimal order to Laos for the nourishment of minimal political stability seemed likely to require military intervention, and accordingly the President asked the Joint Chiefs to prepare appropriate American forces for possible intervention. Now that the armed forces were being refashioned for a strategy of flexible response, intervention in Laos could presumably be accomplished to good effect. It was of this very part of the world that such a strategic critic as General Gavin had written, it will be remembered: "And, if in the past ten years we had spent even a small part of what we have spent in readying our forces for a one-strategy war, in developing and procuring the means of dealing with limited war, we could have settled Korea and Dien Bien Phu quickly in our favor."[23] One-strategy planning now presumably was gone from the Pentagon, and except for the administration's reluctance to use tactical nuclear weapons, Secretary McNamara was building the very kinds of forces that Gavin had said could strike and succeed swiftly in a local Asian war.

When President Kennedy asked them, however, the Joint Chiefs proved reluctant to provide ground, amphibious, and tactical air forces for intervention in Laos. The President discovered that the dominant conviction among the military planners currently established in the Pentagon, and inherited from the Eisenhower years, was that the lesson of the Korean frustrations of 1950–53 decreed that there should be no more limited, local wars fought by American forces on the Asian continent without freedom to use any weapons in the American arsenal, including nuclear ones. Before they would willingly dispatch military forces to Laos, the military leaders seemed to want from the President assurances against their misgivings concerning any Asian land war, in the form of a commitment that if fighting developed, all weapons would be permissible. Either they should be assured that they might employ nuclear weapons of whatever dimensions they thought they needed, or they preferred not to go into Laos at all.[24]

Premier Khrushchev, not knowing all about the misgivings in the Pentagon, may have concluded from President Kennedy's public statements on Laos that an American military intervention was about to occur. For that or other reasons, the Soviet premier made known his willingness to settle for a truce and a coalition under neutralist leadership in Laos, and the President was able to avoid a showdown with his military chiefs by arranging a precarious but at least temporarily satisfactory Laotian agreement with the Soviets. Still, the combination of persisting "one-strategy" sentiment in the Pentagon with the Joint Chiefs' earlier support for the Bay of Pigs adventure convinced Kennedy that he must rearrange the military high command. Within a year after the Bay of Pigs, all the Joint Chiefs except General David M. Shoup of the Marine Corps were replaced, and Maxwell Taylor became Chairman of the Joint Chiefs.

The Laos settlement was so tenuous, and at best it favored the neutralists, that President Kennedy was still far from enjoying what the American public would consider a clear-cut success in foreign policy. Worse, he continued to be in this embarrassing situation into the autumn of 1962, after nearly two years in office and with the mid-term Congressional elections in prospect. Having promised during the 1960 campaign to try to do something to remove Fidel Castro from the Cuban scene, and having failed in his major effort, at this juncture the President could scarcely afford any further unfavorable developments in Cuba, which might tie Cuba still more closely to Soviet Communism or make Castro seem still more of a threat to the stability of the rest of the hemisphere or to the composure of the United States. President Kennedy's political situation and the hopes of the Democratic party for the coming Congressional elections would not permit any further Cuban discomfiture, nor would the President's deep and genuine conviction that the momentum assumed by world events during the 1950s had to be reversed.

But at this juncture the Soviets proceeded to emplace medium-range and intermediate-range ballistic missiles in Cuba, and to assemble there Soviet IL-28 bombers capable of carrying nuclear weapons. Thus began the Cuban missile crisis of October, 1962.

The quantitative and qualitative superiority of the American nuclear force probably helped produce the crisis. In late 1962, the

United States had about 200 to 250 ICBMs, Russia probably only 50 to 75. There were some 144 missiles in American Polaris submarines. The United States had 600 or more intercontinental bombers on fifteen-minute alert, the Soviets only about 200. Probably having anticipated that their massive rockets of the late 1950s would give them a period of strategic dominance, the Russians may have been loath to acquiesce in a renewed period of marked inferiority. After the Bay of Pigs affair, Fidel Castro may have importuned the Russians to supply him with missiles to ensure him against American attack; his own various accounts differ as to whether he or the Soviets first suggested the emplacement of Russian strategic missiles on Cuban soil. In July and December, 1960, Premier Khrushchev had publicly pledged to defend Cuba, though while he mentioned rockets he was careful to say that the rockets were symbolic. Still, the Soviet Union would have been hard put to fulfill Khrushchev's pledge by non-nuclear means, since it concerned an island so close to the United States. The Soviets may well have decided that the best way to back up the pledge was with nuclear rockets. But they chose to send to Cuba not merely short-range rockets which would have provided Castro with nuclear defensive power without making Cuba seem to be a Soviet offensive threat against the United States. They sent instead both medium-range ballistic missiles which could reach up to 1,000 miles and, most strangely if their motive was only to defend Cuba, intermediate-range ballistic missiles which could reach up to 2,200 miles. Their IL-28 bombers had a 700-mile range. It would appear, consequently, that in addition to defending Cuba, the Soviets intended to bring within reliable nuclear range much of the United States that the existing nuclear imbalance left otherwise far less exposed to Soviet nuclear power.

On the other hand, the Soviet buildup in Cuba was not enough to threaten a drastic alteration in the nuclear imbalance. The Russians moved to establish in Cuba six battalions of MRBMs and four battalions of IRBMs. This deployment would give them twenty-four launching pads of MRBMs and sixteen of IRBMs. But the missiles were "soft" and easily targeted from the United States, and thus they were suitable only for a deliberate first-strike attack. When Secretary McNamara received confirmed evidence of the buildup, he accepted the news calmly as not shifting the strategic balance fundamentally. He remarked that it made no difference whether one was killed by a missile from Cuba or an ICBM from the Soviet Union. The total nuclear balance remained overwhelmingly in America's favor.

Nevertheless, President Kennedy and his principal advisers decided they must act to prevent the completion of the Cuban missile deployment and to cause its abandonment. After increasing evidence of various kinds of Soviet military reinforcement of Cuba during the summer and early fall of 1962 and repeated American warnings not to place offensive weapons there, on October 14 a U-2 flight confirmed American suspicions that Soviet MRBMs and IRBMs were about to be installed on the island. The Kennedy administration decided that Soviet strategic advances which could be borne and adjusted to when they occurred gradually over a prolonged period could not be accepted when they were forced upon the United States with the dramatic abruptness of the Cuban missile deployment, with demoralizing effect on the American public. Probably more to the point, President Kennedy and his advisers believed that whatever the strategic consequences, they could not accept the political consequences of Soviet missiles in Cuba—either in the narrowest sense, in terms of the Democratic party's and the President's own electoral prospects, or in the larger sense of the direction they felt they were obliged to give to the momentum of world events. The President's election campaign had offered promise of changing Cuba for the better; after the Bay of Pigs, Kennedy could not accept not betterment but another reversal. Republican Senator Kenneth Keating of New York stridently reminded Kennedy of the political issues with his own charges of Soviet missile deployment in Cuba even before the administration was sure the missiles were there.

The method chosen to terminate the Soviet missile buildup and to secure the removal of the missiles already there contained much of caution, but it also ran the risk of pushing the world over the nuclear brink. It combined President Kennedy's disclosure to the world of the basic intelligence information about the missiles in Cuba, appeals for the support of the Organization of American States and the United Nations, and the restrained employment of force through a naval blockade of Cuba. The naval blockade was highly dangerous in its implication of an unprecedentedly direct Soviet-American collision if the Soviets should attempt to pass it, and the President meanwhile made clear to Premier Khrushchev his intent to take whatever further steps might prove necessary to remove the missiles from Cuba, including invasion of the island whatever the consequences might be. The missiles had Soviet crews and were thoroughly under Soviet control, so an invasion would bring another direct collision of the nuclear powers.

From this challenge the Soviet premier retreated. The Russian ships that were sailing toward Cuba turned back, and in return for an American pledge not to invade Cuba, Khrushchev agreed to dismantle the missile pads and ship the missiles and the IL-28s home under UN inspection. The Cubans then refused to permit the inspection, but American reconnaissance flights and intelligence confirmed that the missiles and bombers left Cuba, along with the bulk of the Soviet troops who had come to the island with them. The Soviets could not match the conventional military power of the American naval blockade or, if it came to that, an American invasion force and its air cover, in an island theater so far from Russia and so close to the United States. Against the strong American strategic deterrent, neither did the Soviets wish to go to general war to trump America's Caribbean strength.[25]

President Kennedy at last had won a kind of international triumph. For the moment Soviet policy had to tread cautiously in the face of assertive American nuclear power, in Berlin as well as in Cuba, and around the world. But the triumph was incomplete—the resolution of the crisis had included Kennedy's pledge not to invade Cuba—and for all the temporary advantages of the United States in the strategic balance, the balance remained too close to prevent such triumph as there was from being more than brief and somewhat illusory.

Because Khrushchev had gambled and failed, he had to pay a price to his rivals within the Soviet Union. Almost certainly the outcome of the missile crisis contributed to Khrushchev's fall from power two years later, in October, 1964. If the verdict has to be mixed on the implications of his fall for Soviet-American relations, the United States can only regard as ominous the price that the Soviet armed forces apparently extracted from Khrushchev and his successors as compensation for their military humiliation: the acceleration of the rise of Soviet naval power, until by the 1970s the Russian fleets became a presence to be reckoned with in almost every ocean of the world, and a threat to the strategic mobility and flexibility hitherto afforded the United States by the possession of unchallenged sea power.[26]

In addition, the Soviet caution and the reciprocal American self-confidence that followed the Cuban missile crisis helped embolden the United States to essay a policy and strategy gamble of its own in southeast Asia.

Before General Maxwell Taylor became Chairman of the Joint Chiefs of Staff, during Taylor's months as personal military adviser to the President, President Kennedy had had him direct his attention especially to paramilitary operations and to "unconventional wars" of guerrilla tactics and subversion. Here was an area of military problems on which even the limited-war strategists of the Eisenhower period, including General Taylor himself, had scarcely touched. But between the election of 1960 and President Kennedy's inauguration, Premier Khrushchev on January 6, 1961, had promised Soviet support for unconventional "wars of national liberation." In doing so, Khrushchev added Soviet endorsement to what had long been Mao Tse-tung's and the Chinese Communists' favorite method of warfare, the type of three-stage war wherewith Mao had won China itself, escalating from propaganda and terrorism to guerrilla war and finally erupting into climactic full-scale war once subversion and guerrillas left the enemy fatally weakened.

Also in the interval between Kennedy's election and inauguration, the Communist leaders in Vietnam had engineered in December, 1960, the establishment of the National Liberation Front of South Vietnam, to head the fight against the anti-Communist regime of President Ngo Dinh Diem in Saigon through a campaign of subversion and guerrilla war that had already been escalating there at least since 1958. Mao's doctrines and Khrushchev's endorsement of wars of national liberation seemed likely to produce a succession of similar Communist-sponsored efforts in underdeveloped nations around the world, wherever lack of national cohesion made states vulnerable to subversive and guerrilla attack.

So President Kennedy feared. While fearing Communist guerrilla wars, however, John F. Kennedy also shared the romantic fascination which many have sensed in the idea of guerrilla war. He had read in Mao's writings on the subject and in those of Fidel Castro's guerrilla theoretician, Che Guevara. Promptly on assuming office, Kennedy urged the Defense Department to accelerate its efforts to deal with the threat of unconventional war, including guerrilla war. When early in the administration the three armed forces were scheduled initially only for an increase of 13,000 men, 3,000 of the 13,000 were planned for the Army's Special Forces. Under the direct prodding of the President, the Army expanded the curriculum and the size of the classes at its Special Warfare School at Fort Bragg. The Special Forces grew from 1,500 to 9,000 men within a year. Over the objections of the Army and a historic Army suspicion of elite forces, Kennedy treated the Special Forces as an elite and gave them their distinctive emblem, a symbol of the romanticism that colored the

President's activities in the area of unconventional war, the green beret.

With Special Forces trained in counterguerrilla warfare, and with all the armed forces skilled enough in counterguerrilla war to give the Special Forces support when necessary, Kennedy believed the United States could check Communist wars of national liberation, not with large commitments of American troops, but through teams of Green Berets sharing their expertise with the defenders of threatened countries. With the Green Berets trained not only in unconventional warfare but also in community organization and leadership, preventive medicine, and construction techniques, the Special Forces could engage in nation building as well, both physically and through inspirational leadership, contributing to the remedy for the underlying national incohesiveness that exposed underdeveloped countries to subversion and guerrilla war.[27]

Guerrilla war, said President Kennedy, requires "a whole new kind of strategy, a wholly different kind of force, and therefore a new and wholly different kind of military training."[28] To begin developing the new strategy, he relied on a high-level interdepartmental "Special Group, Counter-Insurgency," headed by General Taylor, on which Attorney General Robert F. Kennedy was the President's own representative. The interdepartmental group reflected in its composition the President's conviction that unconventional, insurrectionary warfare was never only a military problem, but always a conjoined political and military problem.

In divided Vietnam, American unconventional warfare operations had already been going on before the coming of the Kennedy administration and its special interest in such a mode of war. An American team of unconventional warfare specialists headed by Colonel, later Brigadier General, Edward G. Lansdale, USAF, had been leading and training Vietnamese for covert operations against Ho Chi Minh's North Vietnam regime since the Geneva accords divided the country in 1954, and had been assisting the anti-Communist regime in the South in counterguerrilla operations.[29] Neither the offensive nor the defensive sides of this activity had enjoyed much success, but the attitudes of the Kennedy administration promised an intensified effort. About July, 1961, General Lansdale presented a detailed report on "Resources for Unconventional Warfare, S.E. Asia," to General Taylor.[30]

In October of that year, President Kennedy sent a special mission to South Vietnam, headed by General Taylor, and including Walt

W. Rostow, who was deputy to McGeorge Bundy, Special Assistant to the President on National Security Affairs. The mission was charged with determining how the United States might assist South Vietnam against subversion and guerrillas. It reported back, predictably, that President Diem's South Vietnamese government should be persuaded to carry out political and administrative reforms. But it also recommended a program to help rescue South Vietnam from Communist insurgency, including economic as well as military aid and advisers for the tasks of nation building.

Among the striking features of the mission's recommendations, however, is how little impact the growing flurry of interest in unconventional war had upon them. Despite the President's call for "a whole new kind of strategy," the military recommendations were remarkably reminiscent of the familiar limited-war prescriptions of the 1950s, including General Taylor's own, which had little to do with unconventional war but reflected the frustrations of the conventional war in Korea and proposed how such a war might have been won. The Taylor mission now emphasized the value of freeing the South Vietnamese army from static defense and giving it mobility, especially airborne mobility, with helicopters and American helicopter pilots and mechanics. The mission emphasized also the value of tactical air support for the South Vietnamese army, through slow-flying propeller-driven planes, Douglas B-26s (formerly A-26s) and North American T-28Ds (an armed modification of the T-28 trainer). To stiffen the South Vietnamese, Taylor recommended the dispatch to Vietnam of an American military task force, initially to number about 8,000 men and to be composed mainly of logistical units, but with implications of considerable subsequent involvement: "A bare token [force], however, will not suffice; it must have a significant value."[31]

The old frustrations of Korea seemed especially to color the observations on bringing warfare in Vietnam to an end:

> While the final answer lies beyond the scope of this report, it is clear to me [said General Taylor] that the time may come in our relations to Southeast Asia when we must declare our intention to attack the source of guerrilla aggression in North Vietnam and impose on the Hanoi Government a price for participating in the current war which is commensurate with the damage being inflicted on its neighbors to the south.[32]

"The risks of backing into a major Asian war by way of SVN," General Taylor also wrote, "are present but not impressive. NVN is extremely vulnerable to conventional bombing, a weakness which should be exploited diplomatically in convincing Hanoi to lay off SVN."[33]

Secretary McNamara responded to General Taylor's recommendations with a somewhat ambivalent memorandum, in which he stated that the fall of South Vietnam would lead to rapid extension of Communist control over southeast Asia and Indonesia, that the chances were probably sharply against preventing that outcome "by any measures short of the introduction of U. S. forces on a substantial scale," but that "We do not believe major units of U. S. forces should be introduced in South Vietnam unless we are willing to make an affirmative decision on the issue stated at the start of this memorandum"—that is, on the necessity to save South Vietnam from Communism in order to save southeast Asia. It was not especially indicative of further thinking about President Kennedy's "whole new kind of strategy" that the McNamara memorandum spoke in terms of a maximum commitment of American ground forces in southeast Asia reaching six divisions or about 205,000 men. Nor did the Secretary of Defense's contribution at this or any other point in thinking about the Vietnam problem offer much use of his systems-analysis techniques to try to bring new kinds of strategy and policy options into view. The principal impact of the quantitative approach upon the Vietnam problem seems to have been an unhappy propensity in the Defense Department to try to measure quantitatively successes and setbacks in Vietnam, in terms of kill ratios and desertion and captured weapons statistics.[34]

As for President Kennedy, for the time being he accepted the Taylor-Rostow mission's recommendations only up to and including the one about air support. He wanted to counter the threat of wars of national liberation, and he wanted to make the use of combat once again a practicable instrument of an active foreign policy; but he shied away from the prospect of any substantial American commitment of manpower to land war in Asia. It was implicit in his call for a new strategy that he also felt doubts that large numbers of American troops, trained not primarily for guerrilla war but for warfare similar to World War II and Korea, would counteract suitably an enemy force of elusive, swiftly moving guerrillas who could melt into the local population. Large numbers of American soldiers might also bring the undesired effects of further unsettling the South Vietnamese economy and society and aggravating the nationalist resentments on which the National Liberation Front and its "Viet Cong" guerrillas fed.

President Kennedy perceived all these objections, later so familiar that they became platitudes, to the kind of recommendations offered by the Taylor report. Yet the President also believed the United States must abide by and even reinforce the commitments to support the South Vietnamese government that had been offered on various occasions since the Geneva agreements of 1954. He regarded South Vietnam as something of a test of America's ability to counter Communist wars of national liberation. If the Communists succeeded with such a war in Vietnam, they would be encouraged to stir up insurrectionary wars all through the undeveloped world; if they were dealt a costly reversal in Vietnam, the whole idea of insurrectionary war might be dealt a fatal blow. President Kennedy believed the evidence that Ho Chi Minh's regime in the North was instigating and directing the guerrilla attacks in South Vietnam was conclusive enough to make the war a case of external aggression. Kennedy had endorsed the strategy of flexible response. What did all the voluminous limited-war theorizing point to, what was the strategy of flexible response all about, if the United States was not to bring military rescue to an anti-Communist regime such as Saigon's when it was beleaguered by Communist arms? The limited-war strategists had urged that properly equipped and mobile conventionally armed troops and tactical air support could solve just the sorts of problems that Vietnam presented. The Kennedy administration still lacked an international success commensurate with the implied promises of the 1960 campaign; even after the Cuban missile crisis of 1962, the taste of triumph was flawed by the promise not to invade Cuba. All these considerations were the more persuasive to a President who had chosen as the style of his administration the most strenuous effort to project an image of tough virility since Theodore Roosevelt.

President Kennedy gave South Vietnam the advisers, the arms, the helicopters and airplanes, and the public commitment that the Taylor-Rostow mission recommended. Reluctantly, he also moved further than at first he had wanted to do toward a major manpower commitment; the American presence in South Vietnam grew from 800 personnel at the time of Kennedy's inauguration to 23,000 by November, 1963, about two-thirds of the latter being soldiers of the American Army. With this American presence, Kennedy tied the prestige of the United States to the government in Saigon for all the world to see.[35]

Despite the American support, and despite what had seemed to be surprising initial promise in the 1950s, that government as represented by the regime of President Diem failed to govern effectively. In particular, the Roman Catholic governing elite opened a grievous schism between themselves and the Buddhists, who at least vaguely represented the South Vietnamese majority. American military aid also did not prevent the Communist insurrectionaries from extending their control over wider areas of the countryside and displaying a consistent superiority over the Saigon government's Army of the Republic of Vietnam (ARVN). In these circumstances the Kennedy administration and its missions in Vietnam felt obliged to inform various South Vietnamese generals that they would not frown on a change of regime. On November 1, 1963, a military coup toppled Diem and his *éminence grise*, his brother Ngo Dinh Nhu, and both were murdered. The Diem regime by that time had almost lost the ability to prosecute the war, but the sequel to its collapse was more than a year of instability and rapidly dissolving cabinets in Saigon. The Communists apparently concluded that the fall of Diem, something of a symbol of Vietnamese nationalism in spite of his defects, was a signal for them to quicken their attacks on the outposts of Saigon's power. Through 1964 their offensives mounted in intensity, until early in 1965 they seemed about to gather into a climax that would cut South Vietnam in two at its narrow waist, isolate Saigon from the rest of the country, and complete the triumph of the National Liberation Front. Meanwhile the American role in encouraging the South Vietnamese generals to overthrow President Diem had tied the United States in a guilt-shadowed and therefore all the more irrevocable partnership with Saigon.

The assassination of John F. Kennedy followed by less than a month that of Ngo Dinh Diem. As early as May, 1961, Vice President Lyndon B. Johnson had returned from a visit to South Vietnam saying that the United States must extend itself to assure the defense of southeast Asia, lest a series of successive Communist advances make "the vast Pacific . . . a Red Sea."[36] In the first year of his Presidency, Johnson was much occupied with the problems of simultaneously grasping the reins of executive power and ensuring that he retained them by campaigning for election. He gave enough attention to the mounting Communist successes in Vietnam, however, to permit action on the old recommendation, colored by memories of Communist "sanctuaries" in the Korean War, that North Vietnam ought to be punished for its sponsorship of insurrection in the South by means of attacks on its own territory. The United States inaugurated Operation Plan 34A, consisting of American-sponsored covert attacks on the North, such as commando raids from the sea, sabotage by parachutists, and bombardment of coastal installations by PT boats; there were also bombing raids against the North by T-28s bearing Laotian air force markings, sometimes flown by Thai pilots. These clandestine operations helped produce a clash or clashes between North Vietnamese patrol boats and American destroyers in the Gulf of Tonkin in August, 1964, in response to which President Johnson sought and secured from Congress authorization to take necessary measures to repel attacks against United States forces and to prevent further aggression in southeast Asia.

Armed with this broad mandate, the Johnson administration moved in September toward a decision that direct American participation in the Vietnam War would have to be enlarged, and in particular that the United States would have to begin its own direct aerial attacks against the North.[37] As early as January, 1964, General Taylor had reported to Secretary McNamara that in order to defeat the insurgency in South Vietnam, "the Joint Chiefs of Staff are of the opinion that the United States must be prepared to put aside many of the self-imposed restrictions which now limit our efforts, and to undertake bolder actions which may embody greater risks." The bolder actions and greater risks would be justified because Vietnam presented "the first real test of our determination to defeat the communist wars of national liberation formula." The actions should include aerial bombing of North Vietnamese targets—at first still under South Vietnamese cover—commitment of American combat forces to South Vietnam as necessary, and direct American action against the North as necessary.[38] By August and the time of the Tonkin Gulf events and resolution, Maxwell Taylor had left the Joint Chiefs to become United States Ambassador to Saigon; from there he proposed alternate plans of increased American action, the choice to depend on how much confidence could still be placed on the Saigon government. The Joint Chiefs, now chaired by General Earle D. Wheeler of the Army, recommended the option favoring quick acceleration of United States action.[39] The President's principal civilian advisers tended to agree, and Johnson was not unreceptive to this direction of thought.

The advisers recommended that for any Viet Cong attack on an American or major South Vietnamese base, "a reprisal will be undertaken, preferably with[in] 24 hours, against one or more selected targets in the DRV [Democratic Republic of Vietnam, that is, North Vietnam]. GVN [Government of Vietnam] forces will be used to the maximum extent, supplemented as necessary by U. S. forces."[40] Safely elected in a campaign in which he opposed enlargement of the war, President Johnson accepted the reprisal recommendation after the Viet Cong attacked an American barracks at Pleiku, South Vietnam, on February 7, 1965. On Presidential orders, within fourteen hours carrier-based Navy jets raided a guerrilla training garrison at Donghoi, forty miles inside North Vietnam. A Viet Cong attack on another American barracks at Quinhon precipitated a second reprisal raid into the North on February 11. Having made the commitment to direct bombing of the North, however, President Johnson was not long content with mere tit-for-tat reprisals; the bombing might as well be altogether in earnest, albeit still avoiding the most politically sensitive targets where there was danger of bringing in additional Communist belligerents, such as the harbor of Haiphong. On February 13 the President ordered a sustained American bombing campaign against North Vietnam, called Operation ROLLING THUNDER.[41]

This rapid expansion of the war soon led to still further expansion. Sustaining the bombing campaign seemed to demand American ground troops to protect airfields in South Vietnam. As early as March 8, two battalions of Marines landed at Danang to defend the airfield there. The bombing of the North brought no quick conciliatory response from Hanoi, however, and no relaxation of the Viet Cong assault upon the South. Therefore the American military command in Vietnam, now headed by General William C. Westmoreland, still worried about the ability of the Saigon regime to survive and suggested increased participation in the war in the South by increased numbers of American ground troops. Within a month of their landing, the Marines at Danang were authorized to open offensive operations against the Viet Cong. "I propose to describe the new mission . . . as the use of marines in a mobile counter-insurgency role in the vicinity of Danang for the improved protection of that base and also in a strike role as a reserve in support of ARVN operations anywhere within 50 miles of the base," said Ambassador Taylor. At the same time, President Johnson decided to send ashore two additional Marine battalions and to increase American support forces in South Vietnam by 18,000 to 20,000 men.[42]

If these enlargements of the American role in Vietnam seem

abrupt, they were not so large and so abrupt as the Joint Chiefs of Staff would have liked. Rather:

> The Joint Chiefs of Staff recommend immediate initiation of sharply intensified military pressures against the DRV, starting with a sharp and early attack in force on the DRV, subsequent to brief operations in Laos and U. S. low-level reconnaissance north of the boundary to divert DRV attention prior to the attack in force. This program would be designed to destroy in the first three days Phuc Yen airfield near Hanoi, other airfields, and major POL [petroleum, oil, lubricants] facilities, clearly to establish the fact that the U. S. intends to use military force to the full limits of what military force can contribute to achieving U. S. objectives in Southeast Asia, and to afford the GVN respite by curtailing DRV assistance to and direction of the Viet Cong. The follow-on military program—involving armed reconnaissance of infiltration routes in Laos, air strikes on infiltration targets in the DRV, and then progressive strikes throughout North Vietnam—could be suspended short of full destruction of the DRV if our objectives were earlier achieved.[43]

The President and his civilian advisers were not ready to accept this military program for "full destruction of the DRV" if the enemy did not call off the war in the South. But the insistence of the military that only offensive military operations were doctrinally sound enough to promise success produced further rapid enlargements of the war once President Johnson made the plunge into direct American participation. The history of American military strategy had given no place to static defense in American military doctrine if the means for a more active campaign existed; this fact goes far to explain the shift of the Marines' role at Danang within one month from defense of the airport to "mobile counter-insurgency" within a fifty-mile radius. As additional American troops entered South Vietnam, their mission also fitted briefly into a strategy of creating enclaves fifty miles in radius. The aim of this strategy was to deny the enemy access to key areas. But the strategy remained too defensive to meet the American military's conception of the proper conduct of war. The military, both the Joint Chiefs and General Westmoreland in Vietnam, insisted that the enclave strategy give way to a "search-and-destroy" strategy, aimed at denying the enemy freedom of movement not just in selected areas but throughout South Vietnam, at carrying the war to the enemy, and at winning victory by the means sanctioned by the most deeply rooted historical American conceptions of strategy, the destruction of the enemy's armed forces and of his ability to wage war.[44]

In April, General Westmoreland's requests for addition American troops led to a decision to deploy the Army's 173rd Airborne Brigade, which by the end of June became engaged in the first major ground action of United States forces in Vietnam, the battle of Dongxoai, which resulted from a search-and-destroy mission into Viet Cong base areas. Westmoreland's request that brought the 173rd Airborne to Vietnam and the strategy according to which he employed the brigade promptly produced, before the month of April was out, a government decision to increase the ground forces in Vietnam to thirteen maneuver battalions and 82,000 men. By June 7, Westmoreland was asking for forty-four battalions; by July 30, the government agreed to grant this request, looking to a deployment of 194,000 United States troops in Vietnam. In the course of deciding upon these additional commitments of troops, the government in Washington also revised its strategy, to permit General Westmoreland "to commit U. S. troops to combat, independent of or in conjunction with GVN forces in any situation in which the use of such troops is requested by an appropriate GVN commander and when in [General Westmoreland's] judgment, their use is necessary to strengthen the relative position of GVN forces."[45] To give so free a range to General Westmoreland's judgment was to adopt an offensive strategy aimed at the destruction of the enemy. Westmoreland expected the forty-four-battalion force to establish a favorable balance of power in Vietnam by the end of 1965. He hoped for more troops with which to seize the initiative in 1966. His plan, he told Secretary McNamara in Saigon in July, would involve:

> Phase I—The commitment of U. S./F. W. M. A. [Free World Military Assistance] forces necessary to halt the losing trend by the end of 1965.
>
> Phase II—The resumption of the offensive by U. S./F. W. M. A. forces during the first half of 1966 in high-priority areas necessary to destroy enemy forces, and reinstitution of rural-construction activities.
>
> Phase III—If the enemy persisted, a period of a year to a year and a half following Phase II would be required for the defeat and destruction of the remaining enemy forces and base areas.[46]

Evidently the great world wars and the American military history that had preceded them had so conditioned American military thought that their influence could not be escaped however different the circumstances of new combats might be. While General Westmoreland and the Joint Chiefs opened an offensive strategy of destruction of the enemy armed forces on the ground, the aerial bombardment campaign against North Vietnam attempted a literal application of World War II's presumed lessons. In 1966 Walt Rostow called President Johnson's attention to the effects of sustained aerial attack on Germany's petroleum facilities late in World War II and argued: "With an understanding that simple analogies are dangerous, I nevertheless feel it is quite possible the military effects of systematic and sustained bombing of P.O.L. in North Vietnam may be more prompt and direct than conventional intelligence analysis would suggest."[47] The intelligence analysis in question indicated that North Vietnam depended so little on petroleum and nourished the war in the South with so little economic effort that bombing of the North's petroleum facilities would not much affect the war in the South or compel North Vietnam to make peace—nor would conventional aerial bombing of any targets in North Vietnam, because the country had too little industry and too primitive a transportation network to be susceptible to this kind of campaign. But the Joint Chiefs agreed with Rostow's analogy, and so the aerial campaign against North Vietnam's petroleum was attempted.

Clearly, President Kennedy's "whole new kind of strategy" for unconventional war had long since ceased to receive much attention beyond lip-service in the Vietnam War. But it was not only a possible new strategy for unconventional war that had fallen into the discard; so had much of the limited-war strategic thought of the 1950s. One of the problems that limited-war strategists had failed to face squarely was the difficulty of bringing armed forces with the strategic traditions of the American Army, Navy, and Air Force to conduct campaigns of carefully limited strategic objectives consistent with the presumably carefully limited policy objectives of limited war. The Army seized upon the idea of limited war as a means of keeping itself alive in the massive-retaliation era of the 1950s, and the Army consequently adjusted its tactics and weapons to the prospect of limited war. But it never made the requisite adjustment in its strategy, which the strategic decisions of General Wheeler and General Westmoreland in the Vietnam War showed to be still the historic strategy aimed at destruction of the enemy's armed forces, or if need be, "full destruction of the DRV."

Early in the Kennedy years, when the limited-war strategist General Taylor was at the height of his influence, the February, 1962, edition of the *Army Field Service Regulations* (FM 100-5) had dropped the familiar statement: "The ultimate objective of all military operations is the destruction of the enemy's armed forces and his will to fight."[48] Significantly, General Taylor, the limited-war strategist, objected from his post in Saigon when Washington dropped the enclave strategy for American ground forces in Vietnam and moved toward the search-and-destroy strategy. The decision to bring in the 173rd Airborne Brigade, said Ambassador Taylor, "comes as a complete surprise in view of the understanding reached in Washington [when he had recently visited there] that we would experiment with the marines in a counterinsurgency role before bringing in other U. S. contingents."[49] But experiments with new kinds of strategy and new kinds of war were ending. The Joint Chiefs and General Westmoreland preferred to proceed as though the Field Service Regulations had never changed—"to destroy enemy forces," to invoke again the old strategy of annihilation.

By early 1966, there were 235,000 American soldiers in Vietnam, and in pursuit of his effort "for the defeat and destruction of the remaining enemy forces" General Westmoreland was asking for reinforcements up to 459,000. By February, 1968, American troop strength had reached 495,000; but despite General Westmoreland's promises about the effect of such massive strength upon the enemy's ability to fight or even survive, the Viet Cong that month staged their shocking Tet offensive, and Westmoreland felt obliged to ask for still another 206,000 men. In response, President Johnson decided at length to begin reversing the Vietnam experiment in using World War II-style ground and air campaigns to annihilate elusive little armies in a small and primitive country. The enemy still survived, but further applications of massive American firepower across South Vietnam seemed likely to annihilate all too well the country the Americans had come to save.

The Indochina War brought a bitter dénouement to the long search for a restoration of the use of combat in the service of policy. If the war had been conducted with "a whole new kind of strategy" of counterinsurrectionary war, instead of with old strategies seeking the destruction of the enemy and his logistical systems by means of highly mechanized forces that had a hard time hitting him, conceivably the war might have gone better for the United States. Conceivably, but not probably; counterguerrilla war offers special problems of indecisiveness, and much of the whole larger problem of the use of combat is the persistence in twentieth-century warfare of that inability to produce decisions that overtook war in the nineteenth century, that World War II only superficially appeared to overcome, and that has so painfully reasserted itself in Korea and Indochina.

By the early 1970s, Indochina's renewed demonstration of the indecisiveness of conventionally armed combat had prompted a renewed interest in the option first explored during the middle 1950s, limited war to be fought with tactical nuclear weapons. The United States retained military commitments all over the world from which no likely administration in Washington would easily retreat, yet which might be faced with military challenges despite the disappearance of the bipolar pattern of world politics that had dominated the post-World War II period. On the other hand, all the perils of the doctrine of massive retaliation made that doctrine still seem dubious as a sole reliance in upholding military commitments, while limited war had not worked when restricted to conventional weapons because the costs were too disproportionate to the results. In this dilemma, tactical nuclear weapons again suggested themselves to strategists, as instruments which might conceivably restore decisiveness to combat and thus viability to the use of combat, to sustain American military commitments without going to the extreme of unleashing general nuclear war.

By the 1970s, there had been improvements in tactical nuclear weapons since the original debate of the 1950s. There were now available purely fission, not fusion, warheads whose explosive potential was counted in tons, not kilotons, but whose short-lived radiation effects could destroy enemy troops without causing unrestrained damage to civilian populations. "Fusion-enhanced radiation" or "neutron" warheads with relatively low blast- and heat-collateral effects might be employed with more precision and fewer effects on areas adjacent to impact than American conventional bombing in Indochina. Yet most of the dangers exposed in the earlier debate still clung to tactical nuclear weapons, including the strong possibility that in a confrontation with the Soviets, nuclear weapons might favor them more than the United States. Always, there remained the perils of any crossing of the nuclear threshold.[50]

Nevertheless, in his search for a strategy that would serve American interests over the long run, President Richard M. Nixon looked back to the one strategy that thus far had worked consistently, reliance on the nuclear deterrent. In the Nixon Doctrine of 1969 he announced that even in limited wars of a nonguerrilla character, the United States would expect the country under attack to provide the first line of defense, to hold off at least the first assaults of an aggressor, and perhaps to provide all the ground forces for the war. The Nixon Doctrine obviously implied a heavy reliance on air and sea power employing conventional explosives; but given the limitations of conventional air and sea power, either as deterrents or as weapons of decision, displayed since the North Korean invasion of South Korea in 1950, the doctrine also had to rely for its credibility on a suggestion of willingness to invoke nuclear war.

For the shorter run, President Nixon hoped that conventional air and sea power despite their limitations might serve his immediate military requirements in Vietnam. His predecessor's reversal of course in Vietnam in the last year of his administration, including a curtailment and then a suspension of bombing attacks on North Vietnam, had failed to entice the North Vietnamese and the Viet Cong to make peace by negotiation. Nixon campaigned for the Presidency in 1968 with the pledge that he had a plan to end the war in Vietnam, but his plan proved to include too much intentness on retrieving the huge American investment in a Westward-looking South Vietnam to achieve early progress in the peace negotiations. Thereupon the Nixon plan turned toward ending if not the whole war then at least American participation in ground combat in it. The means was a "Vietnamization" program of gradually transferring responsibility for ground combat to South Vietnamese troops, prepared as well as they could be for an enlarged role by an accelerated schedule of American aid and training, and supported by a reintensification of American aerial operations. In 1969, the administration formally authorized a return to bombing of the North on a limited scale in the form of "protective reaction" raids in response to enemy attacks on American aircraft. The Nixon administration exercised considerably less minute control of aerial operations than the Johnson administration, and it developed that the Seventh Air Force under General John D. Lavelle adopted a very broad interpretation of "protective reaction," including raids on such targets as oil and truck dumps. In June, 1972, however, the President himself responded to an enemy ground offensive with an avowed resumption of bombing of the North, to which was added the mining of Haiphong harbor.

Though the war persisted, and though aerial bombardment and naval interdiction remained as debatable methods of crippling an economically undeveloped country's war effort as they had proved to be in Korea, the aerial bombing campaign nevertheless permitted President Nixon to avoid any appearance of an intent to abandon South Vietnam, while still reducing American troop strength there from 565,000 to 24,000 by December 1, 1972. This plan seemed to suffice to remove from the Indochina War as a political issue much of the emotional voltage it had developed late in Lyndon Johnson's Presidency and in the Presidential campaign of 1968. It did not prevent military policy debates from continuing as a new staple of Presidential politics, as the specific issues of the Indochina War developed into more general debate about the influence of the American military and their characteristic conceptions of strategy upon the prospects for democracy in America and for peace in the world.

While Secretary McNamara, who initially encouraged the Vietnam adventure, had thought the United States should be ready to fight two and a half wars simultaneously, the Nixon administration, engaged in the awkward process of extracting the American military from one war—or officially, a half war—expressed the national disillusionment with such military adventures also by lowering the goal to readiness to fight merely one and a half wars. Eventually the Nixon administration preferred to discourage such a scale for measuring military means altogether. The two-and-a-half war concept, like all the motivations that had carried the Kennedy and Johnson administrations into the Indochina War, was linked to the Cold War perception, still dominant in the American government through most of the 1960s, of the Communist bloc as a monolith. The schism between Russia and China which became evident during the later sixties to all but the truest true believers in monolithic Communism much reduced the likelihood that the United States had to be ready for major wars in Europe and Asia simultaneously, while it also shed a new light on Vietnam of a kind that helped prepare the United States for eventual withdrawal. But these developments and the dilemmas of limited war still left a sufficient impression of confusing perils all over the world to encourage a return to the nuclear deterrent as the one unquestioned pillar of American military policy and strategy.

In his first Presidential press conference, on January 27, 1969, President Nixon defined the nuclear deterrent he sought as a "sufficient" deterrent, significantly looking back again to the Eisenhower administration and to the word Secretary Quarles had used in 1956. "Our objective," said Nixon, "is to be sure that the United States has sufficient military power to defend our interests and to maintain the commitments which this administration determines are in the interest of the U. S. around the world." "Sufficiency," he said, seemed to him a better description of his strategic goal than either "superiority" or "parity."[51] As the administration refined the President's definition of the desired deterrent, a sufficient deterrent came to appear as one that combined a capability to inflict assured destruction on the Soviet Union (though not necessarily retaining the McNamara definition of assured destruction as the capability to destroy 25 percent of Soviet population and industry after riding out a Soviet first strike); stability in a crisis, so that neither the United States nor an opponent would be tempted into a preemptive attack; a guarantee against the Soviet Union's developing an ability to inflict appreciably more damage on the United States than America could impose on Russia; and a capability to deny other nuclear powers than the Soviet Union, specifically China, an ability to damage the United States.[52]

Though by the 1970s the American and Soviet nuclear forces both were far less vulnerable than they had been in the first years of the nuclear rivalry, the balance of terror remained unstable enough to raise additional questions about what constituted sufficiency. In 1967, political and especially Congressional pressures had compelled Secretary McNamara to endorse a limited antiballistic-missile (ABM) system. The pressures sprang partly from illusions about the extent of Soviet ABM building, which might upset the nuclear balance by giving Soviet missiles and cities a high degree of invulnerability. Secretary McNamara was skeptical about what either the Russians or the United States could accomplish with ABMs; he thought that the technical problems that had led him to suspend the Nike/Zeus program still mainly applied, and that ABMs might worsen instability by setting off a race to build missiles to overcome them. Pushed into an ABM program, he may have chosen deliberately the weakest possible rationalization for it, by saying that the "Sentinel" system he was proposing was intended as a protection of cities against the marginal nuclear capabilities of China.[53]

By the time President Nixon took office, critics of the Vietnam War had tended to fix upon the ABM system as another target of their grievances against the military-industrial complex. Since it did not require opposition to the Vietnam War to share McNamara's misgivings that an offensive system cheaper than the ABMs could overcome any ABM system, ABM plans became highly controversial. But President Nixon and his Secretary of Defense, Melvin Laird, argued that the country must proceed with a limited ABM deployment, not primarily to protect cities against the Chinese as McNamara had said, but to protect the Minuteman retaliatory force against Soviet missiles. The increased accuracy of Soviet missiles, the great power of their large SS-9 missiles (how many of which they were deploying became a subsidiary controversy), and the possibility that the Soviets were mounting MIRV (multiple independently targeted reentry vehicle) warheads on their missiles raised the prospect, the administration said, that a Soviet first strike might substantially destroy the Minuteman force. The administration would replace the Sentinel ABM program with a revised "Safeguard" program to shield the American deterrent. Safeguard went forward after a 50-50 vote in the Senate in the summer of 1969 failed to remove it from an authorization bill, and it narrowly survived subsequent Congressional tests.[54]

In September, 1969, meanwhile, the Soviet Union passed the United States in the number of land-based intercontinental ballistic missiles it had deployed. The imminence of this event contributed to the decision for the Safeguard ABM system, and the desire to retain "sufficiency" in the face of it also sealed the American decision to offset Soviet numbers of missiles by beginning in 1970 the deployment of American MIRVs, in the form of Minuteman 3 launchers each of which carries three independently targeted warheads.[55]

Both MIRVs and ABMs illustrated the continuing possibilities for instability and all its dangers in the nuclear balance of terror. More encouragingly, in the winter of 1969 the United States and the Soviet Union opened a series of Strategic Arms Limitation Talks (SALT). The strategy intellectuals of the 1950s in the United States, and the corresponding strategists in the Soviet Union, had begun the discovery that since both superpowers shared an interest in survival and thus in nuclear stability, measures taken either unilaterally or by the two in agreement to impose limits on their arms race might contribute to assuring a peaceful world and enhance the national security of the power or powers initiating the measures at the same time. On the further exploration of this fortunate circumstance the SALT talks were at length founded.[56]

From the talks and the constraints affecting both sides in the Soviet-American nuclear arms race came the SALT agreements signed by President Nixon and the Soviet leadership on Nixon's visit to Moscow in May, 1972. Perhaps the most difficult of these agreements to achieve was the Treaty on the Limitation of Anti-Ballistic Missile Systems, in which the two powers acknowledged the destabilizing dangers in an ABM race but in that acknowledgment rejected the possibility of defending themselves by direct means against nuclear attack. The treaty limited both powers to not more than 200 ABM launchers at two locations in each country, one centered on the national capital and the other on an offensive missile site. It thus compromised the earlier American controversy about whether to defend cities or missile sites by providing for one location for each kind of protection. In doing so the treaty curtailed President Nixon's Safeguard program from fourteen to two sites, a deployment around the Grand Forks, North Dakota, air base and a projected deployment —unlikely ever to be undertaken—around Washington. The Soviet Union was limited to its existing ABM system around Moscow and to another deployment at a missile site of its own choosing.

The ABM treaty left each power dependent on its retaliatory capacity, but assured that the rival power could not defend against that capacity. It thus went a long way toward removing any remaining temptation to prepare for a preemptive strike, since now there would be no adequate defense against the enemy's retaliation. Thus it opened the way to another agreement, the Interim Agreement on Certain Measures with Respect to the Limitation of Strategic Offensive Arms. This executive agreement froze for a five-year period the United States offensive nuclear force at the existing 1,054 land-based missiles and 658 sea-based missiles, the Soviet force at some 1,618 land-based missiles—the number that the American intelligence community attributed to the Soviets at the time of the agreement—and 740 sea-based missiles. The agreement permitted modernizing these existing missile systems (and even certain changes in numbers of missiles if compensatory changes were also made). Although the agreement left the Soviet Union with more missiles and larger individual warheads, it prohibited conversion of launchers for "light" or older ICBMs deployed before 1964 into launchers for "heavy" ICBMs and thus limited deployment of the heavy Soviet SS-9 or larger missiles.

The United States negotiators believed they could accept the ratios also because of the continuing American lead in manned bombers and, more important, the American lead in developing multiple independently targeted warhead missiles. At the time of the agreement, 550 of the 1,000 American Minuteman missiles were or soon would be Minuteman 3s; their MIRV clusters would give the United States 2,204 land-based warheads. During the late 1960s, America's Polaris submarines were being refitted with missile launchers carrying three multiple reentry vehicles (MRVs, unlike MIRVs not independently targeted); and by the time of the SALT agreements, further conversion from Polaris to Poseidon missiles had begun, with the Nixon administration projecting twenty Poseidon submarines for 1973, each with sixteen missile tubes with ten to fourteen MIRV warheads per missile. In warheads, the United States led the Soviet Union by at least 5,200 to 2,500. Eventually, of course, the Soviet Union would overcome the American advantage in MIRV technology; but the Soviets could not test MIRVs sufficiently and deploy enough within the five years of the offensive arms agreement to threaten American sufficiency, and in time, it was to be hoped, qualitative agreements would be added to the initial quantitative ones.[57]

The 1950s were a decade of strategic thought; the 1960s proved to be a decade of military action with relatively little strategic writing, at least compared to the efflorescence of the 1950s. Considering the uncomfortable directness of the line that led from the limited-war strategic thought of the fifties to the Indochina War of the sixties, the relative subsidence of the strategy intellectuals may not have been altogether a misfortune. Amid the comparatively sparse strategic literature of the sixties, perhaps the most notable single work was the economist-strategist Thomas C. Schelling's *Arms and Influence* (1966). In this book Schelling summed up the changes that the nuclear age had worked upon the idea of military strategy by arguing that since nuclear weapons had made the destruction of the enemy too literally possible, the principal aim of strategy had shifted from destroying the enemy to hurting him, enough to coerce him into doing something or refraining from doing something as one might desire. (This observation was only partially accurate for the Indochina War; the notion of punishing North Vietnam enough to persuade Hanoi to cease sponsoring insurrection in the South was an explicit motive of the bombing campaign, especially among President Johnson's civilian advisers, but more grandiose motives of destruction still animated the military command.) When the influence of arms works most satisfactorily, Schelling went on, in deterrence and sometimes in "compellence"—Schelling's term for getting the opponent to do something rather than not do something—the threat of hurting rather than actual hurting produces the desired inaction or action. "Military strategy," said Schelling, "can no longer be thought of, as it could be for some countries in some areas, as the science of military victory. It is now equally, if not more, the art of coercion, of intimidation and deterrence."[58]

"There is a difference," Schelling pointed out, "between taking what you want and making someone give it to you. . . ."[59] The first is accomplished by brute force; it was the manner of most American, and many other, military victories in the past. The second is accomplished by the *diplomacy* of violence, using the threat of hurting an opponent or actually hurting him as a bargaining or negotiating tool to coerce him into helping you get what you want. The United States employed the power to hurt, the diplomacy of violence, occasionally in the past, as in punitive expeditions against unruly Indian tribes. But the main kind of American strategy had remained the strategy of brute force, of using military power to take what was wanted: "To seek out and destroy the enemy's military force, to achieve a crushing victory over enemy armies, was still the avowed purpose and the central aim of American strategy in both world wars. Military action was seen as an *alternative* to bargaining, not a *process* of bargaining."[60] In the nuclear age, in contrast:

> It is the power to hurt, not military strength in the traditional sense, that inheres in our most impressive military capabilities at the present time. . . . And it is pain and violence, not force in the traditional sense, that inheres also in some of the least impressive military capabilities of the present time—the plastic bomb, the terrorist's bullet, the burnt crops, and the tortured farmer.[61]

In Schelling's book, the strategists' search for a viable use of combat, violence, and military force continued, even while American strategy in Indochina was demonstrating how easy it is for sophisticated new strategic ideas such as those that Schelling offered to become blurred into old ideas, enough to vitiate whatever redemptive qualities the new ideas might have. A more modest book published the following year might seem more consistent with the experience of the Indochina War. In *Military Strategy: A General Theory of Power Control*, Rear Admiral J. C. Wylie, Deputy Commander in Chief of United States Naval Forces in Europe, questioned the utility of any military form of strategy and any active use of military violence as a servant of policy except as a final resort, especially for powers seeking essentially to preserve the international status quo as the United States must do. He questioned the utility of military strategy and the use of military violence by questioning the familiar dictum, fundamental to almost all twentieth-century strategic thought, that "war is a continuation of policy." Contrary to that dictum, Admiral Wylie argued, war and the use of military violence inevitably cripple the policies in whose name they are invoked and shape new policies. War creates a momentum of its own; the use of violence cannot be so nicely controlled and restrained as strategists such as Schelling would have it.

> War for a nonaggressor nation [said Admiral Wylie] is actually a nearly complete collapse of policy. Once war comes, then nearly all prewar policy is utterly invalid because the setting in which it was designed to function no longer corresponds with the facts of reality. When war comes, we at once move into a radically different world.[62]

The reader recalling our Civil War chapters may reflect that Abraham Lincoln would have recognized and accepted Admiral Wylie's argument. Lincoln struggled unsuccessfully to prevent the Civil War from generating its own unlimited, revolutionary momentum at the expense of controlled policy long before the age of nuclear weapons. Despite the sophistication of some American strategic thought in the nuclear age, Lincoln's and Wylie's fears of the momentum generated by the unleashing of military violence still seem closer to comprehending reality than do theories calling for the measured control of applications of violence. After the experiences of Indochina, the idea that the United States can work its will in distant parts of the world by means of the measured, controlled application of punitive violence seems especially dubious. America's opponents in the locality involved, like the North Vietnamese, will almost certainly feel too much larger a stake in the outcome of a contest on their home grounds than does the United States itself, to prove susceptible to manipulation by measured applications of violence from distant Washington. The return of American strategy to unlimited, annihilative aims in a contest such as the Vietnam War was predicted by William Howard Gardiner in the Naval Institute *Proceedings* as long ago as the 1920s, because in such a war a resort to unlimited destruction would be implicit in the American problem:

> There is great importance [said Gardiner] in the fact that in a war between the United States and an Asiatic power the latter's aims would seem distinctly "limited" to many Americans, whereas, in order to maintain our position in Asiatic affairs, we might have to aim at "unlimited" reduction of the enemy's country, though not necessarily by invasion in force. In other words, the geographic distribution of interests is such that the inauguration of a "limited" war by an Asiatic power would be likely to compel us to carry through an "unlimited" war to victory as the only alternative to accepting defeat. Conse-

quently, the enemy's combativeness would be aroused to the utmost while some among us probably would rather yield than continue the war.[63]

At no point on the spectrum of violence does the use of combat offer much promise for the United States today. If the nuclear deterrent itself should fail, it is difficult to imagine the strategic nuclear forces as hurting, in Schelling's sense, without destroying. If the Soviet and American deterrent forces should be released into action, they both would be likely to prove all too sufficient. The very hardening of the missile sites of both rivals, which enhanced the deterrent effect of both retaliatory forces and the stability of the nuclear balance during the 1960s, would make controlled and discriminating general war unlikely in the 1970s if deterrence should fail, because destroying the enemy's strategic force would require so overwhelming a weight of nuclear weapons that it would be bound to destroy much or most of his society in the process. It remains difficult also to imagine tactical nuclear war that would not be either a very brief eruption giving way quickly to a different kind of bargaining if the world were very lucky, or the prelude to general war. Because the record of nonnuclear limited war in obtaining acceptable decisions at tolerable cost is also scarcely heartening, the history of usable combat may at last be reaching its end.

Notes

The introductory quotation is from Colonel Ned B. Rehkopf, "Strategy," a lecture delivered at the Army War College, April 11, 1939, copy in the U.S. Army Military History Research Collection, Carlisle Barracks, Pennsylvania. Colonel Rehkopf was Assistant Commandant of the War College. For the quotation within his remarks he cites Rudolf von Caemmerer, *The Development of Strategical Science during the Nineteenth Century*, tr. Karl von Donat (London: Rees, 1905), p. 3.

INTRODUCTION

1. Carl von Clausewitz, *On War*, tr. Col. J. J. Graham, New and Revised Edition with an Introduction and Notes by Col. F. N. Maude (Eighth Impression, 3 vols., New York: Barnes and Noble, 1968 [First Edition, 1873]), I, 86. Subsequent citations refer to this edition. *Cf.* Carl von Clausewitz, *On War*, tr. O. J. Matthijs Jolles (New York: Modern Library, 1943), p. 62: ". . . tactics teaches *the use of the armed forces in engagements*, and strategy *the use of engagements to attain the object of the war*."
2. Alastair Buchan, *War in Modern Society: An Introduction* (Colophon Edition, New York: Harper & Row, 1968), pp. 81–82. Strategy in this large sense, called by Americans "national strategy," in Great Britain is likely to be called "grand strategy." For the nonmilitary usage of "strategy" in the theory of games, see Thomas C. Schelling, *The Strategy of Conflict* (Galaxy Edition, New York: Oxford University Press, 1968), especially pp. 3–6.
3. Earl Wavell, *Soldiers and Soldiering* (New York: Jonathan Cape, 1953), p. 47, quoted in Bernard Brodie, *Strategy in the Missile Age* (Paperback edition, Princeton: Princeton University Press, 1965), p. 12. Wavell of course was a British soldier, but he expressed aptly the sense of "strategy" which abounds in American military literature.

   Under the conditions prevailing during the long wars of Louis XIV, the expense of Europe's newly invented professional armies rendered it especially desirable to obtain military victories by means as bloodless as possible. Then, as Colonel F. N. Maude of the British army put it (*The Evolution of Modern Strategy: From the XVIIIth Century to the Present Time* [London: William Clowes and Sons, 1905], pp. 20–22):

   > . . . the skill and cunning of the leader in feints, ruses, and the dissemination of false intelligence, practically alone decided the result, and it was at this time that the word "Strategy" first made its appearance as a generic term to cover all these manifestations of intellectual activity on the part of the general. . . .
   >
   > Be that as it may, the net result of nearly half a century of continuous fighting was to establish a new word in all dictionaries, embodying a meaning which the philologist will hardly unreservedly sanction. For "Strategy" from its root means only the "Art of the leader," and in that "Art" a knowledge of and aptitude for tricks and chicane plays a very subordinate part indeed, as I propose in this and the following chapters to show.

4. Albert C. Wedemeyer, *Wedemeyer Reports!* (New York: Holt, 1958), p. 49. The Navy, long accustomed to participation in diplomacy, would have taken a somewhat broader view. The Naval War College and the Naval Institute *Pro-*

ceedings gave much attention to the advancement and protection of American business interests as a purpose of naval policy and strategy.

Nevertheless, the narrower conception of strategy that General Wedemeyer encountered at Leavenworth was prevalent consistently enough through American military history that it would be burdensome to encumber the text with examples of the evolution of the American military's definition of strategy. The evolution may be followed up to World War II in: H. Wager Halleck, *Elements of Military Art and Science* . . . (Third Edition, New York: D. Appleton, 1862 [First Edition, 1846]), p. 37; James Mercur, Professor of Civil and Military Engineering, United States Military Academy, *Elements of the Art of War. Prepared for the Use of the Cadets of the United States Military Academy* (Second Edition, Revised and Corrected, New York: Wiley, 1889), pp. 16, 272; Joseph M. Califf, First Lieutenant, 3rd U.S. Artillery, *Notes on Military Science and the Art of War* (Second Edition, Washington: James J. Chapman, 1891), p. 31; John Bigelow, *The Principles of Strategy Illustrated Mainly from American Campaigns* (New York: Greenwood Press, 1968, reprint of Second Edition, Revised and Enlarged, Philadelphia: Lippincott, 1894), p. 17; James S. Pettit, Captain, 1st U.S. Infantry, *Elements of Military Science, For the Use of Students in Colleges and Universities* (Revised Edition, New Haven: The Tuttle, Morehouse & Taylor Press, 1895), p. 84; Arthur L. Wagner, *Strategy. A Lecture Delivered by Colonel Arthur L. Wagner, Assistant Adjutant-General, U.S.A., to the Officers of the Regular Army and National Guard at the Maneuvers at West Point, Ky., and at Fort Riley, Kansas, 1903* (Kansas City: Hudson-Kimberly, 1904), pp. 3–5, 37–38, 54; Lieutenant Colonel G. J. Fiebeger, Professor of Engineering, United States Military Academy, *Elements of Strategy* (n.p., [1906?]), pp. 5–6; Commander Bradley A. Fiske, U.S.N., "Strategy," United States Naval Institute *Proceedings*, XXXIII (June, 1907), 489; Colonel William K. Naylor, General Staff, Director of the General Staff School, The General Service Schools, *Principles of Strategy with Historical Illustrations* (Fort Leavenworth: The General Service Schools Press, 1921), pp. 13, 29, 40; George J. Meyers, Captain, U.S.N., *Strategy* (Washington: Byron S. Adams, 1928), p. xiv; Oliver Prescott Robinson, Lieutenant Colonel, Infantry, U.S.A., *The Fundamentals of Military Strategy* (Washington: United States Infantry Association, 1928), p. 2; Command and General Staff School, Fort Leavenworth, Kansas, 1935–36, *The Principles of Strategy for an Independent Corps or Army in a Theater of Operations* (Fort Leavenworth: The Command and General Staff School Press, 1936), pp. ,-8, 37; Colonel Hollis LeR. Muller, Coast Artillery Corps, U.S.A., *Technique of Modern Arms* (Harrisburg: Military Service Publishiing Co., 1940), pp. 39–40.

5. Emory Upton, *The Military Policy of the United States* (Washington: Government Printing office, 1904).
6. Clausewitz, *op. cit.*, I, xxiii.
7. *Ibid.*, p. 2.
8. *Ibid.*, p. 5.
9. *Ibid.*, pp. 44–45, 284.
10. Gordon A. Craig, "Delbrück: The Military Historian," in Edward Mead Earle, ed., *Makers of Modern Strategy: Military Thought from Machiavelli to Hitler* (Paperback edition, New York: Atheneum, 1966), pp. 272–75. Delbrück's terms are *Niederwerfungsstrategie* and *Ermattungsstrategie*. The former, the strategy of annihilation, said Delbrück, "has only one pole, the battle," whereas the latter, the strategy of exhaustion, "has two poles, battle and maneuver."
11. Clausewitz, *op. cit.*, III, 115.

Part One. Waging War with Limited Resources, 1775–1815

1. Jan. 19, 1777, John C. Fitzpatrick, ed., *The Writings of George Washington* (39 vols., Washington: Government Printing Office, 1931–44), VII, 35.

CHAPTER ONE. A STRATEGY OF ATTRITION: GEORGE WASHINGTON

1. Sept. 8, 1776, John C. Fitzpatrick, ed., *The Writings of George Washington* (39 vols., Washington: Government Printing Office, 1931–44), VI, 28.
2. Even after the conclusion of the French alliance, Washington warned against resting hopes in it, lest the British take advantage of American relaxation to destroy the Continental Army before French help became sufficient to assure against defeat. *Ibid.*, XI, 352.
3. Maurice Matloff, *Strategic Planning for Coalition Warfare, 1943–1944 (United States Army in World War II: The War Department*, Washington: Office of the Chief of Military History, 1959), p. 5.
4. Douglas Southall Freeman, *George Washington: A Biography* (7 vols., New York: Scribner, 1948–57), III, 417, 451–52, 515.
5. Fitzpatrick, *op. cit.*, III, 436–39; IV, 494; *Journals of the Continental Congress* (34 vols., Washington: Government Printing Office, 1904–37), II, 339–41; Edmund Cody Burnett, *The Continental Congress* (New York: Macmillan, 1941), chap. VI; Christopher Ward, *The War of the Revolution*, ed. John Richard Alden (2 vols., New York: Macmillan, 1952), I, 135–50.
6. June 24, 1776, Fitzpatrick, *op. cit.*, V, 171.
7. Freeman, *op. cit.*, III, 458; Ward, *op. cit.*, I, 73–98.
8. Fitzpatrick, *op. cit.*, III, 379–89; V, 259; Freeman, *op. cit.*, IV, 83–85; Dudley W. Knox, *The Naval Genius of George Washington* (Boston: Houghton Mifflin, 1932), pp. 13–14; Piers Mackesy, *The War for America, 1775–1783* (Cambridge: Harvard University Press, 1965), pp. 57–60.
9. July 22, 1776, Fitzpatrick, *op. cit.*, V, 326.
10. Aug. 9, 1776, *ibid.*, p. 406.
11. Sept. 2, 1776, *ibid.*, VI, 6.
12. Freeman, *op. cit.*, IV, 194n; Fitzpatrick, *op. cit.*, VI, 6.
13. Sept. 8, 1776, Fitzpatrick, *op. cit.*, VI, 28–29.
14. April 5, 1776, *ibid.*, IV, 451n.
15. July 25, 1777, *ibid.*, VIII, 470.
16. July 9, 1776, *ibid.*, V, 239; May 9, 1776, *ibid.*, p. 27.
17. March 12, 1777, *ibid.*, VII, 272–73. For Washington's acquaintance with military literature, see Oliver L. Spaulding, Jr., "The Military Studies of George Washington," *American Historical Review*, XXIX (April, 1924), 675–80.
18. Dec. 22, 1777, Fitzpatrick, *op. cit.*, X, 188.
19. June 25, 1777, *ibid.*, VIII, 299.
20. Dec. 5, 1776, *ibid.*, VI, 330; Dec. 14, 1776, *ibid.*, p. 373.
21. Dec. 25, 1776, *ibid.*, pp. 440–41
22. Dec. 21, 1776, *ibid.*, p. 415. On Washington and the gathering of intelligence, see also Freeman, *op. cit.*, IV, 100; V, 482.
23. Fitzpatrick, *op. cit.*, XIX, 189.
24. Jan. 29, 1778, *ibid.*, X, 368. For a critical essay on Washington's use of cavalry, see Charles Francis Adams, *Studies Military and Diplomatic* (New York: Macmillan, 1911), pp. 59–113.
25. Aug. 4, 1775, Fitzpatrick, *op. cit.*, III, 386–87.
26. March 3, 1777, *ibid.*, VII, 223–34.

CHAPTER TWO. A STRATEGY OF PARTISAN WAR: NATHANAEL GREENE

1. Quoted in George Washington Greene, *The Life of Nathanael Greene* (3 vols., New York: Hurd and Houghton, 1867–71), III, 265.
2. Quoted in Allan French, "General Haldimand in Boston," Massachusetts Historical Society *Proceedings*, LXVI (1942), 91.
3. For remarkably perceptive comments on the early divergence of American war from European patterns of war, as well as on many related topics, see John Shy, "The American Military Experience: History and Learning," *Journal of Interdisciplinary History*, I (Winter, 1971), 205–28.
4. Jan. 20 and Jan. 19, 1777, John C. Fitzpatrick, ed., *The Writings of George Washington* (39 vols., Washington: Government Printing Office, 1931–44), VII, 43, 35.
5. For Howe's initial pronouncements in favor of pursuing a decisive battlefield victory, see Ira D. Gruber, *The Howe Brothers and the American Revolution* (New York: Atheneum, 1972), pp. 83, 104–107. Gruber suggests that in abandoning this aggressive design, General Howe may have been influenced by Admiral Howe's belief that peace depended on conciliatory overtures to the rebels, unmarred by excessive military ruthlessness. On the Howes' strategy, see also Sir William Howe, *The Narrative of Lt. Gen. Sir William Howe in a Committee of the House of Commons on 29th April 1779 . . .* (London: H. Baldwin, 1780); Troyer S. Anderson, *The Command of the Howe Brothers during the American Revolution* (New York: Oxford University Press, 1936); Gerald S. Brown, *The American Secretary: The Colonial Policy of Lord George Germain, 1775–1778* (Ann Arbor: University of Michigan Press, 1963), chap. V; Worthington C. Ford, "Parliament and the Howes," Massachusetts Historical Society *Proceedings*, XLIV (Oct., 1910), 120–43; Maldwyn A. Jones, "Sir William Howe: Conventional Strategist," and Ira D. Gruber, "Richard Lord Howe: Admiral as Peacemaker," in George Athan Billias, ed., *George Washington's Opponents: British Generals and Admirals in the American Revolution* (New York: Morrow, 1969), pp. 39–72, 233–59; Piers Mackesy, *The War for America, 1775–1783* (Cambridge: Harvard University Press, 1965), pp. 80–93, 109–12, 116–18, 121–30; Eric Robson, *The American Revolution: In Its Political and Military Aspects, 1763–1783* (Hamden, Conn.: Archon Books, 1965), pp. 93–122; Alan Valentine, *Lord George Germain* (Oxford: Clarendon Press, 1962), pp. 135–49.
6. Lieutenant General Burgoyne, *A State of the Expedition from Canada as Laid before the House of Commons by Lieutenant-General Burgoyne* (London: J. Almon, 1780); Sir Henry Clinton, *The American Rebellion: Sir Henry Clinton's Narrative of His Campaign, 1775–1782, with an Appendix of Original Documents* (Yale Historical Publications, Manuscripts and Edited Texts, XXI, New Haven: Yale University Press, 1954), pp. 60–84; George Athan Billias, "John Burgoyne: Ambitious General," in Billias, *op. cit.*, pp. 142–92; Brown, *op. cit.*, chaps. VI–VII; Jane Clark, "Responsibility for the Failure of the Burgoyne Campaign," *American Historical Review*, XXXV (April, 1930), 543–59; Mackesy, *op. cit.*, pp. 103–109, 112–24, 130–44; Hoffman Nickerson, *The Turning Point of the Revolution* (Boston: Houghton Mifflin, 1928); Valentine, *op. cit.*, chaps. XII–XX; William B. Willcox, *Portrait of a General: Sir Henry Clinton in the War of Independence* (New York: Knopf, 1964), pp. 142–96, and "Too Many Cooks: British Planning before Saratoga," *Journal of British Studies*, II (Nov., 1962), 56–90.
7. John Richard Alden, *The South in the Revolution, 1763–1789* (Baton Rouge: Louisiana State University Press, 1957); Edward McCrady, *The History of South*

Carolina in the Revolution, 1775–1780 (New York: Macmillan, 1901); David Ramsay, *History of the Revolution of South-Carolina . . .* (2 vols., Trenton, N.J.: Isaac Collins, 1785); Paul H. Smith, "The American Loyalists: Notes on Their Organization and Numerical Strength," *William and Mary Quarterly*, third series, XXV (April, 1968), 259–77, and *Loyalists and Redcoats: A Study in British Revolutionary Policy* (Chapel Hill: University of North Carolina Press, 1964).

8. For the beginnings of partisan warfare in the South, see Robert D. Bass, *Gamecock: The Life and Campaigns of General Thomas Sumter* (New York: Holt, Rinehart and Winston, 1961), pp. 53–73, and *The Green Dragoon: The Lives of Banastre Tarleton and Mary Robinson* (New York: Holt, 1957), pp. 84–94; Mark Mayo Boatner III, *Encyclopedia of the American Revolution* (New York: McKay, 1966), pp. 486–87, 941; Clinton, *op. cit.*, pp. 173–87; McCrady, *op. cit.*, pp. 525–64; Christopher Ward, *The War of the Revolution*, ed. John Richard Alden (2 vols., New York: Macmillan, 1952), II, 704–11. On the tactics of the southern partisans, see Robert C. Pugh, "The Revolutionary Militia in the Southern Campaigns, 1780–1781," *William and Mary Quarterly*, third series, XIV (April, 1957), 154–75; Jac Weller, "Irregular But Effective: Partisan Weapons Tactics in the American Revolution," *Military Affairs*, XXI (April, 1957), 118–31, and "The Irregular War in the South," *ibid.*, XXIV (April, 1960), 124–36.

9. Contemporary accounts of Camden include Otho Holland Williams's narrative in William Johnson, *Sketches of the Life and Correspondence of Nathanael Greene* (2 vols., Charleston, S.C.: A. E. Miller, 1822), I, 485–510; R. Lamb, *Original and Authentic Journal of Occurrences during the Late American War . . .* (Dublin: Wilkinson & Courtney, 1809), pp. 302–306; Ramsay, *op. cit.*, II, 146–49; William Seymour, "A Journal of the Southern Expedition, 1780–1783," *Historical and Biographical Papers of the Historical Society of Delaware*, II (Wilmington, 1896), 3–7; Banastre Tarleton, *A History of the Campaigns of 1780 and 1781 in the Southern Provinces of North America* (New York: Arno Press, 1968 [first published 1787]), pp. 100–11, 149–50.

10. Mackesy, *op. cit.*, p. 384. For Fishing Creek, Bass, *Gamecock*, pp. 96–111; Bass, *Green Dragoon*, pp. 100–26; Boatner, *op. cit.*, pp. 79–80; Tarleton, *op. cit.*, pp. 112–16, 149–50.

11. Robert D. Bass, *Swamp Fox: The Life and Campaigns of General Francis Marion* (New York: Holt, 1959), pp. 29–31, 36–92; Boatner, *op. cit.*, pp. 367–69, 575–83; Lyman C. Draper, *King's Mountain and Its Heroes* (Cincinnati: Peter G. Thomason, 1881; Spartanburg, S.C.: The Reprint Co., 1967); George Washington Greene, *op. cit.*, III, 34–134; Don Higginbotham, "Daniel Morgan: Guerrilla Fighter," in George Athan Billias, ed., *George Washington's Generals* (New York: Morrow, 1964), pp. 291–313; Johnson, *op. cit.*, I, 328–56; McCrady, *op. cit.*, pp. 651–702; George C. Mackenzie, *King's Mountain National Military Park, South Carolina* (National Park Service Historical Handbook Series No. 22, Revised Edition, Washington: Government Printing Office, 1956); Hugh F. Rankin, "Cowpens: Prelude to Yorktown," *North Carolina Historical Review*, XXXI (July, 1954), 336–69; Tarleton, *op. cit.*, pp. 211–22; Theodore Thayer, *Nathanael Greene: Strategist of the American Revolution* (New York: Twayne, 1960), pp. 279–99; Ward, *op. cit.*, II, 731–36. Thayer's is the modern biography of Greene; there is also an interesting sketch by Fletcher Pratt, "Nathanael Greene: The Quaker Turenne," in that author's *Eleven Generals: Studies in American Command* (New York: Sloane, 1949). For Greene's campaigns there is M. F. Treacy, *Prelude to Yorktown: The Southern Campaigns of Nathanael Greene* (Chapel Hill: University of North Carolina Press, 1963). My own

longer account is *The Partisan War: The South Carolina Campaign of 1780–1782* (Tricentennial Booklet No. 2, Columbia: University of South Carolina Press, 1970).

12. Boatner, *op. cit.*, pp. 1023–1029, is judicious in untangling disputed dates of incidents in the race to the Dan. Burke Davis, *The Cowpens-Guilford Court House Campaign* (Philadelphia: Lippincott, 1962); G. W. Greene, *op. cit.*, III, 148–209; Johnson, *op. cit.*, I, 386–474; Lamb, *op. cit.*, pp. 343–57; Henry Lee, *Memoirs of the War in the Southern Department of the United States* (Revised Edition, New York: University Publishing Co., 1869), pp. 232–88; Charles Stedman, *History of the Origins, Progress and Termination of the American War* (2 vols., Dublin: Byrne, Moore and Jones, 1794), II, 334–47; Tarleton, *op. cit.*, pp. 222–79, 303–25; Thayer, *op. cit.*, pp. 321–34; Franklin and Mary Wickwire, *Cornwallis: The American Adventure* (Boston: Houghton Mifflin, 1970), pp. 268–310.
13. Rawdon was governor general and commander in chief in India when he was in his sixties, under his later titles of Earl of Moire and First Marquess of Hastings; see "Hastings, Francis Rawdon-Hastings," *The Encyclopædia Britannica* (11th Edition, New York: Encyclopædia Britannica Co., 1910), XIII, 53–55. For Cornwallis's departure and the campaign from Guilford Court House through Hobkirk's Hill, see Bass, *Gamecock*, pp. 129–57; Bass, *Swamp Fox*, pp. 169–81; G. W. Greene, *op. cit.*, III, 233–53; Johnson, *op. cit.*, II, 44–45, 68–95, 99–119; Lee, *op. cit.*, pp. 315–33; Tarleton, *op. cit.*, pp. 279–86, 325–29; Thayer, *op. cit.*, pp. 341–48; Ward, *op. cit.*, II, 798–808; Wickwire, chap. XIV.
14. Bass, *Gamecock*, pp. 141–78; Bass, *Swamp Fox*, pp. 126–210; Boatner, *op. cit.*, pp. 50–51, 310–11, 376, 377, 384, 420, 677, 804–808; G. W. Greene, *op. cit.*, III, 254–320, 325–27; Johnson, *op. cit.*, II, 120–56; Lee, *op. cit.*, pp. 341–60, 371–80; Thayer, *op. cit.*, pp. 355–63; Ward, *op. cit.*, II, 809–24.
15. Bass, *Gamecock*, pp. 193–205; Boatner, *op. cit.*, pp. 350–56, 420, 678, 909–10, 1078; G. W. Greene, *op. cit.*, III, 327–405; Johnson, *op. cit.*, II, 156–57, 206–37; Lee, *op. cit.*, pp. 380–94, 446–74; Thayer, *op. cit.*, pp. 363–81; Ward, *op. cit.*, II, 824–34.
16. Greene to Thomas Jefferson, March 10, 1781, quoted in Thayer, *op. cit.*, p. 326; Greene to Henry Knox, July 18, 1781, quoted *ibid.*, p. 367; Greene to the Chevalier de la Luzerne, June 22, 1781, quoted in G. W. Greene, *op. cit.*, III, 253; Mao Tse-tung quoted in Peter Paret and John W. Shy, *Guerrillas in the 1960's* (Revised Edition, paperback, New York: Praeger, 1962), p. 14; for second Mao quotation, Mao Tse-tung, *Strategic Problems of China's Revolutionary War* (Peking: Foreign Languages Press, 1954), p. 69.
17. Clinton, *op. cit.*, chap. XXII; Mackesy, *op. cit.*, pp. 401–404, 406–12; Hugh F. Rankin, "Charles Lord Cornwallis: Study in Frustration," in Billias, *George Washington's Opponents*, pp. 202–204, 213; Wickwire, *op. cit.*, pp. 318–21; Willcox, *op. cit.*, pp. 381–91.
18. Clinton, *op. cit.*, pp. 301–24; Don Higginbotham, *The War of American Independence: Military Attitudes, Policies, and Practice, 1763–1789* (New York: Macmillan, 1971), pp. 376–79; Mackesy, *op. cit.*, pp. 409–11; Benjamin F. Stevens, ed., *The Campaign in Virginia, 1781: An Exact Reprint of Six Rare Pamphlets on the Clinton-Cornwallis Controversy* . . . (2 vols., London: J. Murray, 1889); Wickwire, *op. cit.*, chap. XV; Willcox, *op. cit.*, pp. 395–408.
19. July 15, 1780, Fitzpatrick, *op. cit.*, XIX, 174.
20. Mackesy, *op. cit.*, pp. 190–211, 225–32, 242–52, 261–66, 272–78, 281–97, 323–37, 375–400; G. J. Marcus, *A Naval History of England*, I, *The Formative Centuries* (Boston: Little, Brown, 1961), pp. 421–46.
21. For an appreciation of Admiral Lord Howe as a strategist, see Commander C.

F. Goodrich, U.S.N., "Howe and D'Estaing: A Study in Coast Defense," United States Naval Institute *Proceedings*, XXII (1896), 577–86, especially p. 586:

> Howe . . . in command of the defense fleet, exhibited at all stages a professional ability and a personal example well worthy of emulation. His preparation for guarding the channel at Sandy Hook, his manœuvring outside of Newport, his promptness in attacking such French ships as could be engaged on favorable terms are admirable. The essence of coast defense strategy is exhibited by him in using his fewer and weaker vessels at all times so as to impede and harass the enemy, hanging on his flanks, observing him, ready at any moment to profit by a temporary advantage and to strike quickly and sharply.

See also Ira D. Gruber, "Richard Lord Howe: Admiral as Peacemaker," in Billias, *George Washington's Opponents*, pp. 233–59.

22. Fitzpatrick, *op. cit.*, XXII, 103–107, 111–20, 143–44, 170–71, 204–209, 229–30, 400–403, 432–34, 450–51, 499–500; XXIII, 6–11, 33–34; Freeman, *op. cit.*, V, 286–321; Harold A. Larrabee, *Decision at the Chesapeake* (New York: Bramhall House, 1964), pp. 152–54; Mackesy, *op. cit.*, pp. 413–14.
23. Burke Davis, *The Campaign That Won America: The Story of Yorktown* (New York: Dial, 1970); Freeman, *op. cit.*, V, 322–91; Ward, *op. cit.*, II, 884–96.

CHAPTER THREE: THE FEDERALISTS AND THE JEFFERSONIANS

1. "Efficiency of Gunboats in Protecting Ports and Harbors, Communicated to Congress, February 10, 1807," *American State Papers, Naval Affairs* (4 vols., Washington: Gales and Seaton, 1834–60), I, 163.
2. Marion Mills Miller, ed., *Great Debates in American History* (14 vols., New York: Current Literature Publishing Co., 1913), II, 162.
3. Russell F. Weigley, *History of the United States Army* (New York: Macmillan, 1967), pp. 84–88. *The Federalist*, Numbers 4 (Jay), 5 (Jay), 8 (Hamilton), 13 (Hamilton), 14 (Madison), 16 (Hamilton), 22 (Hamilton), 23 (Hamilton), 24 (Hamilton), 25 (Hamilton), 26 (Hamilton), 28 (Hamilton), 29 (Hamilton), 30 (Hamilton), 41 (Madison), 45 (Madison), 69 (Hamilton), 72 (Hamilton), and 74 (Hamilton), in particular, touch on questions of national defense, Numbers 4, 23, 24, 25, 26, 28, 29, and 41 at some length. See Jacob E. Cooke, ed., *The Federalist* (Middletown, Conn.: Wesleyan University Press, 1961).
4. Weigley, *op. cit.*, pp. 88–93.
5. *Statutes at Large of the United States*, I, 350–59, 453–54; *American State Papers, Military Affairs* (7 vols., Washington: Gales and Seaton, 1832–61), I, 61–65, 68; *American State Papers, Naval Affairs*, I, 5–17, 25–28; John F. Callan, *The Military Laws of the United States* (Philadelphia: Childs, 1863), pp. 102–105; James D. Richardson, ed., *A Compilation of the Messages and Papers of the Presidents* (20 vols., New York: Bureau of National Literature, 1897–1917), I, 185; Emanuel Raymond Lewis, *Seacoast Fortifications of the United States: An Introductory History* (Washington: Smithsonian Institution Press, 1970), pp. 3, 14–25; Harold and Margaret Sprout, *The Rise of American Naval Power, 1776–1918* (Paperback edition, Princeton: Princeton University Press, 1966), pp. 28–38.
6. On the advantages of forts over ships, see H. Wager Halleck, *Elements of Military Art and Science . . .* (Third Edition, New York: D. Appleton, 1862), pp. 158–209; Lewis, *op. cit.*, pp. 3–12.
7. *U. S. Statutes at Large*, I, 552, 553–54, 556, 575–76; *Naval Documents Related to the Quasi-War between the United States and France* (7 vols., Washington:

Government Printing Office, 1935–38), I, 46, 58, 59–60, 64, 87; Sprout, *op. cit.*, pp. 38–39.

8. Report of Dec. 29, 1798, *American State Papers, Naval Affairs*, I, 65–68; *Naval Documents Related to the Quasi-War*, II, 129–34. Report of Jan. 12, 1801, *American State Papers, Naval Affairs*, I, 74–78; quotation from p. 75. The most important portions of the report of Dec. 29, 1798, are reprinted in Walter Millis, ed., *American Military Thought* (Indianapolis: Bobbs-Merrill, 1966), pp. 74–78.
9. *U. S. Statutes at Large*, I, 621–22; Sprout, *op. cit.*, pp. 43–49.
10. Eugene S. Ferguson, *Truxton of the Constellation: The Life of Commodore Thomas Truxton, U. S. Navy, 1755–1822* (Baltimore: Johns Hopkins Press, 1956), pp. 130–206; Dudley W. Knox, *The History of the United States Navy* (New York: Putnam, 1936), chaps. V–VIII; Fletcher Pratt, *The Navy: A History, The Story of a Service in Action* (Garden City: Garden City Publishing Co., 1941), pp. 86–135, and *Preble's Boys: Commodore Preble and the Birth of American Sea Power* (New York: Sloane, 1950).
11. *American State Papers, Naval Affairs*, I, 161–68; Howard I. Chapelle, *The History of the American Sailing Navy: The Ships and Their Development* (New York: Norton, 1949), chap. IV; Pratt, *The Navy*, pp. 144–46; Sprout, *op. cit.*, pp. 58–66.
12. *American State Papers, Naval Affairs*, I, 163, 194.
13. Chapelle, *op. cit.*, pp. 242–44; Weigley, *op. cit.*, pp. 104, 109, 114–15, 566.
14. Irving Brant, *James Madison: Commander in Chief, 1812–1816* (Indianapolis: Bobbs-Merrill, 1961), chap. IV; Harry L. Coles, *The War of 1812* (Chicago: University of Chicago Press, 1965), pp. 38–45.
15. Chapelle, *op. cit.*, pp. 252–54, 268–74; Coles, *op. cit.*, pp. 38–70, 107–35; Alex R. Gilpin, *The War of 1812 in the Old Northwest* (East Lansing: Michigan State University Press, 1958), chaps. V–XI; A. T. Mahan, *Sea Power in Its Relation to the War of 1812* (2 vols., New York: Scribner, 1903), II, chap. XI; Charles O. Paullin, *Battle of Lake Erie* (Cleveland: Rowfant Club, 1918).
16. C. S. Forester, *The Age of Fighting Sail: The Story of the Naval War of 1812* (Garden City: Doubleday, 1956), pp. 48–58; Knox, *op. cit.*, pp. 82–84; Mahan, *op. cit.*, I, 314–28; Charles O. Paullin, *Commodore John Rodgers, 1773–1838* (Cleveland: Clark, 1910); Pratt, *The Navy*, pp. 148–50.
17. Coles, *op. cit.*, pp. 71–76; Knox, *op. cit.*, pp. 94–95.
18. Coles, *op. cit.*, pp. 81–85; Forester, *op. cit.*, chaps. IX–X, XII; Knox, *op. cit.*, pp. 88–95, 100–108; Mahan, *op. cit.*, I, 407–22; II, 1–9; Pratt, *The Navy*, pp. 157–65, 184–93.
19. *American State Papers, Naval Affairs*, I, 278–79.
20. Coles, *op. cit.*, pp. 88–89; Knox, *op. cit.*, pp. 95–98.
21. Charles B. Brooks, *The Siege of New Orleans* (Seattle: University of Washington Press, 1961); Wilburt S. Brown, *The Amphibious Campaign for West Florida and Louisiana, 1814–1815: A Critical Review of Strategy and Tactics at New Orleans* (University, Alabama: University of Alabama Press, 1969); Chapelle, *op. cit.*, pp. 274–76, 298–99; Coles, *op. cit.*, pp. 149–86, 203–36; Mahan, *op. cit.*, II, chaps. XV–XVII; Neil Swanson, *The Perilous Fight . . . The Battle of Baltimore* (New York: Farrar and Rinehart, 1945).
22. Chapelle, *op. cit.*, p. 292; George Coggeshall, *History of the American Privateers, and Letters of Marque, during our war with England in the years 1812, '13 and '14* (New York: n.p., 1856); Coles, *op. cit.*, pp. 95–106; John Philips Cranwell and William B. Crane, *Men of Marque: A History of Private Armed Vessels out of Baltimore during the War of 1812* (New York: Norton, 1940); Forester, *op. cit.*, pp. 92–96; Mahan, *op. cit.*, II, chap. XIV; Sprout, *op. cit.*, pp. 79–85.

23. *American State Papers, Naval Affairs*, I, 278–79, quotation from p. 279; *U. S. Statutes at Large*, II, 789; Chapelle, *op. cit.*, pp. 279, 283–86; Sprout, *op. cit.*, p. 87.
24. Quoted in Russell F. Weigley, ed., *The American Military: Readings in the History of the Military in American Society* (Reading, Mass.: Addison-Wesley, 1969), pp. 9–15, quotations from pp. 12, 10. The principal parts of Calhoun's plan are also reprinted in Millis, *op. cit.*, pp. 91–102, and the plan appears in *American State Papers, Military Affairs*, II, 188–93, and in Richard K. Crallé, ed., *Reports and Public Letters of John C. Calhoun* (6 vols., New York: D. Appleton, 1866), V, 80–93.

Part Two. Young America as a Military Power, 1815–1890

1. U. S. Grant, *Personal Memoirs of U. S. Grant* (2 vols., New York: Webster, 1885), II, 140.

CHAPTER FOUR. THE AGE OF WINFIELD SCOTT

1. Winfield Scott, *Memoirs of Lieut.-General Scott, LL.D. Written by Himself* (2 vols., New York: Sheldon, 1864), II, 488.
2. J. F. Callan, *The Military Laws of the United States* (Philadelphia: Childs, 1863), pp. 266–67; *Statutes at Large of the United States*, III, 321; Emanuel Raymond Lewis, *Seacoast Fortifications of the United States: An Introductory History* (Washington: Smithsonian Institution Press, 1970), pp. 36–37. With the vagaries of subsequent legislation and naval construction, the ships-of-the-line eventually completed were *Franklin*, 74; *Columbus*, 74; *Washington*, 74; *Independence*, 74; *North Carolina*, 86; *Delaware*, 86; *Ohio*, 86; *Pennsylvania*, 120; *Vermont*, 86. *Alabama*, *Virginia*, and *New York*, all 86s, were begun but never completed.
3. *American State Papers, Military Affairs* (7 vols., Washington: Gales and Seaton, 1832–61), II, 304–13; III, 245–60. Much of the 1821 report is reprinted in Walter Millis, ed., *American Military Thought* (Indianapolis: Bobbs-Merrill, 1966), pp. 102–11.
4. *U. S. Statutes at Large*, III, 330; Lewis, *op. cit.*, pp. 25–66; Russell F. Weigley, *History of the United States Army* (New York: Macmillan, 1967), pp. 139–43, 163–64.
5. James Morton Callahan, *The Neutrality of the American Lakes and Anglo-American Relations* (Johns Hopkins University Studies in Historical and Political Science, XVI, Baltimore: Johns Hopkins University Press, 1898); Albert B. Corey, "Canadian Border Defense Problems after 1814 to Their Culmination in the 'Forties," *Report* of the Annual Meeting of the Canadian Historical Association, 1938 (Toronto: University of Toronto Press, 1938), pp. 111–20.
6. Howard I. Chapelle, *The History of the American Sailing Navy: The Ships and Their Development* (New York: Norton, 1949), pp. 312–18, 340–46; Dudley W. Knox, *A History of the United States Navy* (New York: Putnam, 1936), chaps. XIII–XIV; Harold and Margaret Sprout, *The Rise of American Naval Power, 1776–1918* (Paperback edition, Princeton: Princeton University Press, 1966), pp. 94–96; *U. S. Statutes at Large*, IV, 170.
7. Frank M. Bennett, *The Steam Navy of the United States* (Pittsburgh: Warren, 1896), chap. II; Chapelle, *op. cit.*, pp. 308, 367; Knox, *op. cit.*, p. 140; Samuel Eliot Morison, "*Old Bruin*": *Commodore Matthew C. Perry, 1794–1858* (Boston: Little, Brown, 1967), pp. 81–82; Sprout, *op. cit.*, pp. 111–12.

8. *American State Papers, Military Affairs*, IV, 105; Chapelle, *op. cit.*, pp. 412–13; Sprout, *op. cit.*, pp. 112–13.
9. Bennett, *op. cit.*, chaps. III–IV; Philip Cowburn, *The Warship in History* (New York: Macmillan, 1965), pp. 191, 194–95; Morison, *op. cit.*, pp. 127–32; Sprout, *op. cit.*, pp. 113–15, 124–26.
10. Bennett, *op. cit.*, chaps. III–IV; Cowburn, *op. cit.*, pp. 206–207; Morison, *op. cit.*, pp. 127, 130; F. L. Robertson, *The Evolution of Naval Armament* (London: Constable, 1921), chap. VII.
11. Bennett, *op. cit.*, chap. VIII; Morison, *op. cit.*, pp. 131–32, 274.
12. Sprout, *op. cit.*, p. 180, from 27th Congress, 2nd Session, Senate Documents, I (serial 395), 381.
13. Dobbins's most important statement of policy, his annual report for 1853, is reprinted in large part in Millis, *op. cit.*, pp. 137–42, from 33:1 House Executive Documents, I, pt. 3 (serial 712), pp. 297–319; *U. S. Statutes at Large*, X, 273; XI, 246–47, 318, 319.
14. *American State Papers, Naval Affairs* (4 vols., Washington: Gales and Seaton, 1834–60), IV, 160; Cowburn, *op. cit.*, pp. 209–14; Sprout, *op. cit.*, pp. 126, 145.
15. Scott, *op. cit.*; Charles Winslow Elliott, *Winfield Scott, The Soldier and the Man* (New York: Macmillan, 1937); James W. Silver, *Edmund Pendleton Gaines: Frontier General* (Baton Rouge: Louisiana State University Press, 1949).
16. Virgil Ney, *Evolution of the United States Army Field Manual, Valley Forge to Vietnam* (Combat Operations Research Group, CORG Memorandum, CORG-M-244, Prepared by Technical Operations, Incorporated, Combat Operations Research Group, for Headquarters United States Army Combat Developments Command, Fort Belvoir, Virginia, January 1966), pp. 8–9; Winfield Scott, *Infantry Tactics, or Rules for the Exercise and Manœuvres of the United States Infantry* (3 vols., New York: Harper, 1961); William J. Hardee, *Rifle and Light Infantry Tactics: For the Exercise and Manœuvres of Troops When Acting as Light Infantry or Riflemen* (2 vols., Philadelphia: Lippincott, Grambo, 1855). On the British army in the Napoleonic period, see John W. Fortescue, *A History of the British Army* (13 vols., London: Macmillan, 1899–1930), IV–X; J. F. C. Fuller, *Sir John Moore's System of Training* (London: Hutchinson, 1924); R. Glover, *Peninsular Preparation: The Reform of the British Army, 1795–1809* (Cambridge, England: Cambridge University Press, 1963); C. W. C. Oman, *History of the Peninsular War* (7 vols., Oxford: Clarendon Press, 1902–30); Peter Paret, *Yorck and the Era of Prussian Reform* (Princeton: Princeton University Press, 1966), pp. 204–208.
17. By such means, for example, Anthony Wayne routed the Indians of the Old Northwest at the battle of Fallen Timbers, August 29, 1794; see James Ripley Jacobs, *The Beginning of the U. S. Army, 1783–1812* (Princeton: Princeton University Press, 1947), pp. 173–76.
18. John K. Mahon, *History of the Second Seminole War, 1835–1842* (Gainesville: University of Florida Press, 1967), pp. 140–43, 150–67; Francis Paul Prucha, *The Sword of the Republic: The United States Army on the Frontier, 1783–1846* (New York: Macmillan, 1969), pp. 280–81.
19. Mahon, *op. cit.*; Prucha, *op. cit.*, chap. XIV; John T. Sprague, *The Origin, Progress, and Conclusion of the Florida War* (Facsimile Edition, Gainesville: University of Florida Press, 1964 [first published 1848]).
20. *American State Papers, Military Affairs*, IV, 2; Francis Paul Prucha, *A Guide to the Military Posts of the United States, 1789–1895* (Madison: State Historical Society of Wisconsin, 1964); Prucha, *Sword of the Republic*, pp. 134–37, 147–49, and endpaper maps.
21. Annie H. Abel, "The History of Events Resulting in Indian Consolidation

West of the Mississippi," *Annual Report of the American Historical Association for the Year 1906* (Washington: Government Printing Office, 1908), I, 233–450; Ralph K. Andrist, *The Long Death: The Last Days of the Plains Indian* (New York: Macmillan, 1964), pp. 3–12; Francis Paul Prucha, *American Indian Policy in the Formative Years: The Indian Trade and Intercourse Acts, 1790–1834* (Cambridge: Harvard University Press, 1962), pp. 224–49; *idem.*, "Andrew Jackson's Indian Policy: A Reassessment," *Journal of American History*, LVI (December, 1969), 527–39, especially pp. 536–39; *idem.*, "Indian Removal and the Great American Desert," *Indiana Magazine of History*, LIX (December, 1963), 299–322; *idem.*, *Sword of the Republic*, chap. XIII.

22. *American State Papers, Military Affairs*, VI, 149–55; 24:1 House Reports, II (serial 294), No. 401; Prucha, *Sword of the Republic*, pp. 339–47.

23. *American State Papers, Military Affairs*, VII, 779–86; 25:2 House Documents, II (serial 322), No. 59; 25:2 House Documents, IX (serial 329), No. 311; 26:1 Senate Documents, VI (serial 359), No. 379; Prucha, *Sword of the Republic*, pp. 342–57; Silver, *op. cit.*, pp. 216–57.

24. Prucha, *Sword of the Republic*, pp. 347–48, 357–64; 27:2 Senate Documents, I (serial 395), No. 1, pp. 61–62; 27:3 Senate Documents, I (serial 413), No. 1, pp. 188–89.

25. 29:1 Senate Executive Documents, I (serial 470), No. 1, p. 212; Robert M. Utley, *Frontiersmen in Blue: The United States Army and the Indian, 1848–1865* (New York: Macmillan, 1967), p. 54.

26. Francis B. Heitman, *Historical Register and Dictionary of the United States Army* . . . (2 vols., Washington: Government Printing Office, 1903), I, 65, 66, 141.

27. Alfred Hoyt Bill, *Rehearsal for Conflict: The War with Mexico, 1846–1848* (New York: Cooper Square Publishers, 1969 [first published 1947]), pp. 207–303; Robert Selph Henry, *The Story of the Mexican War* (Indianapolis: Bobbs-Merrill, 1950), chaps. XVI–XXII; Otis A. Singletary, *The Mexican War* (Chicago: University of Chicago Press, 1960), chap. IV; Justin H. Smith, *The War with Mexico* (2 vols., New York: Macmillan, 1919), II, chaps. XXII–XXVIII.

28. Bill, *op. cit.*, pp. 83–100, 119–61, 186–204; Brainerd Dyer, *Zachary Taylor* (Baton Rouge: Louisiana State University Press, 1946), chaps. VII–XI; Holman Hamilton, *Zachary Taylor: Soldier of the Republic* (Indianapolis: Bobbs-Merrill, 1941), chaps. XII–XVII; Henry, *op. cit.*, chaps. II–V, IX, XI–XII, XV; Edward J. Nichols, *Zach Taylor's Little Army* (Garden City: Doubleday, 1963); Singletary, *op. cit.*, chap. II; Smith, *op. cit.*, I, chaps. VIII–XIII, XVIII–XX.

29. Scott, *op. cit.*, II, 404, summed up the strategic purpose of his campaign to Mexico: "To compel a people, singularly obstinate, *to sue for peace*, it is absolutely necessary, as the sequel in this case showed, to strike, effectively, at the vitals of the nation." The decision to wage the campaign from Veracruz to the City of Mexico was made by President James K. Polk in consultation with his cabinet; but the strategy of the conduct of the campaign was Scott's. On Scott's policy in Mexico, see also Smith, *op. cit.*, II, 220–21.

30. Scott, *op. cit.*, II, chaps. XXXI–XXXIII; Bill, *op. cit.*, chap. IX; Douglas Southall Freeman, *R. E. Lee: A Biography* (4 vols., New York: Scribner, 1934), I, 253–70; Henry, *op. cit.*, pp. 337–45, 365–69, 379–81; Smith, *op. cit.*, II, chaps. XXV–XXVIII and pp. 226–32; Edward S. Wallace, "The United States Army in Mexico City," *Military Affairs*, XIII (Fall, 1949), 158–66. Elliott, *op. cit.*, interprets Scott's strategy differently, arguing that his first object was to see the enemy army "thoroughly beaten"—that is, that Scott pursued a strategy of destruction or annihilation against Santa Anna's army. Elliott argues that Scott fought the battle of Churubusco because "the fundamental principle that an

enemy's field army must be crushed before his fortresses are assailed was as sound as ever" (pp. 518–20). The future Confederate maritime raider Raphael Semmes, who accompanied the army to Mexico as a young naval officer, argued rather that the battle of Churubusco was a mistake inconsistent with "The object of General Scott's campaign [which] was to strike a vital blow at the enemy, by reaching, and possessing himself of his capital." Lieut. Raphael Semmes, U.S.N., *The Campaign of General Scott in the Valley of Mexico* (Cincinnati: Moore & Anderson, 1852), pp. 297–300. I think that Semmes is nearer the mark than Elliott, and that an interpretation attributing to Scott a strategy of annihilation does not square with the nature of the Mexican resistance or with Scott's campaign of maneuver. "The capital of an ancient empire, now of a great republic; or an early peace, the assailants were resolved to win," Scott says of his object, *op. cit.*, II, 488. He spoke of his desire, as he said at Chapultepec, "To economize the lives of our gallant officers and men . . ."; *ibid.*, p. 510.

31. Quoted in Henry, *op. cit.*, p. 320.
32. K. Jack Bauer, *Surfboats and Horse Marines: U. S. Naval Operations in the Mexican War, 1846–48* (Annapolis: United States Naval Institute, 1969), and "The Vera Cruz Expedition of 1847," *Military Affairs*, XX (Fall, 1956), 162–69; Morison, *op. cit.*, pp. 206–18.
33. Quoted in Henry, *op. cit.*, p. 344.

CHAPTER FIVE. THE FOUNDING OF AMERICAN STRATEGIC STUDIES: DENNIS HART MAHAN AND HENRY WAGER HALLECK

1. H. Wager Halleck, *Elements of Military Art and Science . . .* (Third Edition, New York: D. Appleton, 1862), p. 37.
2. Quoted in Crane Brinton, Gordon A. Craig, and Felix Gilbert, "Jomini," in Edward Mead Earle, ed., *Makers of Modern Strategy: Military Thought from Machiavelli to Hitler* (Paperback edition, New York: Atheneum, 1966), p. 77.
3. Quoted in David G. Chandler, *The Campaigns of Napoleon* (New York: Macmillan, 1966), p. 142.
4. Quoted *ibid.*, p. 141.
5. *Ibid.*, p. 138; Stanley L. Falk, "Artillery for the Land Service; The Development of a System," *Military Affairs*, XXVIII (Fall, 1964), 98; Albert Manucy, *Artillery through the Ages: A Short Illustrated History of Cannon, Emphasizing Types Used in America* (National Park Service Interpretive Series History No. 3, Washington: Government Printing Office, 1949), pp. 11–12; Harold L. Peterson, *Round Shot and Rammers* (Harrisburg: Stackpole, 1969), pp. 51–54.
6. Carl von Clausewitz, *On War*, tr. Col. J. J. Graham, New and Revised Edition with an Introduction and Notes by Col. F. N. Maude (Eighth Impression, 3 vols., New York: Barnes & Noble, 1968), I, 39, 40. Clausewitz was speaking here of war in the absolute, and elsewhere he qualifies such remarks; but his dramatic encomiums to the battle have always tended to overshadow the qualifications. A still useful introduction to Napoleonic strategy is F. N. Maude, "Strategy," *Encyclopædia Britannica* (Eleventh Edition, 29 vols., New York: Encyclopædia Britannica Co., 1911), XXV, 986–97, especially pp. 988–93. See also Chandler, *op. cit.*, especially Part Three, "Napoleon's Art of War"; Jean Lambert Alphonse Colin, *The Transformations of War*, tr. L. H. R. Pope-Hennessy (London: Rees, 1912); B. H. Liddell Hart, *The Ghost of Napoleon* (New Haven: Yale University Press, 1935); Maximilian Graf Yorck von Wartenburg, *Napoleon as a General* (London: K. Paul, Trench, Trübner, 1902).
7. Stephen E. Ambrose, *Duty, Honor, Country: A History of West Point* (Balti-

more: Johns Hopkins Press, 1960); R. Ernest Dupuy, *Where They Have Trod: The West Point Tradition in American Life* (New York: Stokes, 1940); Sidney Forman, *West Point: A History of the United States Military Academy* (New York: Columbia University Press, 1950). For a less laudatory view of Thayer than is customary in West Point histories, questioning whether the sort of professionalism he instilled in the officer corps was altogether desirable either for the Army or the country, see Marcus Cunliffe, *Soldiers and Civilians: The Martial Spirit in America, 1775–1865* (Boston: Little, Brown, 1968), pp. 156–62, 170–76. On military officership as a profession, see Samuel P. Huntington's already classic *The Soldier and the State: The Theory and Politics of Civil-Military Relations* (Vintage Books Edition, New York: Random House, 1964), especially chaps. I–II, and on the American military profession before the Civil War, chap. VIII. Huntington argues that there prevailed before the Civil War in the American officer corps not professionalism but "technicism," not military but various specialized technical skills. Nevertheless, the Military Academy went remarkably far toward establishing a military profession in a not especially congenial national environment.

8. Halleck, *op. cit.*, p. 37.
9. S. F. Gay de Vernon, *A Treatise on the Science of War and Fortification . . . to which Is Added a Summary of the Principles and Maxims of Grand Tactics and Operations* (2 vols., New York: J. Seymour, 1817); the excerpt from Jomini appears II, 385–490, and is based on Jomini's *Traité des grandes opérations militaires* (8 vols., Paris, 1804–16). See Forman, *op. cit.*, pp. 57–58; Douglas Southall Freeman, *R. E. Lee: A Biography* (4 vols., New York: Scribner, 1934), I, 76–77. As late as 1886, for example, the first section of a text prepared for the United States Artillery School was a translation from Jomini: John H. Calef, Captain 2nd Artillery, Instructor, Department of Military Art, United States Artillery School, *Part I. Military Policy and Institutions, Part II. Ancient and Modern Armies* (Fort Monroe: United States Artillery School, 1886), Part I, pp. 1–17.
10. Baron de Jomini, *Précis de l'art de la guerre* (2 vols., Paris: Librairie Militaire de L. Baudoin, 1894 [First Edition, 1838]), I, 173–74, 472–73. This became Jomini's most influential work. A popular nineteenth-century American translation was Capt. G. W. Mendell and Lieut. W. P. Craighill, trs., *The Art of War . . .* (Philadelphia: Lippincott, 1862). This edition has been reprinted (Westport, Conn.: Greenwood Press, 1971).
11. Jomini, *Précis*, I, 247–51.
12. *Ibid.*, pp. 249, 293–309.
13. See the interpretations by Brinton, Craig, and Gilbert, *loc. cit.*, especially pp. 90–92, and Michael Howard, "Jomini and the Classical Tradition in Military Thought," in Michael Howard, ed., *The Theory and Practice of War: Essays Presented to Captain B. H. Liddell Hart* (London: Cassell, 1965), pp. 3–20; the latter essay is reprinted in Michael Howard, *Studies in War and Peace* (New York: Viking, 1971), pp. 21–36. Of Jomini's doctrines of concentration and interior lines, Colonel F. N. Maude remarked in his *Britannica* article on "Strategy," *loc. cit.*, p. 992:

> These ideas are, after all, elementary, and readily grasped even by the average intellect, though many volumes have been devoted to proving them, and yet they are all that Jomini and his followers have to offer us—a fact that both explains and justifies the contempt with which military study was so long regarded by practical soldiers in England.

14. As translated by Brinton, Craig, and Gilbert, *loc. cit.*, p. 88.

15. Halleck, *op. cit.*, p. 37. Note that in 1936 the Command and General Staff School stated that the fundamental law of strategy is "BE STRONGER AT THE DECISIVE POINT"; Command and General Staff School, *The Principles of Strategy for an Independent Corps or Army in a Theater of Operations* (Fort Leavenworth: Command and General Staff School Press, 1936), p. 37.
16. Halleck, *op. cit.*, pp. 39–40.
17. *Ibid.*, especially pp. 42–43, 56–58, 61–87, 151–234, 327–41, 343–48.
18. *Ibid.*, pp. 155–234. The value of seacoast fortifications continued to be a prime tenet of American military thought to the Civil War; see Capt. E. B. Hunt, Corps of Engineers, U.S.A., *Modern Warfare: Its Science and Art. Read before the American Association for the Advancement of Science, at Newport, R. I., August 4, 1860. From the Advance Sheets of the New Englander, for Nov., 1860* (New Haven: Thomas J. Stafford, 1860). This work is concerned mainly with fortification.
19. Halleck, *op. cit.*, pp. 62–87.
20. *Ibid.*, pp. 89–92.
21. *Ibid.*, p. 116.
22. D. H. Mahan, *An Elementary Treatise on Advanced-Guard, Out-Post, and Detachment Service of Troops . . .* (Revised Edition, New York: Wiley, 1864), p. 30. On Mahan, see Thomas E. Griess, "Dennis Hart Mahan: West Point Professor and Advocate of Military Professionalism, 1830–1871," Ph.D. dissertation, Duke University, 1968.
23. Mahan, *op. cit.*, p. 200, quoted in R. Ernest and Trevor N. Dupuy, *Military Heritage of America* (New York: McGraw-Hill, 1956), p. 193, and in Russell F. Weigley, *Towards an American Army: Military Thought from Washington to Marshall* (New York: Columbia University Press, 1962), p. 51.
24. Mahan, *op. cit.*, p. 78.
25. *Ibid.*, pp. 30–31.
26. Clausewitz, *op. cit.*, I, 25, 23–24.
27. U. S. Grant, *Personal Memoirs of U. S. Grant* (2 vols., New York: Webster, 1885), I, 95; Mark Mayo Boatner III, *The Civil War Dictionary* (New York: McKay, 1959), pp. 860–61; Arcadi Gluckman, *United States Muskets, Rifles and Carbines* (Buffalo: Otto Ulbrich, 1948).
28. Charles Francis Atkinson, "Artillery," *Encyclopædia Britannica* (Eleventh Edition), II, 688–89; Manucy, *op. cit.*, pp. 19–20.
29. Stephen E. Ambrose, *Upton and the Army* (Baton Rouge: Louisiana State University Press, 1964), pp. 28–34, 56–60; A. F. Becke, *An Introduction to the History of Tactics* (London: Rees, 1909), pp. 57–108; John K. Mahon, "Civil War Infantry Assault Tactics," *Military Affairs*, XXV (Summer, 1961), 57–68.

CHAPTER SIX. NAPOLEONIC STRATEGY: R. E. LEE AND THE CONFEDERACY

1. *The War of the Rebellion: A Compilation of the Official Records of the Union and Confederate Armies* (4 series, 70 vols. in 128 vols., Washington: Government Printing Office, 1880–1901), Series One, XI, pt. 2, p. 497; hereafter cited as *O.R.*, with all citations referring to Series One.
2. John G. Nicolay and John Hay, *Abraham Lincoln: A History* (10 vols., New York: Century, 1890), IV, chap. XVII.
3. Roy P. Basler, ed., *The Collected Works of Abraham Lincoln* (9 vols., New Brunswick: Rutgers University Press, 1953), V, 98–99, Lincoln to Brigadier General Don Carlos Buell, Jan. 13, 1862, summarizes Lincoln's view of a broad-front strategy; in part it states:

> . . . I state my general idea of this war to be that we have the *greater* numbers, and the enemy has the *greater* facility of concentrating forces upon points of collision; that we must fail, unless we can find some way of making *our* advantage an over-match for *his*; and that this can only be done by menacing him with superior forces at *different* points, at the *same* time; so that we can safely attack, one, or both, if he makes no change; and if he *weakens* one to strengthen the other, forbear to attack the strengthened one, but seize, and hold the weakened one, gaining so much. . . . Applying the principle to your case, my idea is that Halleck shall menace Columbus, and "down river" generally; while you menace Bowling-Green, and East Tennessee. If the enemy shall concentrate at Bowling-Green, do not retire from his front; yet do not fight him there, either, but seize Columbus and East Tennessee, one or both, left exposed by the concentration at Bowling Green.

But Halleck, having been sent a similar document, said of Lincoln's plan: "To operate on exterior lines against an enemy occupying a central position will fail, as it has always failed, in ninety-nine cases out of a hundred. It is condemned by every military authority I have ever read." *O.R.*, VII, 533. Pedantry such as Halleck's will bring to mind the comment of Colonel F. N. Maude quoted in Chapter Five, note 13, above.

4. Of this campaign Lincoln said in his letter to Buell: "To illustrate [my propositions], suppose last summer, when [the Confederates at] Winchester ran away to re-inforce Mannassas, we had forborne to attack Mannassas, but had seized and held Winchester. I mention this to illustrate, and not to criticize." Basler, *op. cit.*, V, 98.
5. H. J. Eckenrode, *Jefferson Davis: President of the South* (New York: Macmillan, 1923), pp. 151–56, 161–66; Archer Jones, *Confederate Strategy from Shiloh to Vicksburg* (Baton Rouge: Louisiana State University Press, 1961), pp. 16–22; Frank E. Vandiver, *Rebel Brass: The Confederate Command System* (Baton Rouge: Louisiana State University Press, 1956), pp. 15–17, 23–28; *idem.*, *Their Tattered Flags: The Epic of the Confederacy* (New York: Harper's Magazine Press, 1970), pp. 88–94.
6. Douglas Southall Freeman, *R. E. Lee: A Biography* (4 vols., New York: Scribner, 1934), I, 431–33, 463–526, 633–38, and chaps. XXXII–XXXV.
7. *Ibid.*, pp. 606–607; *Official Records of the Union and Confederate Navies in the War of the Rebellion* (2 series, 31 vols., Washington: Government Printing Office, 1894–1927), Series One, VI, 119–44; hereafter cited as *O.R.N.*, with citations referring to Series One.
8. Freeman, *op. cit.*, I, 608.
9. John D. Hayes, ed., *Samuel Francis Du Pont: A Selection from His Civil War Letters* (3 vols., Ithaca: Cornell University Press, 1969), I, lxx–lxxi, 212–31; II, 33; *O.R.N.*, XII, 259–319.
10. *O.R.*, VI, 312–404, *passim*; Freeman, *op. cit.*, I, 609–31.
11. Hayes, *op. cit.*, I, lxxiv–lxxv, 224–25, 235, 254, 256–58, 263–64, 266–78, 285, 289, 296, 314n, 320n, 328n, 335–36, 346–58, 360–70, 374n, 375, 377–84, 408–409, 415–16, 418, 424; *O.R.*, VI, 133–67; Freeman, *op. cit.*, I, 623–24, 626, 629; Ralston B. Lattimore, *Fort Pulaski National Monument, Georgia* (National Park Service Historical Handbook Series No. 18, Washington: Government Printing Office, 1954). Not only did rifled artillery have longer ranges than smooth-bore guns, but it was highly pertinent to the bombardment of fortifications that rifles fired conical projectiles rather than the spheres fired by smooth-bores. Thus rifled projectiles had a greater weight in proportion to diameter, and the increased weight of the

bombarding projectiles was too much for the masonry walls of Fort Pulaski to bear under repeated blows.

12. Hayes, *op. cit.*, I, lxxiii, lxxx, xc, xcvi–xcvii, cv; II, 61, 74, 82, 150–51, 275–76, 353–54, 443–45, 450, 488, 544.
13. Freeman, *op. cit.*, I, 621.
14. *Ibid.*, p. 622.
15. *Ibid.*, pp. 625, 628; II, 1–14.
16. Lee made these statements at other times, Nov. 4, 1863, and June 8, 1863, but they reflect his consistent strategy; *ibid.*, IV, 176, 172; *O.R.*, XXIX, pt. 2, p. 819; XXVII, pt. 3, p. 868.
17. Clifford Dowdey, ed., and Louis H. Manarin, assoc. ed., *The Wartime Papers of R. E. Lee* (Boston: Little, Brown, 1961), pp. 151, 155–57, 159–61, 162–64, 167–69, 174–75; Douglas Southall Freeman, ed., *Lee's Dispatches, Unpublished Letters of General Robert E. Lee, C.S.A., to Jefferson Davis and the War Department of the Confederate States of America, 1862–65* . . . (New Edition, With Additional Dispatches and Foreword by Grady McWhiney, New York: Putnam, 1957), pp. 5–7; Douglas Southall Freeman, *Lee's Lieutenants: A Study in Command* (3 vols., New York: Scribner, 1942–44), I, 329–46.
18. *O.R.*, XII, pt. 3, p. 865.
19. Freeman, *Lee*, II, 35–40, 52–57, 61–66, 83–85, 94–96.
20. *O.R.*, XI, pt. 2, pp. 489–90; Freeman, *Lee*, II, 92–116; Thomas L. Livermore, *Numbers and Losses in the Civil War in America, 1861–65* (Boston: Houghton Mifflin, 1901), p. 86.
21. Dowdey and Manarin, *op. cit.*, pp. 198–99, 211–12; *O.R.*, XI, pt. 2, pp. 489–90, 498–99; Freeman, *Lee*, II, 86, 110–16.
22. For Lee's purposes, see his report, *O.R.*, XI, pt. 2, pp. 489–98, especially p. 497, or in Dowdey and Manarin, *op. cit.*, pp. 211–22, especially p. 221; Freeman, *Lee*, II, 230–32.
23. *O.R.*, XI, pt. 2, pp. 490–91, 498–99, 552–53, 623–24, 756, 834–36; Freeman, *Lee*, II, 122–35, 232–41; Freeman, *Lee's Lieutenants*, I, chaps. XXX–XXXI; G. F. R. Henderson, *Stonewall Jackson and the American Civil War* (2 vols. in one, New York: Grosset & Dunlap, 1949), pp. 344–57; Frank E. Vandiver, *Mighty Stonewall* (New York: McGraw-Hill, 1957), pp. 287–303.
24. *O.R.*, XI, pt. 2, pp. 491–94, 553–56, 624–27, 756–58, 836–37; Freeman, *Lee*, II, chap. XIII; Freeman, *Lee's Lieutenants*, I, chap. XXXII; Henderson, *op. cit.*, pp. 357–70; Vandiver, *Mighty Stonewall*, pp. 303–309.
25. *O.R.*, XI, pt. 2, pp. 494–98, 556–59, 562–65, 627–30, 659–88, 758–61, 837–40; Freeman, *Lee*, II, chaps. XIV–XVIII; Freeman, *Lee's Lieutenants*, I, chaps. XXXIII–XLII; Henderson, *op. cit.*, chap. XIV; Vandiver, *Mighty Stonewall*, pp. 309–22.
26. Freeman, *Lee*, II, 230–31, from E. P. Alexander, *Military Memoirs of a Confederate* (With an Introduction and Notes by T. Harry Williams, Bloomington: Indiana University Press, 1962 [First Edition, 1907, with the subtitle *A Critical Narrative*]), p. 171. For other calculations of casualties in the Seven Days, see *O.R.*, XI, pt. 2, pp. 24–41, 502–10; Livermore, *op. cit.*, p. 86.
27. *O.R.*, XI, pt. 2, p. 497.
28. Freeman, *Lee's Dispatches*, p. 56.
29. *O.R.*, XII, pt. 2, pp. 551–54; pt. 3, pp. 940–41; Freeman, *Lee*, II, 280, 298–301. Freeman stresses that Lee wished to avoid a general engagement *if* it had to be fought against the combined armies of Pope and McClellan, because then "the [numerical] odds against the Army of Northern Virginia would be hopeless . . ." (*Lee*, II, 298). Freeman goes on to say: "If, luckily, a part of Pope's army could be caught, it would of course be attacked, but an offensive leading to a battle

between the whole of the two armies would entail losses to the Confederates that could not then be replaced, even if a victory were gained" (*ibid.*).

30. Livermore, *op. cit.*, pp. 88–89. Freeman, *Lee*, II, 344, from *O.R.*, XII, pt. 2, pp. 250–62, 810–14, gives 14,462 Federal casualties, 9,112 Confederate for the campaign.
31. According to Livermore's figures, the Federals lost 10,096 killed and wounded out of 75,696 engaged; the Confederates, 9,108 killed and wounded out of 48,527. It was the large number of Federals missing that turned the total casualty count markedly in Lee's favor. Boatner, *op. cit.*, p. 105, from Livermore, *op. cit.*, pp. 88–89. Freeman points out that an exceptionally large number of the Confederate casualties were reported only slightly wounded; *Lee*, II, 344, from *O.R.*, XII, pt. 2, p. 657.
32. Freeman, *Lee*, II, 348–49.
33. *O.R.*, XIX, pt. 1, p. 144; pt. 2, pp. 590–92, 593–94, 596–99, 600–603, some of this material appearing also in Dowdey and Manarin, *op. cit.*, pp. 292–96, 297–301; Freeman, *Lee*, II, 350–52.
34. Freeman, *Lee*, II, 358–60, based in part on a conversation of Lee's reported by J. G. Walker in Robert Underwood Johnson and Clarence Clough Buel, eds., *Battles and Leaders of the Civil War* (4 vols., New York: Century, 1884–88), II, 604–605.
35. Livermore, *op. cit.*, p. 92, estimates Federal strength at Antietam at 75,316 effectives and Confederate strength at 51,844 effectives. Confederate writers tend to estimate Confederate strength as much lower. Freeman puts it at less than 40,000; *Lee*, II, 383.
36. Livermore, *op. cit.*, pp. 92–94. The higher losses of the army that fought on the tactical defensive can be explained by the desperation with which Lee's army had to struggle against heavy numerical odds, so that much of the time their last-minute reinforcements were counterattacking to retrieve crumbling positions or engaged in hand-to-hand combat.
37. Boatner, *op. cit.*, p. 20; Freeman, *Lee*, II, 408–409; Freeman, *Lee's Lieutenants*, II, 199. About 1,300 cavalrymen of the Federal garrison escaped.
38. *O.R.*, XIX, pt. 2, p. 627. The letter quoted in Freeman, *Lee*, II, 425, and written about the same time also implies Lee's discontent with the defensive, for he said: "No sooner is one [Federal] army scattered than another rises up. This snatches from us the fruits of victory and covers the battlefields with our dead. Yet what have we to live for if not victorious?"
39. Freeman, *Lee*, I, 621.
40. Livermore, *op. cit.*, p. 96.
41. Edwin B. Coddington, *The Gettysburg Campaign: A Study in Command* (New York: Scribner, 1968), pp. 8–9; Freeman, *Lee*, II, 483, 499–502. Coddington points out, p. 8, that in February, 1863, Lee and Jackson directed Jackson's chief engineer, Jedediah Hotchkiss, to draw up a map of the Valley of Virginia "extended to Harrisburg Pa. and then on to Philadelphia—wishing the preparation to be kept a profound secret"; his source is Hotchkiss's Memorandum Book, Feb. 23, 1863, Hotchkiss Papers, Library of Congress.
42. John Bigelow, Jr., *The Campaign of Chancellorsville* (New Haven: Yale University Press, 1910). This book is one of the best campaign studies in American military literature.
43. *O.R.*, XXV, pt. 2, pp. 791–92, 841–43; XXVII, pt. 2, pp. 302–303, 305, 313; for the same material, Dowdey and Manarin, *op. cit.*, pp. 482, 483–84, 495–97, 502–503, 569–70; William Allen, "The Strategy of the Gettysburg Campaign: Objects, Progress, Results," "Campaigns in Virginia, Maryland and Pennsylvania, 1862–

1863," Military Historical Society of Massachusetts *Papers*, III (Boston: Griffith-Stallings, 1903), 415–48; Jefferson Davis, *The Rise and Fall of the Confederate Government* (2 vols., New York: Appleton, 1881), II, 437–38; Coddington, *op. cit.*, pp. 4–9 (including a notice of conflicting testimony of contemporaries as to whether Lee intended to fight a battle in the North, p. 601n); Jones, *op. cit.*, chap. XI. For criticism of Lee's failure to aid the West and of Lee's strategy generally, see Thomas L. Connelly, "Robert E. Lee and the Western Confederacy: A Criticism of Lee's Strategic Ability," *Civil War History*, XV (June, 1969), 116–32.

44. Longstreet wrote three versions of his understanding of the Pennsylvania campaign and of Lee's supposed pledge to fight on the tactical defensive: "Lee in Pennsylvania," in *The Annals of the War Written by Leading Participants North and South, Originally Published in the Philadelphia Weekly Times* (Philadelphia: Times Publishing Co., 1879), pp. 416–17; "Lee's Invasion of Pennsylvania," in Johnson and Buel, *op. cit.*, III, 244–47; and in *From Manassas to Appomattox: Memoirs of the Civil War in America*, James I. Robertson, Jr., ed. (Bloomington: Indiana University Press, 1960 [First Edition, 1896]), pp. 358–59. Freeman, *Lee*, III, 61–62, 80–85; Freeman, *Lee's Lieutenants*, III, chap. III.
45. Freeman, *Lee*, III, 161.
46. Coddington, *op. cit.*, gives overdue credit to Meade for directing the Army of the Potomac to victory. On the Confederate ammunition shortage, see *ibid.*, p. 791n; Alexander, *op. cit.*, pp. 421–23, 431–32; *O.R.*, XXVII, pt. 2, p. 321.
47. Coddington, *op. cit.*, chap. XIX; Freeman, *Lee*, III, chap. VIII; Freeman, *Lee's Lieutenants*, III, chap. VIII and pp. 178–87.
48. Livermore, *op. cit.*, p. 103.
49. *O.R.*, XXIX, pt. 1, pp. 609–33; Boatner, *op. cit.*, pp. 680–81; Freeman, *Lee*, III, 189–94; Freeman, *Lee's Lieutenants*, III, 264–69.
50. Connelly, "Robert E. Lee and the Western Confederacy," *loc. cit.*, p. 119; Richard D. Goff, *Confederate Supply* (Durham: Duke University Press, 1969). Confederate strategy in the West recalls the comment of Colonel William K. Naylor in his *Principles of Strategy with Historical Illustrations* (Fort Leavenworth: General Service Schools Press, 1921), p. 29: "There are three decisions to be made [in strategy]—the right one, which is best, the wrong one, which is next best, and no decision, which is the worst of all."
51. *O.R.*, VII, 131–44, 254–337; Charles P. Roland, "Albert Sidney Johnston and the Loss of Forts Henry and Donelson," *Journal of Southern History*, XXIII (February, 1957), 45–69.
52. *O.R.*, X, pt. 2, pp. 361, 365, 370–71, 381, 387, 389; Thomas L. Connelly, *Army of the Heartland: The Army of Tennessee, 1861–1862* (Baton Rouge: Louisiana State University Press, 1967), pp. 141–42, 145–57; Charles P. Roland, "Albert Sidney Johnston and the Shiloh Campaign," *Civil War History*, IV (Dec., 1958), 355–82, and *Albert Sidney Johnston: Soldier of Three Republics* (Austin: University of Texas Press, 1964), pp. 305–25.
53. *O.R.*, X, pt. 1, pp. 384–99; pt. 3, pp. 398–401; Connelly, *Army of the Heartland*, pp. 77–80; Livermore, *op. cit.*, pp. 79–80.
54. *O.R.*, X, pt. 1, pp. 762–79; Connelly, *Army of the Heartland*, pp. 175–78; T. Harry Williams, *P. G. T. Beauregard: Napoleon in Gray* (Baton Rouge: Louisiana State University Press, 1955).
55. *O.R.*, XVI, pt. 1, pp. 1087–1108; Connelly, *Army of the Heartland*, pp. 187–267; Livermore, *op. cit.*, p. 95; Grady McWhiney, *Braxton Bragg and Confederate Defeat*, I, *Field Command* (New York: Columbia University Press, 1969), pp. 261–62, 266–74, 281–336; Kenneth P. Williams, *Lincoln Finds a General: A*

Military Study of the Civil War (5 vols., New York: Macmillan, 1950–59), III, 428–31.

56. Unity of command in the West was of course basically a good idea, and if exercised vigorously it might have removed some of the problems that plagued Bragg's invasion of Kentucky. According to Archer Jones, *op. cit.*, pp. vi–viii, 84–88, 92–95, 97–122, 124–37, 219–28, Johnston would have liked to carry out a policy of concentration (including forces from the trans-Mississippi) to defeat Grant's army and to advance to the Ohio River, but he never received enough cooperation from above or below. Johnston's own accounts of his command are *Narrative of Military Operations, Directed, during the Late War between the States, by Joseph E. Johnston, General, C.S.A.* (With an Introduction by Frank E. Vandiver, Bloomington: Indiana University Press, 1960 [First Edition, 1874]), and "Jefferson Davis and the Mississippi Campaign," in Johnson and Buel, *op. cit.*, III, 473–75. See also Gilbert E. Govan and James W. Livingood, *A Different Valor: The Story of General Joseph E. Johnston* (Indianapolis: Bobbs-Merrill, 1956), pp. 162–74; McWhiney, *op. cit.*, pp. 338–41, 344–45; Vandiver, *Rebel Brass*, pp. 51–54, 56–60.
57. *O.R.*, XX, pt. 1, pp. 661–84; Livermore, *op. cit.*, p. 97.
58. *O.R.*, XXX, pt. 2, pp. 21–43; Livermore, *op. cit.*, pp. 105–106; Glenn Tucker, *Chickamauga: Bloody Battle of the West* (Indianapolis: Bobbs-Merrill, 1961).
59. *O.R.*, XXXVIII, pt. 3, pp. 612–27; Johnston, *Narrative of Military Operations*, pp. 297–350, and "Opposing Sherman's Advance to Atlanta," in Johnson and Buel, *op. cit.*, IV, 260–76; Govan and Livingood, *op. cit.*, chaps. XVIII–XXII; Livermore, *op. cit.*, pp. 119–21.
60. *O.R.*, XXXVIII, pt. 3, pp. 628–31; pt. 5, pp. 887–89; Govan and Livingood, *op. cit.*, pp. 316–22.
61. Johnston's accounts, especially "Opposing Sherman's Advance to Atlanta," *loc. cit.*, p. 276, exaggerate his success in depleting Sherman's numbers relative to his own and Confederate prospects for success at the time of his removal from command, but that does not detract from the merit of his strategy. John Bell Hood, *Advance and Retreat: Personal Experiences in the United States and Confederate States Armies*, Richard N. Current, ed. (Bloomington: Indiana University Press, 1959 [First Edition, 1880]) is Hood's statement of his case. For the casualties in Hood's campaigns, Vincent J. Esposito, ed., *The West Point Atlas of American Wars* (2 vols., New York: Praeger, 1958), I, Map 147; Livermore, *op. cit.*, pp. 131–33. The numbers of Confederate killed and wounded at Nashville are unknown.
62. Dowdey and Manarin, *op. cit.*, pp. 690–91.
63. Connelly, "Robert E. Lee and the Western Confederacy," *loc. cit.*; for a critical reply, defending Lee, see Albert Castel, "The Historian and the General: Thomas L. Connelly versus Robert E. Lee," *Civil War History*, XVI (March, 1970), 50–63. Although Castel scores some debating points against Connelly, I believe Connelly's basic charge that Lee was parochial must stand; Lee was first and last a Virginian, and his strategy reflected the fact. See also Jones, *op. cit.*, chap. XI and pp. 233–39. Other recent appraisals of Lee's generalship included J. F. C. Fuller, *Grant and Lee: A Study in Personality and Generalship* (Bloomington: Indiana University Press, 1957 [First Edition, 1933]); Louis H. Manarin, "Lee in Command: Strategical and Tactical Policies," Ph.D. dissertation, Duke University, 1965; Charles P. Roland, "The Generalship of Robert E. Lee," in Grady McWhiney, ed., *Grant, Lee, Lincoln and the Radicals: Essays on Civil War Leadership* (Evanston: Northwestern University Press, 1964), pp. 35–66.

64. Freeman, *Lee*, III, 398, from J. William Jones, *Personal Reminiscences, Anecdotes, and Letters of Gen. Robert E. Lee* (New York: D. Appleton, 1874), p. 40.
65. He began fortifying the length of his Rappahannock lines after Fredericksburg. Freeman, *Lee*, II, 480–81. See also Edward Hagerman, "From Jomini to Dennis Hart Mahan: The Evolution of Trench Warfare and the American Civil War," *Civil War History*, XIII (Sept., 1967), 197–220.

CHAPTER SEVEN. A STRATEGY OF ANNIHILATION: U. S. GRANT AND THE UNION

1. Adam Badeau, *Military History of U. S. Grant* (3 vols., New York: Appleton, 1882), III, 644.
2. U. S. Grant, *Personal Memoirs of U. S. Grant* (2 vols., New York: Webster, 1885), II, 345, 167.
3. Mark Mayo Boatner III, *The Civil War Dictionary* (New York: McKay, 1959), pp. 602–603; Thomas L. Livermore, *Numbers and Losses in the Civil War in America, 1861–65* (Boston: Houghton Mifflin, 1901), pp. 1–70; U. S. Department of Commerce, Bureau of the Census, *Historical Statistics of the United States, Colonial Times to 1957* (Washington: Government Printing Office, 1960), pp. 9, 12–13.
4. Grant, *op. cit.*, II, 505; William T. Sherman, *Memoirs of General William T. Sherman by Himself*, Foreword by B. H. Liddell Hart (2 vols. in one, Bloomington: Indiana University Press, 1957 [First Edition, 1875]), II, 15.
5. Edwin B. Coddington, *The Gettysburg Campaign: A Study in Command* (New York: Scribner, 1968), chap. VII; George Edgar Turner, *Victory Rode the Rails: The Strategic Place of the Railroads in the Civil War* (Indianapolis: Bobbs-Merrill, 1953); Thomas Weber, *The Northern Railroads in the Civil War, 1861–1865* (New York: King's Crown Press, 1952). For the growing complexity of logistics, see James A. Huston, *The Sinews of War: Army Logistics, 1775–1953* (*Army Historical Series*, Washington: Office of the Chief of Military History, 1966).
6. Annual Message to Congress, Dec. 3, 1861, Roy P. Basler, ed., *The Collected Works of Abraham Lincoln* (9 vols., New Brunswick: Rutgers University Press, 1953), V, 48–49.
7. *Ibid.*, IV, 271.
8. *Ibid.*, p. 332.
9. *The War of the Rebellion: A Compilation of the Official Records of the Union and Confederate Armies* (4 series, 70 vols. in 128 vols., Washington: Government Printing Office, 1880–1901), Series One, XI, pt. 3, p. 316; hereafter cited as *O.R.*, with all citations referring to Series One.
10. George B. McClellan, *McClellan's Own Story . . .* (New York: Webster, 1887), pp. 487–89.
11. *O.R.*, II, 197.
12. *Ibid.*, p. 199.
13. For a sympathetic defense of McClellan's generalship, see Warren W. Hassler, Jr., *General George B. McClellan: Shield of the Union* (Baton Rouge: Louisiana State University Press, 1957). Kenneth P. Williams, *Lincoln Finds a General: A Military Study of the Civil War* (5 vols., New York: Macmillan, 1950–59), I, chaps. IV–IX, XII–XIII; II, chap. XIV, is a caustic criticism. Peter S. Michie, *General McClellan* (New York: Appleton, 1901) is a gentlemanly work of criticism in the West Point tradition of strategic study. A brief evaluation can be found in T. Harry Williams, *McClellan, Sherman and Grant* (New Brunswick: Rutgers University Press, 1962).

14. Halleck's career is reviewed in Stephen E. Ambrose, *Halleck: Lincoln's Chief of Staff* (Baton Rouge: Louisiana State University Press, 1960). The often censorious Kenneth P. Williams is not unsympathetic to Halleck; for his discussion of Halleck's controversial decisions after Corinth, see *op. cit.*, III, 428–31.
15. K. P. Williams, *op. cit.*, II, chap. VII. For favorable appraisals of Lincoln's military judgment, see Colin R. Ballard, *The Military Genius of Abraham Lincoln* (Cleveland: World, 1952), and T. Harry Williams, *Lincoln and His Generals* (New York: Knopf, 1952).
16. To Congress, Basler, *op. cit.*, V, 145–46.
17. To Reverdy Johnson, July 26, 1862, *ibid.*, pp. 342–43.
18. *O.R.*, XII, pt. 2, pp. 50–53. For discussions, see Freeman, *Lee*, II, 263–64; K. P. Williams, *op. cit.*, I, 253–54. Pope had no legal right to consider oaths given under duress as binding. His order for his troops to live off the country was watered down within a few weeks; *O.R.*, XII, pt. 3, p. 573.
19. To Cuthbert Bullitt of New Orleans, July 28, 1862, Basler, *op. cit.*, V, 346.
20. Grant, *op. cit.*, I, 325–28, 377; Sherman, *op. cit.*, I, 250, 255–56; Bruce Catton, *Grant Moves South* (Boston: Little, Brown, 1960), pp. 186–88, 193–99, 202–204, 206, 266, 271, 274; K. P. Williams, *op. cit.*, III, 210, 218–19, 234, 266–67, 301–306, 335–36, 405, 410–11, 439.
21. *O.R.*, XXIV, pt. 1, p. 38; Shelby Foote, *The Civil War: A Narrative* (2 vols. to date, New York: Random House, 1958–), II, 381.
22. *O.R.*, XXIV, pt. 1, pp. 5, 58–59; Foote, *op. cit.*, II, 613; K. P. Williams, *op. cit.*, IV, 420.
23. Grant, *op. cit.*, II, 491–93, 499.
24. Catton, *op. cit.*, chaps. XX–XXIII; K. P. Williams, *op. cit.*, IV, chaps. XII–XIII.
25. Grant, *op. cit.*, I, 154, 164–66.
26. *Ibid.*, II. 177–78.
27. *Ibid.*, p. 135n; *O.R.*, XXXIII, 828.
28. Grant, *op. cit.*, II, 318; *O.R.*, XXXVII, pt. 2, pp. 558, 582.
29. Grant, *op. cit.*, II, 129.
30. *Ibid.*
31. *Ibid.*, p. 505.
32. *Ibid.*, p. 130.
33. *Ibid.*, pp. 140–41.
34. Boatner, *op cit.*, p. 165.
35. Grant, *op. cit.*, II, 131n; *O.R.*, XXXII, pt. 3, p. 246.
36. Freeman, *Lee*, II, 264, from *O.R.*, XI, pt. 2, p. 936.
37. Grant, *op. cit.*, I, 368–69.
38. *Ibid.*, p. 507.
39. *O.R.*, XLIII, pt. 1, p. 917.
40. *Ibid.*, pt. 2, p. 308.
41. H. Wager Halleck, *Elements of Military Art and Science . . .* (Third Edition, New York: D. Appleton, 1862), p. 91.
42. Sherman, *op cit.*, II, 128; *O.R.*, XXXIX, pt. 2, p. 503.
43. Sherman, *op. cit.*, II, 145; *O.R.*, XXXIX, pt. 3, p. 3.
44. Sherman, *op. cit.*, II, 227, 111–12.
45. DeB Keim, "Our Moral Weakness," *United States Service Magazine*, III (1865), 372.
46. Sherman, *op. cit.*, II, 111; *O.R.*, XLIV, 799.
47. Sherman, *op. cit.*, II, 227; *O.R.*, XLIV, 799.
48. Badeau, *op. cit.*, III, 642–44.
49. Sherman, *op. cit.*, II, 249.
50. B. H. Liddell Hart, *Sherman: Soldier, Realist, American* (New York: Praeger, 1958), pp. vii–viii.

51. B. H. Liddell Hart, *Strategy* (Second Revised Edition, paperback, New York: Praeger, 1967), p. 153.
52. Sherman himself minimized his departures from Grant's strategy. In his memoirs he made himself seem a much less distinctive strategist than Liddell Hart later made him out to be, and he did not emphasize much the indirect approach. He described his campaign against Joe Johnston in front of Atlanta as having evolved from an exchange of letters between Grant and himself, in which Grant's brief instructions reflected an identity of agreement between the two of them on a strategy aimed directly at the destruction of the enemy army:

> These [Sherman's] armies were to be directed against the rebel army commanded by General Joseph E. Johnston, then lying on the defensive, strongly intrenched at Dalton, Georgia; and I was required to follow it up closely and persistently, so that in no event could any part be detached to assist General Lee in Virginia; General Grant undertaking in like manner to keep Lee so busy that he could not respond to any calls of help by Johnston. Neither Atlanta, nor Augusta, nor Savannah, was the objective, but the "army of Jos. Johnston," go where it might. (Sherman, *op. cit.*, II, 25–26.)

Sherman in his memoirs did not treat his famous marches through Georgia and the Carolinas as a departure from the direct approach which made Johnston's army his first objective. He insisted that he would not have undertaken the marches if he had not considered that army, now commanded by Hood, already substantially destroyed and the force under George H. Thomas which he left to deal with it more than ample for the task. He held, however, that after the capture of Atlanta he could not yield the initiative to the enemy, and that to have followed Hood's army after it had degenerated into a band of raiders would have been just such a surrender of the initiative. At first, he said he hoped that when he struck out from Atlanta toward the sea Hood would have to follow him. (*Ibid.*, p. 154; Sherman's version of the evolution of the idea of the march to the sea, from which the reader may judge for himself the sincerity of his concern that Thomas should be capable of coping with Hood, may be followed *ibid.*, pp. 137–77.) When that hope failed, nevertheless:

> I then finally resolved on my future course, which was to leave Hood to be encountered by General Thomas, while I should carry into full effect the long-contemplated project of marching for the sea-coast, and thence to operate toward Richmond. But it was all-important to me and to our cause that General Thomas should have an ample force, equal to any and every emergency. (*Ibid.*, p. 162.)

Hood's army still remained Sherman's first responsibility; only after he was sure that that objective had been adequately provided for, he said, did he feel free to march through the back door of the Confederacy toward some other objective.

The whole of Sherman's memoirs suggests that he himself regarded the marches of his mobile columns through Georgia and the Carolinas less in the light in which Liddell Hart saw them than in the terms expressed by the late-nineteenth-century American military writer Captain John Bigelow in his textbook *Principles of Strategy*:

> As a rule [said Bigelow], the primary object of military operations should be to overpower, and, if possible, to capture or destroy, the hostile army. This is done by the use mainly of tactical strategy (outnumbering the enemy in battle) and subordinately of regular strategy (depriving the enemy of sup-

plies) and political strategy (embarrassing the enemy's government and carrying the war home to the people). (John Bigelow, *The Principles of Strategy Illustrated Mainly from American Campaigns* [New York: Greenwood Press, 1968, reprint of Second Edition, Revised and Enlarged, Philadelphia: Lippincott, 1894], p. 263.)

Bigelow was an admirer of Sherman and one of the first military writers to attempt to incorporate Sherman's marches into a textbook on strategy; but to him the marches remained subsidiary to the effort to overthrow the hostile army by direct confrontation. (*Ibid.*, pp. 144–47, 224–26, 229.)

53. Sherman as quoted in Keim, *loc. cit.*, p. 375; Sherman, *op. cit.*, II, 126; *O.R.*, XXXIX, pt. 2, p. 418.

CHAPTER EIGHT. ANNIHILATION OF A PEOPLE: THE INDIAN FIGHTERS

1. To Colonel Ranald S. Mackenzie, in instructions for a campaign across the Mexican border against the Kickapoos in 1873; quoted in Clarence C. Clendenen, *Blood on the Border: The United States Army and the Mexican Irregulars* (New York: Macmillan, 1969), p. 66, from Robert Goldthwaite Carter, *On the Border with Mackenzie, Or Winning West Texas from the Comanche* (New York: Antiquarian Press, 1959), pp. 399–406.
2. Francis Paul Prucha, *The Sword of the Republic: The United States Army on the Frontier, 1783–1846* (New York: Macmillan, 1969), especially chaps. II and XI.
3. Annie H. Abel, "The History of Events Resulting in Indian Consolidation West of the Mississippi," *Annual Report of the American Historical Association for the Year 1906* (Washington: Government Printing Office, 1908), I, 233–450; Grant Forman, *Indian Removal* (Norman: University of Oklahoma Press, 1932); Ralph C. Morris, "The Notion of a Great American Desert East of the Rockies," *Mississippi Valley Historical Review*, XIII (Sept., 1926), 190–220; Prucha, *op. cit.*, chap. XIII; Richard G. Wood, *Stephen Harriman Long, 1784–1864: Army Engineer, Explorer, Inventor* (Glendale, Calif.: Arthur H. Clark, 1966), pp. 116–17.
4. Francis Paul Prucha, *American Indian Policy in the Formative Years: The Indian Trade and Intercourse Acts, 1790–1834* (Cambridge: Harvard University Press, 1962), pp. 53–57.
5. Robert M. Utley, *Frontiersmen in Blue: The United States Army and the Indian, 1848–1865* (New York: Macmillan, 1967), pp. 60, 69–70, 262, and *passim.*
6. Stan Hoig, *The Sand Creek Massacre* (Norman: University of Oklahoma Press, 1961); C. M. Oehler, *The Great Sioux Uprising* (New York: Oxford University Press, 1959); Utley, *op. cit.*, pp. 264–69.
7. Ralph K. Andrist, *The Long Death: The Last Days of the Plains Indian* (New York: Macmillan, 1964), p. 95; David Lavender, *Bent's Fort* (Garden City: Doubleday, 1954), pp. 340–44, 362–63.
8. Quoted in Robert G. Athearn, *William Tecumseh Sherman and the Settlement of the West* (Norman: University of Oklahoma Press, 1956), p. 99, from Sherman to U. S. Grant, Dec. 28, 1866, in 39:2 Senate Executive Documents, II (serial 1277), No. 16, p. 4; the letter appears also in 40:1 Senate Executive Documents (serial 1308), No. 13, p. 27. For the contest along the Bozeman Trail, see the former document and the latter, pp. 24–38, 55–74; Andrist, *op. cit.*, chap. IV; Dee Brown, *Fort Phil Kearny: An American Saga* (New York: Putnam, 1962); Fairfax Downey, *Indian-Fighting Army* (Paperback edition, New York: Bantam, 1963), chap. III; Alvin M. Josephy, Jr., *The Patriot Chiefs: A Chronicle*

of *American Indian Leadership* (New York: Viking, 1961), pp. 281–85; Paul I. Wellman, *Death on Horseback: Seventy Years of War for the American West* (Philadelphia: Lippincott, 1947), pp. 49–68.

9. 39:2 Senate Reports (serial 1279), No. 156, "Condition of the Indian Tribes," pp. 3–10; Andrist, *op. cit.*, pp. 125–26, 132–34; National Park Service, *Soldier and Brave: Indian and Military Affairs in the Trans-Mississippi West Including a Guide to Historic Sites and Landmarks*, introduction by Ray Allen Billington (New York: Harper & Row, 1963), pp. 30–31, 35, 36.
10. The treaty is reprinted in Donald Jackson, *Custer's Gold: The United States Cavalry Expedition of 1874* (New Haven: Yale University Press, 1966), pp. 127–36, from *Statutes at Large of the United States*, XV, 635–40.
11. Quoted in Athearn, *op. cit.*, p. 228, from *New York Times*, Oct. 16, 1868.
12. Sherman to John Sherman, Sept. 23, 1868, quoted in Athearn, *op. cit.*, p. 223; Sherman to Generals Philip Sheridan, William B. Hazen, and Benjamin H. Grierson, Dec. 23, 1868, quoted *ibid.*, p. 274. For the fall-winter campaign of 1868, see also Andrist, *op. cit.*, pp. 155–64; Downey, *op. cit.*, pp. 69–83; Wellman, *op. cit.*, pp. 88–96.
13. Andrist, *op. cit.*, pp. 178–201; Downey, *op. cit.*, pp. 117–21; Virginia Weisel Johnson, *The Unregimented General: A Biography of Nelson A. Miles* (Boston: Houghton Mifflin, 1962), pp. 46–72; Wellman, *op. cit.*, pp. 103–23.
14. Andrist, *op. cit.*, pp. 239–45; Jackson, *op. cit.*
15. Andrist, *op. cit.*, pp. 245–48; Jackson, *op. cit.*, chap. VI.
16. The literature of the climactic Sioux war is immense; the war is covered in the histories of the Plains Indian wars already cited and, among many other works, in W. A. Graham, *The Story of the Little Big Horn* (Harrisburg: Military Service Publishing Co., 1941); Josephy, *op. cit.*, chap. VIII, "Crazy Horse, Patriot of the Plains"; Mari Sandoz, *The Battle of the Little Big Horn* (Philadelphia: Lippincott, 1966).
17. The lessons about guerrilla war learned by General Crook were of the kind that seemingly have to be learned anew with each American experience in guerrilla warfare. See Martin F. Schmitt, ed., *General Crook: His Autobiography* (Norman: University of Oklahoma Press, 1960); also Odie B. Faulk, *The Geronimo Campaign* (New York: Oxford University Press, 1969), and Jack C. Lane, ed., *Chasing Geronimo: The Journal of Leonard Wood, May-September, 1886* (Albuquerque: University of New Mexico Press, 1970).

Part Three. Introduction to World Power, 1890–1941

1. A. T. Mahan, *From Sail to Steam: Recollections of Naval Life* (New York: Harper, 1907), p. 283.

CHAPTER NINE. A STRATEGY OF SEA POWER AND EMPIRE: STEPHEN B. LUCE AND ALFRED THAYER MAHAN

1. Rear-Admiral S. B. Luce, U.S.N., "On the Study of Naval Warfare as a Science," United States Naval Institute *Proceedings*, XII (1886), 546.
2. Emanuel Raymond Lewis, *Seacoast Fortifications of the United States: An Introductory History* (Washington: Smithsonian Institution Press, 1970), pp. 66–72; Harold and Margaret Sprout, *The Rise of American Naval Power, 1776–1918* (Paperback edition, Princeton: Princeton University Press, 1966), p. 167, from United States Navy Department, *Regulations for the Government of the United States Navy, 1870*, pp. 36–37.

3. Russell F. Weigley, *Towards an American Army: Military Thought from Washington to Marshall* (New York: Columbia University Press, 1962), chaps. VII, IX.
4. *Report of the Secretary of War, 1884*, p. 49; quoted in John Bigelow, *The Principles of Strategy Illustrated Mainly from American Campaigns* (New York: Greenwood Press, 1968, reprint of Second Edition, Revised and Enlarged, Philadelphia: Lippincott, 1894), p. 55.
5. Bigelow, *op. cit.*, pp. 54–55.
6. Stephen E. Ambrose, *Upton and the Army* (Baton Rouge: Louisiana State University Press, 1964), pp. 147–48.
7. 65th Congress, 3rd Session, Senate Documents, VII (serial 7463), No. 418, *Navy Yearbook 1917 and 1918*, pp. 10–11, 15, 26, 53, 738; hereafter cited as *Navy Yearbook 1917 and 1918*.
8. *Statutes at Large of the United States*, XXIII, 434.
9. *Report of the Secretary of War, 1887*, pp. 118–21, 123–24; *1889*, pp. 68–74; *1890*, pp. 17, 46; and subsequent reports.
10. 49:1 Senate Executive Documents, XXVIII (serial 2395–96), No. 49, p. 6; Lewis, *op. cit.*, pp. 75–84. The report of the Endicott Board is reprinted in part in Walter Millis, ed., *American Military Thought* (Indianapolis: Bobbs-Merrill, 1966), pp. 196–207. James Mercur, Professor of Civil and Military Engineering, United States Military Academy, set forth a conception of war similar to that of the Endicott Board in his *Elements of the Art of War. Prepared for the Use of the Cadets of the United States Military Academy* (Second Edition, Revised and Corrected, New York: Wiley, 1889), pp. 273–74:

> When a powerful nation makes war upon a weaker, to avenge a national insult or commercial injury, the objective is generally the capital of the country, by the capture of which, the payment of the expenses of the war, and the humiliation of the ruler, the object sought is accomplished. When an indemnity has been demanded and refused, the chief commercial cities are frequently selected instead of the capital, and being captured are held until the proper satisfaction is rendered.
>
> When the nations are more nearly equal in strength, and one or both has an extensive commerce either on land or sea, the merchant marine or some important commercial city may be selected for an objective, with a view to threatening great commercial damage by sudden attack, and thus forcing the country into a satisfactory settlement of differences.

11. Samuel Flagg Bemis, *A Diplomatic History of the United States* (Third Edition, New York: Holt, 1950), pp. 451–52; Dudley W. Knox, *A History of the United States Navy* (New York: Putnam, 1936), p. 326.
12. Theodore Ropp, "Continental Doctrines of Sea Power," in Edward Mead Earle, ed., *Makers of Modern Strategy: Military Thought from Machiavelli to Hitler* (Paperback edition, New York: Atheneum, 1966), pp. 446–56. For "Mahanite" ideas of sea power before Mahan, see Peter Karsten, *The Naval Aristocracy: The Golden Age of Annapolis and the Emergence of Modern American Navalism* (New York: Free Press, 1972), pp. 305–16; Robert Seager II, "Ten Years before Mahan: The Unofficial Case for the New Navy," *Mississippi Valley Historical Review*, XL (Dec. 1953), 491–512.
13. Karsten, *op. cit.*, *passim*, especially pp. 250–317; Henry Schindler and E. E. Booth, *History of the Army Service Schools* (Fort Leavenworth: Army Service Schools, 1918); Russell F. Weigley, *History of the United States Army* (New York: Macmillan, 1967), pp. 273–74, 617–18n.

14. John D. Hayes, ed., *Samuel Francis Du Pont: A Selection from His Civil War Letters* (3 vols., Ithaca: Cornell University Press, 1969), I, lxxvi–xciii, xcvi–xcvii; II and III, *passim*; *Official Records of the Union and Confederate Navies in the War of the Rebellion* (2 series, 31 vols., Washington: Government Printing Office, 1894–1927), Series One, XIII–XVI, especially XIV, 3–31.
15. Albert Gleaves, *Life and Letters of Rear Admiral Stephen B. Luce* (New York: Putnam, 1925), pp. 101–103 and chap. X; John A. S. Grenville and George Berkeley Young, *Politics, Strategy, and American Diplomacy: Studies in Foreign Policy, 1873–1917* (New Haven: Yale University Press, 1966), chap. I, "The Admiral in Politics: Stephen B. Luce and the Foundation of the Modern American Navy," especially pp. 15–18.
16. Commodore Stephen B. Luce, U.S.N., "War Schools," United States Naval Institute *Proceedings*, IX (1883), 656.
17. Luce, "On the Study of Naval Warfare as a Science," *loc. cit.*, p. 529.
18. Stephen B. Luce, *Seamanship* . . . (Second Edition, Newport, R.I.: J. Atkinson, 1863).
19. Luce, "On the Study of Naval Warfare as a Science," *loc. cit.*, p. 546. The expectation that the study of warfare and strategy could become a science, so characteristic of the late nineteenth century, was especially strong in Luce. By the closing decade of the century, the expectation was entering upon a slow decline, but military fondness for precision long postponed its demise. "*War is a science and an art*," wrote Captain James S. Pettit of the 1st Infantry in 1895:

> . . . as a science it organizes and administers the affairs of armies and puts them into action. The art lies in the application of the principles laid down in the science. War is an experimental science; its rules are based upon the experiences of past wars and upon observations made in time of peace. Great generals have furnished the facts upon which lesser lights have based the science. (*Elements of Military Science, For the Use of Students in Colleges and Universities* [Revised Edition, New Haven: Tuttle, Morehouse & Taylor, 1895], p. 2.

By 1928, Lieutenant Colonel Oliver Prescott Robinson was much more cautious about calling war scientific:

> ART OF WAR. Art is skill, dexterity, an especial facility in performing any operation, intellectual or physical, acquired by experience or study. The conduct of war is an art, and even the most profound study of the science of war is only to be regarded as an essential part of the preparation of those charged with the conduct of military operations. (*The Fundamentals of Military Strategy* [Washington: United States Infantry Association, 1928], p. 13.)

As late as 1940, however, Colonel Hollis LeR. Muller wrote: "Undoubtedly, *strategy is the art of war* in the fullest sense of the term. But its principles must be regarded as a *science* which controls every detail of the military system." (*Technique of Modern Arms* [Harrisburg: Military Service Publishing Co., 1940], p. 9.)

20. Karsten, *op. cit.*, pp. 34, 48n, 326–34; A. T. Mahan, *The Gulf and Inland Waters* (New York: Scribner, 1883); Mahan, *From Sail to Steam*, *passim*, to p. 273; Commander A. T. Mahan, "Naval Education," United States Naval Institute *Proceedings*, V (June, 1879), 345–76; W. D. Puleston, *Mahan: The Life and Work of Alfred Thayer Mahan* (New Haven: Yale University Press, 1939), chaps. I–XII.

21. A. T. Mahan, *The Influence of Sea Power upon History, 1660–1783* (Boston: Little, Brown, 1890); *The Influence of Sea Power upon the French Revolution and Empire, 1793–1812* (2 vols., Boston: Little, Brown, 1892); *Sea Power in Its Relation to the War of 1812* (2 vols., Boston: Little, Brown, 1905).
22. Puleston, *op. cit.*; Margaret Tuttle Sprout, "Mahan: Evangelist of Sea Power," in Earle, *op. cit.*, pp. 415–45.
23. A. T. Mahan, *The Problem of Asia and Its Effect upon International Politics* (Boston: Little, Brown, 1900), pp. 18–20, 82–86, 124–39; A. T. Mahan, *The Influence of Sea Power upon the French Revolution and Empire, 1793–1812* (2 vols., Fifth Edition, London: Sampson Low, 1920), I, 95–96, 184; II, 106; A. T. Mahan, *Lessons of the War with Spain and Other Articles* (Boston: Little, Brown, 1899), pp. 300–301; Allan Westcott, ed., *Mahan on Naval Warfare: Selections from the Writings of Rear Admiral Alfred T. Mahan* (Boston: Little, Brown, 1942), pp. 50–60, 75–78. On the influence of Mommsen and Jomini, Mahan, *From Sail to Steam*, pp. 277–78, 282–83, 304, 305; Puleston, *op. cit.*, chaps. XI–XII, XV.
24. Mahan, *Influence of Sea Power upon the French Revolution and Empire*, II, 118–20; A. T. Mahan, *Naval Strategy, Compared and Contrasted with the Principles and Practice of Military Operations on Land* (Boston: Little, Brown, 1911), pp. 31–53, 130–66; Mahan, *Problem of Asia*, pp. 82–86, 124–39, 179–84; Westcott, *op. cit.*, pp. 50–60, 68–78.
25. Mahan, *From Sail to Steam*, p. 283; A. T. Mahan, *The Influence of Sea Power upon History, 1660–1783* (Twelfth Edition, Boston: Little, Brown, 1947), p. 288 (subsequent citations refer to this edition).
26. Mahan, *Influence of Sea Power upon History*, p. 138.
27. *Ibid.*, p. 89, and Mahan, *From Sail to Steam*, p. 283, for quotations. See also *Influence of Sea Power upon History*, pp. 288–89, 532–40. On the economic ends of Mahanian sea power, see Walter LaFeber, *The New Empire: An Interpretation of American Expansion, 1860–1898* (Cornell Paperbacks, Ithaca: Cornell University Press, 1967), pp. 85–93, and "A Note on the 'Mercantilistic Imperialism' of Alfred Thayer Mahan," *Mississippi Valley Historical Review*, XLVIII (March, 1962), 674–85.
28. Mahan, *Influence of Sea Power upon History*, p. 132.
29. Mahan, *From Sail to Steam*, p. 276.
30. *Ibid.*, p. 283.
31. Mahan, *Influence of Sea Power upon History*, pp. 62–64.
32. A. T. Mahan, "The United States Looking Outward," *Atlantic Monthly*, LXVI (Dec., 1890), 816–24; reprinted in Raymond G. O'Connor, ed., *American Defense Policy in Perspective: From Colonial Times to the Present* (New York: Wiley, 1965), pp. 118–24, quotation from p. 124.
33. Richard Hofstadter, *Social Darwinism in American Thought* (Revised Edition, Boston: Beacon Press, 1955), chap. IX, especially pp. 184–92; LaFeber, *The New Empire*, pp. 93–101; William L. Langer, *The Diplomacy of Imperialism, 1890–1902* (Second Edition, New York: Knopf, 1965), chap. XIII; Julius W. Pratt, "Alfred Thayer Mahan," in William T. Hutchinson, ed., *The Marcus W. Jernegan Essays in American Historiography* (New York: Russell and Russell, 1958), pp. 207–26; Sprout, "Mahan," *loc. cit.*, pp. 440–45.
34. Westcott, *op. cit.*, p. 315, from A. T. Mahan, "Considerations Regarding the Disposition of Navies," *The National Review*, XXXIX (July, 1902), 711.
35. Mahan, *Lessons of the War with Spain*, pp. 82–84; Mahan, *Problem of Asia*, pp. 179–201; Mahan, "The United States Looking Outward," in O'Connor, *op. cit.*, pp. 123–24.
36. Sprout, "Mahan," *loc. cit.*, pp. 424–25, 428–29. For a different view arguing that Mahan recognized modern technological and strategic changes, see W. D.

Puleston, "A Re-examination of Mahan's Concept of Sea Power," United States Naval Institute *Proceedings*, LXVI (Sept., 1940), 1229–36: "Mahan was convinced that no one nation could ever again exert the unlimited control over the seas that England had during most of the eighteenth and nineteenth centuries, but he did think that together the British and American nations could exercise such control" (p. 1233).

37. Captain A. T. Mahan, U.S.N., "Blockade in Relation to Naval Strategy," United States Naval Institute *Proceedings*, XXI (Nov., 1895), 851–66; Ropp, "Continental Doctrines of Sea Power," *loc. cit.*, pp. 446–50. But see also Puleston, "Re-examination," *loc. cit.*, pp. 1233–36.

38. Mahan, *Lessons of the War with Spain*, pp. 75–90. See also Lieutenant-Commander Richard Wainwright, U.S.N., "Our Naval Power," United States Naval Institute *Proceedings*, XXIV (1898), 63, "Fleet in Being."

39. Mahan, "The United States Looking Outward," in O'Connor, *op. cit.*, p. 121. See William E. Livezey, *Mahan on Sea Power* (Norman: University of Oklahoma Press, 1947); this work includes a bibliography of Mahan's writings.

40. 51:1 House Executive Documents, VIII (serial 2721), 4; Walter R. Herrick, Jr., *The American Naval Revolution* (Baton Rouge: Louisiana State University Press, 1966), chaps. II–IV; Sprout, *The Rise of American Naval Power*, pp. 207–209. Secretary Tracy's annual report for 1889 is reprinted in part in Millis, *op. cit.*, pp. 226–35.

41. *Navy Yearbook 1917 and 1918*, pp. 64, 739, 758, 766; Herrick, *op. cit.*, pp. 71–77. *Dictionary of American Naval Fighting Ships* (2 vols., Washington: Government Printing Office, 1959–63), I, Appendix 1, lists all United States battleships and gives their characteristics.

42. *Navy Yearbook 1917 and 1918*, pp. 79, 99, 111, 739–40, 758, 766; Herrick, *op. cit.*, pp. 143–44, 154–92; Sprout, *The Rise of American Naval Power*, pp. 218–21.

43. Brayton Harris, *The Age of the Battleship, 1890–1922* (New York: Watts, 1965), p. 22. The previous record for a voyage around Cape Horn was eighty-nine days from New York to San Francisco, set by the clipper ship *Flying Cloud* in 1851 and 1854 and by the *Andrew Jackson* in 1860. *Ibid.*; Samuel Eliot Morison, *The Maritime History of Massachusetts, 1783–1860* (Boston: Houghton Mifflin, 1941), p. 341.

44. Grenville and Young, *op. cit.*, pp. 291–94; Knox, *op. cit.*, pp. 334–35, 342–63; Walter Millis, *The Martial Spirit* (New York: Literary Guild, 1931), pp. 167–71, 201–207, 300–15; Raymond G. O'Connor, ed., *Readings in the History of American Military Policy* (mimeograph, Lawrence, Kansas, 1963), chap. XIV, letter, A. T. Mahan to President, General Board, October 29, 1906, from Records of the Navy General Board.

45. A. T. Mahan to President, General Board, in O'Connor, *Readings*, chap. XIV.

46. Philip Cowburn, *The Warship in History* (New York: Macmillan, 1965), pp. 204, 208–209, 220–24, 238–43; Herrick, *op. cit.*, pp. 78–81; D. Macintyre, *The Thunder of the Guns: A Century of Battleships* (New York: Norton, 1960), pp. 9–152; Arthur J. Marder, *The Anatomy of British Sea Power: A History of British Naval Policy in the Pre-Dreadnought Era, 1880–1905* (New York: Knopf, 1940); Elting E. Morison, *Admiral Sims and the Modern American Navy* (Boston: Houghton Mifflin, 1942), pp. 61–65; F. L. Robertson, *The Evolution of Naval Armament* (London: Constable, 1921), chap. VIII.

47. Harris, *op. cit.*, pp. 27–28, 101, 121–30; E. E. Morison, *op. cit.*, pp. 77–111, 156–75; Gordon C. O'Gara, *Theodore Roosevelt and the Rise of the Modern American Navy* (Princeton: Princeton University Press, 1943), pp. 40–64; Sprout, *The Rise of American Naval Power*, pp. 270–80.

48. Daniel J. Costello, "Planning for War: A History of the General Board of the

Navy, 1900–1914," Ph.D. dissertation, Fletcher School, 1969; Grenville and Young, *op. cit.*, pp. 291–336; Raymond G. O'Connor, "Origins of the Navy's 'General Staff,'" in O'Connor, *American Defense Policy in Perspective*, pp. 139–44; O'Gara, *op. cit.*, pp. 18–27.

49. Bernard Brodie, *Strategy in the Missile Age* (Paperback edition, Princeton: Princeton University Press, 1965), p. 25; Major E. S. Johnston, Infantry, "A Science of War," *Review of Current Military Literature*, XIV (June, 1934), 94–95; Sprout, *The Rise of American Naval Power*, pp. 283–84.

50. *Navy Yearbook 1917 and 1918*, pp. 193, 206, 220, 230, 247, 261, 281, 299, 741–43, 758, 766; Cowburn, *op. cit.*, pp. 261–71; Damon E. Cummings, *Admiral Richard Wainwright and the United States Fleet* (Washington: Government Printing Office, 1962), Part III; Macintyre, *op. cit.*, pp. 153–68; Marder, *op. cit.*, Chap. XXVII, and *From the Dreadnought to Scapa Flow: The Royal Navy in the Fisher Era*, I, *The Road to War, 1904–14* (London: Oxford University Press, 1961), pp. 43–45, 56–69; E. E. Morison, *op. cit.*, pp. 163–75; O'Gara, *op. cit.*; Sprout, *The Rise of American Naval Power*, pp. 259–69.

51. Grenville and Young, *op. cit.*, pp. 312–14; Louis Morton, *Strategy and Command: The First Two Years (United States Army in World War II: The War in the Pacific*, Washington: Office of the Chief of Military History, 1962), pp. 23–24; Henry F. Pringle, *Theodore Roosevelt: A Biography* (Harvest Books Edition, New York: Harcourt, Brace, 1956), p. 287.

52. William R. Braisted, *The United States Navy in the Pacific, 1897–1909* (Austin: University of Texas Press, 1958) and *The United States Navy in the Pacific, 1909–1922* (Austin: University of Texas Press, 1971); Richard A. Hart, *The Great White Fleet: Its Voyage around the World, 1907–1909* (Boston: Little, Brown, 1965); E. E. Morison, *op. cit.*, pp. 40–42, 50, 79, 81–86, 106–47, 235–59; O'Gara, *op. cit.*, pp. 82–93.

53. Cummings, *op. cit.*, pp. 183, 189; Hart, *op. cit.*, pp. 54–55, 176–78; Sprout, *The Rise of American Naval Power*, pp. 280–82. The naval interests of the Roosevelt years were accompanied by a renewed modernization of the seacoast fortifications and their extension to the new possessions. Though the Navy became more clearly than ever before the first line of military defense, coastal fortifications seemed necessary for the protection of the Navy's bases and to assure that the Navy would not be scattered and immoblized in static defense. Lewis, *op. cit.*, pp. 89–100.

54. Lieutenant-Commander James H. Sears, "The Coast in Warfare," United States Naval Institute *Proceedings*, XXVII (Sept., 1901), 472.

55. Howard K. Beale, *Theodore Roosevelt and the Rise of America to World Power* (Paperback edition, New York: Collier Books, 1962), pp. 335–39, 344–54; Grenville and Young, *op. cit.*, pp. 309–11; Arthur S. Link, *Woodrow Wilson and the Progressive Era, 1910–1917* (New York: Harper, 1954), p. 178. J. Bernard Walker, *America Fallen* (New York: Dodd, Mead, 1915), whose scenario is that of a successful German invasion of the United States, received a favorable review in the *Infantry Journal*, XII (July-Aug., 1915), 163–65.

56. Commander Bradley A. Fiske, "The Naval Profession," United States Naval Institute *Proceedings*, XXXIII (Sept., 1907), 503; Captain A. T. Mahan, "Reflections, Historic and Other, Suggested by the Battle of the Japan Sea," *ibid.*, XXXII (June, 1906), 447–71; Lieutenant-Commander Wm. S. Sims, "The Inherent Tactical Qualities of All-Big-Gun, One-Caliber Battleships of High Speed, Large Displacement and Gun-Power," *ibid.* (Dec., 1906), 1337–66; Captain Richard Wainwright, "Big Battleships with All Big Guns," *ibid.*, XXXI (Dec., 1905), 801–805, a section of "The Battle of the Sea of Japan," by Wainwright, *ibid.*, 779–805; *idem.*, "A Further Argument for the Big Ship," *ibid.*,

XXXII (Sept., 1906), 1057–63. For further discussion of Mahan's critics, see Harold D. Langley, "Coping with Enlarged Responsibilities: The Navy since 1898," a paper delivered at the annual meeting of the Southern Historical Association, Houston, Texas, November 19, 1971, pp. 6–7. On the beginnings of war gaming at the Naval War College, see Lieutenant John B. Hattendorf, "Technology and Strategy: A Study in the Professional Thought of the U. S. Navy, 1900–1916," *Naval War College Review*, XXIV, No. 3 (Nov., 1971), 25–48. Examples of the reverence in which Mahan again came to be held between the world wars, among students of naval strategy both in and outside the Navy, are Puleston's laudatory biography, *op. cit.*, and the Sprouts' *The Rise of American Naval Power.* The Sprouts retract some of their previous acceptance of Mahan's ideas in an unpaginated introduction to the 1966 edition of that book.

CHAPTER TEN. STRATEGY AND THE GREAT WAR OF 1914–1918

1. Tasker H. Bliss, draft of an article, Jan., 1923 (?), Bliss Papers, Library of Congress, Box 274, pp. 15–16.
2. John Bigelow, *The Principles of Strategy Illustrated Mainly from American Campaigns* (New York: Greenwood Press, 1968, reprint of Second Edition, Revised and Enlarged, Philadelphia: Lippincott, 1894), p. 185.
3. *Infantry Journal*, XII (Nov., 1915), 485–86.
4. Viscount Jellicoe, *The Crisis of the Naval War* (New York: Doran, 1920), chap. II; Tracy Barrett Kittredge, *Naval Lessons of the Great War: A Review of the Senate Naval Investigation of the Criticisms by Admiral Sims of the Policies and Methods of Josephus Daniels* (Garden City: Doubleday, Page, 1921), pp. 196–205; Philip K. Lundeberg, "The German Naval Critique of the U-Boat Campaign, 1915–1918," *Military Affairs*, XXVII (Fall, 1963), 105–18; Elting E. Morison, *Admiral Sims and the Modern American Navy* (Boston: Houghton Mifflin, 1942), chap. XIX; William Sowden Sims, with Burton J. Hendrick, *The Victory at Sea* (Garden City: Doubleday, Page, 1919), chap. I and pp. 374–401; Sir Llewellyn Woodward, *Great Britain and the War of 1914–1918* (London: Methuen, 1967), pp. 338–39.
5. On April 6, 1917, when Congress declared war, one-half of the forty-four new destroyers and 67 percent of all the Navy's ships were in need of repair; they went into shipyards for an average of fifty-six days. Brayton Harris, *The Age of the Battleship, 1890–1922* (New York: Watts, 1965), pp. 158–59. See also Dudley W. Knox, *A History of the United States Navy* (New York: Putnam, 1936), pp. 386–89; Morison, *op. cit.*, pp. 355–56; Harold and Margaret Sprout, *The Rise of American Naval Power, 1776–1918* (Paperback edition, Princeton: Princeton University Press, 1966), p. 363.
6. Jellicoe, *op. cit.*, chaps. IV–VI; David Lloyd George, *The War Memoirs of David Lloyd George* (6 vols., Boston: Little, Brown, 1933–37), III, chap. III; Morison, *op. cit.*, pp. 347–53; Sims, *op. cit.*, chap. III; Woodward, *op. cit.*, pp. 339–46, 491–97.
7. Harris, *op. cit.*, pp. 162–64, 169, 173–75; Knox, *op. cit.*, pp. 414–18; Sims, *op. cit.*, chaps. VI, IX, XI.
8. The statistics of industrial production are from A. J. P. Taylor, *The Struggle for Mastery in Europe, 1848–1918* (Oxford: Clarendon Press, 1954), p. xxx. For the European strategic thought that mostly ignored such prosaic matters, see Ardant du Picq, *Battle Studies: Ancient and Modern*, tr. from the Eighth Edition by John N. Greely and Robert C. Cotton (Harrisburg: Stackpole, 1947); Ferdi-

nand Foch, *The Principles of War*, tr. J. de Morinni (New York: Fly, 1918); Bernard Brodie, *Strategy in the Missile Age* (Paperback edition, Princeton: Princeton University Press, 1965), pp. 45–55; Hajo Holborn, "Moltke and Schlieffen: The Prussian-German School," in Edward Mead Earle, ed., *Makers of Modern Strategy: Military Thought from Machiavelli to Hitler* (Paperback edition, New York: Atheneum, 1966), pp. 172–205; B. H. Liddell Hart, *Foch: The Man of Orleans* (London: Eyre & Spottiswoode, 1929); Jay Luvaas, *The Military Legacy of the Civil War: The European Inheritance* (Chicago: University of Chicago Press, 1959); Stefan T. Possony, "Du Picq and Foch: The French School," in Earle, *op. cit.*, pp. 206–33; Gerhard Ritter, *The Schlieffen Plan: Critique of a Myth*, tr. Andrew and Eva Wilson (New York: Praeger, 1958); Theodore Ropp, *War in the Modern World* (New Revised Edition, New York: Collier Books, 1959), pp. 200–206, 215–22; Woodward, *op. cit.*, chap. III.

9. Bigelow, *op. cit.*, p. 156.
10. John M. Schofield, note on J. H. Chalmers's sketch of "Forrest and His Campaigns," 1879, Schofield Papers, Library of Congress, Box 93.
11. "Franklin," Miscellaneous Notes, Schofield Papers, Box 93.
12. Greene to W. T. Sherman, March 13, 1878, W. T. Sherman Papers, Library of Congress, Box 47A. For a relatively unusual American expression of the view that hard fighting might not be necessary for military victory, see Joseph M. Califf, *Notes on Military Science and the Art of War* (Second Edition, Washington: James J. Chapman, 1891), p. 69: "They [battles] are simply incidents to a campaign, which may be won by strategy without firing a hostile shot."
13. Capt. Carl Reichmann, 17th Infantry, "Chances in War," *Infantry Journal*, III (July, 1906), 26–28. The numerous American textbooks on strategy of the pre-World War I era still, with the exception of Califf's, emphasized the destruction of the enemy army as the goal of strategy. See Lieutenant Colonel G. J. Fiebeger, Professor of Engineering at West Point, *Elements of Strategy* (n.p., [1906?]), pp. 18–19; Captain James S. Pettit, *Elements of Military Science, For the Use of Students in Colleges and Universities* (Revised Edition, New Haven: Tuttle, Morehouse & Taylor, 1895), pp. 140–83; Colonel Arthur L. Wagner, *Strategy* (Kansas City: Hudson-Kimberly, 1904), pp. 43, 45, 54.
14. It should be noted, however, that the French Colonel Jean L. A. Colin stated as the lesson of the Franco-Prussian War: "Well-chosen and well-arranged defensive positions, even when very weakly held, could not be carried." Quoted in Brodie, *op. cit.*, p. 51. But this lesson was widely ignored.
15. Lieutenant Commander Dudley W. Knox, U.S.N., "The Rôle of Doctrine in Naval Warfare," United States Naval Institute *Proceedings*, XLI (March-April, 1915), 338. Despite the title, Knox was referring in this passage to French and German military doctrine in general, not only naval doctrine.
16. John A. S. Grenville and George Berkeley Young, *Politics, Strategy, and American Diplomacy: Studies in Foreign Policy, 1873–1917* (New Haven: Yale University Press, 1966), pp. 334–35.
17. Winston S. Churchill, *The World Crisis* (New York: Scribner, 1949), pp. 272–74; Woodward, *op. cit.*, chaps. V–VI and pp. 176–77.
18. John J. Pershing, *My Experiences in the World War* (2 vols., New York: Stokes, 1931), I, 83–84.
19. Edward M. Coffman, *The War to End All Wars: The American Military Experience in World War I* (New York: Oxford University Press, 1968), pp. 262–84; Harvey A. DeWeerd, *President Wilson Fights His War: World War I and the American Intervention* (New York: Macmillan, 1968), chap. XVI; Pershing, *op. cit.*, II, chap. XLIII.

20. Coffman, *op. cit.*, chaps. IX–X; DeWeerd, *op. cit.*, chaps. XVI–XVII; Pershing, *op. cit.*, II, chaps. XLI–L.
21. William Mitchell, *Memoirs of World War I: "From Start to Finish of Our Greatest War"* (New York: Random House, 1960), p. 10; this and subsequent quotations reprinted by permission of Random House, Inc.
22. Tasker H. Bliss, draft of an article, Jan., 1923 (?), Bliss Papers, Library of Congress, Box 274, pp. 1, 4–5, 15–16.
23. Lieutenant Commander H. H. Frost, U.S.N., "National Strategy," United States Naval Institute *Proceedings*, LI (Aug., 1925), 1347, 1351–52, reprinted from *Proceedings* by permission; Copyright © 1925 U. S. Naval Institute. On Frost, see Edwin A. Falk, "Prefatory Note," in Holloway H. Frost, *The Battle of Jutland* (Annapolis: United States Naval Institute, 1936), pp. ix–xi.
24. Frost, "National Strategy," *loc. cit.*, p. 1368; reprinted from *Proceedings* by permission; Copyright © 1925 U. S. Naval Institute.
25. Commander G. J. Meyers, U.S.N., "General Strategic Considerations," Course at the Army War College, 1923–24, Miscellaneous Course No. 7, p. 1, copy in U.S. Army Military History Research Collection, Carlisle Barracks, Pennsylvania.
26. George J. Meyers, *Strategy* (Washington: Byron S. Adams, 1928), p. xiv.
27. Lt. Col. A. L. Conger, Infantry, "The Estimate of the Economic Situation," lecture delivered at the General Staff College, Washington, Sept. 10 and 11, 1920, Intelligence Course No. 5, p. 2, copy in U.S. Army Military History Research Collection. The Army War College was called the General Staff College from June, 1919, to August, 1921. On its history and the expansion of the scope of its strategic studies, see George S. Pappas, *Prudens Futuri: The Army War College, 1901–1967* (Carlisle, Pa.: Alumni Association of the U.S. Army War College, 1967).
28. William L. Langer and S. Everett Gleason, *The Challenge to Isolation, 1937–1940* (New York: Harper, 1952), pp. 40–41; Mark Skinner Watson, *Chief of Staff: Prewar Plans and Preparations (United States Army in World War II: The War Department*, Washington: Historical Division, United States Army, 1950), p. 121.
29. *Statutes at Large of the United States*, XXXIX, pt. 2, pp. 213–16, 649–50; American Academy of Political and Social Science, *Mobilizing America's Resources for War* (Philadelphia, 1918); Arthur Bullard, *Mobilizing America* (New York: Macmillan, 1917); Grosvener B. Clarkson, *Industrial America in the World War* (Cambridge: Harvard University Press, 1923); Benedict Crowell, *America's Munitions, 1917–1918* (Washington: Government Printing Office, 1919), and with Robert F. Wilson, *The Armies of Industry* (2 vols., New Haven: Yale University Press, 1921) and *The Giant Hand* (New Haven: Yale University Press, 1921).
30. Marvin A. Kreidberg and Merton G. Henry, *History of Military Mobilization in the United States Army, 1775–1945* (Washington: Department of the Army, 1955), pp. 499–502.
31. *Statutes at Large of the United States*, XLI, 764.
32. R. Elberton Smith, *The Army and Economic Mobilization (United States Army in World War II: The War Department*, Washington: Office of the Chief of Military History, 1959), chaps. I–III; Harold W. Thatcher, *Planning for Industrial Mobilization, 1920–1940* (Quartermaster Corps Historical Studies No. 4, Washington: Government Printing Office, 1943); Harry B. Yoshpe, "Economic Mobilization Planning between the Two World Wars," *Military Affairs*, XV (Winter, 1951), 199–204; XVI (Summer, 1952), 71–96.
33. See again Conger, "The Estimate of the Economic Situation," *loc. cit.*

34. Oliver Prescott Robinson, *The Fundamentals of Military Strategy* (Washington: United States Infantry Association, 1928), p. viii. On the influence of Clausewitz, see also H. Wager Halleck, *Elements of Military Art and Science . . .* (Third Edition, New York: D. Appleton, 1862), p. 60; R. M. Johnston, *Clausewitz to Date, With Selected Quotations from Military Writers and New Material* (Cambridge: The Military Historian and Economist, 1917); T. D. Pilcher, ed., *War According to Clausewitz, with Commentary* (New York: Cassell, 1918). Johnston was a Harvard historian specializing in military history and criticism; Pilcher was a British major general. See also Carl von Clausewitz, *On War*, tr. O. J. Matthijs Jolles (New York: Modern Library, 1943); Peter Paret, "Clausewitz and the Nineteenth Century," in Michael Howard, ed., *The Theory and Practice of War: Essays Presented to Captain B. H. Liddell Hart* (London: Cassell, 1965), pp. 21–42; H. Rothfels, "Clausewitz," in Earle, *op. cit.*, pp. 93–113.
35. Carl von Clausewitz, *On War*, tr. Col. J. J. Graham, New and Revised Edition with an Introduction and Notes by Col. F. N. Maude (Eighth Impression, 3 vols., New York: Barnes & Noble, 1968 [First Edition, 1873]), I, xxiii, 23, 4, 2; III, 100–103. Subsequent citations refer to this edition.
36. *Ibid.*, I, 2.
37. *Ibid.*, p. 246.
38. *Ibid.*, p. 288. Despite the type of encomium quoted from Colonel Robinson, suggestions about Clausewitz's influence on English-speaking soldiers should never be pushed too far. The turgid Graham translation does nothing to mitigate Clausewitz's Teutonic obscurities, and anyone who has tried to grapple with this translation must respond with the satisfaction of recognition to Field Marshal Montgomery's remarks: "I did make attempts to read the writings of Clausewitz, a Prussian, and of Jomini, a Swiss. Both were well-known military writers, but I couldn't take them in, and I turned to historians of my own nation and language." Clausewitz's "language is exceedingly difficult to understand; indeed . . . I couldn't understand him myself, and turned to historians of my own nation and language." Viscount Montgomery of Alamein, *A History of Warfare* (Cleveland: World, 1968), pp. 20, 415.
39. Stephen B. Luce, "War Schools," United States Naval Institute *Proceedings*, IX (1883), 656; "Naval Strategy," *ibid.*, XXXV (March, 1909), 93–94, 96.
40. Tasker H. Bliss, draft of an article, Jan., 1923 (?), Bliss Papers, Library of Congress, Box 274, p. 1.
41. Editorial, "Doctrine, Conception, and History of War," *Infantry Journal*, IX (Sept.-Oct., 1912), 255–61; Captain Albert Gleaves, U.S.N., "Some Foreign and Other Views of War and the Study and Conduct of War," United States Naval Institute *Proceedings*, XL (Sept.-Oct., 1914), 1301–21; Knox, "The Rôle of Doctrine in Naval Warfare," *loc. cit.*, pp. 325–54; Captain Wm. S. Sims, U.S.N., "Naval War College Principles and Methods Applied Afloat," United States Naval Institute *Proceedings*, XLI (March-April, 1915), 382–403, the latter being a Naval War College lecture endorsing Knox's ideas on doctrine and discussing efforts to apply them in Sims's command, the Atlantic Torpedo Flotilla. Both Knox and Major George H. Shelton, the editor of the *Infantry Journal*, referred to recent articles in the *Edinburgh Review* on "The British Army and Modern Conceptions of War" and "The Place of Doctrine in War." Knox pointed out that according to the *Edinburgh Review*, "a sound, comprehensive, all-pervading doctrine of war is as important to an army as its organization." ". . . It is, therefore, somewhat extraordinary," Knox went on, "that both the American military services as a whole are unfamiliar even with the meaning of the term 'doctrine' when used in its purely military sense, and fail to com-

prehend its importance as well as its rôle in bringing about timely and united action in the midst of hostilities."

> The object of military doctrine [Knox said] is to furnish a basis for prompt and harmonious conduct by the subordinate commanders of a large military force, in accordance with the intentions of the commander-in-chief, but without the necessity for referring each decision to superior authority before action is taken. More concisely stated the object is to provide a foundation for mutual understanding between the various commanders during hostile operations. (*Loc. cit.*, pp. 333–34.)

This is an excellent explanation of the term. The *Infantry Journal* pointed out that the recent report of the General Staff on "The Organization of the Land Forces" of the United States (largely written by the uncommonly capable Captain John McAuley Palmer; *Report of the Secretary of War, 1912*, I, 69–128) had stated in its draft version (though not in the printed version) that one of the purposes of the General Staff was to provide officers with an opportunity for reflection and study, so that "Returning to the line they revivify it and spread *a common doctrine* as to the purposes and ends of training, the means to be employed, and results to be attained." "It is to this idea of a common doctrine," said the *Infantry Journal*, "that it is desired to attract attention. This is likely its first official appearance with us. It is almost a new term even within the military establishment itself. Doctrine, of course, is not an end. It is no more than a means to some national conception of war." (*Loc. cit.*, pp. 256–57, quotation from p. 257.)

By 1940, "doctrine" could be defined as follows:

> Nature of Doctrine. Uniformity of thought and action throughout an army is the difference between victory and defeat. This uniformity is secured by strict adherence on the part of all military men to approved *policy*, *regulations*, and authorized *training* and *operating methods*, or what collectively are called "doctrine of war." An understanding of doctrine is the foundation of an officer's professional knowledge. (Colonel Hollis LeR. Muller, Coast Artillery Corps, U.S.A., *Technique of Modern Arms* [Harrisburg: Military Service Publishing Co., 1940], p. 47.)

Much study and effort in the American services from World War to World War went into the development of American military doctrine in this sense. Part of the process can be traced in Virgil Ney, *Evolution of the United States Army Field Manual, Valley Forge to Vietnam* (Combat Operations Research Group, CORG Memorandum, CORG-M-244, Prepared by Technical Operations, Incorporated, Combat Operations Research Group, for Headquarters United States Army Combat Developments Command, Fort Belvoir, Virginia, January, 1966).

42. *War Department Training Regulations No. 10-5, Series 1921* (23 December 1921), offered the first printing of the American list of the principles of war. The early discussion of them referred to here is Col. W. K. Naylor, Inf., "The Principles of War," Army War College, Command Course No. 12, Part I, Jan. 5, 1922, copy in Bliss Papers, Library of Congress, Box 277 (a smiliar discussion by Col. Naylor was given Jan. 3, 1923; copy in Bliss Papers, Box 279). There is a discussion of the process by which the principles of war came to be codified in Charles Andrew Willoughby, *Maneuver in War* (Harrisburg: Military Service Publishing Co., 1939), pp. 25–32. For the principles of war as they appeared on the eve of World War II, see Muller, *op. cit.*, pp. 71–95. For the current version, see the latest editions of *FM 100-5, Field Service Regulations: Operations*.

43. *Infantry in Battle* (Second Edition, Washington: Infantry Journal, 1939), pp. 1, 14. For similar criticism of excessive reliance on "principles," see Major E. S. Johnston, Infantry, "A Science of War," *Review of Current Military Literature*, XIV (June, 1934), 89–140, especially pp. 94–95.
44. Kenneth Macksey and John H. Batchelor, *Tank: A History of the Armoured Fighting Vehicle* (New York: Ballantine, 1971), pp. 20–50; Richard M. Ogorkiewicz, *Armoured Forces: A History of Armoured Forces and Their Vehicles* (New York: Arco, 1970), pp. 11–13, 55–56.
45. Brigadier General S. D. Rockenbach, U.S.A., "The Tank Corps," lecture delivered at the General Staff College, Washington, D.C., Oct. 3, 1919, in Army War College 1919–20, Vol. II, Intelligence, Part I, Lectures, Miscellaneous, p. 181, copy in U.S. Army Military History Research Collection.
46. Major Ned B. Rehkopf, F. A., "The Army Commander (The Machine which the Army Commander Operates) (. . . Tanks . . .)," Army War College, Command Course No. 15, Feb. 16, 1925, p. 1, copy in Bliss Papers, Library of Congress, Box 281; Ogorkiewicz, *op. cit.*, pp. 189–90.
47. *Report of the Secretary of War, 1931*, p. 43; Mildred Harmon Gillie, *Forging the Thunderbolt: A History of the Development of the Armored Force* (Harrisburg: Military Service Publishing Co., 1947), chap. II.
48. Gillie, *op. cit.*, chaps. II–III; Macksey and Batchelor, *op. cit.*, pp. 39, 68–69; Ogorkiewicz, *op. cit.*, pp. 190–95.
49. B. H. Liddell Hart, *The Liddell Hart Memoirs* (2 vols., New York: Putnam, 1965–66), I, 135; also *passim*, especially I, 166–68; *idem.*, *Strategy* (Second Revised Edition, New York: Praeger, 1967), pp. 143, 145, 149–54; Jay Luvaas, *The Education of an Army: British Military Thought, 1815–1940* (Chicago: University of Chicago Press, 1964), Part V.
50. Naylor, "The Principles of War," Army War College, Command Course No. 12, Part I, Jan. 5, 1922, pp. 4–6; *idem.*, *Principles of Strategy with Historical Illustrations* (Fort Leavenworth: General Service Schools Press, 1921), especially p. 49.
51. Naylor, "The Principles of War," Army War College Command Course No. 12, Part I, Jan. 5, 1922, p. 25.
52. Captain Reuben E. Jenkins, Infantry, I Section, Command and General Staff School, "Offensive Doctrines: Opening Phase of Battle," *Military Review*, XX (June, 1940), 5, 16, with quotations from *FM 100-5, Field Service Regulations (Tentative): Operations, 1939*. Similar statements are frequent in American military literature between the world wars; e.g., Meyers, *Strategy*, pp. 74, 178; Robinson, *op. cit.*, pp. 16–18, 67; Command and General Staff School, *The Principles of Strategy for an Independent Corps or Army in a Theater of Operations* (Fort Leavenworth: Command and General Staff School Press, 1936), pp. 22, 26, 70; Lieutenant Colonel John G. Burr, U.S.A. (Retired), *The Framework of Battle* (Philadelphia: Lippincott, 1943), p. 20.
53. Kreidberg and Henry, *op. cit.*, pp. 378–80, 394–96, 463–65; John McAuley Palmer, *America in Arms: The Experience of the United States with Military Organization* (New Haven: Yale University Press, 1941), *Statesmanship or War* (Garden City: Doubleday, 1927), and *Washington, Lincoln, Wilson: Three War Statesmen* (Garden City: Doubleday, 1930); Russell F. Weigley, *Towards an American Army: Military Thought from Washington to Marshall* (New York: Columbia University Press, 1962), pp. 225–41.
54. Ray S. Cline, *Washington Command Post: The Operations Division (United States Army in World War II: The War Department*, Washington: Office of the Chief of Military History, 1951), pp. 242–47.

CHAPTER ELEVEN. A STRATEGY OF AIR POWER: BILLY MITCHELL

1. William Mitchell, *Skyways: A Book on Modern Aeronautics* (Philadelphia: Lippincott, 1930), pp. 255–56.
2. F. Lee Benns, *European History since 1870* (Third Edition, New York: Appleton-Century-Crofts, 1950), p. 390. Some estimates of the total military and naval deaths approach thirteen millions. C. R. M. F. Cruttwell, *A History of the Great War, 1914–1918* (Second Edition, Oxford: Clarendon Press, 1936), pp. 630–32.
3. William Mitchell, *Memoirs of World War I: "From Start to Finish of Our Greatest War"* (New York: Random House, 1960), p. 59.
4. *Ibid.*, pp. 234–48, 268; James J. Hudson, *Hostile Skies: A Combat History of the American Air Service in World War I* (Syracuse: Syracuse University Press, 1968), pp. 139, 302; Alfred F. Hurley, *Billy Mitchell: Crusader for Air Power* (New York: Watts, 1964), pp. 35–36.
5. The statistics given by various writers differ slightly. George H. Quester, *Deterrence before Hiroshima: The Airpower Background of Modern Strategy* (New York: Wiley, 1966), pp. 17–27, 30–38, 45–49; Theodore Ropp, *War in the Modern World* (New, Revised Edition, New York: Collier Books, 1959), p. 269; Sir Llewellyn Woodward, *Great Britain and the War of 1914–1918* (London: Methuen, 1967), pp. 370–75.
6. The bombing to which Smuts referred actually occurred on July 7, not July 11. The Smuts Committee " 'Magna Carta' of British Air Power" is reprinted in part in Eugene M. Emme, ed., *The Impact of Air Power: National Security and World Politics* (Princeton: Van Nostrand, 1959), pp. 33–37, quotation on p. 35. See also F. W. Lanchester, *Aircraft in Warfare: The Dawn of the Fourth Arm* (London: Constable, 1916); Robin Higham, *The Military Intellectuals in Britain, 1918–1939* (New Brunswick: Rutgers University Press, 1966), chaps. VI–VIII and Appendices A–C.
7. Hurley, *op. cit.*, pp. 25–27; Mitchell, *Memoirs*, pp. 104–11.
8. Boone L. Atkinson, "Italian Influence on the Origins of the American Concept of Strategic Bombardment," *Air Power Historian*, IV (July, 1957), 142–44; Hurley, *op. cit.*, pp. 31–32, 75–77, 168–69; Edward Warner, "Douhet, Mitchell, Seversky: Theories of Air Warfare," in Edward Mead Earle, ed., *Makers of Modern Strategy: Military Thought from Machiavelli to Hitler* (Paperback edition, New York: Atheneum, 1966), pp. 487–88.
9. Giulio Douhet, *Il Dominio dell' Aria: saggio sul' arte della guerra aerea* (Rome: Per l'amministrazione della Guerra, 1921; Second Edition [considerably expanded], Rome: Instituto Nazionale Fascista di Cultura, 1927); *idem.*, *Scritti inediti*, ed. Antonio Monti (Milan: Scuola di Guerra Aerea, 1950). The standard English translation is *The Command of the Air*, tr. Dino Ferrari (New York: Coward-McCann, 1942). Excerpts, summaries, and comments can be found in Bernard Brodie, *Strategy in the Missile Age* (Paperback edition, Princeton: Princeton University Press, 1965), chap. III; Louis A. Sigaud, *Douhet and Aerial Warfare* (New York: Putnam, 1941); F. Vauthier, *La doctrine de guerre du Général Douhet* (Paris: Berger-Levrault, 1935); Warner, *loc. cit.*, pp. 489–97.
10. William Mitchell, *Winged Defense: The Development and Possibilities of Modern Air Power, Economic and Military* (New York: Putnam, 1925), p. 199; Burke Davis, *The Billy Mitchell Affair* (New York: Random House, 1967), pp. 144–45; Hurley, *op. cit.*, pp. 76–77, 81–83; Warner, *loc. cit.*, pp. 497–99.
11. Quoted in Davis, *op. cit.*, p. 118. *Ibid.*, chaps. V–IX and pp. 151–57; Hurley, *op. cit.*, chap. IV; Isaac Don Levine, *Mitchell: Pioneer of Air Power* (Forum Books

Edition, Cleveland: World, 1944), pp. 168–72, 201–66, 287–90; Harry H. Ransom, "The Battleship Meets the Airplane," *Military Affairs*, XXIII (Spring, 1959), 21–27; Archibald D. Turnbull and Clifford L. Lord, *History of United States Naval Aviation* (New Haven: Yale University Press, 1949), chap. XVIII.

12. Quoted in Davis, *op. cit.*, p. 118.
13. *Ibid.*, pp. 159–81, based on "Report of Inspection of U. S. Possessions in the Pacific and Java, Singapore, India, Siam, China and Japan," Oct. 24, 1924, in Mitchell's personal military file (201 file), U.S. Army Records Administration Center, St. Louis, Mo., and at U.S. Air Force Academy; Hurley, *op. cit.*, pp. 86–89.
14. Quoted in Davis, *op. cit.*, p. 118. Until transoceanic bombers should become available, Mitchell wanted the Army Air Service to have aircraft carriers; Hurley, *op. cit.*, pp. 44, 49.
15. Hurley, *op. cit.*, p. 123.
16. Davis, *op. cit.*, pp. 178–79; Hurley, *op. cit.*, pp. 52–53, 87, 117–18, 123.
17. Davis, *op. cit.*, chaps. XII–XIV, especially pp. 173–76, quoting extensively from Mitchell, "Report of Inspection. . . ."
18. Davis, *op. cit.*, chaps. XIV–XV; Hurley, *op. cit.*, pp. 90–98; Levine, *op. cit.*, pp. 300–17.
19. Quoted in Davis, *op. cit.*, p. 218. *Ibid.*, pp. 207–22; Hurley, *op. cit.*, pp. 98–101; Levine, *op. cit.*, pp. 318–29.
20. Davis, *op. cit.*, chaps. XVIII–XXIII, is the most detailed account of the trial, the first book to be based on the court-martial transcript.
21. See especially William Mitchell, "Aircraft Dominate Seacraft," *Saturday Evening Post*, Jan. 24, 1925, pp. 22–23.
22. The problem of the evolution of Mitchell's ideas is discussed by Hurley, *op. cit.*, especially pp. 42–44, 76–77, 93–95, 111–13, 168–69. Hurley says:

> There can be no doubt that Mitchell encountered at least the first indications of the strategic bombardment idea during World War I, that he did not begin to pursue it in earnest until after his European trip in 1921 and then only privately, and that he had refrained from mentioning the topic publicly until 1924 in deference to American public opinion. There is no evidence, so far, to show that he had fully developed his "vital centers" conception until 1926. (*Ibid.*, pp. 168–69.)

To a degree, the evolution of Mitchell's ideas can be traced by contrasting his earlier books, *Our Air Force: The Keystone of National Defense* (New York: Dutton, 1921) and *Winged Defense*, with the later *Skyways* and the posthumously published *Memoirs*, which though apparently based on now-lost war diaries incorporates and emphasizes post-1926 ideas. "American Leadership in Aeronautics," *Saturday Evening Post*, Jan. 10, 1925, pp. 18–19, 148, 153, sets forth the theory of strategic bombing as an independently decisive weapon of war more clearly than any of Mitchell's earlier work, but then sharply qualifies it by stating that the resolution of war ultimately occurs on the ground and that the applicability of strategic bombing varies with each nation's geographic position. Immediately after the court-martial, the "vital centers" idea appeared more boldly stated in "Let the Air Service Crash!" *Liberty*, Jan. 30, 1926, pp. 43–46. A convenient bibliography of Mitchell's publications appears in Levine, *op. cit.*, pp. 401–405.

23. The articles published soon after the trial, in addition to the *Liberty* piece just cited, include a series in the Sunday New York *American*, April 4–May 23, 1926, "How Asiatic Aerial Army Could Strike Quick, Ravaging Blow"; "When

the Air Raiders Came," *Collier's*, May 1, 1926, pp. 8–9; "Airplanes in National Defense," *Annals* of the American Academy of Political and Social Science, CXXXI (May, 1927), 38–42; "Look Out Below!" *Collier's*, April 21, 1928, pp. 8–9; "The Next War—What About Our National Defense?" *Liberty*, July 27, 1931, pp. 40–44. There are numerous more technical, anecdotal, and reminiscent articles.

24. Mitchell, *Skyways*, pp. 255–56; *Memoirs*, pp. 3–4.
25. Mitchell, *Memoirs*, p. 6.
26. *Ibid.*, p. 10.
27. *Ibid.*, p. 15.
28. *Ibid.*, p. 23.
29. B. H. Liddell Hart, *Paris: Or the Future of War* (New York: Dutton, 1925). Britons and British governments tended to grasp the strategic bombardment theory of air power more wholeheartedly than did Americans, in part because the RAF was an independent service and thus less inhibited in official sponsorship of the theory than the American Army Air Corps, to a greater extent because the economic limitations upon British military power and remembrance of the Somme and Passchendaele created a far deeper need to believe in an escape from future Western Fronts.
30. B. H. Liddell Hart, *The Liddell Hart Memoirs* (2 vols., New York: Putnam, 1965–66), I, 142.
31. Mitchell, *Skyways*, p. 262.
32. Quoted in Harvey A. DeWeerd, *President Wilson Fights His War: The American Military Experience in World War I* (New York: Macmillan, 1968), p. xx.
33. Typical Navy and Army attacks on the strategic bombardment idea as proposing the violation of international law are in the Secretary's Notes, United States Naval Institute *Proceedings*, LIII (June, 1927), 737–38, and Captain Elbridge Colby, U.S.A., "Aerial Annihilation," *ibid.*, LV (Aug., 1929), 686–89. Typical also is the view of Lieutenant Colonel Oliver Prescott Robinson, Infantry, in *The Fundamentals of Military Strategy* (Washington: United States Infantry Association, 1928), p. 4:

> To illustrate more fully, no nation will use its air forces to bomb cities, just for the purpose of destroying the morale of the people by instilling them with fear, any more than it will gas women and children. Why? Because *strategy* knows that such action could only bring on the nation the active resentment of the rest of the civilized world, a thing that no nation can afford.

Interestingly, in the United States Military Academy Library copy of this book, the latter four words are underlined in pencil and there is a marginal pencilled note, written it appears during the "phony war" of 1939–40 (see similar note on p. 51): "This seems to hold today even contrary to lay opinion."

34. Douhet, *The Command of the Air*, pp. 57–58.
35. Alexander P. De Seversky, *Victory through Air Power* (New York: Simon & Schuster, 1942), p. 145; this and subsequent quotations reprinted by permission of Simon & Schuster, Inc.
36. *Ibid.*, pp. 146, 151.
37. *Ibid.*, pp. 146–47.
38. *Ibid.*, pp. 101, 103–16.
39. *Ibid.*, pp. 107–108.
40. *Ibid.*, p. 101.
41. *Ibid.*, p. 104.

42. H. H. Arnold, *Global Mission* (New York: Harper, 1949), p. 149. See also Brodie, *op. cit.*, p. 73n; Thomas H. Greer, *The Development of Air Doctrine in the Army Air Corps, 1917–1941* (Montgomery: Air University, 1955); R. Earl McClendon, *The Question of Autonomy for the United States Air Arm* (Revised Nov., 1950, Montgomery: Air University, 1952).
43. General Henry H. Arnold, "Air Strategy for Victory," *Flying*, XXXIII, No. 4 (Oct., 1943), 50.
44. Army Air Force Historical Studies, No. 6, *The Development of the Heavy Bomber, 1918–1944* (Montgomery: Air University, 1951); Wesley Frank Craven and James Lea Cate, eds., *The Army Air Forces in World War II* (7 vols., Chicago: University of Chicago Press, 1948–58), I, *Plans and Early Operations, January 1939 to August 1942*, chaps. II, IV; and VI, *Men and Planes*, pp. 202–206; Alfred Goldberg, ed., *A History of the United States Air Force, 1907–1957* (Princeton: Van Nostrand, 1957), pp. 40–45; Charles B. Van Pelt, "The B-17, 'An Airplane You Could Trust,'" *American History Illustrated*, IV, No. 6 (Oct., 1969), 25–26; Ray Wagner, *American Combat Planes* (New Revised Edition, Garden City: Doubleday, 1968), pp. 108–17.

CHAPTER TWELVE. A STRATEGY FOR PACIFIC OCEAN WAR: NAVAL STRATEGISTS OF THE 1920S AND 1930S

1. "The Navy War Plans Division: Naval Plans and Planning," Army War College, War Plans Division Course No. 10, March 11, 1924, p. 6, copy in Tasker H. Bliss Papers, Library of Congress, Box 280.
2. 65th Congress, 3rd Session, Senate Documents, Vol. VII (serial 7463), No. 418, *Navy Yearbook 1917 and 1918*, pp. 378–79, 396, 745, 756, 766; Harold and Margaret Sprout, *The Rise of American Naval Power, 1776–1918* (Paperback edition, Princeton: Princeton University Press, 1966), pp. 312–20.
3. *Navy Yearbook 1917 and 1918*, pp. 399–467; Sprout, *op. cit.*, pp. 334–46.
4. Arthur S. Link, *Woodrow Wilson and the Progressive Era, 1910–1917* (New York: Harper, 1954), p. 190.
5. 66:3 Senate Documents, Vol. XIV (serial 7792), *Navy Yearbook 1920–1921*, pp. 871, 874, 875; *Report of the Secretary of the Navy, 1922*, p. 230; Fletcher Pratt, *The Navy: A History: The Story of a Service in Action* (Garden City: Garden City Publishing Co., 1941), p. 451.
6. The Washington Naval Treaty can be found in *Statutes at Large of the United States*, XLIII, pt. 2, pp. 1655–85, and 67:2 Senate Documents, Vol. X (serial 7976), *Conference on the Limitation of Armament*, pp. 871–85. Dudley W. Knox, *A History of the United States Navy* (New York: Putnam, 1936), pp. 425–31; Samuel Eliot Morison, *The Two-Ocean War: A Short History of the United States Navy in the Second World War* (Boston: Little, Brown, 1963), pp. 5–6, 24–25; Merlo J. Pusey, *Charles Evans Hughes* (2 vols., New York: Macmillan, 1961), II, chaps. XLIV–XLVI; Harold and Margaret Sprout, *Toward a New Order of Sea Power* (Princeton: Princeton University Press, 1940), chaps. IX–XIII (pp. 298–307 for another reprinting of the principal provisions of the treaty).
7. Phrase from Captain Yates Stirling, Jr., U.S.N., "Some Fundamentals of Sea Power," United States Naval Institute *Proceedings*, LI (June, 1925), 911. For the London Naval Conference of 1930, Raymond G. O'Connor, *Perilous Equilibrium: The United States and the London Naval Conference of 1930* (Lawrence: University of Kansas Press, 1962); Gerald E. Wheeler, *Prelude to Pearl Harbor: The United States Navy and the Far East, 1921–1931* (Paperback edition, Columbia: University of Missouri Press, 1968), chap. VII.

8. E.g., Commander C. C. Gill, U.S.N., "The New Far East Doctrine," United States Naval Institute *Proceedings*, XLVIII (Sept., 1922), 1479–86; *ibid.*, XLIX (May, 1923), an issue devoted to the impact of the Washington Conference; Captain O. L. Cox, U.S.N., and Commander C. A. Jones, U.S.N., "The Problem of the Naval Design Engineer as Affected by the Limitation of Armament Treaty," *ibid.*, LIV (Oct., 1928), 875–78; Dudley W. Knox, *The Eclipse of American Sea Power* (New York: Army and Navy Journal, 1922). See also William Reynolds Braisted, *The United States Navy in the Pacific, 1909–1922* (Austin: University of Texas Press, 1971), and Thaddeus J. Tuleja, *Statesmen and Admirals: Quest for a Far Eastern Naval Policy* (New York: Norton, 1963); Wheeler, *op. cit.*, pp. 56–60.
9. Contemporary analysis of Elmer Davis, Washington correspondent of the *New York Times, New York Times*, Feb. 6, 1922, p. 8, partly reprinted in Ruhl J. Bartlett, ed., *The Record of American Diplomacy: Documents and Readings in the History of American Foreign Relations* (Second Edition, New York: Knopf, 1950), p. 493; Sutherland Denlinger and Charles B. Gray, *War in the Pacific: A Study of Navies, Peoples and Battle Problems* (New York: R. M. McBride, 1936); Sprout, *Toward a New Order of Sea Power*, chap. XV.
10. Mark Skinner Watson, *Chief of Staff: Prewar Plans and Preparations (United States Army in World War II: The War Department*, Washington: Historical Division, United States Army, 1950), pp. 79, 87.
11. Coffey, "The Navy War Plans Division: Naval Plans and Planning," *loc. cit.*, p. 6. See also Commander G. J. Meyers, U.S.N., "Strategy—From a Naval Viewpoint," Army War College, 1923–24, Miscellaneous Course No. 7, "General Strategic Considerations," copy in U.S. Army Military History Research Collection, Carlisle Barracks, Pa., and *idem.*, "The Strategy of the Atlantic—The Strategy of the Pacific," lecture delivered at the Army War College, Dec. 12 and 14, 1928, G-3 Course No. 25, 1928–29, copy in U.S. Army Military History Research Collection; also Louis Morton, *Strategy and Command: The First Two Years (United States Army in World War II: The War in the Pacific*, Washington: Office of the Chief of Military History, 1962), chap. I; *idem.*, "War Plan ORANGE: Evolution of a Strategy," *World Politics*, XI (Jan., 1959), 221–50.
12. Army Strategical Plan ORANGE, 1928, National Archives and Records Service, Record Group 94.
13. Capt. H. F. Schofield, U.S.N., "Some Effects of the Washington Conference on American Naval Strategy," Army War College, G-3 Course No. 3, Sept. 22, 1923, p. 7, copy in Tasker H. Bliss Papers, Library of Congress, Box 280.
14. Preliminary paper prepared by Professor Sadao Asada for Conference on Japanese-American Relations, 1931–41, held at Kawaguchiko, Japan, July 14–18, 1969, and discussions with him at the conference; Kitaro Matsumoto and Matsataka Chihaya, "Design and Construction of the *Yamato* and *Musashi*," United States Naval Institute *Proceedings*, LXXIX (Oct., 1953), 1102–13; Mark Sufrin, "The 'Yamato,'" *American History Illustrated*, IV, No. 1 (April, 1969), 4–6; Rear Admiral Toshiyuki Yokoi, former Imperial Japanese Navy, "Thoughts on Japan's Naval Defeat," United States Naval Institute *Proceedings*, LXXXVI (Oct., 1960), 72–73.
15. Bernard Brodie, *A Guide to Naval Strategy* (Fifth Edition, New York: Praeger, 1965), p. 43; Samuel Eliot Morison, *The Battle of the Atlantic, September 1939–May 1943* (Vol. I, *History of United States Naval Operations in World War II*, Boston: Little, Brown, 1951), pp. lx, 64.
16. In the text, Japanese names are given in the Japanese fashion, surname first; in

the notes, to conform to the usual style of the English-language translations cited, surnames are given in the Western fashion.

17. Preliminary paper of Sadao Asada.
18. *Ibid.*; Richard Hough, *Death of the Battleship* (New York: Macmillan, 1963), pp. 73–75; Samuel Eliot Morison, *The Rising Sun in the Pacific, 1931–April 1942* (Vol. III, *History of United States Naval Operations in World War II*, Boston: Little, Brown, 1948), pp. 23, 38, 40, 45–46, 61, 80–86; Morison, *Two-Ocean War*, p. 13; Clark G. Reynolds, *The Fast Carriers: The Forging of an Air Navy* (New York: McGraw-Hill, 1968), pp. 4–9, 25, 27.
19. Philip Cowburn, *The Warship in History* (New York: Macmillan, 1965), p. 329; Pratt, *op. cit.*, pp. 451, 453, 455; Reynolds, *op. cit.*, pp. 4–9, 13, 14–21; Archibald D. Turnbull and Clifford L. Lord, *History of United States Naval Aviation* (New Haven: Yale University Press, 1949), pp. 206–208, 270, 284–85, 301–302. *Dictionary of American Naval Fighting Ships* (2 vols., Washington: Government Printing Office, 1959–63), II, Appendix 1, lists all United States carriers, 1922–62. The Navy began numbering its vessels in 1920. "C" stands for "carrier," "V" for heavier-than-air craft. CV-1 was *Langley*.
20. Lieutenant Commander H. T. Bartlett, U.S.N., "Mission of Aircraft with the Fleet," United States Naval Institute *Proceedings*, XLV (May, 1919), 729–41, quotations from pp. 729, 730; Henry Woodhouse, "The Torpedoplane: The New Weapon Which Promises to Revolutionize Naval Tactics," *ibid.*, pp. 743–52. William Fullam, William S. Sims, and Bradley A. Fiske emerged as admirals who emphasized the importance of naval aviation to the future control of the sea; Fiske had pioneered in pre-World War I experiments with torpedo planes. Elting E. Morison, *Admiral Sims and the Modern American Navy* (Boston: Houghton Mifflin, 1942), pp. 504–10; Turnbull and Lord, *op. cit.*, pp. 186–90. "The battleship is dead," said Sims in 1922. E. E. Morison, *op. cit.*, p. 506.
21. Lieutenant Commander H. B. Grow, U.S.N., "Bombing Tests on the 'Virginia' and 'New Jersey,'" United States Naval Institute *Proceedings*, XLIX (Dec., 1923), 1995–96, reprinted from *Proceedings* by permission; Copyright © 1923 U.S. Naval Institute. See Edward Arpee, *From Frigates to Flat-tops: The Story and Life of Rear Admiral William Adger Moffett, U.S.N., "The Father of Naval Aviation"* (Lake Forest, Ill.: privately published, 1953).
22. Lieutenant F. P. Sherman, U.S.N., discussion of "Control of the Air," *ibid.*, L (July, 1924), 1131, reprinted from *Proceedings* by permission; Copyright © 1924 U.S. Naval Institute; Reynolds, *op. cit.*, p. 17, from Lieutenant J. Grimes, U.S.N.R., "Aviation in the Fleet Exercises, 1923–1939," ms, Navy Department, n.d.; Turnbull and Lord, *op. cit.*, especially chap. XXV, "Aviation in the Fleet Exercises."
23. Lieutenant Franklin G. Percival, U.S.N. (Retired), "The Readjustment to New Weapons," United States Naval Institute *Proceedings*, LV (Aug., 1929), 662–63, reprinted from *Proceedings* by permission; Copyright © 1929 U.S. Naval Institute; Reynolds, *op. cit.*, p. 17.
24. Brodie, *op. cit.*, pp. 24–25, and "Our Ships Strike Back," *The Virginia Quarterly Review*, XXI (Spring, 1945), 186–206; S. E. Morison, *Two-Ocean War*, p. 60.
25. Stirling, "Some Fundamentals of Sea Power," *loc. cit.*, p. 913.
26. Reynolds, *op. cit.*, p. 17.
27. *Ibid.*, p. 18.
28. George Carroll Dyer, *The Amphibians Came to Conquer: The Story of Admiral Richmond Kelly Turner* (2 vols., Washington: Government Printing Office, 1972), I, 124; Lieutenant Commander Thomas B. Buell, U.S.N., "Admiral Raymond A. Spruance and the Naval War College: Part II—From Student to Warrior," *Naval War College Review*, XXIII, No. 8 (April, 1971), 43.

29. Pratt, *op. cit.*, p. 409; Bernard Brodie, *Sea Power in the Machine Age* (Princeton: Princeton University Press, 1941), p. 433. In 1928 Captain George J. Meyers had written in *Strategy* (Washington: Byron S. Adams, 1928), p. 173: "Hence we can say that the battleship is the keystone to the arch of fleet strength and that it will remain so until a type is invented that will equal or surpass it in sustained destructive fire, in defensive qualities, and mobility as measured by speed and range of action." Meyers's qualifications of his first statement are significant and explain what eventually developed.
30. Schofield, "Some Effects of the Washington Conference on American Naval Strategy," *loc. cit.*, p. 8.
31. *Ibid.*
32. Jeter A. Isely and Philip A. Crowl, *The U. S. Marines and Amphibious War: Its Theory and Practice in the Pacific* (Princeton: Princeton University Press, 1951), pp. 24–26, 593n; Major General Charles G. Morton, "Landing in Force," *Infantry Journal*, XVI (May, 1920), 981–88, 1077–83.
33. Robert D. Heinl, Jr., *Soldiers of the Sea: The United States Marine Corps, 1775–1962* (Annapolis: United States Naval Institute, 1962); Isely and Crowl, *op. cit.*, pp. 3–28.
34. Major Dion Williams, U.S.M.C., "Military Landing Operations." *Infantry Journal*, III (July, 1906), 97–128, quotation from p. 97; Isely and Crowl, *op. cit.*, pp. 25–26.
35. Vice Admiral George C. Dyer, U.S.N. (Retired), "Naval Amphibious Landmarks," United States Naval Institute *Proceedings*, XCII, No. 8 (Aug., 1966), 54–55; Isely and Crowl, *op. cit.*, pp. 22–23.
36. Captain Asa Walker, U.S.N., "Combined Maritime Operations," United States Naval Institute *Proceedings*, XXVI (March, 1900), 143–55, quotation from p. 153.
37. Dyer, "Naval Amphibious Landmarks," pp. 55–56; Isely and Crowl, *op. cit.*, pp. 3–5, 7–21; W. D. Puleston, *The Dardanelles Expedition: A Condensed Study* (Second Edition, Annapolis: United States Naval Institute, 1927), p. 168. In the United States, Colonel William K. Naylor said in *Principles of Strategy with Historical Illustrations* (Fort Leavenworth: General Service Schools Press, 1921), p. 335: "Descents upon a hostile coast, if opposed, have a very small chance of success, particularly in modern times. It is true that the landing may be made, but getting away from the coast is the difficulty."
38. Captain W. S. Pye, U.S.N., "Joint Army and Navy Operations," United States Naval Institute *Proceedings*, LI (Feb., 1925), 237, 240, reprinted from *Proceedings* by permission; Copyright © 1925 U.S. Naval Institute. Pye offered an extended study: *ibid.*, L (Dec., 1924), 1965–76; LI (Jan., 1925), 1–14; (Feb., 1925), 233–45; (March, 1925), 386–99; (April, 1925), 589–99; (June, 1925), 975–1000.
39. *Ibid.*, LI (Feb., 1925), 240, reprinted from *Proceedings* by permission; Copyright © 1925 U.S. Naval Institute.
40. *Ibid.* (March, 1925), 387–88, reprinted from *Proceedings by permission*; Copyright © 1925 U.S. Naval Institute.
41. Captain T. C. Hart, U.S.N., "Problems of Combined Expeditions," Army War College, Command Course No. 46, March 10, 1925, pp. 2–3, copy in Tasker H. Bliss Papers, Library of Congress, Box 280.
42. Isely and Crowl, *op. cit.*, pp. 26–28.
43. Dyer, "Naval Amphibious Landmarks," p. 50; Isely and Crowl, *op. cit.*, pp. 29–31, quotation from p. 31; Kenneth Macksey and John H. Batchelor, *Tank: A History of the Armoured Fighting Vehicle* (New York: Ballantine, 1971), p. 68;

Richard M. Ogorkiewicz, *Armoured Forces: A History of Armoured Forces and Their Vehicles* (New York: Arco, 1970), p. 409.

44. Maj. Gen. J. L. Hines, Chief of Staff, "Grand Joint Army and Navy Exercise No. 3," Army War College, Miscellaneous No. 7, June 26, 1925, copy in Tasker H. Bliss Papers, Library of Congress, Box 281; Isely and Crowl, *op. cit.*, pp. 29–34; Neill Macaulay, *The Sandino Affair* (Chicago: Quadrangle, 1967).
45. Major General Eli K. Cole, U.S.M.C., "Joint Overseas Operations," United States Naval Institute *Proceedings*, LV (Nov., 1929), 927–37, quotation on p. 928; Isely and Crowl, *op. cit.*, p. 28.
46. Isely and Crowl, *op. cit.*, p. 35.
47. *Ibid.*, pp. 33–35.
48. *Ibid.*, pp. 37–44; Dyer, *The Amphibians Came to Conquer*, I, 206–208, 213–25.
49. Buell, *loc. cit.*, pp. 43–44; Dyer, *The Amphibians Came to Conquer*, I, 170–71; Isely and Crowl, *op. cit.*, pp. 45–67.
50. Daniel E. Barbey, *MacArthur's Amphibious Navy: Seventh Amphibious Force Operations, 1943–1945* (Annapolis: United States Naval Institute, 1969), pp. 12–20; Dyer, *The Amphibians Came to Conquer*, I, 202–206, 208–13; Dyer, "Naval Amphibious Landmarks," pp. 50–54, 57–60; Isely and Crowl, *op. cit.*, pp. 67–69, 173–74; Richard M. Leighton and Robert W. Coakley, *Global Logistics and Strategy, 1940–1943 (United State Army in World War II: The War Department*, Washington: Office of the Chief of Military History, 1955), pp. 376–82.
51. Isely and Crowl, *op. cit.*, p. 4. Dyer, *The Amphibians Came to Conquer*, I, 223–24, 226–27, and "Naval Amphibious Landmarks," pp. 56–57, traces the evolution of the Navy and Marine Corps manuals.
52. Lieutenant Commander Thomas B. Buell, U.S.N., "Admiral Raymond A. Spruance and the Naval War College: Part I—Preparing for World War II," *Naval War College Review*, XXIII, No. 7 (March, 1971), 36–37, and Part II, *loc. cit.*, pp. 32–37. For the Navy's relative neglect of logistics, see also Dyer, *The Amphibians Came to Conquer*, I, 403–21.
53. Quoted in Buell, "Admiral Raymond A. Spruance . . . Part I," *loc. cit.*, p. 33.

Part Four. American Strategy in Global Triumph, 1941–1945

1. Quoted in Haislip's obituary, *New York Times*, Dec. 27, 1971, p. 31. Haislip commanded the 85th Infantry Division and the XV Corps in the European campaign and became Vice Chief of Staff of the Army, 1949–51.

CHAPTER THIRTEEN. THE STRATEGIC TRADITION OF A. T. MAHAN: STRATEGISTS OF THE PACIFIC WAR

1. Quoted in Samuel Eliot Morison, *Leyte, June 1944–January 1945* (Vol. XII, *History of United States Naval Operations in World War II*, Boston: Little, Brown, 1958), p. 58.
2. Ray S. Cline, *Washington Command Post: The Operations Division (United States Army in World War II: The War Department*, Washington: Office of the Chief of Military History, 1951), pp. 58–59; George Carroll Dyer, *The Amphibians Came to Conquer: The Story of Admiral Richmond Kelly Turner* (2 vols., Washington: Government Printing Office, 1972), I, 157–63, 176–77; Maurice Matloff and Edwin M. Snell, *Strategic Planning for Coalition Warfare, 1941–1942 (United States Army in World War II: The War Department*, Washington: Office of the Chief of Military History, 1953), pp. 32–48; Louis Morton, "Germany First," in Kent Roberts Greenfield, ed., *Command Decisions*

(New York: Harcourt Brace, 1959), pp. 3–38, especially pp. 31–37; Mark Skinner Watson, *Chief of Staff: Prewar Plans and Preparations (United States Army in World War II: The War Department*, Washington: Historical Division, U.S. Army, 1950), pp. 367–82.

3. A. Russell Buchanan, *The United States and World War II* (2 vols., New York: Harper & Row, 1964), I, 218–19; Richard M. Leighton and Robert W. Coakley, *Global Logistics and Strategy, 1940–1943 (United States Army in World War II: The War Department*, Washington: Office of the Chief of Military History, 1955), chaps. VI–VII, XV, XXII, and pp. 659–60, 662–68; Matloff and Snell, *op. cit.*, pp. 78–96, 102, 114–73, 210–26, 256–73, 298–306, 357–62, 367–79, 390; Maurice Matloff, *Strategic Planning for Coalition Warfare, 1943–1944 (United States Army in World War II: The War Department*, Washington: Office of the Chief of Military History, 1959), pp. 319, 398; Louis Morton, *Strategy and Command: The First Two Years (United States Army in World War II: The War in the Pacific*, Washington: Office of the Chief of Military History, 1962), pp. 143–53, 158–66, 179–80, 186–93, 198, 204–12, 217–24, 306–11, 331–51.

4. Masanori Ito with Roger Pineau, *The End of the Imperial Japanese Navy*, tr. Y. Kuroda and Roger Pineau (New York: Norton, 1962), pp. 52–69; Samuel Eliot Morison, *Coral Sea, Midway and Submarine Actions, May 1942–August 1942* (Vol. IV, *History of United States Naval Operations in World War II*, Boston: Little, Brown, 1949), chaps. I–VIII; Samuel Eliot Morison, *The Two-Ocean War: A Short History of the United States Navy in the Second World War* (Boston: Little, Brown, 1963), pp. 140–63; Morton, *Strategy and Command: The First Two Years*, pp. 274–85; Clark G. Reynolds, *The Fast Carriers: The Forging of an Air Navy* (New York: McGraw-Hill, 1968), pp. 6–9, 26–29.

   Under Admiral Chester W. Nimitz, Commander in Chief Pacific Fleet, Rear Admiral Frank Jack Fletcher commanded Task Force 17 in the battle of the Coral Sea and as senior commander of the Carrier Striking Force was in tactical command at Midway. Rear Admiral Raymond A. Spruance, in temporary command of Vice Admiral William F. Halsey's Task Force 16, including *Enterprise* and *Hornet*, nevertheless operated almost autonomously at Midway, while Fletcher directly commanded *Yorktown*, in which he flew his flag. Admiral Halsey, Commander Carriers Pacific Fleet, missed the Coral Sea because he had been away commanding *Hornet* and *Enterprise* for Lieutenant Colonel James H. Doolittle's raid on Tokyo of April 18, 1942, Doolittle's B-25s being launched from *Hornet* some 668 miles away from Tokyo. A skin rash then caused Halsey to miss Midway as well. Spruance had Halsey's staff, headed by Captain Miles Browning, a brilliant though erratic carrier officer whose strategic judgment and sense of timing were largely responsible for the American carrier planes' hitting the Japanese Striking Force carriers just as their aircraft were being refueled and rearmed.

5. Carl von Clausewitz, *On War*, tr. Col. J. J. Graham, New and Revised Edition with an Introduction and Notes by Col. F. N. Maude (Eighth Impression, 3 vols., New York: Barnes & Noble, 1968), III, 62, 67, 63; Ernest J. King and Walter Muir Whitehill, *Fleet Admiral King: A Naval Record* (New York: Norton, 1952), chap. XXXI; Morton, *Strategy and Command: The First Two Years*, chap. XIII.

6. Buchanan, *op. cit.*, pp. 229–31; Dyer, *op. cit.*, I, 229–63, 269–80; Jeter A. Isely and Philip A. Crowl, *The U. S. Marines and Amphibious War: Its Theory and Practice in the Pacific* (Princeton: Princeton University Press, 1951), pp. 87–95; King and Whitehill, *op. cit.*, pp. 386–89; Matloff and Snell, *op. cit.*, pp. 256–65, 298–306; John Miller, Jr., *Guadalcanal: The First Offensive (United States Army in World War II: The War in the Pacific*, Washington: Historical

Division, U.S. Army, 1949), chap. I; Morison, *Coral Sea, Midway and Submarine Operations*, chap. XII; Samuel Eliot Morison, *Strategy and Compromise* (Boston: Little, Brown, 1958), pp. 71–74; Morison, *Two-Ocean War*, pp. 164–66; Morton, *Strategy and Command: The First Two Years*, pp. 298–323.

7. Dyer, *op. cit.*, I, 277–336, 383–95, 404; Frank O. Hough, Verle E. Ludwig, and Henry I. Shaw, Jr., *Pearl Harbor to Guadalcanal* (Vol. I, *History of U. S. Marine Corps Operations in World War II*, Washington: Historical Branch, Headquarters U.S. Marine Corps, 1958); Isely and Crowl, *op. cit.*, pp. 98–118; Robert Leckie, *Strong Men Armed: The United States Marines against Japan* (Paperback edition, New York: Ballantine, 1969), chap. I; Miller, *op. cit.*, chaps. II–IV; Morison, *Coral Sea, Midway and Submarine Actions*, pp. 259–83; Samuel Eliot Morison, *The Struggle for Guadalcanal, August 1942–February 1943* (Vol. V, *History of United States Naval Operations in World War II*, Boston: Little, Brown, 1950), pp. 12–15; Morison, *Two-Ocean War*, pp. 166–72; John L. Zimmerman, *The Guadalcanal Campaign* (Marine Corps Historical Monographs, V, Washington: Historical Division, Headquarters U.S. Marine Corps, 1949), pp. 4–25.
8. Isely and Crowl, *op. cit.*, pp. 118–23; Leckie, *op. cit.*, pp. 17–31; Morison, *Coral Sea, Midway and Submarine Actions*, pp. 283–96; Morison, *Struggle for Guadalcanal*, pp. 15–16; Zimmerman, *op. cit.*, pp. 25–49.
9. Dyer, *op. cit.*, I, 419.
10. Wesley Frank Craven and James Lea Cate, eds., *The Army Air Forces in World War II* (7 vols., Chicago: University of Chicago Press, 1948–58), IV, *The Pacific: Guadalcanal to Saipan, August 1942 to July 1944*, chaps. II–III; Dyer, *op. cit.*, I, 336–434; Isely and Crowl, *op. cit.*, pp. 129–65; Ito and Pineau, *op. cit.*, chap. V; Leckie, *op. cit.*, pp. 31–131; Miller, *op. cit.*, chaps. IV–XIV; Morison, *Struggle for Guadalcanal*, chaps. II–XIV; Morison, *Two-Ocean War*, pp. 167–214; Zimmerman, *op. cit.*, pp. 49–159.
11. Reynolds, *op. cit.*, p. 35.
12. Craven and Cate, *op. cit.*, IV, chaps. IV–VIII; Robert L. Eichelberger, *Our Jungle Road to Tokyo* (New York: Viking, 1950), pp. 8–77, 89–99; Frank O. Hough and John A. Crown, *The Campaign on New Britain* (Marine Corps Historical Monographs, X, Washington: Historical Branch, Headquarters U.S. Marine Corps, 1952); Isely and Crowl, *op. cit.*, pp. 165–91; Matloff, *op. cit.*, pp. 88–99; John Miller, Jr., *CARTWHEEL: The Reduction of Rabaul (United States Army in World War II: The War in the Pacific*, Washington: Office of the Chief of Military History, 1959), pp. 6–287; Samuel Milner, *Victory in Papua (United States Army in World War II: The War in the Pacific*, Washington: Office of the Chief of Military History, 1957); Samuel Eliot Morison, *Breaking the Bismarcks Barrier, 22 July 1942–1 May 1944* (Vol. VI, *History of United States Naval Operations in World War II*, Boston: Little, Brown, 1957); Morison, *Two-Ocean War*, pp. 264–65, 272–94; Morton, *Strategy and Command: The First Two Years*, pp. 385–415, 450–53, 502–83; John N. Rentz, *Bougainville and the Northern Solomons* (Marine Corps Historical Monographs, IV, Washington: Historical Branch, Headquarters U.S. Marine Corps, 1948); John N. Rentz, *Marines in the Central Solomons* (Marine Corps Historical Monographs, XI, Washington: Historical Branch, Headquarters U.S. Marine Corps, 1952); Henry I. Shaw, Jr., and Douglas T. Kane, *Isolation of Rabaul* (Vol. II, *History of U. S. Marine Corps Operations in World War II*, Washington: Historical Branch, Headquarters U.S. Marine Corps, 1963).
13. Daniel E. Barbey, *MacArthur's Amphibious Navy: Seventh Amphibious Force Operations 1943–1945* (Annapolis: United States Naval Institute, 1969), chaps.

VI–XII, especially pp. 88–91; Miller, *CARTWHEEL*, pp. 214–21; Morison, *Bismarcks Barrier*, pp. 269–71.

14. Barbey, *op. cit.*, pp. 42, 57, 70–71, 89; Craven and Cate, *op. cit.*, IV, 92–193; George C. Kenney, *General Kenney Reports: A Personal History of the Pacific War* (New York: Duell, Sloan and Pearce, 1949); Douglas MacArthur, *Reminiscences* (New York: McGraw-Hill, 1964), pp. 166–67; Reynolds, *op. cit.*, pp. 30–31.
15. MacArthur, *op. cit.*, pp. 165–66. Wee Willie Keeler was a third baseman and then an outfielder for the New York Giants (1892–93), Brooklyn Dodgers (1893), Baltimore Orioles (1894–98), Brooklyn again (1899–1902), New York Highlanders (Yankees) (1903–1909), and then the Giants again (1910). *The Baseball Encyclopedia* (New York: Macmillan, 1969), p. 1052. At the time of publication of the latter volume he ranked eleventh among all major league players, at present fourteenth, in total lifetime hits. *Ibid.*, p. 64.
16. MacArthur, *op. cit.*, p. 166.
17. Matloff, *op. cit.*, p. 391.
18. *Ibid.*, pp. 307–308, 373–78; Morton, *Strategy and Command: The First Two Years*, pp. 105–109, 376–411, 434–72, 543–58; Reynolds, *op. cit.*, pp. 10, 156–61; Rear Admiral Toshiyuki Yokoi, former Imperial Japanese Navy, "Thoughts on Japan's Naval Defeat," United States Naval Institute *Proceedings*, LXXXVI (Oct., 1960), 68–75.
19. Quoted in Cline, *op. cit.*, pp. 334–35.
20. Craven and Cate, *op. cit.*, IV, Part IV, and V, *The Pacific: MATTERHORN to Nagasaki, June 1944 to August 1945*, Parts I–II; Leighton and Coakley, *op. cit.*, pp. 40, 76, 85–88, 94–95, 525–50; Matloff and Snell, *op. cit.*, pp. 356–57; Matloff, *op. cit.*, pp. 7–8, 15, 77–88, 139–42, 196–205, 232–39, 342–43, 347–52, 359, 370–73, 440–42; Morton, *Strategy and Command: The First Two Years*, pp. 91, 154–61, 447–48, 451; Forrest C. Pogue, *George C. Marshall: Ordeal and Hope, 1939–1942* (New York: Viking, 1966), chap. XVI; and the three volumes by Charles F. Romanus and Riley Sunderland in the subseries *China-Burma-India Theater* of *United States Army in World War II: Stilwell's Mission to China* (Washington: Office of the Chief of Military History, 1953), especially pp. 23, 29–32, 43–44, 50–57, 61–80; *Stilwell's Command Problems* (Washington: Office of the Chief of Military History, 1956); and *Time Runs Out in CBI* (Washington: Office of the Chief of Military History, 1959).
21. Quoted in Matloff, *op. cit.*, p. 188. See also *ibid.*, pp. 186–88; Philip A. Crowl and Edmund G. Love, *Seizure of the Gilberts and Marshalls* (*United States Army in World War II: The War in the Pacific*, Washington: Office of the Chief of Military History, 1955), pp. 3–4; Morton, *Strategy and Command: The First Two Years*, pp. 28–31, 33–44, 435–44, 447; Henry I. Shaw, Jr., Bernard C. Nalty, and Edwin T. Turnbladh, *Central Pacific Drive* (Vol. III, *History of U.S. Marine Corps Operations in World War II*, Washington: Historical Branch, Headquarters U.S. Marine Corps, 1966), pp. 3–7, 13.
22. Lieutenant Franklin G. Percival, U.S.N. (Retired), "Wanted: A New Naval Development Policy," United States Naval Institute *Proceedings*, LXIX (May, 1943), 655–68, quotation on p. 662, reprinted from *Proceedings* by permission; Copyright © 1943 U.S. Naval Institute; Reynolds, *op. cit.*, pp. 36–59, 63–88.
23. This was the final wartime revision of Marine Corps *Landing Operations Doctrine*. Vice Admiral George C. Dyer, U.S.N. (Retired), "Naval Amphibious Landmarks," United States Naval Institute *Proceedings*, XCII, No. 8 (Aug., 1966), 57. Leckie, *op. cit.*, pp. 135–36, 138–39, for Marine divisions in the Pacific.
24. Duncan S. Ballantine, *U. S. Naval Logistics in the Second World War* (Prince-

ton: Princeton University Press, 1947); Worrall Reed Carter, *Beans, Bullets, and Black Oil* (Washington: Government Printing Office, 1951); Samuel Eliot Morison, *Aleutians, Gilberts and Marshalls, June 1942–April 1944* (Vol. VII, *History of United States Naval Operations in World War II*, Boston: Little, Brown, 1957), chap. II; Reynolds, *op. cit.*, pp. 128–30, 134–35, 306.

25. Crowl and Love, *op. cit.*, pp. 12–25; Matloff, *op. cit.*, pp. 186–95, 205–209; Morison, *Aleutians, Gilberts and Marshalls*, pp. 66–92; Morton, *Strategy and Command: The First Two Years*, pp. 481–90, 512–27; Shaw, Nalty, and Turnbladh, *op. cit.*, pp. 10–13.

26. Quoted in Isely and Crowl, *op. cit.*, p. 254. Crowl and Love, *op. cit.*, pp. 13–25; Matloff, *op. cit.*, pp. 192–93, 206–207; Morton, *Strategy and Command: The First Two Years*, pp. 450–53, 458–72; Shaw, Nalty, and Turnbladh, *op. cit.*, pp. 12–13.

27. Crowl and Love, *op. cit.*, chaps. III–X; Dyer, *The Amphibians Came to Conquer*, II, chaps. XVI–XVIII, and 743–48; Isely and Crowl, *op. cit.*, chap. VI; Leckie, *op. cit.*, pp. 184–218, 221–32; Morison, *Aleutians, Gilberts and Marshalls*, chaps. VII–XI; Morison, *Two-Ocean War*, pp. 297–306; Morton, *Strategy and Command: The First Two Years*, pp. 567–75; Reynolds, *op. cit.*, pp. 84–96; Shaw, Nalty, and Turnbladh, *op. cit.*, Part II; James R. Stockman, *The Battle for Tarawa* (Marine Corps Historical Monographs, II, Washington: Historical Branch, Headquarters U.S. Marine Corps, 1947). A major result of the Tarawa experience was the Navy's creation of Underwater Demolition Teams, to be sent to the sites of subsequent landings, both to gather exact geographical knowledge and to destroy static beach obstacles; Dyer, *The Amphibians Came to Conquer*, II, 744.

28. Crowl and Love, *op. cit.*, chaps. XI–XVIII; Robert D. Heinl, Jr., and John A. Crown, *The Marshalls: Increasing the Tempo* (Marine Corps Historical Monographs, XIV, Washington: Historical Branch, Headquarters U.S. Marine Corps, 1954), chaps. I–VII; Isely and Crowl, *op. cit.*, pp. 253–91; Morison, *Aleutians, Gilberts and Marshalls*, chaps. XIII–XV; Morison, *Two-Ocean War*, pp. 306–12; Reynolds, *op. cit.*, pp. 105–109, 123–35; Shaw, Nalty, and Turnbladh, *op. cit.*, pp. 117–80.

29. Spruance quoted in Isely and Crowl, *op. cit.*, p. 292. Crowl and Love, *op. cit.*, chap. XIX; Dyer, *The Amphibians Came to Conquer*, II, chap. XIX; Heinl and Crown, *op. cit.*, chap. VIII; Isely and Crowl, *op. cit.*, pp. 291–309; Morison, *Aleutians, Gilberts and Marshalls*, chap. XVI; Morison, *Two-Ocean War*, pp. 312–17; Reynolds, *op. cit.*, pp. 135–41; Shaw, Nalty, and Turnbladh, *op. cit.*, pp. 181–227.

30. Barbey, *op. cit.*, chap. XV; Craven and Cate, *op. cit.*, IV, chaps. IX, XVII; Gavin Long, *MacArthur as Military Commander* (Princeton: Van Nostrand, 1969), pp. 138–40; Matloff, *op. cit.*, pp. 453–59; Miller, *CARTWHEEL*, chap. XVI; John Miller, Jr., "MacArthur and the Admiralties," in Greenfield, *op. cit.*, pp. 210–23; Morison, *Bismarcks Barrier*, pp. 324–36, 432–48; Reynolds, *op. cit.*, pp. 96–102, 108, 142.

31. Craven and Cate, *op. cit.*, V, chap. I, and VI, *Men and Planes*, pp. 208–10; Isely and Crowl, *op. cit.*, pp. 254–57, 301–309; Matloff, *op. cit.*, pp. 89–90, 194, 206, 310, 444–45, 450, 453–59; Morison, *Aleutians, Gilberts and Marshalls*, pp. 85, 201–206; Samuel Eliot Morison, *New Guinea and the Marianas, March 1944–August 1944* (Vol. VIII, *History of United States Naval Operations in World War II*, Boston: Little, Brown, 1957), pp. 3–10; Morison, *Two-Ocean War*, pp. 282–83, 322–24; Morton, *Strategy and Command: The First Two Years*, pp. 585–91, 595–96; Reynolds, *op. cit.*, pp. 114–19, 141–42; Shaw, Nalty, and Turnbladh, *op. cit.*, pp. 120–21, 220–21. Lieutenant Percival, "Wanted: A New Naval De-

velopment Policy," *loc. cit.*, with characteristic astuteness advocated a leapfrogging strategy, which he called the *Blitzkreig zur See*. "War at sea," he said, "is actually better suited than is war on land to this swiftly decisive [Blitzkrieg] type of campaign; partly because a fleet has far greater strategic mobility than an army, and partly because the obstacles in naval warfare can be more accurately weighed in advance." Pp. 659–60.

Gavin Long, *op. cit.*, pp. 131–44, rightly stresses that it was only with hesitation that MacArthur accepted "leapfrogging," despite the fervor with which he eventually claimed it as his own special strategy.

32. Matloff, *op. cit.*, pp. 459–61, 464; Louis Morton, *Pacific Command: A Study in Interservice Relations* (U.S. Air Force Academy, 1961); Reynolds, *op. cit.*, p. 156. Long, an Australian writer, *op. cit.*, p. 143, is critical of American strategy and command in the Pacific.
33. MacArthur, *op. cit.*, pp. 197–98; Matloff, *op. cit.*, pp. 479–81; Morison, *Leyte*, pp. 4–7; Samuel Eliot Morison, *The Liberation of the Philippines: Luzon, Mindanao, the Visayas, 1944–1945* (Vol. XIII, *History of United States Naval Operations in World War II*, Boston: Little, Brown 1959), pp. 3–5; Morison, *Strategy and Compromise*, pp. 98–106; Morison, *Two-Ocean War*, pp. 421–22; Reynolds, *op. cit.*, pp. 243–45; Robert Ross Smith, *The Approach to the Philippines* (*United States Army in World War II: The War in the Pacific*, Washington: Office of the Chief of Military History, 1953), pp. 450–53; Robert Ross Smith, "Luzon versus Formosa (1944)," in Greenfield, *op. cit.*, pp. 358–73; Robert Ross Smith, *Triumph in the Philippines* (*United States Army in World War II: The War in the Pacific*, Washington: Office of the Chief of Military History, 1963), chap. I.
34. MacArthur, *op. cit.*, pp. 196–98; Matloff, *op. cit.*, pp. 481–88, 530–31; Morison, *Leyte*, pp. 7–12; Morison, *Liberation of the Philippines*, pp. 3–5; Morison, *Two-Ocean War*, pp. 421–23; Charles S. Nichols, Jr., and Henry I. Shaw, Jr., *Okinawa: Victory in the Pacific* (Marine Corps Historical Monographs, XV, Washington: Historical Branch, Headquarters U.S. Marine Corps, 1955; reprinted Rutland, Vt., and Tokyo: Charles E. Tuttle, 1966), pp. 13–17; Reynolds, *op. cit.*, pp. 245–49; Smith, "Luzon versus Formosa," *loc. cit.*, pp. 363–73; Smith, *Triumph in the Philippines*, pp. 7–17.
35. H. H. Arnold, *Global Mission* (New York: Harper, 1949), pp. 476–80; Craven and Cate, *op. cit.*, V, 3–175, 507–76, 608–702; Matloff, *op. cit.*, pp. 118–19, 205–10, 231–34, 308–12, 328–33, 336–38, 373–78, 385, 451–52, 487–89; Morison, *Strategy and Compromise*, pp. 83–91, 96–106, 114–20; Morton, *Strategy and Command: The First Two Years*, pp. 592–605.
36. A. T. Mahan, *The Influence of Sea Power upon History, 1660–1783* (Boston: Little, Brown, 1890), p. 288.
37. Holloway H. Frost, *The Battle of Jutland* (Annapolis: United States Naval Institute, 1936), pp. v–vi, ix–xi (Prefatory Note by Edwin A. Falk), 108–16, 515, 517, quotations from pp. 110, 517. "Jellicoe was a McClellan," Frost goes on to say, p. 517.
38. *Ibid.*, p. 516.
39. Lieutenant Commander H. H. Frost, U.S.N., "National Strategy," United States Naval Institute *Proceedings*, LI (Aug., 1925), 1353, reprinted from *Proceedings* by permission; Copyright © 1925 U.S. Naval Institute.
40. *Ibid.*
41. Lieutenant Commander H. H. Frost, U.S.N., "The Spirit of the Offensive," *ibid.*, XLIX (Feb., 1923), 285.
42. Philip A. Crowl, *Campaign in the Marianas* (*United States Army in World War II: The War in the Pacific*, Washington: Office of the Chief of Military History,

1955); Dyer, *The Amphibians Came to Conquer*, II, chap. XXI; Carl W. Hoffman, *Saipan: The Beginning of the End* (Marine Corps Historical Monographs, VI, Washington: Historical Branch, Headquarters U.S. Marine Corps, 1950), pp. 1–71; Isely and Crowl, *op. cit.*, pp. 310–20; Morison, *New Guinea and the Marianas*, pp. 149–99; Morison, *Two-Ocean War*, pp. 322–29; Reynolds, *op. cit.*, pp. 161–77; Shaw, Nalty, and Turnbladh, *op. cit.*, pp. 231–79.

43. Quotation in Leckie, *op. cit.*, p. 326. Ito and Pineau, *op. cit.*, pp. 92–95; Morison, *New Guinea and the Marianas*, pp. 10–14, 213–21; Morison, *Two-Ocean War*, pp. 330–33; Reynolds, *op. cit.*, pp. 156–61, 179.
44. Quoted in Lieutenant Commander Thomas B. Buell, U.S.N., "Admiral Raymond A. Spruance and the Naval War College: Part I—Preparing for World War II," *Naval War College Review*, XXIII, No. 7 (March, 1971), 32, from Morison, *Rising Sun in the Pacific*, p. 158. Ito and Pineau, *op. cit.*, pp. 95–102; Morison, *New Guinea and the Marianas*, pp. 222–40; Morison, *Two-Ocean War*, pp. 333–38; Reynolds, *op. cit.*, pp. 170–73, 177–81.
45. Lieutenant Commander Thomas B. Buell, U.S.N., "Admiral Raymond A. Spruance and the Naval War College: Part II—From Student to Warrior," *Naval War College Review*, XXIII, No. 8 (April, 1971), 35.
46. Morison, *Two-Ocean War*, p. 336.
47. J. J. Clark with Clark G. Reynolds, *Carrier Admiral* (New York: McKay, 1967), pp. 166–68; Reynolds, *op. cit.*, pp. 180–83.
48. Frost, *Jutland*, p. 516; Morison, *New Guinea and the Marianas*, pp. 240–56; Morison, *Two-Ocean War*, pp. 203–205, 336–38; Reynolds, *op. cit.*, pp. 182–83.
49. Quoted in Reynolds, *op. cit.*, p. 183.
50. E. P. Forrestel, *Admiral Raymond A. Spruance, USN: A Study in Command* (Washington: Government Printing Office, 1966), pp. 131–39; Morison, *Leyte*, pp. 58–59; Morison, *New Guinea and the Marianas*, p. 256; Morison, *Two-Ocean War*, pp. 336–38, 345; Reynolds, *op. cit.*, pp. 183–89, 205–10.
51. Forrestel, *op. cit.*, pp. 139–46; Ito and Pineau, *op. cit.*, pp. 102–109; Charles A. Lockwood and Hans Christian Adamson, *Battles of the Philippine Sea* (New York: Crowell, 1967); Morison, *New Guinea and the Marianas*, pp. 256–321; Morison, *Two-Ocean War*, pp. 338–45; Reynolds, *op. cit.*, pp. 184–205; Theodore Taylor, *The Magnificent Mitscher* (New York: Norton, 1954).
52. Matloff, *op. cit.*, pp. 480–81.
53. M. Hamlin Cannon, *Leyte: The Return to the Philippines* (*United States Army in World War II: The War in the Pacific*, Washington: Office of the Chief of Military History, 1954), chap. I; Morison, *Leyte*, pp. 12–18; Morison, *Two-Ocean War*, pp. 326, 421–23; Reynolds, *op. cit.*, pp. 246–48.
54. Cannon, *op. cit.*, chaps. III–V; Frank O. Hough, *The Assault on Peleliu* (Marine Corps Historical Monographs, VII, Washington: Historical Branch, Headquarters U.S. Marine Corps, 1950); Isely and Crowl, *op. cit.*, chap. IX; Leckie, *op. cit.*, pp. 394–98, 401–27; Morison, *Leyte*, pp. 30–43; Morison, *Two-Ocean War*, pp. 425–27; Smith, *Approach to the Philippines*, chaps. XIX–XXIV.
55. Quoted in Morison, *Leyte*, p. 58. Stanley L. Falk, *Decision at Leyte* (New York: Norton, 1966), pp. 42–90; Hajima Fukaya, ed. by Martin E. Holbrook and Gerald E. Wheeler, "Japan's Wartime Carrier Construction," United States Naval Institute *Proceedings*, LXXXI (Sept., 1955), 1031–43; Ito and Pineau, *op. cit.*, pp. 110–23; Lynn Lucius Moore, "*Shinano*: The Jinx Carrier," United States Naval Institute *Proceedings*, LXXIX (Feb., 1953), 142–49; Morison, *Leyte*, chap. IV; Morison, *Two-Ocean War*, pp. 432–41; Reynolds, *op. cit.*, pp. 253–63; C. Vann Woodward, *The Battle for Leyte Gulf* (New York: Macmillan, 1947), pp. 7–31.

56. Bernard Brodie, *A Guide to Naval Strategy* (Fifth Edition, New York: Praeger, 1965), p. 46.
57. William F. Halsey, Jr., and J. Bryan III, *Admiral Halsey's Story* (New York: McGraw-Hill, 1947), p. 217; Reynolds, *op. cit.*, p. 268.
58. Bernard Brodie, "The Battle for Leyte Gulf," *Virginia Quarterly Review*, XXIII (Summer, 1947), 455–60; Falk, *op. cit.*, chaps. XI–XIV; Fleet Admiral William F. Halsey, Jr., U.S.N., "The Battle for Leyte Gulf," United States Naval Institute *Proceedings*, LXXVIII (May, 1952), 487–95; Halsey and Bryan, *op. cit.*, pp. 211–27; Captain Andrew Hamilton, U.S.N.R., "Where Is Task Force Thirty-four?" United States Naval Institute *Proceedings*, LXXXVI, No. 10 (Oct., 1960), 76–80; Ito and Pineau, *op. cit.*, pp. 123–79; Morison, *Leyte*, chaps. X–XIV; Morison, *Two-Ocean War*, pp. 436–70; Reynolds, *op. cit.*, pp. 256–86; Woodward, *op. cit.*, chaps. II–VI.
59. Reynolds, *op. cit.*, p. 282. Mitscher at least wanted to strike Ozawa at earliest dawn. Morison, *Leyte*, pp. 320, 322–24.
60. MacArthur, *op. cit.*, p. 198.
61. Charles W. Boggs, Jr., *Marine Aviation in the Philippines* (Marine Corps Historical Monographs, IX, Washington: Historical Branch, Headquarters U.S. Marine Corps, 1951); Cannon, *op. cit.*, chaps. VI–XXII; Craven and Cate, *op. cit.*, V, chap. XII; Vincent J. Esposito, ed., *The West Point Atlas of American Wars* (2 vols., New York: Praeger, 1959), II, Section 2, maps 145–46, 148; Walter Krueger, *From Down Under to Nippon: The Story of the Sixth Army in World War II* (Washington: Combat Forces Press, 1953); Long, *op. cit.*, pp. 153–58; Morison, *Leyte*, chaps. XV–XVI; Morison, *Two-Ocean War*, pp. 470–74; Reynolds, *op. cit.*, pp. 285–88; Robert Sherrod, *History of Marine Corps Aviation in World War II* (Washington: Combat Forces Press, 1952), pp. 271–89.
62. Rikihei Inoguchi and Todashi Nakajima, with Roger Pineau, *The Divine Wind: Japan's Kamikaze Force in World War II* (Annapolis: United States Naval Institute, 1958); Ito and Pineau, *op. cit.*, pp. 180–83; Morison, *Leyte*, pp. 300–306, 358–59, 366–68; Morison, *Two-Ocean War*, pp. 462–63; Reynolds, *op. cit.*, pp. 263, 285–90; Sherrod, *op. cit.*, pp. 272–74.
63. Craven and Cate, *op. cit.*, V, chaps. XIII–XV; Morison, *Liberation of the Philippines*, pp. 174–79; Morison, *Two-Ocean War*, pp. 476–93, 514–15; Samuel Eliot Morison, *Victory in the Pacific, 1945* (Vol. XIV, *History of United States Naval Operations in World War II*, Boston: Little, Brown, 1960), pp. 14, 17, 23–24; Smith, *Triumph in the Philippines*, pp. 24–26.
64. Craven and Cate, *op. cit.*, V, chap. XVI; Morison, *Coral Sea, Midway and Submarine Operations*, chaps. X–XI; Morison, *Leyte*, pp. 398–414; Morison, *Two-Ocean War*, pp. 493–512; Theodore Roscoe, *United States Submarine Actions in World War II* (Annapolis: United States Naval Institute, 1949); Reynolds, *op. cit.*, pp. 298–300.
65. Whitman S. Bartley, *Iwo Jima: Amphibious Epic* (Marine Corps Historical Monographs, XIII, Washington: Historical Branch, Headquarters U.S. Marine Corps, 1954); Craven and Cate, *op. cit.*, V, chap. XIX; Dyer, *The Amphibians Came to Conquer*, II, chap. XXIII; Isely and Crowl, *op. cit.*, chap. X; Leckie, *op. cit.*, pp. 432–71; Morison, *Two-Ocean War*, pp. 513–24; Morison, *Victory in the Pacific*, pp. 5–75; Reynolds, *op. cit.*, pp. 320–22, 324–36; Sherrod, *op. cit.*, chap. XXIII.
66. Roy E. Appleman, James M. Burns, Russell A. Gugeler, and John Stevens, *Okinawa: The Last Battle* (*United States Army in World War II: The War in the Pacific*, Washington: Historical Division, U.S. Army, 1948); Dyer, *The Amphibians Came to Conquer*, II, 1059–1107; Benis M. Frank and Henry I. Shaw, Jr., *Victory and Occupation* (Vol. V, *History of U. S. Marine Corps*

Operations in World War II, Washington: Historical Branch, Headquarters U.S. Marine Corps, 1968), Parts I–II; Isely and Crowl, *op. cit.*, chap. XI; Leckie, *op. cit.*, pp. 472–527; Morison, *Two-Ocean War*, pp. 525–36; Morison, *Victory in the Pacific*, chaps. VI–IX; Nichols and Shaw, *op. cit.*; Reynolds, *op. cit.*, pp. 330, 332–34, 336–40; Sherrod, *op. cit.*, chaps. XXIV–XXVII.

67. Ito and Pineau, *op. cit.*, chap. X; Morison, *Two-Ocean War*, pp. 537–57; Morison, *Victory in the Pacific*, chaps. XII–XVII; Reynolds, *op. cit.*, pp. 340–50; Rear Admiral Toshiyuki Yokai, former Imperial Japanese Navy, "*Kamikazes* and the Okinawa Campaign," United States Naval Institute *Proceedings*, LXXX (May, 1954), 505–13.
68. Morison, *Two-Ocean War*, pp. 511–12.
69. Arnold, *op. cit.*, pp. 595–98; K. Jack Bauer and A. C. Coox, "OLYMPIC vs. KETTSU-GO," *Marine Corps Gazette*, XLIX (Aug., 1965), 33–44; Craven and Cate, *op. cit.*, V, chaps. XVII–XXII.
70. Works dealing with the controversy about the decision to use the atomic bomb and its effects include Gar Alperovitz, *Atomic Diplomacy: Hiroshima and Potsdam: The Use of the Atomic Bomb and the American Confrontation with Soviet Power* (London: Secker & Warburg, 1966); J. C. Butow, *Japan's Decision to Surrender* (Stanford: Stanford University Press, 1954); Craven and Cate, *op. cit.*, V, chap. XXIII; Herbert Feis, *Japan Subdued: The Atomic Bomb and the End of the War in the Pacific* (Princeton: Princeton University Press, 1961; new and revised edition published in 1966 under the title *The Atomic Bomb and the End of World War II*); Toshikazu Kase, *Journey to the Missouri* (New Haven: Yale University Press, 1950); Morison, *Two-Ocean War*, pp. 568–73; Morison, *Victory in the Pacific*, Part III; Louis Morton, "The Decision to Use the Atomic Bomb," in Greenfield, *op. cit.*, pp. 388–410; Harry S. Truman, *Memoirs*, Vol. I, *Year of Decisions* (Garden City: Doubleday 1955), pp. 415–23. See also United States Strategic Bombing Survey, *Summary Report (Pacific War)*, July 1, 1946 (excerpts are reprinted in Eugene M. Emme, ed., *The Impact of Air Power: National Security and World Politics* [Princeton: Van Nostrand, 1959], pp. 329–44).
71. Morison, *Leyte*, p. 412. For an early postwar assessment, see W. D. Puleston, *The Influence of Sea Power in World War II* (New Haven: Yale University Press, 1947).

CHAPTER FOURTEEN. THE STRATEGIC TRADITION OF U. S. GRANT: STRATEGISTS OF THE EUROPEAN WAR

1. Diary note, January 22, 1942. Alfred D. Chandler, Jr., ed., *The Papers of Dwight David Eisenhower: The War Years* (5 vols., Baltimore: Johns Hopkins Press, 1970), I, 66.
2. Ray S. Cline, *Washington Command Post: The Operations Division* (*United States Army in World War II: The War Department*, Washington: Office of the Chief of Military History, 1951), pp. 34–37, 55–60; George Carroll Dyer, *The Amphibians Came to Conquer: The Story of Admiral Richmond Kelly Turner* (2 vols., Washington: Government Printing Office, 1972), I, 157–66; Maurice Matloff and Edwin M. Snell, *Strategic Planning for Coalition Warfare, 1941–1942* (*United States Army in World War II: The War Department*, Washington: Office of the Chief of Military History, 1953), pp. 1–48; Louis Morton, "Germany First," in Kent Roberts Greenfield, ed., *Command Decisions* (New York: Harcourt, Brace, 1959), pp. 3–38; Louis Morton, *Strategy and Command: The First Two Years* (*United States Army in World War II: The War in the*

Pacific, Washington: Office of the Chief of Military History, 1962), pp. 31–33; Mark Skinner Watson, *Chief of Staff: Prewar Plans and Preparations* (*United States Army in World War II: The War Department*, Washington: Historical Division, U.S. Army, 1950), pp. 87–97, 103–104.

The ancient tradition of seacoast fortification retained vitality in the 1920s and 1930s with a program that included 14-inch and 8-inch railway-mounted guns and fixed emplacements of guns up to 16-inch caliber. Some of the post-Endicott-program coastal fortifications in the Philippines were used in combat, notably those on Corregidor. An accelerated coastal fortification program was continued for about a year after Pearl Harbor but suspended when it became apparent that the current war was not likely to involve attacks against the continental United States or further attacks on Hawaii. Some batteries whose construction was then deferred resumed building in 1945, but none was completed after 1948. In 1949 the old concepts of harbor defense at last were abandoned and the guns scrapped. The age of airplanes, missiles, and nuclear weapons terminated what may be considered the oldest expression of American military strategy, the coastal fortifications. Emanuel Raymond Lewis, *Seacoast Fortifications of the United States: An Introductory History* (Washington: Smithsonian Institution Press, 1970), pp. 100–25.

3. Albert C. Wedemeyer, *Wedemeyer Reports!* (New York: Holt, 1958), pp. 70–74, quotation from pp. 73–74; Richard M. Leighton and Robert W. Coakley, *Global Logistics and Strategy, 1940–1943* (*United States Army in World War II: The War Department*, Washington: Office of the Chief of Military History, 1955), chap. V; Watson, *op. cit.*, pp. 331–43.
4. Wedemeyer, *op. cit.*, pp. 66 (for quotation), 74–75; Leighton and Coakley, *op. cit.*, p. 135.
5. Cline, *op. cit.*, pp. 60–61; Leighton and Coakley, *op. cit.*, pp. 130–32; Matloff and Snell, *op. cit.*, pp. 58–62; Watson, *op. cit.*, pp. 343–62; Wedemeyer, *op. cit.*, pp. 74–75.
6. Quoted in Winston S. Churchill, *The Hinge of Fate* (Vol. IV, *The Second World War*, Boston: Houghton Mifflin, 1950), pp. 198–99. Leighton and Coakley, *op. cit.*, pp. 137–40, 195–96, 353–56; Matloff and Snell, *op. cit.*, pp. 99–102, 166–67.
7. Quotation from Chester Wilmot, *The Struggle for Europe* (New York: Harper, 1952), p. 103. Chandler, *op. cit.*, I, 205–208; Leighton and Coakley, *op. cit.*, pp. 357–60; Matloff and Snell, *op. cit.*, pp. 177–87.
8. Arthur Bryant, *The Turn of the Tide: A History of the War Years Based on the Diaries of Field-Marshal Lord Alanbrooke, Chief of the Imperial General Staff* (Garden City: Doubleday, 1957), pp. 277–91; J. R. M. Butler, *Grand Strategy*, Vol. III, Part II, *June 1941–August 1942* (*History of the Second World War, United Kingdom Military Series*, London: Her Majesty's Stationery Office, 1964), pp. 565–81; Churchill, *op. cit.*, pp. 314–25; Kent Roberts Greenfield, *American Strategy in World War II: A Reconsideration* (Baltimore: Johns Hopkins Press, 1963), pp. 4–5, 8–9, 12–13; Gordon Harrison, *Cross-Channel Attack* (*United States Army in World War II: The European Theater of Operations*, Washington: Office of the Chief of Military History, 1951), pp. 13–19; Leighton and Coakley, *op. cit.*, pp. 360–62; Matloff and Snell, *op. cit.*, pp. 187–90; Forrest C. Pogue, *George C. Marshall: Ordeal and Hope, 1939–1942* (New York: Viking, 1966), chap. XIV; Robert E. Sherwood, *Roosevelt and Hopkins: An Intimate History* (Revised Edition, New York: Harper, 1950), chap. XXIII; Wedemeyer, *op. cit.*, pp. 97–131; Wilmot, *op. cit.*, pp. 103–104.
9. Herbert Feis, *Churchill, Roosevelt, Stalin: The War They Waged and the Peace They Sought* (Paperback edition, Princeton: Princeton University Press, 1967), pp. 51–52, 61–67, 69–72; Matloff and Snell, *op. cit.*, pp. 231–32; Sherwood, *op. cit.*, pp. 563–69.

10. Bryant, *op. cit.*, pp. 313–14; Butler, *op. cit.*, pp. 595–98, 617–34; Churchill, *op. cit.*, pp. 341–438; Feis, *op. cit.*, pp. 51–57; Leighton and Coakley, *op. cit.*, pp. 152–54, 383–87; Matloff and Snell, *op. cit.*, pp. 102–108, 111–14, 167, 175–77, 231–81; Pogue, *op. cit.*, pp. 326–36, 340–41; Sherwood, *op. cit.*, pp. 556–79, 582–600; Wedemeyer, *op. cit.*, pp. 136–49, 153–58.
11. Dwight D. Eisenhower, *Crusade in Europe* (Garden City: Doubleday, 1948), pp. 53–54. Butler, *op. cit.*, pp. 636–37; Chandler, *op. cit.*, I, chaps. I–III; Cline, *op. cit.*, pp. 145–63; Eisenhower, *op. cit.*, pp. 49–71; Harrison, *op. cit.*, pp. 26–27; Leighton and Coakley, *op. cit.*, pp. 356–76; Matloff and Snell, *op. cit.*, pp. 196–97; Samuel Eliot Morison, *The Battle of the Atlantic, September 1939–May 1943* (Vol. I, *History of United States Naval Operations in World War II*, Boston: Little, Brown, 1951), p. 412; Samuel Eliot Morison, *Strategy and Compromise* (Boston: Little, Brown, 1958), pp. 23–30; Pogue, *op. cit.*, pp. 336–40; Wilmot, *op. cit.*, p. 107.
12. Eisenhower, *op. cit.*, p. 70. Richard M. Leighton, "OVERLORD Revisited: An Interpretation of American Strategy in the European War, 1942–1944," *American Historical Review*, LXVIII (July, 1963), 919–37, rejects the view that interprets the strategy of World War II as the outcome of a well-defined debate between British peripheralists and American concentrationists. For that view, either as held by those who think the British peripheral strategists were right, *e.g.*, Hanson W. Baldwin, *Great Mistakes of the War* (New York: Harper, 1950), or by those who think the American concentrationists were right, *e.g.*, Maurice Matloff in the works cited herein, Leighton would substitute an interpretation emphasizing compromise, adjustment, and opportunism on both sides, with fundamental agreement between both on the ultimate necessity for a cross-channel invasion. Leighton's interpretation is spoken of approvingly by the dean of United States Army World War II historians, Kent Roberts Greenfield, in his *American Strategy in World War II*, pp. 24–48.

    Yet in an earlier work, *The Historian and the Army* (New Brunswick: Rutgers University Press, 1954), Professor Greenfield said of the Anglo-American discussions on strategy preceding June 6, 1944, p. 34: "The outlook of the [United States] Army on strategy became clearly defined in the inter-Allied discussions in which its representatives tried, in vain, to get the British to accept their view." Admitting that there was much, and necessary, compromise, adjustment, and opportunism and that American strategy was not monolithic—some American planners flirted ardently with a Mediterranean strategy for a time in 1943—the difference between the American and British strategists in their World War II discussions still seems a fundamental one and the debates dividing them very real. As Greenfield put it, also in *The Historian and the Army*, p. 46: "It was evident that the British still [as late as the QUADRANT Conference in Québec, August, 1943] had no desire for a power-drive against the Nazis. They wanted a mop-up." "But," as Greenfield continues, p. 59, "when Overlord came, it was no mop-up. It was the power play for which the Americans had always contended."

    TORCH was to have barely begun when on November 22, 1942, Eisenhower expressed his impatience to Marshall: "We still have to defeat the German armies in Europe, and it will have to be ROUNDUP or a similar operation—that we cannot forget. Dispersion must cease!" Chandler, *op. cit.*, II, 760. Yet as the British writer Anthony Verrier says of the Allied conference that occurred shortly thereafter: ". . . no British account of Casablanca shows the slightest conviction of the cross-channel operation's supreme importance and necessity if Germany was to suffer defeat at other than Russian hands." *The Bomber Offensive* (New York: Macmillan, 1969), pp. 160–61.
13. Wedemeyer, *op. cit.*, pp. 132–33.

14. Eisenhower, *op. cit.*, pp. 70–71; Feis, *op. cit.*, pp. 52–54; Matloff and Snell, *op. cit.*, pp. 234–44, 266–72; Pogue, *op. cit.*, pp. 327–42.
15. Matloff and Snell, *op. cit.*, pp. 273–78, quotation from p. 278.
16. Chandler, *op. cit.*, I, 407–14, quotation from pp. 412–13. Bryant, *op. cit.*, pp. 339–47; Butler, *op. cit.*, pp. 634–38; Cline, *op. cit.*, pp. 180–87; Eisenhower, *op. cit.*, pp. 69–73; Greenfield, *American Strategy in World War II*, pp. 5–6, 15; Harrison, *op. cit.*, pp. 28–32; Leighton and Coakley, *op. cit.*, pp. 385–87; Matloff and Snell, *op. cit.*, pp. 273–327; Leo J. Meyer, "The Decision to Invade North Africa (TORCH) (1942)," in Greenfield, *Command Decisions*, pp. 129–53; Pogue, *op. cit.*, pp. 341–49; Sherwood, *op. cit.*, pp. 600–15.
17. Quoted in Matloff and Snell, *op. cit.*, p. 282. Stephen E. Ambrose, *The Supreme Commander: The War Years of General Dwight D. Eisenhower* (Garden City: Doubleday, 1970), pp. 74–75; Chandler, *op. cit.*, I, 417–19; Feis, *op. cit.*, pp. 55–57; Matloff and Snell, *op. cit.*, pp. 280–84; Pogue, *op. cit.*, pp. 346–49.
18. Ambrose, *op. cit.*, pp. 78–79; Chandler, *op. cit.*, I, 436–38; Eisenhower, *op. cit.*, pp. 71–72; Pogue, *op. cit.*, p. 348.
19. Chandler, *op. cit.*, II, chaps. VI–VIII; Eisenhower, *op. cit.*, chaps. V–VIII; George F. Howe, *Northwest Africa: Seizing the Initiative in the West* (*United States Army in World War II: The Mediterranean Theater of Operations*, Washington: Office of the Chief of Military History, 1957); Leighton and Coakley, *op. cit.*, chaps. XVI–XVII; Charles B. MacDonald, *The Mighty Endeavor: American Ground Forces in the European Theater in World War II* (New York: Oxford University Press, 1969), chaps. VI–VIII; Samuel Eliot Morison, *Operations in North African Waters, October 1942–June 1943* (Vol. II, *History of United States Naval Operations in World War II*, Boston: Little, Brown, 1950).
20. Quoted in Maurice Matloff, *Strategic Planning for Coalition Warfare, 1943–1944* (*United States Army in World War II: The War Department*, Washington: Office of the Chief of Military History, 1959), pp. 106–107.
21. Bryant, *op. cit.*, pp. 439–59; Chandler, *op. cit.*, II, 927–29; Churchill, *op. cit.*, chap. XV; Cline, *op. cit.*, pp. 213–19; Robert W. Coakley and Richard M. Leighton, *Global Logistics and Strategy, 1943–1945* (*United States Army in World War II: The War Department*, Washington: Office of the Chief of Military History, 1968), chaps. I–II; Eisenhower, *op. cit.*, pp. 159–60; Feis, *op. cit.*, pp. 93–108; Greenfield, *American Strategy in World War II*, p. 13; Trumbull Higgins, *Soft Underbelly: The Anglo-American Controversy over the Italian Campaign, 1939–1945* (New York: Macmillan, 1968), pp. 38–41, 45–51; Leighton and Coakley, *op. cit.*, pp. 668–76, 682–86; Matloff, *op. cit.*, chaps. I–III; Samuel Eliot Morison, *The Two-Ocean War: A Short History of the United States Navy in World War II* (Boston: Little, Brown, 1963), pp. 237–44, 384–85; Sherwood, *op. cit.*, chap. XXVII; Wedemeyer, *op. cit.*, chaps. XII–XIII, XV.
22. On the military aspects of "unconditional surrender," see Matloff, *op. cit.*, pp. 38–42.
23. Quoted in Churchill, *op. cit.*, p. 810, Wedemeyer, *op. cit.*, p. 229. Wesley Frank Craven and James Lea Cate, eds., *The Army Air Forces in World War II* (7 vols., Chicago: University of Chicago Press, 1948–58), II, *Europe: TORCH to POINTBLANK, August 1942 to December 1943*, pp. 563–70, 725–27.
24. Martin Blumenson, *Salerno to Cassino* (*United States Army in World War II: The Mediterranean Theater of Operations*, Washington: Office of the Chief of Military History, 1969), pp. 8–24; Bryant, *op. cit.*, pp. 491–95, 501–16, 548–57; Chandler, *op. cit.*, II, 1096–97, 1173–75, 1224–29, 1230–33, 1247–49, 1250–51, 1256–73, 1287–93, 1296–1301; Coakley and Leighton, *op. cit.*, pp. 57–76, 173–81, 189–205; John Ehrman, *Grand Strategy*, Vol. V, *August 1943–September 1944* (*History*

of the Second World War, United Kingdom Military Series, London: Her Majesty's Stationery Office, 1956), pp. 58–66; Eisenhower, *op. cit.*, pp. 183–84; Higgins, *op. cit.*, pp. 63–95; Matloff, *op. cit.*, pp. 126–35, 152–61, quotation from p. 160; Samuel Eliot Morison, *Sicily—Salerno—Anzio, January 1943–June 1944* (Vol. IX, *History of United States Naval Operations in World War II*, Boston: Little, Brown, 1964), pp. 227–33, 237–46.

25. Quotation from Matloff, *op. cit.*, p. 164. Blumenson, *op. cit.*, chaps. IV–IX; Chandler, *op. cit.*, II, 1035–III, 1441; Craven and Cate, *op. cit.*, II, chap. XV; Eisenhower, *op. cit.*, pp. 184–90; Higgins, *op. cit.*, pp. 96–117; MacDonald, *op. cit.*, pp. 177–87; Matloff, *op. cit.*, pp. 162–67, 174–79, 211–16, 220–30, 242–53; Morison, *Sicily—Salerno—Anzio*, pp. 233–36, 246–304.

26. In the most judicious account by a British writer, Michael Howard warns against stressing the "soft underbelly" idea: ". . . the Combined Chiefs did not see the Mediterranean as a 'soft underbelly' through which Europe could be invaded, but as an area where the Germans could be brought to battle: not under particularly favourable circumstances, perhaps, but a great deal more favourable than the beaches of North-West Europe." *The Mediterranean Strategy in the Second World War* (New York: Praeger, 1968), p. 36. But of Churchill's enthusiasm for the Italian campaign, Howard says: "The prestige of British arms, it appears, demanded that the triumphal progress of the Eighth Army must continue, unchecked by the cold calculations of planners in Washington." *Ibid.*, p. 40. For the issues of Mediterranean strategy, see also Coakley and Leighton, *op. cit.*, pp. 222–26; Ehrman, *op. cit.*, chap. II; Eisenhower, *op. cit.*, pp. 194–95; Greenfield, *American Strategy in World War II*, pp. 16–23; Harrison, *op. cit.*, chap. III; Trumbull Higgins, *Winston Churchill and the Second Front* (New York: Oxford University Press, 1957); Matloff, *op. cit.*, pp. 2, 30, 162–79, 220–30, 240–43; Wedemeyer, *op. cit.*, pp. 120–21, 132–35, 228–33; Wilmot, *op. cit.*, chap. VI. On the Dodecanese, see Blumenson, *op. cit.*, pp. 184, 247–48; Arthur Bryant, *Triumph in the West: A History of the War Years Based on the Diaries of Field-Marshal Lord Alanbrooke, Chief of the Imperial General Staff* (Garden City: Doubleday, 1950), pp. 30–33, 55–56; Coakley and Leighton, *op. cit.*, pp. 226–29, 280–84, 290–94; Ehrman, *op. cit.*, pp. 88–103; 185–92, 213, 215, 221; Higgins, *Soft Underbelly*, pp. 117–19, 121, 129–30; Matloff, *op. cit.*, pp. 253–62, 353–55.

27. Bryant, *Triumph in the West*, pp. 58–67; Winston S. Churchill, *Closing the Ring* (Vol. V, *The Second World War*, Boston: Houghton Mifflin, 1951), pp. 344–407; Coakley and Leighton, *op. cit.*, pp. 271–90; Ehrman, *op. cit.*, pp. 173–83; Feis, *op. cit.*, pp. 257–66; Harrison, *op. cit.*, pp. 123–27; Richard M. Leighton, "OVERLORD versus the Mediterranean at the Cairo-Tehran Conference," in Greenfield, *Command Decisions*, pp. 182–209; Matloff, *op. cit.*, pp. 356–59; Sherwood, *op. cit.*, pp. 776–99.

28. Chandler, *op. cit.*, III, 1585–91; Eisenhower, *op. cit.*, pp. 206–209; Matloff, *op. cit.*, pp. 362, 381–82.

29. Eisenhower, *op. cit.*, p. 62.

30. Bryant, *Triumph in the West*, pp. 61–67; Chandler, *op. cit.*, III, 1606, 1652–56, 1676–77, 1707–1708, 1712–15, 1732–36, 1743–44; Churchill, *Closing the Ring*, pp. 344–45, 354–55, 366, 372, 382, 410–12; Coakley and Leighton, *op. cit.*, pp. 284–90; Ehrman, *op. cit.*, pp. 175–84; Eisenhower, *op. cit.*, pp. 231–32, 281–84; Maurice Matloff, "The ANVIL Decision: Crossroads of Strategy," in Greenfield, *Command Decisions*, pp. 285–302; Matloff, *Strategic Planning*, pp. 361, 365–66, 370–71, 378–79, 412–26.

31. Bryant, *Triumph in the West*, pp. 72, 75–76, 103–11, 125–26; Chandler, *op. cit.*, III, 1707, 1732–36; Coakley and Leighton, *op. cit.*, pp. 229–70, 297–368; Ehrman,

op. cit., pp. 184, 187, 189, 191, 213–23, 231–47; Eisenhower, *op. cit.*, pp. 230–32; Matloff, *Strategic Planning*, pp. 397–401, 412–13; Samuel Eliot Morison, *The Invasion of France and Germany* (Vol. XI, *History of United States Naval Operations in World War II*, Boston: Little, Brown, 1964), chap. XXIII; Morison, *Strategy and Compromise*, pp. 54–60; Forrest C. Pogue, *The Supreme Command* (*United States Army in World War II: The European Theater of Operations*, Washington: Office of the Chief of Military History, 1954), chap. VI. The shortage of landing vessels was especially a shortage of LSTs.

32. Churchill, *Closing the Ring*, p. 488. Martin Blumenson, *Anzio: The Gamble That Failed* (Philadelphia: Lippincott, 1963); Martin Blumenson, "General Lucas at Anzio," in Greenfield, *Command Decisions*, pp. 244–72; Blumenson, *Salerno to Cassino*, chaps. XVII–XX, XXII, XXIV; Bryant, *Triumph in the West*, pp. 91, 93–94, 99–111, 125; Chandler, *op. cit.*, III, 1611, 1645, 1652–53, 1707–1708, 1712; Churchill, *Closing the Ring*, pp. 427–29, 479–91; Coakley and Leighton, *op. cit.*, pp. 310–17, 330–31, 336–46; Ehrman, *op. cit.*, pp. 208–11, 214–31, 245–47; Eisenhower, *op. cit.*, pp. 212–14; Matloff, *Strategic Planning*, pp. 415–16, 422; Morison, *Sicily—Salerno—Anzio*, chaps. XVI–XVII; Morison, *Two-Ocean War*, pp. 358–62; Pogue, *Supreme Command*, pp. 218–27.

33. Winston S. Churchill, *Triumph and Tragedy* (Vol. VI, *The Second World War*, Boston: Houghton Mifflin, 1953), pp. 65–66, 721–23, and all of chap. IV, quotations from p. 65; Ehrman, *op. cit.*, chap. VII; Howard, *op. cit.*, pp. 48–68; Higgins, *Soft Underbelly*, pp. 170–79; Matloff, "ANVIL Decision," *loc. cit.*, pp. 291–302; Matloff, *Strategic Planning*, pp. 424–26, 467–74.

34. Howard, *op. cit.*, pp. 59–68; Matloff, *Strategic Planning*, p. 472; Wedemeyer, *op. cit.*, pp. 211–12, 214, 228–34.

35. Wedemeyer, *op. cit.*, pp. 133, 126.

36. Matloff, *Strategic Planning*, pp. 427–28.

37. *Ibid.*, p. 427.

38. Quoted in Frank Futrell, "Commentary," in William Geffen, ed., *Command and Commanders in Modern Warfare: Proceedings of the Second Military History Symposium U. S. Air Force Academy, 2–3 May 1968* (U.S. Air Force Academy, 1969), p. 314.

39. Craven and Cate, *op. cit.*, I, *Plans and Early Operations, January 1939 to August 1942*, pp. 64–65; also chap. II, James Lea Cate and Wesley Frank Craven, "The Army Air Arm between Two Wars, 1919–39," pp. 17–71; chap. III, E. Kathleen Williams, "Air War, 1939–41," pp. 75–100; chap. IV, James Lea Cate and E. Kathleen Williams, "The Air Corps Prepares for War, 1935–41," pp. 101–50. See also James Lea Cate, "Development of United States Air Doctrine, 1917–41," reprinted in Eugene M. Emme, ed., *The Impact of Air Power: National Security and World Politics* (Princeton: Van Nostrand, 1959), pp. 186–91, from *Air University Quarterly Review*, I (Winter, 1947); Futrell, *loc. cit.*, pp. 313–15; Thomas H. Greer, *The Development of Doctrine in the Army Air Arm, 1917–1941* (Montgomery: Air University, 1955).

40. Cline, *op. cit.*, chap. VI; Craven and Cate, *op. cit.*, I, 257–67, and VI, *Men and Planes*, chap. I, William A. Goss, "Origins of the Army Air Forces," and chap. II, *idem.*, "The AAF," pp. 3–77; R. Earl McClendon, *The Question of Autonomy for the United States Air Arm* (Revised Nov., 1950, Montgomery: Air University, 1952), Part II, especially pp. 220–29.

41. Craven and Cate, *op. cit.*, I, 590, 138; see in general chap. XVI, James Lea Cate, "Plans, Policies, and Organization [for the air war against Germany]," pp. 557–611; chap. XVII, Alfred Goldberg, "Establishment of the Eighth Air Force in the United Kingdom," pp. 612–54.

42. Denis Richards, *The Fight at Odds* (Vol. I, *Royal Air Force, 1939–1945*, Lon-

don: Her Majesty's Stationery Office, 1953), especially chap. VI; Verrier, *op. cit.*, chaps. II–V; Sir Charles Webster and Noble Frankland, *The Strategic Air Offensive against Germany, 1939–1945* (4 vols., *History of the Second World War, United Kingdom Military Series*, London: Her Majesty's Stationery Office, 1961), I, 65–81, 86–352.

43. Craven and Cate, *op. cit.*, I, 131–32, 146–50, 236–37, 246–47; Giulio Douhet, *The Command of the Air*, tr. Dino Ferrari (New York: Coward-McCann, 1942); Futrell, *loc. cit.*, pp. 315–16.

44. General H. H. Arnold, "Air Strategy for Victory," *Flying*, XXXIII, No. 4 (Oct., 1943), 50.

45. Craven and Cate, *op. cit.*, I, 598–601, for the Norden bombsight; Futrell, *loc. cit.*, p. 316, for the hopes of the authors of AWPD-1.

46. Quoted in *Target: Germany, The Army Air Forces' Official Story of the VIII Bomber Command's First Year over Europe* (New York: Simon & Schuster, 1943), p. 27. For B-17 bombloads, see John Kirk and Robert Young, Jr., *Great Weapons of World War II* (New York: Walker, 1963), p. 75; Ray Wagner, *American Combat Planes* (New Revised Edition, Garden City: Doubleday, 1968), pp. 123–25.

47. Quotation from directive of May 14, 1943, in Verrier, *op. cit.*, p. 330. A. Russell Buchanan, *The United States and World War II* (2 vols., New York: Harper & Row, 1964), I, 196–97, 200–202; Craven and Cate, *op. cit.*, II, Part II, Arthur B. Ferguson, "Origins of the Combined Bomber Offensive," pp. 209–411; Verrier, *op. cit.*, pp. 156–70; Webster and Frankland, *op. cit.*, II, 10–15. As early as October, 1942, Eisenhower instructed the VIII Bomber Command to strike at enemy submarine pens and airfields for the protection of the forthcoming North African invasion. Craven and Cate, *op. cit.*, II, 237–41.

48. Craven and Cate, *op. cit.*, I, 641–45; *Target: Germany*, pp. 27–28; Charles B. Van Pelt, "The B-17: 'An Airplane You Could Trust,'" *American History Illustrated*, IV, No. 6 (Oct., 1969), 29.

49. Craven and Cate, *op. cit.*, I, 655–58; II, 209–10, 213–41, 246–58; Harrison, *op. cit.*, p. 47; Verrier, *op. cit.*, pp. 121–27.

50. Craven and Cate, *op. cit.*, II, 323–24.

51. *Ibid.*, pp. 324–47, 678–89, 696–706; Verrier, *op. cit.*, pp. 172–73, 181–82; Webster and Frankland, *op. cit.*, II, 36–40, 74–75.

52. The Combined Bomber Offensive Directive of May, 14, 1943, is printed in Verrier, *op. cit.*, pp. 330–38, quotation from p. 331. For an extended discussion of the effort toward scientific target selection, see Craven and Cate, *op. cit.*, II, 348–76, 665–69, 729–30; III, *Europe: ARGUMENT to V-E Day, January 1944 to May 1945*, pp. 8–9, 26–48; B. H. Liddell Hart, *History of the Second World War* (New York: Putnam, 1971), p. 602; MacDonald, *op. cit.*, pp. 238–39.

53. Craven and Cate, *op. cit.*, III, 8.

54. *Ibid.*, II, 696–706; III, 9–13, 22–26, 49; VI, 195, 211–21; Wagner, *op. cit.*, pp. 194–202, 207–33; Webster and Frankland, *op. cit.*, II, 40–45, 75–82, 195–209.

55. Craven and Cate, *op. cit.*, III, 47–56; Kirk and Young, *op. cit.*, pp. 23, 28–31; MacDonald, *op. cit.*, pp. 236–37; Webster and Frankland, *op. cit.*, II, 87–88.

56. Quoted in Lieutenant General Ira C. Eaker, "Comments," in Geffen, *op. cit.*, p. 357. See also Futrell, *ibid.*, pp. 317–19, on the importance of auxiliary fuel tanks. As Futrell points out, with auxiliary tanks the P-47N in the Pacific eventually flew longer bomber-support missions than the P-51 in Europe. See also Craven and Cate, *op. cit.*, II, 229–30, 654–55, 679–81.

57. Ambrose, *op. cit.*, pp. 363–76, 395; Omar N. Bradley, *A Soldier's Story* (New York: Holt, 1951), pp. 244–46; Chandler, *op. cit.*, III, 1690–92, 1776; Craven and Cate, *op. cit.*, II, chap. XXII; III, chaps. III–VII; Eisenhower, *op. cit.*, pp. 230–

31, 232–34, 237, 244; Harrison, *op. cit.*, pp. 207–30, 265–67, 334–35; Pogue, *Supreme Command*, chap. VII; Hilary St. George Saunders, *The Fight Is Won* (Vol. III, *Royal Air Force, 1939–1945*, London: Her Majesty's Stationery Office, 1954), chaps. IV–V; Webster and Frankland, *op. cit.*, III, 9–41.

58. Ambrose, *op. cit.*, pp. 394–95 and Book Two, chap. VI; Harrison, *op. cit.*, chaps. IV, VII; MacDonald, *op. cit.*, pp. 257–62; Pogue, *Supreme Command*, pp. 175–80; Wilmot, *op. cit.*, chap. VII; Lieutenant General Bodo Zimmerman, "France, 1944," in Seymour Freidin and William Richardson, eds., *The Fatal Decisions* (New York: Sloane, 1956), pp. 200–13.
59. Bradley, *op. cit.*, pp. 232–36, 275–76; Chandler, *op. cit.*, III, 1673–74, 1715, 1717, 1728, 1881–82, 1894–95, 1915–17; Eisenhower, *op. cit.*, pp. 240, 245–47, 253; Harrison, *op. cit.*, pp. 75, 183–86, 269, 278–300, 345–48; Pogue, *Supreme Command*, pp. 111, 118–22, 171–73; Matthew B. Ridgway, *Soldier: The Memoirs of Matthew B. Ridgway* (New York: Harper, 1956), pp. 1–36, 100–103; Wilmot, *op. cit.*, pp. 135, 175, 213, 219–20, 233–48, 261–62, 277–80, 292.
60. Ambrose, *op. cit.*, pp. 401, 420, 460; Bradley, *op. cit.*, pp. 286–88; Chandler, *op. cit.*, III, 1949, 1989–90; Eisenhower, *op. cit.*, pp. 231, 257–58, 288; Harrison, *op. cit.*, pp. 330–35, 348–51, 369–79, 442–49; MacDonald, *op. cit.*, pp. 281–82; Pogue, *Supreme Command*, pp. 180, 193–96; Wilmot, *op. cit.*, pp. 318–20, 324–27, 332–35; Zimmerman, *loc. cit.*, pp. 212–23.
61. Eisenhower, *op. cit.*, p. 449.
62. Martin Blumenson, *Breakout and Pursuit* (*United States Army in World War II: The European Theater of Operations*, Washington: Office of the Chief of Military History, 1961), chaps. I–XIII; Bradley, *op. cit.*, pp. 278–358; Chandler, *op. cit.*, III, chaps. XIX–XX; IV, chap. XXI; Eisenhower, *op. cit.*, pp. 255–75; Harrison, *op. cit.*, chaps. IX–X; MacDonald, *op. cit.*, pp. 282–310; Pogue, *Supreme Command*, pp. 171–75, 183–201; Roland G. Ruppenthal, *Logistical Support of the Armies* (2 vols., *United States Army in World War II: The European Theater of Operations*, Washington: Office of the Chief of Military History, 1953–59), I, chap. XI; Wilmot, *op. cit.*, pp. 294–365, 383–95.
63. Blumenson, *Breakout and Pursuit*, chaps. XIV–XXIII; Bradley, *op. cit.*, pp. 358–406; Eisenhower, *op. cit.*, pp. 275–304; John S. D. Eisenhower, *The Bitter Woods* (New York: Putnam, 1969), pp. 46–78; MacDonald, *op. cit.*, pp. 310–31; Pogue, *Supreme Command*, pp. 201–17, 227–30, 244–49, 261–78; Ruppenthal, *op. cit.*, I, chaps. XII–XIV.
64. For the Russian campaign, see especially Alan Clark, *Barbarossa: The Russian-German Conflict, 1941–45* (New York: Morrow, 1965); Liddell Hart, *op. cit.*, chaps. XII–XIII, XVIII, XXVIII, XXXII, XXXVI; General Gunther Blumentritt, "The State and Performance of the Red Army, 1941," chap. XII, and Field-Marshal Erich von Manstein, "The Development of the Red Army, 1942–1945," chap. XIII, in B. H. Liddell Hart, ed., *The Red Army* (New York: Harcourt, Brace, 1956), pp. 134–52; Alexander Werth, *Russia at War, 1941–1945* (New York: Dutton, 1964).
65. Bradley, *op. cit.*, pp. 407–26; Chandler, *op. cit.*, IV, 2126, 2133–35, 2158, 2160, 2169, and chap. XXIII; Craven and Cate, *op. cit.*, III, 598–612; D. D. Eisenhower, *op. cit.*, pp. 288–93, 302–12, 315–16, 321–23; J. S. D. Eisenhower, *op. cit.*, pp. 75–84; Charles B. MacDonald, "The Decision to Launch Operation MARKET-GARDEN (1944)," in Greenfield, *Command Decisions*, pp. 329–41; Charles B. MacDonald, *The Siegfried Line Campaign* (*United States Army in World War II: The European Theater of Operations*, Washington: Office of the Chief of Military History, 1963), pp. 14–19 and chaps. VI–IX; Viscount Montgomery of Alamein, *The Memoirs of Field-Marshal the Viscount Montgomery of Alamein* (Cleveland: World, 1958), chap. XVI; Pogue, *Supreme Command*, pp. 250–56, 278–88, 296–301; Ruppenthal, *op. cit.*, II, 104–10; Wilmot, *op. cit.*, 487–92, 498–533.

66. Stephen E. Ambrose, "Eisenhower as Commander: Single Thrust Versus Broad Front," in Chandler, *op. cit.*, V, 39–48; Ambrose, *Supreme Commander*, pp. 492–97, 506–35; Bradley, *op. cit.*, pp. 418–47; Bryant, *Triumph in the West*, chap. VIII; Chandler, *op. cit.*, IV, 2090–94, 2100–2101, 2115–28, 2133–38, 2143–49, 2152–55, 2164–69, 2175–76, 2323–32, 2341–42, 2444–45; Hugh M. Cole, *The Lorraine Campaign* (*United States Army in World War II: The European Theater of Operations*, Washington: Historical Division, U.S. Army, 1950), pp. 6–13; D. D. Eisenhower, *op. cit.*, pp. 284–94, 298–341; J. S. D. Eisenhower, *op. cit.*, pp. 72–75, 88–98; Francis Wilfred de Guingand, *Operation Victory* (London: Hodder & Stoughton, 1947), pp. 329–30; Liddell Hart, *History of the Second World War*, pp. 557–67; MacDonald, *Mighty Endeavor*, chaps. XX–XXI; MacDonald, *Siegfried Line Campaign*, pp. 4–14, 207–15, 377–403, 616–22; Montgomery, *Memoirs*, chaps. XV–XVII; Pogue, *Supreme Command*, pp. 249–60, 279–81, 288–98, 302–18; Ruppenthal, *op. cit.*, II, chaps. I–II; Roland G. Ruppenthal, "Logistics and the Broad-Front Strategy (1944)," in Greenfield, *Command Decisions*, pp. 320–28; Walter Bedell Smith, *Eisenhower's Six Great Decisions: Europe 1944–1945* (New York: Longmans, Green, 1956), pp. 121–32; Wilmot, *op. cit.*, chaps. XXIV–XXV, XXVII–XXIX.
67. Ambrose, *Supreme Commander*, pp. 553–56; Bradley, *op. cit.*, pp. 441–64; Chandler, *op. cit.*, IV, 2331, 2335–36, 2346–48, 2446–47; Hugh M. Cole, *The Ardennes: Battle of the Bulge* (*United States Army in World War II: The European Theater of Operations*, Washington: Office of the Chief of Military History, 1965), chaps. I–IV; Craven and Cate, *op. cit.*, III, 672–82; D. D. Eisenhower, *op. cit.*, pp. 337–41; J. S. D. Eisenhower, *op. cit.*, pp. 99–176; Charles P. von Luttichau, "The German Counteroffensive in the Ardennes," in Greenfield, *Command Decisions*, pp. 342–57; MacDonald, *Mighty Endeavor*, pp. 356–67; Pogue, *Supreme Command*, pp. 359–72; Wilmot, *op. cit.*, pp. 573–82. Maurice Matloff, "The 90-Division Gamble," in Greenfield, *Command Decisions* (Second Edition, Washington: Office of the Chief of Military History, 1960), pp. 365–81, is relevant to the question of the adequacy of American troop reserves.
68. Bradley, *op. cit.*, pp. 455–95; Chandler, *op. cit.*, IV, chap. XXV and chap. XXVI to p. 2483; Cole, *The Ardennes*, chaps. V–XXV; Craven and Cate, *op. cit.*, III, 682–711; D. D. Eisenhower, *op. cit.*, chap. XVIII; J. S. D. Eisenhower, *op. cit.*, chaps. X–XVII, XIX; MacDonald, *Mighty Endeavor*, pp. 367–405; Montgomery, *Memoirs*, chap. XVIII; Pogue, *Supreme Command*, pp. 372–97, 404; Wilmot, *op. cit.*, pp. 580–614.
69. Ambrose, *Supreme Commander*, pp. 571–76, 579–89, 606–12; Chandler, *op. cit.*, IV, 2450–54, 2510–11, 2537, 2539–42, 2551–53, 2557–58; D. D. Eisenhower, *op. cit.*, pp. 370, 395–96.
70. Gavin Long, *MacArthur as Military Commander* (Princeton: Van Nostrand, 1969), p. 143. Wilmot, *op. cit.*, p. 528, calls "the American reluctance to concentrate" one of the two major weaknesses of the Allied high command once ashore in Europe (the other being "the British caution about casualties"). While he generally reiterates this criticism throughout his history of the European campaign, however, German weakness in early 1945 leads Wilmot to say of the crossing of the Rhine, p. 665: "This was the argument of the autumn once again—'single thrust or broad front?'—with the difference that this time events were to prove that Eisenhower's plan was sound and that the British fears were groundless."
71. Ambrose, *Supreme Commander*, pp. 609–12, 625–27; Bradley, *op. cit.*, pp. 495–97, 511–14, 535; D. D. Eisenhower, *op. cit.*, pp. 395–98; Pogue, *Supreme Command*, pp. 434–36, 443.
72. Chandler, *op. cit.*, IV, 2592.
73. Stephen E. Ambrose, *Eisenhower and Berlin, 1945: The Decision to Halt at the*

Elbe (New York: Norton, 1967); Ambrose, *Supreme Commander*, pp. 626–42, 646–48; Bradley, *op. cit.*, pp. 530–54; Chandler, *op. cit.*, IV, 2549–53, 2557–63, 2565–71, 2572–74, 2576–77, 2579–80, 2583–84, 2587–95, 2604–2606, 2609–18, 2632–36, 2640–41, 2649–52, 2655–56, 2662, 2663–64, 2679–81; Craven and Cate, *op. cit.*, III, 768–82; D. D. Eisenhower, *op. cit.*, pp. 397–426; MacDonald, *Mighty Endeavor*, chaps. XXIX–XXXI; Pogue, *Supreme Command*, chaps. XXII–XXIV.

74. Craven and Cate, *op. cit.*, I, 597–600; III, 638, 725–27; Futrell, *loc. cit.*, pp. 315–16; George H. Quester, *Deterrence before Hiroshima: The Airpower Background to Modern Strategy* (New York: Wiley, 1966), pp. 149–50.

75. Winston S. Churchill, *Their Finest Hour* (Vol. II, *The Second World War*, Boston: Houghton Mifflin, 1949), pp. 330–32, 342–43, quotation from p. 331; Quester, *op. cit.*, pp. 82–122; Richards, *op. cit.*, pp. 182–83; Webster and Frankland, *op. cit.*, I, 3–152; Wilmot, *op. cit.*, pp. 48–49, Hitler quotation from p. 49; Gordon Wright, *The Ordeal of Total War, 1939–1945* (Torchbooks Edition, New York: Harper & Row, 1968), p. 176. On pp. 117–18 Quester stretches Churchill's account of the decision to bomb Berlin into the somewhat dubious conclusion that because it was advantageous to the survival of the RAF for the Germans to divert their attacks from the air defenses to London, Churchill in ordering the bombing of Berlin was deliberately baiting them into turning their main attentions to the capital.

76. Craven and Cate, *op. cit.*, I, 591–93, 596–97; Quester, *op. cit.*, pp. 136–44; Richards, *op. cit.*, chap. XIII; Verrier, *op. cit.*, pp. 18–22, 28–30, 88–102; Webster and Frankland, *op. cit.*, I, 152–352, especially pp. 331–52; Wright, *op. cit.*, pp. 176–78, 180–82. On the RAF theory of strategic bombing and its application, see also Noble Frankland, *The Bombing Offensive against Germany* (London: Faber & Faber, 1965), and Sir Arthur Harris's memoirs, *Bomber Offensive* (New York: Macmillan, 1947), especially chapter IV. Lord Cherwell is the bête noire of C. P. Snow's rather overdrawn *Science and Government* (New York: Oxford University Press, 1961) and *A Postscript to Science and Government* (New York: Oxford University Press, 1962). For a balanced study of Cherwell's principal rival among British scientists in government, see Ronald W. Clark, *Tizard* (London: Methuen, 1965).

77. Craven and Cate, *op. cit.*, I, 595, 600–603; II, 371–76, 712–30; Noble Frankland, "The Combined Bomber Offensive: Classical and Revolutionary, Combined and Divided, Planned and Fortuitous," in Geffen, *op. cit.*, pp. 292–96; Quester, *op. cit.*, pp. 141–45; Denis Richards and Hilary St. George Saunders, *The Fight Avails* (Vol. II, *Royal Air Force, 1938–1945*, London: Her Majesty's Stationery Office, 1954), chaps. VI–VIII; Saunders, *op. cit.*, chaps. I–II; Verrier, *op. cit.*, pp. 163–70, 175–80, 189–248; Webster and Frankland, *op. cit.*, I, Part III; II; Wright, *op. cit.*, pp. 178–79.

78. Churchill, *Triumph and Tragedy*, pp. 540–41; Frankland, "The Combined Bomber Offensive," *loc. cit.*, pp. 292–300; David Irving, *The Destruction of Dresden* (New York: Holt, Rinehart and Winston, 1963); Quester, *op. cit.*, pp. 146–51; Saunders, *op. cit.*, chaps. XII–XIII, XVIII; Verrier, *op. cit.*, pp. 263–64, 274–301; Webster and Frankland, *op. cit.*, III, chaps. XII–XIII.

79. Craven and Cate, *op. cit.*, III, 725–27; Verrier, *op. cit.*, pp. 302–304.

80. Field Marshal Erhard Milch, German Air Force (Ret.), "Comment," in Geffen, *op. cit.*, p. 336. Bernard Brodie, *Strategy in the Missile Age* (Paperback edition, Princeton: Princeton University Press, 1965), pp. 110–12, 119–20; Chandler, *op. cit.*, III, 1960–61; Craven and Cate, *op. cit.*, III, 279–308, 640–46, 669–71, 715, 722–24, 728–29, 731–32, 736–47, 751–55; Verrier, *op. cit.*, pp. 269–73; Webster and Frankland, *op. cit.*, III, 225–43.

81. Brodie, *op. cit.*, pp. 112–13; Chandler, *op. cit.*, IV, 2247–49; Cravin and Cate, *op.*

cit., III, 293–94, 646–57, 669–71, 718–19, 722, 728–47, 751–55; Lord Tedder, *With Prejudice: The War Memoirs of Marshal of the Royal Air Force Lord Tedder* (London: Cassell, 1966), pp. 605–15; Webster and Frankland, *op. cit.*, III, 244–62.

82. Milch, *loc. cit.*, pp. 334.
83. Quoted in Webster and Frankland, *op. cit.*, IV, 383.
84. For further discussion, see Brodie, *op. cit.*, pp. 107–20, 124–27; Craven and Cate, *op. cit.*, III, 785–808; Greenfield, *American Strategy in World War II*, pp. 112–17; Carl A. Spaatz, "Strategic Air Power in the European War," in Emme, *op. cit.*, pp. 226–36, reprinted from *Foreign Affairs*, April, 1946; United States Strategic Bombing Survey, *Summary Report (European War)*, Sept. 30, 1945 (excerpts reprinted in Emme, *op. cit.*, pp. 268–80, 322–24); Webster and Frankland, *op. cit.*, III, 208–24, 262–311; IV, Annex V, "The British and United States Surveys of the Strategic Bombing Offensive."
85. Craven and Cate, *op. cit.*, III, 801.

Part Five. American Strategy in Perplexity, 1945–

1. J. C. Wylie, *Military Strategy: A General Theory of Power Control* (New Brunswick: Rutgers University Press, 1967), p. 80.

CHAPTER FIFTEEN. THE ATOMIC REVOLUTION

1. Carl von Clausewitz, *On War*, tr. Col. J. J. Graham, New and Revised Edition with an Introduction and Notes by Col. F. N. Maude (Eighth Impression, 3 vols., New York: Barnes and Noble, 1968), I, 86.
2. H. H. Arnold, *Global Mission* (New York: Harper, 1949), pp. 595–99; Bernard Brodie, *Strategy in the Missile Age* (Paperback edition, Princeton: Princeton University Press, 1965), pp. 127–31, 138–43; A. Russell Buchanan, *The United States and World War II* (2 vols., New York: Harper & Row, 1964), II, 568–85; Wesley Frank Craven and James Lea Cate, eds., *The Army Air Forces in World War II* (7 vols., Chicago: University of Chicago Press, 1948–58), III, *Europe: ARGUMENT to V-E Day, January 1944 to May 1945*, p. 727; V, *The Pacific: MATTERHORN to Nagasaki, June 1944 to August 1945*, chaps. XX–XXIII; Kent Roberts Greenfield, *American Strategy in World War II: A Reinterpretation* (Baltimore: Johns Hopkins Press, 1963), pp. 118–20.
3. Richard G. Hewlett and Oscar E. Anderson, Jr., *A History of the United States Atomic Energy Commission*, I, *The New World, 1939–1946* (University Park: Pennsylvania State University Press, 1962).
4. X [George F. Kennan], "The Sources of Soviet Conduct," *Foreign Affairs*, XXV (July, 1947), 566–82, reprinted in George F. Kennan, *American Diplomacy, 1900–1950* (Chicago: University of Chicago Press, 1951), pp. 89–106.
5. Brodie, *op. cit.*, pp. 272–73.
6. Lloyd C. Gardner, *Architects of Illusion: Men and Ideas in American Foreign Policy, 1941–1949* (Chicago: Quadrangle, 1970), pp. 68, 89, quoting Stimson MS Diary entries for May 13, 15, and September 4, 1945 (quotation from p. 68 and the latter entry). Gar Alperovitz, *Atomic Diplomacy: Hiroshima and Potsdam: The Use of the Atomic Bomb and the American Confrontation with Soviet Power* (London: Secker & Warburg, 1966), bases much of its interpretation that the atomic bomb was used primarily as a bargaining weapon against the Soviet Union upon such testimony from Stimson, but overdraws the case. To believe that the atomic bomb seemed a useful bargaining counter in relations

with Russia does not require belief that it was used against Japan for other than the evident military reasons.

7. Henry A. Kissinger, *Nuclear Weapons and Foreign Policy* (New York: Harper, 1957), p. 12.
8. James M. Gavin, *War and Peace in the Space Age* (London: Hutchinson, 1959), p. 114.
9. R. Alton Lee, "The Army 'Mutiny' of 1946," *Journal of American History*, LIII (Dec., 1966), 555–71.
10. C. Joseph Bernardo and Eugene H. Bacon, *American Military Policy: Its Development since 1775* (Second Edition, Harrisburg: Stackpole, 1961), p. 448; U.S. Department of Commerce, Bureau of the Census, *Historical Statistics of the United States: Colonial Times to 1957* (Washington: Government Printing Office, 1961), p. 736; Harry S. Truman, *Memoirs* (2 vols., Garden City: Doubleday, 1955), I, *Year of Decisions*, pp. 506–509.
11. War Department Circular 347 is printed in The President's Advisory Commission on Military Training, *A Program for National Security* (Washington: Government Printing Office, 1947), pp. 397–99, and Frederick Martin Stern, *The Citizen Army: Key to the Defense of the United States* (New York: St. Martin's, 1957), pp. 353–56. Truman, *op. cit.*, I, 510–12; Russell F. Weigley, *Towards an American Army: Military Thought from Washington to Marshall* (New York: Columbia University Press, 1962), pp. 242–46.
12. Bernardo and Bacon, *op. cit.*, pp. 448–50; President's Advisory Commission, *op. cit.*, pp. 393–97, 401–404; Truman, *op. cit.*, II, *Years of Trial and Hope*, pp. 53–55.
13. Vincent Davis, *Postwar Defense Policy and the U. S. Navy, 1943–1946* (Chapel Hill: University of North Carolina Press, 1966); Clark G. Reynolds, *The Fast Carriers: The Forging of an Air Navy* (New York: McGraw-Hill, 1968), pp. 109–10, 213–18, 233–35, 324, 351–55, 384–98.
14. Ray Wagner, *American Combat Planes* (New Revised Edition, Garden City: Doubleday, 1968), pp. 357–58.
15. *Ibid.*, pp. 134–43.
16. Samuel P. Huntington, *The Common Defense: Strategic Programs in National Politics* (Paperback edition, New York: Columbia University Press, 1966), p. 372; Walter Millis, ed., *The Forrestal Diaries* (New York: Viking, 1951), pp. 374, 378, 388–89; Arnold A. Rogow, *James Forrestal: A Study of Personality, Politics, and Policy* (New York: Macmillan, 1963), pp. 283–86.
17. Huntington, *op. cit.*, pp. 41–42, quotation from p. 42; Millis, *op. cit.*, pp. 374, 418–21, 429–33, 466–67; Rogow, *op. cit.*, pp. 285–87.
18. *Statutes at Large of the United States*, LXI, 495–510, reprinted in part in Walter Millis, ed., *American Military Thought* (Indianapolis: Bobbs-Merrill, 1966), pp. 463–79; Ray S. Cline and Maurice Matloff, "Development of War Department Views on Unification," *Military Affairs*, XIII (Spring, 1949), 65–74; Paul Y. Hammond, *Organizing for Defense: The American Military Establishment in the Twentieth Century* (Princeton: Princeton University Press, 1961), pp. 186–226; Millis, *Forrestal Diaries*, pp. 146–49, 151–53, 159–70, 200–206, 246–47, 269–72, 274, 291–95; Rogow, *op. cit.*, pp. 210–34; Truman, *op. cit.*, II, 46–52.
19. Millis, *Forrestal Diaries*, p. 390.
20. Rogow, *op. cit.*, p. 287.
21. Millis, *Forrestal Diaries*, p. 393.
22. *Ibid.*, pp. 390–98, 400–404, 412–21, 425–39, 464–68, 475–79; Rogow, *op. cit.*, pp. 286–300, quotation from Spaatz on p. 292.
23. *U.S. Statutes at Large*, LXIII, 578–92; Bernardo and Bacon, *op. cit.*, pp. 460–61, 471; Millis, *Forrestal Diaries*, pp. 548–55; Rogow, *op. cit.*

24. Bernardo and Bacon, *op. cit.*, pp. 473–76; Paul Y. Hammond, "Super Carriers and B-36 Bombers: Appropriations, Strategy and Politics," in Harold Stein, ed., *American Civil-Military Decisions: A Book of Case Studies* (University, Ala.: University of Alabama Press, 1963), pp. 465–564.
25. Wagner, *op. cit.*, pp. 142–48, 152.
26. Quoted in Kissinger, *op. cit.*, p. 35, from 81st Congress, 1st Session, U.S. House, *The National Defense Program—Unification and Strategy*, Hearings before the Committee on Armed Services, pp. 50–51.
27. Dean Acheson, *Present at the Creation: My Years in the State Department* (New York: Norton, 1969), pp. 344–49; Huntington, *op. cit.*, pp. 47–49, 298–304; Warner R. Schilling, "The H-Bomb Decision: How to Decide without Actually Choosing," *Political Science Quarterly*, LXXIX (March, 1961), 24–46.
28. Huntington, *op. cit.*, pp. 39–40; Millis, *Forrestal Diaries*, p. 508.
29. Quoted in Acheson, *op. cit.*, p. 349, from David E. Lilienthal, *The Journals of David E. Lilienthal*, II, *The Atomic Energy Years, 1945–1950* (New York: Harper & Row, 1964), p. 624.
30. Acheson, *op. cit.*, pp. 371, 373–74; Paul Y. Hammond, "NSC-68: Prologue to Rearmament," in Warner R. Schilling, Paul Y. Hammond, and Glenn H. Snyder, *Strategy, Politics, and Defense Budgets* (New York: Columbia University Press, 1962), pp. 271–378; Huntington, *op. cit.*, pp. 49–52.
31. Acheson, *op. cit.*, p. 375.
32. Quoted in Kissinger, *op. cit.*, p. 40, from 82nd Congress, 1st Session, U.S. Senate, *Military Situation in the Far East*, Hearings before the Committee on Armed Services and the Committee on Foreign Relations, p. 2083.
33. Quoted in Kissinger, *op. cit.*, pp. 38–39, from 81:1, *The National Defense Program*, pp. 520–22. Acheson, *op. cit.*, p. 374; Huntington, *op. cit.*, pp. 51–53.

CHAPTER SIXTEEN. OLD STRATEGIES REVISITED: DOUGLAS MACARTHUR AND GEORGE C. MARSHALL IN THE KOREAN WAR

1. Douglas MacArthur, *Reminiscences* (New York: McGraw-Hill, 1964), p. 349.
2. Samuel P. Huntington, *The Common Defense: Strategic Programs in National Politics* (Paperback edition, New York: Columbia University Press, 1966), p. 59.
3. Roy E. Appleman, *South to the Naktong, North to the Yalu* (*United States Army in the Korean War*, Washington: Office of the Chief of Military History, 1961), pp. 69–73, 113–14, 180; Malcolm W. Cagle and Frank A. Manson, *The Sea War in Korea* (Annapolis: United States Naval Institute, 1957), pp. 30–33; J. Lawton Collins, *War in Peacetime: The History and Lessons of Korea* (Boston: Houghton Mifflin, 1969), chap. I; T. R. Fehrenbach, *This Kind of War: A Study in Unpreparedness* (New York: Macmillan, 1963), pp. 101–103, 109, 220; James A. Field, Jr., *History of United States Naval Operations: Korea* (Washington: Government Printing Office, 1962), pp. 39–50, 68–71.
4. Appleman, *op. cit.*, chaps. II–XXIV; Cagle and Manson, *op. cit.*, pp. 39–74; Collins, *op. cit.*, chaps. III, V; Fehrenbach, *op. cit.*, chaps. VII–XIV; Field, *op. cit.*, pp. 50–121; Robert Frank Futrell, Lawson S. Moseley, and Albert F. Simpson, *The United States Air Force in Korea, 1950–1953* (New York: Duell, Sloan and Pearce, 1961), pp. 23–34; Lynn Montross and Nicholas A. Canzona, *U. S. Marine Operations in Korea* (4 vols., Washington: Historical Branch, G-3, Headquarters, U.S. Marine Corps, 1954–62 [Vol. IV by Lynn Montross, Hubard D. Kuokka, and Norman W. Hicks]), I; David Rees, *Korea: The Limited War* (New York: St Martin's, 1964), chap. III.
5. Collins, *op. cit.*, p. 113. Appleman, *op. cit.*, pp. 255–62, 329–30, 350–53, 376–79;

Cagle and Manson, *op. cit.*, pp. 47–51, 71–74; Robert Frank Futrell, chap. XXIV, "The Korean War," in Alfred Goldberg, ed., *A History of the United States Air Force, 1907–1957* (Princeton: Van Nostrand, 1957), pp. 243–47; Futrell, Moseley, and Simpson, *op. cit.*, pp. 46–69, 73–139. Later in the war the F-80 was joined by the North American F-86 Sabre, a faster plane which defeated the Soviet-built MIG-15 to retain mastery of the skies over Korea. Ray Wagner, *American Combat Planes* (New Revised Edition, Garden City: Doubleday, 1968), pp. 252–54, 261–63; Ray Wagner, *North American Sabre* (Garden City: Doubleday, 1963).

6. Cagle and Manson, *op. cit.*, pp. 47–67, 71–74, quotation from p. 67; Field, *op. cit.*, pp. 108–27; Montross and Canzona, *op. cit.*, I, 89–90, 98–99, 179–81, 201–206, and *passim.* After World War II, "A" was added to the "CV" designation of all large carriers to indicate "attack." Both *Valley Forge* and *Philippine Sea* were *Essex*-class carriers.
7. Quoted in Cagle and Manson, *op. cit.*, pp. 77–78. Appleman, *op. cit.*, pp. 488–98; Cagle and Manson, *op. cit.*, pp. 75–78; Collins, *op. cit.*, pp. 114–18, 120–29; Field, *op. cit.*, pp. 171–77; Robert Debs Heinl, Jr., *Victory at High Tide: The Inchon-Seoul Campaign* (Philadelphia: Lippincott, 1968), chap. II; MacArthur, *op. cit.*, pp. 346–51; Montross and Canzona, *op. cit.*, II, chaps. I, III–IV; Rees, *op. cit.*, pp. 77–83.
8. Appleman, *op. cit.*, pp. 498–501; Cagle and Manson, *op. cit.*, pp. 78–101; Collins, *op. cit.*, pp. 118–19, 130–37; Field, *op. cit.*, pp. 177–79; Heinl, *op. cit.*, pp. 24–30; Montross and Canzona, *op. cit.*, II, 59–65; Rees, *op. cit.*, pp. 80–81, 83–88, 94–97.
9. MacArthur, *op. cit.*, p. 357n.
10. Appleman, *op. cit.*, pp. 501–637; Collins, *op. cit.*, pp. 137–63; Fehrenbach, *op. cit.*, pp. 247–83; Field, *op. cit.*, pp. 179–218; Heinl, *op. cit.*, chaps. III–VIII; Montross and Canzona, *op. cit.*, II, 74–248; Rees, *op. cit.*, pp. 82–94 and chap. VIII.
11. Appleman, *op. cit.*, pp. 609–21; Cagle and Manson, *op. cit.*, pp. 107–109, 111–15, 118–21, 146–51; Collins, *op. cit.*, pp. 157–71; Field, *op. cit.*, pp. 219–42; Montross and Canzona, *op. cit.*, III, chaps. II–III.
12. Quoted in Collins, *op. cit.*, p. 199. Dean Acheson, *Present at the Creation: My Years in the State Department* (New York: Norton, 1969), pp. 451–52, 456–57, 461–64; Collins, *op. cit.*, pp. 153–54, 172–77, 179–200; Field, *op. cit.*, pp. 242–64; MacArthur, *op. cit.*, pp. 359–68; Rees, *op. cit.*, pp. 115–22, 129–36; Harry S. Truman, *Memoirs* (2 vols., Garden City: Doubleday, 1955), II, *Years of Trial and Hope*, pp. 361–73.
13. Collins, *op. cit.*, p. 199.
14. Cagle and Manson, *op. cit.*, p. 222.
15. *Ibid.*, pp. 222–29; Field, *op. cit.*, pp. 254, 257–62, 280; Futrell, Moseley, and Simpson, *op. cit.*, pp. 209–14.
16. Acheson *op. cit.*, pp. 464–77, 480–81, 512; Collins, *op. cit.*, pp. 200–57; MacArthur, *op. cit.*, pp. 365–84; Rees, *op. cit.*, pp. 130–42, 147–66, 171–85; Matthew B. Ridgway, *The Korean War* (Garden City: Doubleday, 1967), pp. 59–108; Matthew B. Ridgway, *Soldier: The Memoirs of Matthew B. Ridgway* (New York: Harper, 1956), pp. 192–95, 198–216; Allen S. Whiting, *China Crosses the Yalu* (New York: Macmillan, 1960).
17. To the Senate hearings on MacArthur's dismissal, *Military Situation in the Far East*, p. 732.
18. Bernard Brodie, *Strategy in the Missile Age* (Paperback edition, Princeton: Princeton University Press, 1965), pp. 319–21; Field, *op. cit.*, pp. 262–63.
19. MacArthur, *op. cit.*, pp. 386, 404.
20. There is much material on the Truman-MacArthur controversy in the works of Truman, MacArthur, Acheson, Collins, and Ridgway, among the principals,

already cited, and in Rees, *op. cit.* See also Trumbull Higgins, *Korea and the Fall of MacArthur: A Précis in Limited War* (New York: Oxford University Press, 1960); Arthur M. Schlesinger, Jr., and Richard Rovere, *The General and the President* (New York: Farrar, Straus and Young, 1951); John W. Spanier, *The Truman-MacArthur Controversy and the Korean War* (Paperback edition, New York: Norton, 1965).

21. Cagle and Manson, *op. cit.*, pp. 229–39; Field, *op. cit.*, pp. 305–57; Futrell in Goldberg, *op. cit.*, pp. 250–57; Futrell, Moseley, and Simpson, *op. cit.*, chaps. IX–XIV.
22. Alexander P. De Seversky, *Victory through Air Power* (New York: Simon & Schuster, 1942), p. 102. Cagle and Manson, *op. cit.*, pp. 239–40, 269–74; Field, *op. cit.*, pp. 335–38, 343, 358; Futrell, Moseley, and Simpson, *op. cit.*, pp. 285–89, 295, 287–313.
23. Quoted in Cagle and Manson, *op. cit.*, p. 279. *Ibid.*, pp. 241–43, 247–80; Field, *op. cit.*, pp. 357–61 and chap. XII; Futrell, Moseley, and Simpson, *op. cit.*, pp. 296–97, 302, 308, and chaps. XIV–XVI, XVIII–XX. For the closing campaigns, see also Mark W. Clark, *From the Danube to the Yalu* (New York: Harper, 1954); Walter G. Hermes, *Truce Tent and Fighting Front* (*United States Army in the Korean War*, Washington: Office of the Chief of Military History, 1966).
24. Quoted in Huntington, *op. cit.*, pp. 56–57. *Ibid.*, pp. 53–57; Acheson, *op. cit.*, pp. 420–22, 441–42, 451, 491–93; Truman, *op. cit.*, II, 341, 419–32, 437.
25. Quotation in Huntington, *op. cit.*, p. 58. *Ibid.*, pp. 57–59; Bernardo and Bacon, *op. cit.*, pp. 450–51.
26. Quoted in Huntington, *op. cit.*, p. 55, from *New York Times*, July 25, 1950, p. 25.
27. Huntington, *op. cit.*, pp. 59–62; Wagner, *op. cit.*, pp. 147–48, 150–51.
28. Acheson, *op. cit.*, pp. 482–88, 493–94, 608–10, 622–27; Huntington, *op. cit.*, pp. 62, 315–26.

CHAPTER SEVENTEEN. STRATEGIES OF DETERRENCE AND OF ACTION: THE STRATEGY INTELLECTUALS

1. Henry A. Kissinger, *Nuclear Weapons and Foreign Policy* (New York: Harper & Row, for the Council on Foreign Relations, 1957), pp. 430–31.
2. Dwight D. Eisenhower, *The White House Years: Mandate for Change, 1953–1956* (Garden City: Doubleday, 1963), chap. VII; David Rees, *Korea: The Limited War* (New York: St Martin's, 1964), chaps. XXII–XXIII.
3. Samuel P. Huntington, *The Common Defense: Strategic Programs in National Politics* (Paperback edition, New York: Columbia University Press, 1966), pp. 62–66; Ray Wagner, *American Combat Planes* (New Revised Edition, Garden City: Doubleday, 1968), p. 148.
4. Eisenhower, *op. cit.*, pp. 445–47, 452; Robert J. Donovan, *Eisenhower: The Inside Story* (New York: Harper, 1956), chap. IV; Huntington, *op. cit.*, pp. 64–69; Glenn Snyder, "The 'New Look' of 1953," in Warner R. Schilling, Paul Y. Hammond, and Glenn Snyder, *Strategy, Politics, and Defense Budgets* (New York: Columbia University Press, 1962), pp. 400–406, 470–75.
5. Eisenhower, *op. cit.*, pp. 451–52; Huntington, *op. cit.*, pp. 70–71; Snyder, *loc. cit.*, pp. 386–410, 457–64.
6. Eisenhower, *op. cit.*, pp. 452–55; Huntington, *op. cit.*, pp. 71–74; Snyder, *loc. cit.*, pp. 410–36.
7. Huntington, *op. cit.*, p. 74; Snyder, *loc. cit.*, pp. 436–40.
8. Huntington, *op. cit.*, pp. 74–76; Snyder, *loc. cit.*, pp. 436–56.

9. Huntington, *op. cit.*, p. 83; Snyder, *loc. cit.*, pp. 459–60; Wagner, *op. cit.*, pp. 152–53.
10. Department of State *Bulletin*, Vol. XXX, No. 761 (Jan. 25, 1954), pp. 107–10, quotations from pp. 107–108, reprinted in Raymond G. O'Connor, ed., *American Defense Policy in Perspective: From Colonial Times to the Present* (New York: Wiley, 1965), pp. 326–30, quotations from pp. 327–28; and in Dale O. Smith, *U.S. Military Doctrine: A Study and Appraisal* (New York: Duell, Sloan and Pearce, 1955), pp. 226–36, quotations from pp. 228–31. This latter book is a survey history of American military strategy and policy by an Air Force brigadier general; it ends by approving Dulles's strategy. See also Snyder, *loc. cit.*, pp. 464–70, 520.
11. Eisenhower, *op. cit.*, pp. 332–57; Donovan, *op. cit.*, chap. XIX; Bernard B. Fall, *Hell in a Very Small Place: The Siege of Dien Bien Phu* (Paperback edition, New York: Vintage Books, 1968), pp. 25–26, 35–52, 293–314; Matthew B. Ridgway, *Soldier: The Memoirs of Matthew B. Ridgway* (New York: Harper, 1956), pp. 275–78.
12. Eisenhower, *op. cit.*, pp. 455–56; Huntington, *op. cit.*, pp. 88–89.
13. Vannevar Bush, *Modern Arms and Free Men: A Discussion of the Role of Science in Preserving Democracy* (New York: Simon and Schuster, 1949), chaps. I–III; Robert G. Gilpin, *American Scientists and Nuclear Weapons* (Princeton: Princeton University Press, 1962); A. Rupert Hall, "Science, Technology, and Warfare, 1400–1700," and David D. Bien, "Military Education in 18th Century France; Technical and Non-Technical Determinants," with commentary and discussion, in Monte D. Wright and Lawrence J. Paszek, eds., *Science, Technology, and Warfare: The Proceedings of the Third Military History Symposium, United States Air Force Academy, 8–9 May 1969* (Office of Air Force History, Headquarters USAF, and United States Air Force Academy, n.d.), pp. 3–84. For a collective profile of one type of the new strategists, see Roy E. Licklider, *The Private Nuclear Strategists* (Columbus: Ohio State University Press, 1971).
14. Quoted in Robert L. Perry, "Commentary," in Wright and Paszek, *op. cit.*, p. 111, from B. H. Liddell Hart, *Thoughts on War, 1919–39* (London: Faber, 1944), p. 125.
15. Leroy A. Brothers, "Operations Analysis in the United States Air Force," *Journal of the Operations Research Society of America*, II (Feb., 1954), 17–30; I. B. Holley, Jr., "The Evolution of Operations Research and Its Impact on the Military Establishment; The Air Force Experience," with commentary by Robert L. Perry, in Wright and Paszek, *op. cit.*, pp. 89–121; Joseph P. McCloskey, "Of Horseless Carriages, Flying Machines, and Operations Research: A Tribute to Frederick William Lanchester (1868–1946)," *Operations Research: The Journal of the Operations Research Society of America*, IV (April, 1956), 141–47.
16. Holley, *loc. cit.*, pp. 92–98, 107–109; Perry, *loc. cit.*, pp. 110–19.
17. John W. Abrams, "Military Applications of Operational Research," *Operations Research*, V (June, 1957), 434–40 (a letter to the editor, largely historical in content); Robert A. Bailey, "Application of Operations-Research Techniques to Airborne Weapon System Planning," *Journal of the Operations Research Society of America*, I (Aug., 1953), 187–99; Erwin Biser and Martin Meyerson, "The Application of Design of Experiments and Modeling to Complex Weapons Systems," *Operations Research*, V (Feb., 1957), 210–21; A. W. Boldyreff, ed., "A Decade of Military Operations Research in Perspective—A Symposium," *ibid.*, VIII (Nov.-Dec., 1960), 798–860; Douglas L. Brooks, "Choice of Pay-Offs for Military Operations of the Future," *ibid.* (March-April, 1960), 159–68 (especially focuses on the evolution of operations research into systems analysis);

G. H. Fisher, "Weapon-System Cost Analysis," *ibid.*, IV (Oct., 1956), 558–71; Richard B. Foster and Francis P. Hoeber, "Cost-Effectiveness Analysis for Strategic Decisions," *Journal of the Operations Research Society of America*, III (Nov., 1955), 482–93; Charles Hitch, "An Appreciation of Systems Analysis," *ibid.*, pp. 466–81; Norman Precoda, "Air Weapons System Analysis," *Operations Research*, IV (Dec., 1956), 684–98; Walter J. Strauss, "The Nature and Validity of Operations-Research Studies, With Emphasis on Force Composition," *ibid.*, VIII (Sept.-Oct., 1960), 675–93.

18. Gene M. Lyons and Louis Morton, *Schools for Strategy: Education and Research in National Security Affairs* (New York: Praeger, 1965), pp. 239–57, 264; Bruce L. R. Smith, *The Rand Corporation: Case Study of a Nonprofit Advisory Corporation* (Cambridge: Harvard University Press, 1966).
19. Bernard Brodie, ed., *The Absolute Weapon: Atomic Power and World Order* (New York: Harcourt, Brace, 1946); Bernard Brodie, "Unlimited Weapons and Limited War," *The Reporter*, XI, No. 9 (Nov. 18, 1954), 16–21.
20. William W. Kaufmann, "The Requirements of Deterrence," in William W. Kaufmann, ed., *Military Policy and National Security* (Princeton: Princeton University Press, 1956), pp. 12–38. See also *idem.*, "Limited Warfare," *ibid.*, pp. 102–36.
21. Morton H. Halperin, *Defense Strategies for the Seventies* (Boston: Little, Brown, 1971), pp. 43–45 (essentially the same discussion as in Halperin's *Contemporary Military Strategy* [Paperback edition, Boston: Little, Brown, 1967], pp. 48–50); Huntington, *op. cit.*, p. 348; Maxwell D. Taylor, *The Uncertain Trumpet* (New York: Harper, 1960), p. 25.
22. Eisenhower, *op. cit.*, pp. 453–55; Donovan, *op. cit.*, pp. 329–31; Snyder, *loc. cit.*, pp. 442–43, 486–91, 499–500, 504–16, 522–24.
23. Robert Endicott Osgood, *Limited War: The Challenge to American Strategy* (Chicago: University of Chicago Press, 1957), p. 146.
24. *Ibid.*, p. ix.
25. *Ibid.*, p. 1.
26. *Ibid.*, p. 189.
27. *Ibid.*, p. 4.
28. *Ibid.*, p. 18.
29. *Ibid.*, p. 26.
30. *Ibid.*, p. 240. Osgood also wrote, p. 238:

    However, this does not mean that we must necessarily confine our war objectives to the exact territorial boundaries and the other political conditions that existed prior to aggression. This kind of mechanical requirement, making no allowance for the dynamic, unpredictable elements of war, would impose rigid political constraints, unrelated to the actual balance of military power and the enemy's response. Moreover, if potential aggressors could count upon ending a war in at least no worse position than they began it, they might come to regard this situation as an irresistible invitation to launch a series of limited incursions at a minimal risk in proportion to the possible gain.

31. Kissinger, *op. cit.*, pp. 4–5.
32. *Ibid.*, p. 11.
33. *Ibid.*, p. 12.
34. *Ibid.*, p. 53.
35. *Ibid.*, p. 29.
36. *Ibid.*, p. 9.
37. *Ibid.*, pp. 9–13, 43–51.
38. *Ibid.*, pp. 48–49.

39. *Ibid.*, p. 26.
40. *Ibid.*, p. 7.
41. *Ibid.*, p. 18 and chap. VI.
42. *Ibid.*, pp. 244–45.
43. *Ibid.*, p. 22.
44. *Ibid.*, p. 171.
45. *Ibid.*, p. 146.
46. *Ibid.*, pp. 429–30.
47. *Ibid.*, pp. 430–31.
48. Taylor, *op. cit.*, p. 26. Eventually the strategic critics were to develop a huge bibliography of works on limited war; for titles, see Morton H. Halperin, *Limited War: An Essay on the Development of the Theory and an Annotated Bibliography*, Occasional Papers in International Affairs No. 3, May 1962, Harvard University Center for International Affairs, and *idem.*, *Limited War in the Nuclear Age* (New York: Wiley, 1963), which includes a bibliography to September, 1962.
49. Ridgway, *op. cit.*, pp. 268–73, 286–332; Snyder, *loc. cit.*, pp. 442–43, 486–91, 499–500, 504–16, 522–24.
50. Ridgway, *op. cit.*, pp. 296–97.
51. *Ibid.*, p. 324.
52. *Ibid.*, p. 293.
53. Huntington, *op. cit.*, pp. 91–94; Taylor, *op. cit.*, pp. 26–37.
54. John Foster Dulles, "Challenge and Response in United States Policy," *Foreign Affairs*, XXXVI (Oct., 1957), 25–43, quotation from p. 31.
55. Huntington, *op. cit.*, pp. 92–95; Taylor, *op. cit.*, pp. 38–53.
56. Taylor, *op. cit.*, pp. 43–46, 73–79; quotation from I Corinthians on p. vii. For a later account by Taylor and his reflections after more than a decade and much subsequent government service, see Maxwell D. Taylor, *Swords and Plowshares* (New York: Norton, 1972), pp. 156, 164–67, 169–78.
57. Taylor, *Uncertain Trumpet*, p. 5.
58. *Ibid.*, pp. 6–7.
59. *Ibid.*, p. 146.
60. *Ibid.*, p. 151.
61. *Ibid.*, p. 64.
62. *Ibid.*, p. 146.
63. James M. Gavin, *Airborne Warfare* (Washington: Infantry Journal Press, 1947). There is much autobiographical material in James M. Gavin, *War and Peace in the Space Age* (New York: Harper, 1958).
64. James M. Gavin, *War and Peace in the Space Age* (British edition, London: Hutchinson, 1959), *passim*, especially pp. 110–14, 128, 137–38, 168–69, 210, 217–20.
65. *Ibid.*, pp. 218, 124.
66. *Ibid.*, pp. 217–18, 257.
67. *Ibid.*, p. 122.
68. *Ibid.*, pp. 143–46, 151–52, 157, 163–64, 209, 257–58, 261–62.
69. *Ibid.*, p. 128.
70. *Ibid.*, pp. 200–201.
71. *Ibid.*, p. 198.
72. *Ibid.*, p. 190.
73. Albert J. Wohlstetter, "The Delicate Balance of Terror," *Foreign Affairs*, XXXVII (Jan., 1959), 211–34, especially pp. 221–30, 233–34. A longer version of the paper is Albert J. Wohlstetter, *The Delicate Balance of Terror*, RAND Publication P-1472, Dec., 1958. Wohlstetter had begun to develop these themes in *Selection and Use of Strategic Air Bases*, RAND R-266, April, 1954, a study

sometimes considered the first landmark contribution of the civilian strategy intellectuals. See E. S. Quade, "The Selection and Use of Strategic Air Bases: A Case History," in E. S. Quade, ed., *Analysis for Military Decisions* (Chicago: Rand McNally, 1966), pp. 24–63.

74. Excerpts from Quarles's statement appear in "How Much Is Enough?" *Air Force*, XXXIX (Sept., 1956), 51–53; for discussion see Huntington, *op. cit.*, pp. 101–102.
75. On the Air Force preoccupation with cruise missiles, see the appendix to Robert L. Perry's commentary in Wright and Paszek, *op. cit.*, pp. 119–20. On the Missile Evaluation Committee headed by John von Neumann, see Urs Schwarz, *American Strategy: A New Perspective: The Growth of Politico-Military Thinking in the United States* (Garden City: Doubleday, 1966), p. 82.
76. Gavin, *op. cit.*, pp. 27, 151; Huntington, *op. cit.*, pp. 96–97, 108–13; Taylor, *Uncertain Trumpet*, pp. 53–54; *Statutes at Large of the United States*, LXII, 514–24.
77. Morton H. Halperin, "The Gaither Committee and the Policy Process," *World Politics*, XIII (April, 1961), 360–84; Huntington, *op. cit.*, pp. 106–13.
78. *Prospect for America: The Rockefeller Panel Reports* (Garden City: Doubleday, 1961), pp. 93–153; first published as Rockefeller Brothers Fund, *International Security: The Military Aspect* (Garden City: Doubleday, 1958).
79. Huntington, *op. cit.*, pp. 94–97; Taylor, *Uncertain Trumpet*, pp. 53–79.
80. Oskar Morgenstern, *The Question of National Defense* (New York: Random House, 1959), p. 286.
81. *Ibid.*, p. 27.
82. *Ibid.*, p. 39.
83. *Ibid.*, chap. IV.
84. *Ibid.*, pp. 292–93.
85. *Ibid.*, pp. 22–23, quotation from p. 23.
86. *Ibid.*, p. 22.
87. *Ibid.*, pp. 83, 96.
88. *Ibid.*, p. 279.
89. Bernard Brodie, *Strategy in the Missile Age* (Paperback edition, Princeton: Princeton University Press, 1965; first published 1959), pp. 19–20.
90. *Ibid.*, pp. 256–57, quotation from p. 257.
91. *Ibid.*, p. 245.
92. *Ibid.*, pp. 241–48, quotation from p. 247.
93. *Ibid.*, p. 281.
94. *Ibid.*, pp. 42–55 and chap. VI.
95. *Ibid.*, chap. IX, quotation from p. 307.
96. *Ibid.*, p. 321.
97. *Ibid.*, pp. 324–25.
98. *Ibid.*, pp. 328–29.
99. *Ibid.*, p. 332.
100. *Ibid.*, pp. 323–24.
101. *Ibid.*, p. 409.
102. Henry A. Kissinger, *The Necessity for Choice: Prospects of American Foreign Policy* (London: Chatto and Windus, 1961 [American edition, New York: Harper, 1961]), p. 15.
103. *Ibid.*, p. 26.
104. *Ibid.*, p. 35.
105. Huntington, *op. cit.*, pp. 103–105.
106. Quoted in Jack Raymond, *Power at the Pentagon* (New York: Harper & Row, 1964), p. 257, from *New York Times*, Jan. 24, 1960.

107. Theodore H. White, *The Making of the President 1960* (New York: Atheneum, 1961), pp. 180–88, 191–98.
108. Quoted in Theodore C. Sorensen, *Kennedy* (New York: Harper & Row, 1965), p. 612. Kennedy had warned of the missile gap since 1958; see "The Missile Gap," speech delivered in the Senate Aug. 14, 1958, in John F. Kennedy, *The Strategy of Peace*, ed., Allan Nevins (New York: Harper & Row, 1960), pp. 33–45.
109. Quoted in Chester L. Cooper, *The Lost Crusade: America in Vietnam* (New York: Dodd, Mead, 1970), pp. 173, from *Saturday Review*, Sept. 3, 1960, p. 17.
110. Sorensen, *op. cit.*, p. 205, for quotation about Cuba; White, *op. cit.*, pp. 256–57, for other quotations.
111. Herman Kahn, *On Thermonuclear War* (Princeton: Princeton University Press, 1960); see also Herman Kahn *et al.*, *Some Specific Suggestions for Achieving Early Non-Military Defense Capabilities and Initiating Long-Range Programs*, RAND Corporation RM-2206-RC, July 1, 1958.
112. Kahn elaborated upon some of his ideas, condensed some, and generally rang the changes upon *Thermonuclear War* in *Thinking about the Unthinkable* (New York: Horizon Press, 1962) and *On Escalation: Metaphors and Scenarios* (New York: Praeger, 1965).
113. Herman Kahn, "Afterword to the Avon/Discus Edition," *Thinking about the Unthinkable* (Paperback edition, New York: Avon Books, 1971), p. 268. This edition contains excerpts from some of Kahn's critics, some friendly reviews, and Kahn's response. See also Herman Kahn, "The Arms Race and Some of Its Hazards," in Donald G. Brennan, ed., *Arms Control, Disarmament, and National Security* (New York: Braziller, 1961), pp. 89–121. Michael Howard wrote aptly of the "grim jocularity" of Kahn's style in "The Classical Strategists," in Howard's *Studies in War and Peace* (New York: Viking, 1971), p. 173.

CHAPTER EIGHTEEN. STRATEGIES OF ACTION ATTEMPTED: TO THE VIETNAM WAR

1. Quoted in Neil Sheehan *et al.*, *The Pentagon Papers as Published by the New York Times* (Paperback edition, New York: Bantam Books, 1971), p. 463.
2. Quoted in Henry L. Trewhitt, *McNamara* (New York: Harper & Row, 1971), p. 21. See Edgar M. Bottome, *The Missile Gap: A Study of the Formulation of Military and Political Policy* (Rutherford, N.J.: Fairleigh Dickinson University Press, 1971).
3. Roger Hilsman, *To Move a Nation: The Politics of Foreign Policy in the Administration of John F. Kennedy* (Paperback edition, New York: Dell, 1968), pp. 162–64; Trewhitt, *op. cit.*, p. 21.
4. Robert S. McNamara, "National Security and NATO," Department of State *Bulletin*, Vol. XLVII, No. 1202 (July 9, 1962), pp. 64–69, quotation from p. 67.
5. Morton S. Halperin, *Defense Strategies for the Seventies* (Boston: Little, Brown, 1971), p. 49; Jack Raymond, *Power at the Pentagon* (New York: Harper & Row, 1964), p. 233; Trewhitt, *op. cit.*, pp. 23, 119–24.
6. Halperin, *op. cit.*, pp. 49, 73–76; Trewhitt, *op. cit.*, pp. 112–17. For a friendly discussion of the early phases of McNamara's strategic thought, see William W. Kaufmann, *The McNamara Strategy* (New York: Harper & Row, 1964). For sophisticated thinking about deterrence as it had evolved by the early 1960s, see Glenn H. Snyder, *Deterrence and Defense* (Princeton: Princeton University Press, 1961); for further thinking by the strategy intellectuals on exercising

control over nuclear war, Klaus Knorr and Thornton Read, eds., *Limited Strategic War* (New York: Praeger, 1962).

7. *Public Papers of the Presidents of the United States: John F. Kennedy . . . 1961* (Washington: Government Printing Office, 1962), p. 232.
8. *Ibid.*, p. 230.
9. Henry A. Kissinger, *The Necessity for Choice: Prospects of American Foreign Policy* (London: Chatto and Windus, 1961 [American edition, New York: Harper, 1961]), pp. 75–94. The argument appears in a somewhat different form in Henry A. Kissinger, "Limited War: Conventional or Nuclear? A Reappraisal," in Donald G. Brennan, ed., *Arms Control, Disarmament, and National Security* (New York: Braziller, 1961), pp. 138–52.
10. Charles J. Hitch and Roland N. McKean, eds., *The Economics of Defense in the Nuclear Age* (Cambridge: Harvard University Press, 1960).
11. Trewhitt, *op. cit.*, pp. 4–12, 34–56.
12. Quoted *ibid.*, p. 17.
13. Quoted in Hilsman, *op. cit.*, p. 55.
14. Samuel A. Tucker, ed., *National Security Management: A Modern Design for Defense Decision: A McNamara-Hitch-Enthoven Anthology* (Washington: Industrial College of the Armed Forces, 1966), Foreword, p. iii. For systems analysis and cost-effectiveness measurement, see also David B. Bobrow, ed., *Weapons Systems Decisions: Political and Psychological Perspectives on Continental Defense* (New York: Praeger, 1969), especially David B. Bobrow, "Improving the Bases for Decisions," pp. 3–18, and Philburn Ratoosh, "Defense Decision-Making: Cost-Effectiveness Models and Rationality," pp. 21–34; E. S. Quade, *Analysis for Military Decisions* (Chicago: Rand-McNally, 1966).
15. Quoted in Tucker, *op. cit.*, p. 9.
16. U.S. Department of Commerce, Bureau of the Census, *Historical Statistics of the United States, Colonial Times to 1957: Continuation to 1962 and Revisions* (Washington: Government Printing Office, 1965), p. 98, Series Y 358a; Adam Yarmolinsky, *The Military Establishment: Its Impacts on American Society* (Paperback edition, New York: Harper & Row, 1971), pp. 9–10. The figures in my text unlike Yarmolinsky's charts include total Atomic Energy Commission expenditures.
17. Robert J. Art, *The TFX Decision* (Boston: Little, Brown, 1968); James M. Roherty, *Decisions of Robert S. McNamara: A Study of the Role of the Secretary of Defense* (Coral Gables: University of Miami Press, 1970); Trewhitt, *op. cit.*, pp. 24–25, 111–12, 120–22, 133–54, 283–85, 293; Ray Wagner, *American Combat Planes* (New Revised Edition, Garden City: Doubleday, 1968), p. 155; Yarmolinsky, *op. cit.*, pp. 42, 216–18, 272–73, 381.
18. David Novick, ed., *Program Budgeting: Program Analysis and the Federal Budget* (Cambridge: Harvard University Press, 1965); Trewhitt, *op. cit.*, pp. 85–87; Yarmolinsky, *op. cit.*, pp. 381–82.
19. Kissinger, *Necessity for Choice*, pp. 177–78.
20. *Ibid.*, p. 179.
21. *Ibid.*, p. 180.
22. Hilsman, *op. cit.*, chap. III; Arthur M. Schlesinger, Jr., *A Thousand Days: John F. Kennedy in the White House* (Boston: Houghton Mifflin, 1965), chaps. X–XI; Theodore C. Sorensen, *Kennedy* (New York: Harper & Row, 1965), pp. 205–206 and chap. XI; Hugh Thomas, *Cuba: The Pursuit of Freedom* (New York: Harper & Row, 1971), chaps. CIII, CVI. After the failure, the President brought General Maxwell Taylor from retirement to head a study of the causes of failure; for a summary of Taylor's findings, see Maxwell D. Taylor, *Swords and Plowshares* (New York: Norton, 1972), pp. 180–94. On the CIA

and the problems of the intelligence community, see Hilsman, *op. cit.*, Part III, and especially and more broadly, Harry Howe Ransom, *The Intelligence Establishment* (Cambridge: Harvard University Press, 1970).

23. James M. Gavin, *War and Peace in the Space Age* (London: Hutchinson, 1959), p. 128.

24. Hilsman, *op. cit.*, Part IV, especially pp. 128–29, 143–49; Schlesinger, *op. cit.*, pp. 320–40; Sorensen, *op. cit.*, pp. 639–48.

25. Robert A. Divine, ed., *The Cuban Missile Crisis* (Chicago: Quadrangle, 1971) combines a judicious review of the crisis with reprintings of various interpretations of Kennedy's handling of it, both friendly and hostile to the administration. Hilsman, *op. cit.*, Part V; Schlesinger, *op. cit.*, chap. XXX; Sorensen, *op. cit.*, chap. XXIV; and Taylor, *op. cit.*, pp. 262–81, present standard accounts from inside the Kennedy administration, Hilsman, pp. 161–65, 201–202, being an especially full account of the Soviet motives as the administration came to see them. Robert F. Kennedy, *Thirteen Days: A Memoir of the Cuban Missile Crisis* (New York: Norton, 1969) gives the Attorney General's view of a crisis in which his influence upon the policies of his brother the President was even greater than usual. Adam B. Ulam presents the missile crisis as the product of a Soviet effort to solve all the major political and military problems of the Soviet Union across the world in one bold stroke: to negotiate a settlement regarding the missiles in return for a German peace treaty with an absolute prohibition of nuclear weapons for West Germany and a similar arrangement for a nuclear-free zone in the Pacific. *Expansion and Coexistence: A History of Soviet Foreign Policy, 1917–67* (New York: Praeger, 1968), pp. 661–77, and *The Rivals: America and Russia since World War II* (New York: Viking, 1971), chap. X. Elie Abel, *The Missile Crisis* (Philadelphia: Lippincott, 1966) is a standard account; Thomas, *op. cit.*, chaps. CVIII–CIX, may be the best brief account.

A subsidiary controversy has developed over the range of the missiles that the Soviets were installing in Cuba. At the time of the crisis, the Kennedy administration not surprisingly made their potentialities seem as horrendous as possible. The subsequent efforts to make such alarums appear completely absurd neglect the point that strategists of the early 1960s feared IRBMs as much more difficult to intercept than ICBMs, because the IRBMs would be in flight for a much shorter period and their trajectories could be more variable. For an expression of such concern, written before the Cuban missile crisis, see Gordon B. Turner and Richard D. Challener, "Strategic and Political Implications of Missiles," in Turner and Challener, eds., *National Security in the Nuclear Age: Basic Facts and Theories* (New York: Praeger, 1960), p. 89.

26. Ulam, *Expansion and Coexistence*, p. 686, and *The Rivals*, pp. 337–40, on the ouster of Khrushchev. For the rise of Soviet naval power and American naval concern about it, see Lieutenant Commander Jack L. Roberts, USN, "The Growing Soviet Naval Presence in the Caribbean: Its Politico-Military Impact upon the United States," *Naval War College Review*, XXIII, No. 10 (June, 1971), 31–42; Commander Robert B. Rogers, USN, "Trends in Soviet Naval Strategy," *ibid.*, XXI, No. 11 (Feb., 1969), 13–29; Lieutenant Commander Gary G. Sick, USN, "Russia and the West in the Mediterranean: Perspectives for the 1970's," *ibid.*, XXII, No. 10 (June, 1970), 48–69; Drew Middleton, "Cuts in U. S. Sea Power Worry Admirals," *New York Times*, Oct. 11, 1971, pp. 1, 70.

27. Hilsman, *op. cit.*, pp. 52–53, 415; Maurice Matloff, general ed., *American Military History* (*Army Historical Series*, Washington: Office of the Chief of Military History, 1969), pp. 609–10; Schlesinger, *op. cit.*, pp. 340–42; Sorensen, *op. cit.*, pp. 631–33; Taylor, *op. cit.*, pp. 184, 200–203.

28. *Public Papers of the Presidents of the United States: John F. Kennedy . . . 1962* (Washington: Government Printing Office, 1963), p. 454.
29. Chester L. Cooper, *The Lost Crusade: America in Vietnam* (New York: Dodd, Mead, 1970), pp. 170–71, 174; Hilsman, *op. cit.*, pp. 415–20; Sheehan, *op. cit.*, pp. 15–21, 53–66. Edward Geary Lansdale, *In the Midst of Wars: An American's Mission to Southeast Asia* (New York: Harper & Row, 1972), is Lansdale's unilluminating memoir.
30. Sheehan, *op. cit.*, pp. 91–92, 130–38.
31. Cooper, *op. cit.*, pp. 178–81; Hilsman, *op. cit.*, pp. 421–24; Schlesinger, *op. cit.*, pp. 544–50; Sheehan, *op. cit.*, pp. 99–106, 141–48, quotation (Nov. 1, 1961) from p. 142; Taylor, *op. cit.*, pp. 220–44.
32. Quoted in Cooper, *op. cit.*, p. 181.
33. Nov. 1, 1961, Sheehan, *op. cit.*, p. 143.
34. *Ibid.*, pp. 105–106, 148–50, quotation from p. 149.
35. Cooper, *op. cit.*, pp. 180–81, 191–220; Hilsman, *op. cit.*, pp. 423–523; Matloff, *op. cit.*, pp. 618–21; Schlesinger, *op. cit.*, pp. 547–50, 981–98; Sheehan, *op. cit.*, pp. 104–14, 150–232; Sorensen, *op. cit.*, pp. 654–61; Taylor, *op. cit.*, pp. 288–301.
36. May 23, 1961, Sheehan, *op. cit.*, p. 128.
37. *Ibid.*, pp. 232–318, 345–62. See also Eugene G. Windchy, *Tonkin Gulf* (Garden City: Doubleday, 1971).
38. Jan. 22, 1964, Sheehan, *op. cit.*, pp. 274–77, quotations from pp. 274–75.
39. *Ibid.*, pp. 312–13, 354–55.
40. Nov. 29, 1964, *ibid.*, p. 377.
41. Cooper, *op. cit.*, pp. 259–62; Sheehan, *op. cit.*, pp. 343–44.
42. Cooper, *op. cit.*, pp. 270–71; Matloff, *op. cit.*, p. 623; Sheehan, *op. cit.*, pp. 382–403, 405–409, 418–43, quotation (April 4, 1964) from p. 402.
43. Deleted from final draft position paper of President Johnson's civilian advisers, Nov. 29, 1964; Sheehan, *op. cit.*, p. 378.
44. *Ibid.*, pp. 402–408.
45. Matloff, *op. cit.*, p. 623; Sheehan, *op. cit.*, pp. 408–14, quotation from pp. 411–12.
46. Sheehan, *op. cit.*, pp. 462–64, quotation from p. 463.
47. May 6, 1966, *ibid.*, p. 478. For the Joint Chiefs' similar analysis, see pp. 475–76.
48. J. C. Wylie, *Military Strategy: A General Theory of Power Control* (New Brunswick: Rutgers University Press, 1967), p. 51, points out this change.
49. April 14, 1965, Sheehan, *op. cit.*, p. 404. Taylor in his memoirs, *op. cit.*, p. 338, says: "It was curious how hard it had been to get authority for the initiation of the air campaign against the North and how relatively easy to get the marines ashore. Yet I thought the latter a more difficult decision and concurred in it reluctantly."
50. On developments in nuclear weapons, see C. L. Sulzberger, "The New Nuclear Look: I," *New York Times*, Jan. 8, 1971, sec. 4, p. 11.
51. *Public Papers of the Presidents of the United States: Richard Nixon . . . 1969* (Washington: Government Printing Office, 1971), p. 19.
52. Halperin, *op. cit.*, pp. 72–83; Herman S. Wolk, "Formulating a National Strategy for the 1970's," *Air University Review*, XXII (Nov.–Dec., 1970), 45–50.
53. Halperin, *op. cit.*, p. 83; Trewhitt, *op. cit.*, pp. 123–32.
54. William Beecher, "Report on Safeguard ABM Testimony Finds Unprofessional and Misleading Statements on Both Sides," *New York Times*, Oct. 1, 1971, p. 23; Halperin, *op. cit.*, pp. 53, 83–86. An extensive literature on the ABM controversy includes American Security Council, *U.S.S.R. vs. U.S.A.: The ABM and the Changed Strategic Balance* (Second Edition, Washington: Acropolis, 1969); Center for the Study of Democratic Institutions, *Anti-Ballistic Missile: Yes or No?* (New York: Hill & Wang, 1969); Abram Chayes and Jerome B.

Wiesner, *ABM: An Evaluation of the Decision to Deploy an Anti-ballistic Missile System* (New York: Harper & Row, 1969); Johan J. Holst and William Schneider, Jr., *Why ABM? Policy Issues in the Missile Defense Controversy* (New York: Pergamon, 1969).

55. Halperin, *op. cit.*, pp. 3–5, 83–86.
56. During the 1960s, the mutuality of interest between the two principal nuclear powers made possible the Limited Test Ban Treaty, prohibiting the testing of nuclear weapons in the atmosphere, under the sea, and in outer space; the Outer Space Treaty, prohibiting the stationing of nuclear weapons in outer space; the Antarctica Treaty, demilitarizing Antarctica; the Nuclear Non-proliferation Treaty, intended to prevent the spread of nuclear weapons beyond the five existing nuclear powers; and, in 1971, a Convention on Prohibition of Biological Weapons and a United States-Soviet agreement for the exchange of information to reduce the risks of an outbreak of nuclear war. Halperin, *op. cit.*, chap. XI; text of Draft Convention on Prohibition of Biological Weapons, *New York Times*, Oct. 1, 1971, p. 10; texts of pacts on averting atomic war and on the hot line, *ibid.*, p. 14.
57. For an early analysis, see Morton H. Halperin, "Light through 'The Cloud of Doom,'" *New York Times*, May 28, 1972, sec. 4, p. 1.
58. Thomas C. Schelling, *Arms and Influence* (New Haven: Yale University Press, 1966), *passim*, especially chap. I; quotation from p. 34.
59. *Ibid.*, p. 2.
60. *Ibid.*, p. 16.
61. *Ibid.*, p. 7.
62. Wylie, *op. cit.*, pp. 80–81, quotation from p. 80.
63. William Howard Gardiner, "National Policy and Naval Power," United States Naval Institute *Proceedings*, LII (Feb., 1926), 238, reprinted from *Proceedings* by permission; Copyright © 1926 U.S. Naval Institute.

Select Bibliography of American Writings on Military Strategy, Theoretical and Historical

Historical works are listed under the time period with which they are concerned, theoretical strategic writings by time of publication. Military histories and memoirs have been included only if they accord strategic issues a substantial emphasis. Professional military journals are not listed; many of their major articles dealing with strategy appear individually in the notes.

Pre-Civil War

Billias, George Athan, ed. *George Washington's Generals.* New York: Morrow, 1964.

Elliott, Charles Winslow. *Winfield Scott, The Soldier and the Man.* New York: Macmillan, 1937.

Freeman, Douglas Southall. *George Washington: A Biography.* 7 vols. New York: Scribner, 1948–57.

Halleck, H. Wager. *Elements of Military Art and Science. . . .* New York: Appleton, 1846.

Hunt, E. B. *Modern Warfare: Its Science and Art.* New Haven: Thomas J. Stafford, 1860.

Knox, Dudley W. *The Naval Genius of George Washington.* Boston: Houghton Mifflin, 1932.

Mahan, A. T. *Sea Power in Its Relation to the War of 1812.* Boston: Little, Brown, 1905.

Mahan, D. H. *An Elementary Treatise on Advanced-Guard, Out-Post, and Detachment Service of Troops. . . .* Revised Edition. New York: Wiley, 1864. First published 1847.

Mahon, John K. *History of the Second Seminole War.* Gainesville: University of Florida Press, 1967.

Prucha, Francis Paul. *The Sword of the Republic: The United States Army on the Frontier, 1783–1846.* New York: Macmillan, 1969.

Scott, Winfield. *Memoirs of Lieut.-General Scott, LL.D. Written by Himself.* 2 vols. New York: Sheldon, 1864.

Semmes, Raphael. *The Campaign of General Scott in the Valley of Mexico.* Cincinnati: Moore & Anderson, 1852.

Smith, Justin H. *The War with Mexico.* 2 vols. New York: Macmillan, 1919.

Thayer, Theodore. *Nathanael Greene: Strategist of the American Revolution.* New York: Twayne, 1960.

Utley, Robert M. *Frontiersmen in Blue: The United States Army and the Indian, 1848–1865.* New York: Macmillan, 1967.

Civil War

Alexander, E. P. *Military Memoirs of a Confederate.* Introduction and Notes by T. Harry Williams. Bloomington: Indiana University Press, 1962.

Bigelow, John. *The Campaign of Chancellorsville.* New Haven: Yale University Press, 1910.

Coddington, Edwin B. *The Gettysburg Campaign: A Study in Command.* New York: Scribner, 1968.

Connelly, Thomas L. "Robert E. Lee and the Western Confederacy: A Criticism of Lee's Strategic Ability." *Civil War History*, XV (June, 1969), 116–32.

Freeman, Douglas Southall. *Lee's Lieutenants: A Study in Command.* 3 vols. New York: Scribner, 1942–44.

———. *R. E. Lee: A Biography.* 4 vols. New York: Scribner, 1934.

Grant, U. S. *Personal Memoirs of U. S. Grant.* 2 vols. New York: Webster, 1885.

Hassler, Warren W., Jr. *General George B. McClellan: Shield of the Union.* Baton Rouge: Louisiana State University Press, 1957.

Johnson, Robert Underwood, and Clarence Clough Buel, eds. *Battles and Leaders of the Civil War.* 4 vols. New York: Century, 1884–88.

Johnston, Joseph E. *Narrative of Military Operations. . . .* Introduction by Frank E. Vandiver. Bloomington: Indiana University Press, 1960.

Jones, Archer. *Confederate Strategy from Shiloh to Vicksburg.* Baton Rouge: Louisiana State University Press, 1961.

Longstreet, James. *From Manassas to Appomattox: Memoirs of the Civil War in America.* James I. Robertson, Jr., ed. Bloomington: Indiana University Press, 1960.

Luvaas, Jay. *The Military Legacy of the Civil War: The European Inheritance.* Chicago: University of Chicago Press, 1959.

McClellan, George B. *McClellan's Own Story. . . .* New York: Webster, 1887.

McWhiney, Grady. *Braxton Bragg and Confederate Defeat.* I, *Field Command.* New York: Columbia University Press, 1969.

Michie, Peter S. *General McClellan.* New York: Appleton, 1901.

Sherman, William T. *Memoirs of General William T. Sherman by Himself.* Foreword by B. H. Liddell Hart. 2 vols in one. Bloomington: Indiana University Press, 1957.

Vandiver, Frank E. *Rebel Brass: The Confederate Command System.* Baton Rouge: Louisiana State University Press, 1956.

Williams, Kenneth P. *Lincoln Finds a General: A Military Study of the Civil War.* 5 vols. New York: Macmillan, 1950–59.

Williams, T. Harry. *Lincoln and His Generals.* New York: Knopf, 1952.

Civil War to 1917

Adams, Charles Francis. *Studies Military and Diplomatic.* New York: Macmillan, 1911.

Bennett, Frank M. *The Steam Navy of the United States.* Pittsburgh: Warren, 1896.

Bigelow, John. *The Principles of Strategy Illustrated Mainly from American Campaigns*. New York: Greenwood, 1968. Reprint of Second Edition, Revised and Enlarged. Philadelphia: Lippincott, 1894.

Braisted, William Reynolds. *The United States Navy in the Pacific, 1909–1922*. Austin: University of Texas Press, 1971.

Calef, John H. Part I, *Military Policy and Institutions*. Part II, *Ancient and Modern Armies*. Fort Monroe: United States Artillery School, 1886.

Califf, Joseph M. *Notes on Military Science and the Art of War*. Second Edition. Washington: James J. Chapman, 1891.

Cummings, Damon E. *Admiral Richard Wainwright and the United States Fleet*. Washington: Government Printing Office, 1962.

Fiebeger, G. J. *Elements of Strategy*. N. p. [1906].

Gleaves, Albert. *Life and Letters of Rear Admiral Stephen B. Luce*. New York: Putnam, 1925.

Grenville, John A. S., and George Berkeley Young. *Politics, Strategy, and American Diplomacy, 1873–1917*. New Haven: Yale University Press, 1966.

Herrick, Walter R., Jr. *The American Naval Revolution*. Baton Rouge: Louisiana State University Press, 1966.

Mahan, A. T. *From Sail to Steam: Recollections of Naval Life*. New York: Harper, 1907.

———. *The Influence of Sea Power upon History, 1660–1783*. Boston: Little, Brown, 1890.

———. *The Influence of Sea Power upon the French Revolution and Empire, 1793–1812*. Boston: Little, Brown, 1892.

———. *Lessons of the War with Spain and Other Articles*. Boston: Little, Brown, 1899.

———. *Naval Strategy, Compared and Contrasted with the Principles and Practice of Military Operations on Land*. Boston: Little, Brown, 1911.

———. *The Problem of Asia and Its Effect upon International Politics*. Boston: Little, Brown, 1900.

Mercur, James. *Elements of the Art of War. Prepared for the Use of the Cadets of the United States Military Academy*. Second Edition, Revised and Corrected. New York: Wiley, 1889.

Morison, Elting E. *Admiral Sims and the Modern American Navy*. Boston: Houghton Mifflin, 1942.

O'Gara, Gordon C. *Theodore Roosevelt and the Rise of the Modern American Navy*. Princeton: Princeton University Press, 1943.

Pettit, James S. *Elements of Military Science, For the Use of Students in Colleges and Universities*. Revised Edition. New Haven: Tuttle, Morehouse & Taylor, 1895.

Puleston, W. D. *Mahan: The Life and Work of Alfred Thayer Mahan*. New Haven: Yale University Press, 1939.

Steele, Matthew F. *American Campaigns*. Washington: Government Printing Office, 1901.

Wagner, Arthur L. *Strategy. A Lecture Delivered by Colonel Arthur L. Wagner, Assistant Adjutant-General, U.S.A., to the Officers of the*

Regular Army and National Guard at the Maneuvers at West Point, Ky., and at Fort Riley, Kansas, 1903. Kansas City: Hudson-Kimberly, 1904.

1914 to 1941

Brodie, Bernard. *Sea Power in the Machine Age*. Princeton: Princeton University Press, 1941.

Burr, John G. *The Framework of Battle*. Philadelphia: Lippincott, 1943.

Command and General Staff School. *The Principles of Strategy for an Independent Corps or Army in a Theater of Operations*. Fort Leavenworth: Command and General Staff School Press, 1936.

Earle, Edward Mead, ed. *Makers of Modern Strategy: Military Thought from Machiavelli to Hitler*. Princeton: Princeton University Press, 1941.

Frost, Holloway H. *The Battle of Jutland*. Annapolis: United States Naval Institute, 1936.

Greer, Thomas H. *The Development of Air Doctrine in the Army Air Corps, 1917–1941*. Montgomery: Air University, 1955.

Isely, Jeter A., and Philip A. Crowl. *The U. S. Marines and Amphibious War: Its Theory and Practice in the Pacific*. Princeton: Princeton University Press, 1951.

Johnston, R. M. *Clausewitz to Date, With Selected Quotations from Military Writers and New Material*. Cambridge: The Military Historian and Economist, 1917.

McClendon, R. Earl. *The Question of Autonomy for the United States Air Arm*. Revised. Montgomery: Air University, 1952.

Meyers, George J. *Strategy*. Washington: Byron S. Adams, 1928.

Mitchell, William. *Memoirs of World War I: "From Start to Finish of Our Greatest War."* New York: Random House, 1960.

———. *Our Air Force: The Keystone of National Defense*. New York: Dutton, 1921.

———. *Skyways: A Book on Modern Aeronautics*. Philadelphia: Lippincott, 1930.

———. *Winged Defense: The Development and Possibilities of Modern Air Power, Economic and Military*. New York: Putnam, 1925.

Morton, Louis. "War Plan ORANGE: Evolution of a Strategy." *World Politics*, XI (Jan., 1959), 221–50.

Muller, Hollis LeR. *Technique of Modern Arms*. Harrisburg: Military Service Publishing Co., 1940.

Naylor, William K. *Principles of Strategy with Historical Illustrations*. Fort Leavenworth: General Service Schools Press, 1921.

O'Connor, Raymond G. *Perilous Equilibrium: The United States and the London Naval Conference of 1930*. Lawrence: University of Kansas Press, 1962.

Pershing, John J. *My Experiences in the World War*. 2 vols. New York: Stokes, 1931.

Puleston, W. D. *The Dardanelles Expedition: A Condensed Study*. Second Edition. Annapolis: United States Naval Institute, 1927.

Quester, George H. *Deterrence before Hiroshima: The Airpower Background of Modern Strategy*. New York: Wiley, 1966.

Robinson, Oliver Prescott. *The Fundamentals of Military Strategy*. Washington: United States Infantry Association, 1928.

Seversky, Alexander P. De. *Victory through Air Power*. New York: Simon and Schuster, 1942.

Sims, William Sowden, with Burton J. Hendrick. *The Victory at Sea*. Garden City: Doubleday, Page, 1919.

Sprout, Harold and Margaret. *The Rise of American Naval Power, 1776–1918*. Princeton: Princeton University Press, 1939.

———. *Toward a New Order of Sea Power*. Princeton: Princeton University Press, 1940.

Tuleja, Thaddeus J. *Statesmen and Admirals: Quest for a Far Eastern Naval Policy*. New York: Norton, 1963.

Wheeler, Gerald E. *Prelude to Pearl Harbor: The United States Navy and the Far East, 1921–1931*. Columbia: University of Missouri Press, 1963.

Willoughby, Charles Andrew. *Maneuver in War*. Harrisburg: Military Service Publishing Co., 1939.

World War II

Ambrose, Stephen E. *The Supreme Commander: The War Years of General Dwight D. Eisenhower*. Garden City: Doubleday, 1970.

Arnold, H. H. *Global Mission*. New York: Harper, 1949.

Baldwin, Hanson W. *Great Mistakes of the War*. New York: Harper, 1950.

Ballantine, Duncan S. *U.S. Naval Logistics in the Second World War*. Princeton: Princeton University Press, 1947.

Barbey, Daniel E. *MacArthur's Amphibious Navy: Seventh Amphibious Force Operations, 1943–1945*. Annapolis: United States Naval Institute, 1969.

Bradley, Omar N. *A Soldier's Story*. New York: Holt, 1951.

Brodie, Bernard. *A Layman's Guide to Naval Strategy*. Princeton: Princeton University Press, 1942. Third and later editions, from 1944, entitled *A Guide to Naval Strategy*.

Carter, Worrall Reed. *Beans, Bullets, and Black Oil*. Washington: Government Printing Office, 1951.

Chandler, Alfred D., Jr., ed. *The Papers of Dwight David Eisenhower: The War Years*. 5 vols. Baltimore: Johns Hopkins Press, 1970.

Cline, Ray S. *Washington Command Post: The Operations Division. (United States Army in World War II: The War Department.)* Washington: Office of the Chief of Military History, 1951.

Coakley, Robert W., and Richard M. Leighton. *Global Logistics and Strategy, 1943–1945*. (*United States Army in World War II: The War Department*.) Washington: Office of the Chief of Military History, 1968.

Craven, Wesley Frank, and James Lea Cate, eds. *The Army Air Forces in World War II.* 7 vols. Chicago: University of Chicago Press, 1948–58.

Dyer, George Carroll. *The Amphibians Came to Conquer: The Story of Admiral Richmond Kelly Turner.* 2 vols. Washington: Government Printing Office, 1972.

Eisenhower, Dwight D. *Crusade in Europe.* Garden City: Doubleday, 1948.

Emme, Eugene M., ed. *The Impact of Air Power: National Security and World Politics.* Princeton: Van Nostrand, 1959.

Feis, Herbert. *The Atomic Bomb and the End of World War II.* Princeton: Princeton University Press, 1966.

———. *Churchill, Roosevelt, Stalin: The War They Waged and the Peace They Sought.* Princeton: Princeton University Press, 1957.

Forrestel, E. P. *Admiral Raymond A. Spruance, USN: A Study in Command.* Washington: Government Printing Office, 1966.

Greenfield, Kent Roberts. *American Strategy in World War II: A Reconsideration.* Baltimore: Johns Hopkins Press, 1963.

———, ed. *Command Decisions.* New York: Harcourt Brace, 1959.

———. *The Historian and the Army.* New Brunswick: Rutgers University Press, 1954.

Halsey, William F., Jr., and J. Bryan III. *Admiral Halsey's Story.* New York: McGraw-Hill, 1947.

Harrison, Gordon. *Cross-Channel Attack.* (*United States Army in World War II: The European Theater of Operations.*) Washington: Office of the Chief of Military History, 1951.

Higgins, Trumbull. *Soft Underbelly: The Anglo-American Controversy over the Italian Campaign, 1939–1945.* New York: Macmillan, 1968.

King, Ernest J., and Walter Muir Whitehill. *Fleet Admiral King: A Naval Record.* New York: Norton, 1952.

Leighton, Richard M., and Robert W. Coakley. *Global Logistics and Strategy, 1940–1943.* (*United States Army in World War II: The War Department.*) Washington: Office of the Chief of Military History, 1955.

Leighton, Richard M. "OVERLORD Revisited: An Interpretation of American Strategy in the European War, 1942–1944." *American Historical Review*, LXVIII (July, 1963), 919–37.

MacArthur, Douglas. *Reminiscences.* New York: McGraw-Hill, 1964.

Matloff, Maurice, and Edwin M. Snell. *Strategic Planning for Coalition Warfare, 1941–1942.* (*United States Army in World War II: The War Department.*) Washington: Office of the Chief of Military History, 1953.

Matloff, Maurice. *Strategic Planning for Coalition Warfare, 1943–1944.* (*United States Army in World War II: The War Department.*) Washington: Office of the Chief of Military History, 1959.

Morison, Samuel Eliot. *History of United States Naval Operations in World War II.* 15 vols. Boston: Little, Brown, 1950–62.

———. *Strategy and Compromise.* Boston: Little, Brown, 1958.

———. *The Two-Ocean War: A Short History of the United States Navy in the Second World War.* Boston: Little, Brown, 1963.

Morton, Louis. *Strategy and Command: The First Two Years.* (*United States Army in World War II: The War in the Pacific.*) Washington: Office of the Chief of Military History, 1962.

Pogue, Forrest C. *George C. Marshall: Ordeal and Hope, 1939–1942.* New York: Viking, 1966.

———. *The Supreme Command.* (*United States Army in World War II: The European Theater of Operations.*) Washington: Office of the Chief of Military History, 1954.

Puleston, W. D. *The Influence of Sea Power in World War II.* New Haven: Yale University Press, 1947.

Reynolds, Clark G. *The Fast Carriers: The Forging of an Air Navy.* New York: McGraw-Hill, 1968.

Roscoe, Theodore. *United States Submarine Actions in World War II.* Annapolis: United States Naval Institute, 1949.

Ruppenthal, Roland G. *Logistical Support of the Armies.* 2 vols. (*United States Army in World War II: The European Theater of Operations.*) Washington: Office of the Chief of Military History, 1953–59.

Sherwood, Robert E. *Roosevelt and Hopkins: An Intimate History.* Revised Edition. New York: Harper, 1950.

Smith, Walter Bedell. *Eisenhower's Six Great Decisions.* New York: Longmans, Green, 1956.

Watson, Mark Skinner. *Chief of Staff: Prewar Plans and Preparations.* (*United States Army in World War II: The War Department.*) Washington: Historical Division, United States Army, 1950.

Wedemeyer, Albert C. *Wedemeyer Reports!* New York: Holt, 1958.

Post-World War II

Appleman, Roy E. *South to the Naktong, North to the Yalu.* (*United States Army in the Korean War.*) Washington: Office of the Chief of Military History, 1961.

Bobrow, David B., ed. *Weapons Systems Decisions: Political and Psychological Perspectives on Continental Defense.* New York: Praeger, 1969.

Brennan, Donald G., ed. *Arms Control, Disarmament, and National Security.* New York: Braziller, 1961.

Brodie, Bernard, ed. *The Absolute Weapon: Atomic Power and World Order.* New York: Harcourt Brace, 1946.

———. *Strategy in the Missile Age.* Princeton: Princeton University Press, 1959.

———. "Unlimited Weapons and Limited War." *The Reporter*, XI No. 9 (Nov. 18, 1954), 16–21.

Cagle, Malcolm W., and Frank A. Manson. *The Sea War in Korea.* Annapolis: United States Naval Institute, 1957.

Clark, Mark W. *From the Danube to the Yalu.* New York: Harper, 1954.

Collins, J. Lawton. *War in Peacetime: The History and Lessons of Korea.* Boston: Houghton Mifflin, 1969.

Cooper, Chester L. *The Lost Crusade: America in Vietnam.* New York: Dodd, Mead, 1970.

Davis, Vincent. *Postwar Defense Policy and the U. S. Navy, 1943–1946.* Chapel Hill: University of North Carolina Press, 1966.

Field, James A., Jr. *History of United States Naval Operations: Korea.* Washington: Government Printing Office, 1962.

Futrell, Robert Frank, Lawson S. Moseley, and Albert F. Simpson. *The United States Air Force in Korea, 1950–1953.* New York: Duell, Sloan and Pearce, 1961.

Gavin, James M. *War and Peace in the Space Age.* New York: Harper, 1958.

Halperin, Morton H. *Contemporary Military Strategy.* Boston: Little, Brown, 1967.

———. *Defense Strategies for the Seventies.* Boston: Little, Brown, 1971.

———. *Limited War: An Essay on the Development of the Theory and an Annotated Bibliography.* Occasional Papers in International Affairs No. 3, May, 1962. Harvard University Center for International Affairs.

———. *Limited War in the Nuclear Age.* New York: Wiley, 1963.

Hermes, Walter G. *Truce Tent and Fighting Front.* (*United States Army in the Korean War.*) Washington: Office of the Chief of Military History, 1966.

Hilsman, Roger. *To Move a Nation: The Politics of Foreign Policy in the Administration of John F. Kennedy.* Garden City: Doubleday, 1967.

Huntington, Samuel P. *The Common Defense: Strategic Programs in National Politics.* New York: Columbia University Press, 1961.

Kahn, Herman. *On Escalation: Metaphors and Scenarios.* New York: Praeger, 1965.

———. *On Thermonuclear War.* Princeton: Princeton University Press, 1960.

———. *Thinking about the Unthinkable.* New York: Horizon Press, 1962.

Kaufmann, William W. *The McNamara Strategy.* New York: Harper & Row, 1964.

———, ed. *Military Policy and National Security.* Princeton: Princeton University Press, 1956.

Kissinger, Henry A. *The Necessity for Choice: Prospects of American Foreign Policy.* New York: Harper, 1961.

———. *Nuclear Weapons and Foreign Policy.* New York: Harper, 1957.

Knorr, Klaus, and Thornton Read, eds. *Limited Strategic War.* New York: Praeger, 1962.

Lyons, Gene M., and Louis Morton. *Schools for Strategy: Education and Research in National Security Affairs.* New York: Praeger, 1965.

Millis, Walter. *Arms and Men: A Study in American Military History.* New York: Putnam, 1956.

Morgenstern, Oskar. *The Question of National Defense.* New York: Random House, 1959.

Ney, Virgil. *Evolution of the United States Army Field Manual, Valley Forge to Vietnam.* Combat Operations Research Group, CORG Memorandum, CORG-M-244, Prepared by Technical Operations, Incorporated,

Combat Operations Research Group, for Headquarters United States Army Combat Developments Command, Fort Belvoir, Virginia, 1966.

Osgood, Robert Endicott. *Limited War: The Challenge to American Strategy*. Chicago: University of Chicago Press, 1957.

Paret, Peter, and John W. Shy. *Guerrillas in the 1960's*. Revised Edition. New York: Praeger, 1964.

Quade, E. S., ed. *Analysis for Military Decisions*. Chicago: Rand McNally, 1966.

Ransom, Harry Howe. *The Intelligence Establishment*. Cambridge: Harvard University Press, 1970.

Ridgway, Matthew B. *The Korean War*. Garden City: Doubleday, 1967.

———. *Soldier: The Memoirs of Matthew B. Ridgway*. New York: Harper, 1956.

Rockefeller Brothers Fund. *International Security: The Military Aspect*. Garden City: Doubleday, 1958.

Schelling, Thomas C. *Arms and Influence*. New Haven: Yale University Press, 1966.

———. *The Strategy of Conflict*. Cambridge: Harvard University Press, 1960.

Schilling, Warner R., Paul Y. Hammond, and Glenn H. Snyder. *Strategy, Politics, and Defense Budgets*. New York: Columbia University Press, 1962.

Sheehan, Neil, *et al. The Pentagon Papers as Published in the New York Times*. Paperback edition. New York: Bantam, 1971.

Shy, John. "The American Military Experience: History and Learning." *Journal of Interdisciplinary History*, I (Winter, 1971), 205–28.

Smith, Dale O. *U.S. Military Doctrine: A Study and Appraisal*. New York: Duell, Sloan and Pearce, 1955.

Snyder, Glenn H. *Deterrence and Defense*. Princeton: Princeton University Press, 1961.

Stein, Harold, ed. *American Civil-Military Decisions: A Book of Case Studies*. University, Ala.: University of Alabama Press, 1963.

Taylor, Maxwell D. *Swords and Plowshares*. New York: Norton, 1972.

———. *The Uncertain Trumpet*. New York: Harper, 1960.

Trewhitt, Henry L. *McNamara*. New York: Harper & Row, 1971.

Tucker, Samuel A., ed. *A Modern Design for Defense Decision: A McNamara-Hitch-Enthoven Anthology*. Washington: Industrial College of the Armed Forces, 1966.

Turner, Gordon B., and Richard D. Challener, eds. *National Security in the Nuclear Age: Basic Facts and Theories*. New York: Praeger, 1960.

Wohlstetter, Albert J. "The Delicate Balance of Terror." *Foreign Affairs*, XXXVIII (Jan., 1959), 211–34.

———. *The Delicate Balance of Terror*. RAND Publication P-1472, Dec., 1958.

Wylie, J. C. *Military Strategy: A General Theory of Power Control*. New Brunswick: Rutgers University Press, 1967.

Index